Foundations
of
Pentecostal
Theology

Guy P. Duffield
and
Nathaniel M. Van Cleave

Foursquare Media

FOUNDATIONS OF PENTECOSTAL THEOLOGY by Guy P. Duffield and Nathaniel M. Van Cleave

Published by Foursquare Media

1910 W. Sunset Blvd., Suite 200

Los Angeles, California 90026

This book is produced and distributed by Creation House, a part of Strang Communications, www.creationhouse.com.

Unless otherwise noted, all Scripture quotations are from the King James Authorized Version of the Bible.

Copyright © 1983, 1987 by L.I.F.E. Bible College at Los Angeles 2006, 2008, Foursquare Media, Los Angeles, CA
All rights reserved

Library of Congress Cataloging in Publication Data

Duffield, Guy P., 1909–2000

Foundations of Pentecostal Theology.

Includes bibliographical references and index.

1. Pentecostal churches—Doctrines. 2. Pentecostalism. 3. Theology, Doctrinal. I. Van Cleave, Nathaniel M., 1907–2002. II. Title.

BX8762.Z5D84 1983 230'.044 83-25611

Library of Congress Control Number: 2008920135

International Standard Book Number-13: 978-1-59979-336-8

08 09 10 11 12 — 9 8 7 6 5 4 3 2 1

Printed in the United States of America

UNLESS OTHERWISE STATED, all Bible quotations are taken from the King James Authorized Version.

TRANSLATIONS AND VERSIONS OF THE BIBLE

AMP—The Amplified New Testament

AV—The Authorized Version; see KJV

ASV—The American Standard Version

BAS—The New Testament in Basic English

BECK—The New Testament in the Language of Today (William F. Beck)

BER—The Modern Language New Testament: The New Berkeley Version (Gerrit Verkuyl)

DOUAI—The Rheims-Douai Version of the Bible

GSPD—The New Testament: An American Translation (Edgar J. Goodspeed)

GNB—Good News Bible (Today's English Version)

GREEN'S—see KJII

IGEB—see Marshall's

JB—The Jerusalem Bible

KJII—The King James II New Testament (Jay P. Green)

KJV—The King James Authorized Version

KNOX—The Holy Bible: Translated by Ronald Knox

LAM—The New Testament According to the Eastern Texts (George N. Lamsa)

LB—The Living Bible Paraphrased (Kenneth J. Taylor)

LXX—The Septuagint Version

MARSHALL—The Interlinear Greek-English New Testament: The Nestle Greek Text With Literal English Translation (Alfred Marshall)

MOFFATT, MOF—The Bible: A New Translation (James Moffatt)

NAB—The New American Bible

NASB—The New American Standard Bible

NEB—The New English Bible

NIV—The New International Version of the Bible

NKJV—The New King James Version of the Bible

PHILLIPS, PHI—The New Testament in Modern English (J. B. Phillips)

RSV—The Revised Standard Version

ROTHERHAM, RHM—The Emphasized New Testament: A New Translation (J. B. Rotherham)

TAY—See LB

TCNT—The Twentieth Century New Testament

TEV—see **GNB**

WEY—The New Testament in Modern Speech (Richard Francis Weymouth)

WILLIAMS, WMS—The New Testament: A Translation in the Language of the People (Charles B. Williams)

WUEST—The New Testament: An Expanded Translation (Kenneth S. Wuest)

YOUNG'S—Young's Literal Translation of the Bible (Robert Young)

BOOKS OF THE BIBLE

OLD TESTAMENT

Gn.—Genesis
Ex.—Exodus
Lv.—Leviticus
Nm.—Numbers
Dt.—Deuteronomy
Jos.—Joshua
Jgs.—Judges
Ru.—Ruth
1 Sm.—1 Samuel
2 Sm.—2 Samuel
1 Kgs.—1 Kings
2 Kgs.—2 Kings
1 Chr.—1 Chronicles
2 Chr.—2 Chronicles
Ezr.—Ezra
Neh.—Nehemiah
Est.—Esther
Jb.—Job
Ps.—Psalms
Prv.—Proverbs

Eccl.—Ecclesiastes
Sg.—Song of Solomon
Is.—Isaiah
Jer.—Jeremiah
Lam.—Lamentations
Ez.—Ezekiel
Dn.—Daniel
Hos.—Hosea
Jl.—Joel
Am.—Amos
Ob.—Obadiah
Jon.—Jonah
Mi.—Micah
Na.—Nahum
Hb.—Habakkuk
Zep.—Zephaniah
Hg.—Haggai
Zec.—Zechariah
Mal.—Malachi

NEW TESTAMENT

Mt.—Matthew
Mk.—Mark
Lk.—Luke
Jn.—John
Acts—Acts
Rom.—Romans
1 Cor.—1 Corinthians
2 Cor.—2 Corinthians
Gal.—Galatians
Eph.—Ephesians
Phil.—Philippians
Col.—Colossians
1 Thes.—1 Thessalonians
2 Thes.—2 Thessalonians

1 Tm.—1 Timothy
2 Tm.—2 Timothy
Ti.—Titus
Phlm.—Philemon
Heb.—Hebrews
Jas.—James
1 Pt.—1 Peter
2 Pt.—2 Peter
1 Jn.—1 John
2 Jn.—2 John
3 Jn.—3 John
Jude—Jude
Rv.—Revelation

A SERIES OF sweeping waves of revival have coursed across the face of the twentieth century already. At least four discernible times of refreshing from the presence of the Lord have been manifest in this era, and all seem to have these two things in common: they have touched every sector of the Church, with all denominations being impacted to some degree, and they have been uniquely marked by an expanded realization of the role of the Holy Spirit—the third person of the Godhead—in the life and task of the Church.

It is neither sectarian nor self-serving for any Pentecostal to observe the now-historical fact that the revival which God used to introduce this succession of revivals bears His own name, one which is drawn from the birth of the Church itself—Pentecost. At the onset of this century, first in Topeka, Kansas, and then at Azusa Street in Los Angeles, California, the manifestation of the Holy Spirit resulted in an awakening which even today continues to affect the Church everywhere. What God did through Luther in recovering the message of salvation and did through Wesley in recovering the message of holy life and service, He did through the early Pentecostal revival in recovering the dynamism of the power and gifts of the Holy Spirit to the Church. Since then, the evidence abounds to the fact that growth in evangelism has been compounded by a broader, warmer response to the Spirit and His workings, as believers everywhere open to seasonal outpourings from heaven.

And now, this book appears at a crucial season: a time in which we stand expectantly anticipating a new outbreak of God's grace across the face of the earth. The renewal of recent decades has receded as a tide, only to prepare us for the rise of a new and mightier wave of blessing. With deep conviction, I view this volume as suited to a new age of Spirit-filled service in the authority of Jesus' name.

But it is not only the timeliness of this book which gives it special value, it is its uniqueness.

This is an unusual and noteworthy book, which I take great joy in being asked to introduce and to commend to the Church at large. It was begun at my request during the years I served as president of L.I.F.E. Bible College at Los Angeles. To now hold the massive manuscript in hand is a thrill, not only by reason of the confidence I have in its content, but to know we have captured the wealth of two lifetimes of scholarship.

There can hardly be found as complete and functional a doctrinal study from within the Pentecostal movement. This is neither to reflect on any of the fine work that has been done by other authors, nor to presume to offer this work as conclusively complete, but there is an unquestionable distinction present in the wedding of two such remarkable scholars and preachers for the formation of so thorough and usable a doctrine textbook and authoritative reference resource. First, the scholarship for which both Guy Duffield and Nathaniel Van Cleave have become known lends a depth and thoroughness to this work, attested to both by its content and sheer size. Each man has an unimpeachable record of faithfulness to the Word and the doctrine in public ministry for more than a half-century. Second, the unshakeable realities of eternal Truth come from their pen with a purity and power verified through decades of study and ministry. These are trustworthy men who handle God's Word with honesty, and who "by manifestation of the truth [commend themselves] to every man's conscience in the sight of God" (2 Cor. 4:2).

Further, it is in the fact that the ministries of the authors have been marked by effective preaching and pastoral work that this book holds promise for all Christian workers. It is a practical book, featuring systematic theology in a form which is readily adaptable to nourishing the flock of God. Both men have equally distinguished themselves as pastors, preachers, college professors, lecturers, and writers. Such a confluence of training and experience, flowing through men of character and faith, warrants the highest expectations of the reader or the student taking this volume in hand. Such expectations will be justified and will be confirmed.

The title of this volume has been thoughtfully chosen, indicating it is answering to a specific need:

Foundations, because we live in a philosophically relativistic culture which has lost any mooring to the steadfast and absolute. The "rooted and grounded" realities of divine revelation need to be freshly asserted, that this generation of believers be firmly planted and built up "according to the pattern" (Heb. 8:5). The plumb line of God's Word is the standard with which all teaching and preaching must align, and it is firmly adhered to throughout this book.

Pentecostal, because all truth must be made alive by the Holy Spirit in order to be reproductive and refreshing. E. M. Bounds warned of truth without life as the "letter which kills," and which, though of excellent scholarship, becomes "as barren as a field sown with pearls." In contrast, the quality inherent in this volume is that same trait which enabled Peter to rise with a text from Joel in hand and to infuse it with contemporary relevance. The Holy Spirit wants to speak to *today*, and the vitality of the Spirit manifest herein makes ancient verities throb with life.

Theology, because all that we ultimately need, now or forever, is summarized in knowing God and in knowing Him in terms of *all* His counsel. It is in that respect that Drs. Duffield and Van Cleave have served us especially well. They not only expound the riches of traditional theological themes, but with depth and balance provide a development of those facets of God's being, working, and power which have become better understood to the Church at large in the century—the working of the Holy Spirit *in* the Church, the gifts of the Spirit distributed *through* the Church, and the healing life of Christ *amid* the Church. These and other related themes deserve to be understood and exercised in all the Church throughout all of the world.

This, then, is not a theology for Pentecostals alone. Its Pentecostal quality does not take its thrust from a movement a short century old, but from that Spirit which brought forth the Church on a day by that name. Here is truth for the body of Christ, which will cause the preaching of the saving Word and the teaching of sound words to glorify Jesus Christ the Lord and to edify His people.

—JACK W. HAYFORD
Founding Pastor, The Church On The Way
Van Nuys, California
August 10, 1983

ACKNOWLEDGEMENTS

Then said Jesus... If ye continue in my word, then are ye my disciples indeed; And ye shall know the truth, and the truth shall make you free.

—JOHN 8:32

THE REALITY OF this scripture was repeatedly impressed upon my soul and spirit as this manuscript progressed toward publication. As editor, numerous tasks required my attention, but none were as pleasurable and inspiring as the repeated readings of the manuscript which necessitated my own confrontation with the truths of God's Word. As a result, my beliefs were both challenged and confirmed, and I was again convinced of the life-changing effects of the living Word.

All of us at L.I.F.E. Bible College who were requested to be a part of this project are grateful to God for His grace to us in this endeavor. A special acknowledgement must go to the administration of the college for their initiative and direction to proceed with this book; and a special thanks to Dr. Dorothy Jean Furlong, who coordinated and facilitated each phase of the project. In addition, we thank all the staff and personnel who contributed their skills and faithful assistance to the various processes of preparing a manuscript for publication.

We are indebted to the following pastors and leaders for their review of various chapters and for the helpful suggestions that were the result of their responses:

Dr. Leslie R. Eno	Dr. Charles L. Hollis
Dr. Clarence E. Hall	Dr. Harold W. Jefferies
Rev. Jack E. Hamilton	Rev. Paul McEachern
Dr. Jack W. Hayford	Rev. Coleman Phillips

May the Lord receive glory for all that has been done as we have united our efforts to proclaim His truths.

—CONNIE R. KINGSBURY
Editor

ACCORDING TO THE *World Christian Encyclopedia*, in 1980 there were over fifty-one billion Christians in Pentecostal denominations throughout the world,[1] plus, some eleven billion more within other denominations who worship in Pentecostal fashion.[2]

As late as 1956, this number was considered to be about ten billion. Thus, this movement appears to be the fastest growing segment of the Christian Church in the world today.

This large group of Christian believers has experienced a significant ministry of the third person of the Trinity, the Holy Spirit, which has not only manifested itself in the realm of blessing and empowerment, but has affected every phase of their lives.

The Pentecostal movement is not just based on an inspirational experience. It is grounded upon the entire Bible as the Word of God. We are a Bible-believing people. We subscribe to "all the counsel of God" (Acts 20:27). Our spiritual blessings are balanced by the doctrinal teachings of the Scriptures, so that we might be "rooted and built up in him, and stablished in the faith" (Col. 2:7), "that the man of God may be perfect, thoroughly furnished unto all good works" (2 Tm. 3:17).

It has been a privilege and a pleasure to compile the scriptural teachings concerning the great doctrines of our faith as contained in this book. It is the earnest desire of the authors that this work may be a means under God to ground and settle (Col. 1:23) our Pentecostal family throughout the world, and to encourage others to receive and enjoy all the blessings of a rich spiritual life in the fullness of the Holy Spirit.

—GUY P. DUFFIELD AND NATHANIEL M. VAN CLEAVE
Los Angeles, California
August 16, 1983

---

1 David B. Barrett, ed., *World Christian Encyclopedia* (Oxford University Press, 1982), 14.
2 Ibid., 64.

CHAPTER THREE: THE DOCTRINE OF MAN/*Anthropology* 121

CHAPTER FOUR: THE DOCTRINE OF SIN/*Hamartiology* 155

CHAPTER FIVE: THE DOCTRINE OF SALVATION/*Soteriology* 183

CHAPTER SEVEN: THE DOCTRINE OF DIVINE HEALING 365

CHAPTER NINE: THE DOCTRINE OF ANGELS/*Angelology* 471

Chapter Ten: The Doctrine of Last Things/*Eschatology* 523

THE DOCTRINE OF THE SCRIPTURES

Bibliology

Introduction

I. The Names of the Scriptures
  A. The Bible
  B. Other names

II. The Divisions of the Scriptures
  A. The two testaments
  B. Divisions in the Old Testament
  C. Divisions in the New Testament
  D. Chapters and verses

III. The Writers of the Scriptures

IV. The Canon of the Scriptures
  A. The canon of the Old Testament
  B. The Apocrypha
  C. The canon of the New Testament
  D. Tests used to determine canonicity
    1. *Apostolicity*
    2. *Spiritual content*
    3. *Doctrinal soundness*
    4. *Usage*
    5. *Divine inspiration*

V. The Inerrancy of the Scriptures
  A. Definition of *inerrancy*
  B. The testimony to inerrancy
    1. *The Bible claims to be the Word of God*
    2. *The Bible is a unique revelation of truth*
    3. *The Bible is an unchanging revelation*
    4. *The Bible is right morally and spiritually*

VI. The Inspiration of the Scriptures
  A. Definition of *inspiration*
  B. Revelation, inspiration, and illumination distinguished
  C. The meaning of inspiration
    1. *Liberal view of inspiration*
    2. *Neo-orthodox views of inspiration*
    3. *The conservative views*

F. Versions
1. *The Septuagint*
2. *The Samaritan Pentateuch*
3. *Syriac versions*
4. *Latin versions*

G. Biblical criticism
1. *Higher criticism*
2. *Lower criticism*

H. Evidences for the biblical text
1. *The Church fathers*
2. *The Dead Sea Scrolls*
3. *The Papyri*
4. *Encouraging statements*

X. The Scriptures in English

A. The earliest beginnings

B. John Wycliffe

C. William Tyndale

D. Other sixteenth-century translations
1. *The Coverdale Bible*
2. *Matthew's Bible*
3. *The Great Bible*
4. *The Geneva Bible*
5. *The Bishop's Bible*
6. *The Rheims-Douai Bible*
7. *The King James Version*

E. Recent translations of the English Bible
1. *English Revised Version*
2. *American Standard Version*
3. *Revised Standard Version*
4. *New American Standard Bible*
5. *New International Version*
6. *Many others*

CHAPTER ONE

THE DOCTRINE OF THE SCRIPTURES

Bibliology

INTRODUCTION

GOD IS A God who desires to reveal Himself. He does not remain silent like the gods of the heathen, both ancient and modern. The Lord takes pleasure in making Himself known to His creatures. He is pictured as a God of love; love must always communicate itself, and that revelation must come from God Himself. The thoughts of a man can only be disclosed by the man himself. Likewise, only God can make Himself known. The God of the Bible is a God who speaks. From Creation all down through history, God revealed Himself by speaking. He spoke and the universe sprang forth. "By the word of the LORD were the heavens made; and all the host of them by the breath of his mouth" (Ps. 33:6). Through the years He had conveyed His will and purposes by speaking to chosen men, with the greatest of all revelations in the person of Jesus Christ, the Word Incarnate: "In the beginning was the Word, and the Word was with God, and the Word was God....And the Word was made flesh, and dwelt among us" (Jn. 1:1, 14). "God, who at sundry times and in divers manners spake in time past unto the fathers by the prophets, Hath in these last days spoken unto us by [lit., in] his Son..." (Heb. 1:1–2).

It has pleased God that all these revelations of Himself should have been preserved for mankind today in the book we call the Bible. Many naturalists have claimed that the only revelation of God they need can be found in nature, and they do not need the special revelation contained in the Bible. It is true that if God is the Creator of all nature, as the Bible declares that He is, then nature will reveal much about the One who brought it into existence. But nature's revelation of God is very limited. Certainly the God who created this amazing world, to say nothing of the vast universe of which it is a minute part, must be a God of great wisdom and power. But here the revelation stops. Nature tells us nothing of the marvelous love of God, nor of His holiness, nor of the grace that has provided salvation through the Lord Jesus Christ. All of God's great purposes and plans for mankind are revealed only in the written Word, the Bible. There is a view, held rather widely in some intellectual circles, that the Bible is the account of man's age-long efforts to find God. If this were so, there would be in it no authority or sense of divine revelation, but merely the account of man's groping for truths far above his abilities to obtain. Rather than the Bible containing man's efforts to find God, it is the account of God's efforts to reveal Himself to man. It is of the greatest importance, then, that we understand something concerning its origin, its formation, its authority, inerrancy, and Divine inspiration. These will be considered under the study of bibliology.

I. THE NAMES OF THE SCRIPTURES

A. The Bible

Our English word *Bible* comes from the Greek word *biblos,* meaning "a book." *Biblos* comes from the word given to the inner pulp of the papyrus reed on which ancient books were written. "The Book [*biblos*] of the generation of Jesus Christ" (Mt. 1:1); also from *biblion,* a diminutive form of *biblos,* meaning "little book." "And there was delivered unto Him the book [*biblion*]...And when he had opened the book [*biblion*]" (Lk. 4:17).

B. Other names

The Bible is also called "the Scripture" (Mk. 12:10; 15:28; Lk. 4:21; Jn. 2:22; 7:38; 10:35; Rom. 4:3; Gal. 4:30; 2 Pt. 1:20), and "the Scriptures" (Mt. 22:29; Mk. 12:24; Lk. 24:27; Jn. 5:39; Acts 17:11; Rom. 1:2; 1 Cor. 15:3–4; 2 Tm. 3:15; 2 Pt. 3:16). These terms signify "holy writings." Once Paul uses *the holy scriptures* (Rom. 1:2), and once *the sacred writings* (2 Tm. 3:15, RSV), and once *the oracles of God* (Rom. 3:2). One of the most descriptive and satisfying names is "the Word of God" (Mk. 7:13; Rom. 10:17; 2 Cor. 2:17; 1 Thes. 2:13; Heb. 4:12).

II. THE DIVISIONS OF THE SCRIPTURES

A. The two testaments

The Bible is divided into two sections known as the Old and the New Testaments. The word *testament* was originally translated "covenant," and signifies the thought that each is a covenant which God made with His people. There are thirty-nine books in the Old Testament and twenty-seven in the New Testament. An easy way to remember these numbers is to count the number of letters in either the words *Old Testament* or *New Testament*—three and nine. Three placed beside nine (thirty-nine) gives the number of books in the Old Testament, while three multiplied by nine (twenty-seven) gives the number of books in the New Testament.

B. Divisions in the Old Testament

The Hebrew Old Testament was commonly divided into three sections:

The Law (*Torah*), five books:
    Genesis, Exodus, Leviticus, Numbers, Deuteronomy

The Prophets (*Nebhiim*), eight books:
    Former Prophets—Joshua, Judges, Samuel, Kings
    Latter Prophets—Isaiah, Jeremiah, Ezekiel, the Twelve

The Writings (*Kethubim*), eleven books:
    Poetical Books—Psalms, Proverbs, Job
    Five Rolls (*Megillot*)—Song of Songs, Ruth, Lamentations, Esther, Ecclesiastes
    Historical Books—Daniel, Ezra-Nehemiah (in the Hebrew canon, the books of Ezra and Nehemiah were combined), Chronicles[1]

These divisions are in keeping with Jesus' words, "These are the words which I spake unto you, while I was yet with you, that all things must be fulfilled, which were written in the law of Moses, and in the prophets, and in the psalms, concerning me" (Lk. 24:44). Sometimes the Old Testament is more briefly referred to as the Law and the Prophets (Mt. 5:17, RSV; 11:13; Acts 13:15). Even more briefly, the term *Law* seems to include the other divisions (Jn. 10:34; 12:34; 15:25; 1 Cor. 14:21).

C. Divisions in the New Testament

Biographical (four books): Matthew, Mark, Luke, John

Historical (1 book): Acts

Pedagogical (twenty-one books): Romans, 1 Corinthians, 2 Corinthians, Galatians, Ephesians, Philippians, Colossians, 1 Thessalonians, 2 Thessalonians, 1 Timothy, 2 Timothy, Titus, Philemon, Hebrews, James, 1 Peter, 2 Peter, 1 John, 2 John, 3 John, Jude

Prophetic (one book): Revelation.

Sometimes the following alternate divisions are suggested:

---

1 This order is suggested in Norman L. Geisler and William E. Nix, *From God to Us— How We Got Our Bible* (Chicago: Moody Press, 1974), 10. They state their source as *The Holy Scriptures According to the Masoretic Text,* and Rudolf Kittel and Paul Kahle, eds., *Biblia Hebraica* (Stuttgart: Wurttembergische Bibelanstalt Stuttgart, 1937).

1   The Gospels: Matthew, Mark, Luke, John
2. The Acts of the Apostles
3. The epistles of Paul (including Hebrews)
4. The General Epistles
5. The Book of Revelation.[2]

D. Chapters and verses

The Bible was not originally divided into chapters and verses as we know it today. For convenience of reference, these were added at comparatively recent dates. It used to be assumed that the chapter divisions were first introduced by Cardinal Hugo, who died in A.D. 1263. Later investigations have attributed them to Stephen Langton, Archbishop of Canterbury, who died in 1228. The New Testament was first published with verse divisions by Robert Stephens in 1551. The first Bible to be published entirely divided into verse was the Geneva Bible of 1560.

It is of considerable importance that the student realize that these divisions were not in the original texts and were not inspired. Most of the divisions are very helpful, but some have proven to be quite misleading, as there is the tendency to think that a new subject is being introduced when a chapter ends and a new one begins, when in reality many such divisions come right in the middle of the subject being dealt with. One must, many times, completely ignore the chapter division. Two simple examples of this are as follows: In Acts 22, Paul's address is cut off from the events that lead up to it, as recorded in the previous chapter. John 7:53 and 8:1, read together without the chapter break, present a significant contrast: "And every man went unto his own house. Jesus went unto the mount of Olives."

According to figures given by William Evans, the English Bible, King James Version: "contains 1,189 chapters; 31,173 verses; and 773,692 words. Of these, 929 chapters; 23,214 verses; and 592,439 words occur in the Old Testament; and 260 chapters; 7,959 verses; and 181,253 words in the New."[3]

III. THE WRITERS OF THE SCRIPTURES

The Bible is one Book, but it is also many books written by at least forty different authors, over a period of not less than fifteen hundred years, many of whom never saw each other. Yet its unity and continuity are so apparent, it is easy to think of it having just one author—and that none other than God Himself.

---

2 William Evans, *The Book of Books: What It Is; How to Study It* (Chicago: The Bible Institute Colportage Association, 1902), 95.

3 Ibid., 96–97.

Of the sixty-six different books in the Bible, the authors of fifty-five are well-identified by history and tradition. The eleven books whose authors are not known are Judges, Ruth, 1 and 2 Samuel, 1 and 2 Kings, 1 and 2 Chronicles, Esther, Job, and Hebrews. Some books, such as Genesis, Judges, 1 and 2 Kings, and 1 and 2 Chronicles, cover such long periods of history it is possible that they are collections of ancient records brought together and edited by some individual chosen by God toward the end of the historical period described in the book. For instance, Moses could be the compiler of the book of Genesis. If this is so, then the actual number of writers contributing to the Bible may be considerably more than forty. Psalms and Proverbs each have several authors. The superscriptions which appear at the head of many of the psalms suggest at least seven different writers. In addition to mentions of Solomon as the author of Proverbs, Agur is named in 30:1 and King Lemuel in 31:1.

All of the authors, possibly excepting Luke, were Jews and wrote in the context of the Jewish religion. Yet, the words they wrote have more universal appeal and interest to people of all nations than any words ever written.

It is most interesting to note the variety of occupational backgrounds which are represented by those authors who are known:

- Two of the writers were kings—David and Solomon.
- Two were priests—Jeremiah and Ezekiel.
- Luke was a physician.
- Two were fishermen—Peter and John.
- Two were shepherds—Moses and Amos.
- Paul was a Pharisee and a theologian.
- Daniel was a statesman.
- Matthew was a tax collector.
- Joshua was a soldier.
- Ezra was a scribe.
- Nehemiah was a butler.

The background and occupations of the others are largely unknown.

IV. THE CANON OF SCRIPTURES

The word *canon* comes from the Greek *kanon*, meaning "a measuring rod, rule," and signifies a rule, a standard. Hence, the canon of the Bible consists of those books considered worthy to be included in the Holy Scriptures. According to authors Selby and West:

Canonization was the result of a centuries-long development, whereby only those writings that proved useful for faith and worship were elevated to such a decisive role. The Canon, that is to say, was determined not so much by Rabbinic or Church decree as by the intrinsic merit of each separate book and its reception by the worshipping community for the inspiration or edification it offered.[4]

Another author expresses it this way: "The various books possessed and exercised divine authority long before men ever made pronouncements to that effect. Ecclesiastical councils did not give the books their divine authority, but merely recognized that they both had it and exercised it."[5]

A. The Canon of the Old Testament

Any consideration of the actual times when the canon of the Old Testament was closed leads to a variety of opinions among biblical scholars. The Old Testament says nothing on the subject, although it does give many suggestions regarding when God's laws began to be written, that they might be kept for the people. Exodus 17 tells of the victory of the children of Israel over Amalek as Moses' hands were held aloft before the Lord. Verse 14 reads, "And the LORD said unto Moses, Write this for a memorial in a book, and rehearse it in the ears of Joshua." Exodus 24:3–4 records the writing of God's words and judgments: "And Moses came and told the people all the words of the LORD, and all the judgments: and all the people answered with one voice, and said, All the words which the LORD hath said will we do. And Moses wrote all the words of the LORD." Deuteronomy 31 gives the account of Moses writing the Law, which was to be kept and read to the people of Israel every seven years:

And Moses wrote this law, and delivered it unto the priests of the sons of Levi...And Moses commanded them, saying, At the end of every seven years, in the solemnity of the year of release, in the feast of tabernacles, When all Israel is come to appear before the LORD thy God in the place which he shall choose, thou shalt read this law before all Israel in their hearing (vv. 9–11).

---

4 Donald J. Selby and James King West, *Introduction to the Bible* (New York: The Macmillan Company, 1971), 2.

5 N. H. Ridderbos, *The New Bible Dictionary*, 187; as quoted in Roland K. Harrison, *Introduction to the Old Testament* (Grand Rapids, MI: Wm. B. Eerdmans Publishing Company, 1969), 263.

This occasion could well mark the very earliest beginning of the Old Testament Canon, for we read: "And it came to pass, when Moses had made an end of writing the words of this law in a book, until they were finished, That Moses commanded the Levites...saying, Take this book of the Law, and put it in the side of the ark of the covenant of the LORD your God, that it may be there for a witness against thee" (Dt. 31:24–26). Joshua, Moses' successor, also wrote words "in the book of the law of God" (Jos. 24:26). Samuel recorded certain events of his day in a book. We read, "Then Samuel told the people the rights and duties of the kingship; and he wrote them in a book and laid it up before the LORD" (1 Sm. 10:25, RSV). Prophets in later times also engaged in writing books. God spoke to Jeremiah and said, "Take a scroll and write on it all the words which I have spoken to you against Israel and Judah and all the nations, from the day I spoke to you, from the days of Josiah until today" (Jer. 36:2, RSV). Later generations are found consulting the writings of their predecessors. Daniel searches in the books and finds that the prophet Jeremiah limited the duration in which Jerusalem was to be ravaged by the enemy to seventy years (Dn. 9:2). Later, when the people were assembled back in Jerusalem after the Babylonian captivity, it was the Law of Moses that was read and honored (Neh. 8:1–8). During the reign of Josiah in Judah, the book of the Law of the Lord, which had been lost, was found: "And Hilkiah the high priest said unto Shaphan the scribe, I have found the book of the law in the house of the LORD" (2 Kgs. 22:8). Josiah gathered the elders of Judah and Jerusalem together, "and he read in their ears all the words of the book of the covenant which was found in the house of the LORD" (2 Kgs. 23:2). Thus, we see the beginnings of what later became the Old Testament Scriptures.

After careful consideration of the many evidences available and following the Hebrew's threefold division of the Old Testament, George L. Robinson concludes that the books of the Law were recognized as canonical during the time of Ezra (444 B.C.), that the Prophets were recognized as such sometime later (around 200 B.C.), and that the Writings received authorization around 100 B.C. Robinson is not saying that there were three separate canons, but that "there were three separate classes of writings, which between 450 B.C. and 100 B.C. doubtless stood on different bases, and only gradually became authoritative."[6]

Other scholars hold to the belief that there were only two periods of canonization corresponding to "the law and the prophets" and that the Old Testament Canon was completed about 400 B.C.[7] Which of these positions is correct is difficult to say. What is important is that the Old Testament Canon was, no doubt, complete at the time

---

6 George L. Robinson, *International Standard Bible Encyclopedia* (Grand Rapids, MI: Wm. B. Eerdmans Publishing Company, 1943) I, 554–563.

7 Geisler and Nix, 85.

of Christ. Jesus referred to it as "the Scriptures," saying, "Search the scriptures; for in them ye think ye have eternal life" (Jn. 5:39). We read: "And beginning at Moses and all the prophets, he expounded unto them in all the scriptures the things concerning himself" (Lk. 24:27). In Luke 11:51 (RSV) Jesus makes an interesting statement in which He speaks of the time "from the blood of Abel to the blood of Zechariah, who perished between the altar and the sanctuary." Jesus was referring to the martyrs of the Old Testament. Abel was the first, as recorded in Genesis 4, and Zechariah was the last, recorded in 2 Chronicles 24:20–21. Furthermore, in the Hebrew Bible, 2 Chronicles is the last book, while Genesis is the first. Thus, Jesus not only put His stamp of approval upon the entire Old Testament, from Genesis to 2 Chronicles, but gave indication that these books were in existence and were approved at the time He was here on Earth.

As further evidence of the completeness of the Old Testament Canon at this time, we have the testimony of the celebrated Jewish historian Flavius Josephus. In his writings, *Against Apion*, he states:

> For we have not an innumerable multitude of books among us, disagreeing from and contradicting one another, (like the Greeks have) but only twenty-two books, which contain the records of all the past times; which we justly believe to be divine...and how firmly we have given credit to these books of our own nation is evident by what we do; for during so many ages as have already passed, no one has been so bold as either to add any thing to them, to take any thing from them or to make any change in them; but it is become natural to all Jews immediately, and from their very birth, to esteem these books to contain Divine doctrines, and to persist in them, and, if occasion be, willingly to die for them.[8]

In our Christian Bibles, there are thirty-nine books in the Old Testament, while the Jewish Old Testament counts only twenty-four. This is explained by the fact that the twelve books of the Minor Prophets (Hosea through Malachi) are counted as only one book. Also, the following are only one book each: 1 and 2 Samuel, 1 and 2 Kings, 1 and 2 Chronicles, and Ezra and Nehemiah. Thus, though there is no difference in the wording, the Hebrew Old Testament lists nine fewer titles. Josephus counted twenty-two because he joined Ruth to Judges and Lamentations to Jeremiah.

---

8 *The Life and Works of Flavius Josephus,* trans. William Whiston (Chicago: The John C. Winston Company, 1936) 861–862.

B. The Apocrypha

The word *Apocrypha*, as usually understood, means "apocryphal books" and refers to fourteen books which have been added to the Old Testament and are held to be part of the sacred Canon, particularly by the Roman Catholic Church. Protestants generally do not include these in the Bible. The word literally has come to mean "hidden" or "concealed." The Septuagint (LXX), the translation of the Old Testament into Greek made between 280 B.C. and 180 B.C., contained the apocryphal books. Jerome included them in his Latin translation of the Old Testament, called the Vulgate. These books are not a part of the Hebrew Bible. The Reformers were largely responsible for eliminating the Apocrypha from the Bible, because they contain passages which are inconsistent with Protestant doctrine (e.g. the doctrines of prayer for the dead and intercession to the saints). The following are the fourteen books which are in the Apocrypha, sometimes scattered throughout the Old Testament and sometimes printed at the end of the Old Testament: 1 and 2 Esdras; Tobit; Judith; The Rest of Esther; The Wisdom of Solomon; Ecclesiasticus; Baruch, with the Epistle of Jeremiah; The Song of the Three Holy Children; The History of Susanna; Bel and the Dragon; The Prayer of Manasses; and 1 and 2 Maccabees. Although parts of almost all the books of the Old Testament Canon are either quoted or directly referred to in the New Testament, there is no quotation or reference to any of the apocryphal books.

C. The Canon of the New Testament

It is much easier to trace the canonization of the twenty-seven books of the New Testament than that of the Old Testament. There is much more evidence available. The books of the New Testament were written during the last half of the first century A.D. The newly formed Christian church had the Old Testament Scriptures as the basis for their faith, but in addition to this, great importance was placed on the words of Jesus and the teachings of the apostles. Thus, it was not long until the Gospels were being placed alongside of the Old Testament. The authority of the apostles is fully attested. John declares, "That which we have seen and heard declare we unto you" (1 Jn. 1:3); Peter says they "were eyewitnesses of his majesty" (2 Pt. 1:16); and of the early believers we read, "And they continued stedfastly in the apostles' doctrine and fellowship" (Acts 2:42).

Because the epistles of Paul were written to meet the specific need of a local Church or individual, they were cherished for their spiritual value and were read in the Churches. On several occasions, Paul gave definite instructions that his letters should be read and circulated. To the Thessalonian Church he wrote, "I charge you by the Lord that this epistle be read unto all the holy brethren" (1 Thes. 5:27). To the Church at Colosse he admonished, "And when this epistle is read among you, cause that it be read also in the Church of the Laodiceans; and that ye likewise read the epistle from Laodicea" (Col. 4:16). In order that this might be done, it is conceivable that a copy of the Colossian and Laodicean letters would have to be made. As this practice spread, it is easy to see that before too many years, compilations of Paul's letters would be available.

The New Testament suggests a rather widespread distribution of these writings. John was instructed: "What thou seest, write in a book, and send it unto the seven churches which are in Asia" (Rv. 1:11). James's letter is addressed "to the twelve tribes which are scattered abroad" (Jas. 1:1). Peter's first epistle was written "to the strangers scattered throughout Pontus, Galatia, Cappadocia, Asia, and Bithynia" (1 Pt. 1:1). There is a strong suggestion of an early compilation of a canon of the New Testament to be recognized with the Old Testament Scripture:

> And account that the long-suffering of our Lord is salvation; even as our be-loved brother Paul also according to the wisdom given unto him hath writ-ten unto you; As also in all his epistles, speaking in them of these things; in which are some things hard to be understood, which they that are un-learned and unstable wrest, as they do also the other scriptures, unto their own destruction.
>
> —2 PETER 3:15–16

During the early years of the second century, the effect of the church fathers began to be felt. These were gifted students, teachers, and church leaders. In their letters to the early churches, they quoted profusely from the books which were to become the New Testament Canon. These letters bear distinct witness to the value of the book from which they quoted, placing them above their own words. Though it is strange to say, the Gnostic Marcion (A.D. 140), a noted heretic, was used to inspire the recognition of some of the New Testament books, particularly the epistles of Paul. Marcion complied his own canon, which included Luke's gospel and ten of the Pauline epistles. He rejected the Pastoral Epistles, Hebrews, Mark, John, Acts, the General Epistles, and Revelation. His actions brought forth much criticism and a closer study of the books which he rejected. By the end of the second century, all but seven of the twenty-seven books of the New Testament were recognized as canonical. The seven books which were not fully recognized at that time were: Hebrews, 2 and 3 John, 2 Peter, Jude, James, and Revelation.

Additional impetus toward the formation of a definite canon of the New Testament came from the persecutions ordered by Emperor Diocletian (302–305), at which time he ordered that the Scriptures should be burned with fire. Thus, it became necessary that a determination be made as to which books were Scripture. Christians needed to decide which books were worth suffering and dying for. The question of the canon soon gained an earnest, practical significance. Within twenty-five years of the

Dioclesian persecutions, Constantine, the new emperor, had embraced Christianity and ordered Eusebius, bishop of Caesarea and church historian, to prepare and distribute fifty copies of the New Testament. Thus, it was necessary to decide which books should be included.

It is not difficult to understand that at the time the canon was being considered, there were many books in existence which would lay claim to consideration. These writings were generally divided into what has been called the Pseudepigrapha and the Apocrypha. In the former are included a group of spurious and heretical books which are considered false writings. They were virtually never recognized by any council, nor quoted by the Church fathers. Many heretical doctrines, such as those held by the Gnostics, who denied the incarnation of Christ; the Docetics, who denied the reality of Christ's humanity; and the Monophysites, who rejected the dual nature of Christ, are found in these books. Over 280 of these have been grouped under the headings: Gospels, Acts, Epistles, Apocalypses, and Others. Geisler and Nix state: "Whatever fragments of truth they preserve are obscured both by their religious fancy and heretical tendencies. The books are not only uncanonical but are not of much value for religious or devotional purposes. Their main value is historical, revealing the beliefs of their composers."[9]

The books listed as the New Testament Apocrypha were those which were held in high esteem by at least one of the fathers. Though they contain much helpful information concerning the history of the early church, they have never been accepted into the canon of the New Testament. Some of the most popular of these are: The Epistle of Pseudo-Barnabas (70–79), The Epistle to the Corinthians (96), Shepherd of Hermas (115–140), The Didache Teaching of the Twelve (100–120), Epistle to the Laodiceans (4th century?), The Epistle of Polycarp to the Philippians (108), and The Seven Epistles of Ignatius (110).

Athanasius (born about A.D. 298), in one of his pastoral epistles, lists all twenty-seven books of the New Testament as Scripture. At the third council of Carthage (A.D. 397), the Western Christian churches settled on the final form of the New Testament Canon. Thus, by the end of the fourth century all twenty-seven books were received. So, Geisler and Nix conclude: "Once discussions resulted in the recognition of the twenty-seven canonical books of the New Testament canon there have been no moves within Christendom to add to it or take away from it."[10]

D. Tests used to determine canonicity

The following principles were used to determine a book's place in the canon:

---

9 Geisler and Nix, 116–117.
10 Ibid., 101.

1. *Apostolicity.* Was the book written by an apostle or one who was closely associated with the apostles? This question was especially important in relation to Mark, Luke, Acts, and Hebrews inasmuch as Mark and Luke were not among the original Twelve and the authorship of Hebrews was not known.

2. *Spiritual content.* Was the book being read in the churches and did its contents prove a means of spiritual edification? This was a most practical test.

3. *Doctrinal soundness.* Were the contents of the book doctrinally sound? Any book containing heresy, or that which was contrary to the already accepted canonical books, was rejected.

4. *Usage.* Was the book universally recognized in the churches, and was it widely quoted by the church fathers?

5. *Divine inspiration.* Did it give true evidence of divine inspiration? "This was the ultimate test; everything finally had to give way to it."[11]

V. THE INERRANCY OF THE SCRIPTURES

A. Definition of *inerrancy*

The inerrancy of the Scripture means that in its original autographs the Bible contains no mistakes. In the original languages in which it was written, it is absolutely infallible—without error whatsoever. This has been the position of all the confessions of the great evangelical churches down through the years.

In contrast to this, atheists, agnostics, and liberal theologians have declared the Bible to be full of errors. Indeed, there are those who teach a "limited inerrancy," claiming the Bible to be inerrant in matters of faith and practice, but not necessarily so in scientific and historical matters. The problem with this position is, who is going to decide what is true and what is not? If one cannot have a positive faith in the infallibility of this Book, how can he speak with final authority when it comes to matters of eternity? Why is this question so vitally important? Why cannot one come to the Bible as he does any other book? When he reads any other book, a man will take what he believes and leave that with which he is not in accord. Why cannot he do the same, as many are advocating, with the Bible?

B. The testimony to inerrancy

1. *The Bible claims to be the Word of God* The doctrine of inerrancy comes from the Scriptures themselves. It claims to be inspired by God. "All scripture is given by inspiration of God" (2 Tm. 3:16). "For the prophecy came not in old time by the will

---

11 Henry Clarence Thiessen, *Introduction to the New Testament* (Grand Rapids, MI: Wm. B. Eerdmans Publishing Company, 1948), 4th edition, 10.

of man: but holy men of God spake as they were moved by the Holy Ghost" (2 Pt. 1:21).

a) Old Testament writers. The writers of the Old Testament are most explicit in claiming they were speaking the Word of God. They claim 3,808 times to be transmitting His very words. Moses declared, "Ye shall not add unto the word which I command you, neither shall ye diminish ought from it" (Dt. 4:2). The psalmist cried, "The law of the LORD is perfect...The testimony of the LORD is sure" (Ps. 19:7, NASB). Samuel declared, "The spirit of the LORD spake by me, and his word was in my tongue" (2 Sm. 23:2). Isaiah wrote, "Hear, O heavens, and give ear, O earth, for the LORD hath spoken" (Is. 1:2). Jeremiah quotes the words of the Lord to him: "Whatsoever I command thee thou shalt speak...Behold I have put my words in thy mouth" (Jer. 1:7, 9). Ezekiel tells of his commission: "Thou shalt speak my words unto them" (Ez. 2:7), and "Speak with my words unto them" (Ez. 3:4). Each and all of these declared that they were speaking God's words. Thus the Old Testament testifies concerning itself.

b) New Testament writers. The New Testament writers also bear witness to the fact that the Old Testament was God speaking.

(1) In the Gospels. "All this was done, that it might be fulfilled which was spoken of the Lord by the prophet" (Mt. 1:22). "As he spake by the mouth of his holy prophets, which have been since the world began" (Lk. 1:70). "For David himself said by the Holy Ghost" (Mk. 12:36).

(2) In the Epistles. The apostles also gave their witness to the perfections of the Old Testament scriptures. Paul said of the Law that it was holy, and "the commandment, holy, righteous and good" (Rom. 7:12, NIV). The writer of Hebrews regarded the Word of God as living and effectual, going so far as to judge even our feelings and innermost thoughts (Heb. 4:12). James describes the Word as "the perfect law of liberty" (Jas. 1:25). He regarded its complete authority when he issued the warning: "Ye think the scripture saith in vain?" (Jas. 4:5). John brings the written revelation to a close with the words:

> For I testify unto every man that heareth the words of the prophecy of this book, If any man shall add unto these things, God shall add unto him the plagues that are written in this book: And if any man shall take away from the words of the book of this prophecy, God shall take away his part out of the book of life, and out of the holy city, and from the things which are written in this book.
>
> —REVELATION 22:18–19

Thus, toward the beginning (Dt. 4:2; 12:32), in the middle (Prv. 30:6), and at the end of the Scriptures (Rv. 22:18–19), God warns against tampering with His Word by adding to or taking from its message.

c) Jesus Christ. Jesus Himself bore witness to the Scripture. Christ specifically confirmed the whole of the Old Testament. He did not find one error or inconsistency in it. He continually based His arguments and exhortations on it. He declared, "One jot or one tittle shall in no wise pass from the law, till all be fulfilled" (Mt. 5:18). Discussing just one word with the Jews, He said, "The scripture cannot be broken" (Jn. 10:35). In Luke 24:44 Jesus said, "These are the words which I spake unto you, while I was yet with you, that all things must be fulfilled, which were written in the law of Moses, and in the prophets, and in the psalms concerning me." These three sections comprise all of the Old Testament.

Jesus referred to many Old Testament persons and events, and thus bore testimony to the authenticity and authority of the Old Testament. It is interesting to note, from the following list, that Jesus put His stamp of approval on some of the events and miracles of the Old Testament which have always been under greatest question by the critics. He approved the account of the following:

- Creation and marriage—Matthew 19:5
- The Deluge and Noah's ark—Luke 17:26–27
- The destruction of Sodom and Gomorrah—Luke 17:28–29
- The destruction of Tyre and Sidon—Matthew 11:21–22
- Circumcision—John 7:22
- The Passover—Matthew 26:2
- The Law—John 7:19
- The Commandments—Matthew 19:7–9
- The Jewish law of divorce—Matthew 19:7–9
- The fact of the burning bush—Mark 12:26
- Jonah and the great fish—Matthew 12:40
- The repentance of Ninevah—Matthew 12:41
- The glory of Solomon—Matthew 6:29
- The wisdom of Solomon—Matthew 12:42
- The Feast of Tabernacles—John 7
- David eating the shewbread—Matthew 12:3
- The priests profaning the Sabbath—Matthew 12:5
- The heavens shut up in Elijah's day—Luke 4:25
- The story of Naaman the leper—Luke 4:27
- The record of the brazen serpent—John 3:14–15
- The murder of Abel and Zacharias—Matthew 23:35
- The mission of Messiah—Luke 4:16–21

- The mission of John the Baptist—Matthew 17:10–13
- The mission of Elias—Matthew 17:10–13
- Daniel and his great prophecy—Matthew 24:15

2. *The Bible is a unique revelation of truth.* Man asks: Who am I? From where did I come? Where am I going? What about immortality, heaven, hell, judgment, eternity? What does man know—what *can* he know—apart from the Bible? Many in contemporary society are virtually making their own god. What good is a god that a man can make himself? If he can make him, then man is bigger than his god, and so, does not need him. No one, or no nation, has ever revealed a god such as the God of the Holy Scriptures. Chafer says the Bible is infinite because it discloses truth concerning the infinite God, infinite holiness, infinite sin, and infinite redemption. It seems to prove itself infinite, for "no human mind has fully comprehended its message or measured its values."[12] The Christian is not embarrassed in the least that he cannot explain everything about God. God would not be God if this were possible. One never worships what he can understand. It is only when he gets beyond the realm of his own comprehension that he bows his head and lifts his hands in worship.

Who is Jesus? What is He like? Can He do anything for the human soul? Does He have anything vital to say to mankind? Does, indeed, the welfare of man's eternal soul depend upon Him? Some would advocate that we should not worry about the infallibility of the Bible—just follow Jesus! Some liberal teachers have said, "Christ alone is the Word of God! We believe without reservation in the Word of God, but it is Jesus alone who is the Word." This sounds very pious, but what does man know about Jesus apart from what is revealed in the Bible? Our total source of information about Him is in this book. If one cannot depend upon the Word for information about other things, then how can he be sure it is correct in what it tells us about Jesus?

3. *The Bible is an unchanging revelation.* Much of the uncertainty and unbelief about the Bible has come from so-called scientists. Because the inerrancy of the Bible is on the level of observable fact, it is most open to attacks from skeptical and unbelieving scholars. Science has assumed an aura of authority and almost infallibility. Many have made a virtual god out of it. The word *science* simply means "knowledge," and is to be neither worshiped nor feared. The significant thing about science is that it is constantly having to change its conclusions as fresh facts come to life. Scientific textbooks only a few years old are virtually out of date today, while the Bible has not had to be altered in the least degree over the thousands of years since it was written. There is no reason to doubt a book that has withstood the centuries—and every attack leveled against it—

___

12 Lewis Sperry Chafer, *Systematic Theology* (Dallas, TX: Dallas Seminary Press, 1947) I, 22.

when scientific theory must be revised every few years. The Bible is not a textbook of science, but it has never been proven wrong in any scientific fact. The Genesis account of Creation still stands.

4. *The Bible is right morally and spiritually.* Most important of all, the Bible is right morally and spiritually. It is not in the scientific realm that the Bible demonstrates its greatest accuracy, but in the moral and spiritual realm. Myer Pearlman concludes his section on bibliology with the words: "Intellectual defenses of the Bible have their place; but after all, the best argument is the practical one. The Bible has worked. It has influenced civilizations, transformed lives, brought light, inspiration and comfort to millions. And its work continues."[13] And Scripture declares, "For this cause also thank we God without ceasing, because, when ye received the word of God which ye heard of us, ye received it not as the word of men, but as it is in truth, the word of God, which effectually worketh also in you that believe" (1 Thes. 2:13).

VI. THE INSPIRATION OF THE SCRIPTURES

The Bible is an inerrant, infallible book, a book of words, phrases, and sentences, which as it was originally written contains no errors whatsoever. This Book was written by man—fallen, weak, sinful man, with all the potential of misunderstanding, misinterpretation, lack of memory, and even the possibility of malicious falsehood. Yet, it is claimed that the Book man wrote contains no evidence whatever of all these natural weaknesses. In fact, it is claimed that not only was all that he wrote perfectly right—nothing must be removed from the record—but he left nothing out that should have been written; nothing must be added to it. It is not easy to believe that such a thing could be possible for one man of a fallen race, but this was accomplished through more than forty different men who lived over a span of more than fifteen hundred years. Many of them never saw nor conversed with each other, yet their writings in no way disagree. Only a miracle, and that, a long-extended miracle, could bring this to pass. How could such a thing be possible? Through the mystery and miracle of divine inspiration!

A. Definition of *inspiration*

The Bible reveals the source of its magnificence: "All Scripture is God-breathed" (2 Tm. 3:16, NIV). This does not mean that God breathed into the writers, but that the Word was produced by the creative breath of God.

---

13 Myer Pearlman, *Knowing the Doctrines of the Bible* (Springfield, MO: The Gospel Publishing House, 1939), 29.

The Greek word in this passage *theopneustos* very distinctly does not mean "inspired of God." ... [it has] ... nothing to say of inspiring or inspiration: it speaks only of "spiring" or "spiration." What it says of Scripture is, not that it is "breathed into by God" or is the product of the Divine "inbreathing" into its human authors, but that it is breathed out by God, "God-breathed," the product of the creative breath of God. In a word, what is declared by this fundamental passage is simply that the Scriptures are a Divine product, without any indication of how God has operated in producing them. No term could have been chosen, however, which would have more emphatically asserted the Divine production of Scripture than that which has been employed. The "breath of God" is in Scripture just the symbol of His almighty power, the bearer of His creative word.[14]

Just as God breathed into Adam the breath of life, so He breathed into the body of Scripture the breath of His life. We also read, in 2 Peter 1:21, "Holy men of God spake as they were moved by the Holy Ghost." This verse literally reads, "For the prophecy was not borne [or brought] by the will of man at any time, but men spoke from God, being borne [or brought] by the Holy Spirit." Benjamin Warfield says:

The term here used is a very specific one. It is not to be confounded with guiding, or directing, or controlling, or even leading in the full sense of that word. It goes beyond all such terms, in assigning the effect produced specifically to the active agent. What is "borne" is taken up by the "bearer," and conveyed by the "bearer's" power, not its own, to the "bearer's" goal, not its own. The men who spoke from God are here declared, therefore, to have been taken up by the Holy Spirit and brought by His power to the goal of His choosing. The things which they spoke under this operation of the Spirit were, therefore, His things, not theirs.[15]

B. Revelation, inspiration, and illumination distinguished

It is important to distinguish between revelation, inspiration, and illumination. Revelation is that act of God by which He directly communicates truth not known before to the human mind—truth which could not have been known in any other manner. Inspiration has to do with the communication of the truth. Evans says: "Revelation discovers new truth, while Inspiration superintends the communication of that truth."[16]

---

14 Benjamin Warfield, *The Inspiration and Authority of the Bible* (Philadelphia, PA: The Presbyterian Reformed Publishing Company, 1948), 132–33.

15 Ibid., 137.

16 Evans, 196.

Not all that is in the Bible was directly revealed to men. There is much history recorded there, as well as many personal observations. What we are assured of is that the record is true. The Holy Spirit directed and influenced the writers so that, by inspiration, they were kept from every error of fact and doctrine. The Bible records the words and acts of God, men, and the devil. It is very important to take careful note of who is speaking. Dr. Wm. Evans has expressed it well:

> Though all Scripture is inspired, it does not stamp with divine authority every sentence which it reports as uttered by the men of whom it speaks, nor does it mark with divine approval every action which it relates as performed by those with whose biographies it deals. In the book of Job, for example, Inspiration gives with equal accuracy the language of Jehovah, the words of Satan, and the speeches of Job and his three friends; but it does not therefore place them all on the same level of authority. Each speaker is responsible for his own utterances. Neither Satan, Job nor his three friends spoke by inspiration of God. They gave utterances to their own opinions; and all that Inspiration vouches for is that no one of them is misrepresented, but that each one spoke the sentiments that are attributed to him in Scripture.[17]

Some confuse inspiration with illumination. Illumination refers to the influence of the Holy Spirit, common to all Christians, which helps them grasp the things of God. "But the natural man receiveth not the things of the Spirit of God: for they are foolishness unto him: neither can he know them, because they are spiritually discerned" (1 Cor. 2:14). This illumination of spiritual things is promised to all believers and can be experienced by them. "In that hour Jesus rejoiced in spirit, and said, I thank thee, O Father, Lord of heaven and earth, that thou hast hid these things from the wise and prudent, and hast revealed them unto babes: even so, Father; for so it seemed good in thy sight" (Lk. 10:21). Peter speaks of an interesting example where prophets were given inspiration to record great truths, but were not given illumination to understand the exact meaning of what they prophesied.

> Of which salvation the prophets have inquired and searched diligently, who prophesied of the grace that should come unto you: Searching what, or what manner of time the Spirit of Christ which was in them did signify...Unto whom it was revealed, that not unto themselves, but unto us they did minister the things, which are now reported unto you.
>
> —1 PETER 1:10–12

---

17 Evans, 196.

Some try to explain the inspiration of the Scriptures as the result of this experience of illumination. They assert that within man there is this spark of divine light which only needed to be fanned, as it were, to enable men of old to write the Bible. Myer Pearlman points out two specific differences between illumination and inspiration:

> (1) As to duration, illumination is, or can be, permanent. "The path of the just is as the shining light, that shineth more and more unto the perfect day" (Prv. 4:18). The anointing that the believer has received of the Holy One abides in him, says John. "But the anointing which ye have received of him abideth in you, and ye need not that any man teach you: but as it hath taught you, ye shall abide in him" (1 John 2:27). On the other hand Inspiration was intermittent; the prophet could not prophesy at will, but was subject to the will of the Spirit. "For the prophecy came not in old time by the will of man," declares Peter (2 Peter 1:21), "but holy men of God spake as they were moved by the Holy Ghost." The suddenness of prophetic inspiration is implied by the common expression, "The word of the Lord came to such an one." A clear distinction is drawn between the true prophets, who speak only as the word of God comes to them, and the false prophets who speak a message of their own devising. (Jer. 14:14; 23:11, 16; Ez. 13:2, 3). (2) Illumination admits of degrees, Inspiration admits of none. People vary as to the degree of their illumination, some possessing a greater degree of insight than others. But in the case of Inspiration, in the Bible sense, a person is either inspired or he is not.[18]

C. The meaning of inspiration

What does this word *inspiration* really mean as it is applied to the Bible? Unfortunately, not all churchmen are agreed. Therefore, we have various theories of inspiration:

1. *Liberal views of inspiration.* The liberal theologian's view is expressed particularly in the statement, The Bible contains the Word of God. This suggests that it also contains a varied admixture of the words of men. Their position may be stated as follows: From place to place within the Book are to be found revelations which God at times gave to pious men, much as He illumines men's minds today with insights into divine truth. The Bible is a sort of religious scrapbook in which are recorded stories, legends, genealogies, and love poems, classified, arranged, and rearranged without any regard to chronological or literary perfection. The dangerous part of this view is that it places into the hands of finite, feeble, and fallible man the power to

---

18 Pearlman, 22.

determine what and where God is speaking. Thus, man is given power over infinite truth rather than taking a place under it.

2. *Neo-orthodox views of inspiration.* The various neo-orthodox views of inspiration may be summarized by the statement that the Bible becomes the Word of God. Let us consider two of these neo-orthodox views:

a) The existential view popularized by Barth. This teaches that there are many human errors and imperfections in the Bible—even in the autographs. But the Bible becomes the Word of God when He chooses to use this imperfect channel to confront man with His perfect Word. This is accomplished by a personal encounter by God with man in an act of revelation. In this existential experience—crisis encounter—the meaningless blobs on the page leap from the Bible to speak to man concretely and meaningfully. At this "moment of meaning," the Bible becomes the Word of God to the believer.

b) The demythologizing view of Bultmann and Niebuhr. The Bible must be stripped of religious myth in order to get at the real meaning of God's self-giving love in Christ. One must look through and beyond the historical record, with all its myth and error, to the super-historical. Events, such as the Fall of man, the Crucifixion, and Resurrection, are not necessarily the objects of verifiable and factual history. Hence, the Bible becomes a revelation when, by the proper (demythological) interpretation, one is confronted with absolute love as set forth in the "myth" of God's selfless love in Christ.

How, we ask, can the Gospel writer be wrong in an area we can check him—history—and right in the area of doctrine, where no checks are possible? These men refuse to believe that God performed the miracle of giving us, by inspiration, an infallible Bible, but are ready to believe that God daily performs the greater miracle of enabling men to find and see the infallible words of God in the fallible writing of men. It is very difficult to see why God would make use of error to teach us truth.

Again, how can a simple believer have faith in a book when he is told only parts of it are true? He is told to sort it out and keep what is good, but how will he go about classifying the pages of the Bible as inspired, partially inspired, or not inspired? By what authority can he say this or that is not the mind of God? To attempt to decide what is not of God is to put oneself above the Scriptures and to lose the divine message entirely. As has been suggested before, in these views there is a confusion between revelation and illumination. The Bible is not merely God's Word when man hears and understands it. It is God speaking, whether man is listening or not. The Bible declares itself to be the Word of God. Any other position is wholly unbiblical.

There are some claiming to be evangelicals today who teach that there are many historical and scientific errors in the Bible. Yet, they quickly assure us that in matters pertaining to the plan of salvation, it is completely inerrant. How can one be so certain that the Bible is correct in soteriological matters when it is in error in historical and

scientific facts? It sounds very much as if it is men, not God, who are telling us what
to believe. If the Bible is not completely inerrant, that is to say, fully infallible, then
there is no final authority to its message.

While the Liberal contends the Bible merely *contains* the Word of God, and the
Neo-orthodox asserts the Bible *becomes* the Word of God in an existential "moment
of meaning," the Orthodox or Conservative position is that the Bible *is* the Word
of God.

3. *The conservative views.* The Bible is the Word of God. Yet, within the conservative school there is a divergence of opinion regarding what is involved in inspiration.
Thus there are the following conservative theories of inspiration:

a) The verbal dictation theory. This theory states that every word, even the punctuation, is dictated by God, much as a business executive would dictate a letter to
his secretary. This is often called "mechanical inspiration" or "verbal dictation."
Fundamentalists are often accused of subscribing to this method of inspiration, but
only a small percentage of them actually do. The great weakness of this theory is that
it eliminates any possibility of a personal style in the writings of the divinely chosen
author—a phenomenon which is clearly observable.

b) The inspired concept theory. In an endeavor to compensate for the dangers of
the verbal dictation theory, some conservatives have adopted the idea that God gave
the thoughts to the men chosen, and left them to record these thoughts in their own
words. Thus, only the thoughts, not the words, are inspired. This has been called
"dynamic inspiration." This explains the Bible's humanity, but weakens its divinity.
The mechanical theory deifies the human aspect of the Bible, while the dynamic
theory humanizes the divinity.

c) The verbal, plenary inspiration view. This view holds that all the words written
are God-breathed (2 Tm. 3:16). *Verbal* signifies the words, and *plenary* means "full,"
or "complete," as opposed to partial. Thus it is held that the words themselves, and all
of them, are inspired. God gave full expression to His thoughts in the words of the
biblical record. He guided the very choice of the words used within the personality
and culture-complex of the writers so that, in some inscrutable manner, the Bible is
the Word of God, while being the words of men.

Charles Hodge has expressed the meaning of verbal inspiration well:

> It is meant that the Divine influence, of whatever kind it may have been,
> which accompanied the sacred writers in what they wrote, extends to the
> expression of their thoughts in language, as well as the thoughts themselves,
> the effect being, that in the original autograph copies, the language express-

es the thought God intended to convey with infallible accuracy, so that the words, as well as the thoughts, are God's revelation to us.[19]

Inspiration, then, is the process whereby Spirit-moved men (2 Pt. 1:21), produced Spirit-breathed writings (2 Tm. 3:16). L. Gaussen gives us an excellent definition of inspiration in the following: "That inexplicable power which the divine Spirit put forth of old on the authors of the Holy Scripture, in order to their guidance even in the employment of the words they used, and to preserve them alike from all error and from all omission."[20]

It is recognized that here we are in an area of mystery. Just how infallible inspiration was brought about is something finite minds cannot comprehend. That there is a divine side to the process cannot be denied. But that there is a human aspect is equally clear. God used men. We recognize both elements, but we cannot reconcile them. Perhaps the best illustration is the incarnation of Jesus Christ. Christ has both a divine and human nature. The Scripture also has a heavenly and earthly aspect. In both Christ and the Scripture, the human side is perfect, as is the divine. It is wrong to try to explain away the divine nature of Christ in order to understand His human nature, as the Arians did. It is equally wrong to sacrifice His true human nature in order to explain that He is divine, as the Docetics did. So, it is wrong to deny that the words of Scripture are both human and divine in their nature.

The mistake is to try to explain the inexplicable and to fathom the unfathomable. The means, or process, of inspiration is a mystery of the providence of God, but the result of this process is a verbal (through words), plenary (extending to all the parts equally), inerrant (errorless), and authoritative record.

VII. THE SYMBOLS OF THE SCRIPTURES

Many times the Bible uses symbolic language in order to teach. Often spiritual truth can be conveyed more realistically by the employment of symbols, which bring a picture to the human mind. Thus, there are a number of symbols used throughout the Scripture for this purpose. We list those which are most apparent.

A. Mirror

"For if anyone is a hearer of the word and not a doer, he is like a man who looks at his natural face in a mirror" (Jas. 1:23–25, NASB). This illustrates the revealing power of the Word.

---

19 Charles Hodge, source unknown.

20 L. Gaussen, *Theopneustia* (Chicago: The Bible Institute Colportage Association, n.d.), as quoted by Thiessen, 107.

B. Critic

"For the word of God...is a discerner of the thoughts and intents of the heart" (Heb. 4:12). The Greek of Hebrews 4:12 reads, "The Word of God is...a critic of the thoughts and intents of the heart."[21]

C. Seed

"Being born again, not of corruptible seed, but of incorruptible, by the word of God, which liveth and abideth forever" (1 Pt. 1:23). (See also: Lk. 8:5–15, note especially v. 11, "The seed is the word of God"; Is. 55:10–11; Jas. 1:18.) This symbol suggests the generative power of the Word. It is a life-giving Word.

D. Laver and water

"That he might sanctify and cleanse it with the washing of water by the word" (Eph. 5:26). "Unto him that loved us, and washed us from ours sins in his own blood" (Rv. 1:5). (Also: Ps. 119:9; Jn. 15:3.) The laver stood between the worshiper and the tabernacle, providing a means of cleansing. The same Word that reveals one's defilement also provides a means of cleansing.

E. Lamp and light

"Thy word is a lamp unto my feet, and a light unto my path" (Ps. 119:105). (See also v. 130.) "For the commandment is a lamp; and the law is light" (Prv. 6:23). These symbols speak of the illuminating, guiding influence of the Word in a darkened world. The Word is that "more sure word of prophecy; whereunto ye do well that ye take heed, as unto a light that shineth in a dark place" (2 Pt. 1:19).

F. Fire

"Is not my word like as a fire? saith the LORD" (Jer. 23:29); "Then I said, I will not make mention of him, nor speak any more in his name. But his word was in mine heart as a burning fire shut up in my bones, and I was weary with forbearing, and I could not stay" (Jer. 20:9). As the word *fire* is used here, it seems to suggest a consuming impulse and energy. "My heart was not within me, while I was musing the fire burned: then spake I with my tongue" (Ps. 39:3).

G. Hammer

"Is not my word...like a hammer that breaketh the rock in pieces?" (Jer. 23:29). This figure suggests the power of the Word, constantly applied, that will eventually break the heart that is as hard as a rock.

---

21 Sidney Collett, *All About the Bible* (New York: Fleming H. Revell Company, 1934), 64.

H. Sword

"And take…the sword of the Spirit, which is the word of God" (Eph. 6:17). "For the word of God is quick, and powerful, and sharper than any twoedged sword" (Heb. 4:12). This is the believer's one offensive weapon in his contest with the "principalities" and "powers" and "rulers of the darkness of this world…[and] spiritual wickedness in high places" (Eph. 6:12).

I. Food

"I have esteemed the words of his mouth more than my necessary food" (Jb. 23:12).

1. *Milk.* "As newborn babes, desire the sincere milk of the word, that ye may grow thereby" (1 Pt. 2:2). (See 1 Cor. 3:1–2.)

2. *Bread.* "man shall not live by bread alone, but by every word that proceedeth out of the mouth of God" (Mt. 4:4).

3. *Meat.* "For when for the time ye ought to be teachers, ye have need that one teach you again which be the first principles of the oracles of God; and are become such as have need of milk, and not of strong meat. For every one that useth milk is unskillful in the word of righteousness: for he is a babe. But strong meat belongeth to them that are of full age, even those who by reason of use have their senses exercised to discern both good and evil" (Heb. 5:12–14).

4. *Honey.* "How sweet are thy words unto my taste! yea, sweeter than honey to my mouth!" (Ps. 119:103).

VIII. THE HOLY SPIRIT AND THE SCRIPTURES

Inspiration accounts for inerrancy, and inerrancy proves inspiration. This miracle of infallible inspiration is said to be the ministry of the Holy Spirit. This might well be the very greatest ministry in which the Spirit is engaged. All Spirit-filled believers have known, to some degree, the miracle of divine inspiration by the Holy Spirit, but never to the extent experienced by the writers of Scripture.

The Pentecostal movement has been accused of being an experience-centered movement, and indeed it is! But it is also a Bible-centered movement. It is beautiful to see how the Holy Spirit and the written Word are always in perfect agreement. This must be so, because the Word is the result of the inspiration of the Spirit. The following list of references where the Holy Spirit and the Word are mentioned together illustrates the importance of recognizing the ministry of both the Spirit and the Word, and demonstrate the harmony between the Word and the Spirit:

- 2 Samuel 23:2—"The Spirit of the LORD spake by me, and His word was in my tongue."

- Proverbs 1:23—"I will pour out my spirit unto you, I will make known my words unto you."
- Isaiah 40:7–8—"The grass withereth, the flower fadeth: because the spirit of the LORD bloweth upon it...The grass withereth, the flower fadeth: but the word of our God shall stand for ever."
- Isaiah 59:21—"My spirit that is upon thee, and my words which I have put in thy mouth, shall not depart out of thy mouth."
- Zechariah 4:6—"This is the word of the Lord...Not by might, nor by power, but by my spirit, saith the LORD."
- Matthew 22:29—"Ye do err, not knowing the scriptures, nor the power of God."
- Mark 16:20—"Confirming the word with signs following."
- Luke 12:12—"The Holy Ghost shall teach you in the same hour what ye ought to say."
- John 3:34—"He speaketh the words of God: for God giveth not the Spirit by measure unto Him."
- John 6:63—"It is the spirit that quickeneth; the flesh profiteth nothing: the words that I speak...they are spirit, and they are life."
- John 14:26—"The Holy Ghost...shall...bring all things to your remembrance, whatsoever I have said unto you."
- Acts 1:16—"Scripture must needs have been fulfilled, which the Holy Ghost by the mouth of David spake."
- Acts 4:31—"They were all filled with the Holy Ghost, and they spake the word of God with boldness."
- Acts 6:10—"They were not able to resist the wisdom and the spirit by which he spake."
- Acts 10:37–38—"The word...which was published throughout all Judea...How God anointed Jesus of Nazareth with the Holy Ghost."
- Acts 10:44—"While Peter yet spake these words, the Holy Ghost fell on all them."
- Acts 11:15—"As I began to speak, the Holy Ghost fell on them."
- Acts 11:16—"Then remembered I the word of the Lord...ye shall be baptized with the Holy Ghost."
- Acts 13:4–5—"Being sent forth by the Holy Ghost....they preached the word of God."
- Acts 15:7–8—"That the Gentiles...should hear the word...giving them the Holy Ghost."
- Acts 16:6—"They...were forbidden of the Holy Ghost to preach the word in Asia."

- Acts 18:25—"Being fervent in the spirit, he spake and taught diligently."
- Acts 28:25—"Paul had spoken one word, Well spake the Holy Ghost by Isaiah."
- Romans 15:18–19—"To make the Gentiles obedient, by word and deed, through mighty signs and wonders, by the power of the spirit of God."
- 1 Corinthians 2:13—"We speak…the words…which the Holy Ghost teacheth."
- 1 Corinthians 12:8—"For to one is given by the spirit the word of wisdom."
- 1 Corinthians 12:8—"To another the word of knowledge, by the same spirit."
- 2 Corinthians 6:7—"By the word of truth, by the power of God."
- Ephesians 1:13—"After that ye heard the word of truth…ye were sealed with that Holy Spirit of promise."
- Ephesians 6:17—"The sword of the Spirit, which is the word of God."
- 1 Thessalonians 1:5—"Our gospel came not unto you in word only, but also in power, and in the Holy Ghost."
- 1 Thessalonians 1:6—"Received the word in much affliction, with joy of the Holy Ghost."
- 1 Timothy 4:12—"Be thou an example of the believers in word [and] in spirit."
- Hebrews 2:3–4—"First began to be spoken…God also bearing them witness…with…gifts of the Holy Ghost."
- Hebrews 6:4–5—"Partakers of the Holy Ghost, And have tasted the good word of God."
- 1 Peter 1:12—"That have preached the gospel unto you with the Holy Ghost."
- 2 Peter 1:21—"The prophecy came not…by the will of man: but holy men of God spake as they were moved by the Holy Ghost."
- 1 John 5:7—"There are three that bear record in heaven, the Father, the Word, and the Holy Ghost."[22]

If any people should be people of the Word of God, it should be those who believe in the Pentecostal baptism with the Holy Spirit. They have an inspirational

---

22 This list of references is through the courtesy of Evangelist Dick Mills of Hemet, California.

ministry. They believe in prophecy, in speaking with other tongues with interpretation, in inspirational revelations. How can one tell if these come from God or not? Just because one claims to have a revelation from the Lord does not mean it should be accepted as if it were from God. There needs to be a norm, a final court of appeal, by which all manifestations of the gifts of the Spirit can be judged. In fact, the Scripture admonishes the judging of all prophecy, which Paul recognizes as perhaps the greatest of the gifts. "Let the prophets speak two or three, and let the other judge" (1 Cor. 14:29). "To the law and to the testimony: if they speak not according to this word, it is because there is no light in them" (Is. 8:20). There is such a "court of appeal" to which one can come—it is the written Word, which the Holy Spirit inspired. Peter calls it "a more sure word of prophecy; whereunto ye do well that ye take heed, as unto a light that shineth in a dark place" (2 Pt. 1:19). Those who minister in any capacity whatever are never so fully in the Spirit as when they are doing so in full accord with the clearly revealed teaching of the Bible, the Word of God. "He that hath an ear, let him hear what the Spirit saith unto the churches," is an admonition which is given seven times in the book of Revelation (2:7, 11, 17, 29; 3:6, 13, 22), and each time it follows a written epistle from the Lord Jesus Christ Himself.

IX. How the Scriptures Came to Us

The story of how our Bible came to us, in the form with which we are familiar, is a long and fascinating one. It begins with the original manuscripts, or as they are sometimes called, "autographs." These original writings were penned by men of old who were moved upon by the Holy Spirit (2 Tm. 3:16; 2 Pt. 1:20–21).

For years, skeptics claimed that Moses could not have written the first part of the Bible because writing was unknown at that time (1500 B.C.). The science of archaeology has since proven that writing was known thousands of years before the time of Moses. The Sumerians were adept at writing in about 4000 B.C., and the Egyptians and Babylonians almost as far back in history.

A. Ancient writing materials

1. *Stone.* Many famous inscriptions have been found in Egypt and Babylon on stone. God gave Moses the Ten Commandments written on tables of stone (Ex. 31:18; 34:1, 28). Two other examples are the Moabite Stone (850 B.C.) and the Siloam Inscription, found in Hezekiah's tunnel by the Pool of Siloam (700 B.C.).

2. *Clay.* The predominant writing material in Assyria and Babylonia was clay, formed into small tablets and impressed with wedge-shaped symbols called cuneiform writing, and then baked in an oven or dried in the sun. Thousands of these have been uncovered by the spade of the archaeologists.

3. *Wood.* Wooden tablets were used quite extensively by the ancients for writing purposes. For many centuries, these were the common writing surface in Greece. Some believe that this type of writing material is referred to in Isaiah 30:8 and Habakkuk 2:2.

4. *Leather.* The Jewish *Talmud* specifically required that the Scriptures should be copied on the skins of animals, on leather. It is most certain, then, that the Old Testament was written on leather. Rolls were made by sewing skins together that were from a few feet to 100 or more feet long. The text was written in columns perpendicular to the roll. The rolls, eighteen to twenty-seven inches high, were rolled on one or two sticks.

5. *Papyrus.* It is almost certain that the New Testament was written on papyrus, inasmuch as it was the most important writing material at that time. Papyrus is made by shaving thin sections of the papyrus reed into strips, soaking them in several baths of water, and then overlapping them to form sheets. One layer of the strips was laid crossways to the first, then these were put in a press, that they might adhere to each other. The sheets were made six to fifteen inches high and three to nine inches wide. Rolls of any length were made by pasting sheets together. These usually averaged about thirty feet long, although one has been found which is 144 feet in length.

6. *Vellum or parchment.* Vellum came into prominence through the efforts of King Eumenes II of Pergamum (197–158 B.C.). He endeavored to build up his library, but the king of Egypt cut off his supply of papyrus, which made it necessary for him to secure some new type of writing material. This he did by perfecting a new process for the treatment of skins. The result is known as vellum or parchment. Though the terms are used interchangeably now, originally vellum was made from the skins of calves and antelopes, while parchment was from the skin of sheep and goats. From these is secured a fine quality leather specially and carefully prepared for writing on both sides. This was used several hundred years before Christ, and about the fourth century A.D. it supplanted papyrus. Almost all the known manuscripts are on vellum.

B. A codex

A codex is a manuscript in book form, rather than a roll. Around the first or second centuries A.D., the sheets of writing material were put together in a book form instead of joining them side-by-side to make a roll. The codex was easier to carry and made it possible to have much more Scripture in one place.

C. Ancient writing instruments

Black ink for writing was made from soot or lampblack and gum, diluted with water. The Essenes, who wrote the Dead Sea Scrolls, used burned lamb bones and oil. It is remarkable how well the writing has been preserved to this day. The writing instruments were a chisel for use on stone, and a stylus made of metal or hard wood for use on the clay tablets. Pens made from the hollow stalks of coarse grass or reeds were used on the papyrus or vellum. The dry reed was cut diagonally with a knife and shaved thin on the point, which was then split. In order to keep these in good condition, scribes carried a knife with them. Thus, the derivation of our word *penknife*.

It must be understood that, as far as we know, none of the original manuscripts are in existence. Some may yet be discovered, but it is doubtful. No material biblical object has yet been found.

D. Languages used

The Bible was originally written in three languages: Hebrew, Aramaic, and Greek. These languages are still spoken in some parts of the world today. Hebrew is the official language of the State of Israel. Aramaic is spoken by a few Christians in the environs of Syria. Greek, though quite different from New Testament Greek, is spoken by millions of people today.

1. *Hebrew.* Almost all the thirty-nine books of the Old Testament were written in Hebrew. The block-like letters were written in capitals without vowels; without spaces between words, sentences, or paragraphs; and without punctuation. Vowel points were added later (between 500 A.D. and 600 A.D.) by the Masoretic scholars. Hebrew is known as one of the Semitic languages.

2. *Aramaic.* A kindred language to Hebrew, Aramaic became the common language of Palestine after the Babylonian captivity (around 500 B.C.). Some portions of the Old Testament were written in this language: one word as a place-name in Genesis 31:47; part of Jeremiah 10:11; about six chapters in the book of Daniel (2:4–7:28); and several chapters in Ezra (4:8–6:18; 7:12–26).

Aramaic continued to be the vernacular of Palestine for several centuries, so we have some Aramaic words preserved for us in the New Testament: *Talitha cumi* ("little girl, get up") in Mark 5:41; *Ephphatha* ("be opened") in Mark 7:34; *Eli eli, lama sabachthani* ("My God, my God, why hast thou forsaken me?") in Matthew 27:46. Jesus habitually addressed God as Abba (Aramaic for "father"). Note the influence of this in Romans 8:15 and Galatians 4:6. Another common Aramaic phrase of early Christians was *maranatha*, which means "our Lord comes" (1 Cor. 16:22).

3. *Greek.* Though the spoken language of Jesus was Aramaic, the New Testament was written in Greek—Koine Greek. The hand of God can be seen in this, because Greek was the universal language of the first century, and this made possible the spread of the Gospel throughout the then-known world.

E. Manuscripts

1. *Definitions.* The word *manuscript*, as it is used today, is restricted to those copies of the Bible which were made in the same language in which it was originally

written. At the time the Bible came to be printed (A.D. 1455), there were over two thousand manuscripts in the possession of certain scholars. Each is by no means complete. Some contain only small portions of the original text, but, put together, a full text can be secured. At present, there are some forty-five hundred manuscripts of the New Testament.

This number is significant when it is considered that scholars are willing to accept ten or twenty manuscripts of classical writings to consider a work genuine. Virgil, for instance, lived and wrote about the time of Christ. No original of his work is in existence. In fact, the earliest copy of his work is dated three hundred years after his death. Yet if ten or twenty manuscripts are found to agree, scholars will accept the work as genuine. Contrast ten or twenty of his works with the thousands of manuscripts of the Bible, all of which were, of course, made by hand.

2. *Classifications.* They are divided into two classes:

a) Uncials (from Latin *uncia*—"inch"). These are so-called because they were written in large capital letters on fine vellum. These are the older manuscripts.

b) Cursives. Later came the cursive manuscripts, which were named for the writing style—a "cursive," or running, hand. These date from the tenth to the fifteenth centuries A.D. Of the forty-five hundred manuscripts extant, about three hundred are uncials and the remainder, cursives. There probably would have been a great many more, had it not been for Diocletian's order to destroy all Christian writings in A.D. 302. Of the three hundred uncials in existence today, about two hundred of them are manuscripts copied on vellum, which date from the fourth to the ninth centuries. In addition to these, there are about seventy papyri documents which date from the second to the fourth century. Broken pieces of pottery, known as *ostraca*, were often used in olden days for writing material, and about thirty of these have been found on which portions of Scripture were written. These papyri and ostraca have only recently come to light, and serve to add considerably to our knowledge of the New Testament text.

3. *Sinaitic Manuscript—Codex Aleph.* One of the earliest of the uncial manuscripts (A.D. 340), the Sinaitic was discovered in 1844 by Dr. Constantine Tischendorf, a German biblical professor and scholar, at the monastery of St. Catherine at Mt. Sinai. Written in Greek, it contains a part of the Septuagint translation of the Old Testament into Greek, all of the New Testament, about half of the Apocrypha, plus the Epistle of Barnabas and much of the Shepherd of Hermas. It contains 364½ leaves of excellent vellum, 131½ inches wide and 14⅞ inches high. Each page has four columns about 2½ inches wide, except the Poetical Books, where there are two wider columns. Each column has forty-eight lines.

Dr. Tischendorf discovered the pages of the manuscript at the monastery, where the monks were using them to light their fires. He rescued forty-three leaves of the vellum, but it was not until fifteen years later that he was able to procure the remaining pages with the help of the czar of Russia, in return for some gifts to the monastery at Sinai. In 1869, the work was deposited in the Imperial Library at St. Petersburg (now Leningrad). In 1933, the Union of the Socialist Soviet Republic (USSR) sold it to the British Museum for one hundred thousand English pounds (about five hundred thousand dollars). There it resides today. A formerly unknown room was discovered in the monastery of St. Catherine in 1975, and thirteen more pages of the Sinaitic were found in it. Along with the Vaticanus, the Sinaitic is considered to be one of the two most important manuscripts in existence. It is the only one which contains the complete New Testament.

4. *Vaticanus Manuscript—Codex B.* This famous uncial is dated from the fourth century (A.D. 350, possibly 325). It is in Greek, and contains: the Septuagint translation of the Old Testament, the Apocrypha (with the exceptions of the books of Maccabees and the Prayer of Manasses), and the New Testament. Genesis 1:1–46:28; 2 Kings 2:5–7, 10–13; and Psalms 106:27–136:6 are missing from the Old Testament. Mark 16:9–20; John 7:53–8:11; and Hebrews 9:14 to the end of the New Testament, including the Pastoral Epistles (1 and 2 Timothy, Titus, and Philemon) and Revelation, are missing from the New Testament. The General Epistles—James; 1 and 2 Peter; 1, 2, and 3 John; and Jude—are included.

As the name suggests, this manuscript is now in the Vatican Library in Rome, where it was first catalogued in 1481. It contains 759 leaves, 617 of the Old Testament and 142 of the New. The pages are ten inches wide and ten and one-half inches high. Each page contains three columns of forty-two lines, except the Poetical Books, which have two columns. It is considered to have the most exact copy of the New Testament known. It is interesting to note that it does not contain Mark 16:9–20, but the scribe left more than a column blank at this place; as though he knew of these verses, but was undecided whether to include them or not.

5. *Alexandrian Manuscript—Codex A.* This, the last of the three greatest uncials being considered here, dates back to the fifth century (around A.D. 450). While it is of both the Old and New Testament, some parts are missing. From the Old Testament: Genesis 14:14–17; 15:1–5, 16–19; 16:6–9; 1 Kings 12:18–14:9; and Psalms 49:19–79:10. From the New Testament: Matthew 1:1–25:6; John 6:50–8:52; 2 Corinthians 4:13–12:6.

This manuscript is comprised of 773 leaves, 639 of the Old Testament and 134 of the New. The size is 10¼ inches wide and 12¾ inches high. Each page has two columns of fifty or fifty-one lines. It was probably written in Alexandria, Egypt. It is said to have been presented to the patriarch of Alexandria and has won for itself the name "Codex Alexandrinus." It is now in the National Library of the British Museum in London, England. It does not quite measure up to the high standard of the Vatican and the Sinaitic Manuscripts.

Only two more of the old uncial manuscripts will be mentioned here. There are many others, mostly smaller portions of the Old or New Testament. However small these portions may be, each adds its testimony to the accuracy of the present Scriptures.

6. *Ephraem Manuscript—Codex C.* This contains portions of both the Old and New Testaments. There are now only sixty-four leaves of the Old Testament and 145 leaves of the New Testament. The pages are 9½ by 12¼ inches. Each page has one wide column of 40–46 (usually 41) lines. It is thought to have been written in Egypt, probably Alexandria, and is dated back to the fifth century (around A.D. 450).

This manuscript is what is called palimpsest, meaning that the original writing was rubbed out so that something else could be inscribed over it or, as in this case, between the original lines. Vellum parchment was scarce and expensive, so this was a common practice. In the twelfth century the original writings of this manuscript were partially erased and the sermons of the Syric Father Ephraem (299–378) were written between the lines. For this reason, it is called the "Ephraem Manuscript."

Near the end of the seventeenth century, a student of the library thought he saw traces of an older writing under the sermons of Ephraem. In 1834, by means of a strong chemical solution, the original writings of the Greek Bible were partially restored. In 1840, Tischendorf brought out the underlying text more fully and was the first to read it successfully. In 1843–1845 he edited and published it.

7. *Beza Manuscript—Codex D.* This dates from the sixth century (around A.D. 550). With some omissions, it contains the Gospels, 3 John 11–15, and the Acts. It is located in the library at Cambridge University, England. It is made up of 406 leaves, each eight by ten inches, with one column of thirty-three lines to a page. This is the oldest known manuscript to be written in two languages. The left hand page is in Greek, while the corresponding text in Latin is on the right side, opposite. In 1562, it was found in the monastery of St. Irenaeus at Lyons, France, by Theodore Beza, the great French biblical scholar who went to Switzerland and became assistant to, and successor of, John Calvin, the famous Protestant reformer in Geneva. In 1581, Beza gave the manuscript to Cambridge University.

8. *Lectionaries.* One further word needs to be added in order to make the story of the New Testament manuscripts complete. Included in the manuscripts is a group of material known as the lectionaries. The term *lection* refers to a selected passage of Scripture designed to be read in public services. Thus a lectionary is a manuscript especially arranged and copied for this purpose. Some were uncials and some cursives. Most of them are from the Gospels, but some are from Acts and the Epistles. Studies have shown that these were copied more carefully than an ordinary manuscript; therefore, they provide excellent copies for comparisons. More than eighteen hundred lectionaries have been enumerated.

F. Versions

After the manuscripts, the next most important form of the Scriptures, which bears its ancient witness, is the version. A version is a translation from the original language of a manuscript into another language. There are many, many versions spread over the years to the present time, but only a few will be considered as examples.

1. *The Septuagint.* This is perhaps the most important of the versions because of its early date and its influence on other translations. The Septuagint Version is a translation of the Hebrew Old Testament into Greek. It was begun about 200 B.C. and finished around 180 B.C. It is probably the oldest attempt to reproduce a book of any language into another language. This is the oldest scriptural document that we have.

Septuagint means "seventy," which explains why the abbreviation of this version is LXX. This notable work is called the Septuagint because of an old legend that seventy-two scholars came from Palestine (six from each of the twelve tribes of Israel) to Alexandria, where they are said to have completed the work in seventy-two days. According to the story, which is certainly pure fiction, the scholars were isolated from each other, placed one or two to a cell, and when their translations were compared they were identical!

It is now believed that the translation was done by Alexandrian Jews rather than Palestinian. Nonetheless, it is sometimes called the "Alexandrian Version," because it was translated in the city of Alexandria in Egypt. The Pentateuch represents the best of the translation. Other portions of the Old Testament are excellent, but some are more of an interpretation or commentary. In addition to the thirty-nine books of the Old Testament, it contains all or part of each of the fourteen books known as the Apocrypha. The Septuagint was commonly used in New Testament times and has been of great use in subsequent translations.

2. *The Samaritan Pentateuch.* The Samaritan race came into being after the Assyrians conquered the Northern Kingdom of Israel in 721 B.C. and carried most of the ten tribes into captivity. Sargon, king of the Assyrians, sent many idolatrous people from his eastern provinces into Israel (2 Kgs. 17:5–6, 24). These intermarried with the Israelites who were still in the land, thus forming the Samaritan race, a mixture of Israelites and heathen. They set up a rival worship to the Jews, building a temple on Mt. Gerizim. The Samaritans accept only the Pentateuch.

The Samaritan Pentateuch is a Hebrew Pentateuch written in Samaritan letters. It is not a translation, but a form of the Hebrew text itself. The date for its writing is about 430 B.C. Second Kings 17:26–28 tells of a priest from among the Jews who was taken captive in Assyria, being sent back to Samaria to teach the people. It is believed he took with him a copy of the Hebrew Pentateuch and that the Samaritan Pentateuch was made from this.

In the work, there are said to be about six thousand variations from the Hebrew text. Most of these are of minor importance, except where the Samaritans deliberately made alterations to suit their particular beliefs. There are probably around one hundred copies of this version in different places in Europe and America. The oldest known dated manuscript (A.D. 1232) is in the New York Public Library. There is a Samaritan roll at Nablus (ancient Shechem) in Israel, which appears to be very old.

~~~

As the message of Christianity spread beyond Palestine, the need for translations of the Scriptures into the languages of those being evangelized became apparent. Thus we have many versions, of which only a few will be dealt with. Compared to the manuscripts, they are of secondary value, but they do help some in the understanding of the original text.

3. *Syriac Versions.* The Syriac language was the chief language spoken in the regions of Syria and Mesopotamia. It is almost identical with Aramaic.

a) The Old Syriac. This has only been known to exist for a little over one hundred years. There are two chief manuscripts of this work:

(1) The Curetan Syriac is a fifth-century copy of the Gospels, consisting of eighty leaves. It is named after Dr. Curetan of the British Museum, who edited it.

(2) The Sinaitic Syriac was discovered at St. Catherine's Monastery at Mt. Sinai. It is a palimpsest and only about three-fourths of it is decipherable. The date assigned is the fourth or the beginning of the fifth century A.D.

b) The Peshitta. The word *peshitta* means "simple" or "common." Thus it has been known as the Syric Vulgate, or the Authorized Version of the church of the East. It has been in use since the fifth century A.D. It contains all of the New Testament, with the exceptions of 2 Peter, 2 and 3 John, Jude, and Revelation. There are about 250 manuscripts in existence. It has been a valuable aid to textual criticism and has had a wide circulation, even in China. There is an English translation done by George Lamsa.

4. *Latin versions.* It is of interest to us to note that the first English Bible was made from the Latin.

a) The Old Latin. This goes back to a very early date, possibly as far as A.D. 150. There are about twenty copies in existence. It is of primary importance as a witness to the genuineness of the Bible text, because of its antiquity and its faithfulness to the text which it translates.

b) The Latin Vulgate

The word *vulgate* means "common" or "current." This is the great version of the Bible in the Latin language. Because of the many mistakes of the copyists of the Old Latin Version, Damascus, the bishop of Rome, secured the services of Jerome to produce a revision as an authoritative standard for the Latin-speaking Churches. This he did in Bethlehem for the New Testament (A.D. 382–383) and the Old Testament (A.D. 390–405).

It is scarcely possible to over-estimate the influence of Jerome's Vulgate on our Bible. For more than a thousand years, every translation of the Scriptures in Western Europe was based on this work. Eventually the Vulgate was made the official Bible of the Roman Catholic Church and is such to this day. Actually, the Roman Catholic Bible in English is a translation of a translation; and is not, as the Protestant Bible, a translation from the original Greek language. After the invention of printing in 1450, the Vulgate was the first book ever printed from moveable type (1455).

G. Biblical criticism

1. *Higher criticism.* There are two types of biblical criticism which come under the topic of Bible introduction. The first of these has often been called "higher criticism" or "historical criticism." This has to do with the examination of the various books of the Bible from the standpoint of their history. For instance, it deals with age, authorship, genuineness, and canonical authority. It traces their origin, preservation, and integrity. It shows their content and general character and value. It is a discipline which has rendered valuable service to the ascertaining of a genuine canon of Scripture. Sometimes the expression "higher criticism" has been considered extremely detrimental to a proper and reverent attitude toward the Holy Scriptures. This is true where the scholar has lost sight of the inspiration of the Word and has inserted his own attitude of skepticism and unbelief.

2. *Lower criticism.* The second type of criticism has been referred to as "lower criticism." This has for its object the ascertaining of the exact words of the original texts of the Bible. Its method is to gather together and compare ancient manuscripts, ancient versions, and ancient quotations of Scripture and determine the true reading of every doubtful passage.

H. Evidences for biblical text

The sincere biblical critic uses three main sources of evidence for the determining of the true wording, that which is closest to the original manuscripts. Two of these have been referred to previously: the manuscripts and the versions. A third valuable source needs to be considered. It is that of the writings of the early church fathers.

1. *The church fathers.* These men were called fathers, which is synonymous with "teachers." These were the great leaders, theologians, teachers, and scholars of the first few centuries after Christ. These men were dedicated Christians who wrote sermons, commentaries, and harmonies. They earnestly contended for the Faith against the inroads of paganism.

The following are some of the better known names from a group that is said to number about two hundred men during the first seven centuries:

- For the period A.D. 96–150: Clement of Rome, Hermas, Ignatius, Polycarp
- For the period A.D 150–325: Justin Martyr, Irenaeus, Clement of Alexandria, Origen, Tertullian, Cyprian, Tatian
- For the period A.D. 325 and after: Eusebius, Athanasius, Jerome, Augustine

These men quoted freely from the Bible, not only citing all twenty-seven books of the New Testament, but virtually every verse in those twenty-seven books. Geisler and Nix assert: "Five Fathers alone, from Irenaeus to Eusebius, possess almost thirty-six thousand quotations from the New Testament."[23]

Some years ago Sir David Dalrymple was at a dinner with a group of scholars, when the question was asked, if the whole New Testament were destroyed at the end of the third century, would it be possible for it to be put together from the writings of the church fathers of the third and second centuries? Two months later he said to one of the company, "That question roused my curiosity, and as I possessed all the existing works of the Fathers of the second and third centuries, I commenced to search, and up to this time I have found the entire New Testament, except eleven verses."[24]

The testimony of the writings of the church fathers to the genuineness of the text is of so great importance, first, because they were careful in their copying of the Scriptures out of devotion to God and His Word; and, secondly, because they lived so close to the apostolic days. It is probable that they had access to manuscripts not in existence today. There is the possibility some had access to the very originals.

2. *The Dead Sea Scrolls.* First discovered in March of 1947 by a young Bedouin goatherd in a cave near the northern end of the Dead Sea, the Dead Sea Scrolls, about 350 rolls in all, have been considered one of the greatest archaeological finds of the twentieth century. Written by the Essenes between the first century before and the first century after Christ, the scriptural portions of these scrolls give us manuscripts hundreds of years older than any other. Portions of every book of the Old Testament, with the exception of Esther, have been found. Of especial interest are the scrolls of the book of Isaiah, because one of the two which has been found gives the entire book of this great prophet. Here is a Hebrew manuscript of Isaiah one thousand years older

---

23 Norman L. Geisler and William E. Nix, *A General Introduction to the Bible* (Chicago: Moody Press, 1969) 357.

24 Josh McDowell, *The New Evidence That Demands a Verdict* (Nashville, TN: Thomas Nelson, 1999) 43–44.

than any other that has come to light. In a remarkable way, the Scrolls confirm the accuracy of the Masoretic text of the Old Testament.

3. *The papyri.* Of great interest to Bible scholars are a number of quite recent discoveries (in 1931) of papyri found in graves in Egypt. These have been often called the most important gain for New Testament text-criticism since Tischendorf announced the discovery of the Sinaitic Codes. These papyri have been acquired by a noted manuscript collector, A. Chester Beatty. Others are in the possession of the University of Michigan and private individuals. They contain parts of the Old Testament in Greek: considerable portions of Genesis, Numbers, and Deuteronomy, and parts of Esther, Ezekiel, and Daniel. Three manuscripts in the group are of New Testament books: portions of thirty leaves of the Gospels and Acts, eighty-six leaves of the Pauline Epistles, and ten leaves out of the middle section of the book of Revelation. This material is of greatest importance, for it dates from the third century or earlier. The text is of such high quality that it ranks with the Vatican and Sinaitic Codices.

The John Rylands Fragment is a small piece of papyrus only 3½ by 2½ inches in size. Though it is so small, it is recognized to be the oldest manuscript of any part of the New Testament. It is written on both sides and contains a portion of the Gospel of John: 18:31–33, 37–38. It was obtained in 1920.

In 1956, Victor Martin, a professor of classical philology at the University of Geneva, published a papyrus codex of the Gospel of John, called the Papyrus Bodmer II. This included chapters 1:1 through 14:26. It is dated A.D. 200 and is probably the oldest book of the New Testament in substantial condition.

4. *Encouraging statements*

a) The doctrines of Scripture. Whatever variant readings the textual critics have discovered, it is a recognized fact that none of these in any way alter any doctrine of the Christian faith.

b) Purity of the text. "Westcott and Hort, Ezra Abbot, Philip Schaff, and A.T. Robertson have carefully evaluated the evidence and have concluded that the New Testament text is over 99 percent pure."[25]

X. THE SCRIPTURES IN ENGLISH

A. The earliest beginnings

The beginnings of the English Bible go back to the seventh century, when an uneducated laborer by the name of Caedmon arranged stories from the Bible in verse form. In the next century, the first actual translation into English was done by Aldhelm, who translated the psalms in A.D. 705. The Venerable Bede, an early

---

25 Geisler and Nix, *From God to Us,* 180

English historian, finished translating the Gospel of John with virtually his last breath in 735. Toward the close of the ninth century, the godly King Alfred translated the Ten Commandments, other laws of the Old Testament, Psalms, and the Gospels, though these were unfinished at his death. About A.D. 1000, Aelfric, Archbishop of Canterbury, translated the Gospels, the first seven books of the Old Testament, Esther, Job, and a part of Kings.

B. John Wycliffe

John Wycliffe, Oxford teacher and scholar, is one of the really important names in the story of the Bible becoming available in the English language. With the help of some of his students, he translated the entire Bible into English from the Latin Vulgate. The work was finished in 1382, the first translation of the entire Bible into English. A revision of this work, done to harmonize the different styles of those who did the translating, was done by John Purvey, who thoroughly corrected and revised Wycliffe's translation in 1388. This revised edition held sway until the sixteenth century.

C. William Tyndale

William Tyndale has been called "the true father of the English Bible." In 1516, the monk-scholar Erasmus published the first printed New Testament in Greek. Tyndale sought to translate this into English, but he found so much opposition from the Roman Catholic Church that he had to flee to Hamburg, Germany. There he finished the translation and sought to have it printed in Cologne. By this time Tyndale had become associated with Martin Luther and the Reformation. Thus, the enemies of the Reformation became Tyndale's enemies also. He had to flee from Cologne with the sheets of his partially printed New Testament.

It should be noted that in 1450 Johann Gutenberg, of Mainz, Germany, invented the printing press, though it had been known for many centuries in China. In 1454, he invented printing from moveable type and the first book from his press was the Latin Vulgate (in 1455), known as the Mazarin Bible, because copies of it were found in the library of Cardinal Mazarin at Paris.

Tyndale found a more friendly environment at Worms, Germany, where the printing of his translation of the New Testament was completed in 1525. Early the next year, copies of his translation were smuggled into England and bought up with enthusiasm. However, the Romish authorities condemned the translation as heresy and copies were bought up and publicly burned. In the meantime, Tyndale continued his work of translating the Old Testament into English. He finished the Pentateuch in 1530, the book of Jonah in 1531, and revised Genesis in 1534. Tyndale was betrayed and imprisoned in 1534. After sixteen months in prison, he was strangled and burned at the stake. His dying words were, "Lord, open the king of England's eyes." The

King James, Authorized Version, is practically a fifth revision of Tyndale's work. A great debt is owed to him, even today.

D. Other sixteenth-century translations

1. *The Coverdale Bible.* In 1535 the Coverdale Bible was printed. It has the distinction of being the first complete Bible printed in English. It was the work of Miles Coverdale, a personal friend of Tyndale. It was a translation of a translation, from the German and Latin. It was the first Bible to have the King of England's approval.

2. *Matthew's Bible.* Matthew's Bible appeared in 1537. This is the work of Tyndale's friend, John Rogers. It was a combined edition of both Tyndale and Coverdale. Actually, Matthew's Bible is the complete version of Tyndale's Bible, as far as his translation went, supplemented by Coverdale's work. It was the first Tyndale revision and forms the basis of all future revisions: the Great Bible, the Geneva Bible, the Bishop's Bible, and the King James Version. It bears the name Matthew's Bible because Rogers was afraid that if Tyndale's name were attached to it there might be greater opposition.

3. *The Great Bible.* Published in 1539, the Great Bible is actually a revision of Matthew's Bible, which was a revision of Tyndale's. The work was done by Coverdale, a very careful reviser. It was called the Great Bible because of its large size, thirteen and one quarter by seven and one half inches. This has been called the Authorized Bible, because King Henry VIII approved of it and issued a proclamation that it be read publicly in every church, and that it be placed in every church throughout the land so that all might have the opportunity to read it. It was chained to the desk of the churches so that none could steal it; thus, it has also been called the Chained Bible. It seems that Tyndales's prayer had been answered and the Lord had opened the king of England's eyes.

4. *The Geneva Bible.* Published in 1560, this was destined to become the most popular Bible of the century. Called the Geneva Bible because it was printed in Geneva, its small size and legible type, with appropriate illustrations and commentaries, made it the popular Bible of homes, just as the Great Bible had been the popular Bible of the churches. It was the first entire Bible to be divided into verses. The New Testament had been printed with the verse divisions by Robert Stevens in 1551. Some attribute the chapter divisions to Cardinal Hugo (c. 1248); others to Stephen Langton, Archbishop of Canterbury, in 1227. The Geneva Bible was the Bible of Shakespeare and of the Pilgrims who came to America.

5. *The Bishop's Bible.* Published in 1568 by authority of Bishop Parker and other bishops who felt that the Geneva Bible undermined their authority, the Bishop's Bible was never a popular edition, being too cumbersome in size and too stiff, formal, and difficult for the common people to appreciate.

6. *The Rheims-Douai Bible.* As a result of the great activity of Bible translation on the part of the Protestant Church, the Roman Catholics were influenced to produce an English translation of their own. Accordingly, in 1582, an edition of the New Testament was produced at the English college at Rheims, France. In 1609–1610 the Old Testament was issued at the same college, which had moved to Douay, France. The Rheims-Douai thus became the first Roman Catholic edition of the English Bible. It was translated, not from the original languages, but from the Latin Vulgate.

7. *The King James Version.* Published in A.D. 1611, it is better known as the Authorized Version. At the Hampton Court Conference, which was comprised of religious leaders from various and diverse groups to discuss the question of religious tolerance, a proposal was made to produce a new translation of the Bible. King James received the suggestion with enthusiasm and laid down the rules: no comments, which had divided the churches, should be included. About forty-eight Greek and Hebrew scholars were selected and divided into six working groups: two to meet at Westminster, two at Oxford, and two at Cambridge. Each group was given certain books to translate, and then the work of each was sent to the other two groups; so, the translation is indeed the work of all, rather than any individual. Actually, it was a revision of the Bishop's Bible, which in turn was a revision of Tyndale's work. The Authorized Version is actually the fifth revision of the Tyndale translation. It was begun in 1607, and after two years and nine months it was sent to the printers and was first presented to the public in 1611, seven years after the convening of the Hampton Court Conference. It has been the most popular and widely accepted version of the Bible for around four hundred years.

E. Recent translations of the English Bible

1. *English Revised Edition.* As fine a work as the King James Version is, and as popular as it continued to be, it was recognized that the King James Version had certain weaknesses. The most valuable witnesses to the original autographs—the Vatican, the Sinaitic, the Alexandrian, and the Ephraem Manuscripts—were not available to the King James translators. Many archaic expressions are found in this translation and some, though not serious, mistakes were observed.

Accordingly, in February 1870, a motion to consider a revision of the King James was passed by the Convocation of the Province of Canterbury. Men of unimpeachable scholarship were chosen in England, and these were joined by the finest men in America. On May 17, 1881, the New Testament was issued, followed by the Old Testament on May 19, 1885. The whole work is known as the English Revised Edition.

2. *American Standard Version.* Published in 1901, it is recognized that the American Standard Version utilized an improved textual base over that which was available to the translators of the King James, along with an advanced knowledge of

the original languages. Many of the archaisms of the King James were cleared up. Yet, it was not without criticism. What it cleared up in the understanding of the Greek, it lost in the beauty of the language. Charles Spurgeon is quoted as saying of it, "Strong in Greek, weak in English."

3. *Revised Standard Version.* In 1929, the Thomas Nelson and Sons Company had given the expiring copyright of the American Standard Version to the International Council of Religious Education, which appointed a committee of scholars to consider the advisability of revising the American Standard. It was agreed to do so, but funds were hard to get; and it was not until September 30, 1952, that the entire Bible was presented. The purpose of the revisers was to take advantage of many new manuscripts and papyri which had come to light since the 1901 Version had been published, while still retaining the beauty of the King James language. It has been widely received, though has not been without its critics, chiefly among conservative scholars.

4. *The New American Standard Bible.* Published on July 31, 1970, it has received the endorsement of many conservatives. It is based on the American Standard Version of 1901.

5. *The New International Version.* This completely new translation has been enthusiastically received. The New Testament was published in 1973 and the complete Bible in 1978. The work was done by scholars from the United States, Great Britain, Canada, Australia, and New Zealand, thus giving it its international flavor. Scholars from more than thirteen denominations participated in the work of translation.

6. *Many others.* During the past decade or two there has been a flood of new translations, too numerous to mention here. Some have endeavored to be literal renderings of the originals, while others are definitely paraphrases into what is considered to be more modern English usage. Still others are in the making and will, no doubt, be seen in the near future.

~~~

Does this flurry of experts clamoring to give us the exact language of the original autographs indicate that we cannot depend upon our present English Bible to declare the true message God would proclaim to mankind? Perhaps the following quotation from Sir Frederic Kenyon, former director of the British Museum, will answer the question best: "It is reassuring at the end to find that the general result of all these discoveries and all this study is to strengthen the proof of the authenticity of the Scriptures, and our conviction that we have in our hands, in substantial integrity, the veritable Word of God."[26]

---

26 Sir Frederick Kenyon, source unknown.

THE DOCTRINE OF GOD

Theology

Introduction

I. The Knowability of God
  A. Incomprehensible
  B. But knowable

II. The Existence of God
  A. The value of argument for God's existence
  B. Arguments for God's existence
    1. *Reason*
    2. *Nature (design and purpose)*
    3. *History*
    4. *The human soul*
    5. *Scripture*

III. The Nature of God (Theism)
  A. God is Spirit.
    1. *Positive—scriptural affirmation*
    2. *Negative—not corporeal, not localized*
  B. God is perfect.
  C. God is personal.
  D. God is One (unity).
  E. Erroneous theories about God
    1. *Atheism*
    2. *Agnosticism*
    3. *Materialism*
    4. *Pantheism*
    5. *Polytheism*
    6. *Deism*
    7. *Dualism*

IV. The Names of God (Dt. 32)
  A. *Elohim* (plural), *Eloah* (singular)
    1. *El (singular)*
    2. *El Elyon*
    3. *El Olam*
    4. *El Shaddai*
  B. *Adonai* (plural), *Adon* (singular)

C. *Jehovah*

D. *Ha Tsur, the Rock*

E. The compound names of *Jehovah*

    1. *Jehovah-Elohim*

    2. *Jehovah-Jireh*

    3. *Jehovah-Rapha*

    4. *Jehovah-Nissi*

    5. *Jehovah-Shalom*

    6. *Jehovah-Raah*

    7. *Jehovah-Tsidkenu*

    8. *Jehovah-Sabaoth*

    9. *Jehovah-Shammah*

F. New Testament names of God

    1. *Theos*

    2. *Kurios*

    3. *Pater*

V. The Attributes of God

A. Absolute attributes

    1. *Self-existence*

    2. *Immutability*

    3. *Eternity*

    4. *Omnipresence*

    5. *Omniscience (wisdom)*

    6. *Omnipotence*

    7. *Sovereignty*

B. Moral attributes

    1. *Holiness*

    2. *Righteousness (justice)*

    3. *Love (mercy, goodness)*

    4. *Truth*

    5. *Faithfulness*

VI. The Works of God

A. Divine purpose

B. Creation

C. Providence

    1. *Governs the physical universe*

    2. *Cares for animal creation*

    3. *Governs the nations*

    4. *Cares for our birth and place in life*

5. *Concerned about our successes and failures*
6. *Provides protection for the righteous*
7. *Supplies the needs and wants of His people*
8. *Provides the answers to our prayers*
9. *Governs the reward of the righteous and the punishment of the impenitent*

VII. The Trinity of God (the Doctrine)
  A. Definition
  B. Its scriptural presentation
    1. *In the Old Testament*
    2. *In the New Testament*

VIII. The Persons of the Trinity
  A. God the Father (see above)
  B. God the Son
    1. *His virgin birth*
    2. *His nature*
    3. *His works*
  C. God the Holy Spirit
    1. *The personality of the Holy Spirit*
    2. *The deity of the Holy Spirit*
    3. *The names of the Holy Spirit*
    4. *The symbols of the Holy Spirit*

CHAPTER TWO

THE DOCTRINE OF GOD

Theology

INTRODUCTION

"THEOLOGY IS THE study of God and the relations between God and the universe; the study of religious doctrines and matters of divinity, 2. a specific form or system of this study."[1]

Theology comes from two Greek words: *theos* meaning "God," and *logos* meaning "discourse" or "reason"; therefore, the term means "discourse or reasoning about God." Generally speaking, there are three categories of theology:

(1) Natural theology—the study of God as revealed in the universe and in nature.

(2) Biblical theology—the study of God as He has revealed Himself to us in the Scriptures.

(3) Systematic theology—the study of God from nature, from philosophical reasoning, and from Scripture, made to fit into a preconceived mold or system.

While the Christian believer bases his knowledge of God primarily upon the Holy Scriptures and upon the revelation of God through His Son Jesus Christ, he welcomes confirming evidence from the universe and from nature. Any attempt to study God and divine truth will of necessity, if it is to be grasped and retained, take some form and system.

The study of God is of very great importance, for God is man's highest good; He is the source of life and sustenance, "For in Him we live, and move, and have our being" (Acts 17:28). The apostle Paul said in his sermon to the Athenians, "And hath made of one blood all nations of men for to dwell on the face of the earth...That they should seek the Lord...and find him, though he be not far from every one of us" (Acts 17:26–27). John Calvin said, "Nearly all the wisdom we possess, that is to say, true and sound wisdom, consists of two parts: the knowledge of God and of

---

1 Webster's New World Dictionary of the American Language, 2nd college edition, s.v. "theology."

ourselves."[2] There is serious doubt that we can really know ourselves and our purpose in life without some degree of knowledge of God and His will.

The term *theology* is used in two ways: (1) it may describe the study of all biblical truth or (2) it may more specifically describe the study of God, His existence, nature, names, attributes, and works. In this book the term *theology* will apply to the second use of the term.

I. THE KNOWABILITY OF GOD

A. Incomprehensible

God is the Infinite One. In one sense He is incomprehensible. After all, how can finite beings comprehend the infinite, limitless God? Zophar, in the book of Job, said, "Canst thou by searching find out God? canst thou find out the Almighty unto perfection?" (Jb. 11:7). Zophar was not an inspired prophet, for some of his reasoning was proved false, but his words are echoed by Paul in Romans: "O the depth of the riches both of the wisdom and knowledge of God! how unsearchable are his judgments, and his ways past finding out!" (Rom. 11:33). (See Is. 40:18, 25; Ps. 36:6.) Obviously, we cannot comprehend the fullness of God's nature, nor can we know completely all His plans and designs.

B. But knowable

On the other hand, Scripture affirms the "knowability" of God: "God, who at sundry times and in divers manners spake in time past unto the fathers by the prophets, hath in these last days spoken unto us by his Son...Who being the brightness of his glory, and the express image of his person" (Heb. 1:1–3). The NIV renders the latter clauses, "The Son is the radiance of God's glory and the exact representation of His being" (Heb. 1:3, NIV). The apostle John, in his Gospel declares: "No one has ever seen God, but God the One and Only, who is at the Father's side, has made Him known" (Jn. 1:18, NIV). While man, unaided, cannot come to know the infinite God, it is clear that God has revealed Himself and that He can be known to the extent of His self-revelation. In fact, it is essential for man to know God in order to experience redemption and to have eternal life: "And this is life eternal, that they might know thee the only true God, and Jesus Christ, whom thou hast sent" (Jn. 17:3). "And we know that the Son of God is come, and hath given us an understanding, that we may know him that is true" (1 Jn. 5:20). During this life, we can and must know God to the extent essential to salvation, fellowship, service, and maturity, but in Heaven's glory we will come to know God more fully: "For now we

---

2 John Calvin, *Institutes of the Christian Religion* (Edinburgh, Scotland: T. & T. Clark, 1845).

see through a glass darkly; but then face to face: now I know in part; but then shall I know even as also I am known" (1 Cor. 13:12). (See also 1 Cor. 1:21; Eph. 1:17; Phil. 3:10; Col. 1:10; Rom. 1:19–23, 28; 2 Pt. 1:2–3.)

II. The Existence of God

A. The value of the argument for God's existence

Some people, with good reason, will question the value of arguments for the existence of God. Nowhere does the Bible argue for God's existence; everywhere the Scriptures assume His existence as an accepted fact. The first verse of Holy Writ affirms: "In the beginning God created the heaven and the earth" (Gn. 1:1). The psalmist further exclaims, "The fool hath said in his heart, There is no God" (Ps. 14:1). The Christian and all worshipers of God have accepted God's existence as an act of faith. Some theologians, such as Soren Kierkegaard and Karl Barth reject all general or natural theology and claim that God can be known only as an act of faith. However, the believer's faith is neither blind nor unreasonable. Faith is a gift of God (Rom. 10:17); however, it is supported by evidences clear to the unbiased mind. The psalmist states as a comfort for believers: "The heavens declare the glory of God; and the firmament sheweth his handywork" (Ps. 19:1). Paul points out in Romans 1 that even those without a scriptural revelation are without excuse for unbelief:

> Because that which may be known of God is manifest in them; for God hath shewed it unto them. For the invisible things of him from the creation of the world are clearly seen, being understood by the things that are made, even his eternal power and Godhead; so that they are without excuse: Because that, when they knew God, they glorified him not as God.
> —Romans 1:19–21

By this, it can be seen that the Bible supports the validity of a natural theology. We must remember, however, that while a natural theology may point to a powerful, wise, and benevolent Creator, it says nothing to solve the problems of man's sin, of pain and suffering, and his need of a Redeemer; nor can it affirm with John the Baptist, "Behold the Lamb of God which taketh away the sin of the world" (Jn. 1:29). Furthermore, it is important to keep in mind that arguments for the existence of God, such as those supplied by a natural theology, fall short of absolute demonstration. Finite beings cannot demonstrate the existence of an infinite God. J. O. Buswell says:

> There is no argument known to us which, as an argument, leads to more than a probable (highly probable) conclusion. For example, most of us believe that the sun will rise tomorrow morning, but if we were to analyze the

evidences, the arguments that lead to such a conclusion, we should be forced to admit that the arguments, good as they are, are characterized by probability. The theistic arguments are no exception to the rule that all inductive arguments about what exists are probability arguments. This is as far as the arguments, qua arguments, claim to go.[3]

The arguments for God's existence that will follow are not a substitute for scriptural revelation of God, nor can they lead to saving faith. They are a comfort to the believer, and they may serve the preacher of the gospel to awaken the hearers and obtain for him an attentive hearing. Only the Holy Spirit will supply true faith in God.

B. Arguments for God's existence

1. *The argument from reason.* The first phase of the argument from reason is that of cause and effect. All around us there are effects, such as matter and motion. For their explanation there are three alternatives: (1) they exist eternally, (2) they emerged from nothing, or (3) they were caused. Let us examine these alternatives in order. First, it is not likely that the universe has existed eternally, for all evidence points to a universe that is running down. According to the second law of thermodynamics, the sun and the stars are losing energy by a measurable rate; if they had existed from eternity, they already would have been depleted. Radioactive materials are losing their radiation. Spectrographic studies of the stars show that all bodies are traveling outward from the center, indicating a beginning. Second, that matter and motion emerged from nothing is a contradiction; it is true that "from nothing, nothing comes." Third, the most reasonable explanation is that matter and motion were created at a point of time. Most scientists presently date the universe between five and twenty billion years old. Some posit a series of emergences or an impersonal creator, but considering the existence of intelligences and the great complexity of creation, it is most likely that the universe is the work of an intelligent Creator, as set forth in the Bible. It is not likely that a fountain will rise higher than its source, or that rational beings will arise from an irrational source.

Another phase of the argument from reason is that man has an innate knowledge of God. This is evidenced by universal belief in a supreme being of some kind. A tribe can hardly be found without a faith in a higher being or force. As is often said, "man is incurably religious." This does not mean that all men have a full-formed belief in God. It does seem to indicate that religious belief and the propensity to worship a deity are natural to man. Even the atheist who denies God's existence demonstrates

---

3 James Oliver Buswell, *Systematic Theology of the Christian Religion* (Grand Rapids, MI: Zondervan Publishing House, 1962–63), 72.

that he is confronted with the idea of God and must in some way actively put away the concept.

2. *The argument from nature.* For almost everything in nature, we find a designed purpose. The universe everywhere displays precise and orderly movement. "He who planted the ear, shall He not hear? He who formed the eye, shall He not see? He who instructs the nations, shall He not correct?" (Ps. 94:9–10, NKJV). All things seem to be a part of the balance of nature. The earth is tilted on its axis in relation to the sun, and thereby provides the seasons and the best distribution of light and heat during the year. The earth is at an ideal distance from the sun to avoid searing heat and freezing cold. The chemical composition of the atmosphere is at an ideal balance for animal and vegetable life. The ratio of land and water on the earth's surface gives proper rainfall and humidity. Wind and sea currents provide air conditioning and warm coastlines. Blessings like musical sound for the ears and the beauty of color show a design not needed for mere utility, and speak of a Creator who designed ears and eyes as receptors. Now, can intelligent beings believe that an impersonal force or process brought this marvelous universe into being?

An illustration is in order. One of the most common substances is water. Most of the other substances become more dense with lowered temperature. Water, fortunately, expands and becomes less dense when frozen. In the form of ice, water floats on top of lakes, rivers, and seas. If water, when frozen, became denser and sank to the bottom, many rivers, lakes, and seas would never thaw; and much of the earth's surface would become glacial and unlivable. Did a wise Creator give to water its different characteristics?

3. *The argument from history.* The argument from history rests upon the foundation of the divine providence. Students of history, unless they are blind or biased, will discover the working of divine providence. This does not mean that a wise purpose is visible in all events. It must be taken into account that man is sinful and rebellious, and, to a degree, a free moral agent. God does not cause every individual event, but God is in control of the stream of events, carrying out His purposes. He fulfills His inspired prophecies that are recorded in His Word. If one will study the Bible together with history, one will discern a divine pattern focused upon Christ Jesus, the Son of God. This focus is not only upon the earthly life of Jesus. God's purpose in Christ is seen in Israel's history and in their hope of a redeemer (Gn. 12:1–3; Is. 52:10–53:12); in Christ's incarnation, life, death, and resurrection; in the Church's triumph through manifold opposition; and in Israel's indestructibility throughout the centuries.

Christ's uniqueness is well expressed by Napoleon in a letter to General Bertrand:

> Divine effects compel me to believe in a divine cause. Yes, there is a divine cause, a sovereign reason, an infinite being. That cause is the cause of causes.... There exists an infinite being, compared with whom you, General,

are but an atom; compared with whom I, Napoleon, with all my genius, am truly nothing; a pure nothing. I perceive Him—God. I see Him, have need of Him, I believe in Him. If you do not believe in Him, well, so much the worse for you. But, you will, General, yet believe in God. I can pardon many things, but I have a honor of an atheist and materialist...The gods, the legislators of India and of China, of Rome, and of Athens, have nothing which can overawe me...It is not so with Christ. Everything in Him astonishes me. His spirit overawes me, and His will confounds me. Between Him and whoever else in the world, there is no possible term of comparison. He is truly by himself. His ideas and His sentiments, the truths which He announces, His manner of convincing, are not explained either by human organization or by the nature of things.

His birth, and the history of His life; the profundity of His doctrine, which grapples with the mightiest difficulties, the most admirable solution; His Gospel...His march across the ages and the realms, everything is for me a prodigy, a mystery insoluble, which plunges me into a reverie from which I cannot escape, a mystery is there before my eyes, a mystery which I can neither deny nor explain...I search in vain in history to find the equal of Jesus Christ.[4]

4. *The argument from the human soul.* The argument from the human soul has two parts: that of God's image in man and that of man's moral nature. The Word of God declares that man is created in the image of God:

> And God said, Let us make man in our image, after our likeness: and let them have dominion over the fish of the sea, and over the fowl of the air, and over the cattle, and over all the earth, and over every creeping thing that creepeth upon the earth. So God created man in his own image, in the image of God created he him; male and female created he them.
>
>   —GENESIS 1:26–27

We are not to look for God's image in the physical man, for God is Spirit (Jn. 4:24); rather, we are to look for the image of God in the spiritual man: "And have put on the new man, which is renewed in knowledge after the image of him [God] that created him" (Col. 3:10). God's image in man is seen in his having dominion over the lower creatures, and especially in his capacity for and yearning for fellowship with God. The other mark of the divine image is seen in man's moral nature, his sense of

---

4 *Abbot's Napoleon* as quoted in A. M. Baten, *Philosophy of Life* (Garden City, NY: Harper and Row Publishing Company, 1930), 381–390.

duty and responsibility, and in his possession of a conscience: "Who show the work of the law written in their hearts, their conscience also bearing witness, and between themselves their thoughts accusing or else excusing them" (Rom. 2:15, NKJV). C. S. Lewis says:

> These then are the two points I wanted to make. First, that human beings, all over the earth, have this curious idea that they ought to behave in a certain way, and cannot really get rid of it. Secondly, they do not in fact behave in that way. They know the Law of Nature; they break it. These two facts are the foundation of all clear thinking about ourselves and the universe we live in.[5]

A personal God holds us responsible for our conduct and our attitude. We must surrender to His will or live with a guilty conscience. One may succeed in searing his conscience or quieting it by self-deception, but he will then invariably work out his own value system. Experience has shown that the Bible system of ethics, after all, best suits man's God-created moral nature.

5. *The argument from Scripture.* The argument from Scripture rests upon its claims and upon its accuracy. The Bible claims to be the inspired Word of God (2 Tm. 3:16–17; 2 Pt. 1:20–21; 1 Cor. 2:12–13; Jer. 1:1–13). No book on Earth has been as widely embraced as being a message from God. Its opponents and the skeptics have launched every conceivable attack against it, but its popularity remains. Its accuracy has been repeatedly impugned, but every turn of the archeologist's spade confirms the accuracy of some doubted passage. Dr. W. F. Albright, the renowned archeologist writes: "Nothing tending to disturb the religious faith of Jew or Christian has been discovered. Discovery after discovery has established the accuracy of innumerable details, and has brought increased recognition of the value of the Bible as a source book of history."[6] No other book compares with the Bible for elevated moral and spiritual teaching; written centuries ago, it is more modern than today's periodicals. It never ceases to speak with power and healing to the deepest problems of the human soul and spirit.

---

5 Clive Staples Lewis, *Mere Christianity* (New York, Macmillan and Company, 1952), 21. C. S. Lewis's writings have been very effective in presenting the Christian message to educated people.

6 William Foxwell Albright, *The Archaeology of Palestine and the Bible* (Old Tappan, NJ: Fleming H. Revell Publishing Company, 1933) 127–128.

III. THE NATURE OF GOD

The study of the nature of God must be approached with humility and reverence. Who can define the nature and essence of the infinite God? Not only are His ways "past finding out" (Rom. 11:33), His nature and being surpass our comprehension. However, God has revealed as much of His essential nature to us as is needed to serve and worship Him. It is especially important to understand the nature of God, as it is revealed in the Bible, for many different concepts of deity are held by those who reject the God of the Scriptures. The Bible does not give us a single comprehensive definition of God. If "the heaven of heavens cannot contain thee" (1 Kgs. 8:27), how can a sentence or paragraph of human words define His being? The following theological definition from the Westminster Catechism serves as well as any: "God is a Spirit, infinite, eternal, and unchangeable, in his being, wisdom, power, holiness, justice, goodness, and truth."[7]

Several statements about God in Scripture define various aspects of His nature, such as: "God is Spirit" (Jn. 4:24), "God is light" (1 Jn. 1:15), "God is love" (1 Jn. 4:8), and "God is a consuming fire" (Heb. 12:29). In this section we will focus our attention upon four aspects of the divine nature.

A. God is Spirit

1. *Positive—scriptural affirmation.* The statement that God is Spirit means that He cannot be confined to a physical body, nor to dimensions of space and time. He is the invisible, eternal God: "No man hath seen God at any time; the only begotten Son, which is in the bosom of the Father, he hath declared him" (Jn. 1:18). Because God is Spirit, He can say, "Lo, I am with you alway, even unto the end of the world" (Mt. 28:20); "For where two or three are gathered together in my name, there am I in the midst of them" (Mt. 18:20); and "I will never leave thee, nor forsake thee" (Heb. 13:5). Jesus pointed out that man must be "born of the spirit" in order to enter the kingdom of God, in order that he may have fellowship with God who is Spirit (Jn. 3:5).

2. *Negative—not corporeal, not localized.* Two problems arise in connection with the affirmation that God is Spirit. First, some Bible passages represent God as having eyes, ears, or an arm (Is. 52:10; Ps. 34:15). These are figures of speech called anthropomorphisms (meaning man-like descriptions). Living in a material world, man has difficulty thinking of God as perceiving or acting without human members; therefore, the Scriptures condescend to our limitation by attributing to God (figuratively

---

7 Westminster Confession of Faith, Shorter Catechism, accessed at http://www.opc.org/confessions.html (January 15, 2008).

speaking) "ears" to hear our cry or an "arm" to help us. God, speaking through the great prophet Isaiah and thinking of our human limitation, said:

> To whom then will ye liken me, or shall I be equal? saith the Holy One. Lift up your eyes on high, and behold who hath created these things, that bringeth out their host by number: he calleth them all by names by the greatness of his might, for that he is strong in power; not one faileth. Why sayest thou, O Jacob, and speakest thou, O Israel, My way is hid from the Lord, and my judgment is passed over from my God? Hast thou not known? hast thou not heard that the everlasting God, the LORD, the Creator of the ends of the earth, fainteth not, neither is weary? there is no searching of his understanding.
>
> —ISAIAH 40:25–28

The eternal Spirit does not need eyes to see our need, nor is He wearied in His redeeming activity.

The second problem with the representation of God's spirituality is that He is sometimes represented as appearing in human form (see Gn. 17–19; Jos. 5:13–15). Although God is in essence Spirit, He who made all beings and things can, for His wise ends, assume any form that suits His purpose. There are a number of instances where God appeared in visible form; for instance, as unto Abraham to assure him of the promised son through whose descendents all nations would be blessed. These appearances are called theophanies. Such appearances, however, do not contradict God's spiritual nature. How wonderful it is that God the Son took upon Himself human form in order to become our Redeemer, High Priest, and eternal King! "Philip saith unto Him, Lord, shew us the Father, and it sufficeth us. Jesus saith unto him...he that hath seen me hath seen the Father" (Jn. 14:8–9). Furthermore, in 1 Corinthians 15:38–54, Paul states that spiritual beings may have spiritual bodies. After the Resurrection, Jesus had a spiritual body not subject to physical limitations (Jn. 20:19–29), and there is some indication that He may, in His spiritual body, eternally bear the marks of Calvary's ordeal.

B. God is perfect

Jesus said to His disciples, "Be ye therefore perfect, even as your Father which is in heaven is perfect" (Mt. 5:48). It is almost impossible to think of the Creator, who is at the same time righteous and loving, holy and merciful, eternal Judge and Father of our Lord Jesus Christ, as being anything but perfect. The Scriptures affirm this, declaring Him to be perfect. God's perfections will be seen in sharper focus when we study His attributes.

C. God is personal

A personal being is one that is self-conscious, who possesses intellect, feeling, and will. It is popular among sophisticates today to believe in an impersonal god, who is something like a life principle who can be referred to as Nature. Such a god neither answers prayer, nor is displeased with evil doing; he is just the universe itself, including its laws. Such an impersonal god may not confront our selfishness, but neither can he help us when our troubles are more than we can handle. The God of Holy Scripture is a personal, transcendent God who stands apart from the universe as its Creator; but who, at the same time, is an immanent God, residing within His creation to preserve it and care for it as a heavenly Father.

The personality of God is revealed in His dealing with Moses, when He declared His name: "And God said unto Moses, I AM THAT I AM: and He said, Thus shalt thou say unto the children of Israel, I AM hath sent me unto you" (Ex. 3:14). Then in Exodus 6:2–3, "I am the LORD: and I appeared unto Abraham, unto Isaac, and unto Jacob, by the name of God Almighty [El Shaddai], but by my name, JEHOVAH was I not known unto them." The Hebrew word *Jehovah*, or *Yahweh*, is derived from the verb "to be." "I AM THAT I AM" may be a kind of interpretation of the name Jehovah. Jehovah God is the One who was, who is, and who eternally shall be. As a person, God is here revealed to have a personal name; He speaks and enters into a covenant as an intelligent being; He answers the inquiries of Moses as one who responds to human anxiety and feels his concern with him. He chooses a man to carry out His will to lead Israel as a witness nation among nations. He declares that He has heard the groanings of His people in Egypt, whose anguish mattered to Him. This is a personal God, and not a mere impersonal soul of the universe.

In the New Testament, the Son of God (who was a person) said, "For just as the Father has life in Himself, even so He gave to the Son also to have life in Himself" (Jn. 5:26, NASB). This implies that the Father is the same kind of person as the Son to whom He gave His life. Since man as a creature of God has intellect, emotion, and volition, and he is able to intelligently contemplate God and His universe as a rational person, surely he is not superior to God in capacities. God has divine personality, far beyond His creatures, but if He made man to commune with Him and to worship Him, He must certainly have endowed him with like characteristics to His nature when He made him in His own image.

The Bible's gospel is God's message to the sinner who has disobeyed a personal God, whom he has offended by his rebellion. This sinner bears a burden of guilt which only a new relationship with God, made possible by the redeeming work of the Son of God, will alleviate: "There is therefore now no condemnation to them which are in Christ Jesus" (Rom. 8:1); "But God commendeth his love toward us, in that, while we were yet sinners, Christ died for us" (Rom. 5:8). Love cannot come from an impersonal principle. Rather, love is a personal characteristic.

D. God is One

The Law of God given on Sinai begins with the declaration, "Hear O Israel: The LORD our God is one LORD" (Dt. 6:4). Nothing is condemned in Scripture more than the worship of other numerous gods: "Ye shall not go after other gods, of the gods of the people which are round about you" (Dt. 6:14). The nations worshiped many gods—gods that corresponded to the forces of nature, gods who were the creation of their own imagination, who were represented by images and idols. These idolatrous nations were a constant thorn in the side of Israel. The downfall of Israel was their continual flirtation with these deities of nature. When Israel's King Ahab had opened the door to the worship of Baal, a false nature god, Elijah spectacularly challenged the priests of Baal and Ashtoreth to a contest with Jehovah, the living God (1 Kgs. 18:21–40). He then prayed, "Hear me, O Lord...that this people may know that thou art the LORD God" (1 Kgs. 18:37). When Jehovah—not the false deities—answered by fire, the people in one accord cried, "The LORD, he is the God" (1 Kgs. 18:39). It was important for the man of God to halt the catastrophic trend toward polytheism. The Bible, therefore, uncompromisingly calls for the worship of ONE true God. The prophet Isaiah sounded the same trumpet call: "Thus saith the LORD, the King of Israel,...the Lord of hosts, I am the first, and I am the last; and beside me there is no God" (Is. 44:6). Championing the same great truth, our Savior said in prayer to the Father, "And this is life eternal, that they might know thee the only true God" (Jn. 17:3). The apostle Paul commends the Thessalonians because they "turned to God from idols to serve the living and true God" (1 Thes. 1:9).

It used to be widely taught that religion evolved from an original animism and polytheism (the worship of many gods) to a monotheism (worship of one God). More recent archeological evidence, together with the finding of modern missionaries, indicates that man was originally monotheistic (from God's revelation of Himself to the first parents), and that the religions of the nations became increasingly corrupted with the passing of time. There will be a section on the Trinity of God later on (see Section VII), but it is important first to establish the unity of God.

E. Erroneous theories about God

The Bible's teaching about God is that He is the all-powerful, all-wise Creator of all things who is just and holy and at the same time loving and merciful. He is transcendent (above and distinct from the creation), while at the same time, He is immanent (resident in and involved with His creation). He is a personal God who seeks fellowship with His redeemed people. He punishes ultimate rebellion with eternal death; He rewards faith and obedience with eternal life through His Son and Mediator, Jesus Christ. He is the Supreme Being who is also the heavenly Father. He spoke into being the immeasurable universe, yet He notes the sparrow's fall and hears the faintest cry. He made the galaxies, but He stooped to Bethlehem's manger. We tremble before His majesty, but we seek solace in His unconditional love. He dwells beyond the remotest galaxy, but He is no farther from us than the reach of faith. This is the Christian's God. There are, however, different views held by those who ignore the scriptural doctrine of God.

1. *Atheism.* The atheist denies the existence of any deity. He believes that the universe came about by chance or that it has always existed, sustained by resident, impersonal laws. But, is any earthbound man reasonable who denies the existence of a maker for a universe, whose vast expanse he can no more explore than a mole can explore St. Paul's Cathedral? There are two kinds of atheists: (1) the philosophical atheist who denies that God exists, and (2) the practical atheist who lives as if God did not exist.

2. *Agnosticism.* The agnostic does not deny the knowledge of God. Thomas Huxley, who coined the word *agnostic*, took the term from the Greek altar in Athens referred to by Paul in Acts 17:23, which had the inscription *Agnosto Theo* ("the unknown god"). But Professor Huxley misunderstood the intent behind the inscription. The Athenian "unknown god" was the real God, above all the lesser deities, who were really only the human heroes from the dawn of history whom the Greeks had elevated to the status of gods. Socrates and Plato gained some insight into the existence of a Supreme Being; they just did not know what to call Him. Agnosticism is popular today. It is a comfortable refuge for those who think of themselves as intellectuals, but who do not want to take a position of faith in the God of the Scriptures. A sincere and humble seeker after God will sooner or later find Him, for He is not far from any of us.

3. *Materialism.* The materialist denies the existence of spirit, or spiritual beings. To him, all reality is merely matter in motion. The human mind and soul are only functions of the physical brain, developed over billions of years by gradual evolution. There is no life after death; heaven or hell are only earthly states of pleasure or pain, success or failure. If the materialist is consistent in applying his philosophy, he has no real basis for morality. Doing good is only doing what brings the greatest pleasure to the greatest number, but there is no reason he feels deep obligation to be moral, other than his own loss of esteem. According to the materialist, there is no judgment above the human level, and sin is only imperfection.

4. *Pantheism.* This is the religion of Hinduism. God is simply nature, the sum total of the universal system. The term comes from *theos*, meaning "god," and *pan* meaning "all." The philosophers Spinoza and Hegel were the best known European pantheists. Some prominent liberal "Christian" theologians of today are really pantheists and are among those who do not believe in a personal, transcendent God. The turn of many to Eastern religions has revived pantheism in America. The Bible makes no room for this ancient but dreary religion. Its best hope is nirvana, the desireless, passionless, soulless state.

5. *Polytheism.* The word *polytheism* again comes from the two Greek words, *poly* meaning "many," and *theos* meaning "god." It describes the belief in many gods. Among ancient nations, the belief that arose from the worship of the forces of nature was that every facet of nature was ruled over by a god or goddess. Later, tribal heroes were elevated to the position of deities and ruled over rivers, rainfall, agriculture, human passions, various planets, seasons of the year, etc. Israel's neighbors were polytheists and often corrupted Israel's worship. The Bible strongly condemns this paganism with its idolatry (Is. 44:9–20). However, after the Babylonian captivity, Israel was virtually cured of idolatrous worship.

6. *Deism.* Deism comes from the Latin *dues,* which means "god." The Deist believes in a transcendent but absentee God. His God made the universe and man, but left His creation to sustain itself by natural laws. Deism denies man's sinful nature and therefore the need of an atonement or a redeemer. Deism rejects all miracles as well as the divine inspiration of Scripture. This view of God is irrational, for why would a personal God create the world and man, yet have no revealed purpose for man? Deists are not numerous today.

7. *Dualism.* Dualism is the doctrine of the existence of two opposite realms opposed to one another: one of spirit and one of matter. It also describes a belief in the rule of the world by two gods: one of evil and darkness, and one of good and light. Zoroaster, a Persian philosopher of Moses' time, first advanced the idea of two gods of equal power, neither of whom ultimately triumphs. The Bible teaches us of good and evil, of Satan and of God. But God and His kingdom will triumph over Satan and evil at the end of the age: "And the seventy returned again with joy, saying, Lord, even the devils are subject unto us through thy name. And he said unto them, I beheld Satan as lightning fall from heaven. Behold I give unto you power...over all the power of the enemy" (Lk. 10:17–19). The book of Job gives us a picture of a kind of dualism, or conflict between the forces of God and Satan, but again God and virtue triumph. The Gnostics and Manicheans in post-Apostolic times were dualists, teaching that all matter was evil and that only spirit was good. In the New Testament, *the world* does not refer so much to physical things, but to the spirit of sin and evil in an unregenerate society dominated by Satan. Material things may be good and useful to God's kingdom when managed with a dedicated stewardship. All things are ours when laid at the feet of Jesus: "For all things are yours; whether...the world, or life, or death, or things present, or things to come; all are yours; And ye are Christ's; and Christ is God's" (1 Cor. 3:21–23), and "Be not highminded, nor trust is uncertain riches, but in the living God, who giveth us richly all things to enjoy" (1 Tm. 6:17).

There is another dualism that teaches that all affliction, calamity, adversity, poverty, and trouble come directly from Satan. No doubt, much of such does derive from Satan's realm, and in fact all such is the result of the Fall; but the theory that all adversity is Satanic is contradicted by the experience of almost all the apostles and martyrs and great leaders of the Church, who made adversity glorify God. Adversity is evil only if we permit Satan to defeat us with it. On the other hand, there is victory in Christ out of all life's experiences. Paul said, writing to the Corinthian Church:

> For we would not, brethren, have you ignorant of our trouble which came to us in Asia, that we were pressed out of measure, above strength, insomuch that we despaired even of life: But we had the sentence of death in ourselves, that we should not trust in ourselves, but in God which raiseth the dead: Who delivered us from so great a death, and doth deliver: in whom we trust that He will yet deliver us.
>
> —2 CORINTHIANS 1:8–10

This is an example of trouble in Paul's life that God used for His purpose, but three times the apostle uses the word *deliver*. There are opposing forces in the world, and the believer is in the midst of the battle, but we are on the winning side: "Greater is he that is in you, than he that is in the world" (1 Jn. 4:4). Amen!

IV. THE NAMES OF GOD

Webster defines *name* as "that by which a person or thing is known."[8] The Hebrews thought of names as being revelatory, as disclosing some attribute or characteristic of the person named. For instance, the name Adam means "of the earth" or "taken out of the red earth"; his name revealed his origin. A number of names for God are found in the Scriptures, for no one name, or even multiplicity of names, can reveal all His attributes. But, we need only know God's attributes to the extent that He is pleased to reveal them and those that pertain to the relationships we have with Him. It is assuring to know that there is some relationship with God, revealed by one of His names, that corresponds to every need of His children. It is the goal of theology to define, as far as possible, what those relationships are. The study of the names of God will significantly help us to attain that goal.

A. *Elohim* (plural), *Eloah* (singular)

The name *Elohim* is the first word used in Scripture to refer to God. "In the beginning God [*Elohim*] created the heaven and the earth" (Gn. 1:1). This name is used around 2,500 times in the Old Testament. Its probable root meaning is "strong and mighty one." E. B. Smick, writing in the *Zondervan Pictorial Encyclopedia of the Bible*, says: "There are many suggestions for the meaning of the root but no

---

8 *Webster's New World Dictionary,* s.v. "name."

consensus, perhaps related to *El* meaning 'mighty' or 'strong'. A most commonly used Hebrew word for God, god, angels, or magistrates." The singular form *Eloah,* in the same reference work, is defined as follows: "('God,' singular of *Elohim,* q.v.). It is used forty-one times in Job (replacing *Elohim)* and sixteen times elsewhere. These occurrences are mainly poetic and refer to the true God except in 2 Chronicles 32:15; Daniel 11:37–39; and Habakkuk 1:11 (cf. Job 12:6)."[9] The name *Elohim,* like the word *God* in English, may refer to the true God, to any object of worship, or even to human dignitaries. Almost always, when used together with the definite article, it is applied to the one true God of Israel.

The use of the plural form for God (*Elohim*) with the singular article needs some explanation. Some scholars define the word as the plural of majesty or completeness. There may be some truth in this explanation, but it falls short of being a fully satisfactory accounting of its use in the whole of Scripture. To most conservative scholars, it gives a clear indication of the Trinity in unity. From an up-to-date Bible reference work: "The plural ending is usually described as a plural of majesty...but a better reason can be seen in Scripture itself where, in the very first chapter of Genesis, the necessity of a term conveying both the unity of the one God and yet allowing for a plurality of persons is found (Gn. 1:2, 26)." And again, "More probable is the view that *elohim* comes from *eloah* as a unique development of the Hebrew Scriptures and presents chiefly the plurality of persons in the Trinity of the godhead."[10] (More will be said about the Trinity in Section VII).

1. El: *meaning "God, god, mighty one, strength" (Dt. 32:4).* This is a very ancient name for God (probably related in origin to *eloah* and *elohim,* but on this scholars are not agreed) that is found in some form in all of the Semitic languages. It can have several meanings, but in the Bible, it usually refers to the true God of Israel. *El,* as a divine name, does not frequently appear alone, but most often it is used in compound with other terms, such as *El Elyon, El Shaddai,* etc. It also occurs in common names, as in Daniel, meaning "God is my judge." It is interesting that this name, as well as most of the common divine names, are found in Deuteronomy 32.

2. El Elyon *(Dt. 32:8): the Most High (from alah, which means "to ascend")*

> And Melchizedek king of Salem brought forth bread and wine: and he was the priest of the most high God *[El Elyon].* And he blessed him, and said, Blessed be Abram of the most high God *[El Elyon],* possessor of heaven and

---

9 Elmer B. Smick, *Zondervan Pictorial Encyclopedia of the Bible,* ed. Merrill C. Tenney (Grand Rapids, MI: Zondervan Publishing House, 1975) 11, s.v. *"ELOHIM."*

10 R. Laird Harris, Gleason L. Archer Jr., and Bruce Waltke, eds., *Theological Wordbook of the Old Testament* (Chicago: Moody Press, 1981) I, s.v. *"elohim."*

earth: And blessed be the most high God *[El Elyon]* which hath delivered thine enemies into thy hand.

—GENESIS 14:18–20

It was the Most High God who so loved the world that He sent His Son to redeem us, who is our High Priest forever after the order of Melchizedek (Heb. 6:20). The Savior lowered Himself to the level of the guiltiest sinner: "Wherefore God hath highly exalted him, and given him a name above every name" (Phil. 2:9). He is at the right hand of the Most High God.

3. El Olam: *the Everlasting God.* The thought conveyed by this name was not only the eternal duration of God, but also His everlasting faithfulness. As recorded in Genesis, Abraham calls on Jehovah, "the everlasting God," who keeps His covenants (Gn. 21:33). The psalmist, thinking of the Lord as a perpetual dwelling place, said, "LORD, thou hast been our dwelling place in all generations. Before the mountains were brought forth, or ever thou hadst formed the earth and the world, even from everlasting to everlasting, thou art God *[El]*" (Ps. 90:1–2). Isaiah, the messianic prophet, exhorted the people in a time of wavering: "Trust in the LORD [Jehovah] forever, for in GOD [Jah] the LORD [Jehovah], we have an everlasting Rock" [lit., "Rock of Ages"] (Is. 26:4, NASB). Adam Clarke remarks on Isaiah 26:4: "Does not this refer to the lasting streams from the rock in the desert? And that rock was Christ."[11]

4. El Shaddai: *the Almighty God.* "And when Abram was ninety years old and nine, the LORD [Jehovah] appeared to Abram, and said unto him, I am the Almighty God *[El Shaddai]*; walk before me, and be thou perfect" (Gn. 17:1). (See also Gn. 28:3; 35:11; 43:14; 48:3; Ex. 6:3; Ez. 10:5.) The compound form, *El Shaddai,* is found seven times; the single word *shaddai,* meaning "the Almighty" is found forty-one times, thirty-one times in Job alone. Some older commentators took the word *shaddai* as being derived from the word *shad* meaning "breast," giving to the divine name the meaning of "the Satisfier" or "All-Sufficient One." This opinion seems to have come from an incorrect translation in the Greek Septuagint Version. Almost all scholars now derive the word *shad* from a word meaning "mountain," thus the modern understanding of "the Almighty," which is its obvious meaning in Genesis 17:1, where the name first occurs. This name emphasizes God's omnipotence.

B. *Adonai* (plural), *Adon* (singular)—Lord, lord, master, owner, ruler

This name is expressed in the following Scriptures: "After these things the word of the LORD [Jehovah] came unto Abram in a vision, saying, Fear not Abram: I am

---

11 *Adam Clarke's Commentary on the Whole Bible,* abridged by Ralph Earle (Grand Rapids, MI: Baker Book House, 1976).

thy shield, and thy exceeding great reward. And Abram said, Lord GOD [*Adonai Jehovah*], what wilt thou give me, seeing I go childless?" (Gn. 15:1–2). The word *adonai* is used in the Old Testament in very much the same way as the word *kurios* is used in the Greek New Testament and in much the same sense as we use the English word *Lord*. It can refer to a person who is a master, owner, or ruler; or it can refer to the Lord God, because He is the master and owner of everything: "And the servant took ten camels of the camels of his master [*adonai*], and departed" (Gn. 24:10). "Therefore Sarah laughed within herself, saying, After I am waxed old shall I have pleasure, my lord [*adonai*] being old also?" (Gn. 18:12). Peter refers to this verse: "Even as Sara obeyed Abraham, calling him lord [*kurion*]" (1 Pt. 3:6). The believer should be reminded that when we call Jesus "Lord," we are recognizing Him as our master. To call Jesus "Lord" and not obey Him is a contradiction in language and in conduct.

C. Jehovah

Jehovah is the personal name of God in His relationship as Redeemer.

> And Moses said unto God, Behold, when I come unto the children of Israel, and shall say unto them, The God of fathers hath sent me unto you; and they shall say to me, What is His name? what shall I say unto them? And God said unto Moses, I AM THAT I AM: and he said, Thus shalt thou say unto the children of Israel, I AM hath sent me unto you. And God said moreover unto Moses, Thus shalt thou say unto the children of Israel, The LORD [Jehovah] God of your fathers, the God of Abraham, the God of Isaac, and the God of Jacob, hath sent me unto you: this is my name for ever, and this is my memorial unto all generations."
>
> —EXODUS 3:13–15

This personal name also appears in Exodus 6:2–3: "And God spake unto Moses, and said unto him, I am the LORD [Jehovah]: And I appeared unto Abraham, unto Isaac, and unto Jacob, by the name of God Almighty [*El Shaddai*], but by my name JEHOVAH was I not known to them."

Jehovah is the name for the Lord God occurring most frequently in the Old Testament (5,321 times). The actual Hebrew form of the word was *YHWH* (the Hebrew alphabet does not have vowels). We really do not know how the Hebrews pronounced the name (probably *Yahweh;* the Greek transliteration is *Iaoue).* Because they were forbidden by the Commandments to take the name of the Lord in vain, they feared to pronounce the name of *Yahweh,* therefore they substituted in reading the word *Adonai.* After centuries transpired, they forgot how to pronounce *Jehovah* or *Yahweh,* and when scholars finally invented vowel points for written Hebrew, they gave to *Jehovah* the vowel points for *Adonai,* not knowing what the original vowel sounds had been.

Scholars differ over the etymology of the name *Jehovah* (YHWH), but quite certainly, it comes from a form of the verb "to be." This seems clear from the Lord's statement to Moses that "I AM" had sent him. "I AM THAT I AM" seems to amplify the name in a way that could mean "the eternally existing One." Jesus seemed to identify with the name when He said to the Jews, "Before Abraham was, *I am*" (Jn. 8:58, emphasis added). Could it mean, "*I am* the way, the truth and the life" (Jn. 14:6, emphasis added), "*I am* the light" (Jn. 8:12, emphasis added), "*I am* the bread of life" (Jn 6:35, emphasis added), and "*I am* the resurrection, and the life" (Jn. 11:25, emphasis added)? With joy we sing, "He's everything to me." An abbreviated form of *Jehovah,* JAH, is found forty-eight times in the Old Testament (first in Ex. 15:2). It has the same meaning as *Jehovah.* It occurs mostly in the Psalms, and it is always used in a context of praise: "Extol him that rideth upon the heavens by His name JAH" (Ps. 68:4).

D. *Ha Tsur*—"the Rock"

The metaphorical name for Jehovah, *Ha Tsur,* is found five times in Deuteronomy 32: "He is the Rock, his work is perfect" (Dt. 32:4). The term stresses the immutability of God, the Rock of Ages. (See also Dt. 32:15, 18, 30–31; Is. 17:10; 26:4; 32:2; 51:1; Ps. 19:14.) Paul said, "And did all drink the same spiritual drink: for they drank of that spiritual Rock that followed them: and that Rock was Christ" (1 Cor. 10:4). (Also Ex. 17:6).

E. The compound names of Jehovah

Since *Jehovah* is the covenant name of God expressing personal relationship (Ex. 19:3–6), it is natural that His name would be compounded with other terms that identify and make specific those relationships.

1. *Jehovah-Elohim.* "These are the generations of the heavens and the earth when they were created, in the day that the LORD God [*Jehovah-Elohim*] made the earth and the heavens" (Gn. 2:4). This name identifies Jehovah with the creation of all things. The triune God of creation is also the redeemer of His people.

2. *Jehovah-Jireh.* "And Abraham called the name of that place The LORD Will Provide [*Jehovah-Jireh*], as it is said to this day, 'In the mount of the LORD it will be provided'" (Gn. 22:14, NASB). God provided a substitute for Isaac, that he might go free. He has likewise provided for us, once for all, a substitute—the Lamb of God. "He that spared not his own Son, but delivered him up for us all, how shall he not with him also freely give us all things?" (Rom. 8:32).

3. *Jehovah-Rapha.* "And He said, 'If you will give earnest heed to the voice of the LORD your God, and do what is right in His sight, and give ear to His commandments,

and keep all His statutes, I will put none of the diseases on you which I have put on the Egyptians; for I, the LORD, am your healer" (Ex. 15:26, NASB). Jehovah here reveals His personal relationship as the healer of His people. Since the promise related to physical diseases, the healing must also be physical healing. There are a significant number of physical healings in the Old Testament which exemplify this attribute. The promise is conditional upon obedience, however, which explains why the physical healings were not more common. A very large part of the ministry of Jesus and His apostles was given to physical healing. The church has been given "gifts of healings" (1 Cor. 12:9) and the conditions of obedience still apply to God's people.

4. *Jehovah-Nissi.* "And Moses built an altar, and named it The LORD is My Banner" (Ex. 17:15, NASB). The Israelites had just been victorious in the battle with Amalek. Aaron and Hur had held up the hands of Moses until sunset, and while they did so Israel prevailed. To commemorate the victory, an altar was built and named "Jehovah Nissi" (Ex. 17:8–15). The Lord is our banner of victory, in the battle, "and his banner over me is love" (Sg. 2:4, NASB).

5. *Jehovah-Shalom.* "Then Gideon built an altar there to the LORD and named it The LORD is Peace [*Jehovah-Shalom*]" (Jgs. 6:24, NASB). When God was calling Gideon to lead Israel to victory over the Midianites, an angel appeared to him and wrought a miracle. Gideon supposed that he would die as a result. Jehovah assured him that he would live and lead Israel to triumph. Jehovah was peace to him, even before the battles began. *Shalom* ("peace") means more than freedom from conflict; it means prosperity, health, well-being, and faith in the face of conflict. Jesus said, "My peace I give unto you." (Jn. 14:27). (See also Eph. 2:15–16).

6. *Jehovah-Raah.* "The LORD is my shepherd; I shall not want" (Ps. 23:1). It was consoling to Israel to think of Jehovah as the great Shepherd of their flock, who provided such rich pastures that none needed to suffer want. What assurance there is to the Christian believer in the words of Jesus, "I am the good shepherd: the good shepherd giveth his life for the sheep" (Jn. 10:11). And, "When the chief Shepherd shall appear, ye shall receive a crown of glory that fadeth not away" (1 Pt. 5:4).

7. *Jehovah-Tsidkenu.* "In his days Judah shall be saved, and Israel shall dwell safely: and this is his name whereby he shall be called, THE LORD OUR RIGHTEOUSNESS" (Jer. 23:6). Paul wrote concerning Jesus our Savior, "But of him are ye in Christ Jesus, who of God is made unto us wisdom, and *righteousness*, and sanctification, and redemption" (1 Cor. 1:30, emphasis added).

8. *Jehovah-Sabaoth.* "Who is this King of glory? The LORD of hosts [*Jehovah-Sabaoth*], he is the King of glory" (Ps. 24:10). (See 1 Sm. 1:3.) Elisha found that the Lord of hosts surrounded His people in times of attacks by the enemy (2 Kgs. 6:13–17).

9. *Jehovah-Shammah.* "It was round about eighteen thousand measures; and the name of the city from that day shall be, The LORD is there" (Ez. 48:35). How strengthening it is to know that the transcendent God who created the vast universe

is also the immanent God, ever present with His people! The writer of Hebrews declared, "For he hath said, I will never leave thee, nor forsake thee. So that we may boldly say, The Lord is my helper, and I will not fear what man shall do unto me" (Heb. 13:5–6).

F. New Testament names of God

1. *Theos.* "In the beginning was the Word [*logos*], and the Word was with God [*Theos*], and the Word was God [*Theos*]" (Jn. 1:1). The Greek word *theos*, like *elohim*, can mean "God" or "gods." It is the usual word for "God" in the New Testament.

2. *Kurios.* "And that every tongue should confess that Jesus Christ is Lord [*Kurios*], to the glory of God [*Theos*] the Father [*Pater*]" (Phil. 2:11). All three New Testament divine names are used in the verse above. *Kurios* is like *adonai* in the Old Testament.

3. *Pater.* "After this manner therefore pray ye: Our Father [*Pater*] which art in heaven, Hallowed be thy name" (Mt. 6:9). Also, "But ye have received the Spirit of adoption, whereby we cry, Abba, Father" (Rom. 8:15). *Abba* was the Aramaic word for "father"; it was the word Jesus used in prayer in the garden of Gethsemane. What a privilege that, because of Christ's work of redemption, we may call upon the omnipotent One as our heavenly father!

V. THE ATTRIBUTES OF GOD

To write about the attributes of the infinite God is a sobering undertaking. However, one can only search the Word of God with the assurance that in the inspired Scriptures we have God's revelation of Himself to us. God has revealed to us those perfections and excellencies of His nature that He deems essential to our redemption, our worship, and our fellowship with Him. This can be one of the most interesting studies in the realm of Bible doctrine. Who is not awed and thrilled at reading words such as the following from the inspired pen of the prophet Isaiah:

> "To whom will you compare me? Or who is my equal?" says the Holy One. Lift your eyes and look to the heavens: Who created all these? He who brings out the starry host one by one, and calls them each by name. Because of His great power and mighty strength, not one of them is missing. Why do you say, O Jacob, and complain, O Israel, "My way is hidden from the Lord; my cause is disregarded by my God"? Do you not know? Have you not heard? The Lord is the everlasting God, the Creator of the ends of the earth. He will not grow tired or weary, and His understanding no one can fathom.
> —ISAIAH 40:25–28, NIV

Such expressions extol Him as both Creator and Provider and reveal His power, wisdom, providence, and immutability. This is but a part of one chapter from the Old Testament. When we add the New Testament and the revelation of God as seen in His Son Jesus Christ, we have a rich and living source from which to understand the properties and virtues of our God.

It is not easy to categorize the attributes of God. There are clearly two general kinds, but proper words to distinguish them are hard to find. One kind, only God possesses; another kind, man may possess to a limited degree. The kind that only God has I will call absolute attributes; the kind that can be shared with us I will call moral attributes.

A. Absolute attributes

1. *Self-existence.* "For as the Father hath life in himself; so hath he given to the Son to have life in himself" (Jn. 5:26).

God is the absolute source of all life and being, the uncaused Cause. He is not one in a series of emanations, as some have mistakenly taught. He is the eternal Living God, Creator of all beings and all things that have ever existed: "And he is before all things, and by him all things consist" (Col. 1:17). God is not dependent for being or essence upon any source outside Himself, thus He is Self-existent.

2. *Immutability.* "For I am the LORD, I change not" (Mal. 3:6). "Every good gift and every perfect gift is from above, and cometh down from the Father of lights, with whom is no variableness, neither shadow of turning" (Jas. 1:17).

Of our Lord Jesus Christ, we love to quote: "Jesus Christ the same yesterday, and to day, and for ever" (Heb. 13:8). The clauses, "with whom is no variableness" and "Jesus Christ is the same," are unqualified; therefore, the invariableness and sameness apply to all the divine attributes. It is very comforting to the believer to know that the covenants and promises of God are as reliable as the foundations of heaven. In Solomon's prayer at the dedication of the temple, he declared, "Blessed be the LORD, that hath given rest unto his people Israel, according to all that he promised: there hath not failed one word of all his good promise, which he promised by the hand of Moses his servant" (1 Kgs. 8:56).

Man changes from day to day; his obedience is not constant. Man's negative actions and attitudes may diminish the experience of conditional blessings for him, but this does not gainsay the faithfulness of God. Through the mouth of Malachi, God spoke with both reproach and entreaty: "Even from the days of your fathers ye are gone away from my ordinances, and have not kept them. Return unto me, and I will return unto you, saith the LORD of Hosts [*Jehovah-Sabaoth*]" (Mal. 3:7). Paul, perhaps more than anyone, expresses the unchanging love of Christ: "For I am persuaded, that neither death, nor life, nor angels, nor principalities, nor powers, nor things present, nor things to come, Nor height, nor depth, nor any other creature, shall be able to separate us from the love of God, which is in Christ Jesus our Lord" (Rom. 8:38–39).

3. *Eternity.* "Now unto the King eternal, immortal, invisible, the only wise God, be honour and glory for ever and ever. Amen" (1 Tm. 1:17).

God's majestic name given to Moses in Exodus 3:14, "I AM THAT I AM," reveals Him as above time. The psalmist exclaimed, "…even from everlasting to everlasting, thou art God" (Ps. 90:2). His existence, to express it from a human perspective, is from everlasting past to everlasting future. John the Apostle quotes the Lord: "I am Alpha and Omega, the beginning and the ending, saith the Lord, which is, and which was, and which is to come, the Almighty" (Rv. 1:8). The same claims of eternity are from the mouth of Jesus in Revelation 22:13. The eternal God is the giver of eternal life through His eternal Son: "He that hath the Son hath life" (1 Jn. 5:12).

4. *Omnipresence.* "Am I a God at hand, saith the LORD, and not a God afar off? Can any hide himself in secret places that I shall not see him? saith the LORD. Do not I fill heaven and earth? saith the LORD" (Jer. 23:23–24).

Solomon was aware of the immensity and omnipresence of God when he prayed, "Behold, the heaven and the heaven of heavens cannot contain thee; how much less this house that I have builded!" (1 Kgs. 8:27). God is everywhere present. However, He is in some specific places in manifestation. He met Moses at the burning bush and on the mount. He is in His temple, yet it cannot hold Him. He is in heaven, yet He fills heaven and Earth. He is on His throne where Jesus intercedes at His right hand, yet He has promised, "Lo, I am with you alway" (Mt. 28:20). He is everywhere, yet He promised to be wherever two or three were gathered in His name. God is everywhere, but not at all points in the same sense. He is not in everything (that is pantheism), but He is everywhere present. What a wonderful blessing it is that everywhere believers pray, worship, or serve, He is there. It is equally true that whoever shall call upon the name of the Lord shall be saved, no matter where he may be on the face of the earth.

The presence of God is in His Church in a special way through the work of the Holy Spirit: "And I will pray the Father, and he shall give you another Comforter, that He may abide with you for ever…He dwelleth with you, and shall be in you" (Jn. 14:16–17). Everywhere the church goes, there the Holy Spirit is present. Wherever the Gospel is preached, the Holy Spirit will "reprove the world of sin, and of righteousness, and of judgment" (Jn. 16:8).

5. *Omniscience*

> O LORD, thou has searched me, and known me. Thou knowest my down-sitting and mine uprising, thou understandest my thoughts afar off. Thou compassest my path and my lying down, and art acquainted with all my

ways. For there is not a word in my tongue, but, lo, O LORD, thou knowest
it altogether.

—PSALM 139:1–4

Two aspects of God's all-knowledge are emphasized in the Scriptures. First, nothing happens anywhere of which He is ignorant. Man cannot hide either his actions or his thoughts from God. If Gehazi's dishonesty and deceit were known to the prophet of God, they were certainly not hidden from the omniscient One (2 Kgs. 5:20–27). God brought to light in judgment the deceitful schemes of Ananias and Sapphira (Acts 5:1–11). In the letters to the seven Churches of Asia, the Lord clearly describes not only their actions, but also their inward spiritual condition (Rv. 2:1–3:22). All things are present to Him.

Secondly, God is also all-wise in His plans and purposes. He knows all things from the beginning. He has, in His wisdom, planned the redemption of His people, the building of His church, and the triumph of His kingdom. For example:

Wherein he hath abounded toward us in all wisdom and prudence; Having made known to us the mystery of his will, according to his good pleasure which he hath purposed in himself: That in the dispensation of the fulness of times he might gather together in one all things in Christ.

—EPHESIANS 1:8–10

And to make all men see what is the fellowship of the mystery, which from the beginning of the world hath been hid in God, who created all things by Jesus Christ: To the intent that now unto the principalities and powers in heavenly places might be known by the church the manifold wisdom of God, According to the eternal purposes which he purposed in Christ Jesus our Lord.

—EPHESIANS 3:9–11

It is encouraging to know that God, in His wisdom, has made plans that He will carry to completion, in spite of the freedom of will and choice He permits man to exercise. And when we love Him, in His wisdom He works all things together for good (Rom. 8:28).

6. *Omnipotence.* "Ah Lord GOD! behold, thou has made the heaven and the earth by thy great power and stretched out arm, and there is nothing too hard for thee" (Jer. 32:17).

Some have tried to find a contradiction in God's omnipotence because it is stated that there are some things that He cannot do, such as to lie, to sin, to deny Himself, and humorously, to make a rock so big that He cannot lift it. This is not a limitation of His power, but a self-limitation of His will. God will not do what is contrary to His nature, nor what is a contradiction in terms.

a) The greatness of God's power is seen in His created works. The vastness of the universe staggers our imagination, and the microscopic and sub-microscopic realms are almost equally complex. If we think how fearfully and wonderfully the human body is made, we stand in awe before the omnipotent God. His creative power is both immeasurable and incomprehensible. But beyond this is the eternal and unseen world. "The things which are seen are temporal [will pass away]; but the things which are not seen [spiritual reality] are eternal" (2 Cor. 4:18).

b) God's power is also seen in His sovereign rule over all. "Behold, the nations are as a drop of a bucket, and are counted as the small dust of the balance" (Is. 40:15). Biblical prophecy concerning the destinies of nations has had marvelous fulfillment, showing that God indeed rules the affairs of kings and human rulers. "And all the inhabitants of the earth are reputed as nothing: and he doeth according to his will in the army of heaven, and among the inhabitants of the earth: and none can stay his hand, or say unto him, What doest thou?" (Dn. 4:35). The book of Daniel is an eloquent commentary on the sovereignty of God over earthly kingdoms, which are represented as beasts or as parts of an image. The Lord's bringing of His people out of Egypt into the land of promise again demonstrates that nothing is too hard for the Lord (Gn. 18:14).

c) Another demonstration of divine power is the Church of Jesus Christ. God took twelve seemingly ordinary disciples, filled them with His Holy Spirit, and with them "turned the world upside down" (Acts 17:6). That Church is alive and well twenty centuries later and on the verge of worldwide revival.

d) The resurrection of Jesus from the dead shows the power of God over the realm of death and the grave. Together with Jesus, God has raised us up and seated us together with Him in heavenly places (Eph. 1:19–2:6) so "that ye may know...what is the exceeding greatness of his power to usward who believe, according to the working of his mighty power, Which he wrought in Christ, when he raised him from the dead" (Eph. 1:18–20).

e) Finally, God is sovereign over angels, principalities and powers, demon spirits, and Satan himself. God rules in heaven, on Earth, and under the Earth. He who made all things and rules all realms can handle any problems that beset His people.

7. *Sovereignty.* We have already, under the previous heading, discussed God's sovereignty over nations and the unseen realm. Some treatment, at this point, should be given to the age-long controversy over God's sovereignty versus man's free will. Paul writes in Ephesians, "According as he hath chosen us in him before the foundation of the world, that we should be holy and without blame before him in love: Having predestinated us unto the adoption of children by Jesus Christ to himself, according to the good pleasure of his will" (Eph. 1:4–5). This passage seems to imply

that everything results from the will of God. On the other hand, John, in Revelation 22, quotes Jesus in His final appeal to man: "And whosoever will, let him take the water of life freely" (Rv. 22:17). This passage clearly says that the water of life is available to any on the basis of choice and human free will. Unquestionably, the doctrines of election and predestination are in the Bible. On the other hand, we have the words of Jesus while He wept over Jerusalem, "O Jerusalem, Jerusalem...how often would I have gathered thy children together...and ye *would* not!" (Mt. 23:37, emphasis added). Again, "And ye *will* not come to me, that ye might have life" (Jn. 5:40, emphasis added). And again, "Whosoever believeth in him should not perish, but have everlasting life" (Jn. 3:16).

In truth, the Bible teaches both positions. God is sovereign, but not arbitrary; man has freedom of choice and will, with certain limitations. Our inability to reconcile the two positions does not make one position or the other untrue. Our inability to see how both can be true at the same time is due to our finite human comprehension. God can be sovereign without violating man's essential freedom. All divine truth is in a sense paradoxical to us, because our vision of reality is only in parts, at the most 180 degrees. Divine truth is a full circle, 360 degrees. Samuel Fisk quotes Charles Spurgeon as saying, "Brethren, be willing to see both sides of the shield of truth. Rise above the babyhood which cannot believe two doctrines until it sees the connecting link. Have you not two eyes, man? Must you needs put one of them out in order to see clearly?"[12]

Dr. R. A. Torrey, in the following, sets forth foreknowledge as the basis for reconciling predestination with man's freedom of choice. He writes:

> The actions of Judas and the rest were taken into God's plan, and thus made a part of it. But it does not mean that these men were not perfectly free in their choice. They did not do as they did because God knew that they would do so, but the fact that they would do so was the basis upon which God knew it. Foreknowledge no more determines a man's actions than afterknowledge. Knowledge is determined by the fact, not the fact by the knowledge...God knows from all eternity what each man will do, whether he will yield to the Spirit and accept Christ, or whether he will resist the Spirit and refuse Christ. Those who will receive Him are ordained to eternal life. If any are lost, it is simply because they will not come to Christ and thus obtain life (John 5:40). Whosoever will may come (Rv. 22:17), and all who come will be received (John 6:37).[13]

---

12 Charles Spurgeon, *Faith and Regeneration,* quoted in Samuel Fisk, *Divine Sovereignty and Human Freedom* (Neptune, NJ: Loizeaux Brothers, 1973) cover.

13 Reuben Archer Torrey, *Practical and Perplexing Questions Answered* (New York: Fleming H. Revell Company, 1909) 61.

B. Moral attributes

Certain attributes we will call moral, because they are shared to a limited degree with redeemed man and pertain to character and conduct. They all speak of the goodness of God.

1. *Holiness*

> For I am the LORD your God: ye shall therefore sanctify yourselves, and ye shall be holy; for I am holy: neither shall ye defile yourselves with any manner of creeping thing that creepeth upon the earth. For I am the LORD that bringeth you up out of the land of Egypt, to be your God: ye shall therefore be holy, for I am holy.
>
> —LEVITICUS 11:44–45

God is a holy God, and He requires holiness of His people.

Webster defines *holiness* as follows: "Dedicated to religious use; belonging to or coming from God; consecrated, sacred; spiritually perfect or pure; untainted by evil or sin; sinless, saintly."[14]

The Hebrew word for *holy* is *qodesh;* it is defined in *Old Testament Word Studies* as follows: "Ascribed to all those things which in any way pertain to God, or His worship; sacred; free from defilement of vice, idolatry, and other impure and profane things."[15]

The Greek word is *hagios,* which is defined as follows by the *Greek Lexicon:* "Dedicated to God, holy, sacred; reserved for God and His service; pure, perfect, worthy of God, consecrated."[16]

The basic idea of holiness, as applied to God, is that of separation and exaltation, as well as absolute perfection of character. Isaiah's vision of God accents these qualities:

> I saw also the Lord sitting upon a throne, high and lifted up, and His train filled the temple. Above it stood the seraphims....And one cried unto another, and said, Holy, holy, holy is the LORD of hosts: the whole earth is full of His glory....Then said I, Woe is me!...because I am a man of unclean lips...for mine eyes have seen the King, the LORD of hosts.
>
> —ISAIAH 6:1–5

---

14 *Webster's Dictionary*, s.v. "holiness."

15 William Wilson, *Old Testament Word Studies* (Grand Rapids, MI: Kregel Publications, 1978), s.v. "qodesh."

16 William F Arndt and F. Wilbur Gingrich. *Greek English Lexicon of the New Testament* (Chicago: University of Chicago Press, 1957), s.v. "hagios."

The holy God was above all, ruling as king and owner of all things. He was revealed as *Jehovah-Sabaoth* in majestic glory, receiving the worship of the seraphim who extol His holiness, before whose perfections the prophet cried out in awe and repentance of sins. Before we contemplate God's other moral attributes, this is the concept we should have of God. Far more mention is made in Scripture of God's holiness than of His all-power, wisdom, and omnipresence combined. The Scriptures establish the holiness of God long before they picture His love. Exodus, Leviticus, and Numbers repeatedly portray the God of holiness. It is not until we come to Deuteronomy 4:37 that we find an outright declaration of His love, and that is given in a context of awe-inspiring holiness.

As applied to men or things, the primary meaning of holiness is dedication and consecration, the quality of being separated to God. Things are holy that are dedicated exclusively to God or His worship and service. Anything is holy which wholly belongs to God, as His temple with its utensils and furnishings. People were holy who were God's people. Israel is called a holy nation. In the New Testament, the Lord's people are called saints, meaning "holy ones" (Rom. 1:7).

Later, holiness also meant separation from all defilement and from all forms of idolatry. By Isaiah's day, injustice became as great a breach of holiness as delinquency in worship and sacrifices (Is. 1:1–20). A holy God was most provoked at Israel for the adultery of worship to pagan deities.

In the New Testament times, the emphasis shifts more to inward purity of life and separation from the world (see Rom. 6:19, 22; 12:1–2; 2 Cor. 7:1; Eph. 4:24; 1 Thes. 3:13; 4:7; Ti. 2:3; Heb. 12:10, 14; 1 Pt. 1:15–16; 2 Pt. 3:11). The believer throughout his Christian life is being sanctified through the Word and the Holy Spirit, for it is the purpose of God to present us unto Himself and to the Father unblameable in holiness. A holy God will have a holy people: "But as he which hath called you is holy, so be ye holy in all manner of conversation [conduct]; Because it is written, Be ye holy; for I am holy" (1 Pt. 1:15–16).

2. *Righteousness (justice; Gn. 18:25; Dt. 32:4; Rom. 3:25–26).* "That be far from thee to do after this manner, to slay the righteous with the wicked…Shall not the Judge of all the earth do right?" (Gn. 18:25). Closely related to the holiness of God are His righteousness and justice. To simplify, it might be said that God's righteousness is His holiness in action, and His justice is His righteousness in rule and government.

The Hebrew word for "righteous" is *tsedek*, which is defined as follows: "rightness, straightness, rectitude; justice of a judge, of a king, of God exhibited in punishing the wicked, or in avenging, delivering, rewarding the righteous."[17] Another Hebrew word is *mishpat*, which means judgment that is right or just.

---

17 Wilson, s.v. "tsedek."

The Greek word for "righteous" is *dikaios*, a definition of which is, "1. of God—just, righteous, with reference to His judgment of men and nations, a righteous judge; 2. of men—upright, just, righteous conforming to the laws of God and man, and living in accordance with them."[18]

God is a righteous God, because He acts at all times in complete conformity with His holy nature and will. One of the greatest chapters of the Bible about God is Deuteronomy 32. In verse four we have a definition of God's righteous actions: "He is the Rock [*Ha Tsur*], his work is perfect: for all his ways are judgment [*mishpat*—just judgment]: a God of truth [*amunah*—faithfulness in fulfilling promises] and without iniquity [*avel*—injustice in dealing with men], just [*tsadik*—righteous] and right [*jashar*—upright] is he" (Dt. 32:4). God's righteousness is immutable; He is a rock. God is referred to as a rock five times in Deuteronomy 32. His righteousness never changes, His justice is unfailing, and He is faithful in dealing with His people according to His nature and His revealed Law and covenants. He will punish in awful judgment as well as reward bountifully, but always according to His promises and covenants. He is completely above any unjust or deceitful treatment. All His ways are upright.

As righteous God, He lays down just laws to govern the dealings men have with one another in society. The first four commandments have to do with the worship and service of God, but the last six pertain to the people's treatment one toward another. Our God deals with us in justice; we must deal one with another in righteousness. God, through the mouth of Isaiah, admonished Israel, "Put away the evil of your doings from before mine eyes…Learn to do well; seek judgment [*mishpat*—justice], relieve the oppressed, judge [righteously] the fatherless, plead for the widow. Come now, and let us reason together, saith the LORD" (Is. 1:16–18).

In the New Testament, the English words *righteousness* and *justice* are translations of the same Greek word. This is seen in the definition of the word *justification*, which means the act of declaring one to be righteous. In the book of Romans, we learn about a righteousness of man apart from the Law. God requires perfect righteousness from man, but man in his fallen state falls short of perfection. In the Law, provision was made for cleansing through the sacrificial system. Paul made the following declaration concerning a new basis for righteousness:

> But now the righteousness of God without the law is manifested, being witnessed by the law and the prophets; even the righteousness of God which is by faith of Jesus Christ unto all and upon all them that believe; for there is no difference: For all have sinned, and come short of the glory of God [the glory of God is his Holiness]; Being justified freely by his grace through

---

18 Arndt and Gingerich, s.v. "dikaios."

the redemption that is in Christ Jesus: Whom God hath set forth to be a propitiation through faith in his blood, to declare his righteousness for the remission of sins that are past, through the forbearance of God; to declare, I say, at this time his righteousness: that he might be just, and the justifier of him which believeth in Jesus.

—ROMANS 3:21–26

Our righteous and holy God is also a God of mercy and forbearance, but He will not act inconsistently with His holiness. In His righteousness He made a way to justify the sinner by sending His infinite Son to be, once for all, the perfect sacrifice for sin. Since as the Last Adam He lived in perfect obedience to the Holy will of the Father, God could bestow upon the believer Christ's righteousness without ceasing to be righteous Himself. The believing sinner becomes righteous in Christ, and at the same time God's righteousness has not been compromised. We must remember, however, that we are righteous in Christ: "Therefore being justified by faith, we have peace with God through our Lord Jesus Christ" (Rom. 5:1).

3. *Love (mercy, goodness)*

He that loveth not knoweth not God; for God is love. In this was manifested the love of God toward us, because that God sent his only begotten Son into the world, that we might live through him. Herein is love, not that we loved God, but that he loved us, and sent his Son to be the propitiation for our sins. Beloved, if God so loved us, we ought also to love one another....And we have known and believed the love that God hath to us. God is love; and he that dwelleth in love dwelleth in God, and God in him.

—1 JOHN 4:8–11, 16

Perhaps all God's moral attributes are encompassed in these two: His holiness and His love. In His holiness He is unapproachable; in His love He approaches us. In His holiness He is transcendent; in His love He is immanent. But there are not two Lords, but One who is both holy and loving. For fallen man, these two apparently irreconcilable attributes are brought together in the finished atoning work of Christ, in which the demands of holiness are satisfied and the outpouring of love is realized.

The Hebrew word for "love" is *àhab,* which has about the same range of meanings as our English word. It can be used to express both divine love and the carnal love of man. The Old Testament does not reveal God's love in words until the book of Deuteronomy. Perhaps it was necessary to establish the holiness of God in advance of the revelation of His love. In Exodus 19:12, we read, "Whosoever toucheth the mount shall be surely put to death." But in Deuteronomy 7:6–8 God expresses His love as the basis of His covenant with the nation Israel:

> For thou art an holy people unto the LORD thy God: the LORD thy God
> hath chosen thee to be a special people unto himself, above all people that
> are upon the face of the earth. The LORD did not set His love upon you, nor
> choose you, because you were more in number than any people; for ye were
> the fewest of all people: But because the LORD loved you, and because he
> would keep the oath which he had sworn unto your fathers, hath the LORD
> brought you out with a mighty hand, and redeemed you out of the house of
> bondmen.

God's love can be seen constantly in Israel's history, in His patience and longsuffering in dealing with His people, even in times of their backslidings and calamities: "Whom the Lord loveth He chasteneth" (Heb. 12:6).

In the New Testament, there are several Greek words for *love*, but when reference is made to God's love, the word used is always *agape*. The lexicon defines *agape* and the verb *agapao* as follows: "To love, value, esteem, feel or manifest generous concern for, be faithful towards, to delight in, to set store upon; whence—love, generosity, kindly concern, devotedness."[19] The noun *agape* is scarcely found in classical Greek. It is one of the words given a new Christian meaning in the New Testament. The apostle John gives us the two greatest statements about the love of God: "For God so loved the world, that he gave his only begotten Son, that whosoever believeth in him should not perish, but have everlasting life" (Jn. 3:16); and, "God is love" (1 Jn. 4:8).

The following are proofs of God's love for the believer: a) securing our salvation and eternal life (Jn. 3:16), b) desiring and providing for us all needed things (Rom. 8:32; Jas. 1:17; Phil. 4:19), c) sending the Comforter, the Holy Spirit (Jn. 14:15–16; 16:7), d) placing us in His body (Eph. 5:25–30), e) making us sons of God (1 Jn. 3:1–2), f) providing means for bodily healing (Jas. 5:14–16; Mt. 8:16–17), and g) providing means for a victorious Christian life (Rom. 8:35–39).

Under the category of love there may be included other virtues such as: mercy, longsuffering, goodness, forgiveness, compassion, etc.

4. *Truth (Dt. 32:4).* "In hope of eternal life, which God, that cannot lie, promised before the world began" (Ti. 1:2). "And the Word was made flesh, and dwelt among us,...full of grace and truth" (Jn. 1:14). "I am the way, the truth, and the life" (Jn. 14:6). "Let God be true, but every man a liar" (Rom. 3:4). The truth of God is a part of His holy nature and could be considered under the heading of holiness and righteousness, but for practical reasons we will treat it apart as a distinct attribute.

Three reassuring applications may be made of the fact that God is truth:

---

19 H.K. Moulton, ed., *Analytical Greek Lexicon,* revised (Grand Rapids, MI: Zondervan Publishing House, 1978), s.v. "agape" and "agapao."

a) Because God is truth, His Word is true. It is the true revelation of His nature, His will and purpose for man, and His plan of salvation. His promises and covenants are made in truth and are unfailingly dependable (Ps. 119:89; Jn. 17:17).

b) God is truth because He is the only true God, Creator of all things, and the only true object of man's worship. All idolatry, therefore, is a lie and deception. God is the only being or goal worthy of top priority in man's life (Jn. 4:23–24).

5. *Faithfulness.* Because God is truth, He is faithful to keep all His promises and covenants. God cannot (and will not) lie (Nm. 23:19). We know that all His promises will be fulfilled because God by nature cannot promise what He does not intend to do, and, being omnipotent, He is able to do what He promises. We must understand, however, that many promises are conditional upon certain obedience on our part. If we disobey, God is not unfaithful in withholding the promised blessing. It may sometimes appear that God is unfaithful to a promise because of delay. When God delays, it is always in our best interest. In His time, dictated by His wisdom, He will faithfully fulfill His promise. (Heb. 10:23; 2 Cor. 1:20; 2 Pt. 3:4; 1 Kgs. 8:56; 2 Pt. 1:4).

VI. The Works of God

A. Divine purpose (Is. 14:26–27; Eph. 1:11)

> This is the purpose that is purposed upon the whole earth: and this is the hand that is stretched out upon all nations. For the LORD of hosts hath purposed, and who shall disannul it? and his hand is stretched out, and who shall turn it back?
>
> —ISAIAH 14:26–27

> In whom also we have obtained an inheritance, being predestinated according to the purpose of him who worketh all things after the counsel of his own will.
>
> —EPHESIANS 1:11

It seems clear from the teaching of Scripture that all events of nations and individuals are known to God from the beginning and that they are taken into account in His plan and purpose. This does not mean that God causes and is responsible for all acts and events, but that they are a part of His purpose in the sense that He works all things to His ultimate glory. "Declaring the end from the beginning, and from ancient times the things that are not yet done, saying, My counsel shall stand, and I will do all my pleasure...I have purposed it, I will also do it" (Is. 46:10–11).

The overruling purpose of God in the affairs of mankind is expressed by Paul in his sermon to the Athenians: "He [God] giveth to all life, and breath, and all things;

And hath made of one blood all nations of men for to dwell on all the face of the earth, and hath determined the times before appointed, and the bounds of their habitation" (Acts 17:25–26). This "before appointed" divine purposing, however, does not deprive them of their freedom of choice, nor personal responsibility "because," as Paul goes on to say, "He hath appointed a day, in which he will judge the world in righteousness by that man whom he hath ordained" (v. 31).

The great miracle of Bible prophecy demonstrates two things: that God is omniscient and knows all things from the beginning, and that He has a plan and purpose which He carries out in His power and wisdom for His glory and for the redemption of His people. It would be a confusing world if every act and happening surprised God and required Him to improvise to rescue His program from disaster. Not even man's original sin surprised God; He created man with freedom of will to obey or disobey. Why God permitted sin and evil, we cannot perfectly explain, but we have strong intimations that a redeemed people will ultimately contribute to God's glory vastly more than a race of conforming automatons. God is not the author of sin. He, in His infinite wisdom which we cannot fully fathom, made man a free moral agent capable of obedience or disobedience. Depravity, pain, and crime resulted from man's disobedience, but God purposed to overrule these. The three Hebrew children in the fiery furnace; Daniel in the lion's den; and Joseph, sold cruelly into Egypt, demonstrate the working of divine purpose: "Ye meant evil against me, but God meant it for good" (Gn. 50:20, NKJV). All of the above events turned out to the blessing of His people and to His own glory. Furthermore, before He created man, He had already purposed to bring redemption by Christ Jesus: "But with the precious blood of Christ, as of a lamb without blemish and without spot: Who verily was foreordained before the foundation of the world, but was manifest in these last times for you" (1 Pt. 1:19–20), and "In hope of eternal life, which God, who cannot lie, promised before the world began" (Ti. 1:2).

It is scriptural that God's purpose includes His Church, as a definite number known to Him from the beginning. "According as he hath chosen us in him before the foundation of the world, that we should be holy and without blame before him in love: Having predestined us unto the adoption of children by Jesus Christ to himself, according to the good pleasure of his will" (Eph. 1:4–5). "For whom he did foreknow, He also did predestinate to be conformed to the image of his Son" (Rom. 8:29). We must not read into this, however, the idea of an arbitrary predestination that elects some and excludes others. This predestination is based upon the foreknowledge of God, as Paul states in the above passage in Romans, and as Peter confirms in his first epistle: "Elect according to the foreknowledge of God the Father" (1 Pt. 1:2). God, knowing from the beginning who would accept salvation and who would disobey the gospel offer, elected those whom He foreknew would obey. J. Sidlow Baxter, world renowned Bible teacher, writes: "It is in the light of His perfect foreknowledge that

He preadapts and prearranges and predetermines. Thus, while He never leaves His ultimate purposes at the mercy of human uncertainty...He recognizes the free will of man all through, and prearranges according to His foreknowledge of what man will do."[20] Herbert Lockyer remarks about predestination: "What must be borne in mind is the fact that 'predestination' is not God's predetermining from past ages who should and who should not be saved. Scripture does not teach this view."[21] In his *Lectures in Systematic Theology,* Henry C. Thiessen, discussing predestination, says: "God foreknew what one would do in response to His common grace; and He elected those whom He foresaw would respond positively."[22]

It seems clear that the divine purpose culminates in God's Son, Christ Jesus, and that it involves the Church, the body of Christ:

> And to make all men see what is the fellowship of the mystery, which from the beginning of the world hath been hid in God, who created all things by Jesus Christ: to the intent that now unto the principalities and powers in heavenly places might be known by the Church the manifold wisdom of God, according to the eternal purpose which He purposed in Christ Jesus our Lord.
>
> —EPHESIANS 3:9–11

B. Creation (Gn. 1:1; Heb. 11:3; Neh. 9:6; Col. 1:15–17; Jn. 1:3)

"In the beginning God created [*bará*] the heaven and the earth" (Gn. 1:1). "Through faith we understand that the worlds were framed by the word [*rhema*] of God, so that things which are seen were not made of things which do appear" (Heb. 11:3). "All things were made by him; and without him was not anything made that was made" (Jn. 1:3). The Bible represents the original Creation, Genesis 1:1, as an immediate Creation. The physical universe as we know it was spoken into being by God. It had not existed previously in some other form, as the pantheists, dualists, and some modern theologians would have us think.

Dr. A. H. Strong defines the Creation as follows: "That free act of the triune God by which in the beginning and for His own glory He made, without the use of pre-existing material, the whole visible and invisible universe."[23]

---

20 James Sidlow Baxter, *Explore the Book* (Grand Rapids, MI: Zondervan Publishing House, 1975) VI, 47–48.

21 Herbert Lockyer, *All the Doctrines of the Bible* (Grand Rapids, MI: Zondervan Publishing House, 1964), 153.

22 Henry Clarence Theissen, *Introductory Lectures in Systematic Theology* (Grand Rapids, MI: Wm. B. Eerdmans Publishing Company, 1961), 157.

23 Augustus Hopkins Strong, *Systematic Theology* (Philadelphia. PA: The Judson Press, 1912), 371

That God created rather than remade everything is borne out by the use of the Hebrew verb *bará*, indeed, to judge from its use in Joshua 17:15, 18, where it occurs in the *piel*, [to hew out] means literally "to cut, or hew," but in *kal* it always means to create, and is only applied to divine creation, the production of that which had no existence before. In this verse...the existence of any primeval material is precluded by the object created: "the heaven and the earth."[24]

We will not endeavor here to explain the first chapters of Genesis beyond the fact that they chronicle the creation of the heaven, the earth, and the human race. Whether Genesis 1:2 represents a catastrophic "gap," with verse three relating a recreation; whether the days of Creation are literal days or indefinite periods; and whether the details can be reconciled with modem science's theories of origin are better left to commentaries and books devoted to the discussion of science and the Bible. It suffices to say that conservatives of equal scholarship are divided in their interpretation of the details of the Creation account. Many reverent men of science will admit that there is no basic conflict between the Genesis account of Creation and the known facts of science. Many modern materialistic scientists begin with a hypothesis that all phenomena can eventually be explained by laws of matter and motion. That is their "faith." We believe the Bible record that states that all things had a divine origin. We believe that more facts support our view than support a materialistic, evolutionary hypothesis. Furthermore, we believe that faith in the Creator-God of the Bible establishes a foundation for a better, more morally sound, more socially concerned, and more ethically responsible society than one based on a godless, materialistic, purposeless "faith."

A word should be said about what existed before Genesis 1:1. God, the Father, the Son, and the Holy Spirit already existed, as all Three were active in the Creation (Jn. 1:1; Gn. 1:2; Col. 1:16). Jesus prayed, as recorded in John chapter 17: "And now, O Father, glorify thou me with thine own self with the glory which I had with thee before the world was" and "Father, I will that...they may behold my glory, which thou has given me: for thou lovedst me before the foundation of the world" (vv. 5, 24). Before the world was, the Trinity was, and love was among the persons of the triune God. John 3:16 speaks of the love of God that commissioned His Son to His work of redemption before Creation, before man, and before the Fall. God's redeeming love was not an afterthought. Peter said about Jesus: "Who verily was foreordained before the foundation of the world, but was manifest in these last times for you" (1 Pt. 1:20). Francis A. Schaeffer writes on this subject:

---

24 C. F. Keil and F. Delitzsch. *Commentary on the Pentateuch* (Grand Rapids, MI: Wm. B. Eerdmans Publishing Company, n.d.), I, 47.

The impersonal answer at any level... does not explain these two basic factors—the universe and its form—But the Judeo-Christian tradition begins with the opposite answer. The universe had a personal beginning on the high order of the Trinity. That is, thought and communication existed prior to the creation of the heavens and the earth.[25]

The result of Creation, ultimately, will be a redeemed multitude that no man can number, forever worshiping and serving and glorifying God. The earth, redeemed and remade into a new earth, will be the scene of God's kingdom; and in the new heavens and the new earth, with sin and Satan cast into the lake of fire, God and the Lamb will reign, whose right it is to reign (Is. 2:1–5; Rv. 19–22).

C. Providence (Mt. 5:45; Acts 14:17; Ps. 37:1–3; Ps. 105)

"For he maketh his sun to rise on the evil and on the good, and sendeth rain on the just and on the unjust" (Mt. 5:45). "Nevertheless he left not himself without witness, in that he did good, and gave us rain from heaven, and fruitful seasons, filling our hearts with food and gladness" (Acts 14:17). "Trust in the LORD, and do good; so shalt thou dwell in the land, and verily thou shalt be fed" (Ps. 37:3). Included together with providence is God's preservation of His creation, which can be viewed as an aspect of His providence. To the Lord Jesus Christ has been given the operation of the preservation of all things. "For by him were all things created, that are in heaven, and that are in earth, visible and invisible...all things were created by him and for him: And he is before all things, and by him all things consist [hold together]" (Col. 1:16–17).

Preservation has been defined as "that continuous agency of God by which He maintains in existence the things He has created together with the properties and powers with which he has endowed them."[26] Thiessen says of providence: "The Christian view affirms that God has not merely created the universe together with all its properties and powers, and that He is preserving all that He has created, but that as a holy, benevolent, wise, and omnipotent Being, He also exercises sovereign control over it. This sovereign control is called providence."[27]

Preservation and providence are denied by the pantheist, who views the universe as eternal and operating by unchanging fates; and by the deists, who teach that after God created the universe and endowed it with intrinsic laws, He left it to run by its own built-in capacities. The modern materialist does not accept the existence of a

---

25 Francis A. Schaeffer, *Genesis in Space and Time* (Glendale, CA: Regal Books and Inter-varsity Press, 1972), 21.

26 Strong, 410.

27 Thiessen, 177.

personal God; therefore he rejects the idea of a personal providence. On the other hand, the Scriptures everywhere give evidence of the continual working of a divine providence and preservation.

Most people today are deeply concerned about the matter of God's care and providential oversight of our lives, our society, our families, our businesses, and our possessions. Men may not want God to inspect their conduct too closely, but they hope, somehow, that He protects their lives and properties. No doubt, much ordinary prayer, day by day, is for divine protection and provision. A common question in times of adversity and national calamity is, "Is God still on the throne?" Let us examine the Word of God to see the areas of God's providential care.

1. *He governs the physical universe.* "The Lord hath prepared his throne in the heavens; and his kingdom ruleth over all" (Ps. 103:19). "He causeth the grass to grow for the cattle, and herb for the service of man: that he may bring forth food out of the earth" (Ps. 104:14). God maintains continual active rule over the nations of the earth; He is not responsible for all the individual actions of men who are free agents. Some leaders like Hitler and Stalin have done unimaginably evil things, but God in His greater providence finally makes wrathful men praise Him and fit into the divine plan of prophecy. While God has given the earth natural conditions, such as the right proportion of sea and land, trade winds and sea currents, evaporation and precipitation to maintain weather congenial to life and agriculture, He still preserves these processes by His oversight. That nature does not always distribute benefits to every man's convenience is a part of the curse upon the earth accompanying the Fall of man (Gn. 3:17–19). But even an earth under the curse displays God's design and care to those who are not blinded by unbelief.

2. *He cares for the animal creation.* "Behold the fowls of the air: for they sow not, neither do they reap, nor gather into barns; yet your heavenly Father feedeth them" (Mt. 6:26). "The young lions roar after their prey, and seek their meat from God" (Ps. 104:21). The animals have been given instincts by God, which enable them by nature to care for themselves, but they also, like man, depend upon the Creator and Sustainer of the earth to provide rain, vegetation, oxygen, and a stable climate.

3. *He providentially governs the nations.* "For the kingdom is the Lord's: and he is the governor among the nations" (Ps. 22:28). "He ruleth by his power forever; his eyes behold the nations" (Ps. 66:7). The book of Daniel, read together with ancient history, will demonstrate how completely the nations, even the world powers, are subject to divine purpose and follow the prophetic Word. Isaiah's naming of Cyrus a century before he walked on the stage of history to expedite God's plan for Israel proves that God foreknows and orders the human drama. Still, the free will of Cyrus was not violated (Is. 44:28, 45:1–4; Ez. 1:1–6).

4. *God cares for our birth and place in life.*

Before I formed you in the womb I knew you; Before you were born I sanctified you; I ordained you a prophet to the nations.

—JEREMIAH 1:5, NKJV

I will praise thee; for I am fearfully and wonderfully made: marvelous are
thy works; and that my soul knoweth right well. My substance was not hid
from thee, when I was made in secret, and curiously wrought...Thine eyes
did see my substance, yet being unperfect; and in thy book all my members
were written, which in continuance were fashioned, when as yet there was
none of them.

—PSALM 139:14–16

But the very hairs of your head are all numbered.

—MATTHEW 10:30

The Lord's providence embraces not only our occupations and major choices of
life, but even the smallest details, such as the hairs of your head and our daily bread.

5. *God is concerned about our successes and failures.* "He hath put down the mighty
from their seats, and exalted them of low degree" (Lk. 1:52). When we have dedicated
our lives to the Lord, we can trust Him to oversee our progress and promotion in
service. Perhaps we should be less anxious about the relative prestige of positions;
God in His wisdom knows just where we belong. Promotion comes from the Lord
(Ps. 75:6–7).

6. *God provides protection for the righteous.* "1 will both lay me down in peace, and
sleep: for thou, LORD, only makest me dwell in safety" (Ps. 4:8). "For we know that
all things work together for good to them that love God, to them who are the called
according to his purpose" (Rom. 8:28).

7. *God supplies the needs and wants of His people.* "Charge them that are rich in
this world, that they be not highminded, nor trust in uncertain riches, but in the
living God, who giveth us richly all things to enjoy" (1 Tm. 6:17). (See Phil. 4:19.)

8. *God provides the answer to our prayers.* "But when ye pray, use not vain repetitions, as the heathen do....Be not ye therefore like unto them: for your Father
knoweth what things ye have need of, before ye ask him. After this manner therefore
pray ye" (Mt. 6:7–9). "But seek ye first the kingdom of God, and his righteousness;
and all these things shall be added unto you" (Mt. 6:33).

9. *The Lord governs the reward of the righteous and the punishment of the impenitent.* "Thou shalt guide me with thy counsel, and afterward receive me to glory" (Ps.
73:24). "For the Lord knoweth the way of the righteous: but the way of the ungodly
shall perish" (Ps. 1:6).

The average man is greatly prone to anxiety. Worry lands too many in a sick bed
or an early grave. John was correct when he said, "Fear hath torment" (1 Jn. 4:18). He

also said, "Perfect love casteth out fear" (1 Jn. 4:18). When we have a strong confidence in divine providence, we are relieved of the tormenting anxiety to which man is so inclined. "Are not two sparrows sold for a copper coin? And not one of them falls to the ground apart from your Father's will....Do not fear therefore; you are of more value than many sparrows" (Mt. 10:29–31, NKJV). Glory to God!

VII. THE TRI-UNITY (TRINITY) OF GOD

A. Definition

We approach the study of the Trinity with a deep sense of awe. All study of the nature of God defies our full comprehension, but the tri-unity of God is the greatest of all the divine mysteries. In it we stand on holy ground. Because it is a mystery, we do not expect to reduce it to logical formulas, any more than we would attempt to transfer the Pacific Ocean into a teacup. We do study the doctrine, however, because it is the center gem of divine revelation. To the finite human mind, the unity of God and the trinity of God are contradictions, but both doctrines are clearly taught throughout the New Testament. The tri-unity of God is, in fact, the foundation stone of the Christian faith. Every time in Church history that the doctrine of the Trinity has been compromised, the other major Bible tenets have also been compromised or abandoned. Those who have denied the Trinity have also denied the deity of Christ, the Virgin Birth, the vicarious Atonement, and the personality of the Holy Spirit. Or else, they have made God a stage player wearing three different masks.

The apostle Paul, in his sermon to the Ephesian elders, said:

> Take heed therefore unto yourselves, and to all the flock, over the which the Holy Ghost has made you overseers, to feed the church of God, which he hath purchased with his own blood. For I know this, that after my departing shall grievous wolves enter in among you, not sparing the flock. Also of your own selves shall men arise, speaking perverse things, to draw away disciples after them....Therefore watch.
>
> —ACTS 20:28–31

Observe the trinitarian statements in the above passage: "Holy Spirit has made you overseers" and "the church of God, which He purchased with His own blood." Paul's prediction of heresies and divisions in the church very soon began to come to pass. In the second century two separatist groups denied the doctrine of the Trinity; one came to be called Monarchianism, the other Sabellianism. The first denied the deity of Christ and the personality of the Holy Spirit; the second denied separate identities of the three persons, declaring that Jesus and the Holy Spirit were only different modes of the one person, or different guises by which He manifested Himself. Both of these, reasoning humanly, thought they were guarding the unity of God. Today we have offspring of these heresies in Unitarianism and in the Jesus-Only or Oneness doctrines.

The mainstream of the Church has persistently rejected these false teachings. By the beginning of the fourth century, it became incumbent upon the Church to convene a council of leaders and pastors to formulate the Apostolic doctrines to which they held. They felt the need for a formal creed to which the Church at large could subscribe. The first council met at Nicea in A.D. 325, where Athanasius prevailed against Arius and the deity of Christ was confirmed. Controversy continued and other councils were held: at Chalcedon in A.D. 351 and at Constantinople in A.D. 381 At this last council, the doctrines of the deity of Christ and that of the Trinity were upheld and formulated into what we call the Nicene Creed:

> I believe in one God....And in one Lord Jesus Christ, the only-begotten Son of God, begotten of the Father...Light of Light, very God of very God, begotten, not made, being of one substance with the Father....And I believe in the Holy Ghost, the Lord and Giver of life, who proceeds from the Father and the Son; who with the Father and Son together is worshiped and glorified; who spoke by the prophets.[28]

The major Protestant bodies have closely followed this ancient creed of the fourth century. The best known of the Reformation creeds is the Westminster Confession, which reads as follows:

> There is but one only, living, and true God....In the unity of the Godhead there be three persons, of one substance, power, and eternity: God the Father, God the Son, and God the Holy Ghost: the Father is none, neither begotten, nor proceeding; the Son is eternally begotten of the Father; the Holy Ghost eternally proceeding from the Father and the Son.[29]

These creeds and confessions rightly do not attempt to remove the mystery of the Trinity or to reconcile the scriptural statements with finite reasoning. The compilers tried to include all that Scripture teaches about the three persons of the Trinity without any effort to show how God can be both One and Three. The creeds are human documents and are not infallible; nevertheless, the mainstream of the

---

28 "Nicene Creed," *Center for Reformed Theology and Apologetics* http://www.reformed. org/documents/index.html?mainframe=http://www.reformed.org/documents/nicene.html (accessed January 17, 2008).

29 Westminster Confession of Faith, accessed at http://www.opc.org/wcf.html (accessed January 17, 2008).

Church has followed the wording of the Nicene and Athanasian creeds with very little variation.

B. Its scriptural presentation.

1. *In the Old Testament.* It was absolutely essential that, in the Old Testament, the unity of God should be clearly revealed and emphasized. Israel was surrounded by tribes and nations which had departed from the original knowledge of God Almighty, the Creator, to embrace polytheism. The Gentile nations worshiped a variety of gods and goddesses represented by images. God revealed Himself to Abraham as God Almighty *(El Shaddai).* To Moses, God revealed Himself by His redemptive personal name of *Jehovah* or *Yahweh,* and in His Law declared, "Hear, O Israel: The LORD our God is one LORD" [lit: *Jehovah* our *Elohim* is One *Jehovah*] (Dt. 6:4). The Law further admonished, "Thou shalt have no other gods before me" (Ex. 20:3). To have introduced the Trinity perceptually at that juncture would have been premature and confusing to a nation in infancy. The Old Testament gives us intimations of the triune nature of God, but they are clear only in the light of the New Testament's fuller revelation in Christ. Revelation is of necessity progressive, and having received the deeper insight provided by the Incarnation and the outpouring of the Spirit at Pentecost, we can recognize the repeated intimations of the Trinity in the Old Testament.

a) In the Old Testament, there are plural names for God, and plural pronouns are used to refer to Him. The names *Elohim* and *Adonai* are plurals. *Elohim,* when used of the true God, has a singular form of the verb. The plurality of the name is explained away by some as a "plural of majesty," but in Genesis 1:26 we read, "Let *us* make man in *our* image" (note the use of plural pronouns). Plural pronouns are also found in Genesis 3:22 and 11:7. God said to Isaiah, "Whom shall I send, and who will go for us?" (Is. 6:8) The very verse that declared God's unity to all Jews, "*Jehovah* our *Elohim* is one *Jehovah*," contains God's plural name, *Elohim.* Here we have plurality in unity—would not this be an intimation of the Trinity?

b) The Angel of Jehovah is called God. The Angel of Jehovah appears a number of times in the book of Genesis and from time to time throughout the rest of the Old Testament. A distinction is made between the Angel of Jehovah and Jehovah, yet they are one. In such events, when God appears as an angel or as a man, we call the appearance a theophany, from the Greek words *theos* ("God") and *phaino* ("to appear"). (See Gn. 16:7–13, when God appears to Hagar.) In Genesis 18:1–19:29 the Lord appears to Abraham as three men, yet Abraham addresses them as "Lord," in the singular. Two of the men appear to Lot in Sodom, but he addresses them as Jehovah. In Genesis 22:1–19, Abraham is ordered to sacrifice Isaac, but the Angel of the Lord speaks from heaven, releasing him from the order. In verse 16, the angel calls Himself Jehovah. In Genesis 32:22–32, Jacob wrestles with an angel and prevails to receive a divine blessing, then says, "I have seen God face to face" (Gn. 32:30). The

Angel of the Lord appeared to Moses at the burning bush, giving him the promise He would lead them out of Egypt; in the conversation, the terms *Angel* and *Jehovah* are used interchangeably.

c) Jesus is the Prophet like unto Moses. In Deuteronomy 18:18–19 (NASB), God prophesies through Moses:

> I will raise up a Prophet from among their countrymen like you, and I will put My words in his mouth, and he shall speak to them all that I command him. It shall come about that whoever will not listen to My words which he shall speak in my name, I Myself will require it of him.

When has such a prophet ever appeared except Jesus? Who else has so spoken God's words that those who did not heed them incurred God's direct judgment? About whom did God speak, saying, "This is my beloved Son…Hear ye him" (Mt. 17:5)?

d) Jesus is the Captain of the Lord's host. In Joshua 5:13–6:2, a man who called himself the Captain of the host of Jehovah, carrying a drawn sword, appeared to Joshua. Joshua was commanded to loosen his shoes, as he was on holy ground. And in verse 6:2 we read, "And the LORD [Jehovah] said unto Joshua."

In view of what we learn in the New Testament about Jesus, this one who appears to Old Testament characters and speaks as Jehovah, receives worship, and exercises divine power cannot be other than Jesus in preincarnate appearance, a Christophany, from the Greek words *christos* and *phaino* ("to appear"). No man has seen God at any time, but Jesus is God "manifest in the flesh" (1 Tm. 3:16).

e) References in Psalms applied to Jesus. "The Lord said unto my Lord, Sit thou at my right hand, until I make thine enemies thy footstool" (Ps. 110:1). Christ applied this psalm to Himself in Mk. 12:35–37.

"Thou art my Son; this day have I begotten thee" (Ps. 2:7). In Acts 13:33, Paul applies this passage to Jesus.

"Thy throne, O God, is for ever and ever" (Ps. 45:6). The writer of Hebrews relates this to Jesus in verse 1:8.

f) Jesus is the Messiah (the Son of David) predicted in the Old Testament. In Isaiah 7:14, we read that He is to be born of a virgin. In Isaiah 9:6–7, He is the Prince of Peace, the mighty God, the everlasting Father, Son of David, etc. In Micah 5:2, He is to be born in Bethlehem. In Isaiah 53, He is the man of sorrows and acquainted with grief, bruised for our iniquities, etc. Jesus is the only reasonable identification for this Servant of Jehovah. Philip applies Isaiah 53 to Jesus (Acts 8:30–35). Several address Jesus as "Thou Son of David" (Mt. 9:27; 21:9). That Jesus is frequently referred to in the Old Testament Scriptures is attested to by the testimony of Jesus Himself after His Resurrection: "And beginning at Moses and all the prophets, he expounded unto them in all the scriptures the things concerning himself" (Lk. 24:27).

2. *In the New Testament.* After the resurrection of Jesus and the descent of the Holy Spirit on the Day of Pentecost, the doctrine of the Trinity was crystal clear to the New Testament Church. Jesus had revealed Himself in all the Scriptures and now the other Comforter had come and brought "all things to [their] remembrance" (Jn. 14:26). When the apostles began to preach the gospel and to write epistles, they did not waver in declaring that Jesus was God and that the Holy Spirit was God; yet, at the same time, they thought of the Father, the Son, and the Holy Spirit as one God (1 Cor. 8:6).

The following are proofs of the Trinity in the New Testament:

a) The three persons are in evidence at one time at the baptism of Jesus. Jesus ascends from the waters of baptism, the Holy Spirit descends from heaven in the visible form of a dove, the Father speaks from heaven saying, "This is my beloved Son, in whom I am well pleased" (Mt. 3:16–17). All Three are in manifestation at the same time. The Father speaks of the Son as another identity in whom He is pleased. The Spirit has an identity separate from the other two. Those who say that the Three are only modes or guises of one person here make Jesus a magician who produces a dove out of thin air and a ventriloquist who projects His voice to the clouds. The Scripture does not give us an illusion, but a clear demonstration of the divine Trinity (Mk. 1:9–11; Lk. 3:21–22; Jn. 1:32–34).

b) In John 14 we have a clear proof of the three distinct persons of the Trinity. First, in verse 9, Jesus says to Philip, "he that hath seen me hath seen the Father." Here it is clear that Jesus and the Father are One. Yet at the same time, they have separate identities, for Jesus says to the disciples:

> And I will pray the Father, and he shall give you another Comforter, that he may abide with you for ever....But the Comforter, which is the Holy Ghost, whom the Father will send in my name, he shall teach you all things, and bring all things to your remembrance, whatsoever I have said unto you.
> —JOHN 14:16, 26

Jesus speaks of the Father as "He," of the Holy Spirit as "He," and of Himself as "I." Jesus refers to the Holy Spirit as "another Comforter," separate in identity. He explains that the Spirit will come when He goes away. Yet Jesus says, "Lo, I am with you always" (Mt. 28:20). Herein is the mystery: there are three separate identities (not individuals), yet there is one God, not three. The Trinity is beyond our comprehension, yet is still part of the unmistakable teaching of Scripture.

c) The baptismal formula given by Jesus in the Great Commission clearly reveals the threeness and the oneness of God: "Baptizing them in the name of the Father, and of the Son, and of the Holy Ghost" (Mt. 28:19). The three identities are explained as

Father, Son, and Holy Spirit, grouped together in equality. The word *name* is not repeated, indicating the unity of the three persons.

d) The apostolic benediction in 2 Corinthians 13:14 shows in capsule form the trinitarian thinking of the early church: "The grace of the Lord Jesus Christ, and the love of God, and the communion of the Holy Ghost, be with you all. Amen." We have a similar trinitarian statement in Jude 20–21: "Praying in the Holy Ghost, Keep yourselves in the love of God, looking for the mercy of our Lord Jesus Christ unto eternal life." While the usual order of the Three is given in the baptismal formula, in the two benedictions given above, Jesus is placed first in one, and the Holy Spirit first in the other. Does this not show that the terms *Son* and *Holy Spirit* are not inferior to God? (See 1 Cor. 12:4–6; Eph. 4:4–6; 5:18–20; 2 Thes. 2:13–14.)

VIII. THE PERSONS OF THE TRINITY

A. God the Father

We will not enlarge upon the general doctrine of God here, as this has already been covered under the sections on the existence, nature, names, and attributes of God. We will briefly consider God as Father of our Lord Jesus Christ. The relationship of Father and Son has to do with their self-revelation to us in the context of redemption. It does not mean that once the Father existed alone and then He begot the Son at a point of time. All the persons of the Trinity are coequal and coeternal. The lexicons give the meaning of the Greek word *monogenes* as "single of its kind" or, in reference to Christ, "only begotten." The term *only begotten* means that Jesus was not created by the Father, therefore making Him different from the Father. We, however, are created and adopted sons, therefore of a different nature from the Father. John said of Jesus as the Word: "In the beginning was the Word, and the Word was with God [lit., face to face with], and the Word was God. The same was in the beginning with God [lit., already was]" (Jn. 1:1–2). In John 17, Jesus prayed that He might be glorified with the glory He had with the Father before the world was (v. 5). Someone asked what God was doing before He created the universe. He was troubled about the idea of an eternally lonely God. But before there was a universe, in the Trinity of God there was love, communication, and purpose (Eph. 1:4–5; 1 Jn. 4:7–8). If God were not triune, the above question could perplex us. But the Three are One in nature, will, and purpose.

B. God the Son

1. *His virgin birth*

> "Joseph, son of David, do not be afraid to take Mary as your wife; for the child who has been conceived in her is of the Holy Spirit. She will bear a Son; and you shall call His name Jesus, for He will save His people from their

sins." Now all this took place to fulfill what was spoken by the Lord through the prophet: "BEHOLD THE VIRGIN SHALL BE WITH CHILD AND SHALL BEAR A SON, AND THEY SHALL CALL HIS NAME IMMANUEL," which translated means, "GOD WITH US." And Joseph awoke from his sleep and did as the angel of the Lord commanded him, and took Mary as his wife, but kept her a virgin until she gave birth to a Son; and he called His name Jesus.

—MATTHEW 1:20–25, NASB

(See also Lk. 1:26–38.)

a) It is worth noting that in Matthew 1:16, the conclusion of Joseph's genealogy, Jesus' Virgin Birth is accented by the use of a feminine pronoun, of which Mary is the antecedent: "And Jacob begat Joseph the husband of Mary, of whom was born Jesus, who is called Christ." The "of whom" in the Greek, *ex hes,* is singular, feminine gender, making the birth of Mary only, even though the genealogy is Joseph's. Only Matthew and Luke relate the birth of Jesus, but John states, "And the Word was made flesh and dwelt among us, (and we beheld his glory, the glory as of the only begotten of the Father,) full of grace and truth" (Jn. 1:14). The apostle Paul says concerning the birth of Jesus, "But when the fulness of the time was come, God sent forth his Son, made [born] of a woman" (Gal. 4:4). Does not "born of a woman" indicate a virgin birth? Those who doubt or deny the virgin birth of Jesus do so because of a presupposition of unbelief. That the Scriptures teach the Virgin Birth is undeniable.

b) The Westminster Catechism defines the doctrine of the Virgin Birth as follows: "Christ the Son of God became man, by taking to himself a true body, and a reasonable soul, being conceived by the power of the Holy Ghost in the womb of the Virgin Mary, of her substance, and born of her, yet without sin."[30] These words from the Apostle's Creed sum up the belief of the early church: "Conceived of the Holy Spirit, born of the Virgin Mary."[31]

c) In the Old Testament there is a progressive revelation of the supernatural Virgin Birth of Jesus:

(1) In Genesis 3:15, we have the earliest prophecy of a Redeemer from sin, in which He is called "the seed of woman" (author's paraphrase).

(2) God promised Abraham a blessing upon his seed and through his seed blessing upon all nations (Gn. 22:15–18). Paul interprets the promise to Abraham's seed as the promise fulfilled in Christ Jesus: "Now to Abraham and his seed were the promises

---

30 Westminster Confession of Faith, Larger Catechism, accessed at http://www.opc.org/lc.html (January 17, 2008).

31 "The Apostles' Creed," accessed at http://www.reformed.org/documents/index.html?mainframe=http://www.reformed.org/documents/apostles_creed.html (January 17, 2008).

made. He saith not, And to seeds, as of many; but as of one, And to thy seed, which is Christ" (Gal. 3:16).

(3) Jesus' birth shall be a "rod out of the stem of Jesse [David], and a Branch...of his roots: And the Spirit of the LORD shall rest upon him" (Is. 11:1–2). (Also 2 Sm. 7:12–13.) Matthew begins his Gospel with the words: "The book of the generation of Jesus Christ, the son of David" (Mt. 1:1).

(4) Isaiah prophesies about a Child to be born who would be called "The mighty God [and] The everlasting Father" (Is. 9:6–7), and He shall occupy the throne of David.

(5) Isaiah clearly predicts the Virgin Birth as the means of the coming of Immanuel (Mt. 1:22–23; Is. 7:14).

(6) Before the birth of Jesus there was the angelic announcement of it. The angel appeared first to Zacharias announcing the birth of John the Baptist, Jesus' fore-runner, by his wife, Elizabeth (Lk. 1:11–17). Then, angelic witness was given to Mary that she would bring forth a child who would be the Son of the Highest. In spite of her knowing not a man, it would happen by the Holy Spirit's overshadowing, for with God nothing is impossible (Lk. 2:27–35).

d) The doctrine of the Virgin Birth is vitally important to the whole structure of fundamental theology. If Jesus were born of a natural father, then...

(1)...He would have inherited the Adamic nature of the human race, and His death would not have been vicarious nor substitutionary. He would have died only for His own redemption.

(2)...He would not have been infinite, and even if some method could have been arranged to avoid a corporate identity with Adam, He could not have died for the world.

(3)...He would have been merely a sincere and zealous, but finite, religious leader, for the denial of the Virgin Birth is a virtual denial of the deity of Christ. If Jesus had a human father, He could not have been the "only begotten" of the Father, the unique, infinite Son of God.

(4)...we have an unreliable Bible. If Jesus was not born of a virgin, as recorded in Matthew and Luke, how can we trust what it records of His death and resurrection? If our Scriptures cannot be trusted on such a crucial matter, then all religious faith is like sailing the sea without chart or compass.

(5)...we would by logical inference have to reject every miraculous aspect of Christianity. If Jesus is the eternal Son of God who became incarnate to identify with and redeem man, then we could not expect other than a miraculous entrance to this world. Did not the angel say to Mary, "With God nothing shall be impossible" (Lk. 1:37)?

(6)...He would have been, at best, only a spiritual genius with unusual religious insight, and not the one infinite Lamb of God who made valid all Old Testament sacrifice. Only a divine and infinite offering can make effective, once for all, every sacrifice for sin. The Old Testament sacrificial system would have been little above paganism if God had not intended to send His infinite Son in the "fullness of time" to fulfill the typology of animal sacrifices, which by themselves were powerless. In Hebrews 10 we read, "For it is not possible that the blood of bulls and goats should take away sins....we are sanctified through the offering of the body of Jesus Christ once for all" (vv. 4, 10). A Christ of completely human parenthood could not be God's Lamb.

(7)...we could not expect Jesus to come again as the King with whom all the redeemed will rule. Only the preexistent Word of God will come as King of kings and Lord of lords. John says of Him, "Behold, he cometh with clouds; and every eye shall see Him....I am Alpha and Omega, the beginning and the ending, saith the Lord, which is, and which was, and which is to come, the Almighty" (Rv. 1:7–8). And again: "And He was clothed with a vesture dipped in blood: and His name is called The Word of God" (Rv. 19:13). It could be shown, if space permitted, that rejection of the doctrine of the Virgin Birth would weaken practically all other basic historic Christian theology. The fact is that the contemporary teachers who deny the Virgin Birth present a gospel that the apostles would not have recognized and that the Scriptures refute.

2. *His nature.* The Westminster Confession gives the following definition of the nature or natures and person of Christ Jesus:

> The Son of God, the second person of the Trinity, being very and eternal God, of one substance and equal with the Father, did, when the fulness of time was come, take upon him man's nature, with all the essential proper- ties, and common infirmities thereof, yet without sin; being conceived by the power of the Holy Ghost, in the womb of the virgin Mary, of her sub- stance. So that the two whole, perfect, and distinct natures, the Godhead and the manhood, were inseparably joined together in one person, without conversion, composition, or confusion. Which person is very God, and very man, yet one Christ, the only Mediator between God and man.[32]

Jesus had a divine nature and a human nature, yet He was one person, not two. He was the Son of God and the Son of Man, but His two natures did not result in a Dr. Jekyll and Mr. Hyde dual personality. He was Christ, the Messiah, and He was Jesus of Nazareth, "For there is one God, and one mediator between God and men, the man Christ Jesus" (1 Tm. 2:5). He subsisted in the form of God and was equal

---

32 Westminster Confession of Faith, Ch. VIII, Sec. 2., accessed at http://www.opc.org/ confessions.html (January 15, 2008).

with God, but He took upon Himself the form of a servant and was made in the likeness of men. (The Greek *homoioma* means "likeness," but His likeness was not merely human.) Jesus was a real man, but not merely man. Jesus was born and died like men, but He was the Ancient of Days who said, "Before Abraham was, I am" (Jn. 8:58). Jesus said, "I thirst"; but also, "I am the water of life." Jesus said, "Give me to drink," yet, on the same occasion, "Whosoever drinketh of the water that I shall give him shall never thirst" (Jn. 4:7, 14). He was beaten with stripes, yet with his stripes we were healed (Is. 53:5). He said, "I do nothing of myself" (Jn. 8:28), but "without him was not anything made that was made" (Jn. 1:3). Another had to carry His cross, but He upholds "all things by the word of his power" (Heb. 1:3). He increased in wisdom and in stature (Lk. 2:52), but He is the same yesterday, and today, and forever. He was sentenced to death by a Roman governor, but He was the King of kings and the Lord of lords. He said, "Now is my soul troubled" (Jn. 12:27), yet He was the Prince of Peace. He cried on the cross, "Why hast thou forsaken me?" (Mt. 27:46), yet He promised His followers, "I will never leave thee nor forsake thee" (Heb. 13:5).

a) The human nature of Jesus. The apostle John warned against a heresy that denied the humanity of Jesus; he stated:

> Many false prophets are gone out into the world. Hereby know ye the Spirit of God: Every spirit that confesseth that Jesus Christ is come in the flesh is of God: And every spirit that confesseth not that Jesus Christ is come in the flesh is not of God: and this is that spirit of antichrist.
>
> —1 JOHN 4:1–3

Some devout and well-meaning believers have been so absorbed in maintaining the deity of Christ Jesus that they have minimized the humanity of Jesus. Jesus did not merely have a brush with humanity; He took to Himself a genuine human nature with every human attribute except sinfulness. His human nature was in submission to His divine nature, without sacrificing any of its humanness. Let us study the proofs of His human nature:

(1) Jesus was born a natural infant in Bethlehem's manger and wrapped in a baby's swaddling clothes (Lk. 2:7).

(2) He grew up in the normal manner of a child (Lk. 2:39–40).

(3) He grew up in subjection to His parents (Lk. 2:51–52).

(4) Jesus was traced through two human genealogies, one of Joseph (Mt. 1), and one of Mary (Lk. 3:23–38).

(5) He is called the Seed of Woman, the Seed of Abraham, and the Son of David, and is in this way linked to the human race.

(6) Jesus was tempted and tested in all points as we are, without sin. It is often asked if Jesus could have sinned. He could not have sinned because He possessed, in

addition to His human nature, a divine nature which was holy. Furthermore, because He was conceived by the Holy Spirit without a human father, His human nature was devoid of sin. In addition to this, His human nature was in perfect submission to His divine nature and divine will. Then, some will say, why was He tempted if He could not sin? Temptation, as applied to Jesus, meant "testing." It was perfectly in order for Him to be tested to demonstrate, as the Last Adam, His perfect obedience; and as the Lamb of God, that He was without spot or blemish (Mt. 4:1–11; Lk. 4:1–13; Mt. 26:36–46; Heb. 2:18; 4:15).

(7) He calls Himself a man (Jn. 8:40). He calls Himself or is called the Son of Man seventy times. First Timothy 2:5 introduces Him as "One mediator between God and men, the man Christ Jesus."

(8) Jesus is our High Priest (Heb. 5:1–10). The qualification of a priest is that he must be taken from among men in order to be their representative. He must share their state. Isaiah saw Jesus in prophetic vision as "a man of sorrows, and acquainted with grief" (Is. 53:3). The true High Priest must also be able to approach the throne of God on His own merit. Jesus the Son of God represents God to man, and conversely man to God. Our High Priest is the God-man; a High Priest after the order of Melchizedek.

(9) Jesus had human attributes such as hunger, thirst, tears, fatigue, etc. He suffered, shed His blood, died, and was buried.

(10) Even after the Resurrection, with a glorified body, He could invite Thomas to touch His hands and side to feel His wounds. He still retained His humanity along with His divinity. In Revelation 19:11–16 He returns to reign on earth, and it is said of Him, "And he was clothed with a vesture dipped in blood" (v. 13). In Revelation 22, we see Jesus with the Father in the New Jerusalem and He is called the Lamb. The threefold positional work of Jesus was to be that of Prophet, Priest, and King; in the coming age Jesus will retain these same distinctions (Acts 3:19–26; Heb. 7:17, 21; Mt. 27:29, 37; Jn. 19:21; 1 Tm. 1:17; 1 Tm. 6:13–16; 2 Pt. 1:11; Heb. 1:8–14). The Son of God became the Son of Man in order that the sons of men might become sons of God.

b) The divine nature of Jesus. If we approach the study of Jesus with human reason, we tend to discover only His humanity; if we approach it with emotional devotion, we tend to find only His divinity; but if we study the Bible with faith, we accept what God's Word reveals—both humanity and deity. We have examined the proofs of His humanity, so let us now look at the evidence of His deity:

(1) In the Old Testament, the prophets prophesy of His coming, and give to Him divine names: (a) Isaiah calls Him the mighty God and the everlasting Father (Is. 9:6–7), and Immanuel, which means "God with us" (7:14). (b) Jeremiah refers to Him as the Lord Our Righteousness (*Jehovah Tsidkenu*) (Jer. 23:6). (c) David speaks of Him as "My Lord" (Ps. 110:1–7).

(2) He is called God and Lord in the New Testament: "And Thomas answered and said unto Him, My Lord and my God" (Jn. 20:28); "And we know that the Son of God is come…This is the true God, and eternal life" (1 Jn. 5:20); "Christ came, who is over all, God blessed forever. Amen" (Rom. 9:5); "And the Word was God" (Jn. 1:1); "The glorious appearing of the great God and our Saviour Jesus Christ" (Ti. 2:13); "Thy throne, O God, is for ever and ever" (Heb. 1:8, quoted from Ps. 45:6).

(3) He is called the unique Son of God. The term *only begotten* (Gr., *monogenes*) means "single of its kind." Jesus was not created as the Son—He was eternally the Son. "Verily, verily, I say unto you, The hour is coming, and now is, when the dead shall hear the voice of the Son of God: and they that hear shall live" (Jn. 5:25); "For what the law could not do, in that it was weak through the flesh, God sending His own Son in the likeness of sinful flesh, and for sin, condemned sin in the flesh" (Rom. 8:3); "He is antichrist, that denieth the Father and the Son. Whosoever denieth the Son, the same hath not the Father: (but) he that acknowledgeth the Son hath the Father also" (1 Jn. 2:22–23).

(4) Jesus declares Himself to be One with the Father: "I and my Father are one" (Jn. 10:30); "He that hath seen me hath seen the Father" (Jn. 14:9). (Also Jn. 14:7–11.)

(5) Jesus had pre-existence: "Before Abraham was I am" (Jn. 8:58); "In the beginning was the Word, and the Word was with God, and the Word was God.…And the Word was made flesh" (Jn. 1:1, 14); "And now, O Father, glorify thou me with thine own self with the glory which I had with thee before the world was" (Jn. 17:5). (See also Phil. 2:5–11; Jn. 1:15; Heb. 1:1–3.)

(6) To Jesus were ascribed divine attributes: (a) Omnipotence, "All power is given unto me in heaven and in earth" (Mt. 28:18); "And without him was not any thing made that was made" (Jn. 1:3); "For by him were all things created, that are in heaven, and that are in earth, visible and invisible; whether they be thrones, or dominions, or principalities, or powers: all things were created by him, and for him; And he is before all things, and by him all things consist" (Col. 1:16–17). (See also Jn. 1:14; 11:25–26; 20:30–31; Col. 2:9). (b) Omniscience, "But Jesus did not commit himself unto them, because he knew all men, And needed not that any should testify of man: for he knew what was in man" (Jn. 2:24–25). (See also, Jn 1:48–51; 16:30; 21:17–18; Col. 2:3). (c) Omnipresence, "Lo, I am with you away, even unto the end of the world" (Mt. 28:20); "And no man hath ascended up to heaven, but he that came down from heaven, even the Son of Man which is in heaven" (Jn. 3:13). (d) Eternity, "He is before all things" (Col. 1:17); "Jesus Christ the same yesterday, and to day, and for ever" (Heb. 13:8). (See also Jn. 1:1–3; 8:58; Mi. 5:2; Rv. 1:17; Heb. 1:8). (e) Immutability (see Hebrews 13:8). (f) Creation (see John 1:3, 10; Col. 1:16; Heb. 1:10; Eph. 3:9.) (g) Holiness, "Ye know that he was manifested to take away our sins; and in him is no sin" (1 Jn. 3:5). (See also 1 Pt. 2:22; Heb. 7:26). (h) Forgiveness of sins, "'He said…Son, thy sins be forgiven thee'" (Mk. 2:5). (Also Lk. 7:48.) (i) All judgment is given Him, "For the

Father judgeth no man, but hath committed all judgment unto the Son" (Jn. 5:22). (See also Acts 17:31; Rv. 22:12; Rom. 2:16; Mt. 16:27; 25:31–33; 2 Cor. 5:10.)

(7) Jesus made statements about Himself that would be absurdly grandiose were He not divine. "I am the resurrection, and the life: he that believeth in me, though he were dead, yet shall he live: And whosoever liveth and believeth in me shall never die" (Jn. 11:25–26). (See also Jn. 4:14, 25–26; 5:20; 6:33–35, 40, 50–51, 53–54, 62; 8:12, 23–24, 56, 58; 9:35–39; 10:7–9.)

(8) Jesus was aware of and declared His unique relationship as the Son of God to the Father and to the Holy Spirit. "When the Comforter is come, whom I will send unto you from the Father, even the Spirit of truth, which proceedeth from the Father, he shall testify of me" (Jn. 15:26). "It is expedient for you that I go away: for if I go not away, the Comforter will not come unto you; but if I depart, I will send him unto you" (Jn. 16:7). (See also Jn. 6:20–27; 7:38–39.)

(9) Worship was ascribed to Jesus. Exodus 34:14 stipulates: "For thou shalt worship no other god: for the LORD, whose name is Jealous, is a jealous God." Worship belongs only unto God Almighty; yet Christ received genuine worship without objection or protest. "They that were in the ship came and worshipped him, saying, Of a truth thou art the Son of God" (Mt. 14:33). At Jesus' birth the wise men came to pay homage unto Him: "We have seen his star in the east, and are come to worship him....And when they were come into the house, they saw the young child with Mary his mother, and fell down and worshipped him" (Mt. 2:2, 11). God commanded concerning His Son, "And again, when he bringeth in the firstbegotten into the world, he saith, And let all the angels of God worship him" (Heb. 1:6). To whomever worship is ascribed, the same is very God of very God. Jesus is very God, second person of the Godhead, coequal and coeternal with the Father. Amen.

In ancient times, the deity of Christ was denied; first by the Ebionites in A.D. 107, then later in A.D. 325 by Arias and his followers. In modern times Christ's deity has been questioned by the Deists, the Unitarians, the Christian Scientists, Jehovah's Witnesses, Mormons, and many liberal theologians. The mainstream of the Church has always held to the doctrines of the Trinity and the deity of Christ. Some, who have professed belief in Christ's deity, actually believed in a created Christ who was above men but less than God, or they believed that He was divine in the sense that all men may be divine.

3. *The works of Christ.* Jesus was a worker. He said, "My Father worketh hitherto, and I work" (Jn. 5:17). Once, when the disciples were concerned about His need for food, Jesus responded by saying, "My meat is to do the will of him that sent me, and to finish his work" (Jn. 4:34). Feeling the urgency of His task, Jesus exclaimed, "I must work the works of him that sent me, while it is day: the night cometh, when no man can work. As long as I am in the world, I am the light of the world" (Jn. 9:4–5).

In Jesus' prayer near the end of His earthly ministry, He said, "I have glorified thee on the earth: I have finished the work which thou gavest me to do" (Jn. 17:4).

It seems quite clear that any study of the Christian Faith must interpret the meaning of Christ's work on earth. At one point in time, God Himself, in the person of His only Son, visited our world to redeem out of it a people for His own possession. What God's Son did while here, and how it accomplished our salvation, must be the most important matter that can occupy our thoughts. The work of Christ must be studied; it only remains to decide how to best organize that study. Many writers have preferred to study the Lord's work under three headings: His work as prophet, His work as a priest, and His work as a king. While this method of study has been criticized, its value from the perspective of the whole Bible seems to recommend it. Therefore, we will follow it. There were three types of leaders in the Old Testament who were commissioned by God and ushered into their offices by the symbolic act of anointing with oil, which signified the fullness of the Holy Spirit. The term *Messiah* means "the anointed one." The name *Christ* also means "the anointed one." It is appropriate that Christ, God's Anointed, should fulfill all three of these ministries as the ultimate Prophet, Priest, and King.

a) Christ the Prophet—A prophet is one commissioned by God to make known His will to man. The greatest prophet in the Old Testament was Moses, who spoke on God's behalf, revealing divine will to God's chosen people in the form of the Law. A secondary work of a prophet was that of predicting future events. In Deuteronomy 18:18–19, Moses predicted the coming of the greatest of all prophets:

> I will raise them up a prophet from among their brethren, like unto thee, and will put my words in his mouth; and he shall speak unto them all that I shall command him. And it shall come to pass, that whosoever will not hearken unto my words that he shall speak in my name, I will require it of him.

After the healing of the lame man at the Beautiful Gate, Peter addressed the people, declaring to them that Jesus was the promised prophet who fulfilled Moses' prophecy. Then he added, "Unto you first God, having raised up his Son Jesus, sent him to bless you, in turning away every one of you from his iniquities" (Acts 3:26).

When Jesus arose to address the synagogue at Nazareth, He quoted a messianic prophecy from Isaiah 61:

> The Spirit of the Lord is upon me; because he hath anointed me to preach the gospel to the poor; he hath sent me to heal the brokenhearted, to preach deliverance to the captives, and recovering of sight to the blind, to set at liberty them that are bruised, To preach the acceptable year of the Lord.
>
> —LUKE 4:18

When all eyes were fastened upon Him, He continued by saying, "This day is this scripture fulfilled in your ears" (Lk. 4:21).

In the New Testament epistles, the passage which expresses most clearly the prophetic mission of Jesus, of speaking to man on God's behalf, is Hebrews 1:1-2, "God, who at various times and in different ways spoke in time past to the fathers by the prophets, has in these last days spoken to us by His Son, whom He has appointed heir of all things" (NKJV).

There were five functions which usually characterized the ministry of a prophet. They were preaching, teaching, discipling, predicting, and miracles. Not every prophet's ministry had all five functions, but we could point to Elijah, Isaiah, Jeremiah, and several others whose ministries included the full range of functions. Most certainly all the above mentioned functions were manifested fully in the ministry of Jesus the Prophet:

(1) Jesus began His prophetic ministry with preaching. Mark 1:14 says of Him, "Now…Jesus came into Galilee, preaching the gospel of the kingdom of God." There are nearly fifty of the discourses of Jesus recorded in the New Testament, the best known of which was His Sermon on the Mount. That Jesus preached with a sense of mission is indicated by His words recorded in Mark 1:38, "Let us go into the next towns, that I may preach [Gr., *kerusso*, "to herald, proclaim openly"] there also: for therefore came I forth." The preaching of Jesus was revolutionary. He called upon men to change their ways. Mark gives us an excerpt of one of His early sermons: "The time is fulfilled, and the kingdom of God is at hand: repent ye, and believe the gospel" (Mk. 1:15). To the ruler Nicodemus, He demanded, "Ye must be born again" (Jn. 3:7). But Jesus did not preach as a doomsday prophet. He always held out hopeful assurance, as in John 3:17, "For God sent not His Son into the world to condemn the world; but that the world through him might be saved." Again, "For the Son of Man is come to seek and to save that which is lost" (Lk. 19:10). However, Jesus did not come merely to preach the word of God. He was the Word of God. He did not come primarily to preach the gospel, but that there might be a gospel to preach.

(2) The Word has much to say about Jesus' ministry of teaching. "And they went into Capernaum; and straightway on the sabbath day he entered into the synagogue, and taught. And they were astonished at his doctrine: for he taught them as one that had authority, and not as the scribes" (Mk. 1:21-22). The disciples usually addressed Jesus as Master. The word *master* is used more than forty times in the Gospels and is usually applied to Jesus. It must be noted, however, that the usual Greek word translated "master" is *didaskalos,* which means "teacher." Two other Greek words translated "master," one of which was *rabbi,* also mean "teacher." In ancient times the title of teacher was one of great prestige. Jesus was the greatest of all teachers. He did not quote authorities; He was the Authority. He was not merely the way-shower; He was the Way. He was not only the truth-teller; He was Truth itself. When He inquired of

His followers if they would also go away, Peter responded, "Lord, to whom shall we go? thou hast the words of eternal life" (Jn. 6:68). After Jesus' discourse at the Feast of Tabernacles, where He said, "He who believes in me...From his innermost being shall flow rivers of living water" (Jn. 7:38, NASB), many cried out, "Of a truth this is the Prophet" (Jn. 7:40). The officers of the Sanhedrin returned, reporting, "Never man spake like this man" (Jn. 7:46). Yet the teaching of Jesus, characterized by His parables (there were thirty-eight), attracted even the children. The parable of the good Samaritan may well be the best-known story in the Western world. John may have said the ultimate word about Jesus the Teacher when He said, "No man hath seen God at any time; the only begotten Son, which is in the bosom of the Father, he hath declared him" (Jn. 1:18).

(3) Closely connected with Jesus' ministry of teaching was that of making disciples, many of whom became the apostles of the church and the first preachers of the message of Christ crucified and risen. On Jesus' very first preaching mission the following is recorded by Mark, "Now as He walked by the sea of Galilee, he saw Simon and Andrew his brother casting a net into the sea: for they were fishers. And Jesus said unto them, Come ye after me, and I will make you to become fishers of men" (Mk. 1:16–17). A very short while later Mark records: "And he ordained twelve, that they should be with him, and that he might send them forth to preach, And to have power to heal sicknesses, and to cast out devils" (Mk. 3:14–15). This passage informs us of the three purposes of making disciples: that they might be with Him, that they might preach, and that they might heal and cast out demons. If these were given in the order of priority, the matter of first importance is that of spending time in the presence of the Master. A disciple is not one who merely learns the content of books and lectures; he is one who is matured by being in the presence of his teacher, following his example, and imbibing his spirit. Later, when Jesus gave His disciples the Great Commission to go and make disciples of all nations, they well understood His meaning. Our task today is still that of making disciples who learn how to follow Jesus by seeing Him in us and observing His power manifested in us. Secondly, He taught them by His example to preach the gospel of the kingdom, not in word only, but also in the power of deliverance. Thirdly, he gave them power to heal the sick and to cast out demons. We are not surprised that Mark concludes his Gospel with these words of prophecy:

> And these signs shall follow them that believe; In my name shall they cast out devils; they shall speak with new tongues...they shall lay hands on the sick, and they shall recover....And they went forth, and preached everywhere, the Lord working with them, and confirming the word with signs following. Amen.
>
> —MARK 16:17–18, 20

(4) A secondary, but important, function of a prophet was that of predicting future events. If the predictions of a prophet came to pass and they were glorifying to God, the prophet was authenticated as one sent from God. While the greater part of Jesus' preaching and teaching was directed to the people of that time, He made a number of predictions of future events that authenticated His deity. Some of His predictions were: (a) His own death and resurrection (Mt. 16:21); (b) the persecution of the Church (Lk. 12:11); (c) the coming of the Comforter, the Holy Spirit, to abide in the Church (Jn. 16:7–11; 14:16–17, 27); (d) the destruction of the temple and the city of Jerusalem in A.D. 70 (Lk. 19:43–44; 21:6); (e) the signs and conditions of the last days (Mt. 24; Mk. 13; Lk. 21); (f) the Church's triumph—the Church has had many enemies and has endured many trials, yet it is reassuring to remind ourselves that Jesus predicted the Church's triumph: "I will build my Church; and the gates of hell shall not prevail against it" (Mt. 16:18); "And this gospel of the kingdom shall be preached in all the world for a witness unto all nations; and then shall the end come" (Mt. 24:14). Jesus was the Prophet par excellence.

(5) A frequent mark of a prophet was that his ministry was attended by the supernatural. Moses' miraculous deeds range from the plagues of Egypt and the parting of the Red Sea to bringing water from the rock. Elijah called down fire from heaven, multiplied the widow's meal and oil, raised her son from the dead, and was caught up to heaven in a whirlwind. Elisha brought healing to Naaman the leper, raised up the Shunammite's son, and numerous other miracles. Isaiah brought healing to King Hezekiah. Daniel stopped the mouths of lions and interpreted impossible dreams. It is only natural then, that the ministry of Jesus would be characterized by the miraculous. He was not only a worker of miracles, He was the Fountainhead of the supernatural. When we consider His person and mission—that He was God incarnate, the world's Savior—it would be unthinkable that He would have hidden His identity completely in a human disguise. His birth was a miracle. His resurrection from the dead was the miracle of all miracles. He demonstrated His deity by such miracles as walking on water, calming the storm, turning water into wine, and multiplying the bread and fishes. These were miracles over nature, wrought by the Creator of all things. By far the greater number of His signs and wonders were miracles of compassion upon the sick, the afflicted, and the demon possessed. Jesus came to destroy the works of the devil. Jesus imparted to the church the power to carry on a ministry of deliverance, which was made obvious in the book of Acts. Jesus gave assurance of the continuance of miracles in the Great Commission when He said, "All power is given unto me in heaven and in earth. Go ye therefore…and, lo, I am with you alway, even unto the end of the world [lit., consummation of the age]" (Mt. 28:18–20). If the risen Lord is with us, He will confirm His Word with signs, beginning, of course, with the great miracle of regeneration: "Greater works than these shall he do; because I go unto my Father" (Jn. 14:12). (See also 2 Pt. 1:3–4.)

b) Jesus our Great High Priest—While the prophet represents God to man, the priest represents man to God. There are three things that characterize the work of the priest: he is one with, and is taken from among, those whom he represents to God (Ex. 28:1; Heb. 5:1–2); he offers to God sacrifices to atone for sin (Lv. 4:13–21; Heb. 10:11–12), and as a mediator, he makes intercession for the people (Is. 53:12; Heb. 7:25; 1 Tm. 2:5).

(1) Jesus emptied Himself of the outward manifestation of equality with God, and took upon Himself the form of a servant, made in the likeness of men (Phil. 2:5–8). This He did to fully identify with those for whom He would make atonement. He goes to God the Father in our behalf, because He made Himself one with us. Herein is the importance of the human nature of Jesus:

> Wherefore in all things it behoved him to be made like unto his brethren, that he might be a merciful and faithful high priest in things pertaining to God, to make reconciliation for the sins of the people. For in that he himself hath suffered being tempted, he is able to succour them that are tempted.
>   —Hebrews 2:17–18

(2) There is the remarkable circumstance that Jesus was both the Priest and Sacrifice in one person: "For there is one God, and one mediator between God and men, the man Christ Jesus" (1 Tm. 2:5). Jesus was introduced by John the Baptist, His forerunner, as "the Lamb of God, which taketh away the sin of the world" (Jn. 1:29). Peter speaks of Jesus as the Sacrifice: "Forasmuch as ye know that ye were not redeemed with corruptible things, as silver and gold….But with the precious blood of Christ, as of a lamb without blemish and without spot" (1 Pt. 1:18–19).

In the final drama (Rv. 5:1–9), one is sought to take the title deed to the kingdom from the hand of Him who occupies heaven's throne. None was found but one called the Lion of the Tribe of Judah and the Root of David. But when He approached the throne to take the document, He was seen as a lamb that had been slain. All of heaven and the church sang a new song, "Thou art worthy…for thou wast slain, and hast redeemed us to God by thy blood out of every kindred, and tongue, and people, and nation" (Rv. 5:9). (See also Rom. 8:6–10.)

(3) Jesus not only died to make an atonement for our sin; He perpetually represents us at the Father's right hand as our Intercessor. In Hebrews 10:12 we are told, "But this man, after he had offered one sacrifice for sins for ever, sat down on the right hand of God." Our High Priest not only saves us from the guilt of sin, He ever intercedes for us, saving us from the power and presence of sin: "But this man, because he continueth ever, hath an unchangeable priesthood. Wherefore he is able also to save them to the uttermost that come unto God by him, seeing he ever liveth to make intercession for them" (Heb. 7:24–25). Paul expresses Christ's intercessory

work clearly in Romans 8:34, "Who is he that condemneth? It is Christ that died, yea rather, that is risen again, who is even at the right hand of God, who maketh intercession for us." To summarize: Jesus is our High Priest who, having identified with us, represents us to the Father. Through Him we have access to the throne of grace. He is also the perfect Sacrifice for sin, through whose blood we have received the Atonement. Finally, He is our Advocate who intercedes for us: "He bare the sin of many, and made intercession for the transgressors" (Is. 53:12).

(4) Something needs to be said here about the Melchizedek priesthood of Jesus. The man Melchizedek is mentioned eleven times in Scripture, nine times in the book of Hebrews: 5:6, 10; 6:20; 7:1, 10–11, 15, 17, 21. The historic account of this celebrated priest is found in Genesis 14:18–20 and is contained in three short verses. How the writer of Hebrews could develop a complete typology of Christ from this priest might make us wonder, if it were not for a remarkable reference to Melchizedek in Psalm 110:4: "The LORD [Jehovah] hath sworn, and will not repent, Thou art a priest for ever after the order of Melchizedek." Psalm 110 is a messianic psalm beginning with the well-known reference to Christ: "The LORD [Jehovah] said unto my Lord [Adonai], Sit thou at my right hand, until I make thine enemies thy footstool." This prophecy is quoted by Jesus Himself, as recorded by Luke in Acts 2:34–35, and by the writer of Hebrews in 1:13. Psalm 110:4 is a prophecy of Christ's priesthood, of which Melchizedek is the perfect type.

Let us see from Hebrews 7 how this priest of the Most High God [El Elyon], the God of Abraham, typifies the perfect priesthood of Christ. His name, Melchizedek, means "king of righteousness," and since he was King of Salem (Jerusalem), his title means "king of peace." The ideal combination of righteousness and peace is accomplished in Jesus Christ, who is the King of Righteousness (Is. 32:1) and the Prince of Peace (Is. 9:6). Only in Jesus the Savior can we be assured, "Therefore being justified [declared righteous] by faith, we have peace with God through our Lord Jesus Christ" (Rom. 5:1) (See Is. 32:17.) Melchizedek was more than a priest; he was a king. While Jesus fulfilled a number of aspects of the Levitical priesthood (i.e., entering within the veil), Levi could not be His type, for priests only came from the tribe of Levi. Jesus was the Son of David, the Lion of the Tribe of Judah (Heb. 7:14), the coming King.

The Melchizedek priesthood was superior to the Levitical, for the following reasons given in Hebrews 7:

(a) Abraham, the great-grandfather of Levi, paid tithes to Melchizedek, his superior (v. 4).

(b) Abraham was blessed by him, "the lesser is blessed by the greater" (vv. 6–7, NASB).

(c) Levitical priests must be able to trace their genealogy. No parentage or genealogy is reckoned for Melchizedek, although the book of Genesis is full of genealogies (v. 3).

(d) The deaths of Levi, Aaron, and Eleazar are recorded. No mention is made of the birth or death of Melchizedek. His priesthood was by direct divine appointment, not depending upon tribal status or parentage, therefore the priesthood of Melchizedek is perpetual (vv. 15–17).

(e) The work of the Levitical priesthood had virtue only because in the "fulness of time" the perfect Priest would come and offer the perfect Sacrifice (Heb. 10:1–12).

(f) The perfect Priest, prophesied by the psalmist in Psalm 110:4, was to be a royal Priest: "The LORD will stretch forth Thy strong scepter from Zion saying, 'Rule in the midst of Thine enemies'" (Ps. 110:2, NASB).

There has been no end of speculation about the identity of Melchizedek. Some have thought that he was a Christophany, a preincarnate appearance of Christ, or an angel. The Bible does not say that Jesus was Melchizedek, but that His priesthood was "after the similitude of [or order of] Melchizedek" (Heb. 7:15–17). If Melchizedek had been a supernatural being and not a man, he would not have typified Jesus in His human nature, which was essential: "For every high priest [is] taken from among men" (Heb. 5:1). Melchizedek was an earthly king of Salem, but he had been appointed to the priesthood of the Most High God by direct revelation, his office not depending upon a priestly dynasty. While he was human, his priesthood was divine and endless in nature.

Since the priesthood of Levi (and Aaron) was not able to take away sin by animal sacrifices (Heb. 10:4), a High Priest must come who is of a perpetual order, who can, by His kingly sovereignty, destroy Satan's kingdom. The Levitical priesthood was under the old Law that was destined to be disannulled (Heb. 7:18). The priesthood of Jesus is under the new covenant of grace: "Wherefore he is able also to save them to the uttermost that come unto God by him, seeing he ever liveth to make intercession for them" (Heb. 7:25).

c) Jesus our King—We have elected to study Christ's works under the categories of prophet, priest, and king. As Prophet, He is the messagebearer; as Priest, He is the sin-bearer; as King, He is the scepter-bearer. Moses prophesied His coming as a Prophet, Isaiah predicted His coming as the Priest and sin-bearer, and Daniel saw him as the coming Messiah and King: "Know therefore and understand, that from the going forth of the commandment to restore and to build Jerusalem unto the Messiah the Prince shall be seven weeks, and threescore and two weeks" (Dn. 9:25). The angel announced the birth of Jesus to Mary as a royal proclamation:

> And behold, thou shalt…bring forth a son, and shalt call His name JESUS.
> He shall be great, and shall be called the Son of the Highest: and the Lord God shall give unto him the throne of his Father David: And he shall reign over the house of Jacob for ever; and of his kingdom there shall be no end.
> —LUKE 1:31–33

Let us examine Christ's kingly work under three headings:

(1) Christ came as a King—"Where is he that is born King of the Jews" (Mt. 2:2)—therefore, He was aware of His royal mission as announced by John the Baptist in Matthew 2:2, "The kingdom of heaven is at hand." He presented Himself to Jerusalem as their King. Zechariah 9:9 prophesied this, saying, "Thy King cometh unto thee: he is just, and having salvation." (See Mk. 11:1–11.) When Pilate asked Him if He were a king, He answered affirmatively, but added, "My kingdom is not of this world" (Jn. 18:36). The cross on which Jesus died bore the title, Jesus of Nazareth, King of the Jews (Jn. 19:19). After the Resurrection, during His forty last days on Earth, Jesus was occupied about His kingdom, as Luke reports, "being seen of them forty days, and speaking of the things pertaining to the kingdom of God" (Acts 1:3).

(2) Christ represented His kingdom as a present kingdom as well as a future one: "Jesus came into Galilee, preaching the gospel of the kingdom of God, And saying, 'The time is fulfilled, and the kingdom of God is at hand'" (Mk. 1:14–15). Jesus said about His kingdom, "For behold, the kingdom of God is in your midst" (Lk. 17:21, NASB). Some scholars insist that the kingdom of God is entirely future, an eschatological kingdom. They overlook two things. First, the Greek word for "kingdom," *basileia*, does not mean the sphere over which Christ rules, but the rule itself. Wherever Christ Jesus is sovereign, there is His rule (kingdom). Wherever Christ is Lord, there His kingdom is present. Second, when men come to Christ, they are being delivered from Satan's kingdom into Christ's kingdom (Col. 1:13). During Jesus' earthly ministry, culminated by the Cross and Resurrection, He was overturning the kingdom of Satan: "But if I with the finger of God cast out devils, no doubt the kingdom of God is come upon you" (Lk. 11:20). Strongest of all is the fact that Jesus, in connection with the founding of the Church, said to the disciples, "And I will give unto thee the keys of the kingdom of heaven: and whatsoever thou shalt bind on earth shall be bound in heaven: and whatsoever thou shalt loose on earth shall be loosed in heaven" (Mt. 16:19). George Eldon Ladd has the following to say about the present manifestation of Christ's kingdom:

> The kingdom has come in that the powers of the future kingdom have already
> come into history and into human experience through the supernatural min-
> istry of the Messiah which has effected the defeat of Satan. Men may now
> experience the reality of the reign of God... The presence of Christ on earth
> had for its purpose the defeat of Satan, his binding, so that God's power may
> be a vital reality in the experience of those who yield to God's reign by becom-

ing the disciples of Jesus. In Christ, the kingdom in the form of its power, has come among men.[33]

(3) As the culmination of Christ's work on Earth, He will come again to reign over His eschatological kingdom as King of kings and Lord of lords (Rv. 19:16; 20:6; 22:5, 16). John beautifully extols Christ in His kingly work:

> And from Jesus Christ, who is the faithful witness, and the first begotten of the dead, and prince of the kings of the earth. Unto him that loved us, and washed us from our sins in his own blood, And hath made us kings and priests unto God and His Father; to him be glory and dominion for ever and ever. Amen.
>
> —REVELATION 1:5–6

Jesus fulfilled the prophecies of the coming Messiah. His kingdom was not a visible realm with a throne and a capitol, but during His earthly ministry, He defeated Satan and initiated a kingdom of righteousness. His subjects, endued with power, are rescuing men from the kingdom of Satan by the preaching of the gospel of the kingdom and leading them into the kingdom of Christ (Acts 28:22, 31; Col. 1:13). At the culmination of this age, Christ the King will come and establish His kingdom on Earth as well as in heaven, and we shall reign with Him. The qualification for sharing Christ's future reign is stipulated in the parable of the talents: "Well done, thou good and faithful servant: thou hast been faithful over a few things, I will make thee ruler over many things" (Mt. 25:21). Faithfulness means not merely dutifulness, but also being full of faith.

C. God the Holy Spirit

About the Holy Spirit, the Nicene Creed says, "We believe in the Holy Ghost, who is the Lord and Giver of life; who proceedeth from the Father [and the Son]; who with the Father and Son together is worshipped and glorified, who spoke by the prophets."[34] Since we live in the dispensation of the Holy Spirit, it is very important that we know as much about Him as the Word reveals to us. Sound doctrine depends upon a clear and accurate understanding of the nature and work of the blessed third person of the Trinity, who dwells in and empowers the Church, the body of Christ.

---

33 George E. Ladd, *Crucial Questions About the Kingdom of God* (Grand Rapids, MI: Wm. B. Eerdmans Publishing Company, 1971), 91.

34 Henry Bettenson, *Documents of Christian Church*, 2nd edition (Oxford University Press, 1976), 26.

1. *The personality of the Holy Spirit.* Some false teachers, beginning in apostolic times, have doubted or denied the personality of the Holy Spirit, thinking of Him as a force or influence exerted by God, rather than a person. This tendency may derive in part from the word *spirit*, from the Latin *spirilus,* which means "breath." The Greek word *pneuma* and the Hebrew word *ruach* both have the same meaning of "breath" or "wind," as well as "spirit." If one thinks of the Holy Spirit as merely the breath or force of God, then He could be conceived of as impersonal and not a Being having a separate identity from the Father. However, divine revelation tells us that God is spirit (not material or physical). Like the wind, God exerts power and force, while being by nature invisible. The spirit of man is his immaterial, invisible self. If God is a person, and man, who is made in God's image, is a person, it should not be illogical to think of the Holy Spirit as a person. Observe the following proofs from Scripture (of which there are many) of the personality of the Holy Spirit, as well as His separate identity from the Father:

a) Personal pronouns are used in relation to Him (Jn. 16:14 and Eph. 1:14). In spite of the fact that the Greek word for "spirit" is in neuter gender, the demonstrative pronoun *ekeinos,* "that one," is used by John to refer to the Holy Spirit: "Howbeit when he [*ekeinos*], the Spirit of truth, is come, he will guide you into all truth...He [*ekeinos*] shall glorify me" (John 16:13–14). In Ephesians 1:13–14 Paul uses a masculine relative pronoun to refer to the Spirit: "You were sealed in Him with the Holy Spirit of promise, who [masc.] is given as a pledge of our inheritance" (NASB). (See also Jn. 15:26; 14:16–17.)

b) Personal characteristics are ascribed to Him. One might define a person as an individual having intelligence, emotion, and will. (1) The Holy Spirit possesses *intelligence*:

> But God hath revealed them unto us by his Spirit: for the Spirit searcheth all things, yea, the deep things of God. For what man knoweth the things of a man, save the spirit of man which is in him? even so the things of God knoweth no man, but the Spirit of God. Now we have received, not the spirit of the world, but the spirit which is of God; that we might know the things that are freely given to us of God.
>
> —1 CORINTHIANS 2:10–12

Furthermore, the word of wisdom and the word of knowledge are gifts given by the Holy Spirit (1 Cor. 12:8). (2) The Spirit possesses *emotion* and *feeling*: the Holy Spirit loves (Rom. 15:30), is vexed (Is. 63:10), and is grieved (Eph. 4:30). (3) The Holy Spirit possesses a *will*: "But all these worketh that one and the selfsame Spirit, dividing to every man severally as he will" (1 Cor. 12:11).

c) Personal actions are attributed to the Holy Spirit. (1) He speaks: Acts 13:2; 21:11; Rv. 2:7, 11, 17, 29. (2) He testifies: Jn. 15:26. (3) He teaches: Jn. 14:26. (4) He intercedes: Rom. 8:26–27. (5) He guides: Jn. 16:13; Acts 16:6. (6) He gives commands and ordains: Acts 13:2; 20:28. (7) He works miracles: Acts 8:39; Rom. 15:19.

d) Personal reactions are ascribed to the Holy Spirit. The Holy Spirit is shown to be a person, according to the feelings which He is said to have as a result of certain human actions. (1) He can be vexed and grieved: Eph. 4:30; Is. 63:10; Gn. 6:3. (2) He may be tempted: Acts 5:9. (3) He may be resisted: Acts 7:51. (4) He may be lied to: Acts 5:3. (5) He may be despited and blasphemed: Mk. 3:29–30; Heb. 10:29.

e) Personal relationships are maintained by the Holy Spirit:

(1)...with the Father (Mt. 28:19). In the baptismal formula, the Spirit is associated on an equal plane in name and personal identity with the Father and the Son.

(2)...with Christ. "He shall glorify me: for he shall receive of mine, and shall shew it unto you" (Jn. 16:14).

(3)...with believers. "For it seemed good to the Holy Ghost, and to us, to lay upon you no greater burden than these necessary things" (Acts 15:28). The apostles sought the will and good pleasure of the Holy Spirit in forming the policies of the local church.

That the Holy Spirit has a separate identity from the Father and the Son within the Trinity is clearly seen from the last discourse of Jesus, recorded in the book of John. In this discourse, several times Jesus makes reference to the coming of the Holy Spirit, whom He calls "another Comforter": "And I will pray the Father, and he shall give you another Comforter, that he may abide with you for ever" (Jn. 14:16). That the Comforter is the Holy Spirit is clear, for Jesus calls Him "the Spirit of truth" (v. 17). In verse 26, Jesus says, "But the Comforter, which is the Holy Ghost," making the identification certain. Jesus uses masculine pronouns, showing that the Holy Spirit is a person. The Comforter will come in answer to Jesus' prayer to the Father, who will send Him (Jn. 14:16). In John 15:26, Jesus says that He would send the Comforter, from the Father, "But when the Comforter is come, whom I will send unto you...which proceedeth from the Father, he shall testify of me." Clearly, Jesus has expressed an I-Thou-He relationship—Jesus prays, the Father sends, the Comforter proceeds. It is impossible to ignore the separate identities described. This is further amplified by the words of Jesus in John 16:7, "It is expedient for you that I go away: for if I go not away, the Comforter will not come unto you; but if I depart, I will send him unto you." One must go for the other to come. When the Comforter comes, it will be the result of the Son's praying and sending, the Father's sending in the Son's name, and the Spirit's proceeding.

The Holy Spirit, then, proceeds (as the creeds declare) from the Father and the Son. A heresy of ancient times called Sabellianism taught that the Father, Son, and Holy Spirit were only different names for the same person and different modalities by which the one person manifested Himself. If this were true, then Jesus' discourse about the Comforter would be meaningless, as would His prayer to the Father, recorded in John 17. Whether the proceeding of the Spirit mentioned in John 15:26 is an eternal relationship (as stated by the creeds), or a proceeding into the Church on the Day of Pentecost in answer to Jesus' prayer, is difficult to determine, for the "proceeding" is nowhere else mentioned. The Roman and Greek churches have disputed for centuries over whether the Spirit proceeds eternally from the Father only, or from the Father and the Son. The Greek church holds that He proceeds only from the Father, but whether the proceeding is eternal or on the occasion of Jesus' prayer, it seems clear that the Holy Spirit was sent both by the Father and the Son. (Compare Jn. 14:26 with 15:26 and 16:7.)

2. *The deity the Holy Spirit.* We will show from Scripture that the Holy Spirit is God, coequal and coeternal with the Father and the Son, the third person of the Trinity. That the Spirit executes the will of the Father and glorifies the Son, not speaking of Himself, does not denote inferiority; it merely indicates the inner working of the triune God. Among men, subordination would denote inferiority, but not in the Tri-unity of God. That is a part of the incomprehensible mystery. In the Trinity there are not three individuals, but three personal identities in the one God. When we contemplate how submission in the Trinity on the part of the Son and the Spirit does not constitute inferiority in position, we can, then, better understand why submission by believers, one to another, does not belittle the believer, but makes him the more pleasing to his Lord. The following are the scriptural proofs of the deity of the Holy Spirit:

a) He is called God. "But Peter said, Ananias, why hath Satan filled thine heart to lie to the Holy Ghost, and to keep back part of the price of the land?...thou hast not lied unto men, but unto God" (Acts 5:3–4). Clearly, what is done to the Holy Spirit is considered as done to God. Their fatal sin was not in withholding the price of the land, but in the deceit of pretending to give it all (1 Cor. 3:16; 2 Cor. 3:17).

b) Divine attributes are ascribed to Him. (1) Eternal: "How much more shall the blood of Christ, who through the eternal Spirit offered himself without spot to God, purge your conscience from dead works to serve the living God?" (Heb. 9:14). The Holy Spirit is not a created being; He always existed as a part of the triune God. He is as eternal as the Father and the Son. (2) Omniscience: "The Holy Ghost, whom the Father will send in my name, he shall teach you all things" (Jn. 14:26); "For the Spirit searcheth all things" (1 Cor. 2:10). (See also Lk. 2:25–32.) (3) Omnipresence: "Whither shall I go from thy spirit? or whither shall I flee from thy presence?" (Ps. 139:7). The psalmist declares that there is no place on Earth, in hell, or in heaven where one could escape the presence of the Holy Spirit. (4) Omnipotence: "The Holy Ghost shall come upon thee, and the power of the Highest shall overshadow thee: therefore also that holy thing which shall be born of thee shall be called the Son of God" (Lk. 1:35). (See also Mi. 3:8; Rom. 15:13–19.) (5) Holiness: This is seen in the name of the Holy Spirit. He is the Spirit of holiness who operates in the Church to consecrate believers to God. He separates us from the world, and unto God (Eph. 4:30). (6) Foreknowledge: "The Holy Spirit by the mouth of David spake before concerning Judas" (Acts 1:16). Only God can know the future. The Holy Spirit, speaking one thousand years before Christ through David, foreknew and predicted the betrayal and fate of Judas Iscariot (Ps. 69:25; 109:8). (See also Acts 11:27–28, concerning the prediction by the Spirit, through Agabus, of the great famine.) (7) Love: "Now I beseech you, brethren, for the Lord Jesus Christ's sake, and for the love of the Spirit [subjective genitive—"love which the Spirit has"] that ye strive together with me in your prayers to God for me" (Rom. 15:30). In the trinitarian benediction of 2 Corinthians 13:14, the grace of Christ and the fellowship of the Holy Spirit are actually aspects of God's love. Since God is love, we expect to find love manifested in the acts of the Trinity.

c) Divine works are attributed to the Holy Spirit: (1) Creation: "The Spirit of God hath made me, and the breath of the Almighty hath given me life (Jb. 33:4). (See also Gn. 1:2; Ps. 104:30.) This creating and life-giving work of the Holy Spirit is seen also in the overshadowing of Mary at the conception of Jesus and in the raising of Jesus from the dead. Is it not also seen in our regeneration, or new birth? (See also Lk. 1:35; Rom. 8:10–11; Jn. 3:5–7.) (2) Prophecy: "The sweet psalmist of Israel, said, The Spirit of the LORD spake by me, and his word was in my tongue. The God of Israel said, the Rock of Israel spake to me" (2 Sm. 23:1–3). Here the Holy Spirit is equated with the God of Israel and the Rock of Israel; the Spirit is the Spirit of Jehovah who is the same as *Eloah* (God of Creation) and the Rock (*Tsur*—metaphorical name for the "eternal, immutable One"). (3) Intercession: "Likewise the Spirit also helps in our weaknesses. For we do not know what we should pray for as we ought, but the Spirit Himself makes intercession for us with groanings which cannot be uttered" (Rom. 8:26–27, NKJV). The Son of God is our intercessor. The Spirit is associated with the Son in representing us at the throne of grace. The Holy Spirit in His omniscience knows the mind of God and the will of God for us, therefore He can direct us in prayer so that we pray "as we ought." (4) Inspiration of Scripture: "For the prophecy came not in old time by the will of man: but holy men of God spake as they were moved by the Holy Ghost" (2 Pt. 1:21). (See also 2 Tm. 3:16, where "inspiration of God" is literally "God-breathed." The breath of God is a metaphor for the Holy Spirit; see Gn. 2:7.) (5) Agent in divine guidance: "But when they shall lead you, and deliver you up, take no thought beforehand what ye shall speak, neither do ye premeditate: but whatsoever shall be given you in that hour, that speak ye: for it is not ye that speak, but the Holy Ghost" (Mk. 13:11). Note that the Spirit has infallible knowledge of what to speak, and He is able to instruct our minds and to guide us so that in practice we say what is proper and according to God's will.

3. *The names of the Holy Spirit.* In our study of the names of God, we observed that His names portrayed His character. The names of God were not mere designations or identifications; they revealed to us something about God's nature, attributes, or works. The same concept holds true with the names of the Holy Spirit. There are about 350 passages in the Scriptures which make reference to the Holy Spirit, in which more than fifty names or titles may be discerned. We will not attempt to analyze every name ascribed to the Spirit, only those titles that add to the total understanding of the Spirit's nature or activity. They are as follows:

a) The Holy Spirit: "How much more shall your heavenly Father give the Holy Spirit to them that ask him?" (Lk. 11:13). The Holy Spirit is the most precious gift that our Father in heaven can give us, which He is abundantly willing to impart.

b) The Spirit of God: "Know ye not that ye are the temple of God, and that the Spirit of God dwelleth in you?" (1 Cor. 3:16). In 1 Corinthians 6:19, the temple of the Spirit is the individual believer, but here it is the Church of Christ (observe the plural pronoun "ye," as in 2 Cor. 6:16).

c) The Spirit: "That which is born of the Spirit is spirit" (Jn. 3:6). The Spirit produces the born-again experience in the believer. It is He who imparts new life (*zoe,* which is spiritual life, in addition to *bios,* or physical life). (See Ps. 104:30; 1 Cor. 2:10; Jn. 3:6–8.)

d) The Spirit of Jehovah: "And there shall come forth a rod out of the stem of Jesse, and a Branch shall grow out of his roots: and the spirit of the LORD [Jehovah] shall rest upon him, the spirit of wisdom and understanding, the spirit of counsel and might, the spirit of knowledge and of the fear of the Lord" (Is. 11:1–2). This is clearly a messianic prophecy. The Spirit of Jehovah will rest upon the Christ, both in His earthly ministry as Redeemer (Is. 42:1; Mt. 3:16; Jn. 3:33–34) and in His millennial reign. (See also Is. 61:1 where the Holy Spirit is also called the Spirit of Jehovah, and where the prophetic particulars point to both of Christ's comings.)

e) The Spirit of the living God: "Ye are…the epistle of Christ…written not with ink, but with the Spirit of the living God" (2 Cor. 3:3). The Church is an epistle, a testimony to Christ before all men, not of human works but written by the Spirit of the living God (the giver of divine life) upon the tables of the heart. In other words, the Spirit will engrave the character of Jesus on our hearts as we function in the body of Christ.

f) The Spirit of Christ: "Now if any man have not the Spirit of Christ, he is none of his" (Rom. 8:9). Possessing the Spirit of Christ identifies us as one of His.

g) The Spirit of His Son: "And because ye are sons, God hath sent forth the Spirit of his Son into your hearts, crying, Abba, Father" (Gal. 4:6). The Son of God became the Son of Man, that the sons of men may become the sons of God, with the privilege of calling Him, *Abba,* or Father.

h) The Spirit of Jesus Christ: "For I know that this shall turn to my salvation through your prayer, and the supply of the Spirit of Jesus Christ" (Phil. 1:19). As we pray for those who minister, God will supply the same Spirit who sustained Christ Jesus in His mission. The use of one definite article with both the "prayer" and the "supply" shows that the two are related.

i) The Spirit of holiness: "And declared to be the Son of God with power, according to the spirit of holiness" (Rom. 1:4). Jesus came as the promised seed of David, who was also the divine Son of God, His deity being declared by His resurrection from the dead by the agency of the Spirit of holiness. Only God is absolutely holy. His Spirit is the Holy Spirit, or Spirit of holiness.

j) The Spirit of burning: Isaiah calls the Spirit, the Spirit of burning and of judgment (Is. 4:4). The Spirit of holiness purges sin and iniquity from Zion by burning and judgment, resulting in salvation. The Holy Spirit's "fan is in his hand, and he will thoroughly purge his floor" (Mt. 3:12).

k) The Spirit of truth: John calls the Holy Spirit the Spirit of truth because He is the agent of divine revelation who will enable the apostles to record the teachings of Jesus and to accurately interpret the redeeming events of sacred history (Jn. 14:17; 15:26; 16:13).

l) The Spirit of life: The principle of the Spirit of life in Christ has replaced the principle of the flesh (selfish ego), so that now this new dynamic can bring forth the righteousness of Christ in us and through us (Rom. 8:2).

m) The Spirit of glory: "If ye be reproached for the name of Christ, happy are ye; for the spirit of glory and of God resteth upon you" (1 Pt. 4:14). When Jesus approached the cross during His last week, He cried, "The hour is come, that the Son of Man should be glorified" (Jn. 12:23–33). Jesus considered His ordeal of crucifixion as His hour of glory. Peter, speaking to persecuted Christians and remembering the words of Jesus about His hour of glory, assured them that their sufferings for Christ were their glory and that the Spirit of glory was resting upon them. They were participating in the sufferings of Christ, and they would also participate in His glory (1 Pt. 2:19; 3:14).

n) The Spirit of grace: "Of how much sorer punishment, suppose ye, shall he be thought worthy, who hath trodden under foot the Son of God, and hath counted the blood of the covenant, wherewith he was sanctified, an unholy thing, and hath done despite unto the Spirit of grace?" (Heb. 10:29). Here is clearly a case of apostasy on the part of one who was formerly sanctified by the blood. We are saved by grace and not of works, but it is possible to despite the Spirit of grace in such a way that we forfeit God's gracious gift and fall into judgment.

o) The eternal Spirit: "Christ, who through the eternal Spirit offered himself without spot to God" (Heb. 9:14). The eternity of the Spirit demonstrates His deity.

The Spirit, who overshadowed Jesus at His conception, His baptism, and His temptation was with Jesus at the cross and with Him up from the grave.

p) The Holy Spirit of promise: "After that ye believed, ye were sealed with the holy Spirit of promise" (Eph. 1:13). In Luke 24:49, Jesus had promised to pour out the Spirit upon the tarrying disciples. This promise is repeated in Acts 1:4–5. Jesus referred to the Spirit as the promise of the Father, taking the promise probably from Joel 2:28, and Ezekiel 36:27–28. The Holy Spirit's empowerment of believers was well anticipated by Jesus and by the Father, through the mouths of Ezekiel and Joel.

q) The Comforter: "If I go not away, the Comforter will not come unto you; but if I depart, I will send him unto you" (Jn. 16:7). (See also Jn. 14:26; 15:26.) "Comforter" is, perhaps, not the best translation for our day because we think of comfort as consolation. In Old English, the word meant "strengthener." The Latin source-word *comfortare* meant "to strengthen much." The biblical Greek word is *parakletos,* meaning one who is "called to one's aid," which has led to the use of the word "advocate" as a translation. The New American Standard Bible renders the word "helper." The New International Version translates it to "counselor." It seems that *helper* is the best general term, which does justice to the Greek word *parakletos.*

4. *The symbols of the Holy Spirit.* In addition to the names and titles ascribed to the Holy Spirit, a number of symbolic figures of speech are employed in Scripture to reveal characteristics of the Spirit. The Jews expressed themselves more by word pictures than by abstract terms. The teaching of Jesus is exceedingly rich in symbols and figures of speech. The study of these symbols of the Spirit should help us better understand the ways and works of the Spirit of God.

a) Wind: One of the meanings of the Greek and Hebrew words for "spirit" is that of "breath" or "wind." "The wind bloweth where it listeth...so is every one that is born of the Spirit" (Jn. 3:8). On the Day of Pentecost, a "rushing mighty wind" is associated with the Holy Spirit's outpouring (Acts 2:2). Wind symbolizes the invisible, everywhere present, powerful, and life-sustaining influence of the Spirit.

b) Oil: Oil was used in the anointing of kings and priests as a symbol of the Holy Spirit's empowerment for their work. All believers have the promise of this anointing (Is. 61:1; Lk. 4:14–18; Acts 10:38; Jas. 5:14; 1 Jn. 2:20, 27).

c) Dove: The dove symbolizes the qualities of gentleness, purity, love, innocence, and beauty. The Holy Spirit descended upon Jesus at His baptism in the form of a dove (Mt. 3:16; Gn. 8:8–12; Mt. 10:16; Ps. 68:13; Gal. 5:22–23).

d) Water: The Scriptures picture water in the form of rain, dew, rivers, and springs. Water symbolizes the Spirit's refreshing, satisfaction, and fertilization. In the application of this symbol, Jesus and the Spirit are closely related, as in John 4:14 and 7:38–39 (1 Cor. 10:4; Ez. 36:25–27; Jl. 2:23–29).

e) Fire: Fire speaks of the Spirit's power and purging. For one to enjoy the power of the Holy Ghost, he must continually experience His cleansing (Is. 4:4; 6:6–7; 1 Kgs. 18:38; Acts 2:3).

f) Wine: Wine seems to call attention to the spiritually stimulating and joy-giving characteristic of the Spirit's indwelling presence (Is. 55:1; Ps. 104:15; Eph. 5:18). Some of the onlookers on the Day of Pentecost, hearing the glossalalia of the apostles, remarked that they were drunk on new wine. Peter said that they were not drunk, but that they were filled with the Spirit prophesied by the prophet Joel (Acts 2:13–15). The world seeks alcoholic wine for stimulation and merriment, but the Christian receives enhancement of his abilities and true joyfulness from the Spirit of God who indwells him. The world's spirits give a lift with a let-down; the believer's anointing with oil and wine brings inspiration without desperation.

THE DOCTRINE OF MAN

Anthropology

Introduction

I. Man, Created by God
  A. Not evolved from lower life forms
  B. Exists by special creation

II. Man, the Result of Divine Purpose
  A. The council of the Trinity
  B. The work of God's creative purpose

III. Man, Created in God's Image
  A. Not a physical image
  B. A personal image
  C. A moral image
  D. A social image

IV. Man, Created a Living Soul (Being)
  A. Given a body (earth)
  B. Given an immaterial life (God-breathed)
    1. *Trichotomy*
    2. *Dichotomy*
  C. Becomes a living soul (being)
    1. *Unity of the person*
    2. *Origin of the soul*

V. Man's Primitive State or Condition
  A. The state of knowledge
  B. The moral state
  C. The psychological state
  D. The social state
  E. The occupational state
  F. The state of life expectancy

VI. Man's Fall
  A. His probation
    1. *Its purpose*
    2. *Its character*
    3. *Its reasonableness*
  B. His temptation
    1. *The agent*

119

    2. *The motives*
- **C.** His fallen state
  1. *The interpretation of the Fall*
  2. *The results of the Fall*
  3. *The consequences of the Fall*

VII. Man's Potential in the State of Grace
- **A.** The believer, a new man in Christ Jesus
- **B.** Christ's incarnation and the believer's new position in Christ
- **C.** The believer's new nature in Christ
- **D.** The believer's new life in Christ
- **E.** The believer's constant renewal
- **F.** The believer's hope of a heavenly home
- **G.** The believer's victory over the old nature
- **H.** The believer's authority in Christ's kingdom

CHAPTER THREE

THE DOCTRINE OF MAN

Anthropology

INTRODUCTION

IT MAY APPEAR that going from the doctrine of God to the study of man is going from the sublime to the ridiculous. Even the psalmist cried, "What is man that thou are mindful of him?" (Ps. 8:4). But when we stop to think that man is a creation of God (Gn. 1:27), that redeemed man is God's handiwork (Eph. 2:10, WEY), and that redeemed humanity is God's inheritance (Eph. 1:18), we become aware of the importance of man as a subject of study.

Carl Henry, a modern scholar of renown wrote, "Who is man? This remarkable creature, whose amazing conquest of space and time has yielded unabridged dictionaries indexing the whole of reality, has fallen into frustration—ironically enough—when defining himself."[1]

Only the Scriptures give a solid and satisfying answer to the age-long question, Who is man? Therefore, any serious work on Bible doctrine must cope with this question. In academic circles, the study of man is called anthropology, which is derived from two Greek words: *anthropos,* which means "man," and *logos,* which means "account" or "reason." Biblical anthropology deals with man as God's creation, man as a sinner alienated from God by voluntary disobedience, and man as the object of God's redeeming grace. Scientific anthropology, according to Webster, is: "The study of man, especially of the variety, physical and cultural characteristics, distribution, customs, social relationships, etc. of mankind."[2]

In this approach to anthropology, we shall study man as he is portrayed in the Scriptures. The psalmist asks the question, What is man? and answers the question as follows, "For thou hast made him a little lower than the angels, and hast crowned him with glory and honour. Thou madest him to have dominion over the works of thy hands; thou hast put all things under his feet" (Ps. 8:5–6).

---

1 Everett F. Harrison, ed., *Baker's Dictionary of Theology* (Grand Rapids, MI: Baker Book House, 1960), 338.

2 *Webster's New World Dictionary of the American Language,* 2nd college edition, s.v. "anthropology."

But then man disobeyed and fell short of the glory of God; therefore, when the writer of Hebrews quoted from Psalm 8, he added: "But now we see not yet all things put under him. But we see Jesus, who was made a little lower than the angels for the suffering of death, crowned with glory and honour; that he by the grace of God should taste death for every man" (Heb. 2:8–9).

The following scriptural study of man will fall under these categories: (1) man was created by God, (2) man was the result of divine purpose, (3) man was created in God's image, (4) man was created a living soul, (5) man's primitive state, (6) the fall of man, and (7) man in the state of grace.

I. MAN WAS CREATED BY GOD

A. Not evolved from lower life forms

The Bible attributes the origin of man to an act of direct creation by God: "So God created man in his own image" (Gn. 1:27). "And the LORD God formed man of the dust of the ground, and breathed into his nostrils the breath of life; and man became a living soul" (Gn. 2:7). In our public school systems, pupils are taught that man evolved from the lower animals and that all life over a vast expanse of time came from a single life form that came into being from an unknown origin. Honest teachers admit that the theory of evolution is, in fact, only a theory or hypothesis advanced to explain origins without introducing the supernatural, which science cannot study. The theory of evolution is generally attributed to Charles Darwin, who first popularized the hypothesis in the middle of the nineteenth century. His theory was received by materialists everywhere. Mendel's law of heredity seemed to prove that species were fixed and that acquired characteristics could not be inherited. Later scientists gave the name "genes" to the remarkable factors that control heredity. Dr. Robert Kofahl has the following to say about genes:

> Research over the past two decades has revealed much about the structure of the gene. A great deal has been learned about the function of the gene at the molecular level. Molecular genetics is a most complicated subject which affords powerful support for the Biblical creation model.[3]

Dr. Paul Brand, world renowned surgeon, Chief of the Rehabilitation Branch of the U.S. Public Health Service and a professor of surgery, has the following to say about the genes' chemical code, DNA, that controls all forms of life, maintaining the

---

3 Robert E. Kofahl and K. L. Seagrave, *The Creation Explanation* (Wheaton, IL: Harold Shaw Publishers, 1975), 78.

species propagating each after its own kind according to Genesis 1, and preventing the evolution of any species into another:

> All living matter is basically alike; a single atom differentiates animal blood from plant chlorophyll. Yet the body senses infinitesimal differences with an unfailing scent; it knows its hundred trillion cells by name...To complicate the process of identity, the composite of Paul Brand—bone cells, fat cells, blood cells, muscle cells—differs entirely from my components ten years ago. All cells have been replaced by new cells (except for nerve cells and brain cells, which are never replaced). Thus, my body is more like a fountain than a sculpture: maintaining its shape, but constantly being renewed. Somehow my body knows the new cells belong, and they are welcomed. What moves the cells to work together?...The secret to membership lies locked away inside each cell nucleus, chemically coiled in a strand of DNA. Once the egg and sperm share their inheritance, the DNA chemical ladder splits down the center of every gene, much as the teeth of a zipper pull apart. DNA reforms itself each time the cell divides: 2, 4, 8, 16, 32 cells, each with the identical DNA. Along the way cells specialize, but each carries the entire instruction book of one hundred thousand genes. DNA is estimated to contain instructions that, if written out, would fill a thousand, six hundred-page books...(The DNA is so narrow and compacted that all the genes in all my body's cells would fit into an ice cube; yet if DNA were unwound and joined together end to end, the strand could stretch from earth to the sun and back more than four hundred times)...A nerve cell may operate according to instructions from volume four and a kidney cell from volume twenty-five, but both carry the whole compendium. It provides each cell's sealed credential of membership in the body. Every cell possesses a genetic code so complete that the entire body could be reassembled from the information in any one of the body's cells...The Designer of DNA went on to challenge the human race to a new and higher purpose: membership in His own Body...In reality, I become genetically like Christ Himself because I belong to His body.[4]

Mendel's law seemed to sound a death knell for Darwin's theory; however, persistent evolutionists found a new basis for evolution in the occasional sudden changes in life forms, called mutations. While nearly all mutations are harmful, some scientists theorize that beneficial mutations could account for the ongoing evolution from

---

4 Dr. Paul Brand and Philip Yancy, *Fearfully and Wonderfully Made* (Grand Rapids, MI: Zondervan Publishing House, 1981), 44–46.

lower species to higher species; however, no evidence for this exists. Evolution by mutations is called by some "neo-Darwinism."

The whole framework of evolutionary theory is coming under sharp criticism. Francis Hitchings, writing in *Life Magazine,* states, "Charles Darwin died one hundred years ago...Today his explanation of evolution is being challenged as never before, not just by Creationists, but by his fellow scientists."[5]

While many scientists work on the assumption of the evolutionary hypothesis, evolution is not scientific fact; it cannot be proved. And unless one has chosen to be a materialist, there is overwhelming logic in a supernatural origin for man, who almost universally seeks an object of worship and who cannot escape from an instinct of responsibility to a higher power. One hundred years beyond Darwin, evolution is still unproven and contributes nothing to the dignity of man. For the materialist, it is a godless faith.

It should be stated in fairness that not all evolutionists are materialists, nor agnostics. There are the theistic evolutionists who believe that evolution was the method God employed to create all life. However, since there is no evidence whatever (either in the fossil record, or in the science of genetics for the transmutation of species) and since the Bible plainly states that the species propagate each after its own kind, it seems truer to Scripture and to reason to accept a direct creation for man.

It is not the purpose of this book to deal with physical science, but with Bible doctrine. However, this quotation by scientists bears consideration:

> The most powerful evidence for creation and against evolution is, in our opinion, to be found in specific evidences of intelligent, purposeful design. This evidence is all around us and is something the layman as well as the scientist can appreciate. The authors of *The Creation Explanation* accept the claim of the Bible to be the Word of God. They accept the opening chapters of Genesis, therefore, to be true to scientific fact. This is their fundamental postulate and they make no apology for it.[6]

Of course, the Bible-believer cannot prove scientifically the divine creation of man, so he accepts the scriptural account by faith. He finds no problem in this, because having accepted the Lord of the Scriptures by faith, his life has been transformed and he has been given a sustaining hope and a powerful meaning to his existence. The

---

5 Francis Hitchings, "Was Darwin Wrong?" *Life Magazine* (April 1982), quoted from Francis Hitchings, *The Neck of the Giraffe: Where Darwin Went Wrong* (New York: Ticknor and Fields, 1982).

6 Kofahl, xii, xiii.

believer's courageous faith informs him of his meaningful origin and his heavenly destiny.

B. Exists by special creation

Three Hebrew words are used in Genesis 1 and 2 to describe man's creation: *bará*—"to create, shape, or form…something new;" *ásah*—meaning "to fashion, accomplish, prepare, to bring about;" and *yatzar*—meaning "to form or shape" (as a potter forming vessels). In Genesis 1:26, the triune God says, "Let us make [*ásah*] man." In Genesis 1:27, we read, "So God created [*bará*] man." Genesis 2:7 states, "And the LORD God formed [*yatzar*] man." The idea in 1:26 is that God constructed man in conformity with His own image; in 1:27, He created man as something new and wonderful in His purpose; and in 2:7, He formed and shaped man from the earth as a potter forms a vessel of clay. The "dust of the ground" (2:7) identifies man with the scene of his fall and his redemption, and the breath of God identifies his origin with his Maker and his intended heavenly destiny. Man is of the earth, but he is intended for fellowship with God.

The declaration of man's creation by God is not confined to two or three verses; it is affirmed or assumed throughout Holy Scripture. Genesis 5:1–2 continues, "In the day that God created [*bará*] man, in the likeness of God made he him; Male and female created he them." In Genesis 6:7, "And the LORD said, I will destroy man whom I have created [*bará*]." Concerning the miraculous deliverance from Egypt, Moses says in Deuteronomy 4:32, "For ask now concerning the days that are past, which were before thee, since the day that God created man upon the earth, and ask from the one side of heaven unto the other, whether there hath been any such thing as this great thing is." From the inspired quill of the prophet Isaiah come the following statements: "But now thus saith the LORD that created thee" (43:1); "Even every one that is called by my name: for I have created him for my glory, I have formed him; yea, I have made him" (43:7); "I have made the earth, and created man upon it" (45:12). And from Malachi 2:10, "Have we not all one father? hath not one God created us?" That man was created by God is clearly stated by New Testament writers. Paul says, "And have put on the new man, which is renewed in knowledge after the image of him that created him" (Col. 3:10). (See also 1 Tm. 2:13; Rom. 9:20; 1 Cor. 15:45; Jas. 3:9.)

II. MAN THE RESULT OF DIVINE PURPOSE

A. The council of the Trinity

Man was not created in the manner of the lower creatures. They were created as a result of God's spoken command. God first formed man out of the earth, then breathed His divine breath into him. There was something from God Himself that was breathed into man, demonstrating that he was intended to be special to the

Creator, above all other earthly creatures. Isaiah gives the Lord's explanation of His purpose in creating man: "I have created him for my glory" (Is. 43:7). Man is the product of God's planned purpose to create a being to glorify Him. In the light of God's deliberate affirmation of Genesis 1:26, there is a hint of a council of the Trinity in which They said, "Let us make man in our image, after our likeness: and let them have dominion…over all the earth." Some have attributed the plural pronouns "us" and "our" to the fact that the name for God (*Elohim*) is a plural form. However, *Elohim*, while it is plural, usually takes a singular verb. Commenting on Genesis 1:26, H. C. Leupold, the great Lutheran Hebrew scholar, says:

> The hortative, "Let us make" *(nacaseh),* is particularly striking because it is plural…Behind such speaking lies the truth of the Holy Trinity which, as it grows increasingly clear in revelation, is in the light of later clear revelation discovered as contained in this plural in a kind of obscure adumbration. The truth of the Trinity explains this passage. The common explanation that God is addressing the angels has been shown up in its deficiencies by Koenig. It cannot be denied that on occasion God addressed the angelic host before His throne…but never once does God actually counsel with them.[7]

B. The work of God's creative purpose

Paul refers to this council of the triune God in Ephesians 1:4–5 when he says, "According as he hath chosen us in him before the foundation of the world, that we should be holy and without blame before him in love." Also in 2 Timothy 1:9, "Who hath saved us, and called us with an holy calling, not according to our works, but according to his own purpose and grace, which was given us in Christ Jesus before the world began." The following remarkable things are said about man's creation: man is created by God, man alone of all created beings received the breath of God, man is formed in God's image, man is created for God's glory, man was planned and designed in a council of the triune God, and man has been redeemed by the God-man Christ Jesus. Writing to Titus, Paul declared, "In hope of eternal life, which God, that cannot lie, promised before the world began" (Ti. 1:2). Since God could not have promised anything to men before the world began, He must have promised to His Son Jesus the redemption and eternal life of man. Jesus, in His intercessory prayer to the Father, clearly implies this truth: "Father, I will that they also, whom thou hast given me, be with me where I am; that they may behold my glory, which thou hast given me: for thou lovedst me before the foundation of the world" (Jn. 17:24).

---

7 Herbert Carl Leupold, *Exposition of Genesis* (Columbus, OH: The Wartburg Press, 1942), 86–87.

The question has been asked, If God in His foreknowledge knew that man would fall, why did He create him? We cannot, of course, discern God's motives, but we can be certain that in the divine purpose it was determined that in spite of their disobedience, a mankind in God's image would justify God's purpose once they were redeemed through the Son, Jesus. This is a mystery that we cannot fathom with our finite minds, but it is clear that redeemed man in Christ—the object of God's love—fulfills a high purpose. He is only "dust of the ground," but he is a potential child of God.

III. MAN CREATED IN GOD'S IMAGE

The Scriptures tell us that man was created in the image of God, which in Hebrew is *tselem Elohim*; in Greek, *eikon tou theou*; and *imago Dei* in Latin. In Genesis 1:26, the term "likeness" is added; but almost all commentators see it as Hebrew parallelism, introducing a synonym for emphasis only, not added meaning. Nowhere in Scripture are we told explicitly what is meant by the term *in the image of God*; therefore, many explanations have been offered. The following is a listing of the more common interpretations of the *imago Dei*: that man was conformed to an ideal form which God possesses; man's dominion over the Earth and its creatures; man's rationality and ability to have communion with his Creator; man's personality of intellect, emotion, and will; man's original holiness, righteousness, and moral nature; and man's triune being of body, soul, and spirit.

A. Not a physical image

God is Spirit; He does not have a physical body (Jn. 4:24). He is invisible, although He may appear in human form as in the case of the angel of Jehovah. (Col. 1:15; 1 Tm. 1:17; Heb. 11:27; Gn. 17–18.) There has been conjecture that man's upright stature indicates that he was patterned after a prototype image represented by the glorified body of Christ. Romans 5:14 does state that Adam was a type of Christ. However, Israel was expressly prohibited from making any graven image of God in human form, as though God were physically like man. It is true that Jesus subsisted in the form of God, however, when He came to Earth, He took the form of a servant and was made in the likeness of men. Therefore, His earthly form must have been a great condescension from His heavenly form (Phil. 2:7–8). Adam's form before the Fall may have been much superior to his post-Edenic image; however, man still retains something of the original *imago Dei* (Jas. 3:9; Gn. 9:6; Jn. 5:37; Is. 6:1).

B. A personal image

We believe in a personal God—One who designs, plans, communicates, wills, and feels pleasure or displeasure. We define personality as comprising intellect, emotion, and will. Genesis 1:26–3:1 attributes these components of personality to God: intellect, in the words "and God said;" will and purpose in the statement "let us make;" and feeling or emotion in the sentence, "Then God saw everything that He had made, and indeed it was very good" (Gn. 1:31, NKJV). We are careful here, because God's nature is vastly beyond our comprehension, but the infinite God is represented everywhere in Scripture as possessing personal characteristics.

If God had a purpose in creating man, He must have desired to communicate with His creation to reveal something of His will and purpose. The God who said, "Let us make," also said to His nation Israel, "Come now, and let us reason together" (Is. 1:18). Man is the only one of Earth's creatures able to reason abstractly, to create, to innovate, to choose as a free agent, to communicate with, and to worship God. The animals' activities, on the other hand, are instinctive, not free. Do man's personal and rational faculties constitute God's image? Or does man's capacity to have dominion and to rule over Earth's creatures constitute the divine image? Do we still see this image portrayed in man's conquest of space, his control of atomic energy, his harnessing of electricity and other of nature's forces, and his employment of animals to do his work? There seems to be some hint of this in Genesis 1:28–3:1 and Psalms 8:4–9.

C. A moral image

Man is a moral being. He was created with a sense of accountability to his Maker. When he does right, his heart assures him; when he does wrong, his heart condemns him (1 Jn. 3:20–21; Rom. 8:1). Because man is a moral creature, God gave to him His Law, recorded in Exodus 20. If man violated the Law, God would not hold him guiltless (Ex. 20:7). Man, who failed the test in the Garden, also failed to keep the Law. He shared Adam's guilt, as well as Adam's acquired sinful nature. Only the last Adam, Jesus Christ, can free man from the condemnation and guilt of his fallen condition (Rom. 8:1).

As a moral being, man has a conscience. There are those who think that the conscience is not a separate faculty, but merely the knowledge of self in relation to a known standard of right and wrong, or the inter-working of intellect, emotion, and will in the face of a moral standard. It seems clear, however, from Scripture and experience that man does indeed possess a faculty of conscience. *Webster's Dictionary* defines conscience as, "A knowledge or sense of right and wrong, with a compulsion to do right; moral judgment that opposes the violation of a previously recognized ethical principle, and that leads to feelings of guilt if one violates such a principle."[8] While the word *conscience* is not found in the Old Testament, its working

---

8 *Webster's Dictionary*, s.v. "conscience."

is described in Leviticus 5:3. In the New Testament, the word *conscience* occurs thirty-one times. It is said about the conscience that it can be good, weak, pure, seared, defiled, evil, and purged. It is said to perform actions, such as to bear witness and to convict. Could such actions and characteristics be attributed to anything other than a distinct faculty? It appears that the conscience is a human instinct which was given to man in the beginning; for as soon as man sinned, he hid himself. Undoubtedly the conscience interacts with intellect, emotion, and will.

D. A social image

God is love. He is love in His essential nature, for love is the expression of the triune God: Father, Son and Holy Spirit. Man was created in God's image as a social creature who is to love. He was immediately given a wife, taken from his side to be his equal, from near his heart to be loved, and from under his arm to be protected by him. He is commanded to multiply and replenish the earth, to be a family and a family of nations. The Law was given to govern man's social relationships. Of the Ten Commandments, six are concerned with man's treatment of his fellow man. Man was made to have communion with God, with his family, and with his neighbors. When man lost communion with God, his human relationships began to break down. (Consider that the first son of Adam became a murderer.) Love, Jesus tells us, is to be the controlling motive of the redeemed man who, when he is born again, becomes a member of a body—the body of Christ (Jn. 13:34–35).

IV. Man Created a Living Soul (Being)

According to inspired Scripture, man, at his creation, was given two gifts from God: a body formed from the dust and the breath of God. "And the Lord God formed man of the dust of the ground, and breathed into his nostrils the breath of life; and man became a living soul" (Gn. 2:7). As a result of the creative combination of an earthly element and a heavenly element, man became a living being in the image of his Creator. He begins life on the earth in a vessel of clay, but his intended destiny is everlasting life in a glorified body.

A. Is given a body

The Greeks and many of the ancients thought of the body as a prison of the soul and the source of all evil. The Gnostics, a false cult, held this low esteem of the body to the extreme of denying that Jesus had a physical body. To counter these Gnostics, John the Apostle warned about those who denied that Jesus had come in the flesh (1 Jn. 4:1–3). The Scriptures teach us to honor and respect the body as God's creation: "Whoso sheddeth man's blood, by man shall his blood be shed: for in the image of God made he man" (Gn. 9:6).

The following are ten facts about the body from Scripture that are important for the Christian believer to know:

1. *It is a mortal body that will return to the dust out of which it was fashioned.* "For dust thou art, and unto dust thou shalt return" (Gn. 3:19). This thought will keep us humble in the presence of our God. When Abraham talked with God, he said, "Behold now, I have taken upon me to speak unto the Lord, which am but dust and ashes" (Gn. 18:27). The psalmist reminds us that without the breath of God, man is but dust: "Thou takest away their breath, they die, and return to their dust" (Ps. 104:29).

2. *Man is made of mere dust; but that dust, in the hands of God, became something wonderfully made:*

> I will praise thee; for I am fearfully and wonderfully made: marvellous are thy works; and that my soul knoweth right well. My substance was not hid from thee, when I was made in secret, and curiously wrought in the lowest parts of the earth. Thine eyes did see my substance, yet being unperfect; and in thy book all my members were written.
>
> —PSALM 139:14–16

Science is just beginning to discover how unimaginably wonderful and complex is the human body.

3. *Man's natural, physical body is only a temporary tabernacle for the real person who inhabits it.* "Knowing that shortly I must put off this my tabernacle, even as our Lord Jesus Christ hath shewed me" (2 Pt. 1:14); and "For we know that if our earthly house of this tabernacle were dissolved, we have a building of God, an house not made with hands, eternal in the heavens" (2 Cor. 5:1).

4. *In the resurrection, man will have a new house not made with hands; however, that new body will have a relationship to this present natural body.* Paul, discussing the resurrection, states, "It is sown a natural body; it is raised a spiritual body....For this corruptible must put on incorruption, and this mortal must put on immortality" (1 Cor. 15:44, 53). This present body that goes back to dust will somehow be changed and transformed into a glorified body. Jesus said, "The dead shall hear the voice of the Son of God: and they that hear shall live" (Jn. 5:25). Paul assured that the dead in Christ would rise first (1 Thes. 4:16). Paul does say that "flesh and blood cannot inherit the kingdom of God" (1 Cor. 15:50). But, as Jesus in the resurrection had a touchable body of flesh and bones but not blood (Jn. 20:27; Lk. 24:39), so the believer's resurrection body will have a relationship to the earthly body, as a new plant is related to the seed from which it springs (1 Cor. 15:44).

5. *The body of redeemed man is a temple of the Holy Spirit. Therefore it must not be an instrument of sin.*

> What? know ye not that your body is the temple of the Holy Ghost which
> is in you, which ye have of God, and ye are not your own? For ye are bought
> with a price: therefore glorify God in your body, and in your spirit, which
> are God's.
>
> —1 CORINTHIANS 6:19–20

6. *Man's body, when dedicated to Christ's service, is reckoned as a living and holy sacrifice.* "I beseech you therefore, brethren, by the mercies of God, that ye present your bodies a living sacrifice, holy, acceptable unto God, which is your reasonable service" (Rom. 12:1). The Old Testament worshiper offered dead sacrifices of animals to God; the New Testament believer in Christ offers not a dead, but a living, offering of consecrated service—employing the body in Christian living and ministry.

7. *The redeemed man may employ his body as a weapon against Satan.* Satan strives to motivate the believer to use his body in a way that would advance Satan's cause, but Paul urges the believer to use his body as a weapon against Satan and for God:

> You must not let any part of your body turn into an unholy weapon fighting
> on the side of sin; you should instead, offer yourselves to God, and consider
> yourselves dead men brought back to life; you should make every part of your
> body into a weapon fighting on the side of God.
>
> —ROMANS 6:13, JB

8. *Redeemed man enjoys certain benefits of Christ's redeeming work in his body, even in this world.* Matthew, writing about the healing ministry of Jesus, said:

> When the even was come, they brought unto him many that were possessed
> with devils: and he cast out the spirits with his word, and healed all that were
> sick: That it might be fulfilled which was spoken by Esaias the prophet, say-
> ing, Himself took our infirmities, and bare our sicknesses.
>
> —MATTHEW 8:16–17

Clearly, the work of the Cross accomplished something for man's physical body, loosening the hold of sickness upon it. Jesus later said about the ministry of those who were to preach the gospel, "They shall lay hands on the sick, and they shall recover" (Mk. 16:18). When the church became established, prayer for physical healing became a sacrament. James instructs, "Is any sick among you? let him call for the elders of the church: and let them pray over him, anointing him with oil in the name of the Lord: And the prayer of faith shall save the sick, and the Lord shall raise him up" (Jas. 5:14–15). That the redeeming work of Christ and the indwelling of the Holy Spirit bring present benefits, even to the body, is brought out in Romans 8: "But if the Spirit of him that raised up Jesus from the dead dwell in you, he that raised up Christ from the dead shall also quicken your mortal bodies by his Spirit that dwelleth in you" (Rom. 8:11). Some would argue that this "quickening" refers to the final resurrection of the body. That it pertains to present experience is seen in the following facts:

a) Paul is speaking of the believer's present victory over the flesh (v. 9).

b) He refers to our mortal bodies, not dead bodies. *Mortal* means "subject to death."

c) Before the quickening of the resurrection, the bodies will be dead in the grave, not "mortal."

d) In verse 12, he says, "Therefore, brethren, we are debtors, not to the flesh, to live after the flesh." The argument pertains clearly to the present walk in the Spirit.

e) If the Spirit delivers from carnal domination through faith, so also can the Spirit deliver from bodily infirmity through faith.

9. *The believer will be judged at the judgment seat of Christ on the basis of things done in the body.* "For we must all appear before the judgment seat of Christ; that every one may receive the things done in his body, according to that he hath done, whether it be good or bad" (2 Cor. 5:10).

The judgment above mentioned (*bema*) is a judgment of works, not of condemnation (1 Cor. 3:11–15). The degree of reward is based upon things done in the body. It is the soul, of course, that sins, but the sin is executed by the body and its members. Paul said, "But I keep under my body, and bring it into subjection: lest that by any means, when I have preached to others, I myself should be a castaway" (1 Cor. 9:27).

10. *Man's body of "dust," which he inherits from Adam, bears the image of Adam as well as the image of God.* Through Christ we will inherit a glorified body in the image of Christ, the Last Adam. This is brought out in 1 Corinthians 15 and made clear in the rendering of the New King James Version:

> "The first man Adam became a living being." The last Adam became a life-giving spirit. However, the spiritual is not first, but the natural, and afterward the spiritual. The first man was of the earth, made of dust; the second man is the Lord from heaven. As was the man of dust, so also are those who are made of dust; and as is the heavenly man, so also are those who are heavenly. And as we have borne the image of the man of dust, we shall also bear the image of the heavenly man.
>
> —1 CORINTHIANS 15:45–49

B. Is given an immaterial life

The Scriptures teach that man's immaterial life and personality are derived from God's creative breath and that our life's breath depends upon the sustaining grace of our Creator (Jb. 12:10; Ps. 33:6; Is. 42:5; Acts 17:25).

Some schools of modern scientific psychology attribute man's personality and intellect to the physical, chemical, and electrical function of the brain. While these schools cannot explain the origin of life nor the life principle, they prefer to entirely eliminate any supernatural basis for man's rational faculty. Psychologists avoid the term *mind*, preferring to concentrate their experiments on the brain and nerve system, seeking a physical explanation for all human behavior. They cannot explain how, in the event of injury to one side of the brain, one's personality is reestablished on the other side. Man as a free, creative, rational, and worshiping being is far too wonderfully complex to be explained as a result of the mere chance action of physical forces. The book of Genesis tells of the divine origin of man's inner self: "And the Lord God... breathed into his nostrils the breath of life" (Gn. 2:7).

The immaterial element in man is referred to in Scripture by the use of at least nine different terms:

1. Life (Mk. 8:35)
2. Soul (Mk. 8:36)
3. Spirit (Ps. 31:5)
4. Mind (Rom. 7:25)
5. Heart (Eph. 6:6)
6. Strength (Lk. 10:27)
7. Self (1 Cor. 4:3–4)
8. Will (1 Cor. 7:37)
9. Affections (Col. 3:2)

This is not to say, of course, that these terms are all synonyms. Each refers to the immaterial self from a discernibly different point of view, or describes a different function of the self. On the other hand, several of the terms could be interchangeable. For instance, the Greek word *psuche* is variously translated by the English words "life" (forty-two times), "soul" (fifty-three times), and "heart" (two times).

The words most frequently used to identify the immaterial self are *soul* and *spirit*. "Soul" translates the Hebrew word *nephesh* and the Greek word *psuche*. "Spirit" is the English translation of the Hebrew *ruach* and the Greek *pneuma*. It is interesting that all four of these words from the original Hebrew and Greek mean basically "breath" or "wind." These terms aptly express the fact that our immaterial self derives from the "breath" of God. When Jesus described the work of the Spirit of God to Nicodemus He said, "The wind [*pneuma*] bloweth [*pneo*] where it listeth" (Jn. 3:8). Some scholars think that the clause should read, "The Spirit breathes where He wills." The Greek words are capable of either translation.[9] The book of Job attributes man's creation to the breath of God: "But there is a spirit in man: and the inspiration of the Almighty giveth them understanding" (32:8). And "The Spirit of God hath made me, and the breath of the Almighty hath given me life" (33:4).

It has often been said that all living creatures have souls, but only man has a spirit. The fact is that Scripture attributes both soul and spirit to the animals (Eccl. 3:21; Ps. 104:25–30). Man is distinguished from the lower creatures by the quality of his faculties, not the number of them. Man is man because he is created in the image of God and because his life is everlasting. It has been taught that unregenerate man has only a body and soul, that the spirit is imparted at the new birth. This confuses the human spirit with the Holy Spirit, who indwells the believer. Ungodly men are said to have spirits (1 Chr. 5:26). Also, it is incorrect to say that soul is the human element, and that spirit is the divine element. Again, this confuses the human spirit with the Holy Spirit. Souls and spirits of men are pictured in heaven (Rv. 6:9; Heb. 12:23). Soul and spirit are both attributed to God the Father and Son (Mt. 12:18; Is. 42:1; Mt. 26:38; Is. 53:11–12; Lk. 23:46).

In regard to the composition of man, there are two classical schools of thought: one that suggests a trichotomy (three parts)—body, soul, and spirit; and another, a dichotomy (two parts)—body and soul (or spirit). The arguments for the two positions are as follows:

1. *Trichotomy*

a) In Genesis 2:7, the combination of a body of dust and the breath of God resulted in a third part, the soul.

b) 1 Thessalonians 5:23 definitely specifies three parts of man: "And the very God of peace sanctify you wholly; and I pray God your whole spirit and soul and body be preserved blameless unto the coming of our Lord Jesus Christ."

c) Hebrews 4:12 declares that soul and spirit are capable of being divided asunder by the Word of God: "For the word of God is quick, and powerful, and sharper than any twoedged sword, piercing even to the dividing of soul and spirit, and of the joints and marrow, and is a discerner of the thoughts and intents of the heart."

d) When Paul speaks of men as "carnal," "natural" (soulish), and "spiritual," he seems to indicate conditions related to body, soul, and spirit, respectively (1 Cor. 2:14–3:1).

2. *Dichotomy*

---

9 See Rotherham's *Emphasized New Testament,* Kregel; Worrell's *New Testament,* Gospel Publishing House; and the *Interlinear Greek—English Bible* by Jay Green.

a) In Genesis 2:7, only two distinct parts are mentioned: the body of earth and the breath of God. The living soul is not a third part, but the result of body and spirit. It does not say that man had a soul, but "became a living soul [being]."

b) The terms *soul* and *spirit* are used interchangeably. For instance, in John 12:27 Jesus said, "Now is my soul troubled"; but in John 13:21, we read: "When Jesus had thus said, he was troubled in spirit." (See also Gn. 41:8; Ps. 42:6; Heb. 12:23; and Rv. 6:9; 20:4.)

c) The terms *soul* and *spirit* are both used of animals as well as men (Eccl. 3:21; Rv. 16:3).

d) The term *soul* is attributed to Jehovah (Jer. 9:9; Is. 42:1; 53:10–12; Heb. 10:38).

e) The highest spiritual exercises are attributed to the soul as well as to the spirit: "And thou shalt love the Lord thy God…with all thy soul" (Mk. 12:30). (See also Lk. 1:46; Heb. 6:18–19; Jas. 1:21.)

f) According to Jesus, to lose the soul is to lose everything: "For what shall it profit a man, if he shall gain the whole world, and lose his own soul?" (Mk. 8:36). (See also Mk. 8:37; Mt. 16:26; Mt. 10:28.)

g) Responding to the argument based on the benediction in 1 Thessalonians 5:23, the dichotomist answers that Paul does not imply that body, soul, and spirit are three distinct and separable parts of man, but uses soul and spirit in the same way Jesus uses the four terms *heart*, *soul*, *mind*, and *strength* in Mark 12:30; and no one ascribes four parts to man on the basis of the words of Jesus. Paul uses the word *mind* (translated from nine different Greek words) more frequently than he uses the term *soul* when referring to the rational part of man.

h) In response to the trichotomist's argument from Hebrews 4:12 regarding "dividing asunder of soul and spirit," the dichotomist points out that the verse does not speak of the Word as dividing the soul from the spirit, but as penetrating into the deepest recesses of one's being, even to "the thoughts and intents of the heart." About Hebrews 4:12–13, W. E. Vine comments:

> The Word of God pierces through all that lies deepest in human nature, not actually separating soul from spirit and joints from marrow, but piercing and laying bare the inmost being, cutting through the most secret recesses of the spirit's life, penetrating the soul and, deeper still, the spirit, as through joints to their very marrow.[10]

i) The dichotomist does not say that there is no difference whatever between the words *soul* and *spirit*. Although they are frequently used to designate the same

---

10 William Edwy Vine, *The Epistle to the Hebrews* (London: Oliphants Ltd., 1961), 64.

immaterial part of man, in their more precise use, they refer to man's inner-self in different relationships. When the words are distinguished in meaning, the soul faces earthward, the spirit heavenward. The soul is man in his earthly relationships; the spirit is man in his spiritual and immortal relationships. However, the two cannot be separated, but together constitute man's immaterial self.

C. Becomes a living soul (being)—Genesis 2:7

The two views of man's composition, trichotomy and dichotomy, have been outlined above. It should be kept in the mind that the difference between the two positions is not really great and that no other major doctrine is affected by the difference.

1. *Man as a unity.* There is a strong tendency among conservative scholars to think of man as a unity rather than as a being of divisible parts. The soul (spirit) is separated from the body at physical death, but only for an interim awaiting the resurrection. Paul speaks of the soul as naked without the body:

> Now we know that if the earthly tent we live in is destroyed, we have a building from God, an eternal house in heaven, not built by human hands. Meanwhile we groan, longing to be clothed with our heavenly dwelling, because when we are clothed, we will not be found naked. For while we are in this tent, we groan and are burdened, because we do not wish to be unclothed but to be clothed with our heavenly dwelling, so that what is mortal may be swallowed up by life.
>
> —2 CORINTHIANS 5:1–4, NIV

The Greeks thought about the soul in the afterlife as being a disembodied spirit. The Christian believer anticipates a union of the spirit with a glorified body, a body like that of Jesus, raised up from the grave and transformed. In Romans 8, the apostle Paul speaks of the redemption of the body, saying, "And not only they, but ourselves also, which have the firstfruits of the Spirit, even we ourselves groan within ourselves, waiting for the adoption, to wit, the redemption of the body" (Rom. 8:23).

Christ's vicarious atoning work redeemed the whole person, not just the soul or spirit. When we think of man as redeemed wholly, we find new meaning in Paul's benediction of 1 Thessalonians 5:23: "And the very God of peace sanctify you wholly; and I pray God your whole spirit and soul and body be preserved blameless unto the coming of our Lord Jesus Christ."

Are not body, soul, and spirit, then, separate functions of one person, rather than separate substances? Did not Jesus have our wholeness in mind when He said, "Thou shalt love the Lord thy God with all thy heart, and with all thy soul, and with all thy mind, and with all thy strength" (Mk. 12:30)?

Speaking of treating man as a unity, Dr. Paul Tournier, Swiss physician and psychiatrist, writes:

> Science, in fact, works only by analysis, by dividing ad infinitum the object of study…What happens then is like what happens when we separate a jigsaw puzzle into its five hundred pieces: The overall picture disappears. This is the state of modern medicine; it has lost the sense of the unity of man. Such is the price it has paid for its scientific progress. It has sacrificed art to science. Its discoveries are true; that is to say, they reveal valid and important facts. But they do not lead to a true understanding of man, because he is a synthesis. We shall not come to understand man by adding up all the items of analytical knowledge that we possess of him, but by comprehending him as a unified whole. Man is not just a body and a mind. He is a spiritual being. It is impossible to know him if one disregards his deepest reality.[11]

2. *The origin of man's soul or spirit.* Since the Scriptures record only one creation by God's direct act of breathing life, from what source does each newly born person's soul come? There are three theories: (a) preexistence, (b) creationism, and (c) traducianism.

a) Preexistence is self-explanatory. This theory of transmigration of souls is held by Hinduism, Theosophy, Rosicrucians, and many occult religions. It has no support in Scripture whatever.

b) Creationism is held by Roman Catholics and many Reformed theologians. According to creationists, the soul is created directly by God in each newly conceived person sometime between conception and birth; only the body is propagated by the parents. Scriptures quoted in defense of this theory are Zec. 12:1; Is. 42:5; 57:16; Eccl. 12:7; and Heb. 12:9. It is urged against this position that it makes God the creator of sinful souls or represents God as putting a pure soul in a depraved Adamic body. It can also be shown that the Scriptures given in support of a direct creation of each soul would with equal force support the indirect agency of God in procreation.

c) Traducianism seems to be the preferred theory among conservative scholars. According to traducianism, the human race was created in Adam, and from him both body and soul were procreated by natural generation. Scriptures supporting this theory, to list a few, are Jb. 14:4, 15:14; Ps. 51:5, 58:3; Jn. 3:6; and Eph. 2:3. Dr. Strong describes the position as follows:

---

11 Paul Tournier, *The Healing of Persons,* trans. Edwin Hudson (New York: Harper and Row Publishers, Inc., 1965), 54–55.

Traducianism holds that man, as a species, was created in Adam. In Adam, the substance of humanity was yet undisturbed. We derive our immaterial as well as our material being, by natural laws of propagation, from Adam—each individual man after Adam possessing a part of the substance that was originated in him.[12]

It is argued in favor of the traducian theory that:

(1) There is no biblical record of God's creating a human being more than once, after which He rested from His work (Gn. 2:2).

(2) It best explains the inherited sinful nature of man as voiced by David: "Behold, I was shapen in iniquity; and in sin did my mother conceive me" (Ps. 51:5).

(3) It is strongly supported by a vital statistic about the family of Jacob: "All the souls that came with Jacob into Egypt, which came out of his loins, besides Jacob's sons' wives, all the souls were threescore and ten" (Gn. 46:26).

(4) In a biblical statement about the birth of Seth, it is said that he was begotten in the likeness of Adam (Gn. 5:3).

(5) It explains personality likenesses between children and parents.

The traducianist, however, does not posit a purely natural origin for new souls; he maintains that all souls since Adam are indirectly created by God as the Sustainer of the process of procreation (Heb. 1:3; Col. 1:17).

V. MAN'S PRIMITIVE STATE

It will be the purpose of this section to examine the primitive state of Adam before the Fall. An attempt will be made to show the psychological, moral, social, occupational, and spiritual condition of Adam and Eve as occupants of their God-given Edenic home.

A. The state of knowledge

God gave to Adam the task of naming all the animals and birds, and perhaps all forms of life, for he was given dominion over all of God's creatures (Gn. 1:28; 2:19–20). This required a vast knowledge. Apparently, Adam's knowledge included an insight into the nature and relative purpose of each species, for in primitive times names did more than identify the holder, they revealed character and destiny. The father of the human race was not a full-grown adolescent; he was the resident scientist of Eden.

---

12 Augustus Hopkins Strong, *Systematic Theology* (Philadelphia: Griffith and Rowland Press, 1907–09), 494.

B. The moral state

Since holiness and righteousness are among the fundamental attributes of God, Adam, created in God's image, must have partaken of a holy and righteous character. When God had completed the Creation, it was perfect: "And God saw every thing that he had made, and, behold, it was very good" (Gn. 1:31). A comparison of Ephesians 4:24 with Colossians 3:9–10 strongly infers the primitive righteousness of Adam. His state is often described as that of mere innocence; however, the word *innocence* is not sufficiently definitive. Adam was created in a state of holiness; and while it was not yet confirmed, because it had not yet been tested, it was a state devoid of evil.

C. The psychological state

Adam seems to have been created with several basic instincts. (Some may prefer to call them needs, drives, or impulses.) These instincts or needs would seem to be the following:

1. *Self preservation:* Adam was warned by God of impending death if he ate of the forbidden tree (Gn. 3:3).

2. *The desire for food:* God provided every kind of plant and tree good for food (Gn. 1:29).

3. *The urge for procreation, or sex:* Adam and Eve were commanded to multiply and replenish the earth (Gn. 1:28). Genesis says about man and woman, "Therefore shall a man leave his father and mother, and shall cleave unto his wife" (Gn. 2:24).

4. *The need for acquisition:* God placed them in their own garden (Gn. 2:15), which they lost with the Fall.

5. *The drive for domination:* Adam was commanded to have dominion over the earth and over every created thing (Gn. 1:28). These instincts were for the good of man. They continue to be for man's good when they are not abused; however, they constitute the desire of the "flesh." Consequently, they must be controlled by the Spirit in the believer. There will be more on this subject in a later section.

D. The social state

Man is a social creature. He was made for companionship. "And the LORD God said, It is not good that the man should be alone; I will make him an help meet for him" (Gn. 2:18). In the garden, Adam had daily communication with the Lord. When Eve was created, he had constant companionship with a being of his own kind. When Adam sinned, he was alienated from God. Then suspicion surfaced between Adam and Eve such that when Adam was addressing God after the Fall, he accursedly referred to Eve as, "The woman whom thou gavest to be with me" (Gn. 3:12).

E. The occupational state

The Garden of Eden was not a place of idleness. "And the LORD God took the man, and put him into the garden of Eden to dress it and to keep it" (Gn. 2:15). Adam was not only a zoologist, he was also a horticulturist. The beauty and productivity of Eden were not the result of God's creative work only; Adam kept and tended the garden, giving it touches of human handiwork. Creative occupation is positively essential for fulfillment. Work became "toil" only when sin entered the scene.

F. The state of life expectancy

Adam was created with the potential of immortality. Death would occur only if Adam disobeyed the command of God relative to eating from the tree of the knowledge of good and evil (Gn. 2:16–17; 3:3). When Adam and Eve sinned, death began to reign. Angels with a flaming sword henceforth guarded the tree of life (Gn. 3:24). Jesus Christ, the last Adam, has removed the sting of death. The Seed of woman has bruised the serpent's head, and through God's Son, paradise is restored.

Adam was created in God's image, in holiness and righteousness. He was placed in an ideal environment, with a fulfilling occupation. He was provided with divine companionship and marital love. His potential was immortality, yet he disobeyed and fell. How could he have forfeited so much, not only for himself, but for the human race? The answer to this question is taken up in the following section.

VI. MAN'S FALL

At the very heart of the Christian gospel is the statement from the Gospel of John: "For God so loved the world, that he gave his only begotten Son, that whosoever believeth in him should not perish, but have everlasting life" (Jn. 3:16). God sent His Son to rescue man from his perishing condition. If God loved man so much, how did man get into a state of perishing? A brief explanation is given in the following paragraph from the *Foursquare Declaration of Faith:*

> We believe that man was created in the image of God, before Whom he walked in holiness and purity, but that by voluntary disobedience and transgression, he fell from the Eden of purity and innocence to the depths of sin and iniquity, and that in consequence of this, all mankind are sinners sold unto Satan, sinners not by constraint but by choice, shapen in iniquity and utterly void by nature of that holiness required by the law of God, positively

inclined to evil, guilty and without excuse, justly deserving the condemnation of a just and holy God.[13]

Although he was created in God's image, placed in an ideal environment, and given everything he needed, Adam rebelled against God and disobeyed His commandment. The result of Adam's sin was shame, guilt, alienation, and death; not only for himself, but for the whole human race. This raises the question, Why would God subject Adam and Eve to temptation? (See Ps. 14:1–3; Rom. 3:10, 23; 5:12–21.)

A. The probation of man

1. *Its purpose.* Man was created in God's image. He was endowed with intelligence, emotion, and will. He was a free moral agent; therefore, he was capable of making a choice. Since man was created for God's glory (Is. 43:7), and since he could best glorify God by freely choosing to worship and serve Him, it was necessary that Adam be given an opportunity to make a choice. For Adam and Eve, the Garden of Eden was not only a home in paradise; it was also a place of probation, a place to test their obedience and loyalty to Jehovah. The probation of Adam and Eve was based upon a clear, direct commandment, a simple law of works. The law had two parts: a positive part, consisting of a glorious provision; and a negative part, consisting of a clear prohibition: "And the LORD God commanded the man, saying, Of every tree of the garden thou mayest freely eat: but of the tree of the knowledge of good and evil, thou shalt not eat of it: for in the day that thou eatest thereof thou shalt surely die" (Gn. 2:16–17).

It needs to be explained how beings who were created with holy natures could sin. Our first parents had holy natures, but they did not yet have holy characters. A holy nature is the result of creation; a holy character is the result of testing in which a choice of good is made, where a choice of evil was possible. A choice of evil results in an evil character. God desired the worship and service of beings with holy moral characters. Free choice, then, was necessary for the development of mature holiness and blessedness. With free choice there is, of necessity, the possibility of a wrong choice. Adam and Eve made the wrong choice with disastrous consequences, both for themselves and for the human race.

2. *Its character.* The probationary commandment given to Adam was personal, not moral. There was no obvious wrong in eating from the forbidden tree. The Fall of Adam and Eve was the result of disobedience, not the result of a clearly immoral act. This test was similar to the later test of Abraham (Gn. 22:1–13). There would have been no intrinsic wrongdoing by Abraham in sparing his son, but he moved

---

13 Aimee Semple McPherson, *Declaration of Faith* (Los Angeles: International Church of the Foursquare Gospel, n.d.), 10.

toward the sacrifice of Isaac as an act of pure obedience to God. The test of Abraham was purely personal, not moral. A moral law should be obeyed because it is inherently right to do so. For instance, the Ten Commandments are not right only because they came from God; God gave the Decalogue because it represented inherently right conduct. On the other hand, the ceremonial law required obedience because God gave it; its rightness was not self-evident. The prohibition of eating from the tree of good and evil was a testing law, because the evil was not self-evident. The evil was in the disobedience of the commandment. The Fall of Adam and Eve resulted from a pure act of willful disobedience.

3. *Its reasonableness.* The reasonableness of the probation of Adam and Eve can be seen in several considerations. First, an all-wise God knew what was necessary to bring man to his highest potential development and to his greatest blessedness. If Adam had obeyed, resisting Satan's temptation, he would have possessed holy moral character and would have risen to a new level of blessing and of fellowship with God. There is a hint of this in the character and in the consequent translation of Enoch to heaven. Enoch developed holy character even after inheriting an Adamic nature. If Adam had obeyed, he would have had heaven on Earth. A loving God would not have subjected Adam to probation had it not been necessary for Adam's highest possible good.

In the second place, God, having foreseen Adam's failure, provided a plan for his redemption. God is not the author of sin. He did not cause Adam to fall, for Adam had every reason to obey. However, God purposed to bring out of human failure a glorious redemption, a redemption wrought through the Incarnation and vicarious death of His own Son, a redemption that would include the final defeat of Satan, who was, after all, the first sinner. Within the very curse pronounced upon the serpent, God gave a promise of a Redeemer, "the seed of woman," and of Satan's defeat, saying, "It shall bruise thy head" (Gn. 3:15). Typical of the Redemption provided through the blood of Jesus were the animals slain to provide a covering of Adam's nakedness and the acceptable offering of a lamb, which Abel brought to God (Gn. 3:21; 4:4). The apostle Peter declares that Christ, as a Lamb, was purposed "before the foundation of the world"; therefore, God in His foreknowledge saw that Adam would fail and determined to bring out of Adam's failure a people gloriously redeemed by the blood of Christ (1 Pt. 1:18–20). It appears that Adam's testing was necessary and reasonable because whichever result the testing would have produced would have led to a final state superior to the original Edenic state.

B. The temptation of man

1. *The agent of temptation.* In Genesis 3, the temptation of Adam and Eve is attributed to the serpent, who is said to have been "more crafty than any beast of the field" (Gn. 3:1, NASB). The real tempter, however, was Satan. This is made clear by a

passage in Revelation 12, "And the great dragon was cast out, that old serpent, called the Devil, and Satan, which deceiveth the whole world" (Rv. 12:9).

A passage from the apostle Paul strengthens this identity of the serpent with Satan, for he suggests that the same tempter who beguiled Eve is present still, seeking to corrupt the minds of believers: "But I fear, lest by any means, as the serpent beguiled Eve through his subtilty, so your minds should be corrupted from the simplicity that is in Christ" (2 Cor. 11:3).

Furthermore, Genesis 3:1 does not state that the serpent was more subtle than any *other* beast, but more subtle than *any* beast of the field. The serpent was the vehicle which Satan used to effect the temptation. Apparently, Satan has the power to disguise himself by assuming the appearance of another being. Paul says about Satan: "For Satan himself is transformed into an angel of light" (2 Cor. 11:14). It seems likely that the serpent was originally an upright animal, as many scholars believe, since the curse upon the serpent reduced him to a crawling creature (Gn. 3:14–15). That the real tempter was Satan, who had previously rebelled against God, is made clear by the prophecy that the "seed of woman" (Christ) would bruise the serpent's head. Satan's rebellious posture and his fall are described in Isaiah 14:12–15 and in Ezekiel 28:12–15. Seldom does Satan appear in his role as God's adversary, except to those who are completely surrendered to him. He normally disguises himself, assuming the form of a benefactor or of one able to fulfill one's selfish ambitions.

2. *The temptation's motives.* What kind of motivation could Satan use that would tempt holy, innocent beings to disobey God? It was mentioned in Section V that Adam and Eve were endowed with certain basic instincts which they needed for their well-being. These instincts or drives seem to have been those of self-preservation, acquisition, desire for food, desire for love and procreation, and the urge for dominion. Before the Fall, their drives were balanced and controlled. However, they constituted a motivational base to which temptation could be directed. Satan aimed his temptation at three of Eve's basic desires:

> And when the woman saw that the tree was good for food, and that it was pleasant to the eyes, and a tree to be desired to make one wise, she took of the fruit thereof, and did eat, and gave also unto her husband with her; and he did eat.
>
> —Genesis 3:6

These were not inherently evil desires. They became evil because they were motivated by Satan and because they constituted disobedience to God's specific commandment. Desire becomes lust when it is contrary to the Spirit. Many scholars believe that John was referring to the pattern of Eve's temptation when he said, "For all that is in the world, the lust of the flesh, and the lust of the eyes, and the pride of life, is not of the Father, but is of the world. And the world passeth away, and the lust thereof: but he that doeth the will of God abideth for ever" (1 Jn. 2:16–17). The term *world* does not refer to the Earth, but to the societal realm ruled by Satan. The term *flesh* has reference not to the body as such, but to the total person dedicated to selfishness and disobedience to God.

At this point, it is important to notice that Satan did not appeal to Eve's desires until he first caused her to doubt the Lord. He began his temptation with the insinuating question, "Hath God said?" (Gn. 3:1), a question contrived to make Eve doubt God's goodness. The question was followed by a statement meant to raise doubts about God's veracity: "Ye shall not surely die" (Gn. 3:4). With the seed of doubt already planted, Satan showed himself to be God's enemy by making the bold accusation that God was depriving Adam and Eve of their rightful privilege of divine status, "For God doth know that in the day ye eat thereof, then your eyes shall be opened, and ye shall be as gods, knowing good and evil" (Gn. 3:5). Once the seed of doubt had been planted and had germinated, the appeal to desire was effective. Eve may have thought, "If the Lord's truth and goodness are suspect, one must pursue one's own best interests." Scholars have differed over the identity of the basic sin. Their opinions have been divided among self, doubt, and pride—any one of which is deadly (2 Pt. 2:10; 1 Tm. 3:6; Jas. 1:5–8, NIV). All three of which, however, appear to have contributed to the fall of Adam and Eve.

C. The fallen state of man

The Scriptures plainly teach that man was created in the image of God. Genesis 3 describes Adam's disobedience and fall; Genesis 4–11 portray Adam's descendants in their calamities and strife. Man still bears enough of God's image to demonstrate his divine origin. At the same time, man's history of war, crime, terrorism, and perversion give indisputable evidence of his Fall. Man, with his noblest ideals, speaks of his creation by God; man, with his greed and inhumanity to other men, speaks of his corruption by Satan. If we did not have an inspired record of man's fall, we would have to assume some such happening at the dawn of history to account for the tragic human drama, which is brightened only by divine intervention and the redeeming events of Christ's incarnation, resurrection, omnipresence, and promised return (Rom. 5:12–14; 1 Tm. 2:13–14; Jb. 31:33; 1 Cor. 15:22, 45).

1. *The interpretation of the Fall.* Is the account of the Fall of Adam and Eve to be taken figuratively or literally? Is it a myth or an allegory to be taken symbolically, or is it sober history, to be taken factually? Liberal and neo-orthodox theologians generally interpret the first eleven chapters of Genesis as a myth. The following facts argue for a literal interpretation:

a) Nowhere in the Bible is the story of Adam interpreted symbolically. If the

Creation and Fall stories were allegories, the spiritualized interpretations would have been numerous.

b) There is no indication in the book of Genesis, between chapters eleven and twelve, that suggests a change from allegory to history. Noah is as much a real character as is Abraham.

c) Parallels between Adam and Christ are made by the apostle Paul. Since Christ is a historical person, it is not likely that He would be an antitype of a non-historical character (Rom. 5:14; 1 Cor. 15:22, 45).

d) In two genealogies recorded in later books of the Bible, the name of Adam is listed along with obviously historical characters (1 Chr. 1-2; Lk. 3:23-38). Adam is included in the genealogy of Christ along with David, Abraham, Isaac, and Jacob.

e) Real geographical locations are included in the story of Adam, such as Assyria and the river Euphrates.

f) The fallen condition of man is very literal. A real fallen state can hardly be attributed to a mythical event. Furthermore, the fact that man has made fantastic progress scientifically while he, at the same time, has made no progress morally, ethically, and socially clearly indicates man's sinful nature. In addition, the persistence of war, crime, terrorism, greed, political corruption, and perversion demonstrate the existence of a supernatural evil force who motivates much of human activity. However, God's Son established a beachhead at Calvary from which He is building His kingdom. Soon He will return to reign in righteousness and to destroy the power of darkness (Rv. 19:11-20).

2. *The results of the Fall*

a) The judicial results of the fall were fourfold: (1) The judgment upon the serpent (Gn. 3:14-15). This apparently upright and likely beautiful creature was doomed to a crawling posture. The eating of dust was a term denoting utter humiliation. According to Isaiah, the serpent will eat dust during the Millennium, but he will be harmless (Is. 65:25). (2) The judgment upon the woman was that of pain and sorrow in childbearing and submission to her husband (Gn. 3:16). The woman's lot in pagan countries is an exaggerated manifestation of the curse. Only in lands reached by the Christian gospel has womanhood experienced a measure of redemption. (3) The judgment upon the man was not that of labor, but of wearisome toil (Gn. 3:17). Work is a boon to man, but seldom is it free from strife and criticism. This curse is evident the world over in the fear of crop failure, the fear of unemployment, labor strife, bankruptcies, and relentless competition. (4) The judgment upon the ground was that of lowered productivity and the introduction of thorns and thistles (Gn. 3:17-18). Jesus used the illustration of thorns and thistles as the opposite of good fruit (Mt. 7:16-17). Thorns became a symbol of evil and were associated with Satan (2 Cor. 12:7). The evil symbolism of the thorn is seen in the fact that evil men, motivated by Satan, placed a crown of thorns upon the brow of Jesus (Jn. 19:2-5). The prophet Isaiah predicted the lifting of the curse and the removal of the thorn during the Millennium (Is. 55:12–13).

3. The consequences of the Fall

a) The immediate consequence of the sin of Adam and Eve was that of a sense of shame. They hid themselves from God because they were suddenly aware of their nakedness. Shame led to fear and alienation. They wanted the experiential knowledge of good and evil, which they were tempted to believe would make them divine. They got only the knowledge of evil, with the knowledge of good out of reach. Had Adam and Eve obeyed, they would have had the experience of the knowledge of good with a knowledge of evil as God knows and abhors it (Gn. 3:7–13).

b) The most disastrous consequence of the Fall was death. God had warned, "For in the day that thou eatest thereof thou shalt surely die" (Gn. 2:17). There were two trees in the garden: the tree of the knowledge of good and evil and the tree of life. Adam and Eve willfully ate from the tree of knowledge, which led them to the knowledge of evil and to the knowledge of death. As God had warned, they were driven from the garden, from the tree of life, and from the presence of God. Adam did not immediately die physically; in fact, he lived 930 years, but the process of disease and mortality began the moment he sinned: "And as it is appointed unto men once to die, but after this the judgment" (Heb. 9:27). Perhaps the psalmist best describes man's mortality:

> You have set our iniquities before You, Our secret sins in the light of your countenance. For all our days have passed away in Your wrath; We finish our years like a sigh. The days of our lives are seventy years; And if by reason of strength they are eighty years, yet their boast is only labor and sorrow; For it is soon cut off, and we fly away.... So teach us to number our days, that we may gain a heart of wisdom.
>
> —PSALM 90:8–12, NKJV

The Bible identifies three categories of death:

(1) Physical death. Physical death occurs when the spirit is separated from the body and the body returns to dust (Gn. 3:19). In the old dispensation, only Enoch and Elijah escaped physical death (Gn. 5:24; 2 Kgs. 2:11). In the new dispensation, only those who are taken up in the Rapture escape physical death (1 Thes. 4:16–17). Jesus raised several persons from the dead, and several others were raised up under the ministry of the apostles. However, we must assume that they later died natural deaths (Jn. 11:43–44; Acts 9:40).

(2) Spiritual death. Spiritual death is separation from God. All the unregenerate are alienated from God by sin (Eph. 2:1–3). They may pass from death unto spiritual life by exercising saving faith in the Lord Jesus Christ (Eph. 2:4–6; 1 Jn. 5:11–12;

Col. 1:13–14, 18–23; 1 Cor. 15:54–57). "For since by man came death, by man came also the resurrection of the dead. For as in Adam all die, even so in Christ all shall be made alive" (1 Cor. 15:21–22). (See also Rom. 5:12–14.)

(3) Eternal death. Eternal death is the condition of those who are spiritually dead, who depart this earthly life without repentance of sin and without faith in the Lord Jesus Christ. Eternal death is the punishment of those who are terminally unbelieving, unrepentant, and disobedient (2 Thes. 1:7–10). The judgment unto eternal death (also called the second death) will take place at the end of the Millennium before the great white throne of God. It will be a judgment for sinners only; the believer's judgment of works will take place at the Rapture (Rv. 20:11–15; 2 Cor. 5:6–11).

VII. Man's Potential in the State of Grace

Lest it appear that the study of man is concerned only with man's Fall, his sinful nature, and the consequent judgments, this final section will portray man in the state of grace.

A. The believer is a new man in Christ Jesus.

> If so be that ye have heard him, and have been taught by him, as the truth is in Jesus: That ye put off concerning the former conversation [conduct] the old man, which is corrupt according to the deceitful lusts; And be renewed in the spirit of your mind; And that ye put on the new man, which after God is created in righteousness and true holiness.
> —Ephesians 4:21–24

(See also Jn. 1:11–13; 2 Cor. 5:17.)

B. As a result of Christ's incarnation and identification with human nature, man was given a new potential in a new humanity in Christ.

> And so it is written, The first man Adam was made a living soul; the last Adam was made a quickening spirit. Howbeit that was not first which is spiritual, but that which is natural; and afterward that which is spiritual. The first man is of the earth, earthy: the second man is the Lord from heaven. As is the earthy, such are they also that are earthy: and as is the heavenly, such are they also that are heavenly.
> —1 Corinthians 15:45–48

(See also Col. 3:9–10; 1 Cor. 15:21–22.)

Adam corrupted human nature by sin, disobedience, and rebellion. Christ, by taking human nature into union with His divine nature and by living sinlessly and in perfect obedience to His Father, redeemed human nature, giving it a new potential. In Adam, we have paradise lost. In Christ Jesus, we have paradise regained. In Adam, man's fate is death, but in Christ Jesus, man's potential is life and eternal fellowship with God. Paul, writing to the Philippian church, greeted the believers, "To all the saints in Christ Jesus" (Phil. 1:1). The believer's position is in Christ. He is a member of the body of Christ and of the new humanity.

C. The believer in Christ has a new nature in Christ.

> Whereby are given unto us exceeding great and precious promises: that by these ye might be partakers of the divine nature, having escaped the corruption that is in the world through lust.
> —2 PETER 1:4

The word translated "promises" in 2 Peter 1:4 means not the promise itself, but the thing or things promised by God (the fulfillments of the promises). The promises themselves—of which the Word is filled—are a great blessing to the believer, but he has been redeemed from corruption and given a new nature by the fulfillment of God's promises in Christ.

D. The believer has new life in Christ.

> Verily, verily, I say unto you, He that heareth my word, and believeth on him that sent me, hath everlasting life, and shall not come into condemnation; but is passed from death unto life.
> —JOHN 5:24

(See also Rom. 6:11; Eph. 2:1–6.)

E. In Christ, the believer experiences constant renewal.

> For which cause we faint not; but though our outward man perish, yet the inward man is renewed day by day.
> —2 CORINTHIANS 4:16

> And be not conformed to this world: but be ye transformed by the renewing of your mind, that ye may prove what is that good, and acceptable, and perfect, will of God.
> —ROMANS 12:2

F. In Christ, the believer has the hope of an eternal heavenly home.

> And the Lord shall deliver me from every evil work, and will preserve me
> unto his heavenly kingdom.
>
> —2 TIMOTHY 4:18

> To an inheritance incorruptible, and undefiled, and that fadeth not away,
> reserved in heaven for you.
>
> —1 PETER 1:4

(See also Jn. 14:2–3.)

G. In Christ, the believer has victory over the old nature.

> Now if we be dead with Christ, we believe that we shall also live with
> him....Let not sin therefore reign in your mortal body, that ye should obey
> it in the lusts thereof....For sin shall not have dominion over you: for ye are
> not under the law, but under grace.
>
> —ROMANS 6:8, 12, 14

H. The believer in Christ is not only freed from the dominion of sin and death, he is given kingdom authority to minister in the name of Jesus and in the power of the Spirit.

> So then after the Lord had spoken unto them, he was received up into heav-
> en, and sat on the right hand of God. And they went forth, and preached
> everywhere, the Lord working with them, and confirming the word with
> signs following.
>
> —MARK 16:19–20

(See also Mt. 16:19; 18:18; Lk. 9:1–2.)

Man, redeemed in Christ and surrendered to Christ, becomes a vehicle of witness
by which God's salvation purpose is extended to all humanity. The atoning work of
Christ has made a state of grace the potential for all mankind: "Whosoever believeth
in him should not perish, but have everlasting life" (Jn. 3:16).

The Doctrine of Sin

Hamartiology

Introduction

I. The Problem of Sin
A. The source of sin

B. The permitting of sin

1. *The divine recognition of the creature's free choice*
2. *The specific value of redeemed beings*
3. *The acquisition of divine knowledge*
4. *The instruction of angels*
5. *The demonstration of the divine hatred of evil*
6. *The righteous judgment of all evil*
7. *The manifestation and exercise of divine grace*

II. The Origin of Sin
A. In the universe

B. In the human race

III. The First Human Sin
A. The necessity of probation

B. The process of temptation

1. *Satan cast doubts on God's Word and His love*
2. *Eve tampered with God's Word*
3. *Satan contradicted God's Word*
4. *Eve succumbed to the temptation*

C. The results of man's first sin

1. *As seen in man's attitude toward himself*
2. *As seen in man's attitude toward God*
3. *As seen in man's attitude toward his fellow man*

D. The curse which the first sin brought

1. *The curse upon the serpent*
2. *The curse upon the woman*
3. *The curse upon the man*
4. *The curse upon the ground*

IV. **The Nature of Sin**
  A. The definition of sin
  B. Sin and God's law
    1. *The nature of God's law*
    2. *The purpose of God's law*
  C. Scriptural expressions for sin
    1. *Missing of a mark or aim*
    2. *Overpassing or trespassing of a line*
    3. *Disobedience to a voice*
    4. *Falling where one should have stood upright*
    5. *Ignorance of what one ought to have known*
    6. *Diminishing of that which should have been rendered in full measure*
    7. *Non-observance of a law—sins of omission*
    8. *Lawlessness or anarchy—utter disregard for the law*
    9. *Debt, failure in duty, or not meeting one's obligations to God*
    10. *Other single words*
  D. Sin is evil
    1. *Sin is a specific type of evil*
    2. *Sin is a positive evil*
  E. The sinful nature of sin
  F. Important considerations regarding sin
    1. *Sins of omission*
    2. *Sins of unbelief*
    3. *Sins of ignorance*
    4. *One sin makes one guilty of all*

V. **The Universality of Sin**

VI. **The Imputation of Sin**

VII. **Original Sin and Depravity**
  A. The meaning of depravity
  B. The results of depravity

VIII. **The Guilt From Sin**
  A. Sin in relation to God
  B. Degrees of guilt
    1. *Sins of nature and sins of personal transgression*
    2. *Sins of ignorance and sins of knowledge*
    3. *Sins of infirmity and sins of presumption*

IX. **The Penalty of Sin**
  A. The significance of penalty
      1. *Upon the unsaved*
      2. *Difference between chastisement and punishment*
  B. The nature of penalty
      1. *Physical death*
      2. *Spiritual death*
      3. *Eternal death*

CHAPTER FOUR

THE DOCTRINE OF SIN

Hamartiology

INTRODUCTION

THE GREEK WORD for "sin" is *hamartia*, while the word *ology* signifies "knowledge." Thus, hamartiology is the knowledge or the doctrine of sin. That sin is a reality in the world hardly needs to be argued. History reveals its dire effects in the wars, tumults, and the evils sin exhibits. Every sound in nature is in the minor key. The conscience of man is often a nagging testimony to his own shortcomings and sin (Rom. 2:15). The Scripture speaks constantly of its reality. "All have sinned, and come short of the glory of God" (Rom. 3:23). "But the scripture hath concluded all under sin" (Gal. 3:22).

I. THE PROBLEM OF SIN

One of the most perplexing questions which comes to the human mind is in relation to the presence and origin of sin. That all men are sinners cannot be denied. This is true of every race and tribe. Nor is it necessary for man to learn to sin. The principle of sin is in his very nature from the earliest days of his life. No child needs to be told how to do wrong, but he must constantly be taught to do that which is right.

A. The source of sin

Let us clearly understand that the Bible did not create the problem of sin. Sin was in the world long before the Bible was written. If the Bible had never been written, or if it were not true, we would still have the problem of sin on our hands. Men may even blame God and say sin was all His fault, but that does not eliminate the problem. The curse of sin is still upon us.

Just because God is the Creator of all things, it does not follow that He is the author of sin. The Scripture entirely excludes such a thing. "Far be it from God, that he should do wickedness; and from the Almighty, that he should commit iniquity" (Jb. 34:10). God could not possibly sin, for He is holy. "And one cried unto another, and said, Holy, holy, holy, is the LORD" (Is. 6:3). There is no unrighteousness in Him. "He is the Rock, his works are perfect, and all his ways are just. A faithful God who does no wrong, upright and just is he" (Dt. 32:4, NIV). "To shew that the LORD is upright: he is my rock, and there is no unrighteousness in him" (Ps. 92:15). He cannot be tempted with evil, neither does He tempt any man. "Let no man say when he is tempted, I am tempted of God: for God cannot be tempted with evil, neither tempteth he any man" (Jas. 1:13). He hates sin. "For all that do such things, and all that do unrighteously, are an abomination unto the LORD thy God" (Dt. 25:16). "And let none of you imagine evil in your hearts against his neighbor; and love no false oath: for all these are things that I hate, saith the Lord" (Zec. 8:17). In the light of all this, it would be blasphemous to make God the author of sin.

In order for sin to be sin, in the sense that there is guilt attached to it, it must be the free act of a responsible being—one who understands the difference between right and wrong. This is what is called a free moral agent.

B. The permitting of sin

One of the great unanswered questions of all time has been why God, in His infinite wisdom and power, allowed sin to come into the universe. Philosophers, theologians, and scientists have struggled with this problem that is obviously beyond their ability to solve. Perhaps the best one can say is that God permitted sin to come into the world for reasons beyond our ability to understand. Certainly, He was not being taken unawares. His holy purposes had not been thwarted, nor was He seeking to salvage something out of the unforseen wreckage. This is not to say that God planned that sin, with all its evil and suffering, should come into the world. It is merely that for good purposes known only to Him—and in spite of the suffering that it would cause, as well as the awful price of the death of His Son which He must pay—God permitted sin to come, first into heaven and then to Earth.

Lewis Sperry Chafer has listed seven reasons, which are here advanced, for the divine permission of sin:

1. *The divine recognition of the creature's free choice*—It is evidently the purpose of God to secure a company of beings for His own glory who are possessed of that virtue which is the result of a free-choice victory over evil. But man cannot make a choice between good and evil unless evil exists.

2. *The special value of redeemed beings*—According to the Scriptures, God is not revealed as One who seeks to avoid the issues which arise because of the presence of sin in the universe. He could have created innocent, unfallen beings possessing no capacity to err, but if He desired redeemed souls purified by sacrificial blood and purchased at an infinite cost, the expression of such love and the exercise of such sacrifice are possible only when sin is present in the world.

3. *The acquisition of divine knowledge*—The creatures of God's hand must, by a process of learning, attain to that knowledge which God has possessed eternally. They can learn only by experience and revelation. Man must learn both good and evil. He must realize the sinfulness of sin if he is to attain in any degree to the knowledge God

possesses, but he cannot attain to such knowledge unless sin exists as a living reality that is ever-demonstrating its sinful character.

4. *The instruction of angels*—"To the intent that now unto the principalities and powers in heavenly places might be known by the church the manifold wisdom of God" (Eph. 3:10). "Unto whom it was revealed, that not unto themselves, but unto us they did minister the things, which are now reported unto you by them that have preached the gospel unto you with the Holy Ghost sent down from heaven; which things the angels desire to look into" (1 Pt. 1:12). From these Scriptures it is possible to conclude that angels are observing men on Earth and learning important facts through the present experience of human beings. It would be as necessary for angels to learn the truth regarding that which is evil as it is for them to learn the truth regarding that which is good, but the acquiring of the knowledge of evil through observing human experience must be denied the angels unless evil is permitted as an active principle in the universe.

5. *The demonstration of the divine hatred of evil*—It is evidently of immeasurable importance for God to demonstrate His hatred of evil. The apostle Paul declares that God was "willing to shew his wrath, and to make his power known" (Rom. 9:22), but no judgment, wrath, or power in relation to sin could be disclosed apart from the permitted presence of sin in the world.

6. *The righteous judgment of all evil*—Far beyond the mere details of the expression of sin is the essential fact of the principle of evil, which if it is to be judged by God, must evidently be brought out into an open demonstration of its actual character. Such a demonstration could not be secured with sin existing as a hypothetical issue. It had to become concrete and prove its actual character.

7. *The manifestation and exercise of divine grace*—Finally, and of the greatest import, there was that in God which no created being had ever seen. The angelic hosts had seen His wisdom, His power, and His glory; but they had never seen His grace. They had no conception of the goodness of God to the undeserving. By one marvelous act of mercy in the gift of His Son as a sacrifice for sinners, He opened the way for the exercise of His grace toward those who, because of their sin, deserved only His wrath. But there could be no exercise of divine grace toward the sinful and undeserving until there were sinful and undeserving beings in the world.[1]

II. THE ORIGIN OF SIN

It must be realized that sin did not have its beginning here on Earth. The first sin was committed in heaven. Heaven was stained before Earth was marred by its dire

---

1 Lewis Sperry Chafer, *Systematic Theology* (Dallas, TX: Dallas Seminary Press, 1947–48) II, 231–233.

presence. Thus, in order to fully understand its reality and nature, we must first study its beginning in the universe and then its beginning upon Earth.

A. The origin of sin in the universe

First, let us consider the being who was responsible for the first sin in the universe:

> Son of Man, take up a lamentation upon the king of Tyrus, and say unto him, Thus saith the Lord GOD; Thou sealest up the sum, full of wisdom, and perfect in beauty. Thou hast been in Eden the garden of God; every precious stone was thy covering, the sardius, topaz, and the diamond, the beryl, the onyx, and the jasper, the sapphire, the emerald, and the carbuncle, and gold: the workmanship of thy tabrets and of thy pipes was prepared in thee in the day that thou wast created. Thou art the anointed cherub that covereth; and I have set thee so: thou wast upon the holy mountain of God; thou hast walked up and down in the midst of the stones of fire. Thou wast perfect in thy ways from the day that thou wast created, till iniquity was found in thee. By the multitude of thy merchandise they have filled the midst of thee with violence, and thou hast sinned: therefore I will cast thee as profane out of the mountain of God: and I will destroy thee, O covering cherub, from the midst of the stones of fire. Thine heart was lifted up because of thy beauty, thou hast corrupted thy wisdom by reason of thy brightness: I will cast thee to the ground, I will lay thee before kings, that they may behold thee.
>
> —EZEKIEL 28:12–17

That the prophet is describing a supernatural being is clear from the passage. The words might apply to a king of Tyre, but they seem to go beyond this application and describe the highest of all created beings. To whom else could these words apply, than to Satan before his fall?

We next look at the sin of which this exalted being was guilty:

> How art thou fallen from heaven, O Lucifer, son of the morning! how art thou cut down to the ground, which did weaken the nations! For thou hast said in thine heart, I will ascend into heaven, I will exalt my throne above the stars of God: I will sit also upon the mount of the congregation, in the sides of the north: I will ascend above the heights of the clouds; I will be like the most High.
>
> —ISAIAH 14:12–14

Five times Lucifer lifts up his will against the will of God. It can thus be seen that the first sin was that of rebellion against and total independence of God.

"I will ascend into heaven"—There are three heavens: the atmospheric heaven; the stellar or astronomic heaven; and the highest or third heaven, where God and the saints abide. (See 2 Cor. 12:1–4, where Paul writes about having been caught up into the "third heaven.") The angels' sphere is in the second heaven.

"I will exalt my throne above the stars of God"—"The stars of God" refers to the angelic hosts, as in: "When the morning stars sang together, and all the sons of God shouted for joy" (Jb. 38:7), and "Raging waves of the sea, foaming out their own shame; wandering stars, to whom is reserved the blackness of darkness for ever" (Jude 13). (See also Rv. 12:3–4; 22:16.) Thus is expressed the desire to secure a rulership over angelic beings.

"I will sit also upon the mount of the congregation, in the sides of the north"— These words have been taken to express a desire for an earthly kingdom also. In scriptural symbolism, a mountain means a kingdom. "And it shall come to pass in the last days, that the mountain of the LORD's house shall be established in the top of the mountains, and shall be exalted above the hills; and all nations shall flow into it" (Is. 2:2). "And the stone that smote the image became a great mountain, and filled the whole earth" (Dn. 2:35).

"I will ascend above the heights of the clouds"—Divine glory is often symbolized by clouds in Scripture. Lucifer wanted to possess this glory.

"I will be like the most High"—This is the climax of the other four desires. All of these statements express independence of and opposition to God, a willful ambition against God. If we wonder how it was possible for sin to come into a perfect environment, the answer seems to be, as far as Lucifer and the angels who fell with him, that their fall was due to their deliberate, self-determined revolt against God.

B. The origin of sin in the human race

Genesis 3 describes how sin first entered the human race. A complete grasp of this chapter's teachings is essential to our understanding of that which follows in the Scriptures. The story of the fall of man, as given here, is an absolute contradiction to the theory of evolution which purports to teach that man began at the very bottom of the moral ladder and is now slowly climbing upwards. On the contrary, this chapter declares that man began at the very top, in the image of God, and proceeded to tumble to the bottom.

Genesis 3 also contradicts the modern theory of heredity and environment. We are told that sin and evil are in the world because of the pollution of the stream of our heredity. If our ancestors had not sinned, we would not have been sinners. We know that Adam and Eve had no polluted ancestry behind them, yet they sinned. Again we are told that the cause of evil in the human heart is due to the sinful environment in which we live. If we could only clean up society, then men would no longer be subject to sin. This is shown to be false by the fact that our first parents lived in a condition of perfection, yet they sinned. No change of environment will rid man of his sin. Arthur W. Pink has said, "What man needs is not a new berth, but a new birth."[2]

The human race was created in such a way that it could receive and reciprocate the love of God. In order for love to be real, it must be bestowed freely. Love is not love if it is given under compulsion. How was God to know whether this first man and woman loved Him? He gave them an opportunity to prove their love by a simple act of obedience. In fact, it was not even as difficult as can be assumed. All they were asked to do was to refrain from committing one act—partaking of the fruit of one of the many trees in the garden—thereby demonstrating their devotion to Him. God was not depriving them of anything. Adam and Eve did not need the fruit of this tree. It was not necessary to either their happiness or well-being. On the other hand, man does not need sin. It has not added one moment of genuine pleasure to his life in any way. Even those who sin against others the most want others to deal honestly with them. The liar expects you to tell him the truth, and the thief who steals your goods wants you to leave his goods alone.

There was no poison or evil in the fruit of that one tree. It was only wrong because God said they were not to eat of it. In the moral economy which God was establishing here on the Earth, sin was a possibility, but not a necessity. Adam and Eve should never have converted that possibility into an actuality. Since they were surrounded with everything for their every need and were duly warned by God as to what the consequences would be, we can only conclude that they were to blame for what they did. "But every man is tempted, when he is drawn away by his own lust, and enticed" (Jas. 1:14).

It is very important to bear this fact in mind: God did not permit Satan to coerce or overpower Adam and Eve. The serpent tempted them, but he did not force them to eat of the forbidden fruit. The manner in which Satan came was a real trial, but it was not of such a nature as to overwhelm the original pair. This is true of all temptation. A successful temptation requires the cooperation of the individual who is tempted. He must yield just as Adam and Eve yielded. They could blame Satan for tempting them; but they must blame themselves for yielding to the temptation. Their sinning was their own responsibility, and thus they bore the penalty.

The difference between Satan's fall and man's fall is that Satan fell without any external tempter. Sin among angels originated in their own beings; man's sin originated in response to a tempter and temptation from without. Thiessen makes a

---

2 Arthur W. Pink, *Gleanings in Genesis* (Swengel, PA: Bible Truth Depot, 1922), 34.

unique statement, "Had man fallen without a tempter, he would have originated his own sin, and would have himself become a Satan."[3]

III. THE FIRST HUMAN SIN

A. The necessity of probation

God had made man perfect, in His own image. He had placed him in a perfect environment, supplying his every need, and had given him a beautiful helpmate in Eve. He was also given a free will. But it was necessary that his free will be tested, in order for him to be confirmed in positive righteousness of character. Character is the sum total of human choices. It can be attained only through choices. Thus man was on probation, until it should be shown how he would use his power of freedom of choice. He could have chosen to resist temptation. Unfortunately, he chose the opposite.

B. The process of temptation, Genesis 3:1–6

1. *Satan cast doubts on God's Word and His love.* "Now the serpent was more subtil than any beast of the field which the LORD God had made. And he said unto the woman, Yea, hath God said, Ye shall not eat of every tree of the garden?" (Gn 3:1) The reason the tempter came to the woman, rather than to Adam, may be due to the fact that God had given the command forbidding them to eat of the tree to Adam directly. Eve received the command from her husband. So Satan very cleverly did not come directly to the man, but to the woman through the serpent; and he came while she was alone. Satan's subtle question, "Yea, hath God said?" is a favorite tactic of his today—calling in question the veracity of God's Word. He also seemed to suggest that God was keeping something back from man, thus His love might be called into question.

2. *Eve tampered with God's Word.* "And the woman said unto the serpent, We may eat of the fruit of the trees of the garden: But of the fruit of the tree which is in the midst of the garden, God hath said, Ye shall not eat of it, neither shall ye touch it, lest ye die" (Gn. 3:2–3). Eve did three things, each of which is tragically dangerous. Note carefully what God had said: "Of every tree of the garden thou mayest freely eat: But of the tree of the knowledge of good and evil, thou shalt not eat of it: for in the day that thou eatest thereof thou shalt surely die" (Gn. 2:16–17). First, Eve added to God's Word. She added, "Neither shall ye touch it." God had not said that, and by adding these words she made it appear as though God were unreasonable in His demands. It is always a dangerous thing to add to God's plain words. "Add thou not

---

3 Henry Clarence Thiessen, *Introductory Lectures in Systematic Theology* (Wm. B. Eerdmans Publishing Company, 1949), 248–249.

unto his words, lest he reprove thee, and thou be found a liar" (Prv. 30:6). Second, she altered God's Word. She said, "Lest ye die." The sharp point of the Spirit's sword was dulled, suggesting that there was only a possibility that they might die. Third, she omitted part of God's Word. Eve completely left out God's solemn threat, "Thou shalt surely die." Revelation 22:19 says, "And if any man shall take away from the words of the book of this prophecy, God shall take away his part out of the book of life, and out of the holy city, and from the things which are written in this book."

3. *Satan contradicted God's Word.* Having sown the seed of doubt in Eve's mind concerning what God had said, Satan was now ready for the flat denial and its plausible explanation. "And the serpent said unto the woman, Ye shall not surely die: For God doth know that in the day ye eat thereof, then your eyes shall be opened, and ye shall be as gods, knowing good and evil" (Gn. 3:4–5). The word *gods* is not expressed in the original Hebrew in the plural! What Satan really said was, "Ye shall be as God." This certainly made a strong appeal to her self-centered ambition—to be as God! Then she began to rationalize as to the attractiveness of the fruit, its satisfying taste, and the intriguing possibility of a whole new experience in knowing both good, which she had known, and evil—an area which must have stirred her curiosity, to say the least.

4. *Eve succumbed to the temptation.* "And when the woman saw that the tree was good for food, and that it was pleasant to the eyes, and a tree to be desired to make one wise, she took of the fruit thereof, and did eat, and gave also unto her husband with her; and he did eat" (Gn. 3:6).

First John 2:16 states: "For all that is in the world, the lust of the flesh, and the lust of the eyes, and the pride of life, is not of the Father, but is of the world." Here are stated what seem to be the three areas of temptation man is subjected to in this world. All sin stems from at least one of these. It can easily be seen that Eve fell for all three: the lust of the eye—"she saw . . . it was pleasant to the eyes"; the lust of the flesh—"that the tree was good for food"; and the pride of life—"a tree to be desired to make one wise." Thus the seed of every sin among men is seen in this, the first sin.

C. The results of man's first sin

1. *As seen in man's attitude toward himself*

a) Adam and Eve immediately became conscious of their own sin. Their consciences were awakened and instantly accused them to themselves. God had not even entered the picture, yet man knew he was a sinner. "And the eyes of them both were opened, and they knew that they were naked" (Gn. 3:7). God later asked them, "Who told thee that thou wast naked?" (v. 11). Man did not need another to tell him; he knew it himself.

Adam and Eve became conscious of two things with relation to their sin: pollution and guilt. The consciousness of their pollution led them to endeavor to cover themselves. The realization of their guilt caused them to flee when God came near. The pollution of sin is a fact. Sin is sinful, and every man bears its stain upon his soul. God does not put it there. It is the inevitable result of sin. There was also the consciousness of guilt, for all sin is in relation to God.

b) Adam and Eve vainly sought to cover their sin.

"And they sewed fig leaves together, and made themselves aprons" (Gn. 3:7). Hardly had the first man and woman sinned and become conscious of their guilt before there was an attempt to cover up. Prior to this time man needed no covering for his body. Many commentators have imagined that they were covered with a garment of light—the glory of God. Whatever their condition was, they were instantly conscious that they had lost something. Some have thought that prior to this the spirit dominated the body, but now the body ruled over the spirit. The inherent tendency in sinful man is to always try to cover up the result of his sin. Thus many attempt to sew for themselves "fig leaves" of self-righteousness. Our first parents soon discovered that these did not even satisfy themselves, let alone a holy God; for when God came near, they fled from His presence.

2. *As seen in man's attitude toward God*

a) Adam and Eve fled from the presence of God. "And they heard the voice of the LORD God walking in the garden in the cool of the day: and Adam and his wife hid themselves from the presence of the LORD God amongst the trees of the garden" (Gn. 3:8). What a difference sin had made in so short a time! Apparently, they had enjoyed God's presence prior to their sin, but now they fled from Him. There is something about sin in the human heart that forms an antipathy toward God, and the sinner will flee from His presence.

b) Adam and Eve falsely thought they could hide from God. What a false sense of security was theirs as they hid behind the trees of the garden! As though they could hide from the all-seeing eye of the Almighty within the confined limits of Eden! As though there were any place in all God's great universe where one might hide from Him who sees and knows all the secrets of men's hearts! (Ps. 139:7–13.) It is gracious indeed to realize that, though He most surely knew what had happened, it was God who sought the fallen pair: Adam, "Where art thou?" (Gn. 3:9). God has been taking the initiative in seeking lost mankind ever since. "For the Son of Man is come to seek and to save that which was lost" (Lk. 19:10). (Also the parable of the lost sheep, Lk. 15:3–7.)

3. *As seen in man's attitude toward his fellow man.* One of the saddest results of sin is its effect upon others. Eve was not content to disobey God herself alone; she also involved her husband. "And when the woman saw that the tree was good for food…she took of the fruit thereof, and did eat, and gave also unto her husband" (Gn. 3:6). The drunkard, the addict, or the immoral person is never satisfied until he has influenced others to join him in his vices.

When God confronted the first sinners and asked them that searching question, "Hast thou eaten of the tree, whereof I commanded thee that thou shouldst not eat?" (Gn. 3:11), there was an immediate attempt on the part of Adam to shift the blame to another: "The woman...she gave me of the tree, and I did eat" (v. 12). Instead of openly admitting his guilt, Adam blamed his wife. Not only did he blame her, but there is the suggestion that Adam also laid some of the blame on God Himself: "The woman whom thou gavest to be with me" (Gn. 3:12). It is the nature of sin that causes man to refuse to take the responsibility on himself. The prayer that brings forgiveness and cleansing is, "God be merciful to me a sinner" (Lk. 18:13).

D. The curse which the first sin brought

Though it was only one sin—one act of disobedience—it manifested the spirit of rebellion that had come into the heart of man and broke fellowship with the holy God. As a result, God pronounced the curses under which all of creation has suffered ever since.

1. *The curse upon the serpent.* "Thou art cursed above all cattle, and above every beast of the field; upon thy belly shalt thou go, and dust thou shalt eat all the days of thy life" (Gn. 3:14)—the curse upon the animal kingdom.

2. *The curse upon the woman.* "I will greatly multiply thy sorrow and thy conception; in sorrow thou shalt bring forth children; and thy desire shall be to thy husband, and he shall rule over thee" (v. 16).

3. *The curse upon the man.* "Cursed is the ground for thy sake; in sorrow shalt thou eat of it all the days of thy life....In the sweat of thy face shalt thou eat bread, till thou return unto the ground; for out of it wast thou taken: for dust thou art, and unto dust shalt thou return" (vv. 17–19). This plainly includes both physical and spiritual death.

A further result of the curse upon man is his expulsion from the garden of Eden.

> And the LORD God said, Behold, the man is become as one of us, to know good and evil: and now, lest he put forth his hand, and take also of the tree of life, and eat, and live forever: Therefore the LORD God sent him forth from the garden of Eden, to till the ground from whence he was taken. So he drove out the man; and he placed at the east of the garden of Eden Cherubims, and a flaming sword which turned every way, to keep the way of the tree of life.
> —GENESIS 3:22–24

Though this seems to be a severe judgment, yet there is the thought of mercy, for God did not want man to eat of the tree of life, lest he should live forever in his sin; thus making redemption impossible.

4. *The curse upon the ground.* "Cursed is the ground for thy sake...Thorns also and thistles shall it bring forth to thee" (vv. 17–18)—the curse upon the vegetable kingdom.

IV. The Nature of Sin

A. What is sin?

Perhaps the best definition is found in the Westminster Larger Catechism, which says, "Sin is any want of conformity unto, or transgression of, any law of God given as a rule to the reasonable creature."[4] Chafer and others think it would be better to substitute the word *character* for *law* in this definition, inasmuch as the law of God may not include all that God's character requires.[5] Anything that contradicts God's character of holiness is sin. The definition might be more comprehensive if both thoughts were included: Sin is any want of conformity unto, or transgression of, the character or law of God given as a rule to the reasonable creature. Sin may be against God's person and thus be godlessness, defilement, or selfhood; or it may be against God's laws or moral government and thus be transgression, rebellion, or lawlessness. The former is illustrated in Isaiah 6, where the prophet was caught a vision of the holiness of God and cried out, "Woe is me! for I am undone; because I am a man of unclean lips" (Is. 6:5). Also, as Job said to God, "I have heard of thee by the hearing of the ear: but now mine eye seeth thee. Wherefore I abhor myself, and repent in dust and ashes." (Jb. 42:5–6). (See also Lk. 5:8; Rv. 1:17.) That sin is a transgression of the law is clear from the following:

> What shall we say then? Is the law sin? God forbid. Nay, I had not known sin, but by the law: for I had not known lust, except the law had said, Thou shalt not covet.
>
> —ROMANS 7:7

> For as many as are of the works of the law are under the curse: for it is written, Cursed is every one that continueth not in all things which are written in the book of the law to do them.
>
> —GALATIANS 3:10

> If ye fulfill the royal law according to the scripture, Thou shalt love thy neighbor as thyself, ye do well: But if ye have respect to persons, ye commit sin, and are convinced of the law as transgressors.
>
> —JAMES 2:8–9

---

4 Assembly of Divines, *Larger Catechism* (Westminster, England: 1723).
5 Chafer, 227.

B. Sin and God's law

1. *The nature of God's law.* Since we define sin as any want of conformity unto or transgression of God's law, it would be good to understand a few things about His laws.

First, there is nothing wrong with the Law itself. We have so emphasized the fact that we are under grace and not under Law, one would almost think the Law were something evil. Paul says, "The law is holy, and the commandment holy, and just, and good" (Rom. 7:12). It is a revelation of God's nature and will; therefore it can only be good.

Second, God's law is not something arbitrary, since it springs from His own nature. God does not declare that something is right simply on the basis that He says it is. Rather, He says it is right because it is right. If this were not so, He would be a despot.

Third, when God gave man His law, did He expect him to keep it? The answer can only be no! Knowing all things, God was fully aware that man would not—indeed, could not—keep His law when He gave it to him. Why then, did an all-wise God give a set of laws to a people He well knew would not and could not keep them? As in everything, God had a wise and good purpose in this giving of the Law. There seems to be at least a threefold purpose.

2. *The purpose of God's law*

a) The Law was given to intensify man's knowledge of sin. A man's conscience will bear inner witness to him that he is a sinner, but through God's published Law he has a clearer knowledge of what sin is. "Now we know that what things soever the law saith, it saith to them who are under the law: that every mouth may be stopped, and all the world may become guilty before God. . . . for by the law is the knowledge of sin" (Rom. 3:19–20). "What shall we say then? Is the law sin? God forbid. Nay, I had not known sin, but by the law: for I had not known lust, except the law had said, Thou shalt not covet" (Rom. 7:7). Having learned through the Law that sin is breaking God's commandments, sin now takes on the character of transgression: "For until the law sin was in the world: but sin is not imputed when there is no law" (Rom. 5:13). "Was then that which is good made death unto me? God forbid. But sin, that it might appear sin, working death in me by that which is good; that sin by the commandment might become exceeding sinful" (Rom. 7:13).

b) The Law was given to reveal the holiness of God. If there is one message that comes to us from the detailed laws, offerings, priestly requirements, etc., it is that God is a holy God and can only be approached in the proper, prescribed way and only at given times. In this way, the Law reveals the holiness of God: "Wherefore the law is holy, and the commandment holy, and just, and good" (Rom. 7:12).

c) The Law was given to lead men to Christ. "For Christ is the end of the law for righteousness to every one that believeth" (Rom. 10:4). The Law is called a schoolmaster: "Wherefore the law was our schoolmaster to bring us unto Christ, that we might be justified by faith" (Gal. 3:24). The word translated "schoolmaster" is *paidagogos,* which has no exact equivalent in the English language. A *paidagogos* was usually a trusted slave in a wealthy Roman family who had the responsibility of superintending the general care of a son from about age six to sixteen, taking him to and from his teacher's houses or the schools of physical training, looking after him in his play hours, and so on. In likening the Law to the believer's *paidagogos,* Paul had in mind the temporary and purely provisional nature of this arrangement until the child became of age and could participate fully in his father's inheritance. The Law could not save, but it served to make men realize their need of Christ, through whom alone they could be justified by faith. The Law, through its offerings, its priesthood, and the tabernacle, pointed to the cross of Christ as the only way of salvation and access to God. Once Christ came and was received as Savior and Lord through faith, the Law, as a means of obtaining salvation, was done away with. Unbelievers, those who do not come to Christ for salvation, are still being judged by the Law.

The Scriptures teach that upon the death of Christ the believer is delivered not only from the curse of the Law—the penalty imposed upon him by the Law—but from the Law itself.

> Christ hath redeemed us from the curse of the law, being made a curse for us: for it is written, Cursed is every one that hangeth on a tree.
>
> —GALATIANS 3:13

> Wherefore, my brethren, ye also are become dead to the law by the body of Christ; that ye should be married to another, even to him who is raised from the dead, that we should bring forth fruit unto God.
>
> —ROMANS 7:4

> Having abolished in his flesh the enmity, even the law of commandments contained in ordinances.
>
> —EPHESIANS 2:15

> Blotting out the handwriting of ordinances that was against us, which was contrary to us, and took it out of the way, nailing it to his cross.
>
> —COLOSSIANS 2:14

This deliverance from Law refers not only to the ceremonial law, but to the moral law (the Ten Commandments) as well. Second Corinthians 3:7–11 makes it clear that it was that Law which was "written and engraven in stones" that passed away. This makes it certain that Paul was writing about the Ten Commandments.

> But if the ministration of death, written and engraven in stones, was glorious, so that the children of Israel could not steadfastly behold the face of Moses for the glory of his countenance; which glory was to be done away: How shall not the ministration of the spirit be rather glorious?... For if that which is done away was glorious, much more that which remaineth is glorious.
> —2 CORINTHIANS 3:7–8, 11

> But if ye be led of the Spirit, ye are not under the law.
> —GALATIANS 5:18

Thus the believer can realize that he is not "under law, but under grace" (Rom. 6:14).

C. Scriptural expressions for sin

Many different words and expressions are used in the Bible to describe sin. The following are some of the most popularly used ones:

1. *Missing of a mark or aim*—expression most used in both the Old and New Testaments (Rom. 3:23)

2. *Overpassing or trespassing of a line*—to transgress, as described in 1 Timothy 2:14

3. *Disobedience to a voice*—Hebrews 2:2–3

4. *Falling where one should have stood upright*—Galatians 6:1, variously translated

5. *Ignorance of what one ought to have known*—Hebrews 9:7

6. *Diminishing of that which should have been rendered in full measure*—1 Corinthians 6:7; Ananias and Sapphira, Acts 5:1–10

7. *Non-observance of a law*—sins of omission, James 4:17

8. *Lawlessness or anarchy (utter disregard for the Law)*—1 John 3:4, where *transgression* should be translated "lawlessness"

9. *Debt, a failure in duty, a not meeting one's obligations to God*—Matthew 6:12

10. *Other single words:* iniquity, Lv. 26:40; godlessness, 1 Pt. 4:18; wickedness, Prv. 11:31; unbelief, Rom. 11:20; unrighteousness, 1 Jn. 1:9; unjustness, Dt. 25:15–16; unholiness, 1 Ti. 1:9

D. Sin is evil

1. *Sin is a specific type of evil.* There are physical evils and moral evils in the world. Physical evils, such as floods, earthquakes, hurricanes, frost, and drought, are not sins.

They are not moral evils, but are sometimes sent by God to punish or chastise those who have broken His law. It is in this sense in that God is said Isaiah 45:7 to "create evil." The Hebrew word *ra'*, which Isaiah uses here for "evil," is never rendered "sin," but "evil, calamity, adversity," etc. God made the Law and its penalties for breaking it. If man sins he will reap the results, and the responsibility for both are man's.

2. *Sin is a positive evil.* The sinner is not simply one who does not keep the Law. He becomes a positive force for evil.

E. The sinful nature of sin

Sin does not merely consist of outward acts. It is a principle or nature within the sinner. While it is true that men are sinners because they sin, it is a fundamental principle that men sin because they are sinners. They are sinners by nature before they become sinners by practice. The first sin of Adam was a personal sin, which resulted in his having a sinful nature. His descendents have all been born with a sinful nature, which has resulted in their sinning. Jesus said that a tree brings forth fruit according to its nature: "Even so every good tree bringeth forth good fruit; but a corrupt tree bringeth forth evil fruit. A good tree cannot bring forth evil fruit, neither can a corrupt tree bring forth good fruit" (Mt. 7:17–18). He was more interested in cutting down the evil tree, rather than trying to destroy the evil fruit. Thus, John the Baptist prophesied of Him, "And now also the axe is laid unto the root of the trees: therefore every tree which bringeth not forth good fruit is hewn down, and cast into the fire" (Mt. 3:10).

This also explains why Jesus condemned the adulterous look, as well as the act of adultery (Mt. 5:27–28); and why He condemned anger as much as murder (Mt. 5:21–22), for it is this principle which leads to murder. In connection with temptation and the adulterous look of which Jesus speaks here, it seems, according to Dake, that He meant that a man would look "with continual longing, with the mind made up to commit the act if at all possible (Jas. 1:13–16). It becomes a state of the heart and is as deadly as the act itself (1 Sm. 16:7; Mk. 7:19–23)."[6] Temptation itself is not sin; thus, if a man looks at a woman and is tempted, that in itself is not sin. It becomes sin if he dwells upon it, fantasizing concerning his desire. James explains it thus: "But every man is tempted, when he is drawn away of his own lust, and enticed. Then when lust hath conceived, it bringeth forth sin: and sin, when it is finished, bringeth forth death" (Jas. 1:14–15).

The New Testament distinguishes between *sin* and *sins*. The former refers to the sin nature, while the latter refers to the results, or expressions, of that nature. Paul says, "For without the law sin was dead...But when the commandment came, sin

---

6 Finis Jennings Dake, *Dake's Annotated Reference Bible* (Grand Rapids, MI: Zondervan Publishing House, 1961), N.T., 4.

revived, and I died" (Rom. 7:8–9). "Whosoever committeth sin is the servant of sin" (Jn. 8:34); "We have before proved both Jews and Gentiles, that they are all under sin" (Rom. 3:9). "Wherefore, as by one man sin entered into the world" (Rom. 5:12). Sin is also seen to be a force within a person, as well as the acts which he commits: "Let not sin therefore reign in your mortal body, that ye should obey it in the lusts thereof" (Rom. 6:12); "For sin shall not have dominion over you: for ye are not under the law, but under grace" (Rom. 6:14).

Those who study criminals with a view to reclaiming them are more interested in what made them commit the crime than in the actual deed itself. Man needs a salvation that will give him a new nature. That is why "ye must be born again" (Jn. 3:7).

Thiessen quotes Charles Hodge as saying, "Sin includes guilt and pollution; the one expresses its relation to the justice, the other to the holiness of God." Then he adds: "In so far as sin is a transgression of the law, it is guilt; in so far as it is a principle, it is pollution."[7]

Pollution as a result of sin is clearly seen in the following Scriptures: "The whole head is sick, and the whole heart faint" (Is. 1:5); "The heart is deceitful above all things, and desperately wicked" (Jer. 17:9); "An evil man out of the evil treasure of his heart bringeth forth that which is evil" (Lk. 6:45).

The following Scriptures, and many others, speak of men needing to be cleansed: "Wash me throughly from mine iniquity, and cleanse me from my sin" (Ps. 51:2); "Purge me with hyssop, and I shall be clean: wash me, and I shall be whiter than snow" (Ps. 51:7); "And the blood of Jesus Christ his Son cleanseth us from all sin" (1 Jn. 1:7).

F. Important considerations regarding sin

1. *Sins of omission.* Failure to do what God's law requires is as much sin as to do contrarily to the requirements of the Law. There are sins of omission as well as of commission. "Therefore to him that knoweth to do good, and doeth it not, to him it is sin" (Jas. 4:17). Israel was accused of robbing God. "Will a man rob God? Yet ye have robbed me. But, ye say, Wherein have we robbed thee? In tithes and offerings" (Mal. 3:8).

2. *Sins of unbelief.* "And when he is come, he will reprove the world of sin....because they believe not on me" (Jn. 16:8–9). "And he that doubteth is damned if he eat, because he eateth not of faith: for whatsoever is not of faith is sin" (Rom. 14:23).

3. *Sins of ignorance.* Ignorance of the law is no excuse. The Levitical law gave specific instructions concerning the type of offering a man should bring to the priest if he were guilty of a sin through ignorance:

---

7 Charles Hodge, as quoted by Thiessen, 245.

> And if any soul sin through ignorance, then he shall bring a she goat of the first year for a sin offering. And the priest shall make an atonement for the soul that sinneth ignorantly.
>
> —NUMBERS 15:27–28

> And if a soul sin, and commit any of these things which are forbidden to be done by the commandments of the LORD; though he wist it not, yet he is guilty, and shall bear his iniquity.
>
> —LEVITICUS 5:17

The idea of a sin of ignorance is also expressed in the New Testament:

> And that servant, which knew his lord's will, and prepared not himself, neither did according to his will, shall be beaten with many stripes. But he that knew not, and did commit things worthy of stripes, shall be beaten with few stripes.
>
> —LUKE 12:47–48

4. *One sin makes one guilty of all.* "For as many as are of the works of the law are under the curse: for it is written, Cursed is every one that continueth not in all things which are written in the book of the law to do them" (Gal. 3:10). "For whosoever shall keep the whole law, and yet offend in one point, he is guilty of all" (Jas. 2:10). This seems to be a most stringent law. Yet if a person were hanging over a high cliff by a chain, it would not be necessary to break every link in the chain to send him headlong to his death on the rocks below. One would need to break only one link—and that could be the smallest of all. It only takes one sin to make a man a sinner.

V. THE UNIVERSALITY OF SIN

The Scriptures bear testimony to the sinfulness of all mankind. The Old Testament declares, "For there is no man that sinneth not" (1 Kgs. 8:46); "For in thy sight shall no man living be justified" (Ps. 143:2); "Who can say, I have made my heart clean, I am pure from my sin?" (Prv. 20:9); "For there is not a just man upon earth, that doeth good, and sinneth not" (Eccl. 7:20).

The New Testament is even more explicit: "There is none righteous, no, not one... there is none that doeth good, no, not one" (Rom. 3:10–12); "For all have sinned, and come short of the glory of God" (Rom. 3:23); "But the scripture hath concluded all under sin" (Gal. 3:22); "We all stumble in many ways" (Jas. 3:2, NIV); "If we say that we have no sin, we deceive ourselves, and the truth is not in us" (1 Jn. 1:8).

The fact that Christ died for all is an indication that all are sinners and need His saving grace: "For the love of Christ constraineth us; because we thus judge, that if one died for all, then were all dead: And that he died for all, that they which live should not henceforth live unto themselves, but unto him which died for them, and rose again" (2 Cor. 5:14–15).

The Scriptures teach that through the sin of Adam and Eve, all his posterity are counted as sinners. "Through the one man's disobedience the many were made sinners" (Rom. 5:19, NASB). The next section will discuss how God can hold every man responsible for a depraved nature because of a sin he himself did not commit.

VI. THE IMPUTATION OF SIN

Imputation means to attribute or ascribe something to a person. A good illustration of the principle is seen in Philemon 1:17–18, where Paul says of Onesimus' debt, "If thou count me therefore a partner, receive him as myself. If he hath wronged thee, or oweth thee ought, put that on mine account."

Three great examples of imputation are seen in the Bible: that of Adam's sin to the human race; that of our sin to Christ, as He died for us; and Christ's righteousness imputed to believers through faith in Christ. The first and third are especially seen in Romans 5:12–21. This is truly one of the greatest passages in the Bible. The key verse in this passage is verse 12: "Wherefore, as by one man sin entered into the world, and death by sin; and so death passed upon all men, for that all have sinned." "As by one man sin entered in to the world"—sin did not begin with Adam; it merely entered into the human race through him. It had its beginning with Lucifer (Ez. 28:12–17). The important expression here is, "For that all have sinned." The Greek *aorist* tense is used, which indicates a single, completed past action. Thus, "all have sinned" is better rendered "all sinned." Chafer says:

> Each member of the race died physically because of his own part in Adam's sin. Since one complete, single, historical act is in view, the words "all sinned" cannot refer to a nature which results from that act, nor can it refer to personal sins of many individuals. It is not that man became sinful. The assertion is that all sinned at one time and under the same circumstances.[8]

"Sinned" is not equivalent to "became sinful." Paul does not say death passed upon all men for that Adam sinned, but "for that *all* sinned" (v. 12, emphasis added).

Adam was the natural head of the human race, so that all men were in him when he sinned. Thus, we all are sinners because we sinned in him. This principle is illustrated in Hebrews 7:9–10: "And as I may so say, Levi also, who receiveth tithes, payed tithes in Abraham. For he was yet in the loins of his father, when Melchisedec met him."

---

8 Chafer, 301.

Levi, the father of the priestly tribe, received tithes of the people. But because he was in the loins of his great-grandfather Abraham when he paid tithes to Melchizedek, the priest of the Most High God, Levi is said to have paid tithes to this ancient priest (Gn. 14:20). In like manner, the whole human race was in Adam, its natural head, when he sinned. God thus imputes the sin of Adam to each member of the race. Chafer again strongly claims, "No one would claim that Levi consciously and purposefully paid tithes to Melchisedec, yet God declares he did. Likewise, no one would claim that each individual in Adam's race consciously and purposefully sinned in Adam, yet there can be no doubt that God reckons that each member of the race sinned in Adam's transgression."[9] In 1 Corinthians 15:22 we read, "For as in Adam all die."

Lest any think that the statement in Romans 5:12, "For all have sinned," is a reference to personal sin, Paul follows the statement with verses 13–14:

> For until the law sin was in the world: but sin is not imputed when there is no law. Nevertheless death reigned from Adam to Moses, even over them that had not sinned after the similitude of Adam's transgression, who is the figure of him that was to come.

No written statement of what God required had been given to man before the Law was given, thus men were not held as guilty of having broken what did not exist; "Nevertheless death reigned from Adam to Moses" (v. 14). We have already been told that death came by sin. If man was not responsible for breaking laws which did not exist, yet he suffered the penalty of sin, which was death, then the sin which caused him to die, even before the Law was given to Moses, could not have been personal sin. Death reigned, from Adam to Moses, even over infants and incompetent people. It would seem then that the "all" who sinned (v. 12) could not have been held guilty of personal sin, but must have been considered sinners because of their being in Adam when he sinned. In verse 14 we are told that Adam was the figure or type "of him that was to come," Christ Jesus. In the following verses, Paul makes several comparisons and contrasts between the first Adam and the Last Adam, Christ: "Therefore as by the offence of one [Adam] judgment came upon all men to condemnation; even so by the righteousness of one [Christ] the free gift came upon all men unto justification of life. For as by one man's disobedience many were made sinners, so by the obedience of one shall many be made righteous" (vv. 18–19).

If any feel that it is unjust that the sin of Adam should be imputed to all his posterity, by the same reasoning it would be unjust to impute the righteousness of Jesus Christ to those who believe in Him. Yet this is the basis of our justification and salvation.

---

9 Ibid., 303.

It might seem to some that there is a contradiction between two sets of statements which are found in the Old Testament. In Exodus 20:5 and Deuteronomy 5:9 (which are identical) and Exodus 34:7, which expresses the same thought as the former verses in almost the same language, are found the words, "I the LORD thy God am a jealous God, visiting the iniquity of the fathers upon the children unto the third and fourth generation of them that hate me." In apparent contradiction to this, we read, "The son shall not bear the iniquity of the father, neither shall the father bear the iniquity of the son: the righteousness of the righteous shall be upon him, and the wickedness of the wicked shall be upon him" (Ez. 18:20). (See also Dt. 24:16; 2 Kgs. 14:6; 2 Chr. 25:4.) The explanation of this difficulty is not hard to find. The former statement has to do with the consequences of the parents' sin and not the sin *per se*. The passage in Ezekiel is referring to the guilt and penalty of the parents' sin, rather than the consequences. We know that children often must bear the consequences of their parents' wrongdoing and wrong living. The following from *The Pulpit Commentary* illustrates this principle:

> God again manifestly does by the laws which obtain in his moral universe, entail on children many consequences of their parents' ill-doing—as the diseases which arise from profligacy and intemperance, the poverty which is the result of idleness or extravagance, the ignorance and evil habits which are the fruit of neglected education. It is this sort of visitation which is intended here.[10]

Nowhere does the Bible teach, as is made clear from Ezekiel 18:20 and the other references given, that a son or grandson is considered guilty of the individual sin or sins of his parents and will thus be judicially or eternally punished.

VII. ORIGINAL SIN AND DEPRAVITY

A. The meaning of *depravity*

Two things are meant by the expression *original sin*: the first sin of Adam and the sinful nature possessed by every man since Adam, due to Adam's first transgression. This sinful nature is called depravity. Depravity consists of four things which are true of every individual when he is born.

1. *He is completely void of original righteousness.* "Behold, I was shapen in iniquity; and in sin did my mother conceive me" (Ps. 51:5).

---

10 H. D. M. Spence and Joseph S. Exell, eds., *The Pulpit Commentary* (Grand Rapids, MI: Wm. B. Eerdmans Publishing Company, 1950), I, sc. 2, 132.

2. *He does not possess any holy affection toward God.* "Who changed the truth of God into a lie, and worshipped and served the creature more than the Creator, who is blessed for ever. Amen" (Rom. 1:25). "For men shall be lovers of their own selves.... Traitors, heady, highminded, lovers of pleasures more than lovers of God" (2 Tm. 3:2, 4)

3. *This depraved nature is within the heart.* As Mark 7:15 states, "There is nothing from without a man that...can defile him: but the things which come out of him, those are they that defile the man." "For from within, out of the heart of men, proceed evil thoughts, adulteries, fornications, murders, Thefts, covetousness, wickedness, deceit, lasciviousness, an evil eye, blasphemy, pride, foolishness: All these evil things come from within, and defile the man" (Mk. 7:21–23).

4. *He has a continuous bias toward evil.* "And God saw that the wickedness of man was great in the earth, and that every imagination of the thoughts of his heart was only evil continually" (Gn. 6:5).

Lest the term *depravity* be misunderstood, it is good to note the following, quoted from *Lectures in Systematic Theology,* by Thiessen:

> From the negative standpoint, it does not mean that every sinner is devoid of all qualities pleasing to men; that he commits, or is prone to commit every form of sin; that he is as bitterly opposed to God as it is possible for him to be...Jesus recognized the existence of pleasing qualities in some individuals (Mark 10:21; Mt. 23:23)....From the positive standpoint, it does mean that every sinner is totally destitute of that love to God which is the fundamental requirement of the law. "Hear, O Israel: the Lord our God is one Lord: and thou shalt love the Lord thy God with all thine heart, and with all thy soul, and with all thy might" (Dt. 6:4–5). See Mt. 22:35–38; that he is supremely given to a preference of himself to God (2 Tm. 3:2–4); that he has an aversion to God which on occasion becomes active enmity to Him: "Because the carnal mind is enmity against God: for it is not subject to the law of God, neither indeed can be" (Rom. 8:7); that his every faculty is disordered and corrupted: "Having the understanding darkened, being alienated from the life of God through the ignorance that is in them, because of the blindness of their heart" (Eph. 4:18); that he has no thought, feeling, or deed of which God can fully approve: "For I know that in me (that is in my flesh,) dwelleth no good thing: for to will is present with me; but how to perform that which is good I find not" (Rom. 7:18); and that he has entered upon a line of constant progress in depravity from which he can in no wise turn away in his own strength (Rom. 7:18).[11]

---

11 Thiessen, 267–268.

B. The result of man's depravity

Sin is willful rebellion against God. Such an attitude cannot but bring forth evil results. It is not surprising that one can look all about and see the awful results of sin. It is just not possible for men to continue sinning and receive anything but a harvest of sorrows of the worst kind. Paul states in Galatians 6:8, "For he that soweth to his flesh shall of the flesh reap corruption." Hosea said concerning Israel, "For they have sown the wind, and they shall reap the whirlwind" (Hos. 8:7). He also declared, "Ye have plowed wickedness, ye have reaped iniquity; ye have eaten the fruit of lies" (Hos. 10:13).

One would have to be blind not to see the result of sinful depravity in the minds and bodies of the human race today. Superstition, barbarity, and the grossest iniquity are seen in every land where the gospel has not gone. Where the message of salvation from sin has been preached and rejected, the condition is almost worse, for here is added the condemnation of light that has been rejected. In our own land, which is probably the greatest Christian country in the world, every institution of correction, every prison of punishment, every sanitarium and asylum is bulging with the results of sin. Every policeman in the nation is a silent tribute to the result of sin. So devastating is the influence of sin upon the human consciousness that now sin is glamorized until it is being recognized in society as the thing to do. Someone wise once said that the greatest defense against sin is to be shocked at it. When this attitude ceases, sin has accomplished its direst results. Paul, in that terrible list of gross iniquities in Romans 1:24–32, climaxed the whole dread situation when he said, "Who knowing the judgment of God, that they which commit such things are worthy of death, not only do the same, but have pleasure in them that do them" (v. 32). When sin loses its sinfulness and men take pleasure in the grossest of sinful practices, there is little hope left.

VIII. THE GUILT FROM SIN

A. Sin in relation to God

Guilt is just desserts of punishment for self-determined violation of law or failure to conform to that law. It is the result of sin in relation to God's wrath. There are natural results of sin in the sinner himself, but wrath brings God into the picture. Every sin is an offense against God and subject to His wrath (Ps. 7:11; Jn. 3:18, 36). David's repentance reached its height when he realized that he had not only sinned against Bathsheba and her husband Uriah, but against God: "Against thee, thee only, have I sinned, and done this evil in thy sight: that thou mightest be justified when thou speakest, and be clear when thou judgest" (Ps. 51:4). The prodigal realized the same when he cried, "I have sinned against heaven" (Lk. 15:21). Romans 3:19 states the case well: "Now we know that what things soever the law saith, it saith to them who are under the law: that every mouth may be stopped, and all the world may become guilty before God." God's holiness reacts against sin; the reaction is the wrath of God: "For the wrath of God is revealed from heaven against all ungodliness and unrighteousness of men, who hold the truth in unrighteousness" (Rom. 1:18). According to Strong, "Not only does sin, as unlikeness to the divine purity, involve pollution—it also, as antagonism to God's holy will, involves guilt."[12]

While guilt is primarily a reaction to God, there is also a secondary reaction in one's conscience. Strong reports, "Progress in sin is marked by a diminished sensitiveness of moral insight and feeling. As 'the greatest of sins is to be conscious of none,' so guilt may be great, just in proportion to the absence of consciousness of it (Ps. 19:12; Eph. 4:18, 19). There is no evidence, however, that the voice of conscience can be completely or finally silenced. The time for repentance may pass, but not the time for remorse."[13] Dr. H. E. Robins is quoted as saying, "To the convicted sinner a merely external hell would be a cooling flame, compared with the agony of his remorse."[14]

B. Degrees of guilt

The Scripture makes it clear that there are degrees of guilt, and thus degrees of punishment, because there are varieties of sin. This principle is recognized by the variety of sacrifices required by different kinds of sins (Lv. 4–7). The New Testament also suggests degrees of guilt: Lk. 12:47–48; Jn. 19:11; Rom. 2:6; Heb. 2:2–3; 10:28–29. There are:

1. *Sins of nature and sins of personal transgression.* Men are sinners because of the principle of inborn sin—sins of nature—but there is greater guilt when the sinner by nature commits acts of personal transgression.

2. *Sins of ignorance and sins of knowledge.* We have already seen that there are sins of ignorance. But sins against knowledge would be accompanied by greater guilt. The greater the knowledge, the greater the guilt. "Woe unto thee, Chorazin! woe unto thee, Bethsaida! for if the mighty works had been done in Tyre and Sidon, which have been done in you, they had a great while ago repented, sitting in sackcloth and ashes. But it shall be more tolerable for Tyre and Sidon at the judgment, than for you" (Lk. 10:13–14). "For as many as have sinned without law shall also perish without law: and as many as have sinned in the law shall be judged by the law" (Rom. 2:12).

3. *Sins of infirmity and sins of presumption.* The psalmist prayed to be kept from presumptuous sins: "Keep back thy servant also from presumptuous sins; let them not have dominion over me" (Ps. 19:13). In contrast, Peter illustrates a sin of infir-

---

12 Augustus Hopkins Strong, *Systematic Theology* (Philadelphia, PA: The Judson Press, 1943), 645.

13 Ibid., 647.

14 H. E. Robbins, as quoted by Strong, 647.

mity. He was determined to be true even if all others denied the Lord, but he found he did not have the strength he thought was his (Mt. 26:35).

Another way of expressing this contrast is to note the difference between sins of impulse and sins of deliberation. David's sin against Bathsheba was one of impulse, but his sin against Uriah was one of deliberation, as he carefully planned for the latter's death.

IX. THE PENALTY OF SIN

A. The significance of penalty

1. *Upon the unsaved.* Penalty is the pain or loss which is directly inflicted by the Lawgiver in vindication of His justice, which has been outraged by the violation of law. There are natural consequences of sin: "For the wages of sin is death" (Rom. 6:23); "The soul that sinneth, it shall die" (Ez. 18:20); "And as it is appointed unto men once to die, but after this the judgment" (Heb. 9:27). Physical death is one of the natural results of sin, but there is an "after this" which represents the penalty to follow. We do not doubt that the natural consequences of sin are part of the penalty. "His own iniquities shall take the wicked himself, and he shall be holden with the cords of his sin" (Prv. 5:22). Immorality takes its toll upon the human body. Ungodliness results in mental and spiritual deterioration, but this is only part of the penalty. In all penalty there is the holy wrath of the Lawgiver. The one may be suffered now, but the other is to be experienced in the future. "Depravity and guilt, as consequences of sin, rest upon mankind now, but penalty in its fulness awaits a future day."[15]

2. *Difference between chastisement and punishment.* It is important to note that there is a vast difference between chastisement and punishment. Chastisement, which is corrective, is never sent as a punishment upon the children of the Lord. Christ bore all the punishment for the believer's sin. Chastisement always proceeds from love: "O LORD, correct me, but with judgment; not in thine anger, lest thou bring me to nothing" (Jer. 10:24); "For whom the Lord loveth he chasteneth, and scourgeth every son whom he receiveth" (Heb. 12:6).

On the other hand, punishment proceeds from justice: "And they shall know that I am the LORD, when I shall have executed judgments in her, and shall be sanctified in her" (Ez. 28:22); "Thus saith the Lord GOD; I do not this for your sakes, O house of Israel, but for mine holy name's sake, which ye have profaned among the heathen, whither ye went" (Ez. 36:22); "And I heard the angel of the waters say, Thou art righteous, O Lord, which art, and wast, and shalt be, because thou hast judged thus" (Rv. 16:5); "For true and righteous are his judgments: for he hath judged the great whore,

---

15 Thiessen, 270.

which did corrupt the earth with her fornication, and hath avenged the blood of his servants at her hand" (Rv. 19:2). Thus chastisement is intended to be corrective, but penalty, or punishment, is not intended to reform the offender. It hardly needs to be said that you cannot reform a murderer by executing him.

B. The nature of penalty

The one word in Scripture which designates the total penalty of sin is *death*. It is threefold: physical, spiritual, and eternal.

1. *Physical death*. Man was created with a capacity for immortality; he did not have to die if he obeyed God's law. But God told Adam, "In the day that thou eatest thereof thou shalt surely die" (Gn. 2:17), referring to the tree of the knowledge of good and evil. Adam did not immediately die, but from that time on, death was working in his physical frame. Some nine hundred years later, death took its final toll upon his body. "It is appointed unto men once to die" (Heb. 9:27). Death is not the cessation of the personality, but the separation of the soul from the body, "including all those temporal evils and sufferings which result from disturbance of the original harmony between body and soul, and which are the working of death in us."[16]

Only through an act of redemption could man again have access to the tree of life. At the time of resurrection, eternal physical life will be restored to those who receive Christ Jesus as their Savior. At that time the soul and spirit will be reunited with the body and man will be a complete being again. Thus, for the Christian, death is no longer the penalty for his sin, since Christ bore that penalty for him. Death becomes a gateway through which the soul enters into the fullest enjoyment of all of the benefits God has wrought in Christ (Eph. 2:7).

2. *Spiritual death*. By spiritual death, we mean the separation of the soul from God, "including all that pain of conscience, loss of peace, and sorrow of spirit, which result from disturbance of the normal relation between the soul and God."[17] Physical death is by no means the chief part of death as the penalty for sin. While Adam did not die physically the moment he disobeyed God, he did die spiritually. He lost that communion with God which is the source of all life. He became "dead in trespasses and sins" (Eph. 2:1). First Timothy 5:6 relates to the widow, but perfectly describes Adam's immediate condition also, as well as that of every unredeemed man: "But she that liveth in pleasure is dead while she liveth." When Jesus said, "And whosoever liveth and believeth in me shall never die" (Jn. 11:26), He was speaking of the restoration of spiritual life through His redeeming grace.

---

16 Strong, 656.
17 Strong, 659.

3. *Eternal death*. Eternal death is the culmination and completion of spiritual death, and speaks of eternal separation of the soul from God. This is called the second death: "But the fearful, and unbelieving, and the abominable, and murderers, and whoremongers, and sorcerers, and idolaters, and all liars, shall have their part in the lake which burneth with fire and brimstone: which is the second death" (Rv. 21:8). "Who shall be punished with everlasting destruction from the presence of the Lord, and from the glory of his power" (2 Thes. 1:9). "Then shall he say unto them on the left hand, Depart from me, ye cursed, into everlasting fire, prepared for the devil and his angels" (Mt. 25:41). "Marvel not at this: for the hour is coming, in the which all that are in the graves shall hear his voice, And shall come forth; they that have done good, unto the resurrection of life; and they that have done evil, unto the resurrection of damnation" (Jn. 5:28–29). Chafer discusses the second death:

> It is true that the "second death," which is eternal, is a separation from God and that eternal estate is an immeasurable penalty in the light of the fact that the lost soul must know what grace might have wrought. The penalty is a definite imposition over and above the natural course of events—a retribution which corresponds to the punishment required. It is as certain as the character of God that whatever is imposed will be just and right, and it will be so recognized by all. God will not in this, any more than in any other undertaking, be the author of that which is evil.[18]

---

18 Chafer, 362.

THE DOCTRINE OF SALVATION

Soteriology

Introduction
I. Provisions That Have Been Made
   A. Death of Christ
      1. *Importance of the death of Christ*
      2. *Misunderstandings concerning the death of Christ*
      3. *True meaning of the death of Christ*
      4. *Those for whom Christ died*
   B. Resurrection of Jesus Christ
      1. *Importance of the resurrection of Christ*
      2. *Nature and manner of the Resurrection*
      3. *Proofs of Christ's resurrection*
      4. *Results or benefits of His resurrection*
   C. Ascension and exaltation of Jesus Christ
      1. *His ascension*
      2. *His exaltation*
      3. *Practical values of the doctrines of the Ascension and Exaltation*
II. The Application of the Provisions
   A. Election
   B. Repentance
      1. *Definition*
      2. *Importance of repentance*
      3. *Manner in which repentance is produced*
      4. *Fruits of repentance*
   C. Faith
      1. *Importance of faith*
      2. *The meaning of faith*
      3. *The elements of faith*
      4. *The source of faith*
   D. Justification
      1. *Definition*
      2. *What is involved in justification?*
      3. *The method of justification*
   E. Regeneration
      1. *What is the new birth?*
      2. *Necessity of the new birth*

CHAPTER FIVE

THE DOCTRINE OF SALVATION

Soteriology

INTRODUCTION

THE WORD *SOTERIOLOGY* is derived from two Greek words, *soteria* and *logos*. The former means "salvation" and the latter, "word, discourse, or doctrine." Having dealt with the doctrine of theology, wherein the holiness of God was emphasized, and having seen the failure and sin of mankind in the study of anthropology and hamartiology, one is brought to realize the utter need for a plan of salvation sufficient to bridge the vast gap between these two infinite extremes—man's sinfulness and God's holiness. Fortunately for all concerned, God foreknew all that was to take place in man's fall, and He planned just such a salvation as was needed before the foundation of the earth. Before the first sin was committed in the universe, before the sad plight brought on by rebellious man, who had been made in the image of God, the Lord planned and provided the way of escape from the snares and condemnation of sin. Our God was not caught unawares. He foreknew the Fall and He foreordained the plan of rescue.

God's plan of salvation is so simple that the least among the sons of men can grasp enough of it to experience its transforming power. At the same time, it is so profound that no inadequacy has ever been discovered in it. In fact, those who know it best are continuously amazed that one, and only one, plan of salvation is needed to meet the vast array of spiritual needs among the almost limitless varieties of the needs of men in every race, culture, and condition among the nations of this world.

The heart of God's plan of salvation centers around the office and function of a mediator—One who could go between an offended God and a helpless sinful creature, man. Job felt the need for just such a One as he found himself (at least he thought) estranged from God: "He is not a man like me that I might answer him, that we might confront each other in court. If only there were someone to arbitrate between us, to lay his hand upon us both" (Jb. 9:32–33, NIV). This is the position which Christ, in His substitutionary sacrifice, came to fill: "For there is one God, and one mediator between God and men, the man Christ Jesus" (1 Tm. 2:5).

This is the reason for the incarnation of the second person of the Godhead. To be a mediator for God, He must be God; to represent mankind, He must be a man. The penalty for the sins of mankind, which had to be done away with if man was to have fellowship with God, was death. But because God cannot die—spirit cannot die—He had to have a body. And so "the Word was made flesh, and dwelt among us" (Jn. 1:14). Also note the following extended explanation:

> Forasmuch then as the children are partakers of flesh and blood, he also himself likewise took part of the same; that through death he might destroy him that had the power of death, that is, the devil; And deliver them who through fear of death were all their lifetime subject to bondage. For verily he took not on him the nature of angels; but he took on him the seed of Abraham. Wherefore in all things it behooved him to be made like unto his brethren, that he might be a merciful and faithful high priest in things pertaining to God, to make reconciliation for the sins of the people.
> —HEBREWS 2:14–17

All this has been made possible through the death, burial, and resurrection of Jesus Christ.

In the study of the doctrine of salvation, there shall be two headings: "The Provisions That Have Been Made," including the death, burial, resurrection, ascension, and exaltation of Jesus Christ; and "The Application of Provisions," including repentance, faith, justification, regeneration, adoption, sanctification, assurance, and security.

I. PROVISIONS THAT HAVE BEEN MADE

A. The death of Christ

In studying the life of Christ, we are struck by the many wonderful works performed by Him. The feeding of the multitudes, making water into wine, healing the sick, making the lame to walk, the dumb to speak, and the blind to see were all evidences that pointed to the fact that He was the Son of God. By these mighty works, He gave ample evidence that He was, in truth, all that He claimed to be. However, His work was not finished by the mighty deeds done in His life, the great truths He preached, and in being a blessing and a benediction to the people of His day. His primary purpose in coming to this earth was to bring salvation to the souls of men. When the angel of God spoke to Joseph about the child to be born of Mary, he said, "And she shall bring forth a son, and thou shalt call his name JESUS: for he shall save his people from their sins" (Mt. 1:21). This requires discussion of the method by which Jesus would save His people from their sins. This leads to the study of His death.

1. *The importance of the death of Christ.* Myer Pearlman says, "The outstanding event and central doctrine of the New Testament may be summed up in the words,

'Christ died (the event) for our sins (the doctrine)' 1 Cor. 15:3."[1] Christianity is unlike all other religions in the place it assigns to the death of its Founder. All other religions base their claim to greatness on the life and teaching of those who founded them, while the gospel of Jesus Christ centers around the person of Jesus Christ, including especially His death at Calvary. It has often been said that there is good in every religion. It may be true that there is some ethical value in many other teachings, but only in Christianity do we have redemption from sin. This is accomplished through the substitutionary death of the Son of God Himself.

a) The importance given to it in the Scriptures

(1) In the Old Testament—The death of Christ is foreseen throughout the Old Testament in many types and prophecies. Only a few of the most outstanding of these can be mentioned here.

(a) Types:

The coats of skins—"Unto Adam also and to his wife did the LORD God make coats of skins, and clothed them" (Gn. 3:21).

Abel's offering—"And Abel, he also brought of the firstlings of his flock and of the fat thereof. And the LORD had respect unto Abel and to his offering" (Gn. 4:4).

The offering of Isaac (Gn. 22)

The Passover Lamb (Ex. 12)

The Levitical sacrificial system (Lv. 1–7)

The brazen serpent (Nm. 21; Jn. 3:14)

The slain Lamb—"All we like sheep have gone astray; we have turned every one to his own way; and the LORD hath laid on him the iniquity of us all. He was oppressed, and he was afflicted, yet he opened not his mouth: he is brought as a lamb to the slaughter, and as sheep before her shearers is dumb, so he opened not his mouth" (Is. 53:6–7).

(b) Prophecies:

The Seed of the woman—"And I will put enmity between thee and the woman, and between thy seed and her seed; it shall bruise thy head, and thou shalt bruise his heel" (Gn. 3:15). This has been called the Protevangelium—"the first gospel."

The crucifixion scene (Ps. 22)

The vicarious suffering (Is. 53)

The cut-off Messiah—"And after threescore and two weeks shall Messiah be cut off, but not for himself" (Dn. 9:26).

The smitten Shepherd—

---

1 Myer Pearlman, *Knowing the Doctrines of the Bible* (Springfield, MO: Gospel Publishing House, 1939), 171.

And one shall say unto him, What are these wounds in thine hands? Then he shall answer, Those with which I was wounded in the house of my friends. Awake, O sword, against my shepherd, and against the man that is my fellow, saith the LORD of hosts: smite the shepherd, and the sheep shall be scattered: and I will turn mine hand upon the little ones.

—ZECHARIAH 13:6–7

In His conversation with the two disciples on the way to Emmaus on the evening of His resurrection, Jesus stated that Moses and all the prophets, indeed all the Scriptures, spoke of His death: "Ought not Christ to have suffered these things, and to enter into his glory? And beginning at Moses and all the prophets, he expounded unto them in all the scriptures the things concerning himself" (Lk. 24:26–27). It is clear from 1 Peter 1:10–11 that the sufferings of Christ were the one great subject into which the Old Testament prophets inquired and searched diligently: "Of which salvation the prophets have inquired and searched diligently, who prophesied of the grace that should come unto you: Searching what, or what manner of time the Spirit of Christ which was in them did signify, when it testified beforehand the sufferings of Christ, and the glory that should follow." When Moses and Elijah appeared with Christ on the Mount of Transfiguration, the subject of which they spoke was the death of the Savior: "And, behold, there talked with him two men, which were Moses and Elias: Who appeared in glory, and spake of his decease which he should accomplish at Jerusalem" (Lk. 9:30–31).

(2) In the New Testament—Torrey says that the death of Jesus Christ is mentioned directly more than 175 times in the New Testament.[2] Since there are 7,957 verses in the New Testament, this would mean that one out of every forty-five verses refers to this subject. Thiessen states, "The last three days of our Lord's earthly life occupy about one-fifth of the narratives in the four Gospels."[3]

b) Its relation to the Incarnation

This subject has been dealt with under that section of theology which deals with Jesus Christ, but a few pertinent Scriptures will be repeated here to emphasize the importance of His death. Jesus partook of flesh and blood in order that He might die: "Forasmuch then as the children are partakers of flesh and blood, he also himself likewise took part of the same; that through death he might destroy him that had the power of death, that is, the devil" (Heb. 2:14); "He was manifested to take away our sins" (1 Jn. 3:5). Christ came into this world for the express purpose of giving Himself

---

2 Reuben Archer Torrey, *What the Bible Teaches* (New York: Fleming H. Revell Company, 1933), 144.

3 Henry Clarence Thiessen, *Introductory Lectures in Systematic Theology* (Grand Rapids, MI: Wm. B. Eerdmans Publishing Company, 1949), 313.

as a ransom for our sins: "Even as the Son of Man came not to be ministered unto, but to minister, and to give his life a ransom for many" (Mt. 20:28); "But now once in the end of the world hath he appeared to put away sin by the sacrifice of himself" (Heb. 9:26). As Theissen well says, "His death was not an afterthought or an accident, but the accomplishment of a divine purpose in connection with the incarnation. The incarnation is not an end in itself; it is but a means to an end, and that end is the redemption of the lost through the Lord's death on the cross."[4]

c) It is one of the two fundamental truths of the gospel. Notice how Paul first emphasizes the death and burial, then the resurrection of Christ as constituting the gospel: "Moreover, brethren, I declare unto you the gospel…how that Christ died for our sins according to the scriptures; And that he was buried, and that he rose again the third day according to the scriptures" (1 Cor. 15:1, 3–4). The gospel is the good news of salvation—the forgiveness of sins through the death, burial, and resurrection of Jesus Christ.

d) Its necessity for man's salvation. Many Scriptures point out the absolute necessity of Christ's death in order that God could pardon sin and grant man His salvation. Note how often the word *must* occurs in the following passages:

> And as Moses lifted up the serpent in the wilderness, even so must the Son of Man be lifted up.
>
> —JOHN 3:14

> From that time forth began Jesus to show unto his disciples. how that he must go unto Jerusalem, and suffer many things of the elders and chief priests and scribes, and be killed, and be raised again the third day.
>
> —MATTHEW 16:21

> But first must he suffer many things, and be rejected of this generation.
>
> —LUKE 17:25

> Saying, The Son of Man must be delivered into the hands of sinful men, and be crucified, and the third day rise again.
>
> —LUKE 24:7

> Opening and alleging, that Christ must needs have suffered, and risen again from the dead.
>
> —ACTS 17:3

---

4 Thiessen, 314.

The only basis upon which a holy God could forgive sin was by His Son bearing the penalty of the sinner's guilt. He cannot forgive merely on the grounds of the sinner's repentance. It can only be because the penalty has been fully paid. God does not, as some preach, forgive sinners because He loves them. His love caused Him to give His only begotten Son to be a ransom for sin, thus the sinner can be forgiven.

George Herbert Morrison has beautifully written the following on this topic:

> Let me say that the cross is not needed and included because of God's unwillingness to pardon. Nowhere in the New Testament is the cross conceived as turning an unwilling God into a willing one, as a compulsion on a reluctant God. It is not the cause of love, it is its consequence; it is the spring of love, it is its outflow, and that is what is so often forgotten. We read in the New Testament of Christ being offered as a propitiation for our sins, and our thoughts go back to pagan faiths, where men tried to appease their angry gods; but the tremendous difference is that in all these faiths man had to provide the propitiation; in the Christian faith God…does not ask men for an atoning sacrifice; He gives the atoning sacrifice…because He loves the world and willeth not that any man should perish…It is because He is so passionately eager to forgive that God sent His Son to die.
>
> Why then was the cross needed if God eternally is love?…to me the old answer is the only answer—God is more than a private Person; God is the moral Ruler of the universe. A father forgives his child freely if the child is penitent; but if the father is a judge he cannot forgive a criminal like that, even though the criminal is his child; it is his duty to uphold and administer the law in the highest interests of the state, and if he pardoned the criminal on the ground that he was penitent, the country would lapse to lawlessness and chaos.
>
> Or again, take it that the father is a schoolmaster, and the son a pupil in the school; can he act as a schoolmaster as he can act as a father, forgiving because the child expresses sorrow? Would not that disintegrate and destroy discipline and steadily lower the morale of the whole school and inevitably lead to license?
>
> These are imperfect illustrations, but they suggest the problem of God: how to forgive, as His heart yearns to do, and at the same time to be the "judge of all the earth"; how to pardon, on the slightest sign of penitence, and yet maintain that law that lives in Him, so that men may live in the sure and splendid confidence "that justice and judgment are the habitation of (His) throne" (Ps. 89:14).
>
> There was "a problem worthy of God," as Martin Luther and Thomas Chalmers used to say: how to cancel sin, and treat it as if it were not, and yet maintain and vindicate His righteousness. And the New Testament with

unvarying iteration tells us that God solved that problem by giving His only begotten Son to die for sin...Any divine pardon that belittled law would make this world an intolerable dwelling place; but when God gave His Son to die for sin, "righteousness and peace have kissed each other" (Ps. 85:10).[5]

2. *Misunderstandings concerning the death of Christ.* In order to more fully appreciate the true scriptural teaching concerning the death of Christ, it might be good to briefly examine some of the false theories that have been advanced over the years.

a) The accident theory. This view sees Christ simply as a man and thus subject to death, as any other man. He died at the hands of a mob who did not agree with His teachings. His death was completely unforseen and had no significance whatever for anyone else. This view is held by extreme rationalists who disregard the plain teachings of Scripture.

This radical idea is easily refuted by the fact that the death of Christ was forseen and foretold throughout the Old Testament, as we have seen (Ps. 22, Is. 53, Zec. 11). Furthermore, Jesus repeatedly spoke of His future death and the manner of it: Mt. 16:21; Mk. 9:30–32; Mt. 20:17–19; and Lk. 22:19–20. John 10:17–18 clearly contradicts this false theory: "Therefore doth my Father love me, because I lay down my life, that I might take it again. No man taketh it from me, but I lay it down of myself. I have power to lay it down, and I have power to take it again. This commandment have I received of my Father."

b) The martyr theory. This theory holds that the death of Christ was no more than that of a noble martyr, such as Huss or Polycarp. Its only value for mankind is in the example which Jesus set in being true to what He believed and taught, even to being willing to die for it. This has sometimes been called the example theory. Man can be saved by repentance and reformation alone.

This idea completely ignores the scriptural teaching that Christ's death was a propitiation of God's wrath and an atonement for man's sin.

> Being justified freely by his grace through the redemption that is in Christ Jesus: Whom God set forth to be a propitiation through faith in his blood, to declare his righteousness for the remission of sins that are past, through the forebearance of God; to declare, I say, at this time his righteousness: that he might be just, and the justifier of him which believeth in Jesus.
>
> —ROMANS 3:24–26

---

5 George Herbert Morrison, *The Significance of the Cross* (New York: George H. Doran Company, 1924) as quoted in *Decision Magazine* (December 1964).

This theory fails to account for Christ's un-martyrlike attitude in asking that the cup pass from Him. (Mt. 26:42.)

c) The moral influence, or love of God theory. This holds that Christ's suffering and death were merely the natural results of His becoming flesh and suffering with, not for, His creatures. In this theory, Thiessen says, "The sufferings and death of Christ are similar to those of the missionary who enters a leper colony for life, in order to save the lepers."[6] He further points out that the theory teaches that "the love of God manifested in the incarnation, the sufferings and death of Christ, are to soften human hearts and lead them to repentance."[7] Here, then, there is no thought of the wrath of God to be propitiated and Christ dying as the substitute for our sins.

It is true that "God so loved the world, that he gave his only begotten Son" (Jn. 3:16), and that "God commendeth his love toward us, in that, while we were yet sinners, Christ died for us" (Rom. 5:8). These passages emphasize the love of God, but they also make it clear what the love of God did. The love of God did not save sinners; it caused God to be willing to give His Son to die for us and thus satisfy the just demands of His own holiness. Again quoting Thiessen, "On this theory it is difficult to explain how Old Testament believers were saved, since they did not have this object-lesson of the love of God."[8]

d) The governmental theory. The principal thought behind this theory is that God made an example of Christ and His sufferings in order to exhibit to man His displeasure with sin. God's government of the world necessitated that He show His wrath against sin. Only thus could He maintain respect for His law. As mankind realizes God's attitude toward sin, shown in the sufferings of Christ, he will be moved to repentance, which alone is necessary for salvation. The main objection which this teaching raises is, why then was the Incarnation necessary? And why must the sufferer be an innocent person? Why could not God's wrath be manifest against any sinner, rather than His only begotten Son?

3. *True meaning of the death of Christ.* In order to grasp the full extent of what was accomplished through the death of Jesus Christ, a number of different words must be used and their meaning fully understood. Man's sin was so great and God's holiness so pure that the gulf between them that had to be spanned required an amazing accomplishment on the part of our Lord. Through His death, He fully met every need of the sinner relative to sin, enabling him to enjoy eternal fellowship with God. At the same time, Christ fully met every requirement necessary for a righteous and just God to freely forgive sin and receive man back into His fellowship. At no time throughout eternity will anyone—man, devil, or angel—be able to challenge

---

6 Thiessen, 316.

7 Ibid.

8 Ibid.

the perfect and full provision of God's great salvation. We shall consider the death of Christ as it is revealed in five different words.

a) It is vicarious—a substitution. The word *vicarious* comes from *vicar*, which means "a substitute, one who takes the place of another and acts in his stead." "All we like sheep have gone astray; we have turned every one to his own way; and the LORD hath laid on him the iniquity of us all" (Is. 53:6). "Even as the Son of Man came not to be ministered unto, but to minister, and to give his life a ransom for many" (Mt. 20:28). "For he hath made him to be sin for us, who knew no sin; that we might be made the righteousness of God in him" (2 Cor. 5:21). "Who his own self bare our sins in his own body on the tree, that we, being dead to sins, should live unto righteousness" (1 Pt. 2:24). "For Christ also hath once suffered for sins, the just for the unjust, that he might bring us to God" (1 Pt. 3:18).

From these and many other Scriptures (1 Cor. 15:3; Rom. 5:8; Jn. 10:11; Gal. 2:20), it is clear that Christ was our substitute in bearing our sins on the cross. It is obvious that He did not bear His own sins: "Who did no sin, neither was guile found in his mouth" (1 Pt. 2:22); "Which of you convinceth me of sin?" (Jn. 8:46). When He died, He died for the sins of others.

It has been objected that it is immoral for God to punish an innocent person for one who is guilty, and therefore the idea of substitution is unbearable. Let it be said, first, that God knows nothing of punishing the innocent for the guilty. Jesus so took upon Himself our sin that He assumed our guilt. Secondly, it is not unlawful for a judge to himself pay the penalty he has imposed. Christ is very God, and thus had the right to pay the penalty for our sin. Thirdly, it could only be considered immoral if Jesus were compelled to be our sacrifice, but if He voluntarily took that position, no injustice was done. This He did: "Therefore doth my Father love me, because I lay down my life, that I might take it again. No man taketh it from me, but I lay it down of myself. I have power to lay it down, and I have power to take it again" (Jn. 10:17–18). Let it be fully realized that we are not saved by the murder of a man, but by One who willingly offered Himself for us.

b) It is an atonement. The word *atonement* is used in a general and a particular manner. As it is popularly used, it refers to the entire provision of salvation which God made for sinners through the sacrifice of our Lord Jesus Christ. This is the meaning as it is usually used. However, the word has a specific meaning in the Scripture. It literally means "a covering." It is an Old Testament word. The only time it occurs in the New Testament is in the Authorized Version of Romans 5:11: "And not only so, but we also joy in God through our Lord Jesus Christ, by whom we have now received the atonement." "Atonement" is universally recognized as a poor translation of the Greek word *katallage*. It should be "reconciliation," as all other translations render it.

In the Old Testament, atonement must be made for individual trespasses: "If a soul sin, and commit a trespass against the LORD....he shall bring his trespass offering unto the Lord...And the priest shall make an atonement for him before the Lord: and it shall be forgiven him for any thing of all that he hath done in trespassing therein" (Lv. 6:2, 6–7). It was also possible to make national atonement for national sins.

> And if the whole congregation of Israel sin...and are guilty...then the congregation shall offer a young bullock for the sin, and bring him before the tabernacle of the congregation. And the elders of the congregation shall lay their hands upon the head of the bullock before the LORD: and the bullock shall be killed before the LORD. ... and the priest shall make an atonement for them, and it shall be forgiven them.
>
> —LEVITICUS 4:13–15, 20

In the laying on of the hands of the elders, the sins of Israel were transferred to the sacrificial animal and he was slain as their substitute. The atonement provided a covering of the guilt of the real criminal, and made it invisible to the eye of a holy God. This thought is suggested in such Scriptures as the following: "Hide thy face from my sins, and blot out mine iniquities" (Ps. 51:9); "Thou hast cast all my sins behind thy back" (Is. 38:17); "Thou wilt cast all their sins into the depths of the sea" (Mi. 7:19). As has been said, this word *atonement* is an Old Testament word, for in Christ we have more than a covering for our sins. They are forgiven; they are completely removed. The blood of the sacrificial animals, brought by the worshiper, could only suffice to cover man's sins until Christ's precious blood should be shed to remove them: "For it is not possible that the blood of bulls and of goats should take away sins. Wherefore when he cometh into the world, he saith, Sacrifice and offering thou wouldest not, but a body hast thou prepared me....By the which will we are sanctified through the offering of the body of Jesus Christ once for all" (Heb. 10:4–5, 10).

c) It is a propitiation.

> Whom God hath set forth to be a propitiation through faith in his blood, to declare his righteousness for the remission of sins that are passed, through the forebearance of God.
>
> —ROMANS 3:25

> For he is the propitiation for our sins: and not for our's only, but also for the sins of the whole world.
>
> —1 JOHN 2:2

> Therefore, He had to be made like His brethren in all things, so that He might become a merciful and faithful high priest in all things pertaining to God, to make propitiation for the sins of the people.
>
> —HEBREWS 2:17, NASB

The word *propitiation* properly signifies the turning away of wrath by a sacrifice; thus, it signifies appeasement. "The idea of the wrath of God is stubbornly rooted in the Old Testament, where it is referred to 585 times."[9] It is also mentioned a number of times in the New Testament: "He that believeth not the Son shall not see life, but the wrath of God abideth on him" (Jn. 3:36); "For the wrath of God is revealed from heaven against all ungodliness and unrighteousness of men" (Rom. 1:18); "Let no man deceive you with vain words: for because of these things cometh the wrath of God upon the children of disobedience" (Eph. 5:6). (See also Rom. 2:5; 5:9; 1 Thes. 1:10; Heb. 3:11; Rv. 19:15.)

In the passages quoted above, it will be seen that Paul views Christ's death as the means of removing God's wrath (Rom. 5:9). The amazing paradox is that God Himself provided the means of removing His own wrath. We also observe that it is the Father's love that "sent his Son to be the propitiation for our sins" (1 Jn. 4:10); that the reason Christ became "a merciful and faithful high priest" was "to make reconciliation for the sins of the people" (Heb. 2:17); and that His propitiation is adequate for all (1 Jn. 2:2). According to Leon Morris, "The consistent Bible view is that the sin of man has incurred the wrath of God. That wrath is averted only by Christ's atoning offering. From this standpoint his saving work is properly called propitiation."[10]

d) It is a reconciliation. The need of reconciliation is apparent because of the enmity between God and man, brought about by man's sin. Through the sacrifice of Jesus Christ, this condition of enmity can be changed into one of peace and fellowship. This is one of the greatest blessings of personal salvation. Again, this new relationship magnifies the grace of God, for no man can reconcile himself to God. God Himself wrought this reconciliation for us through Christ. We were reconciled to God through the death of His Son. "For if, when we were reconciled to God by the death of His Son, much more, being reconciled, we shall be saved by his life" (Rom. 5:10). "And you, that were sometime alienated and enemies in your mind by wicked works, yet now hath he reconciled" (Col. 1:21). Colossians 1:20 tells us that this was accomplished through the blood of His cross: "And, having made peace through the blood of his cross, by him to reconcile all things unto himself."

---

9 Everett F. Harrison, ed., *Baker's Dictionary of Theology* (Grand Rapids, MI: Baker Book House, 1960), 425.

10 Ibid., 425.

The Scripture applies this word of reconciliation to both God and man: "All things are of God, who hath reconciled us to himself by Jesus Christ, and hath given to us the ministry of reconciliation....Now then we are ambassadors for Christ, as though God did beseech you by us: we pray you in Christ's stead, be ye reconciled to God" (2 Cor. 5:18, 20). Theissen explains:

> The thought is something like this: At first God and man stood face to face with each other. In sinning, Adam turned his back upon God. Then God turned his back upon Adam. Christ's death has satisfied the demands of God and now God has again turned His face toward man. It remains for man to turn round about and face God. Since God has been reconciled by the death of his Son, man is now entreated to be reconciled to God.[11]

e) It is a ransom or redemption. The word *redemption* signifies a releasing or liberation from captivity, slavery, or death by the payment of a price, called a ransom. Thus the word has a double significance: it means the payment of a price, as well as the deliverance of the captive. The death of Christ on the cross is seen in Scripture as the price which Jesus paid for the deliverance of the sinner: "Even as the Son of Man came not to be ministered unto, but to minister, and to give his life a ransom for many" (Mt. 20:28). The deliverance which Jesus obtained is called redemption: "Neither by the blood of goats and calves, but by his own blood he entered in once into the holy place, having obtained eternal redemption for us" (Heb. 9:12).

According to the New Testament, we have redemption from the following:

(1) From the penalty of the Law—Paul calls this the "curse of the law": "Christ hath redeemed us from the curse of the law, being made a curse for us: for it is written, Cursed is every one that hangeth on a tree" (Gal. 3:13).

(2) From the Law itself—"Wherefore, my brethren, ye also are become dead to the law by the body of Christ" (Rom. 7:4). We are now under grace: "For sin shall not have dominion over you: for ye are not under law, but under grace" (Rom. 6:14).

(3) From sin as a power in one's life—"Knowing this, that our old man is crucified with him, that the body of sin might be destroyed, that henceforth we should not serve sin" (Rom. 6:6). "How shall we, that are dead to sin, live any longer therein?" (Rom. 6:2). (See also Ti. 2:14; 1 Pt. 1:18–19; Rom. 6:12–14.)

(4) From Satan—"And that they may recover themselves out of the snare of the devil, who are taken captive by him at his will" (2 Tm. 2:26). "Forasmuch then as the children are partakers of flesh and blood, he also himself likewise took part of the same; that through death he might destroy him that had the power of death, that is,

---

11 Theissen, 327.

the devil: And deliver them who through fear of death were all their lifetime subject to bondage" (Heb. 2:14–15).

(5) From all evil, including our present mortal body—"Who gave himself for our sins, that he might deliver us from this present evil world, according to the will of God and our Father" (Gal. 1:4). "Which is the earnest of our inheritance until the redemption of the purchased possession, unto the praise of his glory" (Eph. 1:14). "And not only they, but ourselves also…waiting for the adoption, to wit, the redemption of our body" (Rom. 8:23). This final consummation of our redemption will be realized at our Lord's second coming: "And when these things begin to come to pass, then look up, and lift up your heads; for your redemption draweth nigh" (Lk. 21:28).

To summarize the benefits of Christ's death: When we speak of it as vicarious, we think of substitution. When we speak of it as an atonement, we think of covering. As a propitiation, we think of appeasement. As a reconciliation, we think of enmity. And as a ransom, we think of redemption.

4. *Those for whom Christ died.* This is a very vital question because of the many theories held within the Christian Church. The Calvinistic theory of a limited atonement teaches that Christ died only for the elect, whom He had previously chosen. Let us see what the Bible says.

a) For the Church. There is no doubt that Christ died for those believers who are the members of His body, the Church.

> Husbands, love your wives, even as Christ also loved the church, and gave himself for it; That he might sanctify and cleanse it with the washing of water by the word, That he might present it to himself a glorious church, not having spot, or wrinkle, or any such thing; but that it should be holy and without blemish.
>
> —Ephesians 5:25–27

> As the Father knoweth me, even so know I the Father: and I lay down my life for the sheep.
>
> —John 10:15

> I pray for them: I pray not for the world, but for them which thou hast given me; for they are thine.…Holy Father, keep through thine own name those whom thou hast given me, that they may be one, as we are.
>
> —John 17:9–11

b) For the entire world. There is an even larger volume of Scripture to show that Christ died for the whole world—for each individual: "All we like sheep have gone astray; we have turned every one to his own way; and the LORD hath laid on him the iniquity of us all" (Is. 53:6); "Behold the Lamb of God, which taketh away the sin of the world" (Jn. 1:29); "Who gave himself a ransom for all" (1 Tm. 2:6); "And he is the propitiation for our sins: and not for ours only, but also for the sins of the whole world" (1 Jn. 2:2). Perhaps the strongest verse against the doctrine of a limited atonement is 2 Peter 2:1: "But there were false prophets also among the people, even as there shall be false teachers among you, who privily shall bring in damnable heresies, even denying the Lord that bought them and bring upon themselves swift destruction." Here it is positively said that Christ bought these who are definitely false prophets, who shall be destroyed. Note also the clear implication in the following two verses that Christ died for some, even though they will be lost: "But if thy brother be grieved with thy meat, now walkest thou not charitably. Destroy not him with thy meat, for whom Christ died" (Rom. 14:15); "And through thy knowledge shall the weak brother perish, for whom Christ died?" (1 Cor. 8:11). Not a single individual man or woman or child is excluded from the blessings offered in the Atonement: "But we see Jesus, who was made a little lower than the angels for the suffering of death, crowned with glory and honor; that he by the grace of God should taste death for every man" (Heb. 2:9).

The following question, quite naturally, comes to mind: if Christ died for all, why then are not all saved? The answer lies in the simple but plain fact that each one must experience a believing faith that Christ died for him before he can participate in the benefits of His death for himself. Jesus said, "If ye believe not that I am he, ye shall die in your sins" (John 8:24). Lewis Sperry Chafer says, "The condition indicated by Christ on which they (the unbelievers) may avoid dying in their sins is not based on His not dying for them, but rather their believing on him...The value of Christ's death, as marvelous and complete as it is, is not applied to the unregenerate until they believe."[12] This matter of the necessity of a personal application, by faith, of the saving grace of Jesus Christ is illustrated by the details of the Passover night. The Israelite family was to kill a lamb and sprinkle the blood upon the doorposts and the lintel of their homes, and then they were to abide in the house. God said, "And the blood shall be to you for a token upon the houses where you are: and when I see the blood, I will pass over you, and the plague shall not be upon you to destroy you, when I smite the land of Egypt" (Ex. 12:13). God was not going to look out in the backyard where the lamb was slain. He was going to look upon the doorposts of each individual home. When He saw the blood there, the death angel passed by. Similarly, there must be a personal application, by faith, of the precious blood that was shed for us on Calvary.

---

12 Lewis Sperry Chafer, *Systematic Theology* (Dallas, TX: Dallas Seminary Press, 1947), III, 97.

William Evans sums it up admirably when he says:

> The atonement is *sufficient* for all; it is *efficient* for those who believe in
> Christ. The atonement itself, so far as it lays the basis for the redemptive
> dealing of God with men is *unlimited*; the application of the atonement is
> *limited* to those who actually believe in Christ. He is the Savior of all men
> *potentially*; of believers alone *effectually*. "For therefore we both labor and
> suffer reproach, because we trust in the living God, who is the Saviour of all
> men, specially of those that believe" (1 Tm. 4:10).[13]

c) What about infants?—Does the grace of God cover infants and little children
until they come to the age of accountability, or moral responsibility? If Jesus did indeed
die for all, then it would seem that these little ones would be included in His atonement. If Christ died for all men, then the sins of all are potentially covered because of
the shedding of His precious blood. But there is a special sin which Jesus said the Holy
Spirit would condemn—the sin of unbelief: "And when he is come, he will reprove
[convict] the world of sin...because they believe not on me" (Jn. 16:8–9). The Holy
Spirit gives a whole new dimension to sin. Unbelief is a sin of which conscience will
never convict a man. In not believing on Jesus Christ and thus rejecting His salvation,
man fails to take advantage of the forgiveness which He provided by His death. Thus
the whole guilt of man's sin is heaped back upon himself. This sin is not possible
for a child before he attains the age of accountability; thus, the saving grace of Jesus
Christ still avails for him. It is impossible to state when a child will reach this point
of accountability. With some it is as early as three or four years, while with others it
may be five or six years of age.

B. Resurrection of Jesus Christ

It seems almost incredible that a fair-sized branch of the Christian Church
perceives the resurrection of Jesus Christ to be an act primarily affecting Him only,
rather than as an event with repercussions that are relevant for their own lives. As we
pursue this study we will see how essential and how glorious is the fact of our Lord's
resurrection.

1. *Importance of the resurrection of Christ*

a) It is one of the two primary doctrines of the gospel. "Moreover, brethren, I
declare unto you the gospel....how that Christ died for our sins according to the
scriptures; And that he was buried, and that he rose again on the third day according
to the scriptures" (1 Cor. 15:1, 3–4). It is impossible and useless to try to determine

---

13 William E. Evans, *The Great Doctrines of the Bible* (Chicago: The Bible Institute Colportage
Association, 1912), 79.

which is the more important: His death or His resurrection, for the one without the other could never have been sufficient for the salvation of men. If Christ had remained in the grave, His death would have been no more than that of any martyr for the Christian faith. He could have given us nothing better than a philosophy. Yet, without the vicarious sacrifice of His death, His resurrection would have presented no saving power.

It was His resurrection which demonstrated that He was the Son of God: "Concerning his Son Jesus Christ our Lord, which was made of the seed of David according to the flesh; And declared to be the Son of God with power, according to the spirit of holiness, by the resurrection from the dead" (Rom. 1:3–4). His resurrection proves that His death was of sufficient value to God to cover all our sins, for His sacrifice was the sacrifice of the Son of God.

b) It was the foundation stone on which the Church was built. In the famous passage from 1 Corinthians 15:13–19 is found "one of the most potent negative suppositions that can be made in connection with the Christian faith."[14] Paul lists five negative facts about the Resurrection which, if they were true, would divest the gospel of all its power and blessing.

(1) Our preaching is vain—"If Christ be not risen, then is our preaching vain" (v. 14). Without the Resurrection, our gospel is robbed of its note of joy and is changed into a funeral dirge. It would become a gospel of death, a mere biography of a man that lived an extraordinary life, but died an ordinary, though ignominious, death— "even the death of the cross" (Phil. 2:8). Our gospel would be emptied of its power. Unless Jesus gained a victory at Calvary, as evidenced by His resurrection over death, hell, and the grave, then we are still victims. It took the victory of the open tomb and the power of the risen Lord to give effectuality to the gospel.

(2) Faith is vain—"Your faith is also vain" (v. 14). All that you have accepted by faith as a free gift from God through Jesus Christ—divine sonship, eternal life, justification, sanctification, glorification, and a home in heaven—you did not receive at all if Christ be not risen. Paul repeats the same in verse 17. Faith is always impotent unless its object gives it power.

(3) The apostles are false witnesses—"Yea, and we are found false witnesses of God; because we have testified of God that he raised up Christ: whom he raised not up, if so be that the dead rise not" (v. 15). An essential qualification of apostleship was that he be a witness of Christ's resurrection: "Wherefore of these men which have companioned with us all the time that the Lord Jesus went in and out among us, Beginning from the baptism of John, unto that same day he was taken up from us, must one be ordained to be a witness with us of his resurrection" (Acts 1:21–22).

---

14 Emery H. Bancroft, *Christian Theology* (Grand Rapids. MI: Zondervan Publishing House, 1976), 84.

In selecting a successor to Judas, one of the prerequisites was that he be a witness of Christ's resurrection. These men were false witnesses if Christ is not risen. If Christ be not risen, the whole fabric of scriptural authenticity breaks down and leaves us without a shred of scriptural authority.

(4) Believers are yet in their sins—"Ye are yet in your sins" (v. 17). "For there is none other name under heaven given among men, whereby we must be saved" (Acts 4:12). "Thou shalt call his name JESUS: for he shall save his people from their sins" (Mt. 1:21). But, if Christ is not risen, He possesses no more saving efficacy than that of any other great character from history. It took the resurrection of Jesus Christ to show the justifying value of His death.

(5) Those who have died are perished—"Then they also which are fallen asleep in Christ are perished. If in this life only we have hope in Christ, we are of all men most miserable" (vv. 18–19). It is better to sorrow as those who have no hope than to sorrow as those who have a false hope. The hope that sustained the martyrs in their sacrifice and that sustained multitudes since then who have died in the faith was a false hope "if Christ be not risen." But away with the thought. Paul triumphantly declares, "But now is Christ risen from the dead, and become the firstfruits of them that slept" (1 Cor. 15:20).[15]

One cannot but be impressed as he reads the early chapters of the book of Acts with the prominent place given by the apostles to the truth of the resurrection of Jesus Christ. The very first sermon preached after the outpouring of the Holy Spirit on the Day of Pentecost is almost entirely on the theme of the resurrection of Jesus (Acts 2:22–36). The second great recorded sermon, preached by Peter from Solomon's porch of the temple, again mentions this great fact: "And killed the Prince of life, whom God raised from the dead; whereof we are witnesses" (Acts 3:15). Speaking later before the Sanhedrin, Peter does not let the opportunity pass without bearing witness that Jesus lives again: "Be it known unto you all, and to all the people of Israel, that by the name of Jesus Christ of Nazareth, whom ye crucified, whom God raised from the dead, even by him doth this man stand here before you whole" (Acts 4:10). There was hardly ever a message preached, either to one person or to a multitude, which did not mention Christ's resurrection. Acts 4:33 summarizes the entire early ministry of the apostles: "With great power gave the apostles witness of the resurrection of the Lord Jesus: and great grace was upon them all." See the following as examples of this in the apostles' and Paul's ministry: Acts 2:24, 32; 3:26; 10:40; 13:30–37; 17:31; Rom. 4:24–25; 6:4, 9; 7:4; 8:11; 10:9; 1 Cor. 6:14; 2 Cor. 4:14; Gal. 1:1; Eph. 1:20; Col. 2:12; 1 Thes. 1:10; 2 Tm. 2:8; and 1 Pt. 1:21.

2. *Nature and manner of Christ's resurrection*

---

15 Ibid., 84–87; several thoughts on the passage from 1 Cor. 15:13–19.

a) His resurrection was by the work of the entire Trinity.

(1) By God the Father—"And what is the exceeding greatness of his power to usward who believe, according to the working of his mighty power, Which he wrought in Christ, when he raised him from the dead" (Eph. 1:19–20). "Whom God raised up, having loosed the pains of death: because it was not possible that he should be holden of it" (Acts 2:24). "Him God raised up the third day, and shewed him openly" (Acts 10:40). "But God raised him from the dead" (Acts 13:30). (See Rom. 10:9; Col. 2:12; Rom 6:4.)

(2) By His own power—"Therefore doth my Father love me, because I lay down my life, that I might take it again. No man taketh it from me, but I lay it down of myself. I have power to lay it down, and I have power to take it again" (Jn. 10:17–18). When He speaks of His own body under the image of a temple, He represents its restoration as His own work: "Destroy this temple, and in three days I will raise it up" (Jn. 2:19). This does not mean that Jesus acted separately from the Father, but it does show that in this great miracle He was not passive. Think of the fact of a dead man raising himself!

(3) By the power of the Holy Spirit—"For Christ also hath once suffered for sins, the just for the unjust, that he might bring us to God, being put to death in the flesh, but quickened by the Spirit" (1 Pt. 3:18). "But if the Spirit of him that raised up Jesus from the dead dwell in you, he that raised up Christ from the dead shall also quicken your mortal bodies by his Spirit that dwelleth in you" (Rom. 8:11).

b) It was an actual resurrection. Jesus actually died. The swoon theory says that He merely swooned upon the cross and pitying hands took Him down, thinking that He had died. Then the cool air of the tomb in which He was laid revived Him so that He came forth as though He had really risen from the dead. This theory is obviously completely false. He appeared to His disciples in the full bloom of health and strength, otherwise He could not have had the effect upon them which He did. The results of hanging on a cross for six hours left a human body in such physical condition that it could not have been restored in only three days. Note the following proofs of His actual death:

(1) The soldiers saw that He was dead—"But when they came to Jesus, and saw that he was dead already, they brake not his legs" (Jn. 19:33). These were professional Roman soldiers who were used to conducting crucifixions and could not be deceived that their work was not finished.

(2) The centurion attested to His death—The centurion in charge of the crucifixion brought his personal report to Pilate. He assured the Roman governor that Jesus was indeed dead: "And Pilate marvelled if he were already dead: and calling unto him the centurion, he asked him whether he had been any while dead. And when he knew it of the centurion, he gave the body to Joseph" (Mk. 15:44–45).

(3) Blood and water flowed from His side—In order to ensure that not the slightest possibility would exist that any life remained in the body of Jesus, one of the soldiers pierced the side of Jesus with his lance or spear: "But one of the soldiers with a spear pierced his side, and forthwith came there out blood and water" (Jn. 19:34). Authorities have claimed that the flowing forth of the blood and water is a physiological evidence that His heart was ruptured, making his death almost instantaneous. William Hendriksen in *New Testament Commentary, Exposition of the Gospel of John,* quotes from an article in *Calvin Forum* written by Dr. Stuart Bergsma, a prominent physician in Grand Rapids, Michigan, to the effect that blood and water flowing from a spear wound could have only come from a ruptured heart.[16]

(4) Joseph of Arimathaea believed He was dead—"Joseph of Arimathaea, an honorable counsellor, which also waited for the kingdom of God, came, and went in boldly unto Pilate, and craved the body of Jesus" (Mk. 15:43).

(5) The women who had stood by His cross believed He died—As soon as the Sabbath day was past, they came with spices to anoint the dead body: "And when the sabbath was past, Mary Magdalene, and Mary the mother of James, and Salome, had brought sweet spices, that they might come and anoint him" (Mk. 16:1).

(6) Jesus said He died—Jesus, who is the Truth, declared that He died: "I am he that liveth, and was dead" (Rv. 1:18). Thus we have every reason to believe that Christ's resurrection was a genuine resurrection of One who was indeed dead.

c) It was a bodily resurrection. The word *resurrection*, as it is used of the Lord Jesus Christ about twelve different times in the New Testament, can only signify the resurrection of the body. It is never connected with the spirit, for the spirit never dies. There is abundant proof that the body of our Lord was literally raised to life again.

(1) His resurrection body was composed of flesh and bones—It was not a phantom: "And as they thus spake, Jesus himself stood in the midst of them, and saith unto them, Peace be unto you. But they were terrified and affrighted, and supposed that they had seen a spirit. And he said unto them, Why are ye troubled? and why do thoughts arise in your hearts? Behold my hands and my feet, that it is I myself: handle me, and see; for a spirit hath not flesh and bones, as ye see me have" (Lk. 24:36–39).

(2) His resurrection body could be touched and felt. "And as they went to tell his disciples, behold, Jesus met them, saying, All hail. And they came and held him by the feet, and worshipped him" (Mt. 28:9). "Behold my hands and my feet, that it is I myself: handle me, and see" (Lk. 24:39). "Then saith he to Thomas, Reach hither thy finger, and behold my hands; and reach hither thy hand, and thrust it into my side: and be not faithless, but believing" (Jn. 20:27).

---

16 William Hendriksen, *New Testament Commentary, Exposition of the Gospel of John,* quoted from an article in *Calvin Forum* written by Dr. Stuart Bergsma (see pp. 437–439).

(3) He ate before their eyes—"And while they yet believed not for joy, and wondered, he said unto them, Have ye here any meat? And they gave him a piece of a broiled fish, and of an honeycomb. And he took it, and did eat before them" (Lk. 24:41–43).

(4) The disciples and His followers recognized Him—It is natural to suppose that they recognized Him by His physical features. "And their eyes were opened, and they knew him; and he vanished out of their sight" (Lk. 24:31). "Jesus saith unto her, Mary. She turned herself, and saith unto him, Rabboni; which is to say, Master....Mary Magdalene came and told the disciples that she had seen the Lord, and that he had spoken these things unto her" (Jn. 20:16, 18). "Then were the disciples glad, when they saw the Lord" (Jn. 20:20). "Therefore that disciple whom Jesus loved saith unto Peter, It is the Lord" (Jn. 21:7).

(5) He appeared in the same body into which the nails had been driven and the spear had been thrust—"And when he had thus spoken, he shewed them his hands and his feet" (Lk. 24:40). "And when he had so said, he shewed unto them his hands and his side" (Jn. 20:20). The Scripture indicates that these same wounds will be visible in His body when He comes again: "And they shall look upon [Him] whom they have pierced" (Zec. 12:10); "And one shall say unto him, What are these wounds in thine hands? Then he shall answer, Those with which I was wounded in the house of my friends" (Zec. 13:6); "Behold, he cometh with clouds; and every eye shall see him, and they also which pierced him" (Rv. 1:7).

(6) Jesus, Himself, had foretold His bodily resurrection—"Destroy this temple, and in three days I will raise it up....But he spake of the temple of his body. When therefore he was risen from the dead, his disciples remembered that he had said this unto them; and they believed the scripture, and the word which Jesus had said" (Jn. 2:19, 21–22).

(7) David, through the Spirit, had prophesied that His body would be raised— "For thou wilt not leave my soul in hell; neither wilt thou suffer thine Holy One to see corruption" (Ps. 16:10). The Jews, in keeping with others in eastern lands, believed that corruption of the body set in on the fourth day after death. Jesus was raised on the third day. This gives significance to Martha's words concerning her brother Lazarus, "Lord, by this time he stinketh: for he hath been dead four days" (Jn. 11:39).

d) It was a unique resurrection. Eight incidents of human bodies being raised from the dead are recorded in the Scriptures: the son of the widow at Zarephath (1 Kgs. 17:17–24); the Shunammite woman's son (2 Kgs. 4:17–27); the man who was laid on the bones of Elisha (2 Kgs. 13:21); Jairus' daughter (Mk. 5:22–43); the young man of Nain (Lk. 7:11–17); Lazarus (Jn. 11); Tabitha (Acts 9:36–43); and Eutychus (Acts 20:7–12). We have every reason to believe that these were not raised in an immortal body, but that they died again. Jesus' resurrection was more than a reversal of His death. First Timothy 6:16 tells us that He alone "hath immortality." Paul states, "Knowing that Christ being raised from the dead dieth no more; death hath no more dominion over him. For in that he died, he died unto sin once: but in that he liveth, he liveth unto God" (Rom. 6:9–10). Jesus said, "I am he that liveth, and was dead; and, behold, I am alive for evermore" (Rv. 1:18).

Though the body that was raised from Joseph's tomb was the same body in which Jesus had lived and ministered, it was somewhat different. It was a spiritual body, one not bound by physical limitations. He could enter a room though the doors were shut: "Then the same day at evening, being the first day of the week, when the doors were shut where the disciples were assembled for fear of the Jews, came Jesus and stood in the midst....And after eight days again his disciples were within, and Thomas with them: then came Jesus, the doors being shut, and stood in the midst" (Jn. 20:19, 26).

Jesus' resurrection body was also unique in that it was not recognizable at times, such as during the incident of the two disciples on the way to Emmaus (Lk. 24:13–16; Mk. 16:12–13), the occasion at the tomb when Mary mistook Him for the gardener (Jn. 20:14–15), and the disciples on Galilee after a fruitless night of fishing (Jn. 21:4–6).

3. Proofs of Christ's resurrection

a) The empty tomb. The angel bore witness that the tomb was empty: "He is not here: for he is risen, as he said. Come, see the place where the Lord lay" (Mt. 28:6). The women found the tomb empty: "And they entered in, and found not the body of the Lord Jesus" (Lk. 24:3). Mary Magdalene testified the same: "Then she runneth, and cometh to Simon Peter, and to the other disciple, whom Jesus loved, and saith unto them, They have taken away the Lord out of the sepulchre, and we know not where they have laid him" (Jn. 20:2). That His body had been stolen from the sepulchre was the story told by the soldiers only after they were bribed.

> And when they were assembled with the elders, and had taken counsel, they gave large money unto the soldiers, Saying, Say ye, His disciples came by night, and stole him away while we slept. And if this come to the governor's ears, we will persuade him, and secure you. So they took the money, and did as they were taught: and this saying is commonly reported among the Jews until this day.
>
> —MATTHEW 28:12–15

Such a happening would be entirely unlikely. The disciples were so filled with discouragement and timidity it is doubtful if they would have had the courage to perpetrate such an act. In 1879, archeologists found a Roman edict stating that during Jesus' lifetime it was illegal, under penalty of death, to rob a tomb or to move a body from one place to another. It is amazing that the enemies of Christ remembered what the disciples had forgotten: "Now the next day, that followed the day of the preparation, the chief priests and Pharisees came together unto Pilate, saying, Sir, we remember that deceiver said, while he was yet alive, After three days I will rise again. Command therefore that the sepulchre be made sure until the third day, lest his disciples come by night and steal him away" (Mt. 27:62–64). Note how well the body was secured: a huge stone was rolled over the door to the sepulchre; it was sealed with the official Roman seal; it was watched over by the Roman guard. The guards would have placed their lives in jeopardy if they had allowed the body to be stolen. Furthermore, if they were asleep (Mt. 28:13) how would they have known what took place?

b) The grave clothes. It was customary for the Jews to wind long strips of cloth around a body from the neck to the feet, preparing it for burial. "And he [John] stooping down, and looking in, saw the linen clothes lying; yet went he not in. Then cometh Simon Peter following him, and went into the sepulchre, and seeth the linen clothes lie, And the napkin, that was about his head, not lying with the linen clothes, but wrapped together in a place by itself" (Jn. 20:5–7). Of Lazarus we read, "And he that was dead came forth, bound hand and foot with graveclothes: and his face was bound about with a napkin" (Jn. 11:44). These strips of cloth would become impregnated with the vast weight of spices that were used for embalming so that they would form a sort of cocoon. (Jn. 19:39–40.) Jesus' body apparently slipped out of this, leaving the clothes undisturbed. Only the napkin about the face was removed—possibly to let it be seen that His body was not within. Anyone who attempted to steal the body would be in such haste he would not take time to unroll the cloths from the corpse and then replace the clothes as they were. Besides, why would one wish to have a nude dead body?

If the lie were true and the disciples did steal the body of the Lord, it is incredible that they would be inspired and willing to devote their lives to the propagation of a colossal falsehood. Each one of the disciples, with the possible exception of John, is reputed to have suffered a martyr's death for the message he proclaimed. It might be conceivable that if the disciples were together in a group, they would have had the courage to sustain each other and agree to die for a lie. But each was alone when he sealed his faith with his blood.

c) It was not challenged in the first century. According to Fitzwater:

> The apostles preached the resurrection of Christ immediately after it oc-
> curred, and in the very region where it took place. They placed the guilt of
> the killing of Jesus Christ upon the very ones who had committed the deed.
> If Christ had not really risen from the dead, it could and would have been

disproved; but there is no hint in history, sacred or profane, of anyone's challenging this fact of the apostles' preaching.[17]

All that would have been necessary would have been for them to have produced the dead body of our Lord.

d) Three effects that demand a cause:

(1) The Lord's Day—The fact that the early disciples, being Jews, changed their day of worship from the time-honored Sabbath to the first day of the week—and that that custom has continued down to our times—is an effect that must have had a great cause. The change was made to celebrate the fact that the Lord arose on the first day of the week (Acts 20:7, 1 Cor. 16:2).

(2) The Christian Church—There has never been another institution in all of history that has produced as much good in this life as the Christian Church, as well as giving promise of the life that is to come. The Christian Church stands alone! "The real historical evidence for the resurrection is the fact that it was believed, preached, propagated, and produced its fruit and effect in the new phenomena of the Christian Church, long before any of our gospels was written."[18]

(3) The New Testament—The New Testament is the book of the resurrection of Jesus Christ. Had it not been for this event, the book would never have been written. Evans concludes, "If Jesus Christ had remained buried in the grave, the story of His life and death would have been buried with Him...The resurrection does not grow out of the beautiful story of His life, but the beautiful story of His life grew out of the fact of His resurrection."[19]

4. Results or benefits of His resurrection

a) It provides a firm foundation for our faith. First, it solidifies our faith in God: "Who by him do believe in God, that raised him up from the dead, and gave him glory; that your faith and hope might be in God" (1 Pt. 1:21). Only God can raise the dead. He proved that He is God when He raised up Jesus. Secondly, Jesus' resurrection is a firm affirmation that He is all He claimed to be—the very Son of God: "And declared to be the son of God with power, according to the spirit of holiness, by the resurrection from the dead" (Rom. 1:4). Christ's resurrection did not *make* Him the Son of God, but rather *declared* Him to be such. Had Christ remained in the tomb, there would have been no reason to believe that He was any different from all those who had died before Him. The Jews twice asked Jesus to show them a sign by which

---

17 P. B. Fitzwater, *Christian Theology* (Grand Rapids, MI: Wm. B. Eerdmans Publishing Company, 1956), 160.

18 James Denney, *Jesus and the Gospel,* as quoted by Chafer, V, 243; cited by Everett F. Harrison in *The Christian Doctrine of Resurrection* (unpublished manuscript), 55.

19 Evans, 91.

they might believe. In each case, He gave them a sign that pointed to His death and His resurrection. The first was that of Jonah being three days and three nights in the fish's belly (Mt. 12:38–40). The second pointed to the destruction and rebuilding of the temple of His body (Jn. 2:18–21).

b) It provides an assurance of forgiveness of sins. Those who believe on Him can be assured of forgiveness of sins: "That if thou shalt confess with thy mouth the Lord Jesus, and shalt believe in thine heart that God hath raised him from the dead, thou shalt be saved" (Rom. 10:9). The sinner's justification is confirmed by the resurrection of Jesus Christ, "who was delivered for our offences, and was raised again for our justification" (Rom. 4:25). Only by His resurrection can the believer have confidence that God was satisfied with the sacrifice Christ had made in his behalf. Indeed, the new birth is said to be accomplished because of His resurrection: "Blessed be the God and Father of our Lord Jesus Christ, which according to his abundant mercy hath begotten us again unto a lively hope by the resurrection of Jesus Christ from the dead" (1 Pt. 1:3).

c) We have an understanding, merciful, and faithful High Priest in heaven. "Wherefore in all things it behoved him to be made like unto his brethren, that he might be a merciful and faithful high priest in things pertaining to God, to make reconciliation for the sins of the people" (Heb. 2:17). "Who is he that condemneth? It is Christ that died, yea rather, that is risen again, who is even at the right hand of God, who also maketh intercession for us" (Rom. 8:34). "Wherefore he is able also to save them to the uttermost that come unto God by him, seeing he ever liveth to make intercession for them" (Heb. 7:25).

d) It assures the believer of all needed power for life and service. The apostle Paul expressed the greatest desire of his life when he said, "That I may know him, and the power of his resurrection" (Phil. 3:10). The great miracle that always stirred faith in the followers of God in Old Testament days was the deliverance of the children of Israel from Egypt. Time after time, the prophets stirred faith in the people by reminding them of what God had done for their fathers at the Red Sea. The greatest demonstration of God's power in the New Testament is the raising of Jesus Christ from the dead. Indeed, this seems to be the yardstick by which God's power is measured. Paul prays that the saints at Ephesus might know "what is the exceeding greatness of his power to usward who believe, according to the working of his mighty power, Which he wrought in Christ, when he raised him from the dead" (Eph. 1:19–20). This was the power that defeated death. Note again in Ephesians 1:19 that the "exceeding greatness of his power" is "to usward who believe." This is sufficient for every day and every emergency.

e) The believer has the assurance of resurrection and immortality. "For if we believe that Jesus died and rose again, even so them also which sleep in Jesus will God bring with him" (1 Thes. 4:14). "Knowing that he which raised up the Lord

Jesus shall raise up us also by Jesus, and shall present us with you" (2 Cor. 4:14). "Because I live, ye shall live also" (Jn. 14:19). (See also Jn. 5:28–29; 6:40; Rom. 8:11; 1 Cor. 15:20–23.)

In Romans 5:14 we read, "Death reigned from Adam to Moses." As a dreaded monarch on a sepulchral throne, death had continued to reign over the sons of men. Each succeeding generation had arisen full of hope, only to go down before the same deadly foe. In Hosea 13:14, God had challenged, "O death, I will be thy plagues; O grave, I will be thy destruction," but still death reigned. But now, in the resurrection of Jesus, death was defeated! Christ defeated death, not by avoiding it, but by enduring and conquering it. Through death, He destroyed "him that had the power of death, that is, the devil" (Heb. 2:14). The power of His resurrection conquered the power of death. In one of the last pictures we have of the Savior, He has "the keys of hell and of death" (Rv. 1:18).

> So when this corruptible shall have put on incorruption, and this mortal shall have put on immortality, then shall be brought to pass the saying that is written, Death is swallowed up in victory. O death, where is thy sting? O grave, where is thy victory? The sting of death is sin; and the strength of sin is the law. But thanks be to God, which giveth us the victory through our Lord Jesus Christ.
>
> —1 CORINTHIANS 15:54–57

f) It guarantees the certainty of a day of judgment. There will be a time of judgment for both the godly and the ungodly: "Because he hath appointed a day, in the which he will judge the world in righteousness by that man whom he hath ordained; whereof he hath given assurance unto all men, in that he hath raised him from the dead" (Acts 17:31). Evans declares, "The resurrection of Christ is God's unfailing testimony to the fact of a coming day of judgment. The one is as sure as the other."[20] (See Acts 10:42; Jn. 5:22, 25–29.)

C. Ascension and exaltation of Jesus Christ

1. *His ascension.* By *the ascension of Christ*, we refer to that event when He departed from this earth in His resurrection body and was visibly taken into heaven. Mark and Luke are the only Gospel writers who speak of it: "So then after the Lord had spoken unto them, he was received up into heaven" (Mk. 16:19); "And he led them out as far as to Bethany, and he lifted up his hands, and blessed them. And it came to pass, while he blessed them, he was parted from them, and carried up into heaven" (Lk.

---

20 Evans, 96.

24:50–51). "And when he had spoken these things, while they beheld, he was taken up; and a cloud received him out of their sight" (Acts 1:9).

Jesus predicted the event of His ascension: "What and if ye shall see the Son of Man ascend up where he was before?" (Jn. 6:62). Paul taught Christ's ascension, writing, "Wherefore he saith, When he ascended up on high, he led captivity captive, and gave gifts unto men. (Now that he ascended, what is it but that he also descended first into the lower parts of the earth? He that descended is the same also that ascended up far above all heavens, that he might fill all things)" (Eph. 4:8–10). (See also Jn. 20:17; 13:1; 16:10, 16, 28; Heb. 4:14; 7:26; 1 Tm. 3:16.)

Putting together the words "ascended up far above all heavens" (Eph. 4:10), with "made higher than the heavens" (Heb. 7:26), and "passed through the heavens" (Heb. 4:14, RSV), the picture seems to be that there are several heavens, possibly the atmospheric and astronomic, through which Jesus passed on His way to the Father. William Evans suggests, "This means that He overcame all those evil principalities and powers that inhabit these heavenlies (Eph. 6) and who doubtless tried their best to keep Him from passing through the heavens to present His finished work to the Father."[21] Myer Pearlman reminds us, "Thus the ascension becomes the dividing line of two periods of Christ's life: From birth to the resurrection He is the Christ of human history, the One Who lived a perfect human life under earthly conditions. Since the ascension He is the Christ of spiritual experience, who lives in heaven and touches men through the Holy Spirit."[22]

2. His exaltation

a) The meaning of the exaltation of Christ. By *the exaltation of Christ,* we refer to the Father giving to the risen and ascended Son the place of honor and power at His right hand. This truth is taught in many places in the New Testament.

By Luke: "Therefore being by the right hand of God exalted" (Acts 2:33); "Him hath God exalted with his right hand to be a Prince and a Savior" (Acts 5:31).

By Peter: "Who is gone into heaven, and is on the right hand of God; angels and authorities and powers being made subject unto him" (1 Pt. 3:22).

By Paul: "It is Christ that died, yea rather, that is risen again, who is even at the right hand of God" (Rom. 8:34); "Which he wrought in Christ, when he raised him from the dead, and set him at his own right hand in the heavenly places" (Eph. 1:20); "If ye then be risen with Christ, seek those things which are above, where Christ sitteth on the right hand of God" (Col. 3:1); "But this man, after he had offered one sacrifice for sins for ever, sat down on the right hand of God" (Heb. 10:12).

---

21 Evans, 98.
22 Pearlman, 176.

Jesus implied it in Matthew 22:41–46 and clearly taught it in Revelation 3:21: "To him that overcometh will I grant to sit with me in my throne, even as I also overcame, and am set down with my father in his throne."

Stephen saw the glorified Lord shortly before his death. Thus, he cried, "Behold, I see the heavens opened, and the Son of Man standing on the right hand of God" (Acts 7:56). "The right hand of God" indicates a place of honor and of power. "Wherefore God also hath exalted him, and given him a name which is above every name: That at the name of Jesus every knee should bow, of things in heaven, and things in earth, and things under the earth; And that every tongue should confess that Jesus Christ is Lord, to the glory of God the Father" (Phil. 2:9–11).

b) Results of the exaltation of Christ

(1) He is now our High Priest—He is now, as our High Priest, appearing before God in our behalf: "For Christ is not entered into the holy places made with hands, which are the figures of the true, but into heaven itself, now to appear in the presence of God for us" (Heb. 9:24); "Seeing then that we have a great high priest, that is passed into the heavens, Jesus the Son of God, let us hold fast our profession" (Heb. 4:14).

(2) We are assured of access to God—It assures believers of a free access into the presence of God: "Seeing then that we have a great high priest....Let us therefore come boldly unto the throne of grace, that we may obtain mercy, and find grace to help in time of need" (Heb. 4:14–16); "There is one God, and one mediator between God and men, the man Christ Jesus" (1 Tm. 2:5).

(3) Christ, Head of the Church—"And hath put all things under his feet, and gave him to be the head over all things to the church" (Eph. 1:22). "And he is the head of the body, the church: who is the beginning, the firstborn from the dead; that in all things he might have the preeminence" (Col. 1:18).

(4) Spirit outpoured—He has poured out the Holy Spirit upon those who believe: "Nevertheless I tell you the truth; It is expedient for you that I go away: for if I go not away, the Comforter will not come unto you; but if I depart, I will send him unto you" (Jn. 16:7); "And I will pray the Father, and he shall give you another Comforter, that he may abide with you for ever" (Jn. 14:16); "Therefore being by the right hand of God exalted, and having received of the Father the promise of the Holy Ghost, he hath shed forth this, which ye now see and hear" (Acts 2:33).

(5) He gave gifts to men and to the Church—1 Cor. 12:8–10; Eph. 4:8–13.

(6) He is preparing a place for His own—"I go to prepare a place for you" (Jn. 14:2).

(7) He pledged His return—"And if I go and prepare a place for you, I will come again, and receive you unto myself; that where I am, there ye may be also" (Jn. 14:3).

3. *Practical values of the doctrines of the Ascension and Exaltation.* Myer Pearlman has given us the following five very practical and inspiring results of realizing that

our Lord and Savior has ascended and is seated in the place of honor at the Father's right hand:

a) An incentive to holiness. Consciousness of the ascended Christ, whom we look forward to seeing someday, is an incentive to holiness (Col. 3:1–4). This upward glance will counteract the downward pull of the world.

b) A right conception of the Church. The knowledge of the Ascension makes for a right conception of the Church. Belief in a merely human Christ will cause people to regard the Church as merely a human society, useful for philanthropic and moral purposes, but possessing no supernatural power or authority. On the other hand, a knowledge of the ascended Christ will result in the recognition of the Church as a supernatural organism deriving divine life from its risen Head.

c) A right attitude toward the world. Consciousness of the ascended Christ will produce a right attitude toward the world and worldly things. "For our conversation [literally, citizenship] is in heaven; from whence also we look for the Saviour, the Lord Jesus Christ" (Phil. 3:20).

d) A deep sense of personal responsibility. Faith in the ascended Christ will inspire a deep sense of personal responsibility. Belief in the ascended Christ carries with it the knowledge that an account will have to be rendered to Him someday (Rom. 14:7–9; 2 Cor. 5:9–10). The sense of a responsibility to a Master in heaven acts as a deterrent to sin and an incentive to righteousness (Eph. 6:9).

e) The joyous hope of His return. With faith in the ascended Christ is connected the joyous and blessed hope of His returning: "And if I go and prepare a place for you, I will come again, and receive you unto myself" (John 14:3).[23]

II. THE APPLICATION OF THE PROVISIONS

A. Election

The doctrine of election is one of the most controversial in all theology. Down through the centuries it has continued to divide Christians into various camps. Some books on systematic theology do not even teach this subject.

It has sometimes been presented in such an extreme manner as to make it sound as though those who are elected will certainly be saved, regardless of their response to the gospel and their manner of living. Contrarily, those who are chosen to be lost are said to perish eternally, regardless of any endeavor to come to God through faith in Christ.

This extreme position is based on the so-called doctrines of unconditional election, which teaches that the elect are chosen completely apart from any repentance

---

23 Pearlman, 181.

and faith on their part; and limited atonement, that Christ did not die for all mankind, but only for those whom He chose. It is also based on the teaching that God's general call to all men to come to Christ is not a sincere call—that He only "efficiently calls" (intending to bring to pass) those whom He has previously elected for salvation. However, Scripture shows that Christ did die for all mankind and that He bids all who labor and are heavy laden to come unto Him. (See section I.A., "The death of Christ.")

What is election? Thiessen says that, in its redemptive sense, election is, "That sovereign act of God in grace whereby He chose in Christ Jesus for salvation all those whom He foreknew would accept Him."[24]

Election is a sovereign act of God because, being God, He does not have to consult with, nor ask the opinion of, anyone else. Inasmuch as the Scripture teaches that election took place "before the foundation of the world" (Eph. 1:4), there was none with whom God could consult. All men have sinned and are guilty before God, so He was not under any obligation whatsoever to provide salvation for any.

Election is an act of God in grace for this same reason. All mankind has sinned and deserves nothing but condemnation. Sinful man can do nothing of himself whereby he could be considered worthy of salvation. Thus, any offer of eternal life must be of grace.

It is "in Christ Jesus," as Thiessen says, because He alone could provide the righteousness which man needed. God could not choose man in himself, so He chose him in Christ.

Election is always said to be according to God's foreknowledge.

> And we know that all things work together for good to them that love God, to them who are the called according to his purpose. For whom he did foreknow, he also did predestinate to be conformed to the image of his Son, that he might be the firstborn among many brethren. Moreover whom he did predestinate, them he also called: and whom he called, them he also justified: and whom he justified, them he also glorified.
> —ROMANS 8:28–30

> Peter, an apostle of Jesus Christ, to the strangers scattered throughout Pontus, Galatia, Cappadocia, Asia, and Bithynia, Elect according to the foreknowledge of God the Father, through sanctification of the Spirit, unto obedience and sprinkling of the blood of Jesus Christ.
> —1 PETER 1:1–2

---

24 Thiessen, 344.

We must clearly distinguish between God's foreknowledge and His foreordaining. It is not right to say that God foreknew all things because He arbitrarily determined to bring them to pass. God, in His foreknowledge, looks ahead to events much as we look back upon them. Foreknowledge no more changes the nature of future events than afterknowledge can change a historical fact. There is a difference between what God determines to bring to pass and what He merely permits to happen. Thiessen asserts:

> Certainly only few who hold the view of "unconditional election" would teach that God is the efficient cause of sin: practically all would agree that God merely permitted sin to enter the universe, and all would admit that He foresaw that it would enter, before He created anything. If, then, God could foresee that sin would enter the universe without efficiently decreeing that it should enter, then He can also forsee how men will act without efficiently decreeing how they shall act.[25]

Ephesians 1:3–5 makes it very clear that believers were chosen in Christ Jesus.

> Blessed be the God and Father of our Lord Jesus Christ, who hath blessed us with all spiritual blessings in heavenly places in Christ: According as he hath chosen us in him before the foundation of the world, that we should be holy and without blame before him in love: Having predestinated us unto the adoption of children by Jesus Christ to himself, according to the good pleasure of his will.

Having chosen His own "in Christ," God was not looking at man in himself, but as he is in Christ. Those who were chosen are those who were in Christ. By His foreknowledge, God already saw them there when He made the choice. Those who are in Christ are sinners who have believed in the redeeming blood of Christ, through which they have been united with Him as members of His body.

There is no virtue whatever in this faith. Men are not saved because they believe, but through believing. Believers were forseen by God in Christ when He chose them. How did they get there? Through faith in His dear Son. He did not determine who should be there. He simply saw them there in Christ when He chose them.

The Bible does not teach selection, but election. Nowhere does the Bible teach that some are predestined to be damned. This would be unnecessary, inasmuch as all are sinners and on their way to eternal condemnation.

---

25 Thiessen, 346.

> And you hath he quickened, who were dead in trespasses and sins; Wherein in time past ye walked according to the course of this world, according to the prince of the power of the air, the spirit that now worketh in the children of disobedience: Among whom also we all had our conversation in times past in the lusts of our flesh, fulfilling the desires of the flesh and of the mind; and were by nature the children of wrath, even as others.... at that time ye were without Christ, being aliens from the commonwealth of Israel, and strangers from the covenants of promise, having no hope, and without God in the world.
>
> —EPHESIANS 2:1–3, 12

It is not a man's non-election that leads to eternal ruin; it is his sin and failure to accept Jesus Christ. Every man is free to accept Christ as his personal Savior, if he will. Not only is he invited, he is urged to do so. Christ has made every provision for him. "But we see Jesus, who was made a little lower than the angels for the suffering of death, crowned with glory and honor; that he by the grace of God should taste death for every man" (Heb. 2:9). "The times of this ignorance God winked at; but now commandeth all men every where to repent" (Acts 17:30).

Many of the problems that have arisen in the Church over this doctrine of election have come because some have applied it to the unsaved. It is truth for those who are already in Christ. It is universally recognized, within the body of believers, that the epistle of Paul to the Romans is the most orderly setting-forth of the plan of salvation that we have in the Bible. It will be noticed that the apostle does not deal with the subject of election until he has passed the eighth chapter, which concludes with the truth that there is no separation from Christ.

The story has often been told, as a parable, of the man laboring up the hill laden down with his sin and condemnation. He sees the door of salvation up ahead of him, and over it is written, Whosoever will may come. He rejoices as he enters, and his burden is rolled away. Once inside the gateway of salvation, he looks up on the inside of the arch and discovers the words, Chosen in Him before the foundation of the world. What a glorious truth to discover after one has found the peace of sins forgiven, as he has placed his faith in the redeeming sacrifice of Jesus Christ!

Let no idea with regard to this doctrine of election in any way hinder the preaching of the gospel to all mankind. The Great Commission is still the obligation of the Church of Jesus Christ: "Go ye into all the world, and preach the gospel to every creature. He that believeth and is baptized shall be saved; but he that believeth not shall be damned" (Mk. 16:15–16).

Election, being a doctrine wholly of God's sovereignty, must be followed by those steps toward the personal experience of salvation which are required of the sinner:

repentance and faith. Each of these will be considered in the two sections that follow.

B. Repentance

Repentance is a subject rarely preached on in our Churches today. Some have even taught that it is not necessary, that we are living in a different dispensation which does not require it. They quote Paul's words to the Philippian jailor's question, "Sirs, what must I do to be saved?" Paul's reply was, "Believe on the Lord Jesus Christ, and thou shalt be saved, and thy house" (Acts 16:30–31). Because Paul did not mention repentance, we are told all we need to do is to believe in order to be saved today. Repentance has to do with turning from sin, and unfortunately the sinfulness of sin is something very seldom emphasized in our day. It is doubtful if a person is ever born again if he does not fully realize that the question of his sin has been dealt with by the Lord Jesus Christ. Many are being asked to come to Christ simply on the basis of blessings to be received and the joy to be experienced. Jesus Christ met the sin question for us, and it is of the greatest importance that we turn from our sin before we can believe on Him as our Savior.

1. *Definition.* The root meaning of *repentance* is a change of mind or purpose. It is a "sincere and thorough changing of the mind and disposition in regard to sin." It involves a change of view, a change of feeling, and a change of purpose. Thus we can say it contains three elements: the intellectual, the emotional, and the voluntary.

a) The intellectual element. This involves a change of view. It is a change of view with regard to sin, God, and self. Sin comes to be recognized not merely as a weakness, an unfortunate happening, or a mistake, but as a personal guilt: "For I acknowledge my transgressions: and my sin is ever before me" (Ps. 51:3); "For by the law is the knowledge of sin" (Rom. 3:20). Furthermore, sin is recognized to be a transgression against God. From a human viewpoint, David's sin was against Bathsheba and Uriah, her husband, but David came to realize that it was also against the laws of God. He cried, "Against thee, thee only, have I sinned, and done this evil in thy sight" (Ps. 51:4). Sin is also recognized in its relationship to one's self. Not only is it seen to be as guilt before God, but as that which defiles and pollutes self. Recognizing this, David prays, "Purge me with hyssop, and I shall be clean: wash me, and I shall be whiter than snow" (Ps. 51:7). As Job received a new vision of God, he said, "I have heard of thee by the hearing of the ear: but now mine eye seeth thee. Wherefore I abhor myself, and repent in dust and ashes" (Jb. 42:5–6). This intellectual element of repentance is very important, but if it is not followed by the next two elements, it may only bring fear of punishment with yet no real hatred of sin.

b) The emotional element. Repentance has often been defined as "a godly sorrow for sin." Writing his second letter to the Corinthians, Paul said, "Now I rejoice, not that ye were made sorry, but that ye sorrowed to repentance: for ye were made sorry after a godly manner, that ye might receive damage by us in nothing. For godly sorrow worketh repentance not to be repented of: but the sorrow of the world worketh death" (2 Cor. 7:9–10). In Luke 18:13 Jesus pictured the publican smiting himself upon his breast: "And the publican, standing afar off, would not lift up so much as his eyes unto heaven, but smote upon his breast, saying, God be merciful to me a sinner." There is no way by which we may measure how much emotion is necessary in true repentance, but certainly there is a real stirring of the heart when one is brought face to face with his own dread sin. Not uncommonly, tears accompany a repentant heart. However, one must distinguish between true sorrow because of his sin and the mere feeling of shame for it. There is a vast difference between remorse and repentance. A person may merely be sorry that he was caught in the act of sin and not truly repentant because of his sin. This could simply be remorse. Sorrow for sin must be followed by the voluntary element.

c) The voluntary element. Billy Sunday used to say, "Religion is not something for your handkerchief but for your backbone." There must be the exercise of the will for repentance to be truly effective. This means an inward turning from sin and a whole-hearted turning to Christ for forgiveness. One of the words used for *repentance* means "to turn." This is illustrated in the story of the prodigal who said, "I will arise and go to my father.... And he arose, and came to his father" (Lk. 15:18, 20). As repentance touches the will, it will result in:

(1) Confessing sin—"For I will declare my iniquity; I will be sorry for my sin" (Ps. 38:18). "I have sinned against heaven" (Lk. 15:21).

(2) Forsaking sin—"He that covereth his sins shall not prosper: but whoso confesseth and forsaketh them shall have mercy" (Prv. 28:13). "Let the wicked forsake his way, and the unrighteous man his thoughts" (Is. 55:7).

(3) Turning to God—"Let the wicked forsake his way, and the unrighteous man his thoughts: and let him return unto the LORD" (Is. 55:7). We must not only turn from sin, but unto God (1 Thes. 1:9; Acts 26:18).

d) Not something meritorious. Repentance must never be thought of as something meritorious—a "work" to be done in order that God will grant salvation. Theissen points out that we are not saved for repenting, but if we repent.[26] The Douay Version translates the word *repent* as "do penance," thus the Roman Catholic Church views repentance as a satisfaction which the sinner presents to God. This is a false translation and pictures the sinner as able to do something for his salvation, instead of realizing his helplessness and seeing that his salvation is totally of God's provision through His marvelous grace.

---

26 Thiessen, 354.

2. *Importance of repentance.* The importance of this subject is emphasized by the large place given to it in the Scriptures, both Old and New Testament, as well as in the ministry of Jesus and the early preachers of the gospel.

a) In the Old Testament. The following Old Testament Scriptures highlight the place that repentance should have in Israel's relationship with God:

> If thou shalt hearken unto the voice of the LORD thy God, to keep his commandments and his statutes which are written in this book of the law, and if thou turn unto the LORD thy God with all thine heart, and with all thy soul.
>
> —DEUTERONOMY 30:10

> Turn ye from your evil ways, and keep my commandments and my statutes, according to all the law which I commanded your fathers, and which I sent to you by my servants the prophets.
>
> —2 KINGS 17:13

> I hearkened and heard, but they spake not aright: no man repented him of his wickedness, saying, What have I done? every one turned to his course, as the horse rusheth into the battle.
>
> —JEREMIAH 8:6

> Therefore say unto the house of Israel, thus saith the Lord GOD; Repent, and turn yourselves from your idols; and turn away your faces from all your abominations.
>
> —EZEKIEL 14:6

> Therefore I will judge you, O house of Israel, every one according to his ways, saith the Lord GOD. Repent, and turn yourselves from all your transgressions; so iniquity shall not be your ruin.
>
> —EZEKIEL 18:30

> If my people, which are called by my name, shall humble themselves, and pray, and seek my face, and turn from their wicked ways; then will I hear from heaven, and will forgive their sin, and will heal their land.
>
> —2 CHRONICLES 7:14

b) In the New Testament

(1) John the Baptist—Repentance was the keynote in the preaching of John the Baptist: "Preaching in the wilderness of Judaea, And saying, Repent ye: for the kingdom of heaven is at hand" (Mt. 3:1–2). John the Baptist came as the forerunner

of Jesus to prepare the hearts of the nation of Israel for their Messiah. The preparation that was necessary was repentance, and it is still so in every sinful heart.

(2) Jesus—Repentance occupied a large place in the preaching of Jesus: "From that time Jesus began to preach, and to say, Repent: for the kingdom of heaven is at hand" (Mt. 4:17); "I am not come to call the righteous, but sinners to repentance" (Mt. 9:13); "Then began he to upbraid the cities wherein most of his mighty works were done, because they repented not" (Mt. 11:20); "The men of Ninevah shall rise in judgment with this generation, and shall condemn it: because they repented at the preaching of Jonas; and, behold, a greater than Jonas is here" (Mt. 12:41).

(3) The Disciples—The twelve disciples preached repentance: "And they went out, and preached that men should repent" (Mk. 6:12).

(4) In the Great Commission—"That repentance and remission of sins should be preached in his name among all nations, beginning at Jerusalem" (Lk. 24:47).

(5) Peter—Peter preached repentance: "Then said Peter unto them, Repent and be baptized every one of you" (Acts 2:38). (See also Acts 3:19, 5:31, 8:22, 11:18.)

(6) Paul—Paul preached repentance: "Testifying both to the Jews, and also to the Greeks, repentance toward God, and faith toward our Lord Jesus Christ" (Acts 20:21). (See also Acts 26:20; 2 Cor. 12:21; 2 Tm. 2:25.)

c) Repentance is the will of God for every man. "The Lord is…longsuffering to us-ward, not willing that any should perish, but that all should come to repentance" (2 Pt. 3:9).

(1) The command of the Lord—It is the command of the Lord that all men repent: "And the times of this ignorance God winked at; but now commandeth all men every where to repent" (Acts 17:30).

(2) Failure will result in eternal death—Men will perish eternally if they do not repent: "I tell you, Nay: but, except ye repent, ye shall all likewise perish" (Lk. 13:3).

(3) Brings joy in heaven—Repentance of sinners on Earth brings great joy in heaven: "I say unto you, that likewise joy shall be in heaven over one sinner that repenteth, more than over ninety and nine just persons, which need no repentance" (Lk. 15:7).

3. *Manner in which repentance is produced.* Jesus taught that miracles of themselves will not produce repentance: "Then began he to upbraid the cities wherein most of his mighty works were done, because they repented not: Woe unto thee, Chorazin! woe unto thee, Bethsaida! for if the mighty works, which were done in you, had been done in Tyre and Sidon, they would have repented long ago in sackcloth and ashes" (Mt. 11:20–21).

Our Lord taught that even the coming of one back from the dead would not, of itself, produce repentance: "And he said, Nay, father Abraham: but if one went unto them from the dead, they will repent. And he said unto him, If they hear not Moses and the prophets, neither will they be persuaded, though one rose from the dead" (Lk. 16:30–31).

a) It is a gift of God. "Then hath God also to the Gentiles granted repentance unto life" (Acts 11:18). "In meekness instructing those that oppose themselves; if God peradventure will give them repentance to the acknowledging of the truth" (2 Tm. 2:25). (See also Acts 5:31.) Repentance is not something that a person can bring about of himself. The person who thinks that he can live for self and the world and then repent and turn to God when he decides to is sadly mistaken. Many a sinner has gone out into eternity crying, "It's too late!" while loved ones and ministers have urged him to repent and accept the Lord. If one ever has an urge to repent of his sin and turn to the Lord, he should do so without any delay. The time may come when he would like to do so but cannot: "Lest there be any fornicator, or profane person, as Esau, who for one morsel of meat sold his birthright. For ye know how that afterward, when he would have inherited the blessing, he was rejected: for he found no place of repentance, though he sought it carefully with tears" (Heb. 12:16–17).

b) Through divinely ordained means

(1) In relation to the unsaved

(a) Through believing God's Word—"So the people of Ninevah believed God, and proclaimed a fast, and put on sackcloth, from the greatest of them even to the least of them. For word came unto the king of Ninevah, and he arose from his throne, and he laid his robe from him, and covered him with sackcloth, and sat in ashes" (Jon. 3:5–6).

(b) Through the preaching of the gospel—"Now when they heard this, they were pricked in their heart, and said unto Peter and to the rest of the apostles, Men and brethren, what shall we do?" (Acts 2:37). "The men of Ninevah shall rise in judgment with this generation, and shall condemn it: because they repented at the preaching of Jonas; and, behold, a greater than Jonas is here" (Mt. 12:41).

(c) Through the goodness of God—"Or despisest thou the riches of his goodness and forebearance and longsuffering; not knowing that the goodness of God leadeth thee to repentance?" (Rom. 2:4). "The Lord is not slack concerning his promise, as some men count slackness; but is longsuffering to us-ward, not willing that any should perish, but that all should come to repentance" (2 Pt. 3:9).

(2) In relation to the Christian

(a) Through God's reproof and chastisement

> For whom the Lord loveth he chasteneth, and scourgeth every son whom he receiveth....For they verily for a few days chastened us after their own pleasure; but he for our profit, that we might be partakers of his holiness. Now no chastening for the present seemeth to be joyous, but grievous: never-

theless afterward it yieldeth the peaceable fruit of righteousness unto them which are exercised thereby.

—HEBREWS 12:6, 10–11

God's chastisement leads to repentance: "As many as I love, I rebuke and chasten: be zealous therefore, and repent" (Rv. 3:19).

(b) Through a new vision of God—"I have heard of thee by the hearing of the ear: but now mine eye seeth thee. Wherefore I abhor myself, and repent in dust and ashes" (Jb. 42:5–6).

(c) Through the loving reproof of a brother—"The servant of the Lord must not strive; but be gentle unto all men, apt to teach, patient, In meekness instructing those that oppose themselves; if God peradventure will give them repentance to the acknowledging of the truth; And that they may recover themselves out of the snare of the devil, who are taken captive by him at his will" (2 Tm. 2:24–26).

4. *Fruits of repentance.* One last word should be said regarding the results of repentance. It will definitely lead to:

a) Confession of sin. "And the publican, standing afar off, would not lift up so much as his eyes unto heaven, but smote upon his breast, saying, God be merciful to me a sinner" (Lk. 18:13).

b) Furthermore, a truly repentant attitude will lead one to make restitution for wrongdoing as much as it is possible. "And Zacchaeus stood, and said unto the Lord; Behold, Lord, the half of my goods I give to the poor; and if I have taken any thing from any man by false accusation, I restore him fourfold" (Lk. 19:8). These, however, do not constitute repentance; rather, they are fruits of repentance.

C. Faith

The second essential element, along with repentance, that is necessary to receiving salvation is faith. It is questionable which of these precedes the other in point of experience. It is doubtful if a person can really repent unless he believes, and it is questionable whether one can truly believe for salvation without a sincere repentance from sin. John Calvin once said, "When John Smith goes through a door, who goes first, John or Smith?" Thus it is difficult to be certain which comes first, repentance or faith. We know that both are necessary.

Thiessen observes, "As in the case of repentance so in the case of faith, the doctrine does not receive the attention that it deserves. Great emphasis is laid upon conduct; a man's creed is said to be a matter of indifference. Yet a man's life is governed by what he believes, and in religion by the person in Whom he believes."[27]

---

27 Thiessen, 355.

1. *The importance of faith.* It is probably not possible to overstate the importance of faith in the Christian life. Faith is the only avenue of approach to God: "He that cometh to God must believe that he is, and that he is a rewarder of them that diligently seek him" (Heb. 11:6). Without faith it is not possible to please God (Heb. 11:6). Everything a believer receives from God, he receives through faith.

a) Salvation through faith. That our salvation is gained through faith is proclaimed by the following:

> For by grace are ye saved through faith.
>
> —EPHESIANS 2:8

> He that believeth and is baptized shall be saved.
>
> —MARK 16:16

> Believe on the Lord Jesus Christ, and thou shalt be saved.
>
> —ACTS 16:31

> As many as received him, to them gave he power to become the sons of God, even to them that believe on his name.
>
> —JOHN 1:12

> To him that worketh not, but believeth on him that justifieth the ungodly, his faith is counted for righteousness.
>
> —ROMANS 4:5

> Therefore being justified by faith, we have peace with God through our Lord Jesus Christ.
>
> —ROMANS 5:1

> We are not of them who draw back unto perdition; but of them that believe to the saving of the soul.
>
> —HEBREWS 10:39

> Verily, verily, I say unto you, He that heareth my word, and believeth on him that sent me, hath everlasting life, and shall not come into condemnation; but is passed from death unto life.
>
> —JOHN 5:24

b) The fullness of the Holy Spirit through faith. "That we might receive the promise of the Spirit through faith" (Gal. 3:14). "This spake he of the Spirit, which they that believe on him should receive" (Jn. 7:39).

c) Sanctification through faith. "And put no difference between us and them, purifying their hearts by faith" (Acts 15:9). "That they may receive forgiveness of sins, and inheritance among them which are sanctified by faith that is in me" (Acts 26:18).

d) Security through faith. "Who are kept by the power of God through faith" (1 Pt. 1:5). "Well; because of unbelief they were broken off, and thou standest by faith" (Rom. 11:20). "Not for that we have dominion over your faith, but are helpers of your joy: for by faith we stand" (2 Cor. 1:24).

e) Perfect peace through faith. "Thou wilt keep him in perfect peace, whose mind is stayed on thee: because he trusteth in thee" (Is. 26:3). "We which have believed do enter into rest" (Heb. 4:3).

f) Healing through faith. "And the prayer of faith shall save the sick, and the Lord shall raise him up" (Jas. 5:15). "The same heard Paul speak: who steadfastly beholding him, and perceiving that he had faith to be healed" (Acts 14:9).

g) Victory over adversaries through faith. The chief adversaries of the Christian may be summed up as: the world, the flesh, and the devil.

h) The world overcome through faith. "This is the victory that overcometh the world, even our faith" (1 Jn. 5:4).

i) The flesh overcome through faith. "Reckon"—an act of faith—"ye also yourselves to be dead indeed unto sin, but alive unto God through Jesus Christ our Lord" (Rom. 6:11).

j) The devil overcome through faith. "Put on the whole armour of God, that ye may be able to stand against the wiles of the devil....Above all, taking the shield of faith, wherewith ye shall be able to quench all the fiery darts of the wicked" (Eph. 6:11, 16). "Simon, Simon, behold, Satan hath desired to have you, that he may sift you as wheat: But I have prayed for thee that thy faith fail not" (Lk. 22:31-32).

k) The entire Christian life is lived through faith. Four times in the Scripture we read, "The just shall live by faith" (Hb. 2:4; Rom. 1:17; Gal. 3:11; Heb. 10:38). Faith is the very atmosphere in which the Christian life is lived: "The life which I now live in the flesh I live by the faith of the Son of God, who loved me, and gave himself for me" (Gal. 2:20). Christians are called believers because their lives are lived in continuous faith. It is clear, then, that it must have a great part in the receiving of salvation in its initial experience.

2. *The meaning of faith.* Many Bible scholars believe that the Bible does not give an actual definition of faith. It is agreed, however, that Hebrews 11:1 is probably the closest to such a definition: "Now faith is the substance of things hoped for, the evidence of things not seen." The value of this verse as a definition of faith is more obvious when we closely examine the use of several words. Faith is said to be the "substance". The word *substance* comes from a word that literally means "foundation," or that which underlies our hope. *Foundation* speaks of that covenant relation-

ship of mutual love between the Lord and the believer which is our ground of hope. Faith is no blind groping in the dark, but the certain conviction, born of love and relationship experience, that God's revealed Word is true. Faith is more than a mere hope; it is *substance*, a word which was, in legal affairs, translated "title deed." He who believes divinely—in whose heart love amounts to persuasion—has a title deed to God's full provision. Faith is a persuasion as it applies to the invisible. The realities of God's kingdom are by nature invisible realities, that is, invisible to natural sight. Faith is that faculty by which the spiritual realities are perceived as being real and capable of being realized. He who has faith has eyes for the spiritual. Faith is, to the Christian, real evidence. He needs no other evidence in order to proceed in accord with the revealed will of God. In classical Greek, the word we translate "evidence" often meant "proof." Faith is a foundation and a proof.[28]

3. *The elements of faith.* Faith, like repentance, has three elements: the intellectual, the emotional, and the volitional, or voluntary.

a) The intellectual element. Faith is not a blind leap into the dark. It has been erroneously called "a step in the dark which leads to the light." On the contrary, faith is walking in the light—the light of God's Word. It is utterly unsafe to take even one step in the dark. A man could be on the edge of a deep precipice, and one step would plunge him to his doom. Faith must be based on knowledge. No one can believe in something of which he has no knowledge. One cannot believe in a person with whom he is completely unacquainted. Believing a thing without evidence is impossible. Faith that is needed for salvation is based on the very best of evidence—the Bible, as the Word of God: "So then faith cometh by hearing, and hearing by the word of God" (Rom. 10:17). We need to know the gospel in order to believe on Christ as our Savior.

b) The emotional element. This element is sometimes seen in the joy that accompanies the first realization of God's goodness in providing for one's needs. It is illustrated by Israel's experience, as described in Psalm 106:12: "Then believed they his words; they sang his praise." Unfortunately the feeling of joy soon passed, for in verses 24 and 25 we read, "They believed not his word: But murmured in their tents, and hearkened not unto the voice of the LORD." Jesus described these individuals in the parable of the sower, saying, "And these are they likewise which are sown on stony ground; who, when they have heard the word, immediately receive it with gladness; And have no root in themselves, and so endure but for a time: afterward, when affliction or persecution ariseth for the word's sake, immediately they are offended" (Mk. 4:16–17).

---

28 William F Arndt and F. Wilbur Gingrich, *Greek English Lexicon of the New Testament* (Chicago: University of Chicago Press, 1957), s.v. "elegos."

Dr. A. T. Pierson has said, "Here is the order: Fact leads. Faith with its eye on Fact following. Feeling with its eye on Faith brings up the rear. All goes well as long as this order is observed. But the moment that Faith turns its back on Fact and looks at Feeling the procession wabbles."[29]

This element of faith also includes an assent of the mind to the truth received. The scribes replied to Jesus' explanation of the greatest commandment, "Well, Master, thou hast said the truth" (Mk. 12:32–33).

Thiessen has well summarized this section as follows: "We may define the emotional element of faith as the awakening of the soul to its personal needs and to the personal applicability of the redemption provided in Christ, together with an immediate assent to these truths."[30]

c) The voluntary element. After knowing what God has promised, and after assenting to the truth of that promise, then faith reaches out and appropriates what is provided. Knowledge itself is not enough. A man may have the knowledge that Christ is divine and yet still reject Him as Savior. Knowledge affirms the reality of these things, but it neither accepts or rejects them. Nor is assent enough. There is an assent of the mind which does not convey a surrender of the heart, and it is "with the heart man believeth unto righteousness" (Rom. 10:10). Real faith is in the realm of the will. It appropriates. It takes. Faith always has the idea of action in it; faith has legs. It is the soul leaping up to embrace the promise: "And being fully persuaded that, what he had promised, he was able also to perform" (Rom. 4:21).

Thus, this phase of faith is comprised of two elements: surrender of the heart to God and the appropriation of Christ as Savior. Proverbs 23:26 illustrates the former: "My son, give me thine heart." Also Matthew 11:28–29: "Come unto me, all ye that labor and are heavy laden, and I will give you rest. Take my yoke upon you, and learn of me; for I am meek and lowly in heart: and ye shall find rest unto your souls." Romans 10:9 says, "If thou shalt confess with thy mouth the Lord Jesus." This literally translates, "If thou shalt confess with thy mouth Jesus as Lord." It conveys the thought of surrendering to the lordship of Jesus over your entire life. The appropriation of Christ as Savior means to fully receive all that He has done on Calvary for the redemption of your soul: "But as many as received him, to them gave he power to become the sons of God, even to them that believe on his name" (Jn. 1:12).

This illustrates the important truth that salvation is receiving Jesus Christ Himself. This personal appropriation is a vital necessity. It is not enough that Jesus has died. I must recognize that He died for me. It is true that He died for all, but I must individually accept Him as my Savior. Water is provided for all, but I shall die of thirst

---

29 Arthur T. Pierson, *The Bible and Spiritual Life* (New York: Gospel Publishing House, 1908).

30 Thiessen, 358.

if I do not personally drink of the life-giving flow. Air is provided for all, but I must individually breathe it if I am to survive. There must be an individual commitment of the soul to Christ, and a personal acceptance of Him as both Savior and Lord.

A Christian family was spending an afternoon enjoying winter sports on the frozen lake near their home. One of the girls went a little too far out on the ice and fell through into the freezing water. Clinging to the ice on the surface, she cried for help. Her father, hearing her cry of distress, made his way gingerly out on the still-frozen surface. Slowly crawling to the broken edge of the ice, he reached out and caught one of his daughter's hands. But try as he would, he could not draw her up over the surface of the ice, as she clung with her other hand to the edge. Finally he said to her, "Give me both of your hands." This meant that she must let go of the firm edge of the ice and commit herself completely to her father's care, with nothing to hold on to but him. It was only then that he was able to pull her to safety. Salvation can only be realized as we let go of every earthly handhold and give Him both our hands in utter surrender and commitment. He alone can save.

4. *The source of faith.* Although many other blessings that are received through faith and are relative to the Christian life have been suggested in this section, we are particularly concerned here with the part faith has in the experience of salvation and how this saving faith is received. Many times individuals, when confronted with the gospel and told that all they have to do is to believe, will reply, "But it is so hard to believe." If one is trying to believe in his faith or in something that he is doing, it is difficult, for neither his faith nor his works are sufficient, and he realizes this. Faith is based on what God has done and what He has promised, not on anything in man. It is based entirely on the finished work of Christ, as revealed in the Scripture. In other words, faith is believing God's Word: "Faith cometh by hearing, and hearing by the word of God." (Rom. 10:17). The NIV renders this, "Consequently, faith comes from hearing the message, and the message is heard through the word of Christ." Thus faith comes through hearing the word of Christ: "Howbeit many of them which heard the word believed" (Acts 4:4). Nothing will produce faith more than reading and studying the Bible, the Word of God, and thus becoming acquainted with what God has promised. Faith is simply believing in what God has said. It is taking Him at His Word.

> The word is nigh thee, even in thy mouth, and in thy heart: that is, the word of faith, which we preach; That if thou shalt confess with thy mouth the Lord Jesus, and shalt believe in thine heart that God hath raised him from the dead, thou shalt be saved.
>
> —ROMANS 10:8–9

Verily, verily, I say unto you, He that heareth my word, and believeth on him that sent me, hath everlasting life.

—JOHN 5:24

Believe on the Lord Jesus Christ, and thou shalt be saved, and thy house.

—ACTS 16:31

Granted, the gospel of the grace of God to sinful man sounds too good to be true. But when one considers it is planned by God, brought about by Him, and promised by Him, it should not be difficult to take Him at His word. This is faith!

D. Justification

1. *Definition.* Justification by faith is the foundation truth of God's provision of salvation for guilty and lost sinners. It was the great truth the Protestant Reformation restored to the Christian Church. It is frequently referred to in the Scriptures, yet it is one of the most neglected and misunderstood doctrines in all evangelical theology. It is of such a far-reaching and startling nature that many seem afraid to teach and believe the scriptural declarations concerning it, yet it must be understood if we are to fully understand the "so great salvation" (Heb. 2:3) God has graciously and freely provided.

Regeneration and justification are closely related doctrines. Regeneration has to do with that which takes place in the believer's heart; justification concerns his standing before God. Regeneration refers to the impartation of life; justification to his being declared righteous in the eyes of God. Regeneration is the divine answer to the problem of spiritual death; justification is the divine answer to the problem of guilt.

Justification is a legal term which pictures the sinner before the bar of God to receive condemnation for the sins he has committed, but instead of being condemned he is judicially pronounced as not guilty, being declared by God to be righteous. Justification has been defined as "that act of God whereby He declares righteous him who believes on Christ." Observe it is not that the sinner is righteous, but that he is declared righteous on the basis of his faith in the sacrifice of the Lord Jesus Christ: "Abraham believed God, and it was counted unto him for righteousness" (Rom. 4:3). Justification is more than forgiveness, or pardon of sins, and the removal of guilt and condemnation. Justification is also a positive action—the reckoning of, or putting to one's account, the perfect righteousness of Christ: "But of him are ye in Christ Jesus, who of God is made unto us wisdom, and righteousness." (1 Cor. 1:30); "For he hath made him to be sin for us, who knew no sin; that we might be made the righteousness of God in him" (2 Cor. 5:21). Justification includes the sinner's deliverance from wrath and also his acceptance as righteous in the sight of God. In justifying the sinner, God places him in the position of a righteous man. It is as though he had never sinned.

2. *What is involved in justification.* Outside the city of Kingston, Ontario, Canada, some years ago, a man entered the kitchen door and began to accost the wife of the household just as she was preparing the evening meal. She cried out to her husband, who was in another room of the house, and he immediately came rushing to her assistance, grabbing the man by the collar and thrusting him out the back door. In the morning as he was going out the door, the husband found, to his utter surprise, the intruder lying dead at the bottom of the steps. It was never determined whether the man was killed by the force of his fall, or whether he was merely stunned and then froze to death in the cold of the winter night. The farmer, being an honest man, immediately went into town and gave himself up to the authorities. Several days later a hearing was held. Every bit of evidence that could be accumulated was brought in and duly recorded by the appointed clerk of the court. After every possible witness had been heard from and all records fully transcribed and considered, the judge turned to the farmer and said, "In the eyes of this court, you are justified." That meant that every shred of evidence that had been taken down during that hearing had to be destroyed. If anyone were to go to Kingston today, he could not find one piece of evidence of that case. Every record is gone.

When God justifies the sinner who trusts in the saving grace of Jesus Christ, all evidence of his sin and guilt is completely wiped out: "In those days, and in that time, saith the LORD, the iniquity of Israel shall be sought for, and there shall be none; and the sins of Judah, and they shall not be found: for I will pardon them whom I reserve" (Jer. 50:20). This is a most remarkable declaration, for certainly Israel and Judah had plenty of sins for which they were guilty. But when God forgives, He forgets: "This is the covenant that I will make with them after those days, saith the Lord, I will put my laws into their hearts, and in their minds will I write them; And their sins and iniquities will I remember no more" (Heb. 10:16–17). This, in itself, is amazing, for He is the omniscient God. He knows all things. The only thing we are ever told that God forgets is the sins of the one who trusts in His great salvation. Thus God does not see believers as forgiven sinners. He sees them, rather, as those who have never sinned.

a) Pardon or remission of sins. "Be it known unto you therefore, men and brethren, that through this man is preached unto you the forgiveness of sins: And by him all that believe are justified from all things, from which ye could not be justified by the law of Moses" (Acts 13:38–39). "In whom we have redemption through his blood, the forgiveness of sins, according to the riches of his grace" (Eph. 1:7). "And you, being dead in your sins and the uncircumcision of your flesh, hath he quickened together with him, having forgiven you all trespasses" (Col. 2:13). Because the believer's sins are all forgiven, it follows that the guilt and punishment of those sins is also removed.

b) Restoration to God's favor. The sinner has not merely incurred a penalty but has also lost God's favor and is thus subject to His wrath. "He that believeth not the Son shall not see life; but the wrath of God abideth on him" (Jn. 3:36). "For the wrath of God is revealed from heaven against all ungodliness and unrighteousness of men" (Rom. 1:18). Through justification, all this is changed: "Much more then, being now justified by his blood, we shall be saved from wrath through him" (Rom. 5:9).

One of the great problems in society today has to do with the rehabilitation of those who have served time for a crime committed. Even though he has met his debt to society, it is difficult for such a person to find his place in the community again. He has the mark of a criminal against him and is not easily received by those who knew him before. This is why a large proportion of those who have been incarcerated drift back into the company of the criminal element and very often are arrested and sentenced to another period in prison. Thank God that His grace is so abundant that we are received into His favor as though we had never broken His laws.

> Therefore being justified by faith, we have peace with God through our Lord Jesus Christ: By whom we have access by faith into this grace wherein we stand, and rejoice in hope of the glory of God.
>
> —ROMANS 5:1–2

> But after that the kindness and love of God our Saviour toward man appeared, Not by works of righteousness which we had done, but according to his mercy he saved us, by the washing of regeneration, and renewing of the Holy Ghost; Which he shed on us abundantly through Jesus Christ our Savior; That being justified by his grace, we should be made heirs according to the hope of eternal life.
>
> —TITUS 3:4–7

This restoration to favor is illustrated for us in the parable of the prodigal son: "But the father said to his servants, Bring forth the best robe, and put it on him; and put a ring on his hand, and shoes on his feet: And bring hither the fatted calf, and kill it; and let us eat, and be merry: For this my son was dead, and is alive again; he was lost, and is found. And they began to be merry" (Lk. 15:22–24). This restoration is confirmed by P. B. Fitzwater, who says, "From these texts it is seen that justification is much more than remission of sins or acquittal. The justified man is more than a discharged criminal. He is restored to the position of one who is righteous. God treats him as though he had never sinned."[31]

---

31 Fitzwater, 47.

c) Imputation of Christ's righteousness. Thiessen well says, "The sinner must not only be pardoned for his past sins, but also supplied with a positive righteousness before he can have fellowship with God. This need is supplied in the imputation of the righteousness of Christ to the believer."[32] "Even as David also describeth the blessedness of the man, unto whom God imputeth righteousness without works, Saying, Blessed are they whose iniquities are forgiven, and whose sins are covered. Blessed is the man to whom the Lord will not impute sin" (Rom. 4:6–8). James Buchanan, DD, LLD, and former divinity professor at New College, Edinburgh, wrote an extensive book on the doctrine of justification that was first published in 1867, in which he says, "Indeed Justification consists partly in the 'non-imputation' of sin, which did belong personally to the sinner, and partly in the 'imputation' of righteousness, of which he was utterly destitute before; and the meaning of the one may be ascertained from the meaning of the other, while both are necessary to express the full meaning of Justification."[33] All fellowship with a holy God must be on the basis of righteousness. In the first two and one-half chapters of the epistle to the Romans, Paul deals with every classification of society and shows that they have no righteousness of their own. He sums up his survey with the words, "Now we know that what things soever the law saith, it saith to them that are under the law: that every mouth may be stopped, and all the world may become guilty before God. Therefore by the deeds of the law there shall no flesh be justified in his sight: for by the law is the knowledge of sin" (Rom. 3:19–20). This is a black, hopeless picture indeed! But this is not the end of the story. Paul goes on to say, "But now the righteousness of God without the law is manifested, being witnessed by the law and the prophets; Even the righteousness of God which is by faith of Jesus Christ unto all and upon all of them that believe" (Rom. 3:21–22).

"For he hath made him to be sin for us, who knew no sin; that we might be made the righteousness of God in him" (2 Cor. 5:21). This verse suggests the double imputation that is present in justification: our sins were imputed to Christ, who Himself had no sin, and Christ's righteousness is imputed to the believer, who had none of his own. (To impute means to lay the responsibility or credit for something on another.) Righteousness is absolutely necessary for fellowship with God, but since man has no righteousness of his own, God imputes to the believer the righteousness of Jesus Christ. How often we have heard Romans 1:16 quoted in testimonies: "For I am not ashamed of the gospel of Christ: for it is the power of God unto salvation to every one that believeth." But the testimony usually stops right there. Why is the gospel the power of God unto salvation? Verse 17 supplies the answer: "For therein is the

---

32 Thiessen, 363–364.

33 James Buchanan, *The Doctrine of Justification* (Grand Rapids, MI: Baker Book House, 1955), 323.

righteousness of God revealed from faith to faith." Christ's righteousness is provided, through the gospel, for those who will believe in Him.

A pardoned criminal is never described as a good or righteous man. But when God justifies a sinner, He declares that he is righteous in His sight: "Who shall lay any thing to the charge of God's elect? It is God that justifieth" (Rom. 8:33). If God justified only good people, then there would be no gospel for the sinner. But, thank God, He justifies the ungodly. Justification by faith does not impart Christ's righteousness to the sinner, nor infuse him with it so that it becomes part of his inner nature. That is the result of sanctification, which we will consider later. Justification reckons to the sinner the righteousness of Christ, so that God sees him through the perfect righteousness of His Son. "This righteousness—being the merit of a work, and not a mere quality of character—may become ours by being imputed to us, but cannot be communicated by being infused; and must continue to belong primarily, and in one important respect, exclusively to Him by Whom alone that work was accomplished."[34] But how can God do this? How can a holy and righteous God, who cannot countenance sin, declare righteous one who is born in sin and thus is guilty both by nature and practice?

3. *The method of justification.* It is very important that we understand the method by which God justifies the sinner. Justification is the very basis of our standing before God. It is not something that can simply be taken for granted. God cannot merely overlook sin out of the bigness of His heart. He must preserve His own holiness and justice. He must "be just, and the justifier of him which believeth in Jesus" (Rom. 3:26).

There is a definite and divine way by which sinners can be declared righteous, and apart from this way such a thing cannot be possible. It is a strange commentary on the sinful heart of mankind that, deserving eternal condemnation as he does and being offered so great a gift as justification of his life before God, he should complain at the divine method. There is only one way—God's way! Let us rejoice in it, being careful to note the details as given in God's Word.

a) Not by good works. If there is one truth made clear in the New Testament, it is that no man is justified on the basis of his own righteousness or his own good deeds.

> For if Abraham were justified by works, he hath whereof to glory; but not before God. For what saith the scripture? Abraham believed God, and it was counted unto him for righteousness. Now to him that worketh is the reward not reckoned of grace, but of debt. But to him that worketh not, but believeth on him that justifieth the ungodly, his faith is counted unto him for righteousness.
>
> —ROMANS 4:2–5

---

34 Buchanan, 320.

> Even so then at this present time also there is a remnant according to the election of grace. And if by grace, then it is no more of works: otherwise grace is no more grace. But if it be of works, then it is no more grace: otherwise work is no more work.
>
> —ROMANS 11:5–6

b) Not by endeavoring to keep the Law.

> Now we know that what things soever the law saith, it saith to them who are under the law: that every mouth may be stopped, and all the world may become guilty before God. Therefore by the deeds of the law there shall no flesh be justified in his sight: for by the law is the knowledge of sin.... For all have sinned, and come short of the glory of God.
>
> —ROMANS 3:19–20, 23

> Knowing that a man is not justified by the works of the law, but by the faith of Jesus Christ, even we have believed in Jesus Christ, that we might be justified by the faith of Christ, and not by the works of the law: for by the works of the law shall no flesh be justified.
>
> —GALATIANS 2:16

Theoretically it would be possible to be saved by keeping the Law if one could keep it perfectly. But we have all utterly broken God's law in the past and are unable to keep it perfectly in the future. Paul makes it quite plain that we are helpless in this regard: "For as many as are of the works of the law are under the curse: for it is written, Cursed is every one that continueth not in all things which are written in the book of the law to do them" (Gal. 3:10).

It is not that there is anything wrong with the Law itself. Paul says, "the law is holy, and the commandment holy, and just, and good" (Rom. 7:12). The trouble is with those who cannot keep it. The Law serves to make men realize they are sinners: "By the law is the knowledge of sin" (Rom. 3:20). The Law is like an alarm clock, which has the ability to awaken but does not have the physical power to move an individual out of bed. It is like the flight schedule of an airliner, which can tell you the time the plane leaves but cannot guarantee that you will be at the airport on time. Romans 8:3 says that the Law is "weak through the flesh."

It is sad to see those who are depending on their own good works or sacrifices in the hope of finding forgiveness of sin and peace with God. A missionary observed a little mother in India approaching the holy river with a weak, emaciated child in her arms, while a strong, healthy boy ran along at her side. Some time later he observed her returning from the place of sacrifice with only the weakling in her arms. "Mother of India," he asked, "where is the healthy, beautiful child who was by your side?" She replied, "When we sacrifice to our god, we always give our best."

Lest there should be any misunderstanding of the teachings of Paul and James and thus a contradiction be imagined, note the following: "Therefore we conclude," says Paul, "that a man is justified by faith without the deeds of the law" (Rom. 3:28). "Ye see, then," says James, "how that by works a man is justified, and not by faith only" (Jas. 2:24).

Actually, there can be no contradiction between these two men because they are both being inspired by the same Holy Spirit. They are writing about two different aspects of one subject. Paul is telling us that salvation is by faith alone and not by works, while James is insisting that a faith that is genuine will result in good works. Ephesians 2:8–10 speaks of both of these aspects: "For by grace are ye saved through faith; and that not of yourselves: it is the gift of God: Not of works, lest any man should boast. For we are his workmanship, created in Christ Jesus unto good works, which God hath before ordained that we should walk in them." Thus the faith that saves without works will result in good works. Faith cannot be seen. It can only be judged by what a man does. That is why James says, "Shew me thy faith without thy works, and I will shew you my faith by my works" (Jas. 2:18). Thus Abraham's faith, which "was imputed unto him for righteousness" (Jas. 2:23), was manifested "by faith, when he had offered Isaac his son upon the altar" (Jas. 2:21). The outward act clearly demonstrated the inner faith.

c) By the gift of God's grace. Justification cannot be worked for, nor merited. It is only received through God's grace: "Being justified freely by his grace through the redemption that is in Christ Jesus" (Rom. 3:24); "Being justified by his grace, we should be made heirs according to the hope of eternal life" (Ti. 3:7). What is grace? The word *grace* (in Greek, *charis,* from which we get our word "charismatic") originally meant "loveliness" or "charm." Later it was used to mean any favor granted to another, especially when the recipient had not merited such a favor. The Bible writers borrowed this word and, under God's guidance, clothed it with a new significance so that in the New Testament it usually meant the forgiveness of sins granted entirely out of the goodness of God, completely apart from any merit on the part of the person forgiven. Grace blesses man in the face of all non-merit and positive lack of merit. Someone has said, "To feed a tramp who calls on me is unmerited favor, but scarcely grace. But to feed a tramp who has robbed me would be grace." Grace is favor shown where there is positive demerit.

Grace is not merely something which God expresses. It is an expression of what He is. "Grace is the attitude on God's part that proceeds entirely from within Himself and is conditioned in no way by anything in the objects of His favor."[35] Dr. Henry C. Mabie is quoted as saying, "Grace is a boon purchased for us by the court which found us guilty."[36] Dr. Fitzwater's own definition of grace is, "As applied to salvation, grace means that what the holy and righteous God demands of us was provided by himself...God in his grace is not dealing with innocent creatures, but with sinners under righteous and just condemnation. In grace what God's righteousness demands He supplies."[37] A. W. Pink has written, "Grace is a provision for men who are so fallen that they cannot help themselves, so corrupt that they cannot change their natures, so averse to God that they cannot turn to Him, so blind they cannot see Him, so deaf they cannot hear Him, so dead that He Himself must open their graves and lift them into resurrection."[38]

d) Through the substitutionary sacrifice of Jesus Christ. God cannot forgive our sins just because He is gracious. As a God of justice he cannot merely overlook our sin. His pardon is based upon the strict terms of justice. The penalty of our sins has been paid—paid for by none other than the Lord Jesus Christ. The sins of the believer are put to the account of Christ, "who his own self bare our sins in his own body on the tree, that we, being dead to sins, should live unto righteousness" (1 Pt. 2:24); "For he hath made him to be sin for us, who knew no sin; that we might be made the righteousness of God in him" (2 Cor. 5:21). God can forgive sin because the Law has been kept and the penalty for its breaking has been paid. Not only is the penalty of our sin paid by Christ, but His perfect obedience to the Law provided a righteousness which God could put to our account: "For as by one man's disobedience many were made sinners, so by the obedience of one shall many be made righteous" (Rom. 5:19). Thus we have the amazing situation whereby Christ takes our sin upon Himself, while His righteousness is bestowed upon us. What an unbelievable exchange! Yet that is exactly what God offers to those who will believe.

e) Through faith alone

> Being justified freely by his grace through the redemption that is in Christ Jesus: Whom God hath set forth to be a propitiation through faith in his blood.... To declare, I say, at this time his righteousness: that he might be just, and the justifier of him which believeth in Jesus.
>
> —ROMANS 3:24, 26

---

35 *International Standard Bible Encyclopedia* (Grand Rapids, MI: Wm. B. Eerdmans Publishing Company, 1943), II, 1291.

36 Dr. Henry C. Mabie, as quoted by Fitzwater, 401.

37 Fitzwater, 401, 403.

38 Arthur W. Pink, source unknown.

But to him that worketh not, but believeth on him that justifieth the ungodly, his faith is counted for righteousness.

—ROMANS 4:5

Therefore being justified by faith, we have peace with God through our Lord Jesus Christ.

—ROMANS 5:1

For with the heart man believeth unto righteousness.

—ROMANS 10:10

Knowing that a man is not justified by the works of the law, but by the faith of Jesus Christ, even we have believed in Jesus Christ, that we might be justified by the faith in Christ, and not by the works of the law: for by the works of the law shall no flesh be justified.

—GALATIANS 2:16

When we declare that we are justified through faith, we must realize that faith is not something that we meritoriously offer to God for our salvation. It is only the means through which we receive His gracious provision. Quoting Thiessen, we can say of faith, as we said of repentance, "We are not saved *for* our faith, but *through* our faith."[39]

Two further facts must be born in mind. First, the resurrection of Christ is the guarantee of our justification: "Who was delivered for our offences, and was raised again for our justification" (Rom. 4:25). The fact that God raised Jesus from the dead is a testimony that He was satisfied with the sacrifice Jesus had made and that our sins, which He took upon Himself, are gone. It is the Father's seal of approval upon Christ's atoning death. Second, justification is complete. There are no degrees in justification. The babe in Jesus Christ stands in the same justification as the believer of fifty years. There is no such thing as progress in justification.

E. Regeneration

It is of the greatest importance that we fully understand what Jesus' words to Nicodemus really mean: "Verily, verily, I say unto thee, Except a man be born again, he cannot see the kingdom of God" (Jn. 3:3). Church history clearly shows the tendency of religious organizations, once the initial revival has subsided, to consider conversion as a ceremonial act of the Church or a voluntary act of the human will, rather than as a supernatural act of the Holy Spirit. In this section we shall consider

---

39 Thiessen, 382.

the meaning and importance of what it is to be born again. This expression is being widely used—and used in jest—in many areas where its true meaning has no place whatsoever. Perhaps it would be well to realize that the word *again* in the above-mentioned scripture often means "from above," so that many prefer to translate the words, "Except a man be born from above, he cannot see the kingdom of God."[40] Merely being born a second time would not necessarily put one on a higher plane.

1. *What is the new birth?*

a) Negative. The new birth is not the following:

(1) Not reformation—When you tell the average person that he must be born again, he immediately thinks you mean he must reform, he must mend his ways, or turn over a new leaf. The new birth is not reformation. Reformation, at best, is of human origin and is only outward in its effect. It cannot change the inner man. Imagine that one has a watch with the main spring broken. If it is taken to the jeweler and he puts on a new crystal and polishes the case, will the watch run again? Of course not. All he did was to brighten up the outside, when the trouble is within. Man has a heart that "is deceitful above all things, and desperately wicked" (Jer. 17:9), and he needs something that will bring about a vital transformation within his being.

(2) Not becoming religious—If you should tell the average churchgoer that he must be born again in order to see the kingdom of God, he is not perturbed. He has always been a Christian. He belongs to a certain church and regularly contributes to its support. He may even read his Bible every day and say his prayers each night. He seeks to treat his neighbor as himself. What else does he need? The new birth is not becoming religious. We remind ourselves that when Jesus was talking about the necessity of the new birth, he was speaking to an ultrareligious man, Nicodemus, a sincere Pharisee and a member of Israel's highest ecclesiastical court, the Sanhedrin. If anyone could get to heaven on the basis of his religion, surely Nicodemus could have!

(3) Not a change of heart—Though this expression is often used, it is not scriptural. The new birth is not the changing of something in man, nor the removal of something from man, but the communication of something to man—something which he never before possessed. The new birth is literally the impartation of the divine nature to the heart and life of the sinner, which makes him a new creation. It is brought to pass through a personal union with Jesus Christ: "He that hath the Son hath life; and he that hath not the Son of God hath not life" (1 Jn. 5:12); "Whereby are given unto us exceeding great and precious promises: that by these ye might be

---

40 So translated in *The Emphasized New Testament* by Rotherham, and in Moffatt's *The New Testament: A New Translation*. The NASB shows "born from above" in the margin, as do *The New Scofield Reference Bible* and Worrell's *Translation of the New Testament*. Robertson's *Word Pictures in the New Testament*, V, 45, says: "In the other passages in John (3:31; 19:11, 23) the meaning is 'from above' *(desuper)* and usually so in the Synoptics."

partakers of the divine nature" (2 Pt. 1:4). When I was born the first time, I received from my parents their nature; when I was born the second time, I received from God His nature. No other religion has such a message as this. Christianity is the only religion which professes to take a man, fallen by nature, and regenerate him by bringing into him the life of God. No one would ever dream of saying, "He that hath Buddha hath life."

b) Positive. As described in the New Testament, the new birth is:

(1) A birth—"Whosoever believeth that Jesus is the Christ is born of God: and every one that loveth him that begat loveth him also that is begotten of him" (1 Jn. 5:1). John 3:8 speaks of the Christian as being "born of the Spirit." "As many as received him, to them gave he power to become the sons of God...Which were born...of God" (Jn. 1:12–13).

(2) A cleansing—"According to his mercy he saved us, by the washing of regeneration" (Ti. 3:5). This suggests the cleansing of the soul from the defilements of the old life.

(3) A quickening—We are saved not only "by the washing of regeneration" but also by the "renewing of the Holy Ghost" (Ti. 3:5). (See Col. 3:10; Rom. 12:2; Ps. 51:10.)

(4) A creation—"Therefore if any man be in Christ, he is a new creature [literally, new creation]: old things are passed away; behold, all things are become new" (2 Cor. 5:17). (See Eph. 2:10; 4:24; Gal. 6:15.)

(5) A resurrection—In describing the new birth as a resurrection, we must realize that it is preceded by a death. Believers have been crucified with Christ and have also been raised together with Him. Both of these truths become a spiritual reality through identification with Christ in His death, burial, and resurrection.

> How shall we who died to sin still live in it? Or do you not know that all of us who have been baptized into Christ Jesus have been baptized into his death? Therefore we have been buried with him through baptism into death, so that as Christ was raised from the dead through the glory of the Father, so we too might walk in newness of life. For if we have become united with him in the likeness of His death, certainly we shall be also in the likeness of his resurrection, knowing this, that our old self was crucified with Him, in order that our body of sin might be done away with, so that we should no longer be slaves to sin; for he who has died is freed from sin.
>
> —Romans 6:2–7, nasb

This is symbolized in the ordinance of water baptism by immersion. As the result of this identification with Christ in His death, burial, and resurrection, Paul can say, "And you hath he quickened, who were dead in trespasses and sins" (Eph. 2:1). He adds a further blessed dimension to this gracious identification with Christ when he says, "Even when we were dead in sins, hath quickened us together with Christ...And hath raised us up together, and made us sit together in heavenly places in Christ Jesus" (Eph. 2:5–6).

2. *Necessity of the new birth.* "Marvel not that I said unto thee, Ye must be born again [from above]" (Jn. 3:7). These are the words of Jesus. Yet we do marvel and wonder. Perhaps the chief question that persists in our mind is, why must a man be born from above? This is a legitimate question, and it demands a forthright answer.

a) The kingdom of God cannot be seen without it. Regeneration is not a mere privilege, but an absolute necessity. Jesus said, "Except a man be born again, he cannot see the kingdom of God" (Jn. 3:3). It is not that God will not allow the unregenerate to see the kingdom of God; it is an absolute impossibility: "The natural man receiveth not the things of the Spirit of God: for they are foolishness unto him: neither can he know them, because they are spiritually discerned" (1 Cor. 2:14).

b) Because of the nature of man's first birth, a second birth is necessary. We were all born of sinful parents and, thus, are sinners. One of the unbreakable laws of nature is that like begets like.

> Behold, I was shapen in iniquity; and in sin did my mother conceive me.
>
>   —Psalm 51:5

> That which is born of the flesh is flesh; and that which is born of the Spirit is spirit.
>
>   —John 3:6

> Now the works of the flesh are manifest, which are these; Adultery, fornication, uncleanness, lasciviousness, Idolatry, witchcraft, hatred, variance, emulations, wrath, strife, seditions, heresies, Envyings, murders, drunkenness, revellings, and such like: of which I tell you before, as I have also told you in time past, that they which do such things shall not inherit the kingdom of God.
>
>   —Galatians 5:19–21

> Because the carnal mind is enmity against God: for it is not subject to the law of God, neither indeed can be....But ye are not in the flesh, but in the Spirit, if so be that the Spirit of God dwell in you. Now if any man have not the Spirit of Christ, he is none of his.
>
>   —Romans 8:7, 9

Flesh is flesh, and it does not matter how cultured or even how religious it may become, it is always flesh. The kingdom of God is spiritual, and only spiritual beings can inherit it. Jesus condemned those who rejected Him and declared, "Ye are of your father the devil, and the lusts of your father ye will do" (Jn. 8:44). The widespread teaching of today is of the universal fatherhood of God and brotherhood of man. The only way in which God may be considered the Father of all mankind is that He is mankind's Creator. Otherwise, unless a man has been born again into the family of God, he cannot claim God as his Father. It is not possible to *join* the company of the saints. You have to be born into it. Flesh and spirit are two entirely different realms, and there is no way a sinner by nature can make himself a child of God. The spiritual life, which is necessary in order that we may become sons of God, is only possible through the power of the Holy Spirit.

c) Because man would not be happy in heaven without it. Heaven is a place, but it is also a state or condition, and no one could possibly be happy in the presence of the Lord and the company of the redeemed unless his inner nature was in harmony with God. If it were possible for a man to enter heaven without being born again, one of the first things he would look for, after satisfying his curiosity regarding the heavenly city, would be something to satisfy his sinful nature. If his nature has not been transformed by the power of God, he will have in heaven the same sinful desires that he possessed before coming to heaven. Death is not going to work a transformation equal to the grace of God. Those who do not enjoy the spiritual atmosphere of the presence of the Lord and the company of the saints now will not enjoy it later. That is why the following is such a true test of one's spiritual life: "We know that we have passed from death unto life, because we love the brethren" (1 Jn. 3:14).

d) Because man without the new birth is dead. The natural man is "dead in trespasses and sins" (Eph. 2:1). He is devoid of spiritual life altogether, and the only way in which life may be received is birth. Arthur W. Pink has well said, "Let us realize that the sinner is not ignorant, needing instruction; he is not weak and in need of invigoration; he is not sick and in need of doctoring. He is dead and needs to be made alive."[41] The Bible says of the unregenerated: that he is "alienated from the life of God" (Eph. 4:18); "To be carnally minded is death" (Rom. 8:6); "You have a name that you are alive, but you are dead" (Rv. 3:1, NKJV); "She that liveth in pleasure is dead while she liveth" (1 Tm. 5:6). What is the difference between one who is a Christian and one who is not? The answer in just one word is *life*! One has spiritual life, while the other is absolutely dead. Thus when Jesus said, "Except a man be born again, he cannot see the kingdom of God" (Jn. 3:3), He was not stating a theological dogma, nor laying down a divine edict. He was stating a simple fact—"He cannot see [let alone enter into] the kingdom of God." It is an utter impossibility. Yes, you must be born again!

---

41 Pink, source unknown.

3. *How the new birth is received*

a) The new birth may not be received through human effort. Man cannot in any wise—either by any virtue or effort of his own—bring himself into the position of divine sonship. Just as there is nothing the newly-born child does to bring about his natural birth, so there is nothing the unregenerated can do, of himself, to bring about his spiritual birth. Eternal life is the gift of God: "Not by works of righteousness which we have done, but according to his mercy he saved us" (Ti. 3:5); "For by grace are ye saved through faith; and that not of yourselves: it is the gift of God: Not of works, lest any man should boast" (Eph. 2:8–9); "Which were born, not of blood, nor of the will of the flesh, nor of the will of man, but of God" (Jn. 1:13).

While it is certainly true that the new birth is the gift of God, it is important that we realize that there are certain means and agencies involved in the experience.

b) The Holy Spirit is the agent. That is why it is referred to as the "renewing of the Holy Ghost" (Ti. 3:5). Jesus, in John 3:5–8, refers to our being "born of the Spirit." The Holy Spirit, coming into the heart of the believer, brings the life of God, thus enabling him to be a partaker of the divine nature.

c) The Word of God has a vital part. Indeed the Holy Spirit bears witness to the Word in bringing the new birth to pass: "Of his own will begat he us with the word of truth, that we should be a kind of firstfruits of his creatures" (Jas. 1:18); "Being born again, not of corruptible seed, but of incorruptible, by the word of God, which liveth and abideth for ever" (1 Pt. 1:23). The first creation was brought about by the operation of the Word of God and the Spirit: "And God said" (Gn. 1:3); "And the Spirit of God moved" (Gn. 1:2). Likewise, the creation of new creatures in Christ Jesus is brought to pass by the Word and the Spirit.

d) It is a divine mystery. The actual new birth is clouded in mystery. It is a miracle of God, and we cannot understand just how it takes place. That I live I know, but just how I live, I cannot tell. Nonetheless, this fact will not hinder me from enjoying life fully. So it is with the wonder of my spiritual life.

Concerning this very question, Jesus said to Nicodemus, "The wind bloweth where it listeth, and thou hearest the sound therof, but canst not tell whence it cometh, and whither it goeth: so is every one that is born of the Spirit" (Jn. 3:8). On every stormy day, people bear witness to the fact the wind is blowing, but no one has ever seen the wind itself. One can only observe the results of the wind's fury. Similarly, no one can observe the regenerating of a human soul, but we can easily bear witness to the results that are apparent in this divine operation. We know a little about how to bring this great experience about, but we do not know—nor need we know—how it actually takes place.

4. *How the new birth is brought about.* While we say there is nothing a man can do to regenerate himself, there is something which he must do to obtain the regenerating work of God in his own life. The following two experiences are necessary:

a) Believing the message of the gospel. The sinner must believe that the work of Christ on the cross is sufficient for salvation. There must ever be a close relationship between the doctrines of the cross and regeneration. First Peter 1:17–23 shows that it is on the basis of the "precious blood of Christ" one is born again (vv. 19, 23).

b) Accepting Jesus Christ as Savior. Salvation is an intensely personal experience. By placing our faith in all that Jesus is and has done for us, we receive Him as our Savior. "But as many as received him, to them gave he power to become the sons of God, even to them that believe on his name" (Jn. 1:12); "For ye are all the children of God by faith in Christ Jesus" (Gal. 3:26).

5. *The results of the new birth*

a) The new birth makes the believer a child of God. Thus he has the privilege of calling God his Father: "After this manner therefore pray ye: Our Father" (Mt. 6:9). All the resources of the heavenly Father are now open and available to him: "If ye then, being evil, know how to give good gifts unto your children, how much more shall your Father which is in heaven give good things to them that ask him?" (Mt. 7:11). Being now a child of God, he immediately becomes an heir of God: "The Spirit itself beareth witness with our spirit, that we are the children of God: And if children, then heirs; heirs of God, and joint-heirs with Christ" (Rom. 8:16–17).

b) It makes the believer a new creation and a partaker of the divine nature (2 Cor. 5:17; 2 Pt. 1:4). Thus, his whole attitude is transformed. He now loves the brethren: "Whosoever believeth that Jesus is the Christ is born of God: and every one that loveth him that begat loveth him also that is begotten of him" (1 Jn. 5:1); "For we know that we have passed from death unto life, because we love the brethren" (1 Jn. 3:14). He now loves God in a new and deeper way: "We love him, because he first loved us" (1 Jn. 4:19). He also has a deep love for the Word of God: "O how I love thy law! it is my meditation all the day" (Ps. 119:97); "As newborn babes, desire the sincere milk of the word, that ye may grow thereby" (1 Pt. 2:2). He will also have an inborn love for even his enemies: "But I say unto you, Love your enemies, bless them that curse you, do good to them that hate you, and pray for them which despitefully use you, and persecute you; That ye may be the children of your Father which is in heaven" (Mt. 5:44–45).

c) It enables the believer to live a life of victory over sin and the world. "And be renewed in the spirit of your mind; And that ye put on the new man, which after God is created in righteousness and true holiness" (Eph. 4:23–24). "If ye know that he is righteous, ye know that every one that doeth righteousness is born of him" (1 Jn. 2:29). "Whosoever is born of God doth not commit sin; for his seed remaineth in him: and he cannot sin, because he is born of God" (1 Jn. 3:9). The tense of the verb *doth not commit* [in Greek, *hamartian ou poiei*] used here makes it clear that what

John is saying is that the born-again child of God does not practice sin. He does not make it the habit of his life because he has a new nature within.[42]

F. Adoption

Adoption, as a doctrine, is a phase of our salvation which is seldom stressed, yet it is a great truth which every believer should realize and appropriate. The word *adoption* is used exclusively by Paul in his epistles. It occurs five times in his writings. Once the term is applied to Israel as a nation: "Who are Israelites; to whom pertaineth the adoption, and the glory, and the covenants, and the giving of the law, and the service of God, and the promises" (Rom. 9:4). In another passage, Paul uses it to refer to the full culmination of our experience at the second coming of the Lord: "Even we ourselves groan within ourselves, waiting for the adoption, to wit, the redemption of our body" (Rom. 8:23). The other three references speak of it as a present fact in the life of the Christian: "But when the fullness of the time was come, God sent forth his Son, made of a woman, made under the law, To redeem them that were under the law, that we might receive the adoption of sons" (Gal. 4:4–5); "Having predestinated us unto the adoption of children by Jesus Christ to himself, according to the good pleasure of his will" (Eph. 1:5); "For we have not received the spirit of bondage again to fear; but ye have received the Spirit of adoption, whereby we cry, Abba, Father" (Rom. 8:15).

1. *Definition.* It is important to realize that the manner in which Paul uses the word *adoption* has virtually nothing in common with the way in which it is used in our society today. According to human custom, adoption is a means by which an outsider may become a member of a family. But this is not so in the family of God.

Thus the word *adoption* literally means "to take voluntarily as one's own child." The believer, after becoming a child of God through the new birth, is immediately advanced to maturity of position, being constituted an adult son by this legal placing of adoption. There is therefore no childhood period in the sphere of Christian responsibility. God addresses the same appeal to holiness and service to every Christian, regardless of the length of time he may have been saved. According to Chafer:

> Whatever God says to the old and established saint, He says to every believer—including those most recently regenerated. There should be no misunderstanding respecting the "babe in Christ," mentioned in 1 Corinthians 3:1, who is a babe because of carnality and not because of immaturity of years in the Christian life. In human experience legitimate birth and adoption never combine in the same person. There is no occasion for a father

---

42 Archibald Thomas Robertson, *Word Pictures in the New Testament* (New York: R. R. Smith, Inc., 1930), VI, 223.

to adopt his own child. In the realm of divine adoption, every child born of God is adopted at the moment he is born. He is placed before God as a mature, responsible son.[43]

Adoption does not mean son-making, but son-placing. Thus the child is placed as a son; the minor as an adult. Thiessen summarizes, "In regeneration we receive a new life; in justification, a new standing; and in adoption, a new position."[44] Adoption takes place the moment we are born into the family of God. It is simultaneous with regeneration and justification. In the eternal councils of God, it took place when we were "chosen...in him before the foundation of the world" (Eph. 1:4–5). The full realization and enjoyment of adoption will happen at the time of the resurrection of our bodies when the Lord returns for His own (Rom. 8:23). Then we will be delivered from the bonds of mortality and will have a body "like unto his glorious body" (Phil. 3:21).

2. Results of adoption

a) The witness of the Holy Spirit. "To redeem them that were under the law, that we might receive the adoption of sons. And because ye are sons, God hath sent forth the Spirit of his Son into your hearts, crying, Abba, Father" (Gal. 4:5–6). The Holy Spirit bears witness to our sonship: "The Spirit itself beareth witness with our spirit, that we are the children of God" (Rom. 8:16). This will lead into a gracious fellowship with our heavenly Father: "Ye have received the Spirit of adoption, whereby we cry, Abba, Father" (Rom. 8:15). In keeping with this, the believer will be enabled to walk in the Spirit, for he will be led by the Spirit: "For as many as are led by the Spirit of God, they are the sons of God" (Rom. 8:14).

b) Deliverance from fear. "For ye have not received the spirit of bondage again to fear; but ye have received the Spirit of adoption" (Rom. 8:15). No longer will we be in bondage to the Law: "Wherefore the law was our schoolmaster to bring us to Christ, that we might be justified by faith. But after that faith is come, we are no longer under a schoolmaster" (Gal. 3:24–25). The Holy Spirit, indwelling our spirit, makes the consciousness of divine acceptance so real that all fear is banished.

c) Made heirs and joint-heirs with Christ. "And if children, then heirs; heirs of God, and joint-heirs with Christ; if so be that we suffer with him, that we may be also glorified together" (Rom. 8:17). A child may be an heir of his parents, but until he becomes of age he cannot possess his inheritance. When he becomes of age the inheritance is his.

---

43 Chafer, III, 243.
44 Thiessen, 373.

Now I say, that the heir, as long as he is a child, differeth nothing from a servant, though he be lord of all; But is under tutors and governors until the time appointed of the father. Even so we, when we were children, were in bondage under the elements of the world: But when the fullness of the time was come, God sent forth his Son, made of a woman, made under the law, To redeem them that were under the law, that we might receive the adoption of sons.... Wherefore thou art no more a servant, but a son; and if a son, then an heir of God through Christ.

—GALATIANS 4:1–5, 7

Too many redeemed children of the Lord do not realize their inheritance and are acting as servants rather than sons. The elder brother complained to his father, "Lo, these many years do I serve thee...and yet thou never gavest me a kid, that I might make merry with my friends....And he said unto him, Son, thou art ever with me, and all that I have is thine" (Lk. 15:29, 31). Let us begin to draw on our inheritance in Christ Jesus even now!

G. Sanctification

The doctrine of sanctification is of great importance because it has to do with the Christian's daily life. Thus it is a most practical consideration. A wide variety of teachings have been proclaimed under this heading. It is well to keep very close to the explicit teachings of Scripture in order not to be led into false notions of this great subject. We need to enter into the full benefits made available to us through this provision.

1. *Meaning of sanctification.* In the Scripture, sanctification has both a primary and a secondary meaning. It is important that these are kept in the proper order. The first thought that comes to most minds when this subject is mentioned is that of cleansing, but this is not its primary meaning.

a) The primary meaning—Sanctification entails a dedication, consecration, or setting apart for some specific and holy use. In the Old Testament, many inanimate things were said to be sanctified. A few examples are:

- A house: "And when a man shall sanctify his house to be holy unto the LORD, then the priest shall estimate it, whether it be good or bad: as the priest shall estimate it, so shall it stand" (Lv. 27:14).
- A field: "And if a man shall sanctify unto the LORD some part of a field of his possession, then thy estimation shall be according to the seed thereof: an homer of barley seed shall be valued at fifty shekels of silver" (Lv. 27:16).

- The vessels of the temple: "Moreover all the vessels, which king Ahaz in his reign did cast away in his transgression, have we prepared and sanctified" (2 Chr. 29:19).

This signifies that these vessels were set apart for the use of the worship of the Lord. They could be used for no other purpose. Belshazzar's culminating sin the night God destroyed him was that he took the vessels which had been set apart for the worship of God and drank wine from them in worship of heathen gods (Dn. 5:3–5). The firstborn of Israel were set apart, sanctified, unto the Lord: "Sanctify unto me the firstborn, whatsoever openeth the womb among the children of Israel, both man and of beast: it is mine" (Ex. 13:2). In the sanctification of each of these things, no thought of moral cleansing is implied. They were simply separated to the service of the Lord. It is important for every Christian to realize that he is a chosen vessel, set apart for a very special purpose for the glory of God. In this sense, he is already sanctified.

Jeremiah was sanctified before he was born: "Before thou camest forth out of the womb I sanctified thee, and I ordained thee a prophet unto the nations" (Jer. 1:5). This could not mean that Jeremiah was made perfect, but rather that he was set apart, consecrated, unto the service of Jehovah. Jesus is said to have been sanctified. John 10:36 speaks of "him, whom the Father hath sanctified, and sent into the world." "For their sakes I sanctify myself," said the Lord (Jn. 17:19). Jesus was already perfect, but these verses mean He was specially set apart for the purpose of coming into the world to provide redemption for mankind. The popular Greek word for "church" is *ekklesia,* which means "the called-out ones." Each member of the Church is especially set apart to bring glory to God. He is sanctified unto Him in this initial sense of the word.

It is like a connoisseur of fine brass who was searching through a pile of junk on the outskirts of an Eastern city, when he suddenly spied an old, battered brass pot. It was dirty, stained, and beaten up, but his practiced eye recognized a thing of value. He made his way through the junk and picked up the old pot and set it apart by itself. In so doing, he sanctified that vessel. This is sanctification in its initial application. Of course he must spend many hours cleansing, straightening out the dents, and polishing the old pot until it becomes a thing of beauty to grace his living room table. This process is sanctification in its second application.

b) The secondary meaning of sanctification involves cleansing and purging from moral defilement. This is a progressive experience. Unlike justification, which is a one-time happening only (there is no progress in justification), sanctification is both a crisis and a process. Put in another way, there is a positional justification, but not a progressive aspect. There may be said to be three time-elements in sanctification—three distinct phases or aspects.

2. Three aspects of sanctification

a) The initial act of sanctification is positional. The moment a person is born again he is said to be sanctified: "Such were some of you: but ye are washed, but ye are sanctified, but ye are justified in the name of the Lord Jesus, and by the Spirit of our God" (1 Cor. 6:11); "We are bound to give thanks alway to God for you, brethren beloved of the Lord, because God hath from the beginning chosen you to salvation through sanctification of the Spirit and belief of the truth" (2 Thes. 2:13). This is positional sanctification. At this time, the holiness of Jesus is imputed to the believer. He may not yet be holy in his daily living, but the holiness of Jesus is put to his account, much like the righteousness of Jesus is put to the account of the believer when he is justified. Christ is made unto us both righteousness and sanctification: "But of him are ye in Christ Jesus, who of God is made unto us...righteousness, and sanctification" (1 Cor. 1:30). There seems to be a difference between righteousness and holiness. *Righteousness* is a legal expression and has to do with rightness. It applies to conduct, or what a man does, while holiness is related to character, or what a man is.

Believers are called saints the moment they are saved: "Unto the church of God which is at Corinth, to them that are sanctified in Christ Jesus, called to be saints" (1 Cor. 1:2). This reads literally, "called saints." The *to be* is in italics in some versions, signifying that these words were not in the original text, but supplied by the translators. The Corinthian Christians were not called to be saints; they were saints, but anyone reading the epistle of 1 Corinthians is well aware that this church was far from being a perfect church. In fact, they are accused of being carnal and guilty of numerous dreadful sins. But they illustrate this first aspect of sanctification. They were positionally holy, having the holiness of Christ imputed to them, but they were far from manifesting His holiness in their practical living. In 1 Corinthians 1:8 Paul speaks of them as "blameless," and then he proceeds throughout the remainder of the book to blame them for everything. The following are also examples of Christians being called saints: Eph. 1:1; Col. 1:2; and Jude 1. The basis of this sanctification is the sacrifice of Jesus Christ on the cross: "By the which will we are sanctified through the offering of the body of Jesus Christ once for all" (Heb. 10:10); "Wherefore Jesus also, that he might sanctify the people with his own blood, suffered without the gate" (Heb. 13:12).

b) The process of sanctification is practical. Paul speaks of the Christians at Thessalonica as being sanctified: "We are bound to give thanks alway to God for you, brethren beloved of the Lord, because God hath from the beginning chosen you to salvation through sanctification of the Spirit and belief of the truth" (2 Thes. 2:13). But he also prays for their sanctification: "And the very God of peace sanctify you wholly; and I pray God your whole spirit and soul and body be preserved blameless unto the coming of our Lord Jesus Christ" (1 Thes. 5:23). He recognizes that these Christians were sanctified, in that the holiness of Christ was imputed to them, but now they needed that this imputed holiness should progressively become a practical part of their daily Christian living.

A similar truth is emphasized in Colossians 3:8–12. Here the Christians are said to "have put off the old man with his deeds" and to "have put on the new man, which is renewed in knowledge after the image of him that created him" (vv. 9–10). But in this same passage, they are admonished: "But now ye also put off all these; anger, wrath, malice, blasphemy, filthy communications out of your mouth....Put on therefore, as the elect of God, holy and beloved, bowels of mercies, kindness, humbleness of mind, meekness, longsuffering" (vv. 8, 12). What they had positionally, they must seek experientially.

Thus sanctification is seen to be a continuing process throughout a Christian's entire lifetime. It is not something negative. A man is not considered holy because of the things he does not do. Virtue cannot be judged by the vices from which a person abstains. There must be a positive conformation to the image of Christ. This is seen as a gradual growth in, not into, grace: "But grow in grace, and in the knowledge of our Lord and Savior Jesus Christ" (2 Pt. 3:18); "But we all, with open face beholding as in a glass the glory of the Lord, are changed into the same image from glory to glory, even as by the Spirit of the Lord" (2 Cor. 3:18); "For whom he did foreknow, he also did predestinate to be conformed to the image of his Son, that he might be the firstborn among many brethren" (Rom. 8:29); "Being confident of this very thing, that he which hath begun a good work in you will perform it until the day of Jesus Christ" (Phil. 1:6).

There is no promise in the Scripture that a Christian, in this life, will ever reach the place where he will no longer sin: "If we say that we have no sin, we deceive ourselves, and the truth is not in us" (1 Jn. 1:8). There are those who teach that it is possible to have an experience of sanctification, which they call a second work of grace. It is described in the following quotation:

> The heart is purified, cleansed and made holy. It is purged of that inbred sin nature; and from that time on, temptation comes only from without, not from within a heart that is sanctified. No one ever becomes so completely perfected that he is not subject to temptation. But one has greater and more glorious victory after he is sanctified because he no longer has to contend with the carnal nature. It has been removed.[45]

How wonderful that would be if it were true! The carnal nature, the flesh, never becomes sanctified: "That which is born of the flesh is flesh; and that which is born of the Spirit is spirit" (Jn. 3:6). God never builds on the old, fleshly, sinful nature. He

---

45 Source unknown.

always begins with something new. That is why Jesus said, "Ye must be born again" (Jn. 3:7). The flesh never becomes spiritual. Do not expect it to do so. The flesh in the most saintly person is the same flesh that is in the worst of sinners.

Paul likens the two sons of Abraham to the two natures of the believer: the fleshly nature and the new spiritual nature that he receives in the new birth. "For it is written, that Abraham had two sons, the one by a bondmaid, the other by a freewoman. But he who was of the bondwoman was born after the flesh; but he of the freewoman was by promise.... But as then he that was born after the flesh persecuted him that was born after the Spirit, even so it is now" (Gal. 4:22–23, 29). The flesh always opposes the Spirit. What are we to do? "Cast out the bondwoman and her son: for the son of the bondwoman shall not be heir with the son of the freewoman" (v. 30). Ishmael could not be corrected. He had to be cast out (Gn. 21:10). This is the way to deal with the flesh. Thus Paul admonishes, "Likewise reckon ye also yourselves to be dead indeed unto sin, but alive unto God through Jesus Christ our Lord" (Rom. 6:11). The flesh cannot be overcome by *eradication*. It will always be there as long as we are in this earthly body, neither can it be overcome by *suppression*. Some have earnestly tried to gain victory by the power of their will and the energy of the flesh. The victory is seen to be only through *identification* with Christ. Paul said, "I am crucified with Christ; nevertheless I live; yet not I, but Christ liveth in me: and the life which I now live in the flesh I live by the faith of the Son of God, who loved me, and gave himself for me" (Gal. 2:20).

The apostle sees himself identified with Christ in His death on the cross. He says in essence, "When Christ died, I died," meaning his old, fleshly nature: "I have been put to death on the cross with Christ" (Gal. 2:20, BAS.). Not only was he identified with Christ in His death but also in His resurrection, so he could say, "Nevertheless I live." This is a new victorious, resurrected life. But Paul hastens to explain, "It is no longer I who live, but Christ lives in me; and the life which I now live in the flesh I live by faith in the Son of God, who loved me gave Himself up for me" (Gal. 2:20, NASB). Paul states the facts plainly when he says, "Or do you not know that all of us who have been baptized into Christ Jesus have been baptized into His death? Therefore we have been buried with Him through baptism into death, so that as Christ was raised from the dead through the glory of the Father, so we too might walk in newness of life" (Rom. 6:3–4, NASB).

The key to this whole marvelous truth is found in Romans 6:11: "Even so consider yourselves to be dead to sin, but alive to God in Christ Jesus" (NASB). This is the practical point. Each believer is to consider himself to be dead to sin. If he is dead to sin, then he can no longer sin. But how can one consider, or reckon, himself to be dead to sin? He can consider it to be so because it is so. The admonition of verse 11 is based on the fact recorded in verses 6 and 7: "Knowing this, that our old self was crucified with Him, that our body of sin might be done away with, that we should no longer be slaves to sin; for he who has died is freed from sin" (Rom. 6:6, NASB). There is no Bible teaching to the effect that some Christians have died to sin and others have not. All believers have died unto sin in Christ's sacrifice, but all have not claimed the riches which were provided for them by that death. They are not asked to die experimentally; they are urged only to "reckon" themselves to be dead indeed unto sin. Note the tense of the verb: "Our old self was crucified with Him." This is considered to be an accomplished fact. Let us not forget that death is followed by resurrection: "For if we have become united with Him in the likeness of His death, certainly we shall be also in the likeness of His resurrection" (v. 5, NASB). What triumph this suggests! Now for the final, practical, every day admonition: "Therefore do not let sin reign in your mortal body that you should obey its lusts, and do not go on presenting the members of your body to sin as instruments of unrighteousness; but present yourselves to God as those alive from the dead, and your members as instruments of righteousness to God" (Rom. 6:12–13, NASB). This is progressive sanctification!

It is true that the New Testament speaks of the perfectness of the child of God: "Having therefore these promises, dearly beloved, let us cleanse ourselves from all filthiness of the flesh and spirit, perfecting holiness in the fear of God" (2 Cor. 7:1); "Be ye therefore perfect, even as your Father which is in heaven is perfect" (Mt. 5:48). We need, however, to understand the scriptural use of this word *perfect*. It has the sense of maturity and implies growth in spiritual stature, not sinless perfection. Noah is said to have been "a just [righteous] man and perfect in his generations" (Gn. 6:9). But his later drunkenness and shame shows that he was not sinlessly perfect (Gn. 9:20–27), nor was Job sinlessly perfect, even though his description reads, "That man was perfect and upright, and one that feared God, and eschewed evil" (Jb. 1:1). He later confessed, "Wherefore I abhor myself, and repent in dust and ashes" (Jb. 42:6). Maturity depends on constant growth. A green apple may be said to be perfect for that stage of its development, but it is not mature. So the fruit of the Spirit (Gal. 5:22–23) may be said to be perfect in the life of the young Christian, although it has not yet come to full maturity. Paul holds out before us that final maturity: "Till we all come in the unity of the faith, and of the knowledge of the Son of God, unto a perfect man, unto the measure of the stature of the fulness of Christ" (Eph. 4:13).

First John 3:9 has caused considerable misunderstanding: "Whosoever is born of God doth not commit sin; for his seed remaineth in him: and he cannot sin, because he is born of God." The question is cleared up when one notices that the verbs here are all in the present tense, and what John is saying is that he that is born of God does not practice sin. It is not the usual experience of his life. Sinning is the usual life of the sinner; it is the unusual experience of the Christian.

c) Complete and final sanctification. Sinless perfection and being wholly sanctified await the coming of the Lord Jesus. At that time we will be delivered from the body of this flesh: "For our conversation is in heaven; from whence also we look for the Saviour, the Lord Jesus Christ: Who shall change our vile body, that it may be fashioned like unto his glorious body, according to the working whereby he is able to subdue all things unto himself" (Phil. 3:20–21); "To the end he may stablish your hearts unblameable in holiness before God, even our Father, at the coming of our Lord Jesus Christ with all the saints" (1 Thes. 3:13). We have been saved from the penalty of sin. We are being saved from the power of sin. We shall yet be saved from the presence of sin. "Beloved, now are we the sons of God, and it doth not yet appear what we shall be: but we know that, when he shall appear, we shall be like him; for we shall see him as he is" (1 Jn. 3:2). In the meantime we are encouraged to "grow in grace, and in the knowledge of our Lord and Savior Jesus Christ" (2 Pt. 3:18). Beholding the glory of the Lord as in a glass, we are "changed into the same image from glory to glory, even as by the Spirit of the Lord" (2 Cor. 3:18).

3. *The means of sanctification.* As in so many phases of the Christian's experience, there is both a divine and a human side to the means of sanctification.

a) The divine side—the triune God

(1) The Father—Jesus prayed to the Father concerning His disciples, "Sanctify them through thy truth: thy word is truth" (Jn. 17:17). Paul prayed to the Father, "And the very God of peace sanctify you wholly; and I pray God your whole spirit and soul and body be preserved blameless unto the coming of our Lord Jesus Christ. Faithful is he that calleth you, who also will do it" (1 Thes. 5:23–24). The Father reckons the holiness of Jesus to the account of believers: "But of him are ye in Christ Jesus, who of God is made unto us wisdom, and righteousness, and sanctification, and redemption" (1 Cor. 1:30). The perfection of the believer is most certainly an important work of the Father: "Now the God of peace, that brought again from the dead the Lord Jesus, that great shepherd of the sheep, through the blood of the ever-lasting covenant, Make you perfect in every good work to do his will, working in you that which is wellpleasing in his sight" (Heb. 13:20–21). Sometimes the Father finds it necessary to use disciplinary measures to further the Christian's sanctifica-tion: "Furthermore we have had fathers of our flesh which corrected us, and we gave them reverence: shall we not much rather be in subjection unto the Father of spirits, and live? For they verily for a few days chastened us after their own pleasure; but he for our profit, that we might be partakers of his holiness" (Heb. 12:9–10).

(2) The Son, the Lord Jesus Christ—Jesus accomplished our sanctification through the shedding of His own precious blood: "By the which will we are sanc-tified through the offering of the body of Jesus Christ once for all" (Heb. 10:10); "Wherefore Jesus also, that he might sanctify the people with his own blood, suffered without the gate" (Heb. 13:12); "Husbands, love your wives, even as Christ also loved the Church, and gave himself for it; That he might sanctify and cleanse it with the washing of water by the word, That he might present it to himself a glorious Church,

not having spot, or wrinkle, or any such thing; but that it should be holy and without blemish" (Eph. 5:25–27).

(3) The Holy Spirit— The indwelling power and anointing of the Holy Spirit is perhaps the greatest agency to give us victory over the flesh: "If ye live after the flesh, ye shall die: but if ye through the Spirit do mortify the deeds of the body, ye shall live" (Rom. 8:13); "Being sanctified by the Holy Ghost" (Rom. 15:16); "Elect according to the foreknowledge of God the Father, through sanctification of the Spirit" (1 Pt. 1:2); "For the flesh lusteth against the Spirit, and the Spirit against the flesh" (Gal. 5:17). The works of the flesh are enumerated in Galatians 5:19–21: "Adultery, fornication, uncleanness, lasciviousness, Idolatry, witchcraft, hatred, variance, emulations, wrath, strife, seditions, heresies, Envyings, murders, drunkenness, revellings, and such like." But in verses 22 and 23 the characteristics of the fruit of the Spirit are depicted: "Love, joy, peace, longsuffering, gentleness, goodness, faith, Meekness, temperance." What an amazing contrast! How important that each Christian learn to abide in Christ, the Vine, that he may bring forth this fruit upon the branch of his life (Jn. 15:4–5)!

What a wonderful sanctifier the Holy Spirit is! How many have found that when they have received the fullness of the Spirit, the things of the world and of the flesh have simply dropped off. There is what has been called "the expulsive power of a new affection." When the Spirit fills the heart there is little relish for that which is displeasing to the Lord: "Walk in the Spirit, and ye shall not fulfil the lusts of the flesh" (Gal. 5:16).

b) The human side—It is abundantly true that God is the One who sanctifies the believer. No one can do it himself. Paul tells us, "For it is God that worketh in you both to will and do of his good pleasure" (Phil. 2:13). But at the same time, we are told in a number of Scripture passages that the Christian must sanctify himself: "Sanctify yourselves therefore, and be ye holy: for I am the LORD your God" (Lv. 20:7); "For they could not keep it at that time, because the priests had not sanctified themselves sufficiently" (2 Chr. 30:3). Hezekiah had discovered in the Law that Israel was to keep the Passover in the first month of every year. They had not been doing so, so the king gave commandment that the feast be kept. However, the priests had not sanctified themselves sufficiently in time for the observance in the first month. So the king gave them thirty more days in which to sanctify themselves. "And Joshua said unto the people, Sanctify yourselves: for to morrow the LORD will do wonders among you" (Jos. 3:5). "Having therefore these promises, dearly beloved, let us cleanse ourselves from all filthiness of the flesh and spirit, perfecting holiness in the fear of God" (2 Cor. 7:1). "But in a great house there are not only vessels of gold and of silver, but also of wood and of earth; and some to honor, and some to dishonor. If a man therefore purge himself from these, he shall be a vessel unto honor, sanctified, and meet for the master's use, and prepared unto every good work" (2 Tm. 2:20–21).

What can a man do to sanctify, cleanse, and purge himself? He can, by employing the means that God has put at his disposal, take advantage of the cleansing, sanctifying ministry of God in his behalf. What are these means which are at his disposal?

(1) Faith— It is by faith that the believer lays hold of the sanctifying blood of Jesus Christ, referred to above: "That they may receive forgiveness of sins and inheritance among those who have been sanctified by faith in Me" (Acts 26:18, NASB); "And put no difference between us and them, purifying their hearts by faith" (Acts 15:9).

(2) Obedience to the Word—The Word of God is said to be a great medium of sanctification: "Now ye are clean through the word which I have spoken unto you" (Jn. 15:3); "Sanctify them through thy truth: thy word is truth" (Jn. 17:17); "That he might sanctify and cleanse it with the washing of water by the word" (Eph. 5:26); "If we walk in the light, as he is in the light, we have fellowship one with another, and the blood of Jesus Christ his Son cleanseth [keeps on cleansing] us from all sin" (1 Jn. 1:7). Walking in the light is walking according to the Word of God: "Thy word is a lamp unto my feet, and a light unto my path" (Ps. 119:105). The only way the Word of God can be a cleansing agent in our lives is through obedience. This we must provide.

(3) Yielding to the Holy Spirit—The Holy Spirit never forces Himself upon anyone. There must be a surrender and a yielding of our members to His anointing. How graciously He takes the Word and makes its message plain, giving the believer the desire and the power to obey it: "Howbeit when he, the Spirit of truth, is come, he will guide you into all truth: for he shall not speak of himself; but whatsoever he shall hear, that shall he speak: and he will shew you things to come" (Jn. 16:13).

(4) Personal commitment—In the initial experience of sanctification, which takes place at conversion, God sets the believer apart as a chosen vessel for His use and glory. But there comes a time in the life of every sincere follower of the Lord Jesus Christ when he, by an act of deep personal commitment, sets himself apart for whatever service God would have him fulfill. At that time he separates himself from the things of the world and the flesh, and dedicates himself to God's perfect will for his life. The individual has recognized and received Jesus Christ as his Savior, but now he crowns Him as King and Lord over his life. This is a real act of sanctification. This is what Paul is referring to when he urges, "I beseech you therefore, brethren, by the mercies of God, that ye present your bodies a living sacrifice, holy, acceptable unto God, which is your reasonable service. And be not conformed to this world: but be ye transformed by the renewing of your mind, that ye may prove what is that good, and acceptable, and perfect will of God" (Rom. 12:1–2).

The definite surrender of the life to God constitutes the supreme condition to practical sanctification. This involves the yielding of all our members to His will: "Neither yield ye your members as instruments of unrighteousness unto sin: but yield yourselves unto God, as those that are alive from the dead, and your members as instruments of righteousness unto God" (Rom. 6:13); "I speak after the manner of men because of the infirmity of your flesh: for as ye have yielded your members servants to uncleanness and to iniquity unto iniquity; even so now yield your members servants to righteousness unto holiness" (Rom. 6:19); "If a man therefore purge himself from these, he shall he a vessel unto honor, sanctified, and meet for the master's use, and prepared unto every good work" (2 Tm. 2:21). How many times we have prayed, "Lord, purge me." Perhaps if we would listen carefully we might hear Him say, "Purge yourself!" There is much that we can do to keep our feet out of paths that would lead to sin and our eyes from that which would bring temptation. We can read and study God's Word, pray and seek His face, and keep ourselves in the place and company of spiritual fellowship. If we will do all we can in this sense to sanctify ourselves, certainly God will more than do His part. "Since God must make a man holy, if he is ever to be holy, man must yield himself to God that He may accomplish this work in him."[46]

H. Assurance

The greatest necessity in life is to believe on the Lord Jesus Christ and find eternal life: "For there is none other name under heaven given among men, whereby we must be saved" (Acts 4:12); "I am the way, the truth, and the life: no man cometh unto the Father, but by me" (Jn. 14:6). It is equally important that when one has come to believe he has a real and abiding assurance of having received eternal life. Many are filled with uncertainty as to their standing before God. They think they are saved, yet lack the positive ring of assurance. Others are afraid to be too positive on the subject, fearing perhaps to presume on the grace of God. As a result, their Christian life is apologetic and lacks the reality of true fellowship with God through Jesus Christ.

Surely God wants us to know we are saved. We believe that one of the chief reasons behind God's eternal plan of salvation is the re-establishing of fellowship between Himself and man. The foundation of fellowship is assurance. The former is utterly impossible without the latter. How can you have fellowship with someone when you have no confidence or understanding regarding your relationship with him? It is imperative that we know we are saved. Everything else in the Christian life depends on this assurance.

If, as we most surely believe the Scriptures teach, salvation must be obtained in this life, and it is impossible to receive it after having died an unbeliever, then surely there must be some means by which a seeking soul may know when he has found this most treasured possession. If assurance is not possible, then eternal life is but a chance.

---

46 Thiessen, 384.

1. *Reasons for the lack of assurance*

a) Sought through the keeping of the Law, through their own good works. God has said, "All our righteousnesses are as filthy rags" (Is. 64:6). If this is the picture of our righteousness, what must the Lord think of our sins? And, "All have sinned and come short of the glory of God" (Rom. 3:23). Salvation is by grace alone: "For by grace are ye saved through faith; and that not of yourselves: it is the gift of God: Not of works, lest any man should boast" (Eph. 2:8–9); "Now we know that what things soever the law saith, it saith to them who are under the law: that every mouth may be stopped, and all the world may become guilty before God. Therefore by the deeds of the law there shall no flesh be justified in his sight" (Rom. 3:19–20). Be it the initial experience or in the realm of assurance, we must ever look away from self to Christ, to what He has accomplished for us on Calvary. The Gospel is not a question of what we do, but of what Christ has done.

b) Have not been born again. They have substituted religious ceremony for a vital experience with God. Many have joined the church without having experienced the miracle of grace in their hearts by the Holy Ghost. Jesus said, "Ye must be born again" (Jn. 3:7), and no outward ordinance of religious ceremony will suffice.

Others have seen the folly of their sinful way and have decided to live a different kind of life. Morally they have definitely improved themselves, but this is not the new birth, which leads to a positive, lasting assurance of one's spiritual position.

c) Have not faced and dealt with the matter of sin in their lives. Too many have sought salvation merely as a panacea for sorrow, disappointment, or frustration. That which must be dealt with is the guilt of a soul that has broken God's laws. Man needs to be reconciled to God, and Jesus came to accomplish that reconciliation.

John the Baptist, introducing Jesus to the world at the beginning of His public ministry, said, "Behold the Lamb of God, which taketh away the sin of the world" (Jn. 1:29). A person cannot have real assurance of eternal life until he knows through accepting Jesus Christ as his personal Savior that his sins have been forgiven.

d) Lack of faith in what God says in His Word. Some are afraid to trust the promise of God. They look within themselves to discover if they feel saved instead of to God's Word and its positive declaration. They examine their conduct to assure themselves that they are living what they think is a Christian life. If their conduct is correct they feel they have assurance, but if they discover weaknesses and failure their assurance is gone. If God has been satisfied and has seen fit to receive us, it should be our joy to believe that we have been received and to rest upon His Word.

e) Thinking it is impossible to have an absolute assurance of salvation in this life. Some tell us we cannot know until the Judgment Day. Thank God, this waiting is not necessary. The judgment day for sin is passed when one accepts Jesus as His Savior. Sin was judged on Calvary. It is all in the past: "Verily, verily, I say unto you, He that heareth my word, and believeth on him that sent me, hath everlasting life, and shall not come into condemnation [judgment]; but is [already] passed from death unto life" (Jn. 5:24).

2. *Five positive means of assurance*

a) By the witness of the Spirit. When a sinner is born again, there comes to his heart a witness that something definite has been transacted between him and God. That this witness within is a true, scriptural experience is borne out abundantly by the following passages: "He that believeth on the Son of God hath the witness in himself" (1 Jn. 5:10); "The Spirit itself beareth witness with our spirit, that we are the children of God" (Rom. 8:16); "And hereby we know that he abideth in us, by the Spirit which he hath given us" (1 Jn. 3:24); "And because ye are sons, God hath sent forth the Spirit of his Son into your hearts, crying, Abba, Father" (Gal. 4:6).

What is this witness of the Spirit? How does it manifest itself? What does it feel like? It is not easy to put into words just exactly how this witness is manifested, for it is a witness not in the flesh but in the spirit. This is not a matter of feelings, but the witness of a new relationship. In Romans 8:15 we read, "For ye have not received the spirit of bondage again to fear; but ye have received the Spirit of adoption, whereby we cry, Abba, Father." The witness that is borne to us is that we are in the family of God. We are sons of God. A new relationship has been established and there need be no mistake about it. Can you imagine a son ever mistaking another woman for his mother? Though he may not have seen her for many years and she has changed with the passage of time, there is something within which responds to her, and he would be able to pick her out from among hundreds of others. There is a kinship, a witness, that never fails. And so, the Holy Spirit witnesses within our being when the new relationship with God becomes a reality in our life.

Notice that it is not our relationship to God, but—far better—His relationship to us, to which the Spirit bears witness. The blessed truth which is witnessed to our hearts is that God, the mighty Lord of glory, is our Father.

b) By the testimony of the Word of God. In John 3:36 we read, "He that believeth on the Son hath everlasting life." That is the simple statement of God's truth. If you believe on the Son, you have eternal life. The Father says it. After all, salvation is of and from God, and if He says I am saved, that should be enough. It is His holiness which has been abused by my sin, and when He is satisfied, I am too.

Notice Romans 10:9–10: "That if thou shalt confess with thy mouth the Lord Jesus, and shalt believe in thine heart that God hath raised him from the dead, thou shalt be saved. For with the heart man believeth unto righteousness; and with the mouth confession is made unto salvation." There are two requirements here. There must be an outward confession of the faith, which can only begin in the heart. Faith is not in the head, but in the heart. This implies a surrender to the One in whom we believe.

Another verse that gives positive faith to the believer is John 5:24: "Verily, verily, I say unto you, He that heareth my word, and believeth on him that sent me, hath everlasting life, and shall not come into condemnation; but is passed from death unto life." There are conditions to be fulfilled here, and when they are fulfilled, the promise is sure. Note particularly the use of the present tense: "hath everlasting life," "is passed from death unto life." Here is something experienced and assured right now; it is not a future blessing, but is ours now.

Perhaps the finest and most definite verse of all is 1 John 5:13: "These things have I written unto you that believe on the name of the Son of God; that ye may know that ye have eternal life, and that ye may believe on the name of the Son of God."

c) By the possession of love toward the brethren. If one loves the children of the Lord, it is a real proof that God has wrought a work of grace in his heart.

> For this is the message that ye heard from the beginning, that we should love one another. Not as Cain, who was of that wicked one, and slew his brother. And wherefore slew he him? Because his own works were evil, and his brother's righteous. Marvel not, my brethren, if the world hate you. We know that we have passed from death unto life, because we love the brethren. He that loveth not his brother abideth in death.
>
> —1 JOHN 3:11–14

There is a real fundamental principle behind this indication of salvation. It is brought out in the reference made in these verses to Cain and his attitude toward his righteous brother Abel. Why did Cain hate, or not love, his brother? We are told that it was "because his own works were evil, and his brother's righteous." In other words, if Cain's works had been righteous, he would have loved his brother Abel; but because they were evil, the very presence of Abel convicted him and made him miserable, and of course hatred toward his brother filled his heart. One can only love the children of the Lord when his own life has been transformed through Jesus Christ. Otherwise the life and experience of the Christian become a source of condemnation to his soul and he does not enjoy the company, nor love the fellowship, of those who have been made clean through Calvary.

This thought is clearly shown in the following words of Jesus:

> And this is the condemnation, that light is come into the world, and men loved darkness rather than light, because their deeds were evil. For every one that doeth evil hateth the light, neither cometh to the light, lest his deeds should be reproved. But he that doeth truth cometh to the light, that his deeds may be manifest, that they are wrought in God.
>
> —JOHN 3:19–21

Then again, love is a positive thing and is obtained only from Him who is the source of love. If we have that love, it proves we are in fellowship with Him: "Beloved, let us love one another: for love is of God; and every one that loveth is born of God, and knoweth God. He that loveth not knoweth not God; for God is love" (1 Jn. 4:7–8).

d) By the desire to obey God's commandments. "And hereby we do know that we know him, if we keep his commandments. He that saith, I know him, and keepeth not his commandments, is a liar, and the truth is not in him. But whoso keepeth his word, in him verily is the love of God perfected: hereby know we that we are in him" (1 Jn. 2:3–5).

Notice the definite statements in the text: "Hereby we do know that we know him…hereby know we that we are in him." This is the very certainty which we desire. If we keep His commandments, if we keep His Word, we shall know that we know Him, and the love of God will be perfected in us.

Why should obedience be a test of relationship? Is it not possible to obey God without a spiritual transformation of our life—without being saved? What fundamental principle is at stake? Without the transforming grace of God, it is impossible for man to adequately obey the commands of the Lord. It is not that it is improbable that unregenerate man will do the will of God; it is absolutely impossible. Paul tells us in Romans 8:7, "The carnal mind is enmity against God: for it is not subject to the law of God, neither indeed can be." The simple fact is that it is not possible for the carnal man to keep the Law of God.

There are several reasons why this is so. In the first place, man in himself does not have the power to keep the commands of the Lord. At the giving of the Law, the Israelites of old, in all good faith, said, "All the words which the LORD hath said will we do" (Ex. 24:3). However, they overestimated their ability, for it was not but forty days before they had broken the most important of these commands and were worshiping a golden image made from their very own trinkets. Man just cannot do the will of God of his own power. If the unsaved should set out to obey the commands of God, he would soon come face to face with 1 John 3:23, which says, "And this is his commandment, That we should believe on the name of his Son Jesus Christ." If he refused to do that, he would not be obeying the commands of God. So it is either a case of surrendering in saving faith to Jesus or admitting that one cannot be subject to the will of God.

Another reason why the carnal man cannot do the will of God is that the commandments of the Lord are spiritual. There are spiritual principles behind everything God asks us to do, and to these the natural man is utterly blind: "The natural man receiveth not the things of the Spirit of God: for they are foolishness unto him: neither can he know them, because they are spiritually discerned" (1 Cor. 2:14). Thus he fails to appreciate the will of God and consequently cannot obey it.

Then, the unsaved is not one who is uninformed concerning the things of God and who only needs to be instructed in order to accept and live in harmony with God's every desire. The unsaved man is depraved by nature. He has within him a rebellious spirit which says, as Pharaoh did, "Who is the Lord that I should obey him?" Before an unregenerate man even wants to do the will of God, there must be a change of his nature—a positive transformation.

If this natural, sinful man suddenly finds that he delights in the Law of the Lord and desires to do that which is pleasing to God, he can rightly believe that he has become a partaker of the divine nature.

Going a step further, we read in John 14:23, "If a man love me, he will keep my words." The manifestation of love will be obedience. The converse is equally true, that the basis of obedience is love: "He that hath my commandments, and keepeth them, he it is that loveth me" (Jn. 14:21). Thus, when a Christian delights to do the will of God, there is a positive evidence that he loves the Lord. As the text at the beginning of this section says, "In him verily is the love of God perfected" (1 Jn. 2:5).

Such a one finds that "His commandments are not grievous" (1 Jn. 5:3), and he can say, "I delight to do thy will, O God" (Ps. 40:8). So we conclude that "he that keepeth his commandments dwelleth in him, and he in him" (1 Jn. 3:24).

e) The transformation of life and desires. "If any man be in Christ, he is a new creature: old things are passed away; behold, all things are become new" (2 Cor. 5:17). It is difficult to explain how the process takes place, but we know when it happens. "The wind bloweth where it listeth, and thou hearest the sound thereof, but canst not tell whence it cometh, and whither it goeth: so is every one that is born of the Spirit" (Jn. 3:8).

A man knows the wind is blowing, not because he sees the wind, but because he sees the result of the wind. So it is with the Spirit in regeneration. We cannot see Him perform His wondrous work of regeneration, but we can see the result of it. We know salvation has come by the glorious transformation of life and desires. What are some of these indications that show salvation has come?

(1) Repentance—Repentance, a real turning from sin, is as much a work of the Spirit of God in the human heart as is the final inflow of the saving grace which transforms the life of the sinner. Certainly all the believing in the world will not bring assurance without a real turning from sin, and man needs God's help to do that.

If one is willing to forsake sin and truly repent, he can know the reality and everlasting assurance of God's salvation: "If ye know that he is righteous, ye know that every one that doeth righteousness is born of him" (1 Jn. 2:29).

(2) Peace—The redeemed soul can rightly expect a deep, settled peace in his soul: "Therefore being justified by faith, we have peace with God through our Lord Jesus Christ" (Rom. 5:1). Man was made for God. There was placed within his being a

spiritual faculty that is capable of communion with God. As long as sin separates and man is estranged from God, he can expect no real and lasting peace in his soul: "The wicked are like the troubled sea, when it cannot rest, whose waters cast up mire and dirt. There is no peace, saith my God, to the wicked" (Is. 57:20–21). But what an inexplicable peace comes the moment the burden of sin is rolled away—a "peace...which passeth all understanding" (Phil. 4:7). The enmity of our rebellious heart is gone, and we have become reconciled to God through our Lord Jesus Christ (Rom. 5:1, 11, 21; 6:11, 23).

(3) Power—When the guilt and condemnation of sin are gone, the bondage to the habits of sin will also go, and in its place will be a new power and joy in righteousness. For the first time, the soul will realize it is free. The sinner supposes that he is free because he can indulge in whatever he desires, but the fact is, he so indulges because he cannot resist temptation. He is bound, and must submit. The Christian, on the other hand, is free. He is free to say no to that which is unprofitable, and free to choose that which he knows is right and pleasing to God.

(4) Fear of death removed—The fear of death will be completely removed and an anticipation of seeing the Savior in glory will fill its place. The question of sin has been settled. Judgment and condemnation are passed, and to be absent from the body is now "to be present with the Lord." Earth is now the dressing room for heaven, and eternal life has begun.

> For we know if our earthly house of this tabernacle were dissolved, we have a building of God, an house not made with hands, eternal in the heavens. For in this we groan, earnestly desiring to be clothed upon with our house which is from heaven: If so be that being clothed we shall not be found naked. For we that are in this tabernacle do groan, being burdened: not for that we would be unclothed, but clothed upon, that mortality might be swallowed up of life.
>
> —2 CORINTHIANS 5:1–4

3. *What this assurance will mean to the believer*

a) It will stabilize his entire Christian experience. Whenever there is doubt and uncertainty there is instability. Until we realize that our experience is founded on that which is certain and unchanging, we will be like the man in the parable who built his house on the shifting sand. Emotional exultation and self-centered evidence make poor foundations for eternal life, but once one gains an assurance of salvation based on God's Word and His eternal work, it is as rock under the pillars of the soul. On this, one can build well, and build eternally.

A positive knowledge and assurance of salvation will stabilize the Christian in the hours of temptation. When others might look back and turn back, he will be kept by divine power. Without a settled surety, the blessing of the Christian life will fluctuate with every passing circumstance, but the sure knowledge of an eternal relationship with God will anchor all both sure and firm. Hear the words of Hebrews 6:17–20:

> Wherein God, willing more abundantly to shew unto the heirs of promise the immutability of his counsel, confirmed it by an oath: That by two immutable things, in which it was impossible for God to lie, we might have a strong consolation, who have fled for refuge to lay hold upon the hope set before us: Which hope we have as an anchor of the soul, both sure and stedfast, and which entereth into that within the veil; Whither the forerunner is for us entered, even Jesus, made an high priest for ever after the order of Melchisedec.

b) It will enable him to enjoy a positive life of prayer, giving faith that will appropriate the promises of God. The prayer that accomplishes things in the kingdom is founded on relationship to God. Jesus said, "When ye pray, say, Our Father" (Lk. 11:2), thus introducing us to a gracious place of assurance within the family of God.

c) It will give him power over Satan. The success of a conflict depends so much upon the ground upon which it is fought. If the devil can cause the Christian to forsake the high tower that is the name of Jesus and to do battle in his own strength, that arch-enemy of righteousness is sure to win a victory, for if he can cause a doubt in the midst of the fray, he knows he has the upper hand. But let that same Christian insist that his life is "hid with Christ in God" (Col. 3:3) and steadfastly refuse to meet the tempter apart from his relationship to the mighty Conqueror, and the devil will be a defeated foe. There is a conflict of faith wherein the Christian must boldly claim his position in Christ and refuse to take a backward step when the enemy assails. To do this, he must be sure of his relationship to God.

d) It will give power to his testimony and his influence over others. There are enough uncertainties in the world today. Religion has already offered too many vague and vain philosophies. Men are looking for something positive and real. They want a Christ who meets their needs, a Christ who can reveal Himself to them and make them know His presence in their lives, a Christ who can save and cause one to know he has been redeemed.

The Church today needs the rallying call of men and women who are sold out to God, who know whereon they stand, and who are not afraid to go ahead for God. Who knows how many about us in a world of sin are only waiting for that sincere and urgent call from those who know that salvation is real to cause them to forsake the ranks of sin and yield themselves to Jesus Christ?

The first essential and irreplaceable fact that must ring in every heart with an undoubted assurance is this: you must know that you have been born again. All else springs from this glorious knowledge. Here is the beginning of eternity: "For I know whom I have believed, and am persuaded that he is able to keep that which I have committed unto him against that day" (2 Tm. 1:12).

I. The security of the believer

1. *The problem.* If there is one heart-rending fact in our nation today, it is the multitude of men and women all about us who have once served the Lord in the church, professed a vital experience of salvation, given evidence of having received the baptism with the Holy Spirit—many even having preached the Word of God—who today never darken the door of the church, nor make any pretense of serving the God whom they once professed to love with all their hearts.

The more one contemplates the situation, the more he is convinced that we must be in that time the apostle Paul referred to when he wrote, "That day shall not come, except there come a falling away first, and that man of sin be revealed, the son of perdition" (2 Thes. 2:3). This is not reserved to what we like to refer to as the old line denominations.

Maybe this can be dismissed by saying these were never really saved in the first place or by believing that someday, even in the last moment of life, they will repent and return to the Lord. That these statements are true of many, we do not doubt, but we cannot blithely dismiss the whole matter in so simple a way. One great preacher who believed strongly in unconditional eternal security admitted this vast group of former witnesses to Christ, and he invented a virtual purgatory where they might be punished and purged from their backslidings before being admitted to the eternal reward of the saints. Such additions to the Scriptures are not wise.

2. *Assurance possible.* Note carefully that this subject is not being dealt with under the topic of the insecurity of the believer, but rather of the security of the believer. Above all else in our Christian life, we must have a positive assurance of our salvation. It is certainly God's will that men be saved—and that they know it. Every spiritual experience, every conflict with the enemy, every prayer that is uttered, and every promise that is pleaded is based on an assurance of one's position in Christ. Whenever a Christian endeavors to do anything for God, he must be able to stand on the firm foundation of the positive assurance that he is His child. He can have this assurance now: "Our gospel came not unto you in word only, but also in power, and in the Holy Ghost, and in much assurance" (1 Thes. 1:5).

3. *Two sides to the subject.* This subject constitutes an age-old battleground. The controversy has been waged for years, and there have been those who have gone to extremes on both sides of this question. Friends have parted. Churches have split. Denominations have started. Whole schools of theology have been formulated. There is only one way to settle the disagreement—by the Word of God. The only thing wrong with that statement is that both sides say exactly the same thing. The Calvinist

brings a long list of proof texts, each asserting that salvation is an eternal work and, once wrought in an individual heart it can never be undone. But the Arminianist comes along with an equally long list of Scriptures that prove the very opposite. "O, but," the Securityist says, "you interpret those wrongly;" and the Non-securityist says, "So do you."

The fact that this difference has continued for so many hundreds of years and that so many good men are on each side of the question proves that there must be Scripture and good reasoning for both positions. There are two sides to every theological question. This is because every doctrine has to do with God and man. There is no easy, simple way of proving one side right and the other wrong—or else it would have been done long ago. The Bible must be the answer, but the Bible must be interpreted by the Bible. The conclusion that must be reached is that there is truth in both positions, but to carry either to the extreme is either to destroy the believer's sense of assurance and security or to comfort the apostate in his apostasy.

Salvation—and every spiritual blessing—comes from God. But it has to do with man, and because of the manner in which God has made him as a free moral agent, he has a part to play in every spiritual transaction. Had God made him a mere automation, without a will or mind of his own, this would not be. But it is so. Therefore, in every theological matter there is God's side and man's. This simple fact helps us understand why it is possible to list two arrays of Scripture. They seem to contradict each other, but in reality they do not. One has to do with what God promises to do. The other has to do with what man must do. Actually they do not contradict, but compliment each other.

4. *The balance of Scripture.* Note these blessed promises of the keeping power of God: "And I give unto them eternal life; and they shall never perish, neither shall any man pluck them out of my hand. My Father, which gave them to me, is greater than all; and no man is able to pluck them out of my Father's hand. I and my Father are one" (Jn. 10:28–30). "For I am persuaded, that neither death, nor life, nor angels, nor principalities, nor powers, nor things present, nor things to come, Nor height, nor depth, nor any other creature, shall be able to separate us from the love of God, which is in Christ Jesus our Lord" (Rom. 8:38–39).

These glorious promises must not be minimized, but they must be understood in proper relation to such passages as:

> Let no man say when he is tempted, I am tempted of God: for God cannot be tempted with evil, neither tempteth he any man: But every man is tempted, when he is drawn away of his own lust, and enticed. Then when lust hath conceived, it bringeth forth sin: and sin, when it is finished, bringeth forth death.
>
> —JAMES 1:13–15

> For it is impossible for those who were once enlightened, and have tasted
> of the heavenly gift, and were made partakers of the Holy Ghost, and have
> tasted of the good word of God, and the powers of the world to come, If they
> shall fall away, to renew them again unto repentance; seeing they crucify to
> themselves the Son of God afresh, and put him to an open shame. For the
> earth which drinketh in the rain that cometh oft upon it, and bringeth forth
> herbs meet for them by whom it is dressed, receiveth blessing from God: But
> that which beareth thorns and briars is rejected, and is nigh unto cursing:
> whose end is to be burned.
>
> —HEBREWS 6:4–8

One of the basic rules of hermeneutics is that the obvious meaning of a passage
is probably closest to the true meaning. One can hardly read verses 4 and 5 of this
passage without believing that these expressions are describing one who has experienced salvation.

While this passage warns of the danger of turning away from Christ, it must not
be used to teach that there is no hope for one who falls away. The Scriptures make it
clear that if one who has turned away from Christ and has rejected Him will humble
himself and return to faith in Christ, there is forgiveness.

> Do ye think that the scripture saith in vain, The spirit that dwelleth in us
> lusteth to envy? But he giveth more grace. Wherefore he saith, God resisteth
> the proud, but giveth grace unto the humble. Submit yourselves therefore to
> God…Draw nigh to God, and he will draw nigh to you. Cleanse your hands,
> ye sinners; and purify your hearts, ye double minded. Be afflicted, and mourn,
> and weep: let your laughter be turned to mourning, and your joy to heaviness.
> Humble yourselves in the sight of the Lord, and he shall lift you up.
>
> —JAMES 4:5–10

> Take heed, brethren, lest there be in any of you an evil heart of unbelief,
> in departing from the living God. But exhort one another daily, while it
> is called To day; lest any of you be hardened through the deceitfulness of
> sin. For we are made partakers of Christ, if we hold the beginning of our
> confidence stedfast unto the end. While it is said, To day if ye will hear his
> voice, harden not your hearts, as in the provocation. For some, when they
> had heard, did provoke: howbeit not all that came out of Egypt by Moses.
> But with whom was he grieved forty years? was it not with them that had
> sinned, whose carcases fell in the wilderness? And to whom sware he that
> they should not enter into his rest, but to them that believed not? So we see
> that they could not enter in because of unbelief.
>
> —HEBREWS 3:12–19

> Brethren, if any of you do err from the truth, and one convert him; Let him
> know, that he which converteth the sinner from the error of his way shall
> save a soul from death, and shall hide a multitude of sins.
>
> —JAMES 5:19–20

Remember, this last passage was written to Christians (Jas. 1:2). To say that they were Jews is beside the point, for in Christ there is neither Jew nor Greek (Gal. 3:28). This verse speaks of a Christian who sins, but if one "convert him" (literally, turn him back from his sin) he "shall save a soul from death." It is possible then for the soul—not merely the body—of a Christian to die. Note also 1 John 5:16, "If any man see his brother sin a sin which is not unto death, he shall ask, and he shall give him life for them that sin not unto death. There is a sin unto death: I do not say that he shall pray for it."

The Christian is distinctly told, "Work out your own salvation with fear and trembling" (Phil. 2:12). But the Scripture hastens to add, "For it is God which worketh in you both to will and to do of His good pleasure" (v. 13). God put two great principles here in these verses, and the Bible says, "What therefore God hath joined together, let not man put asunder" (Mt. 19:6). The Bible presents and enforces both truths, and it never tones down the emphasis of one for fear of clashing with the other. In this very connection, Alexander McLaren says, "The short cord of my plummet does not quite go down to the bottom of the bottomless, and I do not profess to either understand God, or to understand man, both of which I should want to do before I understand the mystery of their conjoint action."[47] Here we have this positive setting forth of both of these lines of truth—what God says, He will do; and what He says, we must do: "Work out your own salvation…For it is God which worketh in you" (Phil. 2:12).

It certainly is not God's will that any of His children should be lost. We are also assured that He is able to keep them from falling. But these things are not automatic. God does not save a man against his will, nor does He keep him against his will. Just as faith and repentance are necessary for salvation, so they are necessary for the continuance of that salvation in the Christian's life. The scriptural condition for salvation is believing: "He that believeth on the Son hath everlasting life" (Jn. 3:36); "He that believeth on him is not condemned: but he that believeth not is condemned already, because he hath not believed in the name of the only begotten Son of God" (Jn. 3:18); "Verily, verily, I say unto you, He that heareth my word, and believeth on him that sent me, hath everlasting life, and shall not come into condemnation; but is passed from death unto life" (Jn. 5:24); "Verily, verily, I say unto you, He that believeth on me hath everlasting life" (Jn. 6:47). It is important to note that the word *everlasting* (literally, "eternal") in these last two verses is not an adverb but an adjec-

---

47 Alexander McLaren, source unknown.

tive. It is the life that is eternal, not one's possession of it. The word *believe* in these and other passages (Jn. 3:16; 6:40) is in the present tense and means "to believe and to continue to believe." It is the continuous or progressive present tense and implies not only an initial act of faith, but a maintained attitude. Assurance of security, therefore, is for the believing ones. The elect "are kept by the power of God through faith" (1 Pt. 1:5). Moody calls attention to the literal translation of John 10:28, and says:

> Not for one moment do I doubt this literal translation: "My sheep keep on hearing my voice, and I keep on knowing them, and they keep on following me: and I keep on giving them eternal life, and they shall never perish, and no one shall snatch them out of my hand." Some read the passage as if it says: "My sheep heard my voice, and I knew them, and they followed me, and I gave to them eternal life." The verbs are present linear, indicating continuous action by the sheep and by the Shepherd, not the punctiliar fallacy of the past tense.[48]

There is no promise in the Bible that God will keep the man who willfully turns away from the provisions of salvation which Christ has made. In fact, we are plainly told, "If we sin willfully after that we have received the knowledge of the truth, there remaineth no more sacrifice for sins, But a certain fearful looking for of judgment and fiery indignation" (Heb. 10:26–27). These verses describe an apostate who willfully turns away from, or rejects, Christ. "He that despised Moses' law died without mercy under [at the testimony of] two or three witnesses: Of how much sorer punishment, suppose ye, shall he be thought worthy, who hath trodden under foot the Son of God, and hath counted the blood of the covenant, wherewith he was sanctified, an unholy thing, and hath done despite unto the Spirit of grace" (Heb. 10:28–29). Such a one who turns from Christ most certainly has no hope, because he willfully turns from the only source of forgiveness and cleansing.

5. *Scriptural warnings.* The Word of God contains enough warning to preclude any thought of presuming on the grace of God. Followers of Christ are exhorted to "watch and pray, that ye enter not into temptation" (Mt. 26:41); to "beware lest ye also, being led away with the error of the wicked, fall from your own steadfastness" (2 Pt. 3:17); to "give diligence to make your calling and election sure" (2 Pt. 1:10); to hold "faith, and a good conscience" in order to avoid shipwreck (1 Tm. 1:19); to "be careful to maintain good works" (Ti. 3:8); to "stand fast in the Lord" (Phil. 4:1).

The Christian is warned of mortal danger through salt losing its savor (Lk. 14:34–35); through failing to abide in Christ (Jn. 15:6); in being moved away from the hope

---

48 Dale Moody, *The Word of Truth* (Grand Rapids, MI: Wm. B. Eerdmans Publishing Company, 1981), 356.

of the gospel (Col. 1:23); in erring from the faith (1 Tm. 6:10); in being taken captive by the devil (2 Tm. 2:24–26); in neglecting so great salvation (Heb. 2:3); in departing from the living God (Heb. 3:12); in being hardened through the deceitfulness of sin (Heb. 3:13); in willfully sinning (Heb. 10:26–31); in erring from the truth (Jas. 5:19–20); in being overcome by the world (2 Pt. 2:20–22); and in leaving one's first love (Rv. 2:4–5).

6. *The believer's responsibility.* However, in recognizing the possibility of the union with Christ being broken, we must not think of returning to a legalistic position where we are kept by our own efforts. A Christian can no more keep himself in the power of the flesh than he can save himself by this means. We are "kept by the power of God through faith unto salvation" (1 Pt. 1:5). Our part is to believe Him; His part is to keep us. The believer's responsibility is to continually take advantage of the means of grace which God has provided for His children. He cannot keep himself, but the Christian must submit himself to the mighty keeping power of God within him. The only way he can work out his own salvation is as God works within him (Phil. 2:12–13). The believer's part is to constantly feed on God's Word, to yield to the ministry of the Holy Spirit, and to maintain unbroken fellowship with God through prayer. Through faith, obedience, and yieldedness to His will, he avails himself of all God's grace has supplied. We are not saved because of our faith and obedience, nor are we kept saved by these. But it is faith and obedience that keeps us in fellowship with Christ, who is faithful to keep that which we have committed unto Him: "For I know whom I have believed, and am persuaded that he is able to keep that which I have committed unto him against that day" (2 Tm. 1:12).

If the follower of Christ will do these things, he is eternally secure. If through flagrant unbelief; unconfessed, willful sinning; or apostasy he does not abide in Christ, he has no promise that he will be kept. Nowhere in the Scripture are we given license to presume against God's grace. We have a High Priest who is "touched with the feeling of our infirmities" (Heb. 4:15) and who "is able also to save them [us] to the uttermost that come unto God through him, seeing he ever liveth to make intercession for them [us]" (Heb. 7:25). But we are enjoined to "draw near with a true heart in full assurance of faith," and to "hold fast the profession of our faith without wavering" (Heb. 10:22–23). Maintaining our salvation is not a neat balancing act that we must perform as we endeavor to walk a narrow path with a deep chasm on either side. There is a chasm, to be sure; but by faith, obedience, and faithful communion with our Lord we are privileged to walk farther and farther from it as we make our way up the headlands toward the city of God.

7. *An illustration.* Some years ago a great jet airliner was coming through a storm, getting tossed and buffeted with the elements. Finally, when the troubled area was passed, a little lady passenger sighed with great relief and settled down to rest with the words, "Well, *we* made it." She had done her part. Little did she think, or possibly

even know, of the planning behind that great plane: the years of experience with past models, the thousands of hours skilled technicians had spent over the drawing boards, the almost endless tests in the wind tunnels with every conceivable kind of model, the thousands of men who had labored on all the component parts, the skill and precision with which it was put together with every stress minutely calculated. She did not consider the experience of the pilot and his crew, with perhaps a million or more miles of successful flight behind them. She had been filled with worry and apprehension, thinking she must do something. If only someone had said, "Settle down, little lady. Your security does not lie in your fear and concern. It rests in the great ship and her skillful crew."

So the eternal destiny of our souls! When the storms of temptation, doubt, and fear would buffet the ship of your experience, do not forget the loving faithfulness of your heavenly Father, who, before the world was, laid the foundation of your salvation. Do not forget all the divine skill, labor, and sacrifice that have gone into it. Remember the Pilot has taken many a soul through storms worse than you will ever have to endure. He experienced all these tempests Himself: "For it became Him, for whom are all things, and by whom are all things, in bringing many sons into glory, to make the captain of their salvation perfect through sufferings....that he might be a merciful and faithful high priest" (Heb. 2:10, 17). He made it! And He is able to help all who trust in Him.

Only, do not forsake the ship. Do not get out and trust your parachute or endeavor to fly your flimsy plane through the storm. Stay in the ship of His salvation. Fasten the seatbelt of His promises a little tighter. Cheer your heart with worship and praise to Him who is at the controls. Keep close to Jesus. Remember His faithfulness—"Being confident of this very thing, that he which hath begun a good work in you will perform it until the day of Jesus Christ" (Phil. 1:6). Keep close to Him and you will touch down with the softest, most perfect landing on the shore of eternity. Keep close to Jesus!

The Doctrine of the Holy Spirit

Pneumatology

Introduction

I. The Work of the Holy Spirit
  A. In relation to the world in general
    1. *With regard to the material universe*
    2. *With regard to humanity as a whole*
  B. In relation to Jesus Christ
    1. *Concerning Christ's person*
    2. *Concerning Christ's earthly ministry*
    3. *Concerning Christ's death and resurrection*
    4. *Concerning Christ's ministry to the church*
  C. In relation to the Christian believer
    1. *The Spirit's work in salvation*
    2. *The Holy Spirit's work subsequent to salvation*
    3. *The Holy Spirit's work in connection with ministry or service*
    4. *The Holy Spirit's work in connection with resurrection*

II. The Ministry of the Holy Spirit as the Comforter
  A. He is our Teacher—the Spirit of truth who "shall teach you all things" (Jn. 14:26).
    1. *He guides into truth.*
    2. *He acts as God's mouthpiece for revealing His words and desires.*
    3. *He reveals things that are yet to come.*
  B. He is our reminder.
    1. *Reminding of the Word of God*
    2. *Reminding of a special promise God has given in the past*
    3. *Bringing to memory thoughts and Scriptures when preaching or testifying*
  C. He is the revealer of Jesus.
    1. *Christ revealed to the believer by the Holy Spirit*
    2. *Christ revealed in the believer by the Holy Spirit*
    3. *Christ revealed through the believer by the Holy Spirit*
  D. He is the reprover and convicter of the world.

III. The Fruit of the Spirit
  A. The contrast between the works of the flesh and the fruit of the Spirit
  B. The secrets of fruit-bearing

C. What does it mean to abide in Christ?

D. The difference between the gifts of the Spirit and the fruit of the Spirit

E. The relationship between the gifts of the Spirit and the fruit of the Spirit

F. Detailed characteristics of the fruit of the Spirit

    1. *Love*

    2. *Joy*

    3. *Peace*

    4. *Longsuffering—patience*

    5. *Gentleness—kindness*

    6. *Goodness*

    7. *Faith*

    8. *Meekness*

    9. *Temperance—self-control*

IV. The Baptism With the Holy Spirit

A. The name of the experience

    1. *Negatively*

    2. *Positively—It is the baptism with the Holy Spirit.*

B. What the baptism with the Holy Spirit is

    1. *Negatively*

    2. *Positively*

C. The purpose and necessity of the baptism with the Holy Spirit

    1. *Power for service*

    2. *Power for spiritual warfare*

    3. *Power for overflow*

    4. *Power for ability*

D. For whom is the baptism with the Holy Spirit?

    1. *Negatively*

    2. *Positively—for all who believe*

E. Conditions for obtaining the baptism with the Holy Spirit

    1. *Repentance from sin*

    2. *A definite experience of salvation*

    3. *Water baptism*

    4. *A deep conviction of need*

    5. *A measure of consecration*

F. How to receive the baptism with the Holy Spirit

    1. *By faith*

    2. *By a full yieldedness of the entire being*

    3. *A word about "tarrying" for the baptism with the Holy Spirit*

G. The manner in which the baptism with the Holy Spirit is received

    1. *Suddenly, while sitting and expecting Him to come*

    2. *Instantly and unexpected, while listening to a sermon*

    3. *Through prayer and the laying on of the apostles' hands*

    4. *Through the seeker's personal prayer and faith*

H. The evidence and results of the baptism with the Holy Spirit

    1. *Immediate evidences*

    2. *Permanent evidences*

I. Additional fillings with the Holy Spirit

    1. *For defending the Faith*

    2. *For rebuking the power of the devil*

    3. *To give disciples new boldness and power*

    4. *Grace and power to endure persecutions for the sake of the gospel*

V. Offenses Against the Holy Spirit

A. Offenses committed by the unbeliever

    1. *Resisting the Holy Spirit*

    2. *Insulting or spiting the Holy Spirit*

    3. *Blaspheming the Holy Spirit—the unpardonable sin*

B. Offenses committed by a believer

    1. *Grieving the Holy Spirit*

    2. *Lying to the Holy Spirit*

    3. *Quenching the Holy Spirit*

VI. The Gifts of the Spirit

A. The background for spiritual gifts

    1. *The promise given*

    2. *The promise fulfilled*

B. The vocabulary of spiritual gifts

    1. *Spirituals,* pneumatika

    2. *Spiritual gifts,* charismata

    3. *Administrations,* diakonia

    4. *Operations (inworkings),* energemata

    5. *Manifestations,* phanerosis

    6. *Diversity,* diairesis

C. The purpose of spiritual gifts

    1. *Edification*

    2. *Exhortation*

    3. *Comfort*

D. The gifts enumerated in 1 Corinthians 12

    1. *Word of wisdom*

CHAPTER SIX

THE DOCTRINE OF THE HOLY SPIRIT

Pneumatology

INTRODUCTION

UNDER THE STUDY of the doctrine of theology, the subject of the Trinity of the Godhead has already been covered. Reference was made to the third person of the Trinity, the Holy Spirit. The previous study covered His personality, His deity, His names, and His symbols. In our present section, we will enter more minutely into a consideration of the ministry of the Holy Spirit as the outworking of the characteristics that have been covered. We plan to study the work of the Holy Spirit, the ministry of the Holy Spirit as the Comforter, the fruit of the Spirit, the baptism with the Holy Spirit, offenses against the Holy Spirit, and the gifts of the Spirit.

I. THE WORK OF THE HOLY SPIRIT

One of the first thoughts which must impress itself upon us as we pursue this study is the diversified ministry that is attributed to the Spirit. Let us put out of our minds completely the impression that the Holy Spirit did not come into the world until the Day of Pentecost, described in Acts 2, for it will be noted that the Spirit has been active in every dispensation and has been present wherever God has been revealed.

It is not always possible, nor is it necessary, to minutely distinguish the work of the Spirit from that of the Father and the Son. God is One, and the inter-relationship between the various activities of each person of the Godhead is so close that we cannot always discern one from the other. In many of His activities God works through the Son in the power of the Spirit. As a general principle, it might be said that all the divine workings originate with the Father, are carried out by the Son, and are brought to fruition by the Holy Spirit. We shall study the works of the Holy Spirit as they relate to the physical universe, the unsaved, the Lord Jesus Christ, and the Christian believer.

A. In relation to the world in general

1. *With regard to the material universe*

a) The Holy Spirit as an agent in Creation. Each person in the Godhead is represented as having created all things.

- The Father—"God…Hath in these last days spoken unto us by his Son…by whom also he made the worlds" (Heb. 1:1–2).
- The Son—"All things were made by him; and without him was not any thing made that was made" (Jn. 1:3); "For by him were all things created, that are in heaven, and that are in earth, visible and invisible, whether they be thrones, or dominions, or principalities, or powers: all things were created by him, and for him" (Col. 1:16).
- The Holy Spirit—"Thou sendest forth thy Spirit, they are created: and thou renewest the face of the earth" (Ps. 104:30); "The Spirit of God hath made me, and the breath of the Almighty hath given me life" (Jb. 33:4).

These various passages are not to be thought of as contradictory, but rather a setting forth of the principle which prevails throughout the Bible that all three persons of the Trinity work together for the accomplishing of the divine will. In fact, the opening statement of the Bible—"In the beginning God created the heaven and the earth"—suggests that the entire Trinity was active, for the word *God* is the Hebrew *Elohim*, a uni-plural word indicating more than one personality.

b) Three specific acts of creation. In the account of Creation, as given in Genesis 1:1–27, the Hebrew word *bará*, which means "to create," is used but three times. At other times, God is said to have made certain things, which would imply using something that was already in existence. These three occasions represent the three great distinctive kingdoms: the heavens and the earth (1:1), animal life (1:21), and human life (1:26–27). Evolutionists try to tell us that each kingdom is the result of the gradual development of a lower kingdom, but God's Word emphasizes that a new kingdom was made possible only by a special act of creation. It is interesting to our present study to notice that the Holy Spirit is said to have been active in the creation of each of these three kingdoms:

(1) The heavens and the earth—Gn. 1:2; Jb. 26:13; Ps. 33:6;

(2) Animal life—Ps. 104:30; also vv. 11–12, 14, 17–18, 20–21, 25–26;

(3) Human life—Jb. 33:4.

2. *With regard to humanity as a whole*

a) The Holy Spirit witnesses to the redeeming work of Christ. The Holy Spirit bears witness to God's plan for and method of salvation. None would know it better than the Holy Spirit.

> The God of our fathers raised up Jesus, whom ye slew and hanged on a tree. Him hath God exalted with his right hand to be a Prince and a Saviour, for to give repentance to Israel, and forgiveness of sins. And we are his witnesses

of these things; and so is also the Holy Ghost, whom God has given to them that obey him.

—Acts 5:30–32

b) The Holy Spirit convicts the world of sin, righteousness, and judgment. "And when he is come, he will reprove the world of sin, and of righteousness, and of judgment" (Jn. 16:8). The word *reprove* is variously translated in different versions as "convince," "convict," "expose," and "rebuke." Someone has stated, "These three things are the most difficult to impress on any man, for he can always attempt to justify himself by asserting an excusable motive for evil actions, or by pleading a relative scale of ethical standards in the place of absolute righteousness, or by assuming that judgment is indefinitely deferred so that it is no real threat."[1]

(1) "Of sin, because they believe not on me" (Jn. 16:9)—Here is something impossible for man to accomplish. No one can produce conviction in the heart of another. Only the Holy Spirit can overcome the blindness and deceitfulness of the sinful, human heart and make a man realize the greatness of his own iniquity. Notice the particular sin of which the Holy Spirit will convict. It is not the sin of stealing, drunkenness, or adultery. Conscience will convict a man that such things are wrong, but the Holy Spirit convicts of a sin of which conscience would never convict him— the sin of unbelief: "Of sin, because they believe not on me" (Jn. 16:9). Unbelief of Jesus Christ is the greatest of all sins, for it causes the rejection of God's only means of forgiveness and thus brings all the condemnation of one's every sin upon the one who fails to appropriate Christ's salvation through faith. As George Smeaton has so aptly worded it:

> The sin of unbelief is here described, with all the enormous guilt attached to it, as a rejection of the proposal of reconciliation, as the chief and the supreme sin, because a sin against the remedy—as sinful in itself, and as preventing the remission of all other sins…all other sins, original and actual, with all their guilt, are remissible through faith in Christ. But this sin involves the rejection of the graciously provided remedy; and final unbelief has nothing to interpose between the sinner and righteous condemnation…The sin of unbelief is here described as if it were the only sin, because, according to the happy remark of Augustine, while it continues, all other sins are retained, and when it departs all other sins are remitted.[2]

---

1 The authors are indebted to the unknown source of this quote.

2 George Smeaton, *The Doctrine of the Holy Spirit* (London, the Banner of Truth Trust, 1958), 178.

(2) "Of righteousness, because I go to my Father, and ye see me no more" (Jn. 16:10)—The righteousness of which the Spirit convicts is not any human righteousness, but Christ's righteousness. The righteousness of Christ is attested to by the fact that He was raised from the dead and has ascended to the Father. Had He been an imposter—as the religious world insisted when they cast Him out—the Father would not have received Him. The fact that the Father did exalt Him to His own right hand demonstrates that He is completely innocent of the charges laid against Him. Moreover, it proves that He had paid the full price for the believer's sins, which had been laid upon Him. Again, Smeaton declares:

> To convince the world of righteousness, must mean that the Spirit gives convincing evidence, not merely that His cause was good, and that He is innocent, but that in Him is found the righteousness which the world needs, the imputed righteousness which was graciously provided for us and becomes ours by faith.[3]

His returning to the Father gave evidence that He had fully completed the task for which He was sent into the world—that of providing righteousness for those who would believe on Him.

(3) "Of judgment, because the prince of this world is judged" (Jn. 16:11)—The world stands guilty for refusing to believe in Christ. Its condemnation is acclaimed by the righteousness of Christ exhibited in His going to the Father; therefore, nothing awaits it but judgment. The greatest demonstration of judgment is that the prince of this world is judged: "Now is the judgment of this world: now shall the prince of this world be cast out" (Jn. 12:31). If Christ would judge the prince of this world, then all who follow him will likewise be judged.

It is important for every Christian to realize how this convicting ministry of the Spirit is to be accomplished. The Holy Spirit does not operate in this capacity through the atmosphere, as it were. He ministers through Spirit-filled believers. Jesus said, "If I go not away, the Comforter will not come unto you; but if I depart, I will send him unto you. And when he is come [unto you], he will reprove the world of sin, and of righteousness, and of judgment" (Jn. 16:7–8). This emphasizes the importance of each believer living a Spirit-filled life.

B. In relation to Jesus Christ

Probably the most profound statement of all time is found in the first four words with which our Bible begins: "In the beginning God." No explanation is given. No attempt is made to account for His being. This greatest-of-all-revelations is given

---

3 Smeaton, 179.

simply. Only as God has chosen to reveal Himself can we ever hope to have any insight whatever concerning Him. God has done this through the person of His Son: "God, who at sundry times and in divers manners spake in time past unto the fathers by the prophets, Hath in these last days spoken unto us by [literally, in] his Son" (Heb. 1:1–2). Jesus could say, "He that hath seen me hath seen the Father" (Jn. 14:9), for the Son was the "brightness of his glory, and the express image of his person" (Heb. 1:3). But then we have a further revelation of the Son by the Holy Spirit. Jesus said of the Spirit, "He shall glorify me: for he shall receive of mine, and shall shew it unto you. All things that the Father hath are mine: therefore said I, that he shall take of mine, and shall shew it unto you" (Jn. 16:14–15). Thus we see the progressive revelation: the Father revealed by the Son and the Son revealed by the Spirit. G. Campbell Morgan speaks of Jesus being the revelation of the Father and the Holy Spirit as the interpretation of the revelation.[4]

It will be most profitable, then, to study the closeness of the ministry of the Holy Spirit to the person and ministry of the Lord Jesus, especially as He took upon Himself the lowliness of our human nature. In studying the work of the Holy Spirit in the life of Christ, we recognize that the Holy Spirit has little, if anything, to do with the deity of Christ. That was not necessary, for it was perfect and had always been so. But He had much to do with Christ's human nature. Attention will be called to the work of the Holy Spirit in Christ's person, Christ's earthly ministry, concerning Christ's death and resurrection, and Christ's ministry to the church today.

1. *Concerning Christ's person*

a) He was sent into the world by the Holy Spirit, along with the Father. "And now the Lord GOD, and his Spirit, hath sent me. Thus saith the LORD, thy Redeemer, the Holy One of Israel" (Is. 48:16–17). Christ did not have His beginning in Bethlehem. He existed from all eternity; thus, it could be said that He who already existed was sent into the world.

b) He was conceived, or begotten, by the Holy Spirit. We have this fact confirmed in three passages of Scripture: "And the angel answered and said unto her, The Holy Ghost shall come upon thee, and the power of the Highest shall overshadow thee: therefore also that holy thing which shall be born of thee shall be called the Son of God" (Lk. 1:35); "When as his mother Mary was espoused to Joseph, before they came together, she was found with child of the Holy Ghost" (Mt. 1:18); "The angel of the Lord appeared unto him in a dream, saying, Joseph, thou son of David, fear not to take unto thee Mary thy wife: for that which is conceived in her is of the Holy Ghost" (Mt. 1:20).

---

4 G. Campbell Morgan, *The Gospel According to John* (New York: Fleming H. Revell Company, 1909), 247.

In the conception of Jesus Christ, it was not a new being who was called into life (as in all other cases of human birth), but one who had existed eternally and who, by His conception, now entered into vital relationship with human nature. When Christ was conceived, it was not the conception of a human personality but of a human nature. There is only one personality in Jesus Christ, namely the eternal One, who was and is the Son of God.

c) His reception in the temple was arranged by the Holy Spirit.

> And, behold, there was a man in Jerusalem, whose name was Simeon; and the same man was just and devout, waiting for the consolation of Israel: and the Holy Ghost was upon him. And it was revealed unto him by the Holy Ghost, that he should not see death, before he had seen the Lord's Christ. And he came by the Spirit into the temple: and when the parents brought in the child Jesus, to do for him after the custom of the law, Then took he him up in his arms, and blessed God, and said, Lord, now lettest thou thy servant depart in peace, according to thy word: For mine eyes have seen thy salvation.
>
> —LUKE 2:25–30

This is a remarkable passage in relation to the ministry of the Holy Spirit as He witnessed to Simeon and then arranged the fulfillment of His prophecy to that old saint.

d) His growth is attributed to the Holy Spirit. The Bible attributes the physical, intellectual, and spiritual growth of Jesus to the Holy Spirit: "And the child grew, and waxed strong in spirit, filled with wisdom: and the grace of God was upon him" (Lk. 2:40). In Luke 2:52 we are told, "And Jesus increased in wisdom and stature, and in favour with God and man." Jesus was not created an adult, as Adam was. He grew and developed as any other child grows, except He did not possess any of the detriments of a sinful nature. His development was rapid and beautiful so that when He was only twelve the rabbis in the temple were astonished as they listened to Him. This was due to an operation of the Holy Spirit within Him. Listen to Isaiah: "And there shall come forth a rod out of the stem of Jesse, and a Branch shall grow out of his roots: And the spirit of the LORD shall rest upon him, the spirit of wisdom and understanding, the spirit of counsel and might, the spirit of knowledge and of the fear of the LORD" (Is. 11:1–2). Christ's Godhood could not grow one whit, in any sense; it was perfect and complete. But His humanity did develop and increase in its abilities. Palmer states, "Nor was this due to the fact that the man Jesus was inseparably connected with the divine person, so that as a man He had omniscience. For that would destroy the true humanity of Jesus."[5]

e) He was led by the Holy Spirit into the wilderness to be tempted by the devil. "Then was Jesus led of the spirit into the wilderness to be tempted of the devil" (Mt. 4:1). "And immediately the spirit driveth him into the wilderness. And he was there in the wilderness forty days, tempted of Satan" (Mk. 1:12–13). Palmer comments that Luke:

> ...uses a verbal tense, the imperfect, that indicates not a momentary act, but a period of time. The clear indication, therefore, is that the Holy Ghost not only led Christ into the wilderness, but that all the time Christ was there the Holy Spirit was with Him, guiding and helping Him overcome the temptations. And after they were all over, Luke says that He "returned in the power of the Spirit" (4:14). In other words, that whole period of temptation from beginning to end was under the control of the Holy Spirit, and it was by means of the Spirit that Jesus' human nature was given the strength to overcome the severe temptations placed before Him. He did not have victory because His divine nature infused divine qualities into His human nature, enabling Him to resist. No, for then He no longer would have been a man. Instead, being complete man, He relied upon the indwelling Spirit for the ability to resist evils.[6]

Note carefully that Jesus was not cornered by the devil. He was led out—or as Mark says, "driven"—by the Spirit to meet the enemy. This is instructive to believers today. It strongly teaches that the Christian is not necessarily out of the will of God when he is being subjected to personal testing. Also, he may have the same victory as Christ, for he has the same Holy Spirit abiding within.

2. *Concerning Christ's earthly ministry.* Jesus was indeed very God, but when He came into this world it seems that He subjected Himself to the Father in such a way that His ministry was through the direction and power of the Holy Spirit. Note the following examples of the Spirit's activity in Christ's ministry.

a) The Holy Spirit anointed Jesus with power for His ministry. "And Jesus, when he was baptized, went up straightway out of the water: and, lo, the heavens were opened unto him, and he saw the Spirit of God descending like a dove, and lighting upon him: And lo a voice from heaven, saying, This is my beloved Son, in whom I am well pleased" (Mt. 3:16–17).

---

5 Edwin H. Palmer, *The Person and Ministry of the Holy Spirit: The Traditional Calvinist Perspective* (Grand Rapids, MI: Baker Book House, 1974), 68.

6 Ibid., 71–72.

b) The bestowal of the Holy Spirit officially equipped Him for public ministry.

(1) His preaching ministry—It was not until after this that we read of Him teaching and preaching (Lk. 5:14–15; Mt. 4:17). Jesus quoted the prophet Isaiah in the synagogue, saying, "The Spirit of the Lord is upon me, because he hath anointed me to preach the gospel to the poor" (Lk. 4:18). It is customary to think that the gracious words which proceeded out of His mouth were the result of His own inherent greatness, but Jesus attributes them to the anointing of the Spirit.

(2) His healing ministry—Indeed, it was as the result of the power given Him by the Holy Spirit that He was able to perform miracles: "How God anointed Jesus of Nazareth with the Holy Ghost and with power: who went about…healing all that were oppressed of the devil; for God was with him" (Acts 10:38).

(3) His casting out devils—In Matthew 12:28 Jesus attributes His ability to cast out demons to the Holy Spirit: "But…I cast out devils by the Spirit of God." The Pharisees accused Jesus of casting out demons by Beelzebub, the prince of demons. Jesus showed them the foolishness of Satan casting out himself. He made very plain His source of power for this ministry. In Acts 10:38 we read, "How God anointed Jesus of Nazareth with the Holy Ghost and with power: who went about doing good, and healing all that were oppressed of the devil; for God was with him." Jesus was conscious of this anointing as He read from Isaiah 61:1 in the synagogue at Nazareth: "The Spirit of the Lord is upon me; because he hath anointed me" (Lk. 4:18).

3. *Concerning Christ's death and resurrection*

a) He was enabled by the Holy Spirit to offer the necessary sacrifice for sins. "How much more shall the blood of Christ, who through the eternal Spirit offered himself without spot to God, purge your conscience from dead works to serve the living God?" (Heb. 9:14). It was not enough for Jesus to suffer and die for our sins; He had to do so in the proper manner. As Abraham Kuyper expresses it:

> Christ did not redeem us by His sufferings alone, being spit upon, scourged, crowned with thorns, crucified and slain; but this passion was made effectual to our redemption by His love and voluntary obedience. Hence, there was in Christ's sufferings much more than mere passive, penal satisfaction. Nobody compelled Jesus. He, partaker of the divine nature, could not be compelled, but offered himself quite voluntarily: "Lo, I come to do thy will, O God: in the volume of the book it is written of me."[7]

And Edwin Palmer explains:

---

7 Abraham Kuyper, *The Work of the Holy Spirit* (Grand Rapids, MI: Wm. B. Eerdmans Publishing Company, n.d.), 104.

God always demands a proper relationship between the heart and the overt act. He is not pleased with mere external conformation to His will, but there must be a corresponding attitude of the soul. He does not look only on the lips that say, "Lord, Lord," or the cups that are clean on the outside, but He demands an attitude of perfect love toward Him. If Jesus had gone to the cross unwillingly, sullenly, grudgingly, stoically; and not willingly, with a perfect, ardent zeal, and with faith toward the Father, no atonement could have been made.[8]

Hebrews 9:14, quoted above, indicates that the perfection of Christ's sacrifice was made possible by the Holy Spirit: "Who through the eternal Spirit offered himself without spot to God." Without the enabling of the Holy Spirit, the man Jesus could never have done this. The Spirit enabled Him to offer a perfect sacrifice in the proper, obedient, loving attitude that was acceptable to God. Undoubtedly, the Holy Spirit graciously empowered and sustained Him during the sufferings, both physical and spiritual, of that awful sacrifice!

b) He was raised from the dead by the Holy Spirit. Romans 8:11 speaks of "the Spirit of him that raised up Jesus from the dead." Sometimes the resurrection of Jesus is attributed to the Father. Acts 2:24, speaking of Jesus, says, "Whom God hath raised up." At other times it is said to be the work of the Son Himself. In John 10:17–18, we hear Jesus saying, "I lay down my life, that I might take it again. No man taketh it from me, but I lay it down of myself. I have power to lay it down, and I have power to take it again." But also, in a special way, the resurrection is the work of the Holy Spirit.

4. *Concerning Christ's ministry to the Church*

a) Christ gave commandments to His apostles through the Holy Spirit. Acts 1:1–2 speaks of "all that Jesus began both to do and teach, Until the day in which he was taken up, after that he through the Holy Ghost had given commandments unto the apostles whom he had chosen." The Holy Spirit is so vitally connected with the ministry of the servants of the Lord that it seems quite fitting that it should have been He who inspired the Lord Jesus to give commandments to the disciples as they were being sent forth. As the Spirit guides each Christian today in the service of the Lord, we are blessed to realize that it is the voice of Jesus still speaking to us. In other words, the same Savior who commanded those first disciples through the Holy Spirit is guiding and directing the endeavors of His servants today through the same blessed Holy Spirit. The Church is not dependent upon the bodily presence of the Lord in order to be led by Him. Such leading is accomplished by the Holy Spirit.

---

8 Palmer, 72.

b) Christ is the bestower of the Holy Spirit. In Peter's Day of Pentecost sermon that astounded everyone in Jerusalem and in which he explained the outpouring of the Spirit, he said concerning Jesus, "Therefore being by the right hand of God exalted, and having received of the Father the promise of the Holy Ghost, he hath shed forth this, which ye now see and hear" (Acts 2:33). This was the fulfillment of the promise of the Lord to His disciples, "But when the Comforter is come, whom I will send unto you from the Father" (Jn. 15:26). Perhaps the most important thing Jesus has done for His followers, after having purchased redemption by His death and resurrection, is to baptize them with the Holy Spirit. John the Baptist, moved by the Holy Spirit, in speaking of that which would characterize the coming of Jesus, said, "He shall baptize you with the Holy Ghost, and with fire" (Mt. 3:11). So vitally was the Spirit present in all the ministry of the Savior, it is no wonder He was anxious that those who were to carry on His work would likewise be empowered by the same mighty Spirit. It is indeed wonderful that believers today have this same great privilege! How else could His work be accomplished? This is true New Testament ministry, and Jesus is our great example. This is what Jesus indicated when He said, "He that believeth on me, the works that I do shall he do also; and greater works than these shall he do; because I go unto my Father" (Jn. 14:12).

C. In relation to the Christian believer

We have briefly seen the revelation of the Father through the Son, and then the further revelation of the Son through the Holy Spirit. It now is our task to observe the manner in which the Father and the Son are revealed in and through those who are believers in Christ in the world today. This is a further ministry of the Holy Spirit. We shall consider this phase of our subject under four headings: the Spirit's work in salvation, the Spirit's work subsequent to salvation, the Spirit's work in connection with the believer's ministry and service; and the Spirit's work in relation to resurrection.

1. The Spirit's work in salvation

a) The believer is born again of the Holy Spirit. The subject of the new birth is covered in the section of this book under regeneration. (See chapter 5, The Doctrine of Salvation.) We emphasize here the fact that this experience is wrought through the Holy Spirit. Jesus said to Nicodemus, "Except a man be born of water and of the Spirit, he cannot enter into the kingdom of God. That which is born of the flesh is flesh; and that which is born of the Spirit is spirit" (Jn. 3:5–6). When one is born naturally, natural life is imparted. In some very definite degree, Adam lost spiritual life when he sinned. Many believe he lost the indwelling presence of the Holy Spirit. God had warned that death would follow disobedience to His Word (Gn. 2:17), and as a result of his sin Adam was left in spiritual darkness. Myer Pearlman points out the result of this darkness, or lack of the Holy Spirit, in unregenerated man ever since:

In relation to understanding, the unconverted cannot know the things of the Spirit of God (1 Cor. 2:14); in relation to the will, he cannot be subject to the law of God (Rom. 8:7); in relation to worship, he cannot call Jesus Lord (1 Cor. 12:3); as regards practice, he cannot please God (Rom. 8:8); in regard to character, he cannot bear spiritual fruit (John 15:4); in regards to faith, he cannot receive the spirit of truth (John 14:17).[9]

This new spiritual life is imparted to the believer through the indwelling Holy Spirit, which is the mark of a New Testament Christian: "But ye are not in the flesh, but in the Spirit, if so be that the Spirit of God dwell in you. Now if any man have not the Spirit of Christ, he is none of his" (Rom. 8:9). Again, Pearlman states, "One of the most comprehensive definitions of a Christian is that he is a man in whom the Holy Spirit dwells. His body is a temple of the Holy Ghost, in virtue of which experience he is sanctified as the Tabernacle was consecrated by Jehovah's indwelling."[10] (See 1 Cor. 6:19.)

This is not to be confused with the baptism with the Holy Spirit, which is an outpouring of the Spirit subsequent to salvation. It is not the impartation of spiritual life, but rather power for spiritual service.

b) The Holy Spirit bears witness to the believer's sonship. "He that believeth on the Son of God hath the witness in himself" (1 Jn. 5:10). "The Spirit itself beareth witness with our spirit, that we are the children of God" (Rom. 8:16). "And because ye are sons, God hath sent forth the Spirit of his Son into your hearts, crying, Abba, Father" (Gal. 4:6). It is important to notice that in each of these verses it is the Spirit who takes the initiative. He is the One who bears the witness within the heart of the believer. This is not just an inner feeling. It is a divine witness of a new relationship brought about by the Holy Spirit, and when it is accomplished, He is the One who testifies to its reality.

c) The Holy Spirit baptizes the believer into the body of Christ. "For as the body is one, and hath many members, and all the members of that one body, being many, are one body: so also is Christ. For by one Spirit are we all baptized into one body, whether we be Jews or Gentiles, whether we be bond or free" (1 Cor. 12:12–13). Much confusion has arisen over this verse because some have taught that it is referring to the baptism with the Spirit, which the 120 received on the Day of Pentecost. Thus, it is claimed that all receive the baptism with the Holy Spirit when they are saved. There is a vital difference between the Holy Spirit baptizing believers into the body of Christ, an operation of the Holy Spirit, and being baptized with the Holy Ghost,

---

9 Myer Pearlman, *Knowing the Doctrines of the Bible* (Springfield, MO: The Gospel Publishing House, 1939), 306.

10 Pearlman, 307.

which is an operation of Jesus. John the Baptist said, "I indeed have baptized you with water: but he [referring to Christ] shall baptize you with the Holy Ghost" (Mk. 1:8).

The baptism spoken of in 1 Corinthians 12:13 is conducted by the Holy Spirit and has to do with the believer's position in Christ, while the baptism spoken of by John in Mark 1:8 is conducted by Jesus Christ and has to do with power for service. In the first of these two baptisms—the baptism into the body of Christ—the Holy Spirit is the agent, while the body of Christ, the Church, is the medium. In the second, Christ is the agent and the Holy Spirit is the medium.

First Corinthians 12:12–13 teaches that every believer is made a member of the body of Christ through an operation of the Holy Spirit called a baptism. First Corinthians 10:1–2 states, "Moreover, brethren, I would not that ye should be ignorant, how that all our fathers were under the cloud, and all passed through the sea; And were all baptized unto Moses in the cloud and in the sea." Christian believers are baptized "unto Christ." Baptism signifies death, burial, and resurrection. The sinner is said to be baptized into the body of Christ because by faith he takes the place of dying with Christ on Calvary and rising in newness of life in union with Christ. Water baptism is an outward symbol of that which is actually accomplished by the Holy Ghost.

d) The Holy Spirit seals the believer. "In whom ye also trusted, after that ye heard the word of truth, the gospel of your salvation: in whom also after that ye believed, ye were sealed with that holy Spirit of promise, Which is the earnest of our inheritance until the redemption of the purchased possession" (Eph. 1:13–14). "And grieve not the holy Spirit of God, whereby ye are sealed unto the day of redemption" (Eph. 4:30). The sealing of the believer brings out the thought of ownership. When we are saved, God places His seal of ownership—the indwelling of the Holy Spirit—upon us. This is an earnest pledge that they are His, until the day when He shall return to take them unto Himself: "Nevertheless the foundation of God standeth sure, having this seal, The Lord knoweth them that are his" (2 Tm. 2:19).

2. *The Holy Spirit's work subsequent to salvation.* We have studied the important part the Holy Spirit plays in the salvation of a soul and have realized that without this ministry no one could ever become a child of God. However, after the human heart has been regenerated by the Spirit of God and the life of Christ has been imparted, the Holy Spirit does not leave. Were it so, the new Christian would soon slip back into his former ways, but the Holy Spirit has a continuing ministry He seeks to perform for every believer that is indeed the secret of his strength and progress in his new spiritual life. We shall emphasize here that the Holy Spirit continues to be the active agent in the progressive walk of the child of God.

a) The believer is sanctified by the Holy Spirit. The subject of sanctification is fully dealt with under the study of soteriology, so it will simply be pointed out here that the Holy Spirit has an integral part in this phase of the Christian's development:

"But we are bound to give thanks alway to God for you, brethren beloved of the Lord, because God hath from the beginning chosen you to salvation through sanctification of the Spirit and belief of the truth" (2 Thes. 2:13). (See also 1 Peter 1:2.) In the fuller treatment of the subject of sanctification, to which we have referred, the two phases of sanctification are pointed out: being set apart for the Lord, and the continual cleansing that is needed. These two passages mentioned above emphasize what we might call the progress of salvation: it is through the choosing of the Father, the setting apart or sanctifying of the Holy Spirit, the sprinkling of the blood of Jesus Christ, and belief in the truth of the Word of God. The world, the flesh, and the devil are ever present in the Christian's daily walk. Just as a sinner cannot save himself, so a believer cannot keep himself sanctified apart from the daily strength which the Holy Spirit imparts. The Christian can expect to enjoy this gracious ministry of the Spirit as he believes God's Word and yields to the Holy Spirit.

b) The believer is enabled to mortify the flesh through the Holy Spirit.

> For they that are after the flesh do mind the things of the flesh; but they that are after the Spirit the things of the Spirit. For to be carnally minded is death; but to be spiritually minded is life and peace.... But ye are not in the flesh, but in the Spirit, if so be that the Spirit of God dwell in you... And if Christ be in you, the body is dead because of sin; but the Spirit is life because of righteousness.... Therefore, brethren, we are debtors, not to the flesh, to live after the flesh. For if ye live after the flesh, ye shall die: but if ye through the Spirit do mortify the deeds of the body, ye shall live.
> —ROMANS 8:5–6, 9–10, 12–13

The word *carnal* means "fleshly," and Paul tells us it is impossible to do the will of God with the carnal mind: "For it is not subject to the law of God, neither indeed can be. So then they that are in the flesh cannot please God" (Rom. 8:7–8). It is the Holy Spirit who enables us to mortify—make dead—the flesh and live victoriously in the Spirit. We mortify the deeds of the flesh by reckoning the old man crucified with Christ (Rom. 6:11), and then by choosing to walk under the guidance and power of the indwelling Holy Spirit.

c) The Holy Spirit transforms the believer into the image of Christ. This thought also has to do with the sanctifying influence of the Holy Spirit in transforming the nature of the child of God. "But we all, with open face beholding as in a glass the glory of the Lord, are changed into the same image from glory to glory, even as by the Spirit of the Lord" (2 Cor. 3:18). Weymouth translates this verse, "But all of us, as with unveiled faces we mirror the glory of the Lord, are transformed into the same likeness, from glory to glory, even as derived from the Lord the Spirit."

Earlier in his letter, Paul speaks of the fact that Christians are epistles of Christ: "Written not with ink, but by the Spirit of the living God; not in tables of stone, but in fleshy tables of the heart" (2 Cor. 3:3). He changes the figure in the eighteenth verse and likens the Christian to a mirror, reflecting the image of the glory of the Lord. Moses' face shone as he came down from communing with God on Mt. Sinai (2 Cor. 3:7), and he had to put a veil on his face so that the people could look upon him, because the glory of the Lord was so brilliant. Our faces, says Paul, are not veiled, but open as we reflect the glory of Christ Jesus. The wonderful thing that takes place, though, is that while we are reflecting the glory of the Lord so that others can see it, something is taking place within our lives. We are being changed (the word is literally "transformed") by the operation of the Holy Spirit into the same image of Christ which we are endeavoring to reflect. If we will keep in focus with Jesus, His image is going to be implanted upon our own lives through the inner ministry of the Holy Spirit.

d) The Holy Spirit strengthens the believer for greater revelations of Christ.

> That he would grant you, according to the riches of his glory, to be strength-ened with might by his Spirit in the inner man; [for the purpose] That Christ may dwell in your hearts by faith; that ye, being rooted and grounded in love, May be able to comprehend with all saints what is the breadth, and length, and depth, and height; And to know the love of Christ, which pass-eth knowledge, that ye might be filled with all the fulness of God.
> —EPHESIANS 3:16–19

What Jesus must have had in mind when He said, concerning the Comforter, "He shall glorify me" (Jn. 16:14), is expressed in the above verses. Who but the Spirit of God could make us able to comprehend such gracious revelations of the person and nature of our wonderful Lord? This ministry of revelation, which the Holy Spirit exercises upon the renewed mind of the believer, is for the purpose of bringing him to the place where he can "be filled with all the fulness of God" (Eph. 3:19). It is as He reveals these things that the believer sees the desirability of having them, and then faith and desire reach out to possess them.

e) The Holy Spirit leads the sons of God. "He will guide you," Jesus said of the Holy Spirit (Jn. 16:13). One of the greatest privileges of the children of the Lord is to be led by the omniscient, unerring guidance of the Holy Spirit. We are going a way which we have never gone before. We are passing through unfriendly territory with enemies on every hand. What a blessing to have One who knows all that lies ahead as our Guide: "For as many as are led by the Spirit of God, they are the sons of God" (Rom. 8:14). "But if ye be led of the Spirit, ye are not under the law" (Gal. 5:18).

The Holy Spirit is a person, and His guiding makes life a personally conducted tour. Not only does He lead the sons of God, but the Holy Spirit enables and empowers each one to walk in the path of His choosing.

f) The Holy Spirit performs the office of the Comforter. In four great passages of Scripture in the Gospel of John, Jesus tells of the Holy Spirit as the Comforter. These are: 14:16–18; 14:26; 15:26; and 16:7–15. Because these will be discussed in considerable detail in a future section, they will not be expounded here. (See Section II, The Ministry of the Holy Spirit as the Comforter.)

g) The Holy Spirit brings forth fruit in the believer's life. The subject of the fruit of the Spirit will be dealt with in detail in a later section. (See Section III, The Fruit of the Spirit.) The following scriptures are most pertinent: Gal. 5:22–23; Rom. 14:17; 15:13; 1 Tm. 4:12; 2 Tm. 2:24–25; 3:10; 2 Cor. 6:6; Eph. 5:8–9; and 2 Pt. 1:5–7.

3. *The Holy Spirit's work in connection with ministry or service.* Thus far we have considered the ministry of the Holy Spirit with regard to the imparting and developing of spiritual life within the individual Christian. But the Spirit has a great part in enduing the believer for a life of ministry and service in the work of the kingdom of God. Spiritual ministry and service are always pictured in the Scriptures as being accomplished by the power of the Holy Spirit rather than through human abilities: "This is the word of the LORD unto Zerubbabel, saying, Not by might, nor by power, but by my spirit, saith the LORD of hosts" (Zec. 4:6).

a) The Holy Spirit baptizes and infills believers, giving power for service. The baptism with the Holy Ghost and fire (Lk. 3:16) and the peculiar anointing of power that would come as a result, was to be a new phase in the work of the Holy Spirit. The familiar words of the Great Commission as expressed in Mark 16:15, "Go ye into all the world, and preach the gospel to every creature," are followed by a further command and promise from the Lord: "But tarry ye in the city of Jerusalem, until ye be endued with power from on high" (Lk. 24:49). Again, just before His ascension, He had enlarged upon this promise by telling the disciples, "Ye shall receive power, after that the Holy Ghost is come upon you: and ye shall be witnesses unto me both in Jerusalem, and in all Judea, and in Samaria, and unto the uttermost part of the earth" (Acts 1:8).

This mighty ministry of the Holy Spirit must not be confused with His other activities in relation to the children of the Lord. The baptism with the Holy Ghost is distinct from, and subsequent to, His regenerating work in the hearts of the unsaved. This baptism is especially that men might have the necessary spiritual power to carry on the ministry which has been committed to them. In a later section we will study the entire subject of the baptism with the Holy Ghost. (See Section IV, The Baptism with the Holy Spirit.)

b) The Holy Spirit reveals and gives understanding of the Word of God. The chief tool which the Christian worker needs and uses is the written Word of God—the

Bible. Here is contained God's complete revelation to man, pointing to the means of salvation and giving instructions in how to live the Christian life. One of the most important ministries of the Holy Spirit is to reveal the truths of God's Word to the heart of the believer. Inasmuch as the Word was written by men who were moved upon by the Spirit of God (2 Pt. 1:21), He may rightly be said to be its Author. Certainly the author of a book is best able to explain what is really meant by its contents. The remarkable thing is that every believer can have the Author of the Bible as his own personal teacher and guide. Not only can the Holy Spirit give understanding as to the Scriptures' meaning, but He is also able to lead one to the experience of the truths contained in its pages, making it a Living Word.

c) The Holy Spirit helps the believer to pray. Along with a study of the Word of God, prayer is the chief source of the Christian's strength for his daily life and his constant battle with the enemies of his soul. The Holy Spirit is vitally connected with both these sources of Christian life and power.

> Likewise the Spirit also helpeth our infirmities: for we know not what we should pray for as we ought: but the Spirit itself ["Himself," NASB] maketh intercession for us with groanings which cannot be uttered. And he that searcheth the hearts knoweth what is the mind of the Spirit, because he maketh intercession for the saints according to the will of God.
>
> —ROMANS 8:26–27

> Praying always with all prayer and supplication in the Spirit.
>
> —EPHESIANS 6:18

> But ye, beloved, building up yourselves on your most holy faith, praying in the Holy Ghost.
>
> —JUDE 20

The Spirit's ministry in prayer is very precious. Praying in the strength and wisdom of the flesh can be very difficult and trying. It is hard to realize the presence of God to whom you are praying. It is hard to exercise faith for things you cannot see. It is almost impossible to know how to pray about things that are beyond your human understanding, but all this is changed when the Holy Spirit anoints the heart and mind. The presence of God becomes real, the Spirit opens the understanding, and faith is simple.

As one is lifted up in the Spirit, spiritual things become more real than temporal things, and it is quite natural to become burdened for eternal matters. Added to all this, the Holy Spirit gives wisdom to know how to present petitions to the Father, constantly reminding of the promises which He has given. Many times the Holy

Spirit will enable the intercessor to pray in other tongues concerning problems one could never understand in the natural, but which are wondrously met as the believer prays "with the Spirit" (1 Cor. 14:14–15). Praying under the anointing and guidance of the Holy Spirit becomes one of the Christian's most precious experiences.

d) The Holy Spirit gives power for preaching the Word of God. Paul testified, "And my speech and my preaching was not with enticing words of man's wisdom, but in demonstration of the Spirit and of power" (1 Cor. 2:4). Again he says, "For our gospel came not unto you in word only, but also in power, and in the Holy Ghost" (1 Thes. 1:5). Peter recognized the presence of the Holy Spirit in his preaching as he testified before the Jewish Sanhedrin at Jerusalem. He declared, "And we are his witnesses of these things; and so is also the Holy Ghost" (Acts 5:32).

Effective preaching of the gospel must be under the anointing of the Holy Spirit. Nothing is more impossible than to try to bring men to realize the value and their need of spiritual things, unless the message is delivered in the power of the Holy Spirit. Jesus testified that He was especially anointed for His preaching ministry (Lk. 4:18–19). If this was necessary for Him, it most certainly is for all lesser servants of the Cross.

The signs which were to follow the preaching of the gospel were important, for they demonstrated the authority that the preachers held under God. But the signs were not the preaching of the gospel; they were merely the evidences of the authority. The message they were to preach was the gospel of salvation through the name of the Lord Jesus and the call to repentance. "Now then we are ambassadors for Christ, as though God did beseech you by us: we pray you in Christ's stead, be ye reconciled to God. For he hath made him to be sin for us, who knew no sin; that we might be made the righteousness of God in him" (2 Cor. 5:20–21). This is the message of the preacher, and God has given the Holy Spirit to give power to the preaching. It is the gospel of Jesus Christ, not the miracle accompanying it, that is the power of God unto salvation (Rom. 1:16–17). Let us who thrill to the message of Pentecost never fail to bear this thought in mind!

e) The Holy Spirit gives the believer spiritual gifts for ministry to others. The subject of spiritual gifts is brought before us in 1 Corinthians 12:4–11 and Romans 12:6–8. That they are to be used in spiritual service for ministry to others is clearly taught in 1 Corinthians 12:7: "But to each one is given the manifestation of the Spirit for the common good" (NASB). The subject is thoroughly discussed in a later section but is mentioned here to show its relationship to ministry and service.

4. *The Holy Spirit's work in connection with resurrection*

a) He will raise the bodies of believers in the last day. "But if the Spirit of him that raised up Jesus Christ from the dead dwell in you, he that raised up Christ from the dead shall also quicken your mortal bodies by his Spirit that dwelleth in you" (Rom. 8:11). The body is a definite and important part of man's being. It is included in Christ's redemption (Rom. 8:23). As Christ was raised from the dead and now lives in a glorified body, so each believer who dies in Christ will experience a similar resurrection. This is attributed to the power of the indwelling Holy Spirit. We do not understand the mystery, but we are here told that the Holy Spirit will "quicken," or make alive, our mortal body. "For our conversation is in heaven; from whence also we look for the Savior, the Lord Jesus Christ: Who shall change our vile body, that it may be fashioned like unto his glorious body, according to the working whereby he is able to subdue all things unto himself" (Phil. 3:20–21).

b) The Holy Spirit gives a foretaste of this resurrection by healing our mortal bodies. The expression "shall also quicken your mortal bodies by his Spirit" (Rom. 8:11) seems to also give promise of the Holy Spirit bringing strength and healing to the believer now. Ephesians 1:14 speaks of the Holy Spirit being "given as a pledge [down payment] of our inheritance, with a view to the redemption of God's own possession" (NASB). Thus the pledge, or foretaste, of resurrection life is healing of the mortal body now. Paul speaks about this resurrection life being manifested "in our mortal flesh" (2 Cor. 4:11).

II. THE MINISTRY OF THE HOLY SPIRIT AS THE COMFORTER

The apostle John has recorded a name Jesus gave to the Holy Spirit that is not used in any other book of the New Testament. Apparently he was the inspired writer chosen to reveal the name "Comforter" to the Church. Though not found anywhere else, it has, next to the term *the Holy Spirit*, become the favorite term for designating the third person of the Godhead.

The importance of the ministry of the Holy Spirit as the Comforter can be realized from the words of Jesus: "Nevertheless I tell you the truth; It is expedient for you that I go away: for if I go not away, the Comforter will not come unto you; but if I depart, I will send him unto you" (Jn. 16:7). Apparently, Jesus considered it more important for His disciples that the Holy Spirit be present with them than that He, in His bodily presence, abide with them. Jesus was geographically limited by His incarnation, but the Comforter would dwell in each believer and thus have a worldwide ministry through them.

Two important expressions are used in John 14:16 with regard to the coming of the Comforter that must not be overlooked. First, Jesus spoke of Him as "another Comforter." This word *another* is the clue to the meaning of the word *Comforter*. The word used here means "another of the same kind." The Holy Spirit is not another kind of Comforter, but another of the same kind as Jesus had been. Whatever Jesus was to that little band of disciples, the Holy Spirit would be to them. In fact, Jesus said, "I will not leave you comfortless: I will come to you" (Jn. 14:18). The word translated "comfortless" here literally means "orphans." Jesus did not leave His disciples as orphans. In fact, He did not leave them at all. He departed at the suffering Christ, only to come to them again in the Holy Spirit.

Christ is not restricted to a position in heaven. Instead, He dwells in our hearts, in us in the same way that the Comforter dwells in us. Being full of the Spirit means being full of Jesus. This is not saying that Jesus and the Spirit are the same, but just as Jesus was full of the Spirit, so is the Spirit full of Jesus. Similarly, Jesus was in the Father, and the Father was in Jesus, which means that those who saw the Son saw the Father (John 14:9). Thus we read, "So then after the Lord had spoken unto them, he was received up into heaven, and sat on the right hand of God. And they went forth, and preached everywhere, the Lord working with them, and confirming the word with signs following" (Mk. 16:19–20). The Lord was in heaven, but He was also on Earth in the power of the Spirit, working His same signs and miracles. This is possible only because each member of the Trinity is omnipresent and each is present in the others.

Secondly, Jesus also said of the Comforter in John 14:16, "That he may abide with you for ever." The promised Comforter was given in a permanent sense. He abides with the believer forever. As long as there is a church, there will be a Comforter. We may expect that the Spirit's permanence in the church will result in the same works of power and blessing as in all ages. It is through the Spirit that Jesus is to us "the same yesterday, and to day, and for ever" (Heb. 13:8).

The word translated "comforter" in the Authorized Version is the Greek word *parakletos*. The modern understanding of the word *comforter* is no longer adequate to describe the ministry of the Holy Spirit. We think of a comforter as one who consoles in the time of sorrow. The Spirit does not only console us in our sorrow, but rather gives strength and victory over our sorrows. It is true that the disciples were sorrowful over the announced departure of their Lord, but the other Paraclete was to remove that sorrow by taking the place of Jesus.

Some versions translate the word as "advocate," for the word *parakletos* obviously means "advocate" when applied to Jesus in 1 John 2:1: "And if any man sin, we have an advocate [paraclete] with the Father, Jesus Christ the righteous." We understand that an advocate is one who represents another or pleads the cause of another. That this is one of the real functions of the indwelling Spirit is clear from Romans 8:26: "Likewise the Spirit also helps in our weakness. For we do not know what we should pray for as we ought, but the Spirit Himself makes intercession for us with groanings which cannot be uttered" (NKJV). The Son and the Spirit are both advocates of our cause and intercessors for us. The Spirit intercedes from within us, while the Son intercedes at the throne of grace.

The meaning of the word *helper* is closely akin to the above description: "The Spirit also helpeth our infirmities" (Rom. 8:26). The most literal meaning of *parakletos* is "one called to one's side" to help. The Comforter does not do for us what we ourselves can do, but He does help us do whatever we attempt for God. God has chosen to work through human instruments, but only when such instruments are yielded to the Holy Spirit.

There is yet another meaning of the word *parakletos*. The verb form from which *parakletos* comes means "to summon" or "to exhort." It is used in Romans 12:1: "I beseech you therefore, brethren, by the mercies of God, that ye present your bodies a living sacrifice." The Spirit not only comforts, encourages, intercedes, and helps; but He also entreats, exhorts, and beseeches. He is a persuader. Without the persuasion of the Holy Spirit, no preaching could succeed, nor could sound doctrine long endure uncorrupted. No consideration of the Spirit's work would be complete that did not take into account His beseeching, convicting, and convincing operations.

However, when all definitions have been considered, we will still have to agree with A. J. Gordon, who said:

> The name is the person himself, and only as we know the person can we interpret his name. Why attempt to translate this word any more than we do the name of Jesus?...Certain it is that the language of the Holy Ghost can never be fully understood by an appeal to the lexicon. The heart of the church is the best dictionary of the Spirit. While all the before-mentioned synonyms are correct, neither one is adequate, nor are all together sufficient to bring out the full significance of this great name, "The Paraclete."[11]

The ministry of the Comforter is given in detail in the following four passages from the Gospel of John:

> And I will pray the Father, and he shall give you another Comforter, that he may abide with you forever; Even the Spirit of truth; whom the world cannot receive, because it seeth him not, neither knoweth him: but ye know him; for he dwelleth with you, and shall be in you. I will not leave you comfortless: I will come to you.
>
> —John 14:16–18

> But the Comforter, which is the Holy Ghost, whom the Father will send in my name, he shall teach you all things, and bring all things to your remembrance, whatsoever I have said unto you.
>
> —John 14:26

---

11 Adoniram Judson Gordon, *The Ministry of the Spirit* (Grand Rapids, MI: Baker Book House, 1964), 35.

> But when the Comforter is come, whom I will send unto you from the Father, even the Spirit of truth, which proceedeth from the Father, he shall testify of me.
>
> —JOHN 15:26

> Nevertheless I tell you the truth; It is expedient for you that I go away: for if I go not away, the Comforter will not come unto you; but if I depart, I will send him unto you. And when he is come, he will reprove the world of sin, and of righteousness, and of judgment: Of sin, because they believe not on me; Of righteousness, because I go to my Father, and ye see me no more; Of judgment, because the prince of this world is judged. I have yet many things to say unto you, but ye cannot bear them now. Howbeit when he, the Spirit of truth, is come, he will guide you into all truth: for he shall not speak of himself; but whatsoever he shall hear, that shall he speak: and he will shew you things to come. He shall glorify me: for he shall receive of mine, and shall shew it unto you. All things that the Father hath are mine: therefore said I, that he shall take of mine, and shall shew it unto you.
>
> —JOHN 16:7–15

In these passages, the ministry of the Holy Spirit is divided into four phases. Let us consider them under these four headings: He is our teacher, our reminder, the revealer of Jesus, and the reprover of the world.

A. He is our teacher—the Spirit of truth who "shall teach you all things" (Jn. 14:26).

1. *He guides into truth:* "He will guide you into all truth" (Jn. 16:13).

The Spirit's work is to guide into all truth. Having only half of the truth is sometimes worse than ignorance. Christ desires that we come to a full knowledge of all divine truth relative to redemption and to God's glory.

The Holy Spirit guides into the truth of God's Word, revealing the hidden meaning, making its teachings clear, and causing even the most familiar passages to radiate with new beauty and meaning. Because the Bible is a spiritual book, the reader needs someone to teach him and lead him into its truths (Acts 8:30–31; 1 Cor. 2:14). Who better can guide than He who first inspired its writers?

Note the ignorance of the disciples before they received the infilling of the Spirit. They failed to comprehend what Jesus meant when He referred to the "leaven of the Pharisees and of the Sadducees" (Mt. 16:6–11). They could not grasp the meaning of His parables (Mk. 4:10). They failed to perceive what Jesus referred to when He spoke of the death of Lazarus as a sleep (Jn. 11:11–14). They completely missed the truth concerning His resurrection (Jn. 20:9).

However, after the Day of Pentecost they were like different men, giving wonderful expositions of Old Testament passages, being perfectly familiar with their meaning. They could fully understand the scripturalness of His resurrection (Acts 2:25–31). Before Pentecost, they could not see that Jesus had to suffer; but now they understood the Old Testament prophecies of His crucifixion (Acts 4:25–28). Many of the sermons they preached were but expositions of passages from the Old Testament Scriptures (Acts 2:16–21; 3:12–26; 7:2–53). What a wonderful insight to truth they had!

2. *He acts as God's mouthpiece for revealing His words and desires*: "But whatsoever he shall hear, that shall he speak" (Jn. 16:13).

a) This probably refers, in its largest application, to the Holy Spirit inspiring chosen men to write the New Testament Scriptures. Paul declares that He received the marvelous truths contained in his epistles by revelation (Gal. 1:12–16; Eph. 3:3–5). This was, no doubt, accomplished through the ministry of the Comforter, the Spirit of truth.

b) He also speaks to the hearts of individual Christians, revealing what God would have each to do in his service for the Lord. Note how the Spirit guided Philip to join the Ethiopian eunuch, that he might lead him to Christ (Acts 8:26–29). See also the Spirit leading Paul with regard to where he should minister (Acts 16:6–10).

3. *He reveals things that are yet to come*: "He will shew you things to come" (Jn. 16:13).

a) Blessings ahead in one's own spiritual life. First Corinthians 2:9–12 speaks of the things that lay ahead for the child of God, things he has never imagined. This refers to the fullness of the glorious redemption that is in Christ Jesus. Paul declares, "But God hath revealed them unto us by his Spirit" (1 Cor. 2:10). There are also wondrous spiritual truths in relation to the Lord which have not yet been grasped, and Paul prays that these may be made known (Eph. 1:17–21). The Comforter continually stirs up the heart of each Christian to a fuller endeavor in seeking the fullness of God.

b) Dispensational truth. The Holy Spirit will witness to those who will hear regarding what lies ahead for the world and the church, making the prophetic Scriptures clear (Am. 3:7; Gn. 18:17). Each one should be careful, though, that no personal revelations are accepted that are not perfectly in keeping with the teachings of Jesus and the written Word of God. The Paraclete has no independent teaching. Let no one say that the Spirit has revealed anything that is in conflict with the plain teachings of Christ. Let us beware of any so-called (new) movements of the Spirit where Christ's teachings are said to be outdated or overruled by new revelations. No teaching that belittles the Word of God can possibly come from the Holy Spirit.

c) What lies ahead in the pathway of the believer. When God chooses certain men for specific tasks, His call is brought to their heart by the Holy Spirit. Many times He will make known certain things that lie ahead and prepare the individual worker for unforeseen eventualities. Agabus was sent by the Holy Spirit to tell Paul of the dangers that lay ahead for him at Jerusalem (Acts 21:10–11). Thus, Paul was strengthened and prepared for the coming conflict. It is important that the Christian be sensitive to the leadings of the Spirit in relation to these things.

B. He is our reminder.

"He shall...bring all things to your remembrance" (Jn. 14:26). Man's memory, as every other function of his being, has suffered as the result of the Fall. He needs, and has, a wonderful reminder in the Comforter, the Holy Spirit.

1. *Reminding of the Word of God*: "He shall...bring all things to your remembrance, whatsoever I have said unto you" (Jn. 14:26). Much trouble and heartache would be saved the servant of the Lord if he were more mindful of the Word that has been given. Peter would never have denied his Lord if he had remembered what Jesus had said unto him sooner (Mt. 26:75). If the disciples had only remembered what He had said about His death and resurrection, they would not have had to mourn during those three harrowing days and nights while Jesus was in the grave, nor would they have doubted the women who told of His resurrection (Mt. 16:21; 17:22–23; 20:18–19; Jn. 2:22; Lk. 24:6–11). Peter's prejudices against Gentiles and that of the early church leaders were overcome when they remembered the word of the Lord (Acts 11:15–18). In times of persecution when the devil whispers that one is out of God's will, how precious to remember John 15:18–20:

> If the world hate you, ye know that it hated me before it hated you. If ye were of the world, the world would love his own: but because ye are not of the world, but I have chosen you out of the world, therefore the world hateth you. Remember the word that I said unto you, The servant is not greater than his lord. If they have persecuted me, they will also persecute you; if they have kept my saying, they will keep yours also.

In times of chastening, when one is tempted to think God does not love him or He would not have allowed this, how comforting to remember that it is "whom the Lord loveth he chasteneth, and scourgeth every son whom he receiveth" (Heb. 12:6).

2. *Reminding of a special promise God has given in the past.* How many times Paul must have been encouraged as the Holy Spirit reminded him of that night in the castle in Jerusalem when the Lord stood by him and said, "Be of good cheer, Paul: for as thou hast testified of me in Jerusalem, so must thou bear witness also at Rome" (Acts 23:11), especially in the great storm at sea (Acts 27:24–25). How precious to be reminded of God's faithfulness in all the days that have gone by and to be assured that He will watch over His own now! "Blessed be the LORD, that hath given rest

unto his people Israel, according to all that he promised: there hath not failed one word of all his good promise, which he promised by the hand of Moses his servant" (1 Kgs. 8:56).

3. *Bringing to memory thoughts and Scriptures when one is preaching or dealing with a soul about his spiritual need.* How many times just the right passage has been brought to mind!

C. He is the revealer of Jesus.

"He shall testify of me" (Jn. 15:26). "He shall glorify me" (Jn. 16:14). These promises of Christ were certainly fulfilled in the early Church and whenever the ministry of the Holy Spirit is honored. Whenever the Spirit is powerfully moving, be sure that Jesus is powerfully glorified. Through the operation of the Holy Spirit there is a threefold revelation of Jesus Christ.

1. *Christ is revealed to the believer by the Holy Spirit.* "He shall glorify me: for he shall receive of mine, and shall shew it unto you. All things that the Father hath are mine: therefore said I, that he shall take of mine, and shall shew it unto you" (Jn. 16:14-15). No one knows Jesus as the Holy Spirit does. He was with Christ through the eternities and throughout His earthly ministry, even to His sacrifice on the cross. As the servant of old told Rebekah of the as-yet unknown and unseen bridegroom, Isaac (Gn. 24:35-36), so the Holy Spirit reveals the glories of the Christian's heavenly Bridegroom.

2. *Christ is revealed in the believer by the Holy Spirit.* "But when it pleased God, who separated me from my mother's womb, and called me by his grace, To reveal his Son in me, that I might preach him among the heathen" (Gal. 1:15-16). "My little children, of whom I travail in birth again until Christ be formed in you" (Gal. 4:19). (See also Eph. 4:14; 2 Cor. 3:18.) One of the great purposes of salvation is to restore man to the image of God from which he fell through sin. After conversion, the Holy Spirit seeks to fashion the new babe in Christ into Christ's own image and to implant His likeness within his heart. The fruit of the Spirit (listed in Gal. 5:22-23) is a description of the character of Christ, and as this is found in the life of the believer, so he is growing "unto the measure of the stature of the fulness of Christ" (Eph. 4:13).

3. *Christ is revealed through the believer by the Holy Spirit.* "He will not speak on his own initiative...He shall glorify me" (Jn. 16:13-14, NASB). The Holy Spirit never magnifies Himself, nor the human vessel through whom He operates. He came to magnify the person and ministry of Jesus Christ. Whenever He is truly having His way, Christ, and none other, is exalted. Note the heart of Peter's sermon on the Day of Pentecost: "Therefore let all the house of Israel know assuredly, that God hath made that same Jesus, whom ye crucified, both Lord and Christ" (Acts 2:36). See what Philip, under the guidance of the Holy Spirit, spoke about: "Then Philip opened his mouth, and began at the same scripture, and preached unto him Jesus (Acts 8:35). In

Old Testament times, God was manifested through the Law and the Prophets. In the days of His flesh, Jesus was the manifestation of God to the world. Now, God manifests Himself through the Holy Spirit's revelation of Christ through human vessels.

D. He is the reprover and convicter of the world.

"Of sin, because they believe not on me; Of righteousness, because I go to my Father, and ye see me no more; Of judgment, because the prince of this world is judged" (Jn. 16:9–11). We have studied this ministry of the Holy Spirit in a previous lesson. (See Section I.A.2.b, which begins with "The Holy Spirit convicts…").

III. THE FRUIT OF THE SPIRIT

"But the fruit of the Spirit is love, joy, peace, longsuffering, gentleness, goodness, faith [literally, "faithfulness," NASB], Meekness, temperance: against such there is no law" (Gal. 5:22–23). "For the fruit of the Spirit is in all goodness and righteousness and truth" (Eph. 5:9). "But now being made free from sin, and become servants to God, ye have your fruit unto holiness, and the end everlasting life" (Rom. 6:22).

We have come, now, to the very heart of the practical manifestation of the Christian life. It is by the fruit of character, which is manifested in his daily life, that the Christian gives evidence of the reality of the life of Christ within. Jesus said:

> Do men gather grapes of thorns, or figs of thistles? Even so every good tree bringeth forth good fruit; but a corrupt tree bringeth forth evil fruit. A good tree cannot bring forth evil fruit, neither can a corrupt tree bring forth good fruit.… Wherefore by their fruits ye shall know them.
> —MATTHEW 7:16–18, 20

The fruit of the Spirit is the true characteristic of the Christian life. The "blessed man" of Psalm 1 is said to "be like a tree planted by the rivers of water, that bringeth forth his fruit in his season" (Ps. 1:3).

The principal purpose of a tree is that it may bring forth fruit. Jesus had no place for a tree that did not produce fruit: "Now in the morning as he returned into the city, he hungered. And when he saw a fig tree in the way, he came to it, and found nothing thereon, but leaves only, and said unto it, Let no fruit grow on thee henceforward for ever. And presently the fig tree withered away" (Mt. 21:18–19); "Every branch in me that beareth not fruit he taketh away" (Jn. 15:2).

The true Christian virtues are the fruit of the Spirit, not the fruit of human effort. We have the fruit of the Spirit when we have the Spirit. We can achieve fruit-bearing only by living in cooperation with the indwelling Fruitbearer. The fruit of the Spirit is the character of Christ, which is produced by the Spirit of Christ in the follower of Christ. The more completely one is infused with the Spirit's presence, the more emphatic will be the manifestation of the fruit of the Spirit in his living and working. Only when he is full of the Holy Spirit does he exhibit the full fruition of Christian virtues.

A great many persons are endeavoring to produce the fruit of the Spirit through the entirely natural processes of character building, such as: the exercise of the will, esthetic culture, mental science, the pursuit of philosophy, and education in ethics. All of this is very commendable from the human point of view. It is much better to be moral, ethical, cultured, well-informed, decent, friendly, honorable, and patient than to be the opposite. However, these above-named virtues, achieved by purely human effort, are not the fruit of the Spirit, but an imitation of it. They are wax fruit in contrast with real fruit, just as beautiful as the real to view from a distance, but immeasurably inferior to the taste. When Christ is fully formed in the believer by the indwelling of the Spirit, true Christlike virtues will be the natural result—a result as natural as that of the growth of apples on an apple tree. If he is devoid of fruit, he is obviously devoid of the Spirit of Christ.

Paul's list of the characteristics of the fruit of the Spirit is actually the Sermon on the Mount in a nutshell. It is the ideal of Christian living in its most concentrated expression. First Corinthians 13 is merely an extension of Galatians 5:22–23. Paul emphasizes the same principle of Christian life when, writing to the Philippians, he says, "Finally, brethren, whatsoever things are true, whatsoever things are honest, whatsoever things are just, whatsoever things are pure, whatsoever things are lovely, whatsoever things are of good report; if there be any virtue, and if there be any praise, think on these things" (Phil. 4:8). Any concept of Christianity that does not have as its pattern of character the fruit of the Spirit is a false concept. The greatest treasure of the believer is the fruit of the Spirit, a golden chain composed of nine precious links.

The apostle Peter agrees with the apostle Paul exactly when he says:

> Whereby are given unto us exceeding great and precious promises: that by these ye might be partakers of the divine nature, having escaped the corruption that is in the world through lust. And beside this, giving all diligence, add to your faith virtue; and to virtue knowledge; And to knowledge temperance; and to temperance patience; and to patience godliness; And to godliness brotherly kindness; and to brotherly kindness charity. For if these things be in you, and abound, they make you that ye shall neither be barren nor unfruitful in the knowledge of our Lord Jesus Christ.
>
> —2 PETER 1:4–8

A. The contrast between the works of the flesh and the fruit of the Spirit

The list of the graces of the fruit of the Spirit as recorded in Galatians 5:22–23 is preceded by a list of what Paul calls the "works of the flesh."

> Now the works of the flesh are manifest, which are these; Adultery, fornication, uncleanness, lasciviousness, Idolatry, witchcraft, hatred, variance, emulations, wrath, strife, seditions, heresies, Envyings, murders, drunkenness, revellings, and such like: of the which I tell you before, as I have also told you in time past, that they which do such things shall not inherit the kingdom of God.
>
> —GALATIANS 5:19–21

The fruit of the Spirit is manifest; it cannot be hid. So likewise are the works of the flesh. A Spirit-filled man can be distinguished for his fruit. A carnal man can be identified by his works. The manifestation of the believer's character is called fruit, while that of the carnal unbeliever's character is called works. A fleshly man is one who is not dominated by the indwelling Spirit of God. The struggle in the personality is a struggle between the self and Christ. If self wins, self becomes the center of the personality and the person becomes self-centered. If Christ wins, He becomes the center of the personality and the person is Christ-centered. The result of an ego-centric life is the manifestation of the works of the flesh. The result of a Christ-centered life is the manifestation of the fruit of the Spirit.

The principle of fruit-bearing is the principle of life. Fruit is not made; it grows. Samuel Chadwick, referring to the passage in Galatians 5, has said:

> The most striking feature of the contrast is the emphatic change from works to fruit. Works belong to the workshop; fruit belongs to the garden. One comes from the ingenuity of the factory; the other is the silent growth of abounding life. The factory operates with dead stuff; the garden cultivates living forces to their appointed end. Works are always in the realm of dead things. Every building is built out of dead material. The tree must die before it can be of use to the builder. There is no life in stones and brick, in steel joists and iron girders. They are all dead and in the process of disintegration. Nothing material lasts. Man's best works fail and fade, crumble and pass away...Fruit does not come of man's labor. It requires his diligence, but it is neither his invention nor his product. He does not make the flowers. No skill of his brings the golden harvest of the fields, or the luscious fruit upon the trees. When man has done all he can, then God begins and life proceeds. Fruit is God's work. The phrase "fruit of the Spirit" assigns

the graces of the Christian character to their proper source. They are not of man's producing.[12]

So the difference between the works of the flesh and the fruit of the Spirit is quite apparent. The flesh produces works. The Spirit produces fruit. The one requires self-effort; the other, no effort of the flesh. The one is the product of the factory; the other is of the garden. The one is dead; the other is alive. The one is of the flesh; the other of the Spirit.

B. The secrets of fruit-bearing

In John 15:1–8, Jesus teaches us the importance of fruit-bearing and its secrets. In this passage He speaks of those who have no fruit, saying they are "cast forth as a branch, and [are] withered" (v. 6). Others are described not just as having fruit, but as bearing "more fruit," "much fruit," and fruit that abides. The fruit that He referred to is, without doubt, the fruit of the Spirit—the true essence of spiritual life.

The first secret of fruit-bearing is abiding in Christ: "Abide in me, and I in you. As the branch cannot bear fruit of itself, except it abide in the vine; no more can ye, except ye abide in me. I am the vine, ye are the branches: He that abideth in me, and I in him, the same bringeth forth much fruit: for without me ye can do nothing" (vv. 4–5). Fruit-bearing is the result of the life of Christ, the Vine, flowing through the branch of the life of the believer. Jesus said, "Without me [literally, "apart from me" or "separated from me"] ye can do nothing" (v. 5). Hence, the branch must abide in the Vine.

It is important to realize that the fruit of the Spirit in the life of the believer is not directly the result of the baptism with the Spirit. Every believer has the Holy Spirit abiding in him, and as he continues to abide in Christ, will experience the fruit of the Spirit in his life. Certainly, one who is full of the Holy Ghost will experience "more fruit," "much fruit," and fruit that remains in his life. Again however, this comes from abiding in Christ. The fact that every believer can have the fruit of the Spirit in his life explains why some deeply spiritual Christians have never given evidence of having received a Pentecostal experience. The fruit does not come as the result of the baptism with the Spirit, but of abiding in Christ. This also explains why some who have received the baptism with the Spirit may not be manifesting the qualities of the fruit of the Spirit. Many who are baptized with the Spirit fail to go on to live in the fullness of the Spirit. Many of the Galatians and some of the Corinthians who had received the Pentecostal anointing were at the same time devoid of love. They had experienced the fullness at one time, but they were not living in the fullness. We err

---

12 Samuel Chadwick, *The Way to Pentecost* (New York: Fleming H. Revell Company, 1937), 102–103.

in supposing that being baptized in the Spirit at a single experience is the crowning attainment of the Christian life. The crowning attainment is a daily Spirit-filled life, abundant in the fruit of the Spirit. If the Spirit who abides in us is grieved and quenched, if we walk in the flesh rather than in the Spirit, we can expect a fruitless life. This subject will be enlarged upon later in this study.

It is tremendously important to realize the necessity of abiding in Christ: "Every branch in me that beareth not fruit he taketh away" (v. 2). This refers to Christians or those who once became such, not to mere professing believers. The expression "in me" clearly shows that some who are taken away for failure to produce fruit were originally true branches in the Vine. They were branches, but they did not continue in contact with the Source of life long enough to come to bear fruit.

Note that it is the branch that is taken away, not the fruit. Verse 5 says, "Ye are the branches." The people who say that they who are once saved are always saved would like us to believe that God rejects only the fruit of the apostate, but not that man himself. Nevertheless, the Word says that the reprobate branch is removed and cast into the fire because it bears no fruit. It is not unreasonable to expect fruitfulness of the believer inasmuch as it is God who provides the elements for it. The believer has one sole responsibility, which is to abide in Christ. The fruit is the natural product of abiding. However, if one does not abide, he bears no fruit, and, consequently, he is cast away.

The second secret of fruit-bearing that Jesus gives us in John 15 is found in verse 2: "Every branch that beareth fruit, he purgeth it, that it may bring forth more fruit." This suggests the process of pruning. Every branch that does not bear fruit is taken away, but the branch that does bear fruit is pruned, that it might bear even more fruit. The pruning process in the life of a sincere Christian is never an easy one. Pruning suggests chastening, and "no chastening for the present seemeth to be joyous, but grievous: nevertheless afterward it yieldeth the peaceable fruit of righteousness unto them which are exercised thereby" (Heb. 12:11). Leaves may be very beautiful, but trees that are given to growing excessive leaves seldom produce much fruit. Sometimes the Lord must cut away some of the leaves of self-indulgence from the life of the Christian that he might bear more fruit, and even, as Jesus said, "much fruit." Lest he should have a tendency to draw back from this disciplining of his life, let the believer remember that Jesus said, "My Father is the husbandman" (Jn. 15:1). He is the One who holds the knife and the pruning shears. We may safely trust ourselves to His loving care.

C. What does it mean to abide in Christ?

In answering this question, keep in mind the figure of the vine and the branches. The branch is an integral part of the vine. It grows from it and must never be severed from the vine, so that nothing will ever come between the branch and the source of its life. Considering the believer's relationship to Christ, this would mean an unbroken fellowship with Him. This relationship is sustained first by an unwavering faith in what Christ has done for him and what he is in Christ. The believer must continually rejoice in the saving grace of Jesus Christ and constantly realize that he is redeemed, justified, born into the family of God, and placed as a son and therefore heir and joint-heir with Jesus Christ. As a result of these glorious realizations, he will then remain constant in thanksgiving and praise, communion in prayer, and conscious fellowship with the Lord. There will be an ever-increasing earnest endeavor to yield to His abiding Holy Spirit, to obey His commands, and to walk in His will. He must "live in the Spirit" (Gal. 5:25), be "led of the Spirit" (Gal. 5:18), and "walk in the Spirit" (Gal. 5:16, 25).

D. The difference between the gifts of the Spirit and the fruit of the Spirit

It is of the greatest importance to a vital spiritual life and ministry that these two areas of spiritual blessing be fully understood in their relationship to each other. They are not the same. There must never be any confusion between them. One is not a substitute for the other. No one must ever say, as some have, "I do not believe in the gifts of the Spirit; I believe in love." The gifts have their place and the fruit has its place, but they are in entirely different categories of spiritual blessing.

Note the following differences between these two: The gifts of the Spirit have to do with spiritual capabilities—what one can *do* in the service of the Lord. The fruit of the Spirit has to do with spiritual character—what one *is* in the Lord. The gifts are received as a result of the baptism with the Holy Spirit. The fruit is the result of the new birth and of abiding in Christ. Gifts are received instantly, while the fruit develops gradually. Gifts, of themselves, are not a means of judging the depths of one's spiritual life, but the fruit is the basic criterion of the development of spiritual life and character. There are varieties of gifts, but there is only one fruit of the Spirit. Let us enlarge on these thoughts.

Spiritual gifts indicate spiritual capabilities, while the fruit denotes spiritual character. There are many natural gifts and talents with which people are endowed at birth. Without these inbred tendencies, no one could really excel in any field (i.e., art and music). Jesus used the parables of the talents and the pounds to indicate that certain men were given these talents to use, and for which use they were held responsible. So in the spiritual realm, the Holy Spirit, at His divine choosing, bestows certain spiritual capabilities to be used in spiritual service. The fruit of the Spirit has nothing to do with what a person may be able to do in the service of the Lord. As we shall see, it will not have a great deal to do with what he does for the Lord, but how he does it.

The manifestation of gifts of the Spirit seem to have to do with the outpouring of the Spirit on the Day of Pentecost. Certainly the apostles and others were possessed of abilities that they did not manifest before they were baptized with the Holy Spirit. As recorded in John 15, Jesus plainly indicated that this fruit would come as a result of abiding in Him, the Vine.

The gifts of the Spirit are bestowed by the Holy Spirit, "dividing to every man severally as he will" (1 Cor. 12:11). These divine abilities are apparently given almost instantly. The bestowal of the Holy Spirit on the Day of Pentecost happened suddenly: "And they were all filled with the Holy Ghost, and began to speak with other tongues, as the Spirit gave them utterance" (Acts 2:4). It seems that one moment they were not able to speak with tongues and the next moment they were. Acts 19:6 confirms this fact, for we read of the believers at Ephesus, "And when Paul had laid his hands upon them, the Holy Ghost came on them; and they spake with tongues, and prophesied." Fruit, on the other hand, is always the result of a slow, gradual development. Because fruit suggests character traits, it would of necessity involve a period of development.

There is a tendency to look with awe upon one who has many gifts of the Spirit as though it indicates that he or she is a super-spiritual individual. It is well to realize that gifts are not, of themselves, the indication of the depth of one's spiritual life. Paul said of the Corinthian church that they came "behind in no gift" (1 Cor. 1:7). Rather, they were noted for the exercise of at least some of the gifts of the Spirit. At the same time, the apostle accuses them of being carnal and guilty of allowing many situations within their midst that were not evidences of spiritual advancement. Saul, the first king of Israel, was noted for his possession of the gift of prophecy. We read that just about the time of his anointing as king, "The Spirit of God came upon him, and he prophesied among them. And it came to pass, when all that knew him beforetime saw that, behold, he prophesied among the prophets, then the people said one to another, What is this that is come unto the son of Kish? Is Saul also among the prophets?" (1 Sm. 10:10–11). Later in his reign, Saul dishonored the Lord and disobeyed His word, and God said He would no longer hear Saul's prayers. Thus, the Spirit of the Lord departed from him (1 Sm. 16:14). However, when Saul later got among a group of prophets, the Spirit of the Lord came upon him, and he prophesied (1 Sm. 19:23–24). But this certainly did not indicate that Saul was again a spiritual man. The measure of the development of the fruit of the Spirit in an individual's life is a real indication of the steadfastness of his abiding in Christ. (See also Balaam as an example of one with gifts but little spiritual life [Nm. 22–24].)

There are varieties of gifts, but one fruit of the Spirit. In 1 Corinthians 12:8–10, Paul lists nine different gifts of the Spirit. Other passages, such as Romans 12:6–8, Ephesians 4:11, and 1 Peter 4:10–11, indicate that there may be many more. But there is only one fruit of the Spirit, which is love. It is unscriptural to speak of the *fruits* of the Spirit, plural. What is listed in Galatians 5:22–23 are eight characteristics of love, the fruit of the Spirit. All these other virtues that are mentioned are but facets of love. When the Spirit of God comes into one's life, He invariably sheds abroad His love in the heart. In *Notes From My Bible* by D. L. Moody, this characterization of love is found in terms of all these other virtues, as follows:

> Joy is love exulting.
> Peace is love reposing.
> Longsuffering is love untiring.
> Gentleness is love enduring.
> Goodness is love in action.
> Faith is love on the battlefield
> Meekness is love under discipline.
> Temperance is love in training.[13]

E. The relationship between the gifts of the Spirit and the fruit of the Spirit

While there are certain definite differences between the gifts and fruit of the Spirit, there is also a very vital relationship between these two. It is not by chance that 1 Corinthians 13 comes right between the twelfth and the fourteenth chapters. Chapters 12 and 14 deal with the gifts of the Spirit, while Chapter 13 is all about love, the fruit of the Spirit. This emphasizes the importance of having the fruit of the Spirit in close relation to the gifts. Paul makes it very clear that the gifts without the fruit are powerless and of little use. In fact, he goes as far as to say that they are nothing.

> If I speak with the tongues of men and of angels, but do not have love, I have become a noisy gong or a clanging cymbal. And if I have the gift of prophecy, and know all mysteries and all knowledge; and if I have all faith, so as to remove mountains, but do not have love, I am nothing.
> —1 CORINTHIANS 13:1–2, NASB

As has been stated above, love is the very essence of the fruit of the Spirit. Paul is saying that though he has the gift of speaking with other tongues, of prophecy, wisdom, knowledge, and faith, these gifts mean absolutely nothing if he does not have the fruit of the Spirit. The development of the inner nature of a Christ-like character must be behind any use of the spiritual gift. While he is emphasizing the negative fact that the gift without the fruit is of no value, one must recognize the positive truth that the ministry of the gifts of the Spirit, accompanied by the fruit of a spiritual life, is of great power and usefulness in the work of the Lord. The Holy Spirit is as much interested in character as He is in power. Every Spirit-baptized servant of the Lord

---

13 Dwight Lyman Moody, *Notes From My Bible: From Genesis to Revelation* (New York: Fleming H. Revell Company, 1895), 166.

needs to realize the importance of both of these blessings. (This subject is discussed again in Section VI, The Gifts of the Spirit, see J, "The relationship between the gifts and the fruit of the Spirit.")

F. Detailed characteristics of the fruit of the Spirit

1. *Love:* "But the fruit of the Spirit is love" (Gal. 5:22). It would be impossible to over-emphasize the prominence of this gracious virtue as the chief characteristic of the Christian life: "Beloved, let us love one another: for love is of God; and every one that loveth is born of God, and knoweth God. He that loveth not knoweth not God; for God is love" (1 Jn. 4:7–8). Thus, love is the evidence that one has been born of God. Not only is it the inner evidence, but it is also the outer evidence. Jesus said, "By this shall all men know that ye are my disciples, if ye have love one to another" (Jn. 13:35). He also gave His disciples the command, "Love your enemies, do good to them which hate you, Bless them that curse you, and pray for them which despitefully use you" (Lk. 6:27–28). This is impossible to the natural man; it cannot be produced by human effort. Such love can only be the product of the love of God being shed abroad in one's heart by the Holy Ghost (Rom. 5:5). The love which the Spirit produces is something more than ordinary human affection, however sincere. It comes from abiding in Christ and experiencing His love flowing through the soul. Love is the cement which binds all the other virtues of the fruit of the Spirit together into a united whole. It is the common denominator of all Christian character. One cannot love and fail to have any of the other virtues. To be filled with the Spirit is to be filled with love.

2. *Joy:* "For the kingdom of God is not meat and drink; but righteousness, and peace, and joy in the Holy Ghost" (Rom. 14:17). Joy is love's reaction to God's mercies, blessings, and benefits. Christian joy is not, however, dependent on circumstances. The joy that is a facet of love trusts God even in the most trying circumstances. Human joy looks at things upon Earth and is affected by the condition of Earth. Christian joy—a fruit of the Spirit—looks heavenward and is unaffected by surrounding conditions, because heaven's benefits are unvarying. Joy accepts trials as divine blessing in disguise. The true Christian life is a joyful life. Those who would suppress all emotion in Christian worship and who call all enthusiasm and rejoicing emotionalism do not rightly interpret the Word of God. Not one sentence can be found in God's Word to condemn emotion, but it does not teach emotionalism. Joy is natural to Christianity. Paul uses the words *joy* and *rejoice* seventeen times in the short epistle to the Philippians. Emotionless worship is cold worship. Emotion is the condition of being inwardly moved. Emotionalism is the seeking of emotion as an end in itself—emotion for emotion's sake. We carefully distinguish between emotional extravagance and the true operations of the Holy Spirit. In accordance with the teaching of the Scripture, we exercise control over our feelings so as not to

selfishly interrupt more profitable phases of worship and the ministry of the Word. On the other hand, we believe in singing joyfully, in praying earnestly, in preaching zealously, in testifying forcefully, and in giving cheerfully—"for the joy of the LORD is your strength" (Neh. 8:10). When the Spirit of God fills an individual, the joy of the Lord is bound to be there, for "in thy presence is fulness of joy" (Ps. 16:11).

3. *Peace:* "For the kingdom of God is not meat and drink; but righteousness, and peace, and joy in the Holy Ghost" (Rom. 14:17). Peace is deeper and more constant than joy. Jesus said, "Peace I leave with you, my peace I give unto you: not as the world giveth, give I unto you" (Jn. 14:27). Paul speaks of "the peace of God, which passeth all understanding" (Phil. 4:7). Peace with God is obtained as the result of being justified by faith (Rom. 5:1). But peace, the fruit of the Spirit, is an inner characteristic that manifests itself in peaceableness with others. It signifies freedom from a quarrelsome, contentious, or party spirit. It seeks to live peaceably with all men. Thus the Spirit-filled believer may not only know peace with God, but he may have "the peace of God, which passeth understanding" (Phil. 4:7), because of the promise that "the God of peace shall be with you" (Phil. 4:9).

4. *Longsuffering—patience.* Virtually all modern translators render the word *longsuffering* as meaning "patience." This is not a very prevalent characteristic of the human spirit. Most of us are a little short of that gracious virtue. Patience is, however, a very special characteristic of our loving Lord, and the Christian needs an ever-closer abiding in Christ in order that this grace may become part of his life. The quote from D. L. Moody cited earlier in this chapter reminds us that "longsuffering is love untiring."[14] It is love persevering through the storm and the flood. As each believer realizes how longsuffering the Lord has been with him, it will enable him to be more patient with others. God is patient in seeking to win the unsaved: "The Lord…is longsuffering to us-ward, not willing that any should perish, but that all should come to repentance" (2 Pt. 3:9); "But thou, O Lord, art a God full of compassion, and gracious, longsuffering, and plenteous in mercy and truth" (Ps. 86:15). How much today's Christian needs the Holy Spirit's help in this area of Christlikeness! This may very well be the place where he needs Him the most. James admonishes, "But let patience have her perfect work, that ye may be perfect and entire, wanting nothing" (Jas. 1:4).

5. *Gentleness—kindness.* The NASB, NIV, and numerous other modern versions render *gentleness* as "kindness." This word is nowhere else in the New Testament translated as "gentleness." The word is frequently used to depict God's dealings with His people. They, in turn, bring glory to Him when they manifest this same graciousness to others. Kindness is love dealing with others in their faults. Perhaps nothing

---

14 Moody, 166.

more frequently discredits one's testimony and ministry than unkindness. No conceivable circumstance can possibly justify, on Christian grounds, unkind treatment of others. No matter how firm one must become in reproof, he never needs to become unkind. There is no greater mark of greatness and nobility of character than the ability to reprove in kindness. "Reprove, rebuke, exhort with all longsuffering" (2 Tm. 4:2). "Charity [love] suffereth long, and is kind" (1 Cor. 13:4).

6. *Goodness:* "For the fruit of the Spirit is in all goodness and righteousness and truth" (Eph. 5:9). The goodness mentioned here has reference to works and acts of goodness, to goodness shown to others, and to practical works of love. If a man is truly good at heart, he does good to others. There is a kind of pharisaical, self-righteous goodness which is more a blight to Christianity than a recommendation. Selfish goodness could well be a kind of badness, but, says D. L. Moody, "Goodness is love in action."[15] It is love heaping benefits on others. The Christian does good because he is good. Negative goodness is not sufficient. When the Holy Spirit pervades the being, there is a positive outflow of goodness to all men.

7. *Faith.* The majority of translators render this word "faithfulness," rather than "faith." It has to do with character as it relates to others. J. Lancaster is quoted as saying, "While faith in God and His Word is the basis of our relationship with Him and the avenue through which His blessings flow into our lives, what is in view here is the faithfulness of character and conduct that such faith produces."[16] The fruit of a tree is not for the tree, but for others. Thus, each of these beautiful characteristics indicate the Christian's attitude to those with whom he comes in contact. Two thoughts have been suggested from this particular virtue. The first is expressed in the word *trustworthiness.* Jesus said to the two who multiplied their talents, "Well done, thou good and faithful servant: thou has been faithful over a few things" (Mt. 25:21, 23), suggesting the characteristic of trustworthiness. According to this interpretation, the one who bears the fruit of the Spirit will keep his word with others. He will be faithful to his covenants, promises, duties, and obligations. The true Christian does not shirk responsibility.

The second word is *trustfulness.* In his commentary on Galatians, Martin Luther says:

> In listing faith among the fruits of the Spirit, Paul obviously does not mean faith in Christ, but faith in men. Such faith is not suspicious of people, but believes the best. Naturally the possessor of such faith will be deceived, but

---

15 Moody, 166.

16 J. Lancaster in Percy S. Brewster, ed., *Pentecostal Doctrine* (Cheltenham, England: Grenehurst Publishers, 1976), 71–72. Percy S. Brewster is the late secretary-general of the Elim Church of Great Britain.

he lets it pass. He is ready to believe all men. Where this virtue is lacking, men are suspicious, forward, and wayward and will believe nothing, nor yield to anybody. No matter how well a person says or does anything, they will find fault with it, and if you do not humor them, you can never please them. Such faith in people, therefore, is quite necessary.

What kind of life would this be if one person could not believe another person?[17]

Paul plainly teaches that this characteristic of love "rejoiceth not in iniquity, but rejoiceth in the truth; Beareth all things, believeth all things" (1 Cor. 13:6–7).

Both of these viewpoints are possible, and certainly trustworthiness and trustfulness are both necessary virtues. A true Christian will be neither unfaithful nor suspicious.

8. *Meekness.* Jesus said, "Take my yoke upon you, and learn of me; for I am meek and lowly in heart: and ye shall find rest unto your souls" (Mt. 11:29). Meekness is slowness to anger and to offense. The meek are not boistrous, noisy, or selfishly aggressive. They do not strive, quarrel, or contend. They are not argumentative or boastful. However, meekness must not be confused with shyness, timidity, or weakness, which are characteristics of an inferiority complex. W. E. Vine comments, "It must be clearly understood, therefore, that the meekness manifested by the Lord and commended to the believer is the fruit of power... The Lord was 'meek' because He had the infinite resources of God at His command."[18] Spiritual meekness is not cowardice, nor lack of leadership. Moses was the meekest man in Israel, yet he was their greatest leader. He was humble and patient, but he was also capable of firmness and great courage. Rather than a disqualification for leadership, meekness is an essential to it. Jesus said in the Sermon on the Mount, "Blessed are the meek: for they shall inherit the earth" (Mt. 5:5).

9. *Temperance—self-control.* The word *temperance* means, in reality, "self-control." Among the graces of the Spirit, which are the fruit of abiding in Christ, none is more important than self-control: "He that is slow to anger is better than the mighty; and he that ruleth his spirit than he that taketh a city" (Prv. 16:32). Temperance is true self-love. He who respects himself, who considers his body to be a temple of the Holy Spirit, will exercise control over his own impulses. True temperance is control over not only food and drink, but over every phase of life.

---

17 Martin Luther, *Commentary on Galatians,* trans. Theodore Graebner (Grand Rapids, MI: Zondervan Publishing House, 1939), 232.

18 William Edwy Vine, *An Expository Dictionary of New Testament Words* (Old Tappan, NJ: Fleming H. Revell Company, 1966), III, 56.

Temperance means full self-control. It means control over anger, carnal passion, appetites, desire for worldly pleasure, and selfishness. Before one can rule a city, a community, a club, a church, or a nation, he must first be able to rule his own spirit. Paul treats this subject admirably in his letter to the Corinthians. He says:

All things are lawful unto me, but all things are not expedient [profitable]: all things are lawful for me, but I will not be brought under the power of any. Meats for the belly, and the belly for meats: but God shall destroy both it and them. Now the body is not for fornication, but for the Lord; and the Lord for the body. And God hath both raised up the Lord, and will also raise up us by his power.

—1 CORINTHIANS 6:12–14

What? know ye not that your body is the temple of the Holy Ghost which is in you, which ye have of God, and ye are not your own? For ye are bought with a price: therefore glorify God in your body, and in your spirit, which are God's.

—1 CORINTHIANS 6:19–20

In concluding his remarks concerning the nine graces of the fruit of the Spirit as Paul enumerates them in Galatians 5:22–23, Samuel Chadwick makes this interesting statement:

In newspaper English, the passage would read something like this: The Fruit of the Spirit is an affectionate, lovable disposition, a radiant spirit and a cheerful temper, a tranquil mind and a quiet manner, a forebearing patience in provoking circumstances and with trying people, a sympathetic insight and tactful helpfulness, generous judgment and a big-souled charity, loyalty and reliableness under all circumstances, humility that forgets self in the joy of others, in all things self-mastered and self-controlled, which is the final mark of perfecting.[19]

In summarizing the subject of the fruit of the Spirit, it is emphasized that these characteristics are not imposed upon the Christian from without, but are the result of the life of Christ within. They describe the character of Jesus Christ in the life of the believer. J. Lancaster explains:

---

19 Chadwick, 104.

In some ways the term "Christlikeness" is inadequate, since the Christian is called, not merely to resemble Christ, but to share His very life. With deference to a great Christian classic, the life of the believer is more than the imitation of Christ; it is becoming "a partaker of the divine nature" (2 Peter 1:4). One might be bold enough to suggest that "Christ-ness" would be nearer the mark, since the believer is more than a copy of Christ; he is part and parcel of His very being, "bone of His bone, flesh of His flesh," as Paul daringly puts it in Ephesians 5:30. Our likeness to Christ is therefore not something applied from without—a cosmetic transformation produced by the formulae of some religious make-up department—but a genuine likeness produced by an intimate relationship with Him. Christ's own analogy of the vine and the branches upholds this (John 15). The branches are not merely "vine-like," they are part of the vine; likewise the fruit does not merely resemble grapes, but possesses their inherent structure and taste.[20]

IV. THE BAPTISM WITH THE HOLY SPIRIT

We come now to a study of that powerful experience which was responsible for the miraculous growth of the Christian church in the apostolic and post-apostolic years and which has been the principal cause of the dynamic revival that has swept the world since the turn of the twentieth century—the greatest revival, in terms of numbers, that the world has ever experienced. According to the *World Christian Encyclopedia,* there are in the world today some fifty-one billion believers in Pentecostal churches who have experienced the baptism with the Holy Spirit, beside eleven billion more in other churches who enjoy the fullness of this blessing.[21]

No attempt is made here to exalt the empowering ministry of the Holy Spirit above the redemptive Work of Christ. It is recognized that the principal work of the Holy Spirit is in exalting Christ, but it is also affirmed that Christ's finished work makes provision for a fullness of the Spirit beyond regeneration, of which believers may or may not avail themselves. The greatest promise to the whole world is, of course, "That whosoever believeth in him should not perish, but have everlasting life" (Jn. 3:16); but the greatest promise to the church is, "But ye shall receive power, after that the Holy Ghost is come upon you" (Acts 1:8).

That Jesus Christ is the baptizer with the Holy Ghost is the second of the four cardinal truths upon which the Foursquare Gospel is founded. It is of the most vital importance in connection with the spiritual life and service of every believer. The

---

20 Lancaster in Brewster, 74–75.

21 David B. Barret, ed., *World Christian Encyclopedia* (Oxford, England: Oxford University Press, 1982), 838.

baptism with the Holy Ghost is the secret of the Church's power. It is the greatest need in every sphere of Christian activity that the message of salvation might be proclaimed with the divine unction, which alone can insure its success.

It is now our purpose to deal with the name of this experience; its definition, purpose, and necessity; for whom it is provided; conditions for obtaining it; how to receive it; the manner of its reception; evidences and results; and additional infillings of the Spirit.

A. The name of the experience

It is important in dealing with scriptural truths and experiences that we adhere to scriptural names, otherwise one cannot be sure that he has received the true scriptural experience. It is not wise to tamper with the revelation of God's truths as He has seen fit to give them.

1. *Negatively*

a) It is not "the second definite work of grace." This expression is nowhere used in the Bible, though we hear it a great deal in certain religious circles. We would not say that we do not believe in a second work of grace, for we are anxious to receive all that God has for us. But if there is a second work of grace, perhaps there is a third, fourth, fifth, etc. In other words, we believe in a continual growth in grace (2 Pt. 3:18). This, however, does not describe the baptism with the Holy Spirit.

b) It is not "the second blessing." Here, again, is an expression not used in Scripture. Undoubtedly God has a second, and many other, blessings for His children, but to call a definite, spiritual experience by this name is not biblical. Receive every blessing possible from the Lord, but realize that "the second blessing" is not what God calls the outpouring of the Holy Spirit.

c) It is not sanctification. Sanctification is the scriptural name for something quite different from the baptism with the Holy Spirit. This subject has been dealt with under the discussion of soteriology.

d) It is not holiness. Holiness is a blessed scriptural word, but it describes an attribute of character rather than an experience. It is developed, not received as a gift or single blessing.

2. *Positively—It is the baptism with the Holy Spirit.* The scriptural name for the Holy Spirit coming upon the lives of Christian men and women is the baptism with the Holy Ghost. Notice the explicit language of the following scriptures: "He shall baptize you with the Holy Ghost, and with fire" (Mt. 3:11); "I indeed have baptized you with water: but he shall baptize you with the Holy Ghost" (Mk. 1:8); "For John truly baptized with water; but ye shall be baptized with the Holy Ghost not many days hence" (Acts 1:5).

This great experience must be called by its right name. Others, no doubt, have had the same experience in former days, but have failed to call it by its scriptural name.

As a result, they have failed to pass the truth on to others. To say that these other names mean the same thing is to confuse God's blessings, purposes, and provisions for His own.

B. What the baptism with the Holy Spirit is

1. *Negatively*

a) It is not the new birth. The baptism with the Holy Spirit is subsequent to, and distinct from, His regenerative work. A full Christian experience should certainly contain both, but this distinction must be made, because many are genuinely saved who have never been filled with the Spirit. The following facts prove this distinction.

(1) The apostles were converted under the ministry of Jesus (Jn 1:35–50; Lk. 10:20; Jn. 13:10–11; Jn. 15:3). They were commanded to wait for Christ to send the Comforter and were instantly filled with the Spirit at least two years later (Lk. 24:49; Acts 1:13–14; 2:1–4).

(2) The Samaritans were saved under the ministry of Philip (Acts 8:5–8, 12). They were baptized with the Holy Ghost under the ministry of Peter and John some days later (Acts 8:14–17).

(3) Paul was converted on the road to Damascus by a personal vision of the resurrected Christ (Acts 9:3–9). He was baptized with the Holy Ghost under the ministry of Ananias three days later (Acts 9:17–19).

(4) The twelve men at Ephesus were believers, according to Paul's own words to them: "Have ye received the Holy Ghost since ye believed?" (Acts 19:2). In other words, he was asking, did you receive the Holy Ghost when you believed? These believers were baptized in water and later received the baptism with the Holy Spirit subsequent to the laying on of the apostle's hands (Acts 19:2–7). The second translation of verse 2, as given above, is followed by many other modern versions. Those who teach that all who are saved receive the baptism with the Holy Spirit at the same time as salvation use this translation to seek to prove their point. But the answer of these believing Ephesians to the question, did ye receive the Holy Ghost when you believed? was, "We have not so much as heard whether there be any Holy Ghost" (Acts 19:2). Yet, they were believers. One, then, can be a believer and not have been filled with the Spirit. There need not be a long period of time between salvation and the fullness of the Spirit, but the baptism with the Spirit is an additional experience to the new birth.

b) It is not sanctification. As has been noted under the chapter dealing with the subject of soteriology, sanctification is a manifestation of God's grace entirely different from the baptism with the Holy Ghost. The two augment each other, but are vitally different in character and purpose. Sanctification has to do with separation to God and purification for His service. It is two-fold: instantaneous, as this phase of sanctification refers particularly to the believer's standing in Christ (Jn. 15:3; 1 Cor.

6:11; Heb. 10:10–14); and progressive, which refers to the daily process by which the believer's actual condition is brought up to his standing (1 Thes. 5:23; Heb. 6:1; 12:14).

c) It is not a reward for years of Christian service, nor is it the zenith of Christian experience. This should be clearly understood, for many have adopted the idea that to have received the baptism with the Holy Spirit marks them superior in spirituality and worthy of some special dispensation from God. On the contrary, believers were taught to expect the fullness of the Spirit immediately after conversion and water baptism: "Repent, and be baptized every one of you in the name of Jesus Christ for the remission of sins, and ye shall receive the gift of the Holy Ghost" (Acts 2:38). In other words, the baptism with the Spirit is available to newborn babes in Christ.

The baptism with the Holy Spirit is not something to have, but something to use. It is not the height of spiritual experience, but one of the tremendously essential foundations for further development and service.

d) An error corrected. There are those who teach that the Holy Spirit was poured out once and for all on the Day of Pentecost, and we need to expect no further experiences of this kind, either individually or collectively.

Note, however, that Peter in quoting Joel 2:29 did not say, "Now is fulfilled that which was spoken by the prophet Joel." If he had, there would be nothing more to expect. The prophecy would be fulfilled. But what he did say was, "This is that which was spoken by the prophet Joel" (Acts 2:16). Peter explained to his listeners that this is what Joel was prophesying about; leaving them, and us, to expect further, similar manifestations. Notice the specific wording in Scripture when a prophecy is finally fulfilled: "All this was done, that it might be fulfilled which was spoken by the prophet, saying, Tell ye the daughter of Sion, Behold, thy King cometh unto thee, meek, and sitting upon an ass, and a colt the foal of an ass" (Mt. 21:4–5); "And they crucified him, and parted his garments, casting lots: that it might be fulfilled which was spoken by the prophet, They parted my garments among them, and upon my vesture did they cast lots" (Mt. 27:35). Pentecost was not the fulfillment. There have been many since that day. The full consummation of Joel's prophecy is still in the future, when all the accompanying signs will attend (Joel 2:30–31).

Furthermore, the above-mentioned position is untenable because the book of Acts records at least four other occasions when the Spirit was poured out after the Day of Pentecost: Acts 8:14–17; 9:17; 10:44–46; 19:2–7.

The baptism with the Holy Ghost was given once and for all, as far as the Church in general is concerned. He was made available. The gift of eternal life was offered once and for all at Calvary, but to suggest that every believer is filled with the Spirit is just like asserting that every creature is saved for eternity. There must be a definite, individual acceptance and experience of each.

If the Spirit was poured out only at Pentecost, then those 120 or so were the only ones who received the baptism with the Holy Spirit. Salvation is not by proxy, nor is it handed down from one generation to another; neither is the baptism with the Spirit. Each must be received individually.

2. *Positively*

a) The baptism with the Holy Ghost is a definite experience subsequent to salvation whereby the third person of the Godhead comes upon the believer to anoint and energize him for special service. This experience is designated in the New Testament as the Spirit "falling upon," "coming upon," or being "poured out upon" the yielded believer in a sudden and supernatural manner.

b) The promise of the Father. "And, behold, I send the promise of my Father upon you" (Lk. 24:49). "And being assembled together with them, commanded them that they should not depart from Jerusalem, but wait for the promise of the Father" (Acts 1:4). These promises are of great encouragement to the seeking heart. The baptism with the Holy Spirit is not something which he must persuade the Father to give him. God took the initiative and promised the Holy Spirit to us. This great experience did not originate with men. Furthermore, the Father will not forget that which He has promised. In addition, He is abundantly able to fulfill the promise which He has given.

c) A gift of the Father and the Son. "Repent, and be baptized every one of you in the name of Jesus Christ for the remission of sins, and ye shall receive the gift of the Holy Ghost" (Acts 2:38). "And we are his witnesses of these things; and so is also the Holy Ghost, whom God hath given to them that obey him" (Acts 5:32). If the baptism with the Holy Spirit is a gift, then it is free and cannot be worked for, merited, or deserved in any manner. The Spirit is not received as a reward for hours of prayer, nor because of deep sacrifices made. The Spirit comes as a free gift of God's grace. Receive Him freely!

d) The command of the Lord. "And, being assembled together with them, commanded them that they should not depart from Jerusalem, but wait for the promise of the Father, which, saith he, ye have heard of me" (Acts 1:4). "And we are his witnesses of these things; and so is also the Holy Ghost, whom God hath given to them that obey him" (Acts 5:32). "And be not drunk with wine, wherein is excess; but be filled with the Spirit" (Eph. 5:18). The matter of receiving the fullness of the Spirit is not left to the believer's whim or fancy. Here is a strict command of the Lord, and each one has a responsibility to obey. Failure to do so constitutes disobedience.

C. The purpose and necessity of the baptism with the Holy Spirit

1. *Power for service.* The chief purpose of the baptism with the Holy Spirit is that the believer might have power for Christian service. It may well be that the greatest promise given to the Christian is that given by Jesus to His disciples just prior to

His ascension: "But ye shall receive power, after that the Holy Ghost is come upon you: and ye shall be witnesses unto me both in Jerusalem, and in all Judaea, and in Samaria, and unto the uttermost part of the earth" (Acts 1:8). This power for special service is the distinctive result of having been filled with the Spirit.

Jesus was anointed with the Holy Ghost before He began His public ministry and performed His mighty works by the power of the Spirit. He preached and healed under the anointing of the Holy Spirit.

> The Spirit of the Lord is upon me, because he hath anointed me...to preach deliverance to the captives, and recovering of sight to the blind, to set at liberty them that are bruised.
>
> —LUKE 4:18

> How God anointed Jesus of Nazareth with the Holy Ghost and with power: who went about doing good, and healing all that were oppressed of the devil; for God was with him.
>
> —ACTS 10:38

> But if I cast out devils by the Spirit of God, then the kingdom of God is come unto you.
>
> —MATTHEW 12:28

As great as were the Savior's acts, He promised that His disciples would perform greater works through the power of the Spirit, whom He would send unto them when He returned to the Father. "Verily, verily, I say unto you, He that believeth on me, the works that I do shall he do also; and greater works than these shall he do; because I go unto my Father" (Jn. 14:12). It is probable that Jesus was referring to the disciples' works as being greater in quantity rather than in quality.

The disciples were transformed into different men after the Holy Spirit came upon them at Pentecost. In John 20:19 they are seen huddled together behind closed doors "for fear of the Jews." That very same group of men could not be kept behind closed doors after the Day of Pentecost (Acts 5:17–20), and they became as bold as lions before the Jewish authorities in the power of the Holy Spirit. Hear them say to the Jewish rulers, "Whether it be right in the sight of God to harken unto you more than unto God, judge ye. For we cannot but speak the things which we have seen and heard" (Acts 4:19–20). Hear them pray, "And now, Lord, behold their threatenings: and grant unto thy servants, that with all boldness they may speak thy word....and they were all filled with the Holy Ghost, and they spake the word of God with boldness" (Acts 4:29, 31).

Stephen had power: "And Stephen, full of faith and power, did great wonders and miracles among the people....And they were not able to resist the wisdom and the spirit by which he spake" (Acts 6:8, 10). Paul preached in power: "And my speech and my preaching was not with enticing words of man's wisdom, but in demonstration of the Spirit and of power" (1 Cor. 2:4).

2. *Power for spiritual warfare.* The believer needs the fullness of the power of the Holy Spirit upon his life because of the very nature of the task that has been committed to him. He is sent out to accomplish a spiritual task, and this is not possible without spiritual ability. Moreover, the Christian worker is opposed by great forces from the enemy, and the conflict is in the spiritual realm. Thus, he needs spiritual ability and power to be successful in his work: "For we wrestle not against flesh and blood, but against principalities, against powers, against the rulers of the darkness of this world, against spiritual wickedness in high places" (Eph. 6:12). Spiritual weapons are provided: "For though we walk in the flesh, we do not war after the flesh: (For the weapons of our warfare are not carnal, but mighty through God to the pulling down of strong holds;) Casting down imaginations, and every high thing that exalteth itself against the knowledge of God, and bringing into captivity every thought to the obedience of Christ" (2 Cor. 10:3–5). There is no substitute for the power of the Holy Spirit. He who refuses or resists Him is helpless: "Greater is he that is in you, than he that is in the world" (1 Jn. 4:4).

3. *Power for overflow.* Jesus challenged, "If any man thirst, let him come unto me, and drink. He that believeth on me, as the scripture hath said, out of his belly shall flow rivers of living water. (But this spake he of the Spirit, which they that believe on him should receive: for the Holy Ghost was not yet given; because that Jesus was not yet glorified)" (Jn. 7:37–39). Note particularly the words *out of.* The power is to flow out of the believer. It is not enough that the Lord has the power; the individual worker must have it too. An outflow can only be an overflow. God's servants are more than empty channels—they are vessels. The Lord is looking for those whom He can so fill with His presence and power that they will flow over to others. The only real blessing one can bring to others is that which is the overflow of his own experience with God. It is not how much he can hold, but how much he can overflow.

Note the great promise of Ephesians 3:20: "Now unto him that is able to do exceeding abundantly above all that we ask or think." What a promise! But see the closing statement of the same verse: "According to the power that worketh in us." It is not enough that God has all this exceeding, abundant power; the believer must have it before he can be mightily used of God. Jesus gave His disciples power to heal the sick and to cast out demons (Mt. 10:1). It was His power, to be sure, but He bestowed it on them. Believers today may have the same power through the fullness of God's Holy Spirit.

4. *Power for ability.* Power from on high is ability from heaven—God-given ability to do God-given tasks and to carry out God-given commissions. It is the ability of the person who abides within. It is ability to follow divine guidance into fields known only by God. It is ability to respond to divine providence. It is ability to exalt the Lord Jesus Christ. It is ability to love divinely as Jesus loved. It is ability to preach Christ with conviction and persuasion. It is ability to exercise spiritual gifts for the edification of the Church. It is ability to suffer persecution for the Lord's sake. It is ability to live a holy life above the sordid standards of the world. Finally, it is ability to work for God lovingly, willingly, faithfully, and untiringly. In short, it is the ability to work until Jesus comes or until Earth's race is run.

D. For whom is the baptism with the Holy Spirit?

It has been noted above that the receiving of the baptism with the Holy Spirit was a command of Jesus. It was a promise of the Father and a gift of both Father and Son. The important thing to know is to whom this command, this promise, and this gift applies. No one responds to a command which he is not sure applies to himself, nor does he seek what he is not certain is available. It is important that we know whether the Lord has singled out a special class of people for this outstanding experience or if it applies to a wider group of Christians.

1. *Negatively*

a) The baptism with the Holy Spirit is not simply for those who lived in apostolic days. It is surprising the number of Christians who believe that the Pentecostal outpouring of the Spirit was just for those who lived at that time, as though they needed a supernatural enduement of power which, for some reason or other, the Church does not need today. This idea is certainly not in keeping with the words of Peter on that memorable day of the first outpouring: "Repent, and be baptized every one of you…and ye shall receive the gift of the Holy Ghost. For the promise is unto you, and to your children, and to all that are afar off, even as many as the Lord our God shall call" (Acts 2:38–39). It is hard to imagine one confining such a promise to any sort of limitation as far as time is concerned. Peter referred to the present generation of his day when he said, "The promise is unto you." He specifically included the next generation with the words, "And to your children." One would gather that he was thinking of future generations when he said, "And to all that are afar off." Some might limit that to a few hundred years, but it is hard to say the next words do not mean every Christian of every future day—"Even as many as the Lord our God shall call." The baptism with the Holy Spirit is for the Church of God in all ages. God is no respecter of times within the church age, any more than He is respecter of persons. There were no needs, problems, or urgencies existing in the early Church times that do not still exist today. As long as the Great Commission still is in effect, binding us to the duty of world-wide evangelization, there will still be a provision for power to fulfill the Commission.

b) It is not simply for ministers, missionaries, and those in special service for the Lord. If there is one truth emphasized in the New Testament, it is that of the unity of the body of Christ and the importance of every member to that body. The apostle Paul plainly and emphatically teaches that no one member is of greater importance than another.

> And the eye cannot say unto the hand, I have no need of thee: nor again the head to the feet, I have no need of you. Nay, much more those members of the body, which seem to be more feeble, are necessary: And those members of the body, which we think to be less honourable, upon these we bestow more abundant honor; and our uncomely parts have more abundant comeliness. For our comely parts have no need: but God hath tempered the body together, having given more abundant honor to that part which lacked: That there should be no schism in the body; but that the members should have the same care one for another.
> —1 CORINTHIANS 12:21–25

If this be true, then every Christian is of equal importance to the accomplishing of God's perfect will through His Church. The humblest Christian who is walking in the center of God's will is just as much a servant of the Lord as the most famous preacher of his day. One is called to one ministry, and another to another ministry (Rom. 12:3–8). God is concerned with faithfulness wherever He has placed each one. Often it is more difficult to be faithful in what seem to be small places than it is to be faithful in the larger. Every Christian needs the baptism with the Holy Spirit to be able to fulfill his part in the great scheme of ministering the gospel to a needy world.

c) It is not simply for a special, privileged class. Peter had to learn that the fullness of the Spirit was for Gentiles as well as Jews (Acts 10:34–35, 44–48; 11:15–18). The Lord is no respecter of persons and plays no favorites. Everyone is treated the same, and God's gifts are free to all alike.

Neither must one think that after he has received the baptism with the Spirit he is better than others. All of God's gifts are of grace, and that which is received freely in no wise contributes to the personal glorification of the individual. The glory all belongs to Him—the great Giver. The reception of the fullness of the Spirit never increases one's personal prestige, but rather serves to increase his responsibility. If one has great power, God has a right to expect greater service.

d) It is not simply for matured Christians. There is a good deal of sentiment abroad that the baptism with the Holy Spirit is only for those who are deeply matured in their Christian life, and one must wait until he achieves such a position before he can hope to receive. It is significant that the Lord baptized the Samaritan Christians just a few days after their conversion (Acts 8:14–17). Those in the house of Cornelius were filled with the Spirit almost immediately after believing the word that Peter was preaching to them. In fact, it seems that the sermon was interrupted by the Holy Ghost falling upon them (Acts 10:44–46).

The youngest believer needs—and can have—this gift of God. It is for power for service, and that is needed just as soon as one enlists under the banner of the Lord. Christians were taught to expect the baptism with the Holy Ghost immediately after conversion and water baptism (Acts 2:38).

2. *Positively—for all who believe.* The baptism with the Holy Spirit is for all, in all ages, who believe on Jesus Christ as Savior and Lord and are children of God through Him. It is intended to be the normal divine provision for a fully adequate Christian work and witness, available to all believers of all stations, all times, all races, and all callings.

E. Conditions for obtaining the baptism with the Holy Spirit

What is necessary before one can receive this marvelous experience? Are there some necessary preliminary steps which must be taken? The Scriptures indicate the following conditions must be met:

1. *Repentance from sin.* When the multitude came to Peter on that memorable Day of Pentecost and cried, "Men and brethren, what shall we do?" He replied, "Repent…be baptized…and ye shall receive the gift of the Holy Ghost" (Acts 2:37–38). Repentance, then, is the very first step. The Holy Spirit cannot operate where sin holds sway (Acts 17:30).

2. *A definite experience of salvation.* Repentance must be followed by faith in Jesus Christ for salvation before the new birth takes place. (Luke 11:13 stresses the fact that it is "your heavenly Father" who gives "the Holy Spirit to them that ask." One must be in the family of God before he can expect this gift of the Father. The Holy Spirit is the gift of the Father, and only those who have been saved can call Him Father: "And because ye are sons, God hath sent forth the Spirit of his Son into your hearts, crying, Abba, Father" (Gal. 4:6).

3. *Water baptism.* Again, attention is called to Peter's words to those on the Day of Pentecost who cried, "Men and brethren, what shall we do?" Peter replied, "Repent, and be baptized" (Acts 2:37–38). The order seems to be: repentance, regeneration, water baptism, and then the baptism with the Holy Ghost. Each step of obedience opens the way for the next. It is not dogmatically claimed that one who has not been baptized in water could never receive the fullness of the Spirit, but inasmuch as water baptism is a step of obedience, it is necessary. No one who is knowingly and willingly

disobedient to any of God's commands can have faith to receive the fullness of the Spirit. Faith always follows obedience.

It is interesting, though, to notice that in two cases recorded in the book of Acts, the outpouring of the Holy Spirit preceded water baptism. It seems that Saul of Tarsus, the apostle Paul, was healed of his blindness and filled with the Spirit as Ananias laid his hands on him in the house of Judas on the street called Straight: "Brother Saul, the Lord, even Jesus, that appeared unto thee in the way as thou camest, hath sent me, that thou mightest receive thy sight, and be filled with the Holy Ghost." After this we read: "And immediately there fell from his eyes as it had been scales: and he received sight forthwith, and arose, and was baptized" (Acts 9:18).

We know that those who were gathered in the house of Cornelius at Caesarea believed the word Peter preached and were filled with the Spirit right then. Peter, seeing this, said, "Can any man forbid water, that these should be baptized...in the name of the Lord" (Acts 10:47–48). We note that in both of these cases the Holy Spirit came upon new believers before they had a chance to be baptized in water. However, immediately after their acceptance of Christ, they were baptized. For those who are believers and are seeking the fullness of the Spirit, water baptism would be a necessary step. Many have received the fullness of the Spirit as they were brought up out of the waters of baptism.

4. *A deep conviction of need.* There must be a real hunger and thirst for more of God before one will receive the baptism with the Spirit. God does not give such gracious gifts except as they are sincerely desired and deeply appreciated: "Blessed are they which do hunger and thirst after righteousness: for they shall be filled" (Mt. 5:6); "If any man thirst, let him come unto me, and drink.... (But this spake he of the Spirit, which they that believe on him should receive" (Jn. 7:37, 39); "As the hart panteth after the water brooks, so panteth my soul after thee, O God. My soul thirsteth for God" (Ps. 42:1–2).

5. *A measure of consecration.* Inasmuch as a person is yielding himself for a baptism of power for service, there must be a surrender of the self-will to the will of God. Henceforth, one is willing to be led in the path of His choosing. Do not confuse this yieldedness of the will with a complete abandonment of the will, in which case one becomes will-less. This is dangerous, for it leads to a greater susceptibility to the power of evil spirits. At all times, one is in full possession of his will and all his faculties. It does mean the changing of the center of one's will from the self to Christ. He makes the greatest use of the person who is willing to yield his or her will to the Spirit of God for His direction and control.

F. How to receive the baptism with the Holy Spirit

Having considered the meaning, the purpose, the necessity, as well as some of the main conditions that must be met for the receiving of the baptism with the Holy

Spirit, it is our purpose now to consider just how one obtains this rich blessing from the Lord. This is not an easy question to answer, inasmuch as God is not confined to just one method of fulfilling His promises, nor are any two human beings exactly alike in their reception of spiritual things. There are, however, certain general principles which can be observed and which serve as a guide to the sincere seeking soul. The following basic truths will provide some help in this area.

1. *By faith.* Everything we receive from the Lord comes by faith: "That we might receive the promise of the Spirit through faith" (Gal. 3:14); "(But this spake he of the Spirit, which they that believe on him should receive" (Jn. 7:39); "For he that cometh to God must believe" (Heb. 11:6). There is no other way. The baptism with the Spirit is not primarily a matter of feelings, of signs, or evidences. It is a matter of believing that God will send His promise upon us—that Jesus will baptize with the Holy Spirit.

However, it should be clearly understood that when one takes something from the Lord by faith, he actually gets it. Do not confuse receiving something by faith with merely hoping for it, thinking that you have received, or just taking for granted that the Spirit has come. One can believe, merely from a mental standpoint, that he is saved, yet never experience the transforming power of regeneration in his life. Real faith gets through to an actual experience, and there is an assured witness that one has been truly born of the Spirit. Likewise with the baptism with the Holy Spirit. There is such a thing as believing that one has accepted the fullness of the Spirit by faith without having Him come upon him in mighty power. Keep your heart open before the Lord with an expectant faith until you actually know the Spirit has baptized you. Do not substitute thinking for experiencing. When the Spirit comes in His fullness, no one needs to be told that He is there. Still, it must be kept in mind that the Spirit will come only as one believes the promises of God. Faith operates in the following ways:

a) Faith in the promise of God. Faith is not centered in oneself, but on the fact that God has promised to give the Holy Spirit, and He will keep His word.

> If a son shall ask bread of any of you that is a father, will he give him a stone? or if he ask a fish, will he for a fish give him a serpent? Or if he shall ask an egg, will he offer him a scorpion? If ye then, being evil, know how to give good gifts unto your children: how much more shall your heavenly Father give the Holy Spirit to them that ask him?
>
> —Luke 11:11–13

> What things soever ye desire, when ye pray, believe that ye receive them, and ye shall have them.
>
> —Mark 11:24

b) Faith that the promise is for you. A general belief in the promise of God is not sufficient. There must be a personal appropriation of the promise of the Spirit: "For the promise is unto you" (Acts 2:39); "For every one that asketh receiveth; and he that seeketh findeth; and to him that knocketh it shall be opened" (Lk. 11:10). It is not a case of personal worthiness, but of God's promise to each one individually because of the worthiness of Jesus. He is no respecter of persons, and if He has bestowed the Spirit on others who are saved by grace, He will also hear and meet the cry of each one who comes in sincerity. It is not glorifying to the Lord to believe that He will do for one of His children what He will not do for all.

c) A persistency of faith that will not be denied. The two parables of Jesus in Luke 11:5–10 and 18:1–8 emphasize the importance of a consistency and persistency of faith that will not be denied. Sometimes the Lord may delay the granting of this request because receiving the baptism with the Holy Spirit marks a great turning point in one's Christian experience, and the Lord is concerned that the motives and desires of the seeking heart might be fully tested. Many have been the most discouraged just before the Spirit came in His fullness. Stand on God's promise until it is completely fulfilled.

d) Faith will be manifest in praise and thanksgiving. Realizing the greatness of what God has promised and that which He is about to do should cause the heart to rejoice and overflow with thankfulness. Almost invariably, the Holy Spirit comes as one is praising the Lord. Praise is a manifestation of faith. Praise can be given to God, even when one does not feel like doing so. Thankfulness and praise to God are not to be centered in one's feelings, but in the greatness of God. God is the same, regardless of how one may feel. He is always worthy of the adoration of His own.

2. *By a full yieldedness of the entire being in order that the Holy Spirit might have His own way.* This is often the most difficult condition to fulfill. After one realizes his need of the baptism with the Spirit and comes to the Lord for this blessing, there is still the matter of the yieldedness of his various faculties to the control of the Spirit. It is generally easier to do something for one's self than to yield to another to do it for him. John said concerning Jesus, "He shall baptize you with the Holy Ghost and with fire" (Lk. 3:16). (See also Mk. 1:8; Mt. 3:11.) When the subject of the baptism with the Holy Spirit is mentioned, people usually think of the Holy Spirit—and rightly so. But it must be realized that this mighty experience is primarily an encounter with the Lord Jesus Christ. Peter confirmed our Lord's personal association with this Pentecostal experience when, on the Day of Pentecost, he said, "This Jesus hath God raised up, whereof we all are witnesses. Therefore being by the right hand of God exalted, and having received of the Father the promise of the Holy Ghost, he hath shed forth this, which ye now see and hear" (Acts 2:32–33). When one receives the baptism with the Holy Spirit, he is yielding to Christ. If he rejects the Pentecostal experience, he is rejecting a distinct ministry of Jesus Christ. There must be a baptizer

in order for there to be a baptism. One must yield himself completely to the one who is immersing him in the waters of baptism. Likewise, one must yield to the One who is baptizing him in the Holy Spirit. The baptism with the Holy Spirit, then, is a total yielding to the Lord Jesus Christ. Thus, it brings the recipient into a new and more intimate relationship with Jesus Christ.

This thought of yieldedness is perhaps the fundamental thought behind the entire Spirit-filled life and ministry. Every phase of service after this must be the result of yielding to the power and presence of the Holy Ghost. Thus God seeks to teach, right from the start, the secret of yielding to Him.

Here is something that it is virtually impossible to tell another how to do. Some have sought for the fullness of the Spirit for years and wondered why they did not receive the full anointing. Upon receiving it, they have testified that, had they only known how to yield to the Spirit, they could have received years before. But each must learn this important lesson for himself, for God wants every individual to know how to let Him have His way in the days to come. There is something blessedly individualistic about this great experience with God, and it seems that the Lord has left it so that each may learn for himself.

It is vitally important, however, to realize that at no time does the Lord require a believer to surrender his own personality. Many of the satanic cults of the present day seek to bring a person to the place of the negation of his own personality. This is dangerous, and the Lord does not work this way. He has given each one the personality which he possesses, and He would operate through it. The Holy Spirit does not take the place of the individual. He simply seeks to shine through him, enhancing and glorifying the person's talents and his entire being. He does not supply a new set of functions, but utilizes those which are already there and which are yielded to Him. This, again, emphasizes the individualistic nature of God's dealings with His children.

Moses was amazed as he turned aside to see the bush that was burning on the backside of the desert (Ex. 3:2–3). The thing that impressed him was not that the bush was aglow, but that it was not consumed. Likewise, when the Holy Spirit sets the hearts and lives of believers aglow with the fiery glory of His presence, the individual personality is not consumed. The dross is consumed, but the life itself becomes radiant with God's glory.

3. *A word about "tarrying" for the baptism with the Holy Spirit.* In the early days of the twentieth-century outpouring of the Pentecostal baptism with the Holy Spirit, it was quite customary to speak of "tarrying" for the baptism with the Spirit. The idea of tarrying for the Pentecostal experience came from two verses of Scripture: "And, behold, I send the promise of my Father upon you: but tarry ye in the city of Jerusalem, until ye be endued with power from on high" (Lk. 24:49); "And, being

assembled together with them, commanded them that they should not depart from Jerusalem, but wait for the promise of the Father" (Acts 1:4).

In obedience to these commands, the disciples did tarry a number of days. In fact, they tarried until the Day of Pentecost when the Comforter descended in His initial coming, from which time He was to abide in the Church forever. It was necessary for the disciples to wait for the promise because the advent of the Comforter was set for a certain day, just as the advent of the Son was set for a certain day. Clearly, the disciples could not have received before that set day. Before the Day of Pentecost, it was necessary to wait for the promised Comforter. Since the Day of Pentecost, the abiding Comforter waits for the believer. We conclude, therefore, that it is not now necessary to wait for the Spirit.

An examination of all the passages in the book of Acts that mention the Holy Spirit baptism reveals that, in every case, the believers who received the blessed experience received it in the very first prayer meeting or on the very first occasion when it was sought. The apostles did not hold tarrying meetings; they held receiving meetings. Now, because of the careless use of the word *tarry*, many hungry seekers have been given the impression that the Spirit baptism can only be received after weeks or months of tarrying. Those who have been given this impression find it hard to exercise faith for immediate reception. Seekers should be taught that the Spirit is willing to fill them as soon as they open their hearts, yield their lives, and exercise faith.

There is a distinct difference between a tarrying meeting and a prayer meeting for the reception of the Spirit. He who tarries for the Spirit believes that he will receive when God is ready. He who prays for the Spirit knows that He will come when the seeker is ready. Note the manner in which the Holy Spirit was received in the revival at Samaria:

> Now when the apostles which were at Jerusalem heard that Samaria had received the word of God, they sent unto them Peter and John: Who, when they were come down, prayed for them, that they might receive the Holy Ghost.... Then laid they their hands on them, and they received the Holy Ghost.
>
> —ACTS 8:14–17

When the apostles from Jerusalem came to Samaria, they found a great revival in progress. Many had been gloriously saved, but none had received the Holy Ghost. The apparent reason for this was that they had not heard any teaching on this subject. After Peter and John taught concerning the Holy Spirit, they held a prayer meeting with the new converts, after which they laid hands on them and the Spirit was poured out. In Samaria there was no tarrying, but there was certainly praying.

The question might well be asked in the light of what has been said above, why do so many pray so long before receiving? The Bible does not record one case of a person's seeking for long periods of time before receiving. However, the biblical examples are taken from an era of more or less ideal conditions. Faith was high and doctrinal teachings were quite uniform. The apostles were men of great faith and spiritual power who created high expectancy in those who heard them. Unfortunately, such is not always the case today, as many seek for a deeper experience without fully realizing what they are seeking and with little faith to cause them to expect immediate results. However, Jesus is the same as in those early Church days, and the reception of the Spirit need not differ any today from what it was at that time. This is being witnessed in many Churches where apostolic conditions are present.

In addition to things already mentioned, it should be added that the following conditions, if they existed, would cause delay in receiving the fullness of God's promise: weak faith, unholy living, imperfect consecration, and egocentric motives.

Weak faith could be caused by a meager knowledge of the blessing to be received and the notion that long periods of tarrying are invariably necessary before receiving. Appropriating faith must believe that the blessing is available *now*.

It should not be hard for anyone to understand that the Spirit who is holy would not care to operate through unholy channels. Thus, unholy living could be a real barrier to receiving His fullness. Paul was good to describe the necessity of cleansing before a vessel can be "meet for the master's use" (2 Tm. 2:19–21). There must be an experience of cleansing preceding one's baptism with the Holy Spirit.

Imperfect consecration is, likewise, a hindrance to receiving. The baptism with the Spirit is given to empower one for service. Unless one is willing to yield himself for whatever service the Lord may choose, why should the Lord fill him? Any who seek the fullness of the Spirit without any intention of serving the Lord, whatever He chooses, need to heed Paul's admonition in Roman's 12:1.

Finally, let it be observed that egocentric motives may be a widely prevalent reason for delay in receiving the baptism with the Holy Spirit. Does one seek God's fullness only in order that he may not be behind others in the Church in relation to attainment? Does one seek only for the joy of an emotional experience or that he may be esteemed as spiritual? One's desire to receive the baptism with the Spirit must not be for any selfish purpose, but rather for the purpose of being more useful to God for the winning of souls and the extension of His kingdom. In too many of our churches, the Pentecostal experience is held up as a badge of spiritual prestige, rather than a means of godly living, radiant witnessing, and powerful service.

G. The manner in which the baptism with the Holy Spirit is received

A brief outline shows the various ways in which this great experience was received in the early Church. God is a God of infinite variety, and we must not think that there is any stilted form in which the Spirit is received.

1. *Suddenly, while sitting and expecting Him to come (Acts 2:1–4)*

2. *Instantly and unexpectedly, while listening to a sermon (Acts 10:44–46).* While these men were not specifically expecting the Holy Spirit to come in this manner, they were in an expectant attitude. Their hearts were open to God's truth, whatever that might be.

3. *Through prayer and the laying on of the apostles' hands (Acts 8:14–17; 9:17; 19:6).*

4. *Through the seeker's personal prayer and faith (Lk. 11:9–13; Jn. 7:37–39).*

H. The evidence and results of the baptism with the Holy Spirit

An experience so great and so important as the baptism with the Holy Spirit undoubtedly will be accompanied by unmistakable evidences, so that the recipient will have no doubts whatsoever that he has indeed received the promise of the Father. Some of the evidence is manifested immediately, while others continue on a permanent basis as one walks in the fullness of the Spirit.

1. *Immediate evidences*

a) Speaking with other tongues as the Spirit gives utterance (Acts 2:4; 10:44–46; 19:6). The question of the initial evidence of the reception of the gift of the Holy Spirit is one of paramount importance to all who hunger to be filled with the Spirit. It is logical that the supernatural experience of the baptism with the Holy Spirit would be accompanied by some definite and unmistakable sign by which the seeker would be assured that he had received it. There are many operations of the Spirit, but only one baptism with the Spirit. If there were no particular supernatural evidence of the baptism with the Spirit by which it could be distinguished from all other operations of the Spirit, how could anyone be assured of the experience? We believe that the initial evidence of the baptism with the Holy Spirit is that of speaking with other tongues as the Spirit gives utterance. The evidence of the Spirit's fullness on the Day of Pentecost was that of speaking with other tongues by the prompting of the Holy Spirit: "And they were all filled with the Holy Ghost, and began to speak with other tongues, as the Spirit gave them utterance" (Acts 2:4). The manifestation of the Spirit on the Day of Pentecost was the original outpouring of the empowerment of the Church. It was the pattern for the Pentecostal experience. What the disciples did when they were first filled, we reasonably expect all who are filled in the same sense to do. Inasmuch as the purpose of the anointing was to give power to witness, it is not surprising that the sign of the experience was manifested in their utterance.

In addition to the initial outpouring of the Spirit as recorded in Acts 2:4, we have the account of the reception of the Spirit by the believers in the house of Cornelius, given in Acts 10:44–46:

> While Peter yet spake these words, the Holy Ghost fell on all them that heard the word. And they of the circumcision which believed were astonished, as

many as came with Peter, because that on the Gentiles also was poured out the gift of the Holy Ghost. For they heard them speak with tongues, and magnify God.

It is interesting and important to note how the Jews who came with Peter knew that these Gentiles had received the Holy Ghost experience that the disciples received on the Day of Pentecost. The Scripture says that they knew because "they heard them speak with tongues." This verse reads literally, "For they, hearing them continuing to speak with tongues." Their speaking in tongues was no brief confusion of syllables, but a full and flowing use of a language, which brought amazement to the hearers. Now, if those present were convinced that the Gentiles had an equivalent Holy Ghost experience to that enjoyed by the Jews on the grounds of their speaking with tongues, then tongues must be the unmistakable sign or initial evidence of the Pentecostal experience. One can know today that his baptism is a genuine Pentecostal experience, equivalent to that of the disciples, when he experiences speaking with other tongues by the power of the Spirit. One does not seek the tongues, but the Spirit Himself. However, he does seek such a sign as will make him sure that he has been filled in biblical fashion.

A third such account of believers receiving the fullness of the Spirit where it is specifically mentioned that they spoke with tongues is recorded in Acts 19:6: "And when Paul had laid his hands upon them, the Holy Ghost came on them; and they spake with tongues, and prophesied." This was in the city of Ephesus. The theory that some have advanced is that the Spirit's anointing with the evidence of speaking with other tongues was only given when a new racial group accepted the gospel, such as the Jews at Pentecost, the Samaritans in Philip's revival, and the Gentiles in the house of Cornelius. But this theory breaks down here in Acts 19:6, where no new ethnic group can be distinguished. The same could be said of the Corinthians, who certainly spoke with tongues.

Some oppose tongues as the exclusive initial evidence of this baptism on the grounds that tongues are not always mentioned in the Bible in connection with the baptism with the Holy Spirit. It is true that three accounts say nothing of tongues, but the omission is due to the brevity of those accounts. In the record of the outpouring on the Samaritans (Acts 8:14–19) no mention is made of an accompanying sign, but the fact that Simon was willing to pay money for the power to impart the gift of the Spirit shows that some audible or visible sign made the gift spectacular. It is logical to assume that he heard them speak with tongues.

In Acts 4:31 there is no mention of tongues: "And when they had prayed, the place was shaken where they were assembled together; and they were all filled with the Holy Ghost, and they spake the word of God with boldness." But this could well have been a refilling of those who were initially baptized on the Day of Pentecost.

In Acts 9:17 we do not read that Paul spoke with tongues when he received the Spirit. Nonetheless, that he did is quite certain from his testimony: "I thank my God, I speak with tongues more than ye all" (1 Cor. 14:18).

In this connection, two thoughts should be noted. First, the first and last biblical accounts of the reception of the Holy Spirit (Acts 2:4; 19:6) mention that the recipients spoke with tongues. Secondly, in every account of outpourings of the Holy Spirit where any sign is mentioned, tongues is signified. Where no signs at all are spoken of, there is strong evidence that the recipients did so speak.

The Pentecostal Fellowship of North America is an association of twenty-two of the largest Pentecostal denominations in North America. The statement of faith to which all member groups must agree has as its sixth point: "We believe that the full gospel includes holiness of heart and life, healing for the body and the baptism in the Holy Spirit, with the initial evidence of speaking in other tongues as the Spirit gives utterance."[22]

There are some who teach that the initial evidence of tongues is not always necessary to assure that one has received the fullness of the Spirit, but that any of the other gifts of the Spirit could be the evidence of the Pentecostal experience. These sometimes mention Acts 19:6, where we read, "They spake with tongues, and prophesied."

It is never claimed that all that one will do when filled with the Spirit is to speak with tongues. Other gifts may well be manifested. All that is claimed here is that the newly baptized believers at Ephesus did speak with tongues, as well as prophecy. Why is it claimed that speaking with tongues is the sign of the filling more than any other gift of the Spirit? Because all of the gifts of the Spirit were more or less manifested in Old Testament times, with the lone exception of speaking with other tongues and its accompanying gift of interpretation of tongues.

- The word of wisdom—Joshua (Dt. 34:9) and Solomon (1 Kgs. 3:9–12)
- The word of knowledge—Bezaleel (Ex. 31:3)
- Faith—Abraham (Gn. 15:6)
- Gifts of healing—Elijah (1 Kgs. 17:17–23) and Elisha (2 Kgs. 4:18–37)
- Working of miracles—Elijah (2 Kgs. 1:10), Elisha (2 Kgs. 6:4–7), and Moses (Ex. 7:10, 20)
- Prophecy—Isaiah, David (2 Sm. 23:2), and Balaam (Nm. 24:2)
- Discerning of spirits—Ahijah (1 Kgs. 14:1–6) and Moses (Ex. 32:17–19)

---

22 From the constitution and bylaws of the Pentecostal Fellowship of North America, Art. 3.6. http://www.pccna.org/constitution_bylaws200510.pdf (accessed January 4, 2008).

God was doing a new thing at Pentecost—something never experienced before—and the sign accompanying it was something never witnessed previously. Thus, it was a most significant sign.

b) Important points to note:

(1) Speaking in tongues is not the baptism with the Holy Spirit. It is the initial evidence, but not the only one.

(2) Do not seek to speak with tongues as though it were the baptism with the Holy Spirit—seek more of God and yield to Him. He will take care of the rest.

(3) It may well be true that some have apparently spoken in tongues who have not received the baptism with the Holy Spirit—the word *apparently* is used because it is believed that many of these are not real languages at all. The devil has a counterfeit for this gift, as he does for all others, but the earnest seeker for more of God need have no fear whatever that he is going to receive anything but God's best (Lk. 11:11–13).

c) Other immediate evidences of a new experience of the anointing of the Spirit in the life will include praise to God (Acts 2:11; 2:47; 10:46), an overflowing joy (Acts 2:46), and a deep burden and desire to preach or testify about Jesus (Acts 1:8; 2:14–18; 19:6).

2. *Permanent evidences*

a) Jesus Christ glorified and revealed as never before (Jn. 14:21–23; 15:26; 16:13–15). The Holy Spirit centers all things in Christ. A new love is born for Him that will increase as one follows on in the Spirit-filled life. The Holy Spirit imparts the ability to comprehend the greatness of the Savior—His person and provisions (Eph. 1:17–23). It is recognized that many of these Scriptures are realized through the ministry of the Holy Spirit as the Comforter who indwells all believers, but experience demonstrates that all ministries of the Holy Spirit are enhanced as a result of the Pentecostal baptism with the Spirit.

b) A deeper passion for souls. One cannot read the history of the early Church immediately after Pentecost without realizing how there was a burning desire to proclaim the way of salvation (Acts 2:14–41; 4:19–20; 5:29–33; 6:8–10; 11:22–24; 26:28–29).

c) A greater power to witness (Acts 1:8; 2:41; 4:31–33; Jn. 15:26–27; 1 Cor. 2:4–5).

d) A new power in, and spirit of, prayer (Acts 3:1, 4:23–31; 6:4; 10:9; Rom. 8:26; Jude 20; Eph. 6:18; 1 Cor. 14:14–17).

e) A deeper love for, and richer insight into, the Word of God (Jn. 16:13).

f) The manifestations of the gifts of the Spirit (1 Cor. 12:4–11).

I. Additional fillings with the Holy Spirit

The Pentecostal baptism with the Holy Spirit is a definite experience in a Christian's life, but it is more than an experience—it is a *life*. An experience is of little value if it does not leave a permanent impression on one's life. This is particularly true of the baptism with the Spirit. A short season of spiritual ecstasy is very blessed while it lasts, but its value is questionable if it does not lead to a permanent possession of spiritual power. The baptism with the Holy Spirit should—and does—lead into a Spirit-filled life. Paul admonished the Christians, "And be not drunk with wine, wherein is excess; but be filled with the Spirit (Eph. 5:18). Literally, he said, "Be *being* filled with the Spirit." This is to be a continuous experience. We briefly outline four additional fillings that the disciples received after the Day of Pentecost. The book of Acts seems to indicate that there is one baptism but many infillings.

1. *For defending the Faith.* "Then Peter, filled with the Holy Ghost, said unto them, Ye rulers of the people, and elders of Israel" (Acts 4:8). Following the healing of the lame man at the Beautiful Gate of the temple and the great sermon Peter preached in Solomon's porch, the disciples were imprisoned. The following morning, the Sanhedrin brought them out and asked the question, "By what power, or by what name, have ye done this?" (Acts 4:7). The bold and inspiring answer which Peter gave was the result of his being filled with the Spirit. This was a new experience for humble men, but the Holy Spirit enabled them for the occasion. Jesus had told them that just such times would come, but that the Holy Spirit would teach them what to say in such an hour: "And when they bring you unto the synagogues, and unto magistrates, and powers, take ye no thought how or what thing ye shall answer, or what ye shall say: For the Holy Ghost shall teach you in the same hour what ye ought to say" (Lk. 12:11–12). The results were that the leaders marveled (Acts 4:13).

2. *For rebuking the power of the devil.* "Then Saul, (who also is called Paul,) filled with the Holy Ghost, set his eyes on him, And said, O full of all subtilty and all mischief, thou child of the devil, thou enemy of all righteousness, wilt thou not cease to pervert the right ways of the Lord?" (Acts 13:9–10). On the island of Cyprus, Paul was ministering to the deputy of the country, Sergius Paulus, when the sorcerer Elymas sought to turn the deputy away from the faith. Paul received a special anointing of the Spirit and rebuked him in no uncertain words. When Satan seeks to hinder the Word of God, we may expect special infillings so that he may be overcome and the ministry not be hindered.

3. *To give disciples new boldness and power.* "And when they had prayed, the place was shaken where they were assembled together; and they were all filled with the Holy Ghost, and they spake the word of God with boldness" (Acts 4:31). The Sanhedrin had just commanded the disciples and threatened them, "That they speak henceforth to no man in this name" (Acts 4:17). The disciples resorted to prayer and, as a result, a new filling with the Spirit came upon them. They received divine boldness and power to continue preaching the Word of God.

4. *Grace and power to endure persecutions for the sake of the gospel.* "And the disciples were filled with joy, and with the Holy Ghost" (Acts 13:52). As the result of great

success in preaching the gospel in Antioch of Pisidia, "The Jews stirred up the devout and honorable women, and the chief men of the city, and raised persecution against Paul and Barnabus, and expelled them out of their coasts. But they shook off the dust of their feet against them, and came into Iconium. And the disciples were filled with joy, and with the Holy Ghost" (Acts 13:50–52). No one particularly enjoys being persecuted, but those who were received a special filling of the Holy Spirit at such a time. The Greek verb used here is in the imperfect tense, signifying that they were being constantly—every day—filled with the Holy Spirit. They were being subjected to persecution every day; why not a fresh infilling every day?

V. Offenses Against the Holy Spirit

Although the six offenses against the Holy Spirit that are mentioned in the New Testament have been divided into those committed by unbelievers and those by believers, there may be some overlapping.

A. Offenses committed by the unbeliever

1. *Resisting the Holy Spirit.* "Ye stiffnecked and uncircumcised in heart and ears, ye do always resist the Holy Ghost: as your fathers did, so do ye" (Acts 7:51). These words were spoken by Stephen as he spoke to the unbelieving Sanhedrin. The Holy Spirit seeks to speak to the heart of the unbeliever and lead him to God. The Spirit is patient and persistent, but it is possible to resist all His pleadings. The spiritual leaders of Israel described in Acts 7 were convinced of the truth of what Stephen was telling them, but would not yield their hearts (Acts 6:10).

2. *Insulting or spiting the Holy Spirit.* "Of how much sorer punishment, suppose ye, shall he be thought worthy, who hath trodden under foot the Son of God, and hath counted the blood of the covenant, wherewith he was sanctified, an unholy thing, and hath done despite unto the Spirit of grace?" (Heb. 10:29). It is the office of the Holy Spirit to present the saving work of Jesus Christ to the unsaved. When an individual refuses to accept Jesus Christ, he is really insulting the love of God, manifested in His grace. It is as though he is saying either that he does not need salvation or does not believe Christ can save him. To resist the Spirit's appeal is, therefore, to insult the Godhead and cut off all hope of salvation.

3. *Blaspheming the Holy Spirit—the unpardonable sin*

> Wherefore I say unto you, All manner of sin and blasphemy shall be forgiven unto men: but the blasphemy against the Holy Ghost shall not be forgiven unto men. And whosoever speaketh a word against the Son of Man, it shall

be forgiven him: but whosoever speaketh against the Holy Ghost, it shall not
be forgiven him, neither in this world, neither in the world to come.

            —MATTHEW 12:31–32

This is the most serious offense against the Holy Spirit, for there is no forgiveness for one who commits it. What is the blasphemy against the Holy Spirit? The
Pharisees had accused Jesus of working miracles by the power of the devil, but He
had cast out that demon by the power of the Holy Spirit (Mt. 12:22–30). That is
attributing the work of the Holy Spirit to the devil. Mark 3:28–30 explains that the
sin of blasphemy could be committed by a Christian, as well as an unsaved person, if
he is not careful. In verse 30 the scribes are recorded as having said of Jesus, "He hath
an unclean spirit."

B. Offenses committed by a believer

1. *Grieving the Holy Spirit.* "And grieve not the holy Spirit of God, whereby ye
are sealed unto the day of redemption. Let all bitterness, and wrath, and anger, and
clamour, and evil speaking, be put away from you, with all malice" (Eph. 4:30–31).
Verse 31 gives some examples of that which grieves the Holy Spirit. To grieve means
"to feel sad or show grief over." We do this as individuals when we allow anything
in our heart that is unlike Him or when we do or say anything that does not reflect
Him. One can only be grieved by someone or something that is loved.

2. *Lying to the Holy Spirit.* "But Peter said, Ananias, why hath Satan filled thine
heart to lie to the Holy Ghost, and to keep back part of the price of the land?" (Acts
5:3). When one consecrates a thing to the Lord and then does not follow through on
that consecration, he is lying to the Holy Spirit. It may be money, time, or service. If
a believer does not intend to be faithful to his promise, he had better not make the
consecration in the first place. Peter, in Acts 5:4, tells Ananias, "Thou hast not lied
unto men, but unto God."

3. *Quenching the Holy Spirit.* "Quench not the Spirit" (1 Thes. 5:19). The thought
of quenching suggests a fire. Unbelief and fleshly criticism may serve to put out the
fire of the Holy Spirit's moving. This is usually done in the assembly, when the Spirit
is manifesting Himself in the worship of the congregation. It is better not to criticize
than to risk the danger of hindering the moving of the Spirit.

VI. THE GIFTS OF THE SPIRIT

A thorough treatment of the doctrine of the Holy Spirit cannot be made without a
full discussion of the gifts of the Spirit. Three full chapters of the New Testament,
as well as parts of two other chapters, are devoted exclusively to the subject. There
are approximately one hundred New Testament references to the subject of spiritual

gifts or to the exercise of one or another of those listed in 1 Corinthians 12, and this number is exclusive of the miracles of Jesus recorded in the Gospels. In spite of the frequent manifestation of the Spirit in the New Testament Church, the majority of books on doctrine and theology ignore spiritual gifts or devote a mere paragraph or two to their discussion, much of which is negative, with the inference that gifts would cease at the end of the apostolic age. There is not the slightest inference in the New Testament that any endowment of the Holy Spirit would cease before seeing "face to face" or before "that which is perfect is come" (1 Cor. 13:10–12).

Regarding spiritual gifts, the Foursquare *Declaration of Faith* says:

> We believe that the Holy Spirit has the following gifts to bestow upon the believing church of the Lord Jesus Christ: wisdom, knowledge, faith, healing miracles, prophecy, discernment, tongues, interpretation; that, according to the degree of grace and faith possessed by the recipient, these gifts are divided to every man severally, as He, the Holy Spirit will; that they are to be earnestly desired and coveted, in the order and proportion wherein they prove most edifying and beneficial to the church.[23]

A. The background for spiritual gifts

1. *The promise given.* It was to be expected that special spiritual enablement would be provided in order that the Church might carry out the divine mission committed to her by the Lord Jesus Christ. Jesus instructed His followers to go into all nations with the gospel, but first to wait for enduement with power from on high (Lk. 24:47–49). With the giving of the Great Commission Jesus promised, "These signs shall follow them that believe": casting out demons, speaking with "new tongues," and recovery of sickness by the laying on of hands (Mk. 16:17). When Jesus announced His return to the Father, He promised His followers that He would send the Comforter who would abide forever; teach them all things; bring all His sayings to their remembrance; guide into all truth; convict of sin, righteousness, and judgment; and who would testify of Him.

2. *The promise fulfilled.* Then, on the Day of Pentecost, the promised Holy Spirit was poured out upon the waiting Church with visible and audible signs, and they began to speak in the tongues predicted in the Great Commission. The believers were filled with the Holy Spirit (Acts 2:2–4). They were so thoroughly enabled by the Spirit's power that everywhere their ministry is marked by the supernatural. The apostles were not mere guardians of orthodoxy; they were ambassadors of Christ equipped with divine capabilities. They had a divine work to do and they had divine

---

23 Aimee Semple McPherson, *Declaration of Faith* (Los Angeles, CA: International Church of the Foursquare Gospel, n.d.), 19.

power with which to do it. It must always be thus. The Church's mission is much more than propagating a new philosophy or calling to a new morality. It is delivering men from the bondage of Satan and binding and loosing in the name of Jesus (Mt. 16:19). Philosophizing and moralizing can be done with mere human capabilities— and such is not unimportant—but delivering individuals from bondage and bringing them to repentance and faith require an anointing of the Holy Spirit (2 Cor. 3:4–6). Certainly, God accepts and honors all human talent dedicated to His service, but He enhances that dedicated talent with the Spirit's glow, lifting it to a new level. God can and often does take natural capacities and transform them into spiritual operations. (Ex. 35:29–35; Rom. 15:13–14; Ti. 1:7–9; 2 Tm. 2:2).

B. The vocabulary of spiritual gifts

The nature of spiritual gifts can be determined to a large degree by the vocabulary employed to refer to them. The first reference to the gifts as a general class of phenomena is found in 1 Corinthians, which was written in about A.D. 55 Chapters 12–14 are devoted in their entirety to spiritual gifts. The first seven verses of chapter 12 deal with the gifts as a class and provide a vocabulary for their description. The gifts are called:

1. *Spirituals,* pneumatika. "Now concerning spiritual *gifts,* brethren, I would not have you ignorant." (1 Cor. 12:1, emphasis added). Note that in some versions the word *gifts* is in italics, meaning that it is not found in the original Greek. The first reference to the spiritual phenomena called spiritual gifts classifies them merely as "spirituals" or "things of the Spirit," exactly the same descriptive is used in 1 Corinthians 14:1. The reference probably is to the gifts, although the same word, *pneumatikos* (masc. gender), is used elsewhere to mean "spiritual men." F. F. Bruce, in his commentary on 1 Corinthians, takes *pneumatika* as referring to the "persons endowed with spiritual gifts."[24] The spirituals in one sense are gifts, but they are more than gifts, as will be shown.

2. *Spiritual gifts,* charismata. "Now there are diversities of gifts" (1 Cor. 12:4). The Greek word *charisma,* which is rendered "spiritual gift," comes from the basic word *charis,* which means "grace." A *charisma,* then, is an enablement, an endowment, or a blessing bestowed freely by God. The text in Corinthians refers to the gifts as spirituals because they are capacities freely bestowed by the Holy Spirit. They cannot be merited or earned, and they are of divine origin. They are operated through Spirit-filled persons, but in a real sense they are gifts to the church, the body of Christ (1 Cor. 12:11–27).

---

24 Frederick Fyvie Bruce, *New Century Bible Commentary: First Corinthians* (Grand Rapids, MI: Wm. B. Eerdmans Publishing Company, 1971).

3. *Administrations,* diakonia. "And there are differences of administrations" (1 Cor. 12:5). *Administrations* is better translated "ministries" (NKJV). The spirituals are gifts in regard to their origin and source, but they are ministries in regard to their application. He who exercises his spiritual gift in the body ministers to the body. There are as many kinds of ministries as there are spiritual gifts and spiritual offices. The gifts are not merit awards, nor are they bestowed primarily to benefit the possessor; the Spirit imparts the *charismata* that there might be ministry to the body. Their value resides in their capacity to minister to the body spiritual profit and edification.

4. *Operations (inworkings),* energemata. "And there are diversities of operations" (1 Cor. 12:6). The spirituals are operations in the sense that they are gifts and ministries operated by the Holy Spirit. The Greek word for "operation" is *energema,* which means "thing wrought" or "effect." The English word *energy* comes from the same root. The spiritual gifts are activities of the Spirit, bringing spiritual effects. They are operations energized by the Spirit, producing effects in the body. A gift that does not operate nor minister nor produce an effect is of little value.

5. *Manifestations,* phanerosis. "But the manifestation of the Spirit is given to every man to profit withal" (1 Cor. 12:7). Every operation of the spirituals is a manifestation of the Spirit. *Manifestation* is defined as an "outward evidence." The gifts of the Spirit bring the Holy Spirit into outward evidence in the body. The operation of the gifts causes the believers to be aware of the presence of God, producing the effects of praise and worship. Every Spirit-filled believer is given some capacity for the manifestation of the Spirit. The exercise of a gift is a manifestation of the Spirit primarily, not of the gifted person, and the test of its genuineness is that it profits the whole body.

6. *Diversity,* diairesis. See 1 Corinthians 4–6. The idea behind the word *diversity* is that of distribution. God does not intend that only a few gifts operate through one or two persons. There are many different spiritual gifts, more than the nine chosen for mention in 1 Corinthians 12. There may be as many gifts as there are useful functions in the Church. Every believer should have some manifestation of the Spirit, and there should operate in the body every variety of gift. God is a God of infinite variety. The spirituals are of great variety, but there is one Lord and one Holy Spirit operating in the great variety of spiritual manifestations and ministries.

C. The purpose of spiritual gifts

The purpose of the spiritual gifts is the edification of the Church. If the exercise of the gifts does not edify and build up the body, they are valueless: "Even so ye, forasmuch as ye are zealous of spiritual gifts [spirituals], seek that ye may excel to the edifying of the church" (1 Cor. 14:12). "Let all things be done unto edifying" (1 Cor. 14:26). The words *edify* and *profit* are used eight times in 1 Corinthians with relation to the operation of spiritual gifts. Gifts are bestowed with the purpose of bringing spiritual profit and edification to the whole body. If a gift is exercised without love or merely as a personal display, a golden bell is changed into a clanging, brazen cymbal.

There are said to be three effects of the gift of prophecy: "He that prophesieth speaketh unto men to edification, and exhortation, and comfort" (1 Cor. 14:3). All three of these effects build up and profit the body of Christ.

1. *Edification.* The word *edification* comes from the Greek word *oikodome,* which basically means "the act of building" a structure. The vocal gifts are intended to effect the building of the temple of Christ's body.

2. *Exhortation.* The word *exhortation* translates the Greek word *paraklesis,* which means "exhortation" or "encouragement." It is related to the word *paraclete,* the name Jesus gave to the Holy Spirit. The name Barnabas was said to mean "son of consolation" or "encouragement." The Greek word translated "consolation" is the same, *paraklesis.* What a blessing and profit Barnabas was to the whole church, especially the church at Antioch (Acts 11:22–26)! The verb form of *paraklesis* is frequently translated "I beseech you." He that exhorts the Church may stir and motivate believers to do God's whole will. Hebrews 10:24 provides a good example of this kind of exhortation: "And let us consider one another to provoke unto love and to good works."

3. *Comfort.* The word *comfort* is used as the translation of the word *paramuthia,* which also means "consolation." It was predicted that the Church would suffer persecution. The body often needs the ministry of consolation in a time of sorrow.

There is a process of growth and maturity in the exercise of spiritual gifts. In order that the Church might receive profitable edification, God desires that the gifts be exercised maturely: "Brethren, do not be children in understanding...but in understanding be mature" (1 Cor. 14:20, NKJV). First Corinthians 14 contains the apostle's teaching about the mature use of spiritual gifts. Where the gifts are in operation, this teaching should be diligently given.

D. The gifts enumerated in 1 Corinthians 12

The gifts of the Spirit enumerated in 1 Corinthians 12, according to many, are nine in number. However, in verse 28 of the same chapter, Paul, after repeating the mention of miracles, healings, and tongues, adds the gifts of helps and governments without making any distinction in classification. Nor does the apostle distinguish sharply between the offices of apostles, prophets, and teachers and the endowments of miracles, healings, and tongues. Apparently, when God set apart a person for an office, He bestowed upon him a spiritual enablement that corresponded with the office or ministry. Perhaps the mention of two additional gifts in verse 28 was made for the purpose of showing that the number could be lengthened considerably. Some have seen a need to fix the number of gifts at nine to correspond to the nine ,the Spirit, but a careful search will reveal other fruit of the Spirit in addition to the nine listed in Galatians 5. Paul mentions seventeen works of the flesh, then ends the list with the phrase "and such like." If the flesh can produce seventeen works and more, the Spirit can produce an endless number of virtues that are some aspect of love. In 1 Corinthians 12–14, Paul mentioned the gifts that were well known to the Corinthians, and in Romans he introduces other gifts that illustrated his purpose of discussion. August Hermann Cremer, an eminent theologian and Greek scholar who wrote before the latter-day Pentecostal outpouring, said regarding the gifts, their function, and their number:

> The place, therefore, that each member has in the community he has by virtue of a "charisma," which he is to administer to his brethren (1 Pt. 4:10). Natural powers as such are useless to the life of the body of Christ; what it needs must, like itself, be spiritual. Charismata, then, may be defined as powers and capacities necessary for the edification of the church, bestowed by the Holy Spirit upon its members, in virtue of which they are enabled to employ their natural abilities in the service of the church, or are endowed with new abilities for this purpose. According to 1 Cor. 12:11, 18; Rom. 12:5–8; Eph. 4:11, the "charismata" form the basis of the offices in the church. There can be no office without a charisma; but not all charismata are applicable to the exercise of an office. Those that correspond to the permanent and invariable needs of the church form the basis of offices, the others do not... Since the number of the charismata must correspond to the needs of the church, it follows that the lists in 1 Cor. 12, Eph. 4, and Rom. 12 cannot be taken as exhaustive.[25]

1. *Word of wisdom.* This is not the gift of wisdom in general, but the gift of a word of wisdom. However, by itself it is not necessarily a vocal gift. The Greek word *logos*, translated here as "word," is defined as "speech...[that] embodies a concept or idea," "a weighty saying," "reason," "narrative," or "doctrine." If the idea of "utterance" had been meant, the Greek word *rhema* would probably have been used instead of *logos*. Working together with prophecy, the word of wisdom could function as a vocal gift. It is likely that this is the gift that operated in Stephen in Acts 6:10: "And they were not able to resist the wisdom and the spirit by which he spake." Acts 15 records the first council of the apostolic church to settle a dispute. The conclusion they reached is expressed as follows: "For it seemed good to the Holy Ghost, and to us, to lay upon you no greater burden than these necessary things" (Acts 15:28). The mind of the Holy Ghost was probably conveyed to the apostles by a word of wisdom. While *wisdom* has many meanings, when used in contrast to *knowledge* it probably means an

---

25 August Hermann Cremer, *The New Schaff-Herzog Encyclopedia of Religious Knowledge* (Grand Rapids, MI: Baker Book House, 1949–50), III, 11.

insight for practical conduct or action. In the life of the local church, there are times when important decisions need to be made concerning a course of action to take. The operation of a word of wisdom could provide the Spirit's guidance (1 Cor. 2:13–16).

2. *Word of knowledge.* This gift of a word of knowledge may be referred to by Paul's statement in 1 Corinthians 1:5: "That in everything ye are enriched by him, in all utterance, and in all knowledge." If a word of wisdom gives insight to the Church for practical action, a word of knowledge must bring to light the principles of doctrine that form a basis for the action. This gift may bring scriptural truth to the attention of the Church, or it may reveal facts that are needed for further action. Paul had confidence that spiritual knowledge operated in the Church when he said, "And I myself also am persuaded of you, my brethren, that ye also are full of goodness, filled with all knowledge, able also to admonish one another" (Rom. 15:14). John probably exercised the gift of a word of knowledge to discern the spiritual conditions of the seven churches to which he wrote in Revelation 2–3. These gifts of the word of wisdom and word of knowledge are for the guidance of the Church for knowledge and action. They are not for personal guidance. Silas was a prophet, but it is never recorded that he gave guidance to Paul in his decisions. When Paul did not know which way to turn at Troas, God gave him a vision of the Macedonian man calling him to preach in Greece, yet Silas was with him at the time. Gifts are given to exhort, edify, and comfort the assembled church. Gifts of revelation work in harmony with the Word of God, never contradicting its teaching, for the inspired Word is called a "more sure word of prophecy" (2 Pt. 1:19).

3. *Special faith.* Nearly all writers on the gifts refer to the gift of faith as that of special faith. The reason for this is that the gift of faith differs from saving faith and the normal Christian faith, "without which it is impossible to please God" (Heb. 11:6). All faith is alike in nature, but the gift of special faith differs from other faith in degree and in application. Special faith works often in conjunction with healings and miracles. The gift of faith is seen in operation in the healing of the lame man at the gate of the temple, recorded in Acts 3. Peter had the miraculous faith to command the lame man to rise and walk in the name of Jesus. Donald Gee writes concerning this faith:

> It would seem to come upon certain of God's servants in times of special crisis or opportunity in such mighty power that they are lifted right out of the realm of even natural or ordinary faith in God—and have a divine certainty put within their souls that triumphs over everything.[26]

---

26 Donald Gee, *Spiritual Gifts in the Work of the Ministry Today* (Springfield, MO: Gospel Publishing House, 1963), 65.

Perhaps Jesus was describing this quality of faith when He said to His disciples, "Have faith in God" (Mk. 11:22). The Greek of Mark 11:22 reads literally, "Have the faith of God." Jesus suggested in the next verse that with this divinely imparted faith one might tell a mountain to be removed and cast into the sea, and it would happen. The mountain symbolizes any apparently impossible obstacle to the mission of the church.

4. *Gifts of healings*. While it is inferred that all the spirituals are *charismata* (gifts), the term is actually attached only to this one of healings. In the Greek, both of the terms, *gifts* and *healings*, are plural. This fact would suggest either that there are many gifts of healing for different diseases or that each exercise of the healing power is a separate gift. Nowhere in the New Testament is a person said to have *the* gift of healing. Most of the evangelists and pastors who have had great ministries of prayer for the sick have disclaimed possession of a gift of healing. Certainly no one has had a ministry of healing every sick person. Jesus healed all who came to Him on some occasions, but He was limited on other occasions by lack of faith on the part of the people (Mt. 13:58). What is certain is that God has made provision that physical healing would be a ministry of His church and that gifts of healings would operate along with faith. Healing is so common in the ministry of Jesus and in that of the apostles that a church without gifts of cures would seem far removed from the Bible's pattern. In addition to gifts of healings, all elders (pastors) are to be ready to anoint with oil all the sick who call for them and to pray over them the prayer of faith. In response, God has promised to raise up the sick and to forgive their sins (Jas. 5:14–16).

In the Great Commission, recorded by Mark (Mk. 16:15–18), Jesus promised that signs would follow the ministries of those who witnessed of the saving gospel. One of the signs would be that the sick would recover after the laying on of hands by believers. As long as it took to preach the gospel to every creature, signs were to follow those who believed, including that of the miraculous healing of the sick. The clause "them that believe" in verse 17 would suggest that the signs or gifts were not to be exercised by the apostles only, but by all who had faith. In the command and promise of Jesus, the laying on of hands was to be the outward expression of faith and love on the part of those who would pray, which would also show that God uses faithful believers as a channel of His power. The anointing with oil, according to James 5, involved the laying on of hands as well, with the oil symbolizing the work of the Holy Spirit. When Jesus sent forth the twelve disciples to minister, they, according to Mark, "Anointed with oil many that were sick, and healed them" (Mk. 6:13). The believer is the vehicle of power, but the healing is the Spirit's work.

While on some occasions the sick are healed through the faith of the one who prays, faith on the part of the afflicted person is important, and sometimes essential: "Paul, observing him intently and seeing that he had faith to be healed, said with a loud voice, 'Stand up straight on your feet!' And he leaped and walked" (Acts 14:9–10, NKJV). Paul was exercising the gifts of faith and healings, nevertheless his command to stand up was given after he discerned that the lame man had faith to be healed. The need for the afflicted to have faith suggests that candidates for healing might well benefit from faith-building teaching. The most effective faith-building comes through the Word of God: "So then faith cometh by hearing, and hearing by the Word of God" (Rom. 10:17). Old Testament promises of healing are found in: Ex. 15:26; Ex. 23:25; Dt. 32:39; 2 Kgs. 20:5; Ps. 30:1–2; Ps. 103:3; Ps. 107:17–22; Is. 38:4–5; and 53:5. New Testament healing passages are: Mt. 4:23; 8:8, 16–17; 10:8; Mk. 3:14–15; Lk. 4:40; 9:6; Acts 3:1–11; 4:30; 5:15–16; 8:7; 28:8; 1 Cor. 12:9; Jas. 5:14–16; and 1 Pt. 2:24.

5. *Operations of miracles.* The working of miracles is the translation of the Greek *energemata dunameon,* which literally rendered is "operations of supernatural powers." As with the gifts of healings, the term is plural. This is not a gift that makes one a miracle worker. It seems from the plurality of the two expressions that each miracle or supernatural manifestation of power is operated through one with a gift of faith (Mt. 17:20; 21:20–22). What is a miracle? "An event or action that apparently contradicts known scientific laws and is hence thought to be due to supernatural causes, especially to an act of God."[27] In the New Testament, events of supernatural origin are called "signs, wonders, and miracles" (Acts 2:22, 43; 6:8; 8:13; Heb. 2:4). The Greek words translated "miracles," "wonders," and "signs" are *dunamis, teras, semeion.* Literally, they mean, "events of divine power," "events that cause wonderment," and "events that signify something" (about God or His working). It is noteworthy that the term *wonder* is never used by itself; it is always used together with the term *sign.* God does not manifest His power just to cause wonderment; He always signifies or teaches something with His miracles: "God also bearing them witness, both with signs and wonders, and with divers miracles [acts of power], and gifts of the Holy Ghost, according to His own will" (Heb. 2:4).

Examples of miracles are: supernatural deliverances from imprisonments (Acts 5:18–20; 12:5–10; 16:23–30); the striking with blindness of Elymas the sorcerer (Acts 13:8–12); the instant transportation of Philip from Gaza to Azotus (Acts 8:39–40); the raising from the dead of Dorcas (Acts 9:36–42) and Eutychus (Acts 20:9–12); and Paul's shaking off the poisonous viper without receiving harm (Acts 28:3–5). The healing of the sick and the casting out of demon spirits may be classified as gifts of miracles when there is great sign value, as in the case of Paul in Ephesus, where great soul-winning resulted: "And God wrought special miracles [literally, "not ordinary miracles"] by the hands of Paul: So that from his body were brought unto

---

27 *Webster's New World Dictionary of the American Language* (New York: Collins World Publishing Company, 1976), s.v. "miracle."

the sick handkerchiefs or aprons, and the diseases departed from them, and the evil spirits went out of them" (Acts 19:11–12); and in the case of Peter in Jerusalem, when just his shadow falling upon the sick brought healing (Acts 5:12–15).

6. *Prophecy.* The word *prophet* is a transliteration from the Greek *prophetes,* which is derived from two words: *pro,* which means "before" (in the sense of "in behalf of"); and *phemi,* which means to "declare, say." Together, the word *prophetes* can refer to one who predicts something, "one who solemnly declares," or an individual who speaks in behalf of someone else. Since the office of the prophet begins in the Old Testament, the basic definition should begin there. The Hebrew word for "prophet" is *nabi,* which means "to announce, witness, or testify." The office of a prophet is clearly defined: "I will raise them up a Prophet from among their brethren, like unto thee, and will put my words in his mouth; and he shall speak unto them all that I shall command him" (Dt. 18:18). The prophet is one who speaks to the people on behalf of God the words that God puts in his mouth. This is confirmed by the words of the Lord to Moses when Moses disclaimed ability to speak to Pharaoh: "See, I have made thee a God to Pharaoh: and Aaron thy brother shall be thy prophet. Thou shalt speak all that I command thee: and Aaron thy brother shall speak unto Pharaoh" (Ex. 7:1–2). Aaron is called the prophet of Moses because he spoke in behalf of Moses, delivering Moses' message. The same idea of speaking for God is borne out by the testimony of Jeremiah the prophet: "Then the LORD put forth his hand, and touched my mouth. And the LORD said unto me, Behold, I have put my words in thy mouth" (Jer. 1:9). Sometimes the prophet would speak forth in God's behalf a message to the people for their current situation, while at other times he would predict coming events. In either case, he was simply speaking forth the Lord's message.

Deuteronomy 13 and 18 list several qualifications for a prophet and tests of his authenticity.

- He is one taken from among his brethren (18:18).
- He is to speak to his brethren in the name of the Lord (18:19). He may with his prophecies show signs and wonders (13:1).
- If he prophesies anything contrary to God's Law already revealed (Scripture), he is to be rejected in spite of any signs or wonders (13:1–3). (God may permit false prophets to test our obedience to His Word.)
- If he predicts the future and the prediction fails to come to pass as he prophesied, he is to be rejected (18:20–22).

In the New Testament, there are two kinds of prophets: those who occupy the office of a prophet (Eph. 4:11) and those in the Church who possess the gift of prophecy. Those of the first category are among the ministry gifts; those of the second could include any Spirit-filled believer. Not all can occupy the office of a prophet ("The Lord gave some, apostles; and some, prophets" [Eph. 4:11]), but according to 1 Corinthians 14:31, "Ye may all prophesy one by one." Thus, having the gift of prophecy does not make one a prophet (possessing the ministry gift of that type).

Among the gifts listed by Paul in 1 Corinthians, prophecy is that which is to be desired most earnestly (14:1, 5, 24–25, 39). Its importance is indicated by the fact that some form of the word is found twenty times in 1 Corinthians 12–14. The gift of prophecy is defined as speaking "unto men to edification, and exhortation, and comfort" (1 Cor. 14:3). The Amplified Version renders verse 3: "The one who prophesies…speaks to men for their upbuilding and constructive spiritual progress and encouragement and consolation." Predicting future events is not associated with the gift of prophecy; this is a function of the prophetic office. The gift operates to spiritually build up the local church body. When the church faces a problem of missing facts or a need for wisdom for practical action, a word of knowledge or a word of wisdom may operate in conjunction with the gift of prophecy. A word of wisdom may have assured the apostles in their knotty decision regarding the relationship between circumcision and salvation, recorded in Acts 15. When the conclusion of the council was delivered to the Gentile church in Antioch by Judas and Silas, who were prophets, Luke reports, "Now Judas and Silas, themselves being prophets also, exhorted and strengthened the brethren with many words" (Acts 15:32, NKJV). Normally, in the operation of the gift of prophecy, the Spirit heavily anoints the believer to speak forth to the body not premeditated words, but words the Spirit supplies spontaneously in order to uplift and encourage, incite to faithful obedience and service, and to bring comfort and consolation. The words need not be in archaic English, in a loud and altered voice, nor spoken in first person. More will be written on the practical exercise of vocal gifts in Section E, "Special instructions on the gifts of tongues and prophecy."

7. *Discerning of spirits.* Discerning of spirits comes from the Greek *diakrisis pneumaton.* The Greek word *diakrisis* is defined, "to discern," "to discriminate," or "to distinguish." The verb form is used in Hebrews 5:14: "But strong meat belongeth to them that are of full age, even those who by reason of use have their senses exercised to discern both good and evil." Paul uses the verb several times in 1 Corinthians. In 6:5 he uses it in regard to a dispute to question whether they had anyone wise enough to "judge between his brethren" (as to who was in the right). In 11:29 Paul uses the word to reproach the Corinthian brethren who had not "discerned" the Lord's body (i.e., discerned the meaning of the communion bread for bodily health and healing). Quite clearly, the gift of discerning of spirits is the capacity to discern the source of a spiritual manifestation—whether it is the Holy Spirit, an evil spirit, or merely the human spirit. In 1 Corinthians 14:29, Paul says, "Let the two or three prophets speak, and let the others judge [discern—*diakrino*]" (NKJV). This seems to infer that

someone with the gift of discernment should be present when the gift of prophecy is used. Apparently, in Corinth the gift of discernment was as common as that of prophecy ("let the others [plural] judge"). All Spirit-filled believers are, in a measure, able to judge the operation of vocal gifts on the basis of whether they are spiritually edifying to the body. The exercise of gifts is not infallible. If an utterance (prophecy or interpretation of tongues) is not received, the speaker should not be offended or unteachable, but should humbly pray for better sensitivity to the Spirit and for more wisdom in the use of his gift. On the other hand, believers should heed the admonition of Paul in 1 Thessalonians 5:19–20: "Quench not the Spirit. Despise not prophesyings [literally, prophecies]." Careful scriptural teaching on spiritual gifts will avoid immature and misguided manifestations on one hand and fear, distrust, and quenching the Spirit on the other hand. It should be noted that the gift of discerning of spirits is not that of judging people, but rather of judging the spirit behind the manifestation, whether holy, evil, or human.

8. *Kinds of tongues.* This is literally "kinds of tongues" (Greek—*gene glosson*). The term *kinds* doubtless refers to the fact that there are "new tongues" (Mark 16:17) and "tongues of men and of angels" (1 Cor. 13:1). Some tongues are human languages, as on the Day of Pentecost, which showed that the gospel was for all races and nations. Some tongues are of heavenly origin (of angels, used for praise and prayer where the mind is superseded, as in 1 Cor. 14:2; Rom. 8:26–27). Of these latter category, it is said that the speaker in tongues speaks to God, speaks mysteries, and that no one understands him. Tongues used as a sign (e.g., 1 Cor. 14:22) may be known languages by which witness is given to the unsaved. Since the unsaved may be of any one of a number of languages, there must therefore be various kinds of tongues of this type. If one employs tongues only in private devotion, the kind is not important; they will probably be new tongues or Spirit-given heavenly tongues.

It is very important to observe that there are several different uses of tongues. Paul A. Hamar, in his commentary on 1 Corinthians, remarks:

> There is an acknowledged difference between tongues as the evidence of the baptism of the Holy Spirit and in individual praying, and tongues as a gift (as used here). The difference is basically one of purpose: one is to edify one's own spirit; the other to edify the congregation.[28]

When the apostle asks the question in 1 Corinthians 12:30, "Do all speak with tongues?" admittedly, the form of the question infers a negative answer. Paul is not speaking here of tongues as the initial evidence of the baptism of the Spirit, but of

---

28 Paul A. Hamar, *The Radiant Commentary on the New Testament, The Book of First Corinthians* (Springfield, MO: Gospel Publishing House, 1980), 110.

tongues as the congregational gift, accompanied by interpretation. Not all had the gift of tongues, but all had received tongues as the evidence of their baptism. Those who have the gift of tongues may employ it to speak with God in praise, to pray or sing in the Spirit, or to speak forth in the congregation. However, public tongues speaking must be interpreted. If no interpreter is present, the one with the gift of tongues must hold his peace. Those who have a gift of tongues for public manifestation should pray for the accompanying gift of interpretation of tongues. If the tongues speaker does not know whether an interpreter is present, he must be ready to interpret his own utterance (1 Cor. 14:13, 28). Apparently, tongues together with interpretation are equivalent to prophecy, except that tongues are addressed to God, while prophecy is addressed to the congregation (1 Cor. 14:5, 14–15; Acts 2:11; 10:45–46).

The following is a summary of the discernibly different uses of speaking in tongues:

(1) The initial physical evidence of the baptism in the Holy Spirit (Acts 2:4; 10:45–46; 19:6).

(2) Praying in tongues as a prayer language, when the mind is bypassed and the spirit communes directly with God (1 Cor. 14:2, 14–15; Romans 8:26–27).

(3) Tongues with interpretation, for the spiritual edification of the church body (1 Cor. 14:5, 26–28).

(4) Tongues together with interpretation, as a sign to the unbeliever (1 Cor. 14:22). (The tongues may be a sign of the presence of God, or they may act as a sign when the unbeliever understands the language spoken.)

9. *Interpretation of tongues.* The word "interpretation" translates the Greek word *hermeneia,* from which is derived the English word *hermeneutics* (the science of interpretation). The Greek word may have several meanings, including "translation," "explanation," or "interpretation." The verb form of the word is used several times, where it has the meaning of translation (Jn. 1:38, 42; 9:7; Heb. 7:2). The noun form, *hermeneia,* is found only in 1 Corinthians 12 and 14, where it is used of the spiritual gift. The basic meaning of the word suggests more the idea of explanation or interpretation. It need not, therefore, be expected that the interpretation of an utterance in tongues be a literal, word-by-word translation, but rather an explanation of the meaning. The interpretation may reasonably vary in length from the utterance in tongues. Where the gift of tongues is exercised for the edification of the Church, or as a sign gift, interpretation is essential, for Paul limits the gift of tongues to one's personal prayer language unless accompanied by interpretation (1 Cor. 14:13, 27–28). Those who have the gift of tongues are admonished to pray for the gift of interpretation (1 Cor. 14:13).

The question often arises concerning the number of interpreters to be used in any one service. First Corinthians 14:27 says, "If any man speak in an unknown tongue, let it be by two, or at the most by three, and that by course; and let one interpret."

The Greek word for "one" is *heis,* which is the number one. The Greek word means "someone," but since the numbers two and three are used in the same verse, it would follow that *one* is used here as a number, its usual meaning. Not all the versions and the commentators are in agreement on the clause, "Let one interpret." The NIV renders it, "Someone must interpret." Nevertheless, the KJV, the NKJV, the RSV, the NASB, the AMP, Wiest's Expanded Translation, Rotherham's Emphasized Bible, and Marshall's Interlinear translate *heis* as the number one. Commentators such as Grosheide, Alford, Godet, Clarke, and Plummer take the word *one* as a number. Pentecostal and charismatic writers are not agreed. Therefore, one should not be dogmatic. If one person is to interpret in any one service, it does not follow that the same interpreter will function at all services. More will be said in the next section about prophecy, tongues, and interpretation.

10. *Helps,* antilepsis. That the nine gifts listed in 1 Corinthians 12:8–10 do not constitute the total number of *charismata* is indicated in a summary at the close of the same chapter (vv. 28–30). Paul lists three ministry gifts: apostles, founders of the church; prophets, who exhort and motivate the church; and teachers (or pastors), who instruct the church. After that, six of the *charismata* are listed: miracles, healings, helps, governments, tongues, and interpretation. Two of the *charismata,* helps and governments, are new to the list.

The word *helps* comes from the Greek word *antilempseis,* which is used only once in the New Testament. The verb form (*antilambanomi*) occurs in three passages, one of which gives good indication of the meaning of the gift: "I have shewed you all things, how that so laboring ye ought to support [*antilambanomi*] the weak, and to remember the words of the Lord Jesus, how he said, It is more blessed to give than to receive" (Acts 20:35). Paul was addressing the Ephesian elders, into whose hands the care of the Ephesian church was being placed. They were charged to feed the flock in the Word of God (v. 28) and to fortify against false teachers (vv. 29–30), but they were also instructed to carry on a ministry of helps (*antilepsis*) for the benefit of those who were weak physically and economically, that is, who were sick and needy.

Not everyone can be assigned to a ministry to the sick and poor. One must have a spiritual burden and a God-given love for the needy and afflicted. Human compassion helps, but to this must be added a divine call and the Spirit's anointing, for without such spiritual endowment, one will quickly become discouraged and critical. Besides, a ministry to the weak does not merely administer spiritual sedatives and stop-gap relief. Rather, it leads out of weakness to strength (Heb. 11:34). For every kind of work which the Church must do, God has supplied a corresponding spiritual gift.

11. *Governments,* kubernesis. As in the case of the gift of helps, the Greek word translated "governments" (*kubernesis*) is found only once in the New Testament. However, the noun form *kubernetes* occurs twice, referring each time to a ship-master (Acts 27:11; Rv. 18:17). The verb form means "to steer" or "to be a helmsman."

The gift of governments, then, would seem to describe a spiritual capacity given to certain leaders to steer the church through storms and difficult seas. On the basis of 1 Timothy 5:17, some have reasoned that there were two classes of elders in the churches, teaching elders and ruling elders. It has been suggested that some of the elders who did not minister the Word may have exercised their ministry in the business and structural affairs of the church. Paul Hamar suggests, "It may have involved elders who did not labor in the Word and doctrine, but who were charged with some form of leadership and distribution."[29] The modern term *cybernetics*, which comes from the same Greek word, is the name for the science of control over operations and processes by means of computers. The Church has need of leaders whom the Holy Spirit can use to keep the Church on an even keel.

E. Special instructions on the gifts of tongues and prophecy

The entire fourteenth chapter of 1 Corinthians was written to instruct the church on the proper use of spiritual gifts, especially the vocal gifts of tongues, the interpretation of tongues, and prophecy. Some have inferred that Paul wrote to the Corinthians to discourage the use of tongues. Such cannot be the case because he said in verse 5, "I would like every one of you to speak in tongues" (NIV). The apostle who said, "I thank my God, I speak with tongues more than ye all" (v. 18), was not discouraging tongues, but he was prohibiting uninterpreted tongues in public meetings. He wanted all of them to use tongues as a prayer language (vv. 2, 4). Apparently, the Corinthians thought that when the Spirit moved they were expected to exercise their gift, even if they all spoke at once and even if there was no interpretation. They did not know that the spirit of the gifted person was subject to his personal control (v. 32). They overlooked the fact that God gives believers endowments to use intelligently, in accordance with Scripture and for the sole purpose of the spiritual edification of the whole body. The gifts belong to the Church more than they belong to the individuals who exercise them. Therefore, they must not be used selfishly, ostentatiously, nor without love (see chapter 13). The use of the vocal gifts among members of the body must not be so all-consuming that the ministry of teaching the Word and preaching the gospel are despised or displaced (vv. 27, 29). The opposite, of course, is also true. The gifts are a great blessing when they are in submission to scriptural pattern and to wise spiritual leadership.

1. *The priority of prophecy.* "Follow after charity [love], and desire spiritual gifts, but rather that ye may prophesy" (1 Cor. 14:1). Prophecy is the vocal gift of preference. It is often said that tongues plus interpretation are equal to prophecy, a statement based in Paul's words in 1 Corinthians 14:5. This is not quite true. Verse 39 of the same

---

29 Hamar, 114.

chapter says, "Wherefore, brethren, covet to prophesy, and forbid not to speak with tongues." The tongues referred to must have been with interpretation, for Paul had already forbidden them to speak in tongues without interpretation. The conclusion is that tongues are to be permitted, but prophecy is to be coveted and encouraged. Both gifts belong in the Church, but prophecy is preferred. Prophecy accomplishes its goal in one operation; it is more direct and with less chance for distraction. Tongues are primarily directed to God and are preferred for prayer and praise, but prophecy is still preferred for the edification, exhortation, and comfort of the Church.

2. *The private use of tongues.* The most prevalent use of the gift of tongues is that of tongues as one's prayer language (1 Cor. 14:2, 14–15; Rom. 8:26–27). Some have suggested that Jesus spoke in tongues inwardly when He prayed for the deaf and dumb man in Mark 7:34, for the same Greek word, *stenazo*, is used in this passage and in Romans 8:26, where it says the Spirit intercedes for the believer "with groanings [*stenazo*] which cannot be uttered." Prayer in tongues is normal for a Spirit-filled Christian. Believers are commanded thus to pray "always with all prayer and supplication in the Spirit" (Eph. 6:18). (See also Eph. 5:18–19.) Prayer in the Spirit promotes a deepening of the prayer life and the spiritual development of the personality. Many critics of tongues infer that speaking in tongues may be unsettling to the mind's sanity. The fact is that psychological studies have shown that speaking in tongues tends to integrate and solidify the personality and make possessors of the gift more able to cope with life's problems.[30] In Romans 8:26–27, Paul suggests that the Spirit can help our weakness in prayer, which derives from our lack of knowledge of what to pray for and about. The Spirit, who knows our need better than we know it, prays through us in groanings that cannot be uttered, accomplishing intercession on a higher level than that of our conscious petitioning.

3. *Tongues and interpretation.* There are three uses of the gift of tongues which are in addition to its role as the initial physical evidence of the baptism with the Holy Spirit:

(1) Tongues exercised in worship as a prayer language, which is a powerful channel of communication with God and a vehicle for praise.

(2) Tongues as a sign to unbelievers (1 Cor. 14:22–23). A sign is not necessarily a means of converting the unsaved. According to Paul in verses 22–24, it is prophecy that convinces the unbeliever. Rather, the sign of tongues witnesses to the unbelief and doom of the unrepentant. In verse 21, he said, referring to the quotation from Isaiah, "With men of other tongues and other lips will I speak unto this people; and

---

30 See Arnold Bittlinger, *Gifts and Graces* (Grand Rapids, MI: Wm. B. Eerdmans Publishing Company, 1967), 101; and Morton J. Kelsey, *Speaking with Tongues* (New York: Doubleday Publishing Company, 1965).

yet for all that will they not hear me, saith the Lord." (See Is. 28:11–13.) Nevertheless, the sign, when given by God, is necessary.

(3) Tongues is a vocal gift directed to the Church that must always be interpreted. If the tongues speaker is not certain of the presence of an interpreter, he is to hold his peace or pray that he himself may be enabled to interpret (vv. 13, 28).

4. *Prayer and praise in the Spirit.* Much has already been written on this aspect of tongues as a Spirit-provided vehicle for prayer and praise. However, there is an exercise of tongues in prayer and singing in the Spirit that calls for interpretation: "What is it then? I will pray with the spirit, and I will pray with the understanding also: I will sing with the spirit, and I will sing with the understanding also" (v. 15). Verse 16 indicates that this is ministry to the body (perhaps a smaller group): "Else when thou shalt bless with the spirit, how shall he that occupieth the room of the unlearned [ungifted] say Amen at thy giving of thanks, seeing he understandeth not what thou sayest?" Clearly, this exercise differs from tongues as a private prayer language, as described in 1 Corinthians 14:14 and 28.

5. *Limitations on tongues and prophesyings.* Apparently, the meetings in Corinth were so much given to the exercise of vocal gifts, especially speaking in tongues both with and without interpretation, that all other ministry was reduced or eliminated. First Corinthians 14 was written to put vocal gifts in perspective and to give teaching on the mature exercise of the gifts. Chapter 12 (vv. 4–6) had already emphasized the need for variety in the distribution of gifts. If all the gifts are to be exercised and if all believers are to exercise some gift (as it says in verse 11), the vocal gifts must not occupy the whole body life. Prophecy and tongues with interpretation, exercised in scriptural order, are very edifying, but there must also be anointed teaching, preaching of the gospel, and other ministries. Therefore, utterances with tongues must be held to two or three with proper interpretation. Prophesyings likewise must be restricted to two or three in any one gathering. Supernatural utterances must not be so numerous as to become commonplace. This may have happened in Thessalonica, prompting Paul to write the warning, "Despise not prophesyings" (1 Thes. 5:20). An important fact about the operation of gifts is expressed by the apostle in 1 Corinthians 14:32: "And the spirits of the prophets are subject to the prophets." Then he adds, "For God is not the author of confusion, but of peace, as in all Churches of the saints" (v. 33). All those who exercise vocal gifts should pray for wisdom to recognize those moments in the service when an utterance is edifying. Only in very rare occasions should one who is ministering be interrupted by an utterance. As is often said, the Holy Spirit is a gentleman. There are any number of pauses in a service where a gift for the edification of the Church may be exercised, so there is no need for anyone to be interrupted. There are exceptions, but they are rare.

6. *Not to be considered infallible.* Another principle for the exercise of the gifts is that no operation wrought through human instruments is infallible. The gift of the

discerning of Spirits should be operative in every assembly where the gifts are exercised. This does not mean that a public pronouncement of judgment must be made upon every operation of a vocal gift. Paul wrote, "Let two or three prophets speak, and let the others judge [discern]" (1 Cor. 14:29, NKJV). All Spirit-filled believers have some measure of ability to judge whether utterances are spiritually edifying. If all are to discern, then it must be that each discerns whether the utterance has spiritual value for himself. If it does have value and application, he should receive the message and act upon it in his own life. Not all messages are meant to apply to all individuals present. If the utterance is totally from a human spirit and unedifying, then one with the gift of discernment may declare the utterance unprofitable. If the utterance is from a spirit of evil, then it should be denounced and the believers warned. Leadership ought to covet the gift of discernment. "You must want love more than anything else; but still hope for the spiritual gifts as well, especially prophecy" (1 Cor. 14:1, JB).

F. The gifts of the Spirit listed in Romans 12

1. *Prophecy and ministry.* In the study of the gifts enumerated in 1 Corinthians 12, at least eleven were identified, along with the mention of three of the ministry gifts (to be studied in the next section). In the list in Romans 12, only one gift is common to the list in Corinthians—that of prophecy. Of the vocal gifts operative in Corinth, apparently only prophecy was exercised in Rome. However, since prophecy was the vocal gift of preference, it accomplished the purpose of all edification, exhortation, and comfort. Here Paul adds the fact that faith is the operational principle underlying prophecy and that prophecy must be exercised in proportion to the measure of one's faith. This faith is not the saving faith that all possess as a gift, nor "the Faith" in the sense of Christian doctrine, but the faith associated with works of power (Mt. 9:29).

To the church at Rome, Paul mentions the gift of ministry (*diakonia*), which probably included a number of gifts. In 1 Corinthians 12:5, Paul wrote, "And there are varieties of ministries [*diakonia*] and the same Lord" (NASB); which suggests that all gifts are ministries or vehicles of service to the body. After the mention of prophecy and ministry, the focus is turned away from the gift itself to the person who exercised the gift.

2. *The teacher and his teaching.* God does not impart gifts in the Church merely to satisfy one's instinct for acquisition, but rather that the things of God may be ministered from one to another and that the Church may be built up spiritually. When God provides the teaching of divine truth, He really gives two gifts. He gives to the Church a teacher, and along with the teacher, God gives a divine enablement to teach, a gift of teaching. But a teacher is of little value unless he exercises his gift. In Romans 12:7 Paul is saying, in effect, "If someone is a God-anointed teacher, let him use his gift to teach" (author's paraphrase). The proof that one is a teacher is seen in the fact

that he is practicing constructive teaching. A title does not make one a minister, but rather the fact that he ministers. What authenticates a God-given teacher are pupils who are growing in grace and knowledge under his teaching gift (1 Cor. 2:10–16; 1 Tm. 5:17; 2 Tm. 2:2; 1 Jn. 2:20, 27).

3. *The exhorter and his exhortation.* Exhortation (*paraklesis*) was said by Paul in 1 Corinthians 12 to be one of the exercises of the prophet. Since "he who exhorts" is mentioned in Romans 12 (v. 8), in addition to the one who prophesies (v. 6), it would appear that there were those in Rome who were called exhorters. Barnabas was called "the son of exhortation [*paraklesis*]" (Acts 4:36, ROTHERHAM, ASV). Since Paul frequently uses the verb *to exhort* in the sense of "to implore," "to urge," "to beseech," or "to entreat" (Rom. 12:1), it is probable that the work of the exhorter was that of arousing and motivating the church to patient endurance, brotherly love, and good works. The author of Hebrews was an exhorter when he implored:

> Let us hold fast the profession of our faith without wavering; (for he is faithful that promised;) And let us consider one another to provoke unto love and to good works: Not forsaking the assembling of ourselves together, as the manner of some is; but exhorting one another: and so much the more, as ye see the day approaching.
>
> —HEBREWS 10:23–25

Some religious groups recognize an office of the exhorter and grant a ministerial credential to correspond to it (Acts 11:23; 14:22; 15:31–32; 16:40; 20:2; 1 Thes. 5:14–22).

4. *The giver and his liberality.* In the Church, there are those who have a gift of giving. This is not one who administers the charities of a church. This giver is one who shares his own possessions with others with great liberality. "He that giveth" translates the Greek phrase *ho metadidous.* In addition to Romans 12:8, the term is also found in Ephesians 4:28: "But rather let him labour, working with his hands the thing which is good, that he may have to give [*metadidonai*] to him that needeth." The same word is used in Luke 3:11 by John the Baptist: "He that hath two coats, let him impart [*metadoto*] to him that hath none; and he that hath meat [food], let him do likewise." This is not institutional giving, but personal sharing. The gifted giver may channel his gifts through the church, but he is more than an official who distributes the gifts of others; he is a giver of his own things who, motivated by the Holy Spirit, gives with extraordinary generosity. An example of such giving is found in 2 Corinthians 8. Paul, writing to the Corinthians about the collection for the poor, said, "Moreover, brethren, we make known to you the grace [*charis*] of God bestowed on the churches of Macedonia: that in a great trial of affliction the abundance of their joy and their deep poverty abounded in the riches of their liberality.... And [this

they did] not only as we had hoped, but they first gave themselves to the Lord, and then to us by the will of God" (2 Cor. 8:1–2, 5, NKJV). Then, using the Macedonian churches (Philippi, Thessalonica, Berea) as an example, he urged the Corinthians (the gifted church) to manifest the same gift of giving for the poor. He said further, "Therefore, as ye abound in every thing, in faith, and utterance, and knowledge... see that ye abound in this grace [gift] also" (2 Cor. 8:7). Paul uses the word *grace* (*charis*) here in the same sense as the word *gift* (*charisma*). He calls the gifts (*charismata*) that the Corinthian church possessed "graces." W. E. Vine gives one of the meanings of *grace* as "the power and equipment for ministry."[31] This definition of *grace* as a spiritual gift is borne out by Paul's statement in 1 Corinthians 1:4–5, 7: "I thank my God... for the grace of God which is given you by Jesus Christ; That in every thing ye are enriched by him, in all utterance, and in all knowledge.... So that ye come behind in no gift [*charisma*]; waiting for the coming of our Lord Jesus Christ." All believers, out of love and compassion and a sense of responsibility to Christ's kingdom, will give to the church and to the needy. Beyond this normal giving, there are those who, gifted by the Holy Spirit, give with extraordinary liberality, even out of affliction and poverty.

5. *The leader and his diligence.* Paul hints in 1 Timothy 5:17 that there were elders of the church other than those who ministered the Word of God. The Church has need of a number of different kinds of leadership. In Romans 12:8 the apostle says, "If it [a man's gift] is leadership, let him govern diligently" (NIV). The same Greek word translated "he who leads" in Romans 12:8 is found in 1 Thessalonians 5:12: "And we urge you, brethren, to recognize those who labor among you, and are over you in the Lord and admonish you, and to esteem them very highly in love for their work's sake" (NKJV). Many of God's choice men occupy executive positions of leadership, administration, management of funds, personnel guidance, strategy planning, and missionary oversight. These are often thought of as being outside the realm of the Holy Spirit's moving. But in fact, these leaders are as needful of spiritual endowments as any who preach or teach. Some of the most spiritually powerful people in Church history have also been the leaders of the Church. God has a spiritual gift of leadership which He has bestowed upon the Church. Believers should pray constantly that their leaders, including their pastors, may enjoy a powerful anointing of the Spirit upon their offices (Heb. 13:7, 17, 24; Eph 6:18–20; 2 Cor. 1:11; 1 Tm. 2:1–3).

Some have believed that the gift of leadership listed in Romans 12 is the same as that called "governments" in 1 Corinthians 12:28. This is possible. However, entirely different Greek words with different basic meanings are employed. The gift listed in Romans 12:8 has the meaning of being over others as their leader, while that in

---

31 Vine, s.v. "grace."

1 Corinthians 12:28 has more the meaning of guidance through all kinds of seas (a helmsman). Both kinds of leadership are needed in the Church, and one person very well might have both capacities. It is encouraging to know that the leaders of Christ's Church do not have to exercise their offices with merely human wisdom and ability. The characteristic virtue of spiritual leadership is declared to be diligence. Perhaps the apostle was describing this diligence in 2 Corinthians 11:28 when he spoke of his "care of all the churches."

6. *The cheerful mercy-shower.* It is quite possible that the gift described here in Romans 12:8 (NKJV) as "he who shows mercy" may be the same gift listed in 1 Corinthians 12:28 as "helps." The Greek word for "have mercy" is *eleeo*, which is defined as "to have pity or mercy on," "to have compassion." Mercy is said to be an attribute of God: "But God, who is rich in mercy, for His great love wherewith He loved us" (Eph. 2:4). Nearly always, the sick who cried out to Jesus exclaimed, "Have mercy on me!" It would seem that as a gift in exercise in the Church, showing mercy would be a ministry of care for the sick and afflicted by means of visitation and prayer. In all probability, the gifts of healings were exercised by those with the ministry of showing mercy. All believers have some responsibility to show such mercies to the poor and afflicted, but there are those who by being gifted by the Lord carry out works of compassion as an anointed ministry. There are those who by the Spirit's anointing are "cheerful [Greek, "hilarious"] givers" (2 Cor. 9:7) and who share readily with the needy. There are others with a different gift who share their love, compassion, time, and presence in order to heal and restore the poor and afflicted. It is like the God of all mercy and compassion to place such gifted people in the body of Christ. Such are not vocal gifts, but works of love that speak as loudly as words. The God of variety certainly does administer a blessed variety of Spirit-anointed gifts and ministries, one to match every need in the Church.

G. The ministry gifts inscribed in Ephesians 4

The apostle Paul, writing to the Ephesian Church, declared a remarkable truth concerning the spiritual leaders in the body of Christ:

> But to each one of us grace was given according to the measure of Christ's gift. Therefore it says, "When He ascended on high, He led captive a host of captives, And He gave gifts to men" [Ps. 68:18]....And He gave some as apostles, and some as prophets, and some as evangelists; and some as pastors and teachers, for the equipping of the saints for the work of service, to the building up of the body of Christ.
> —EPHESIANS 4:7–8, 11–12, NASB

The remarkable truth was that spiritual offices in the Church were to be thought of as gifts from Christ to His body. Therefore, men cannot make themselves leaders, nor can they be made such by the whim of others (Rom. 1:5; 1 Cor. 1:1; 2 Cor. 1:1; Gal. 1:1, 16). The Church must set apart as spiritual leaders and ministers those whom God has called and chosen (Acts 13:1–3), because when Christ gives a man to the body of Christ, He first endows the man with a spiritual gift that corresponds to his office. Some Bible teachers draw a sharp distinction between the ministry gifts and the *charismata,* contending that the former are gifts of Christ, while the *charismata* are gifts of the Spirit (*pneumatika*). That all divine offices and enablements are gifts of the triune God is seen in Paul's introduction to the *charismata:* "Now there are diversities of gifts, but the same Spirit. And there are differences of administrations [ministries], but the same Lord. And there are diversities of operations, but it is the same God which worketh all in all [all things in all men]" (1 Cor. 12:4–6). Furthermore, Paul intermingles offices with endowments in his summary of the *charismata:* "And God hath set some in the church, first apostles, secondarily prophets, thirdly teachers, after that miracles, then gifts of healings, helps, governments, diversities of tongues" (1 Cor. 12:28). Three offices are listed, along with five spiritual gifts. In Romans 12, where the apostle lists seven gifts, he mixes two gifts (*charismata*) with five kinds of possessors of gifts. It all adds up to the conclusion that all divinely ordained men are given a gift of enablement, and every spiritual gift equips for some ministry. Of course, not every exercise of a gift makes one a leader over others, as those described in passages such as Ephesians 4:11; Hebrews 13:7, 17, 24; 1 Thessalonians 5:12; Acts 20:28; 1 Peter 5:1–4; or 1 Timothy 5:17. But whether leaders or followers, there are spiritual gifts that divinely equip the saints to build up the body of Christ. The Bible does not put as wide a gulf between leaders and believers in general as men tend to do. Nevertheless, the offices of the Church are a divine gift, without which the Church cannot be adequately matured, directed, and protected from error. The offices and their endowments are as follows:

1. *The apostle.* The apostles were the first leaders of the Church—first in time (Mt. 10:1–2; Lk. 22:14–15; Eph. 2:20), first in authority (Mk. 6:7; Acts 1:21–26), first in ministry (Acts 2:37; 6:1–4), and first in the lists of giftings (Eph. 4:11; 1 Cor. 12:28). The apostles were those commissioned and sent forth by Jesus to initiate and direct the preaching and teaching of the gospel and, together with Him, to found the Church (Eph. 2:20; Rv. 21:14).

The title "apostle" comes from the Greek word *apostolos,* which means "a messenger, one sent forth with orders." The basic idea expressed by the word *apostle* is that of one sent as a representative of another and who derives his authority from the sender. In the classical Greek, *apostolos* also meant "a fleet of ships, an expedition." From the latter, the meaning is extended to "one commissioned and sent to another country," thus "a missionary." The verb *apostello* means "to send away."

Who in the New Testament are called apostles? The first group to be called apostles were the twelve disciples of Jesus (Mt. 10:2–4; Lk. 6:13–16), which number had been reduced to eleven by the fall of Judas (Acts 1:24–26). In addition to the Twelve, several others are called apostles, such as Barnabas (Acts 14:14), Silas and Timothy (1 Thes. 2:6), James (1 Cor. 15:7), Paul (Rom. 1:1), and probably Andronicus and Junias (Rom. 16:7). The last two, who were Paul's kinsmen, may be referred to in 2 Corinthians 8:23 as messengers (Gr., *apostolos)* of the churches. Paul calls Epaphroditus the messenger (apostle) of the Philippian Church (Phil. 2:25). It appears that the term *apostle* was used with several different meanings: the twelve apostles of Jesus (Mt. 10:2; 19:28; Lk. 22:14); all those commissioned by Jesus, including the Seventy and group of 120 (1 Cor. 15:5, 7); Paul as a special apostle to the Gentiles (Gal. 2:7–9); and certain associates of Paul in his ministry to the nations (Acts 14:14; Rom. 16:7).

Different levels of apostleship seem to be set forth in 1 Corinthians 15:4–5, 7–10 (emphasis added):

> He rose again the third day according to the scriptures: And that he was seen of Cephas, then of *the twelve....* After that, he was seen of James; then of *all the apostles.* And last of all he was seen of me also, as one born out of due time. For I am the least of the apostles, that am not meet to be called an apostle, because I persecuted the church of God. But by the grace of God I am what I am: and his grace which was bestowed upon me was not in vain; but I labored more abundantly than they all: yet not I, but the grace of God which was with me.

A comparison between verses 5 and 7 will show that the apostle made a clear distinction between "the twelve" (v. 5) and "all of the apostles" (v. 7). Grosheide comments on verse 7 that "there is thus an analogy with verse 5: there it was Peter first and then the twelve; here James first and then a greater circle of apostles"[32]

Finally, Paul refers to himself as the last and the least of all the apostles. If Paul is the "least of all" the apostles (men who had seen the Lord Jesus, see 1 Corinthians 9:1), then there cannot be apostles in the true sense in later times. The larger circle of apostles probably included the seventy whom Jesus personally commissioned, or even the 120 who received the Spirit's fullness on the Day of Pentecost. That these latter were not considered to be apostles on the same level with the Twelve is borne out by passages such as Acts 1:22–26 and Revelation 21:14. Barnabas, Silas, Andronicus, and Junias could well have been among the seventy or the 120 who were witnesses to

---

32 Frederick Willem Grosheide, *New International Commentary on the New Testament, First Corinthians* (Grand Rapids, MI: Wm. B. Eerdmans Publishing Company, 1953), 352.

Jesus' resurrection (Acts 1:21–22). Paul seems to class himself in a third category of apostles, "one born out of due time," one to whom the risen Lord had appeared after His ascension. He had seen the Lord (1 Cor. 9:1); the signs of an apostle had appeared in his ministry (2 Cor. 12:12); he had received the right hand of fellowship from the Jerusalem apostles and authority from them to carry the gospel to the Gentiles. Subsequent history demonstrated Paul's apostleship in that he was used of the Lord to pen more books of the New Testament than any other human author. Yet, the fact that Paul was forced to contend so strongly for his own apostleship shows that the early Church had set exceedingly high qualifications for the office of an apostle (1 Cor. 9:1; 2 Cor. 12:11–12). Those who claimed apostleship falsely were strongly condemned (2 Cor. 11:13; Rv. 2:2). The apostles are called the foundation of the Church, and a structure can have only one foundation (Eph. 2:20). Around Paul at Antioch, a circle was formed of men such as Barnabas, Silas, Timothy, Titus, and Epaphroditus, who were called apostles in the sense that they were commissioned by the church at Antioch to be missionaries (one meaning of the word *apostolos*). In this last sense, there have been apostles in every age of the Church, men with mighty gifts of the Spirit, men who through the power of the risen Christ have pushed the frontiers of the Church out to the ends of the earth. If they have not called themselves apostles, they have wrought the works of apostles. The title of apostle seems to belong to the first generation of the Church. However, the spiritual endowments needed for apostolic work will continue to be poured out as long as there are unreached peoples on the face of the earth. Jesus is still sending forth with a commission men who are given His authority over powers of darkness, who have authority to bind and loose, and who preach the gospel with the anointing of a prophet. They work among us today.

2. *The prophet.* The prophet, whom Paul lists among the ministry gifts to the Church (Eph. 4:11), is second in importance only to the apostles. The prophet was one who not only exercised the gift of prophecy, but who occupied a place of leadership ministry along with the apostles and teachers (Acts 11:27; 13:1–3; 15:32; Eph. 2:20; 3:5).

In the Early Church, there were two classifications of prophets. Any member of the general body of believers who ministered edification, exhortation, and comfort through the gift of prophecy was called a prophet (1 Cor. 14:24, 31). Another group, consisting of such men as Barnabas, Silas, Judas, Agabus, and others mentioned in Acts 13:1, were spiritual leaders of the Church (Acts 21:22). This prophetic gift is referred to by Paul in Ephesians 4:11 as among the ministry gifts to the Church. Those of the latter group, although they exercised the same gift of prophecy, possessed an additional *charisma* of leadership.

How did the gift of prophecy operate in and through those who exercised it?

a) The prophet speaks as the Lord's agent. He speaks that which the Lord wills him to speak. Peter defines the function of the prophet as follows: "As each one has received a special gift [*charisma*], employ it in serving one another, as good stewards of the manifold grace of God. Whoever speaks, let him speak, as it were, the utterances of God; whoever serves, let him do so as by the strength which God supplies" (1 Pt. 4:10–11, NASB). In all gifted ministry there is a supernatural element.

b) Often the content of the prophet's message will be given extemporaneously at the time of speaking. However, the message may be given beforehand during prayer or meditation. Many of the Old Testament prophets received their message content in a dream, a vision, or during prayer, to be delivered to the people at a later date (Is. 6:9–13).

c) Sometimes, the message content may consist of data well known to the prophet, such as scriptural truth or history. Both Peter, on the Day of Pentecost (Acts 2:14–37), and Stephen, before the Sanhedrin (Acts 7), delivered prophetic messages that were filled with quotations from the Old Testament. That both spoke in the power of the Spirit is clear from the accounts in Acts. The word used to describe Peter's utterance in Acts 2:14, *apophtheggomai,* is the same word used in the clause "and began to speak with other tongues" (Acts 2:4). It is a term used to express the speech of prophets, seers, and oracles. Stephen concluded his message with a vision of Christ "standing on the right hand of God" (Acts 7:56). It appears from this that a prophet may employ Scripture in his messages, in which case the Holy Spirit directs him in the choice of material and in its application to specific situations. A prophet may be moved strongly by the Spirit to set forth a certain scriptural passage, in which instance the Spirit also provides a special boldness and power of communication: "And they were all filled with the Holy Ghost, and they spake the word of God with boldness [*parrhesia*]" (Acts 4:31); "Praying always with all prayer and supplication in the Spirit...for me...that therein I may speak boldly [with *parrhesia*], as I ought to speak" (Eph. 6:18–20). Not all preaching is prophecy by any means, but much preaching becomes prophetic where great unpremeditated truth or application is provided by the Spirit, or where special revelation is given beforehand in prayer and is empowered in the delivery. When one speaks in tongues, the mind is inactive (1 Cor. 14:14), but when one prophesies, the Spirit operates through the mind to supply a message: "However, in the church I desire to speak five words with my mind, that I may instruct others also, rather than ten thousand words in a tongue" (1 Cor. 14:19, NASB). Here the apostle is not contrasting gifted utterance with non-gifted speech; he is contrasting tongues with prophecy, for the entire fourteenth chapter of 1 Corinthians is written to compare uninterpreted tongues with prophecy.

d) Before the New Testament was written, many of the apostolic prophets were used of the Spirit to reveal the gospel plan of salvation, for it was only dimly prefigured in the typology of the Old Testament. This prophetic revelation later became incorporated in the Epistles: "Whereby, when ye read, ye may understand my knowledge in the mystery of Christ) Which in other ages was not made known unto the sons of men, as it is now revealed unto his holy apostles and prophets by the Spirit" (Eph. 3:4–5).

e) While prophecy is more forth-telling than it is foretelling, sometimes it may involve prediction of the future. The book of Acts records two predictive prophecies of Agabus (Acts 11:27–28; 21:10–14), the first relative to the impending famine in Judea and the second pertaining to Paul's soon coming imprisonment in Jerusalem. Both prophecies were fulfilled. It should be noted regarding the second prediction of Agabus in Acts 21:11 that Paul did not change his plans as a result of the prophecy, nor at the entreaty of his friends. This teaches that prophecy may be given to reveal or confirm a coming event, but not to provide personal guidance. Paul respected the prophecy of Agabus, which revealed only what Paul already knew (Acts 20:22–23), but he followed his own understanding of God's will for his future. God may reveal the future, but we are not to inquire of prophets concerning the future. Those who walk by faith live one day at a time, leaving the unknown future to God.

f) It is often asked whether prophetic utterances ought to be phrased in first person ("I, the Lord") or in third person ("Thus saith the Lord" or "The Lord would have…"). When someone exercises a vocal gift, he speaks as the Spirit supplies thoughts. The Spirit reveals, the prophet speaks. God does not speak, but reveals to the prophet what He wants said. Paul said, "Let the prophets speak two or three and let the other[s] judge" (1 Cor. 14:29). Since the messages of the prophets are subject to being judged (discerned), it seems more consistent with humility for the prophet to speak in the third person, as did Agabus in Acts 21:11. Paul declared that the things which he wrote in 1 Corinthians 14 were the commandments of the Lord (1 Cor. 14:37), yet he expressed his precepts in the third person. Myer Pearlman writes on this question, "Many experienced workers believe that interpretations and prophetic messages should be given in the third person."[33] Concerning those who were filled with the Spirit on the Day of Pentecost, Luke declares, "And they…began to speak with other tongues, as the Spirit gave them utterance" (Acts 2:4). God did not speak with tongues. Instead, the believers spoke as they were enabled by the Spirit. God does not normally speak through men as passive megaphones; He reveals to prophets His will, enabling them to speak what He supplies. Often God spoke directly to the prophet; but when the prophet delivered the message to the people, he said, "Thus saith the Lord" or something equivalent to it. Today, many are of the opinion that prophetic utterance is better phrased in contemporary language rather than with archaic words, except where actual Scripture may be incorporated.

---

33 Pearlman, 326.

3. *The evangelist.* The word *evangelist* comes from the Greek word *euaggelistes,* which is defined as a "bringer of good tidings." The English word *gospel* translates another form of the same Greek word. An evangelist, then, is one who devotes himself entirely to preaching the gospel, especially the message of salvation. The term *evangelist* is used only three times in the New Testament (Acts 21:8; Eph. 4:11; 2 Tm. 4:5). Nevertheless, Paul lists the evangelist as one of the ministry gifts to the church (Eph. 4:11). Only Philip is specifically called an evangelist (Acts 21:8), but workers such as Timothy (2 Tm. 4:5), Luke (2 Cor. 8:18), Clement (Phil. 4:3), and Epaphras (Col. 1:7; 4:12) may have functioned as evangelists. Paul's words to Timothy suggest that his true calling was that of the evangelist: "Preach the word; be ready in season and out of season; reprove, rebuke, exhort, with great patience and instruction....But you, be sober in all things, endure hardship, do the work of an evangelist, fulfill your ministry" (2 Tm. 4:2, 5, NASB). (See also 1 Tm. 1:18; 4:14.) Paul quite clearly describes an evangelist when he refers to an unnamed worker (most scholars identify him as Luke) in the following way: "And we have sent with him the brother, whose praise is in the gospel throughout all the churches" (2 Cor. 8:18).

The clearest picture of an evangelist at work is found in Acts 8, which describes the ministry of Philip, who is specifically called an evangelist in Acts 21:8. The following characteristics of Philip's ministry, listed in Acts 8, form a pattern of New Testament evangelism:

a) Philip preached the Word of God, especially declaring the heart of the gospel, which is Christ the Savior. He "preached Christ unto them" (v. 5). (See also vv. 4, 35.)

b) There were many who believed and were baptized (vv. 6, 12).

c) Mighty miracles of healing followed his preaching, and many were delivered from demon spirits (vv. 6–7). The healing miracles gave greater effectiveness to Philip's ministry (vv. 6, 8).

d) Philip was ready to witness about Christ as the Savior to whole cities or to one individual. Leaving Samaria, he was directed to the chariot of the treasurer of Ethiopia (vv. 26–27), whom he led to Christ (vv. 35–38). The true soulwinner has a passion for souls that makes him adaptable to mass evangelism or personal evangelism.

e) Philip's evangelistic ministry took him from city to city (v. 40).

The picture of the evangelist in the New Testament and in the post-apostolic period was that of one preaching the gospel message of salvation from church to church and from city to city. Eusebius, the great church historian of the fourth century described the evangelist as follows: "And they scattered the saving seeds of the kingdom of heaven far and near throughout the whole world...Then starting out on long journeys they performed the office of evangelists, being filled with the desire to preach Christ to those who had not yet heard the word of faith."[34] (See Rom. 15:20–21.)

4. *The pastor-teacher.* In the grammatical structure of Ephesians 4:11, the term *teacher* does not have a definite article, as all the preceding terms for the ministry gifts do. It seems, therefore, that *teacher* is to be taken together with *pastor.* This does not mean that the terms are interchangeable. There may be teachers who are not pastors, but there cannot be pastors who are not teachers (Acts 20:28–30). In churches where there were several elders, some might have had a ministry of leadership who were not teachers (1 Tm. 5:17), but the real pastor was a teacher: "Especially those whose work is preaching and teaching" (1 Tm. 5:17, NIV). One of the necessary qualifications for a bishop (pastor, elder) was that he be "apt to teach" (1 Tm. 3:2; 2 Tm. 2:24). A true pastor, then, will have the *charisma* of teaching (Rom. 12:7; 1 Cor. 12:28).

The words *pastor* and *shepherd* come from the same Greek word, *poimen.* The word *pastor* (Gr., *poimen*), used to refer to the spiritual leader of a local church, is found only once in the New Testament (Eph. 4:11). However, the figure of the pastor as a shepherd, leading the church as a flock (Gr., *poimaino*), is found several times (Jn. 21:15–17; Acts 20:28; 1 Pt. 5:14).

The idea of Israel as the flock of God and of Jehovah as their Shepherd is a common figure in the Old Testament (Ps. 23:4; Ps. 80:1–2; Is. 40:11; Jer. 23:4; 25:34–38; Ez. 34; Zec. 11). In the New Testament, Jesus uses the figure of the shepherd and the sheep in John 10, where He calls Himself the Good Shepherd. Besides the title "Good Shepherd," Jesus is also called the great Shepherd (Heb. 13:20), the chief Shepherd (1 Pt. 5:4), and the gentle Shepherd (Is. 40:11). Pastors of the churches are merely serving as shepherds under the chief Shepherd.

The fact that teaching was the principal goal of the Great Commission as given by Matthew (Mt. 28:19–20) shows the importance of the ministry of the teacher. The book of Acts reinforces this observation: "And daily in the temple, and in every house, they ceased not to teach and preach Jesus Christ" (Acts 5:42). (See also Acts 11:26; 13:1; 15:35; 20:20; 28:31; 1 Cor. 4:17; Col. 3:16; 2 Tm. 2:2.) In view of the importance of teaching, it should not be surprising that one of the special endowments of the Holy Spirit would be the capacity to teach. The prophet inspired, exhorted, comforted, and motivated the Church; the teacher instructed the Church in sound doctrine, guarding the flock from false teachers with their destructive teachings. The Church at Antioch enjoyed a balanced ministry from prophets and teachers who administered anointed exhortation and evangelism and anointed teaching. Some have concluded that the *charisma* of a word of wisdom was the prophet's gift and that the operation of the word of knowledge was the teacher's gift. The apostle John

---

34 Eusebius, *Church History,* Vol. III, Chap. 37, 1–2.

referred to the anointing enjoyed by true teachers: "But ye have an unction from the Holy One, and ye know all things" (1 Jn. 2:20). (See also 1 Jn. 2:27.) There is a tendency to think of the prophet as one who speaks supernaturally and of the teacher as one who imparts the findings of merely natural scholarship, but the difference is not between the supernatural and the natural. The difference between the two is a difference in the manner by which the Holy Spirit operates in the two ministry gifts. The anointing upon the prophet is more sudden and impromptu, with the goal of motivation, while the anointing upon the teacher is more measured, operating to illuminate the Word of Truth and give ability to communicate accurately. For every ministry in the body of Christ there is a spiritual *charisma*.

H. Other probable spiritual gifts

It has already been pointed out that the lists of spiritual gifts in 1 Corinthians 12, Romans 12, and Ephesians 4 are not intended to be exhaustive. The following are phases of ministry that may require a special endowment of the Holy Spirit:

1. *Hospitality.* Peter appears to categorize hospitality as a spiritual gift: "Use hospitality one to another without grudging. As every man hath received the gift [*charisma*], even so minister the same one to another, as good stewards of the manifold grace of God" (1 Pt. 4:9–10). Hospitality was very important to early Christians. It was a necessary qualification for bishops: "A bishop then must be blameless…given to hospitality, apt to teach" (1 Tm. 3:2). Perhaps in the modern world, particularly in the cities, Christian workers are not normally entertained in the people's homes, but hospitality may be manifested in the contemporary world by a loving interest in and concern for the needs of others.

2. *Intercession.* A basic exercise of the Christian life is prayer. Prayer is to the spiritual life what breathing is to physical life. However, prayer in the Spirit "with groanings that cannot be uttered" is a *charisma* of the Spirit (Rom. 8:26–27). Prayer in the Spirit is the potential of all Spirit-filled believers, but most need to "stir up the gift" (2 Tm. 1:6). (See also 1 Tm. 4:14.) Perhaps prayer and praise in the Spirit are aspects of the gift of tongues or interpretation of tongues. In any case, they are charismatic operations of the Spirit in the believer (Eph. 5:18–19; Col. 3:16; 1 Cor. 14:15).

3. *Witnessing.* Witnessing is one of the primary goals of the Church of Jesus Christ. Jesus promised, "But ye shall receive power, after that the Holy Ghost has come upon you: and ye shall be witnesses unto me" (Acts 1:8). Witnessing is not specifically said to be a spiritual gift, but the capacity to witness effectively is clearly declared to be the result of the outpouring of the Holy Spirit upon the believer. Since there are many, like Paul, who have a special ministry of witnessing, God may give a special endowment for it: "Having therefore obtained help of God, I continue unto this day, witnessing both to small and great" (Acts 26:22). (See also Acts 23:11.) Two passages declare that witnessing is a special work of the Spirit: "And we are his

witnesses of these things; and so is also the Holy Ghost, whom God has given to them that obey him" (Acts 5:32); "And it is the Spirit that beareth witness, because the Spirit is truth" (1 Jn. 5:6). It appears that the more one is yielded to the Spirit, the greater will be his ability to witness effectively.

I. Gifts for special abilities

1. *Old Testament spiritual gifts for special skills.* In the Old Testament, special gifts of the Spirit were given to artisans who served in the construction of the tabernacle:

> And Moses said to the children of Israel, "See the LORD has called by name Bezalel the son of Uri, the son of Hur, of the tribe of Judah; and He has filled him with the Spirit of God, in wisdom and understanding, in knowledge and manner of workmanship, to design artistic works, to work in gold and silver and bronze…and to work in all manner of artistic workmanship."
> —EXODUS 35:30–33, NKJV

This passage provides a typology for the work of the Holy Spirit who supplies, in the new dispensation, special endowments for believers who are God's workmen, building the body of Christ.

2. *Spiritual music, prose, and poetry.* If God supplied supernatural gifts for every skill needed in the building of the tabernacle and its furnishings, will He not also supply in this age a spiritual enablement to correspond with every kind of service needed in building the holy temple of which Christ is the foundation and chief Cornerstone? Might this not include the composing of spiritual music, the mastery of musical instruments that aid worship, the writing of Christian literature that edifies spiritually, and even the building of structures that serve for worship and teaching?

3. *Spiritual capacitation for every work in the body of Christ.* If anyone has a service that is useful to Christ's Church, should he not expect that God will endow that service with a special unction so that no work in Christ's body need be done in merely human strength? Therefore, "If any man minister, let him do it as of the ability which God giveth: that God in all things may be glorified through Jesus Christ" (1 Pt. 4:11).

J. The relationship between the gifts and the fruit of the Spirit

1. *The importance of love.* Critics of the operation of spiritual gifts often say they would rather have love than tongues or miracles. Fortunately, they are not mutually exclusive alternatives. One does not have to choose between love and miracles, nor between the gifts of the Spirit and the fruit of the Spirit. The Spirit bestows both the fruit and the gifts; both are essential for a complete Church. First Corinthians 13, called the great love chapter of the Bible, is sandwiched between the two great

gift chapters, not as an alternative to the gifts presented before and after it, but as an undergirding for the gifts. Paul said, "Follow after charity [love], and desire spiritual gifts" (1 Cor. 14:1). It is true that the exercise of the gifts without love has no value (1 Cor. 13:1–3). If the possession of gifts is only an ego trip or a status symbol, then they are less than useful. If he who exercises a gift is unteachable, having no concern to edify the whole body, then he is nothing (1 Cor. 13:2). We do not seek gifts. Instead, the Holy Spirit distributes them as He will. But the fruit of the Spirit should be the quest of every Spirit-filled believer: "Follow after [pursue] charity [love]" (1 Cor. 14:1). When the fruit of the Spirit ripens in the believer's life, the Holy Spirit will, no doubt, bestow gifts upon those who desire them for the edification of the body and for the glory of God.

2. *How all fruit is contained in love.* The apostle, enumerating the fruit of the Spirit, said, "But the fruit of the Spirit is love, joy, peace, longsuffering, gentleness, goodness, faith, Meekness, temperance" (Gal. 5:22–23). He had just declared that the works of the flesh were such as adultery, idolatry, envyings, wrath, strife, etc. The works of the flesh were plural ("works," v. 19). When he enumerated the fruit, he said, "The fruit of the Spirit is love [singular]." All the virtues that follow love are really aspects of love. The flesh manifests many vile works. The Spirit manifests love, which is a spiritual jewel with eight sparkling facets. Love is the basic qualification for the ministry of gifts. It also ought to be the underlying motive for the desire of the gifts. In the vocal gifts, love makes the difference between clanging brass and heavenly music.

The Doctrine of Divine Healing

Introduction

I. The Reasonableness of Divine Healing

   A. God is definitely interested in the human body.

      1. *Man was created in the image of God.*

      2. *The human body is included in Christ's redemption.*

      3. *The body of a Christian is a member of Christ.*

      4. *God is deeply concerned about the sanctity of the body of His children.*

      5. *The human body of the Christian is the temple of the Holy Spirit.*

      6. *Christians are urged to glorify God in their physical bodies.*

      7. *Christians are urged to present their body as a living sacrifice to God.*

      8. *The human body is to be resurrected.*

   B. There is a vital relationship between the soul and spirit of man and his physical body.

   C. Man's needs are twofold.

II. The Origin of Sickness

   A. Historically

      1. *The affliction that came upon Job*

      2. *Those whom Jesus healed were oppressed of the devil*

      3. *The woman who had been bowed over for eighteen years*

      4. *The prophetic outline of Jesus' ministry*

      5. *Enmity between Satan and the seed of the woman*

      6. *The man in Corinth turned over to Satan for the destruction of the flesh*

      7. *Sickness is among the curses of the broken Law*

      8. *Paul's thorn in the flesh*

      9. *Satan bound during the Millennium*

     10. *Jesus rebuked sickness*

   B. Physiologically

      1. *All sickness is the result of sin—ultimately.*

      2. *Some sickness and afflictions are the result of specific sins.*

      3. *The findings of physicians and psychologists*

      4. *The misuse of the body*

   C. Correctively

      1. *Because of man's disobedience or sin*

2. *Because of God's love for His children*
3. *Because of failure to rightly discern the Lord's body*
4. *Because of murmuring against God-appointed leaders*

III. **The Spiritual Nature of Sickness**
   A. Sickness is in the world because of sin.
   B. Certain sickness is the result of specific sin.
   C. Sickness as a form of discipline

IV. **Healing and the Will of God**

V. **The Scripturalness of Divine Healing**
   A. Divine healing in the Old Testament
   B. Healing in the ministry of Jesus
   C. Healing in the ministry of the disciples
      1. *The Twelve given power and sent forth*
      2. *The Seventy given power and sent out*
   D. Healing in the early Church

VI. **Healing Through the Church Age**

VII. **Healing and the Atonement**
   A. Atonement was made for healing in the Old Testament.
   B. Forgiveness of sins and healing of diseases go hand-in-hand in the Bible.
   C. Redemption from the curse of the Law
   D. Isaiah 53
   E. The Passover and the Lord's Supper

VIII. **Why Jesus Healed the Sick**
   A. Because of the promises of His Word
   B. In order to reveal His will
   C. To manifest the works of God
   D. Because of compassion
   E. Because of faith not only in His ability, but also His willingness
      1. *Sometimes the faith of others rather than the sick person*
      2. *Sometimes the faith of those who needed the healing*

IX. **Why Christians Should Seek Divine Healing**
   A. Because it is a solemn command
   B. Because of the spiritual blessing it will bring
   C. Because it is glorifying to God

X. **Methods of Administering Divine Healing**
   A. Pray for yourself.
   B. Ask someone else to pray for you.

C. Call for the elders of the Church.

D. By laying on of hands

E. Special miracles through handkerchiefs and aprons

F. Spiritual gifts of healing

XI. Why Are Some Not Healed?

A. Some seek healing before salvation.

B. Some seek healing for wrong purposes.

C. Some look to the minister rather than to Christ.

D. Disobedience

E. Because of some unconfessed sin

F. Because of unbelief

    1. *In the one who prays*

    2. *In the one prayed for*

G. Failure to stand in faith until the answer comes

XII. How to Retain Divine Healing

A. Keep in an atmosphere of faith.

B. Keep praising the Lord for what He has done.

C. Keep testifying of what God has done.

D. Feed your faith on the Word of God.

E. Contend in faith for your healing.

F. Walk in obedience to God's will—His Word.

G. Start, and continue, service to the Lord.

XIII. Divine Life for the Body

XIV. Answers to Objections

A. The day of miracles has passed.

B. Why are many Christians not healed?

C. Why not also believe in raising the dead and other miracles promised in Mark 16?

D. Now that medical science is perfected, God expects His people to use medicine for healing.

E. If divine healing always worked, no Christian would ever die.

F. There are cases of failure in the New Testament.

G. Divine healing is taught only by false cults.

H. Divine healing puts more emphasis upon the body than upon the soul.

I. If God created herbs and drugs, does He not expect man to use them for healing?

J. The miracles recorded in Matthew 8:16–17 completely fulfilled the prophecy of physical healing in Isaiah 53:4–5.

K. If healing is in the Atonement, Christians who are sick must conclude that they are sinners.

L. Failure by many to receive healing weakens the faith of the whole Church.

CHAPTER SEVEN

THE DOCTRINE OF DIVINE HEALING

INTRODUCTION

SECTION FOURTEEN OF the *Declaration of Faith* of the International Church of the Foursquare Gospel states, "We believe that divine healing is the power of the Lord Jesus Christ to heal the sick and the afflicted in answer to believing prayer; that He who is the same yesterday, and today and forever has never changed but is still an all-sufficient help in the time of trouble, able to meet the needs of, and quicken into newness of life, the body, as well as the soul and spirit, in answer to the faith of them who ever pray with submission to His divine and sovereign will."[1]

This precious doctrine is one-fourth of the Foursquare Gospel and should not be neglected by those who minister the Word of God. In some circles, there is a good deal of misunderstanding and opposition with regard to divine healing. This is due to a failure to accept and comprehend the full teaching of the Word of God on this subject. It will be the purpose of this chapter to deal with the reasonableness of divine healing, the origin of sickness, the spiritual nature of sickness, healing and the will of God, the scripturalness of divine healing, divine healing through the Church age, healing and the atonement, why Jesus healed the sick, why Christians should seek divine healing, methods of administering divine healing, why all are not healed, how to retain divine healing, divine life for the body, and answers to objections.

I. THE REASONABLENESS OF DIVINE HEALING

In the light of all that is revealed in the Scriptures, it is not to be thought unreasonable that the Lord should heal the physical afflictions of those who seek His aid. It is not the purpose of this section to deal with the reasonableness of physical healing merely from an acceptable rational standpoint. The thought to be emphasized is that based on the Word of God and what it reveals about God's will, His purpose, and His power, it is wholly reasonable to believe that God is interested in the physical, human bodies of those who are His children through the new birth. The following facts bear witness to this. It is not necessary for a Christian to try to persuade God to take an interest in his physical needs. From Creation on, God has certainly done

---

1 Aimee Semple McPherson, *Declaration of Faith* (Los Angeles, CA: International Church of the Foursquare Gospel, n.d.), 20.

this. The promises of God and the revelations of His concern for man's physical needs have always far outstripped man's faith to receive them.

A. God is definitely interested in the human body.

The vital relationship of the human body to God's program is set forth in 1 Corinthians 6:9–20. From this passage we quote;

> Meats for the belly, and the belly for meats: but God shall destroy both it and them. Now the body is not for fornication, but for the Lord; and the Lord for the body. And God hath both raised up the Lord, and will also raise up us by his own power. Know ye not that your bodies are the members of Christ? shall I then take the members of Christ, and make them the members of an harlot? God forbid. What? know ye not that he which is joined to an harlot is one body? for two, saith he, shall be one flesh. But he that is joined unto the Lord is one spirit. Flee fornication. Every sin that a man doeth is without the body: but he that committeth fornication sinneth against his own body. What? know ye not that your body is the temple of the Holy Ghost which is in you, which ye have of God, and ye are not your own? For ye are bought with a price: therefore glorify God in your body, and in your spirit, which are God's.
>
> —1 CORINTHIANS 6:13–20

In verse 13, a double assurance is given: "Now the body is...for the Lord; and the Lord [is] for the body." Not only are the soul and spirit of man intended to be for God, but his body also is "for the Lord." But then Paul adds the revealing thought that God has not only provided for the needs of man's spiritual nature, but He has also provided for his physical needs—"The Lord is for the body." Note the following:

1. *Man was created in the image of God.* "And God said, Let us make man in our image, after our likeness...So God created man in his own image, in the image of God created he him" (Gn. 1:26–27). While this applies particularly to the spiritual nature of man, the image of God must have some relation to man's body as well. This is evidenced by a truth suggested in Genesis 9:6: "Whoso sheddeth man's blood, by man shall his blood be shed: for in the image of God made he man." We know that death only affects the life of the body. It does not kill the soul (Lk. 12:4–5). Yet, the reason for this warning of judgment upon one who kills man's body is because "in the image of God made he man." The image of God, then, must have some relationship to man's physical body.

2. *The human body is included in Christ's redemption.* "Even we ourselves groan within ourselves, waiting for the adoption, to wit, the redemption of our body" (Rom. 8:23). The body of a Christian belongs to God because it was purchased by Him.

"What? know ye not that your body is the temple of the Holy Ghost which is in you…and ye are not your own? For ye are bought with a price?" (1 Cor. 6:19–20). Many who never question God's claim upon the soul and spirit practically deny His possession of the body as well. God is definitely interested in both.

3. *The body of a Christian is a member of Christ.* "Know ye not that your bodies are the members of Christ?" (1 Cor. 6:15). Again it is emphasized that it is the body, not the soul or spirit, of man that is here in view.

4. *God is deeply concerned about the sanctity of the body of His children.* Verses 15–18 of the passage in 1 Corinthians 6 make this dramatically clear. Some sins, Paul emphasizes, are particularly against the physical body. God is just as much concerned about these sins as He is about those which touch only the soul.

5. *The human body of the Christian is the temple of the Holy Spirit.* "Know ye not that your body is the temple of the Holy Ghost?" (1 Cor. 6:19). One has only to consider how deeply interested God was in every detail of the tabernacle in the wilderness and the temple in Jerusalem to realize how concerned He is with the physical frame which is the dwelling place of His Holy Spirit.

6. *Christians are urged to glorify God in their physical bodies.* "Therefore glorify God in your body, and in your spirit, which are God's" (1 Cor. 6:20). To glorify God by the right attitude of one's spirit is a commonly accepted truth of the Christian life, but the admonition here is to glorify Him in the physical part of one's being. Both aspects of man's being are said to be God's.

7. *Christians are urged to present their body as a living sacrifice to God.* "I beseech you therefore, brethren, by the mercies of God, that ye present your bodies a living sacrifice, holy, acceptable unto God" (Rom. 12:1). Again, note that it is the body, not the soul or spirit, which is here specified. After Shadrach, Meshach, and Abednego came out of the fiery furnace unscathed, "Nebuchadnezzar spake, and said, Blessed be the God of Shadrach, Meshach, and Abed-nego, who hath sent his angel, and delivered his servants that trusted in him, and have changed the king's word, and yielded their bodies, that they might not serve nor worship any god, except their own God" (Dn. 3:28). The great monarch was impressed with these three faithful followers of the Lord because they "yielded their bodies" in sacrifice to Him.

8. *The human body is to be resurrected.* "And God hath both raised up the Lord, and will also raise up us by his own power" (1 Cor. 6:14). Resurrection is real. Christians will live in the same body, resurrected and glorified, throughout eternity. Because of this, it is important to God what happens to it now. The earnest of the believer's inheritance (Eph. 1:14) of resurrected, immortal life is healing and health for his body now.

B. There is a vital relationship between the soul and spirit of man and his physical body.

Conditions in the body affect the soul. When well in body, one's disposition is almost always cheerful. When sick in body, it is not unusual for a person to be depressed in his spirit.

Likewise, conditions in the soul and spirit will affect the body. Good news will exhilarate the body and cause one to walk with a light step, while sad news often makes one walk as with leaden feet. "Statistics reported in 1948 indicated that two thirds of the patients who went to a physician had symptoms caused or aggravated by mental stress."[2]

There is such a close relationship between the soul and the body of man, it is difficult to see how God could be interested in and make provision for one without the other. Many seem to believe that the spiritual life should be supernatural and the physical life merely natural. There will never be perfect harmony until all is given to God for His care and keeping. God is interested in both soul and body—the whole man. The right thing is always the healthy thing.

C. Man's needs are twofold.

The human being has two distinct natures. He is both a material and spiritual being. When Adam sinned, both parts of his nature were affected by the Fall. This is true of all men ever since, for they have inherited his fallen nature. Man's soul is corrupted by sin, and his body is exposed to disease. The complete plan of Christ's redemption includes both natures of man and provides for the restoration of his spiritual life, at the same time providing for the results of sin that may be seen in his physical being. A complete redemption must offset the full effect of sin and meet the total need of mankind. This is illustrated in the ministry of Jesus, who healed all the sick who came to Him, as well as shed His precious blood for the forgiveness of sin. It is also indicated by the double commission given to the disciples: "Go ye into all the world, and preach the gospel to every creature. He that believeth and is baptized shall be saved....they shall lay hands on the sick and they shall recover" (Mk. 16:15–16, 18).

II. THE ORIGIN OF SICKNESS

A clear understanding of the origin of sickness is absolutely essential to any grasp of the subject of divine healing. No one will ever have the right kind of faith to believe

---

2 *Journal of the American Medical Association* (May 29, 1948), 442, as quoted in Sim I. McMillen. M.D., *None of These Diseases* (Westwood, NJ: Fleming H. Revell Company, 1963), 60.

God for healing until he sees sickness as God sees it. Nor will he be able to see sickness as God sees it until he knows how sickness originated.

In this section of study we shall undertake to show that sickness is the result of sin, and its presence in the world must be traced directly to the influence and power of Satan. We shall look at this fact historically, physiologically, and correctively.

A. Historically

There is little room for disagreement that sickness is the result of the coming of sin into the world. Created as he was in the image of God, if man had not sinned, he certainly would not have suffered pain, weakness, and disease in his body. Paul makes it very clear that death is the result of sin: "Wherefore, as by one man sin entered into the world, and death by sin; and so death passed upon all men, for that all have sinned" (Rom. 5:12). Death is sickness matured, and death is the result of sin. Therefore, sickness must also be the result of sin, since the greater (death) contains the lesser (sickness). This means that if there had been no sin in the world, there would have been no sickness. This general principle—that sickness is the result of sin and may be traced to the influence and power of Satan—is specifically illustrated in the following:

1. *The affliction that came upon Job.* Language could not make it clearer that Job's affliction came from Satan: "So went Satan forth from the presence of the LORD, and smote Job with sore boils from the sole of his foot unto his crown" (Jb. 2:7). It was God who healed him: "And the LORD turned the captivity of Job, when he prayed for his friends" (Jb. 42:10).

2. *Those whom Jesus healed were oppressed of the devil.* "How God anointed Jesus of Nazareth with the Holy Ghost and with power: who went about doing good, and healing all that were oppressed of the devil; for God was with him" (Acts 10:38).

3. *The woman who had been bowed over for eighteen years.* "And ought not this woman, being a daughter of Abraham, whom Satan hath bound, lo, these eighteen years, be loosed from this bond on the sabbath day?" (Lk. 13:16).

4. *The prophetic outline of Jesus' ministry.* As He stood in the synagogue in Nazareth, Jesus opened the scroll of the prophet Isaiah to the sixty-first chapter and began to read the prophetic message which outlined His earthly ministry: "The Spirit of the Lord is upon me, because he hath anointed me to preach the gospel to the poor...to preach deliverance to the captives, and recovering of sight to the blind, to set at liberty them that are bruised" (Lk. 4:18). Mankind was bound, and the prison keeper was Satan.

5. *Enmity between Satan and the seed of the woman.* In the garden of Eden, enmity was pronounced between Satan and the seed of the woman (Gn. 3:15), and he has harassed the human race ever since.

6. *The man in Corinth turned over to Satan for the destruction of the flesh.* Paul advised that the man in the Church at Corinth who was guilty of incest be disciplined that his spirit might be saved: "To deliver such an one unto Satan for the destruction of the flesh, that the spirit may be saved in the day of the Lord Jesus" (1 Cor. 5:5). He delivered him to Satan—no doubt that some physical affliction would come upon him so that he could no longer continue in his sin.

7. *Sickness is among the curses of the broken Law.* Among the curses which God said would come upon Israel because of their sin are a number of physical diseases (Dt. 28:15, 22, 27–28, 35).

8. *Paul's thorn in the flesh.* If Paul's "thorn in the flesh" was a physical affliction, as many believe it was, it is very clear from whence it came, for the text says specifically that it was "the messenger of Satan." (2 Cor. 12:7).

9. *Satan bound during the Millennium.* There will be no sickness on earth during the Millennium: "And the inhabitant shall not say, I am sick" (Is. 33:24); "They shall not hurt nor destroy in all my holy mountain" (Is. 11:9); "The Sun of righteousness [shall] arise with healing in his wings" (Mal. 4:2). It is highly significant that Satan will be bound in the bottomless pit all during this time (Rv. 20:2–3).

10. *Jesus rebuked sickness.* In healing the sick, Jesus sometimes dealt with them as He did with demons, showing that He considered sickness the work of the devil. In the case of demon possession: "And Jesus rebuked him…And when the devil had thrown him in the midst, he came out of him, and hurt him not" (Lk. 4:35). In the case of healing Peter's mother-in-law: "And he stood over her, and rebuked the fever; and it left her (Lk. 4:39).

B. Physiologically

1. *All sickness is the result of sin—ultimately.* Hospitals, asylums, sanitariums, and other institutions throughout the land are tangible evidence to the presence of sin and its manifestation in the human body. This does not mean that every time a person becomes sick he has committed some particular sin. But it does mean that, had there been no sin in the world, there would have been no sickness.

2. *Some sickness and afflictions are the result of specific sins.* Jesus said to the man who was healed at the Pool of Bethesda, "Sin no more, lest a worse thing come unto thee" (Jn. 5:14). The disciples recognized this principle of sin causing sickness when they asked the question, "Master, who did sin, this man or his parents, that he was born blind?" (Jn. 9:2). They were wrong in this case, but the principle remains in others. There are certain sins which are directly against the body and expose one to diseases: "There is no soundness in my flesh because of thine anger; neither is there any rest in my bones because of my sin…My wounds stink and are corrupt because of my foolishness…My loins are filled with a loathsome disease: and there is no soundness in my flesh. I am feeble and sore broken…My heart panteth, my strength faileth

me: as for the light of mine eyes, it also is gone from me" (Ps. 38:3, 5, 7–8, 10); "For my life is spent with grief, and my years with sighing: my strength faileth because of mine iniquity, and my bones are consumed" (Ps. 31:10).

3. *The findings of physicians and psychologists.* Physicians and psychologists are more and more coming to the realization that anger, hatred, fear, and a sense of guilt are responsible for a large percentage of even organic diseases. Stomach ulcers, arthritis, and heart trouble are among those which result from some of the above mentioned attitudes of the soul. Hatred and fear are sin. Jesus condemned hatred as murder, because it is the cause of murder (Mt. 5:21–22). Jesus condemned the seed of murder, not only the full-grown fruit of the outward act. Fear is sin: "For whatsoever is not of faith is sin" (Rom. 14:23). A guilty conscience, the result of unconfessed and unforgiven sin, is the basic cause of many people's physical illnesses.

4. *The misuse of the body.* Misuse of the body, in relation to diet and morals or in not taking proper care of it, is sin. God gave Israel moral and dietary laws, which if disobeyed would be constituted sin. He gave them these laws because He knew they were good for their bodies, and He wanted His people to care for their physical beings. Disregard for these principles often brought sickness or physical weakness.

If the body of the Christian belongs to God, is bought with a price, and is the temple of the Holy Ghost, he should see to its proper care. Overeating, overworking, and lack of proper rest and exercise are sins against the body. Many Christians and ministers are guilty here.

C. Correctively

1. *Because of man's disobedience or sin.* God sometimes allows sickness to come upon His children as a chastening measure because of their disobedience or sin. (Heb. 12:5–13). This, again, points out the relationship between sickness and sin.

The psalmist pictures this chastening process at the hand of the Lord: "Fools because of their transgression, and because of their iniquities, are afflicted. Their soul abhoreth all manner of meat; and they draw near unto the gates of death. Then they cry unto the LORD in their trouble, and he saveth them out of their distresses. He sent his word, and healed them, and delivered them from their destructions" (Ps. 107:17–20).

However, it must be clearly understood that chastening is not punishment; it is correction. All judgment for the sins of a believer were borne by Christ on the cross of Calvary.

2. *Because of God's love for His children.* God does not chasten His children because He is angry with them. Chastening is always administered in love and because He wishes to correct them for their good and His glory.

> And ye have forgotten the exhortation which speaketh unto you as unto children, My son, despise not thou the chastening of the Lord, nor faint when thou art rebuked of him: For whom the Lord loveth he chasteneth, and scourgeth every son whom he receiveth. If ye endure chastening, God dealeth with you as with sons...But if ye be without chastisement, whereof all are partakers, then are ye bastards, and not sons.
>
> —HEBREWS 12:5–8

Unfortunately, parents often chasten their children because they are angry with them. "Furthermore we have had fathers of our flesh which corrected us...For they verily...chastened us *after their own pleasure*" (Heb. 12:9–10, emphasis added). When parents react in this way, it is been because they were taken by surprise by the child's misbehavior and have become angry, resulting in the expression of their anger being taken out on the child. God is never taken by surprise. He knows what His children will do, and thus is prepared ahead of time to deal with them in accordance with His love—however severe the suffering may appear to be. Note again that Paul's purpose in committing the incestuous man at Corinth to Satan was love for his soul: "That the spirit may be saved in the day of the Lord Jesus" (1 Cor. 5:5).

3. *Because of failure to rightly discern the Lord's body.* Paul illustrates the principle by showing that the reason some of the Corinthian saints were weak and sickly, and some had already died, was because they had failed to rightly discern the Lord's body in their observance of the communion ordinance (1 Cor. 11:27–30). He adds, "For if we would judge ourselves, we should not be judged. But when we are judged, we are chastened of the Lord, that we should not be condemned with the world" (1 Cor. 11:31–32).

4. *Because of murmuring against God-appointed leaders.* Disobedience and murmuring on the part of the children of Israel brought plagues upon their bodies. Note the result of Miriam's criticism of her brother Moses, as God's chosen leader (Nm. 12). Also, when the congregation murmured against the leadership of Moses, plagues were sent among the people and thousands died (Nm. 16:46–50).

There can be no doubt that some afflictions which Christians endure are the result of their own disobedience and sin. Many have become physically well the moment they have confessed their sin and asked God for forgiveness. Others who have cherished malice in their hearts toward another have been healed when they forgave the one who had wronged them. Some people have a greater need to repent of their disobedience and sin than to be prayed over for healing.

III. The Spiritual Nature of Sickness

For too long, a wide distinction between sin and sickness has been made. It has been taught or taken for granted that the former must be dealt with from a spiritual point of view, while the latter, being purely physical, must be dealt with through natural means. However, more and more it is being recognized that sickness has a spiritual significance as well. If it can be shown that sickness has a spiritual character, then the reasonableness of a spiritual remedy, divine healing, will be established. The following three facts, which are a summary of what has been presented above, clearly establish the spiritual nature of physical sickness:

A. Sickness is in the world because of sin.

Sickness is in the world because of sin, which is in the spiritual realm, and the activity of Satan, who is a spiritual being. Therefore, its original source is spiritual.

B. Certain sickness is the result of specific sin.

Certain sicknesses are known to be the direct result of certain specific sins. There is, therefore, a close relationship between the sickness and the sin and a spiritual significance to these diseases.

C. Sickness as a form of discipline

God sometimes allows sickness to come upon His children as a disciplinary measure because He loves them. These sicknesses must have a spiritual significance because they have a spiritual purpose—to correct the steps of the child of God.

If, then, sickness is a spiritual thing, a cure must be found which is, itself, spiritual. No remedy that reacts only on the physical will meet the full need. The physician's remedy may be able to alleviate the physical symptoms, but it is not able to deal with the spiritual cause behind the physical symptoms. Many doctors and psychiatrists have admitted that a vast majority of their patients would be well physically if they could have their spiritual needs met. Divine healing treats the physical need through the spiritual realm and thus gets to the very heart of the sick person's need.

The forgiveness of sins and the healing of diseases are related to each other in a number of passages of the Word of God: "Who forgiveth all thine iniquities; who healeth all thy diseases" (Ps. 103:3); "And the inhabitant shall not say, I am sick: the people that dwell therein shall be forgiven their iniquity" (Is. 33:24); "And the prayer of faith shall save the sick, and the Lord shall raise him up; and if he have committed sins, they shall be forgiven him" (Jas. 5:15).

The fact that great spiritual blessing always accompanies physical healing is proof of the interrelationship of the two. In fact, many experience that the spiritual blessing received is even greater than the physical relief which comes by the touch of God's power. Anything that falls short of meeting the spiritual need behind the physical sickness is not a sufficient cure.

IV. HEALING AND THE WILL OF GOD

The greatest hindrance to God's children enjoying divine healing and health is the lack of clear knowledge of God's will in the matter. It centers around the nagging uncertainty as to whether it is God's will to heal all who come to Him today. The question is not one of God's ability to heal. Every professing Christian believes that God has the ability to do anything He chooses to accomplish. The vast majority of those who make no profession of salvation still believe in God and that He can perform the miraculous if He wills to do so. The question, again, is not one of ability but willingness, and we are insulting God when we adopt this attitude. Instead of saying to Him, "I know you would if you could," we are telling Him, "I know you could if you only would." We are casting reflections on God's willingness to do good for His children.

What strange thoughts many have had with regard to God's will. Too long they have looked upon it as something which must be accepted as the final token of sacrifice on their part. Kenneth MacKenzie states:

> The will of God has been a deep shadow on their pathway, obscuring the light of present blessing with its possible decrees of sorrow. It has been a skeleton in their closet, which they have prayed to stay behind closed doors. It has been a presence from whose cold embrace they have pleaded to be released. Their dread of His will has impelled them to school themselves to be ready for its visitation as for the pestilence that sweeps through the land. The will of God is associated with sick rooms, poverty, loss, bereavement, funerals, the open grave. The will of God, to such, is always dressed in black. And this conception of His will gives us sickly Christians, weak faith, empty joy, puny conquests. With many, no thought of the will of God is given, until some calamity presses into their lives, and then they awake to such sad surmisings as we have noted. When we say, in prayer, "Thy will be done," are we always impressed with its significance? God's will is not a vindictive judge, exercising the keen scrutiny of inevitable retribution. Ah, how we have placed a libel upon our Father's great heartedness in all these miserable thoughts of Him! His will is a blessed companion, which illumines our way, cheers our spirits, makes glad our lives and brings fruitfulness to all that we do.[3]

---

3 Kenneth MacKenzie, *Divine Life for the Body* (Brooklyn, NY: Christian Alliance Publishing Company, n.d.), 32–33.

Let us seek to know God's will in this matter of healing for the sick today. Is He willing to do it? Does He think it wise to? Is it part of His plan for us at the present time? The importance of finding the scriptural answers to these questions is emphasized by the fact that, according to F. F. Bosworth, "It is impossible to boldly claim by faith a blessing which we are not sure God offers, because the power of God can be claimed only where the will of God is known...Faith begins where the will of God is known."[4]

Because they have not taken time to learn from God's Word what His will is and what are His provisions for healing, most people add to their petition, "If it be thy will." There was one in Christ's day who had this kind of faith. He was a leper, and he came to Jesus saying, "Lord, if thou wilt, thou canst make me clean. And he [Jesus] put forth his hand, and touched him, saying, I will: be thou clean. And immediately the leprosy departed from him" (Lk. 5:12–13). The "I will" of Christ cancelled the "If thou wilt" of the leper. Thus, the man who had faith that Christ *could* had his faith exercised by the word of Jesus until he believed Christ *would*.

The theology of the leper, when he first came to Jesus, is almost universal today: "If thou wilt, thou canst." The moment we say "If it be Thy will" in prayer for the healing of the sick, we are throwing all the responsibility on God. We are making God responsible for the sickness, for we are saying the Lord could heal if He only would. This is not scriptural. The Lord puts the responsibility on the one who is seeking His healing touch. The father who brought his son to Jesus at the foot of the Mount of Transfiguration cried, "If thou canst do any thing, have compassion on us, and help us. Jesus said unto him, If thou canst believe, all things are possible to him that believeth" (Mk. 9:22–23). The father, by his words, "If thou canst," was putting the responsibility on the Lord, but Jesus immediately returned the responsibility to the father by saying, "If thou canst believe, all things are possible to him that believeth."

The question is often asked whether prayer for the sick should include the statement, "If it be Thy will." Every sincere Christian wants God's will. If it can be shown that sickness is better for him than healing, he should be resigned to sickness. However, if healing is purchased for him and promised to the Church as a divine provision of the unchanging God, as the Word of God declares, then he will boldly ask the Lord to heal him, assuming on the basis of the Scripture that it is His will. Must we doubt the will of God to do something He has promised? Do we pray, "Lord save me, if it be Thy will?" *If*s defeat faith. No one can lay hold of a benefit by faith if he doubts its availability. One ought, however, to discover whether the matter is according to the will of God before he prays. If the sickness is a discipline, then one

---

4 Fred Francis Bosworth, *Christ the Healer: Message on Divine Healing* (Miami Beach, 1948), 7th edition, 33.

ought to pray first for guidance into victory or into maturity, after which he may pray for healing. If one is in doubt about the nature of a sickness, he ought to pray for insight into the trial. If one feels that sickness is a temporary testing, he ought to pray for grace to bear his trial. However, normally, one need not pray on the basis of an *if*, but may assume that God desires to fulfill His promise.

God is good and wills the blessing and the health of all His children. Note His desire, expressed by John, for blessings for the entire man: "Beloved, I wish above all things that thou mayest prosper and be in health, even as thy soul prospereth" (3 Jn. 2). No doubt Paul had this three-fold blessing in mind when he wrote, "And I pray God your whole spirit and soul and body be preserved blameless unto the coming of our Lord Jesus Christ" (1 Thes. 5:23).

If sickness is of the devil, certainly God does not will it upon any of His blood-bought children. For centuries, people have been taught the traditions of men rather than the Word of God, and thus they are not sure whether it is God's will to heal them. God tells us His ways are far above our ways (Is. 55:8–9), and the sooner we dismiss the traditions of men and turn to the Word of God, the better.

The only sure way to learn what God's will is regarding healing for the sick is to search the Word of God and ascertain what it says on the subject. In every age, every plan made by God for His people included physical health and healing. Those who believed fully in His Word and obeyed Him enjoyed this blessing. We will now turn to the Word and see what provision He has made for the healing of His people in every period of human history.

V. The Scripturalness of Divine Healing

A. Divine healing in the Old Testament

It is not possible in this work to undergo an exhaustive study of healing in the Old Testament, but many of the outstanding cases will be referred to and the principal promises studied.

The first case of divine healing recorded in the Bible is, "So Abraham prayed unto God: and God healed Abimelech, and his wife, and his maidservants; and they bare children. For the LORD had fast closed up all the wombs of the house of Abimelech, because of Sarah Abraham's wife" (Gn. 20:17–18).

What has been frequently referred to as the Old Testament divine healing covenant was given to Israel very shortly after their miraculous escape from Egypt and the crossing of the Red Sea. Of the very beginning of those long years of journeying and wandering on their way to the Promised Land, we read:

> There he made for them a statute and an ordinance, and there he proved
> them, And said, If thou wilt diligently hearken to the voice of the LORD

thy God, and wilt do that which is right in his sight, and wilt give ear to his commandments, and keep all his statutes, I will put none of these diseases upon thee, which I have brought upon the Egyptians: for I am the LORD that healeth thee.

—EXODUS 15:25–26

The words from verse 25, "There he made for them a statute and an ordinance," indicate that this was more than a passing promise for an individual situation. This was to be a permanent covenant, to be incorporated into the very life of God's people. There is no record that God ever rescinded the promise He made here. In fact, He put one of His redemptive names, *Jehovah-Rapha,* right into this legal agreement. In verse 26, God said, "I am the Lord thy Healer." This great promise still applies today, for God did not say, "I *was,*" as though to indicate some time past. Nor did He say, "I will," which would indicate some uncertain time in the future. But instead He said, "I am," indicating the great eternally, unchanging nature of God Himself. He used this great name once again when Moses, on the occasion of his call to go to Pharaoh and demand the release of Israel from bondage, asked God:

Behold, when I come unto the children of Israel, and shall say unto them, The God of your fathers hath sent me unto you; and they shall say to me, What is his name? what shall I say unto them? And God said unto Moses, I AM THAT I AM: and he said, Thus shalt thou say unto the children of Israel, I AM hath sent me unto you.

—EXODUS 3:13–14

Jesus said this great name when speaking to the Jews: "Before Abraham was, I am" (Jn. 8:58). The writer of Hebrews expressed it in the familiar words, "Jesus Christ [is] the same yesterday, and to day, and for ever" (Heb. 13:8).

Exodus 15:26 does not leave any doubt that it was God's will to heal all who were sick. That God kept His covenant is shown in Psalm 105:37: "He brought them forth also with silver and gold: and there was not one feeble person among their tribes."

This universal condition of health among the people of Israel continued as long as they kept their part of the covenant, but when Miriam grieved the Lord by criticizing the leadership of her brother, Moses, she was smitten with leprosy (Nm. 12:1–10). She had broken the covenant. When she repented and when Moses prayed to God to heal her, she was delivered (Nm. 12:11–14). Thus God showed that He was still the One who healed.

Numbers 16:41–50 records that the congregation sinned and a plague destroyed a great company of them. However, when they repented and again met the conditions of the covenant God had given them, the Lord healed them and the plague was stayed. Thus, He once again showed that He was *Jehovah-Rapha,* the God who healed not merely some of them, but all those who were afflicted.

Israel continued to enjoy the health that God had promised until, once again, they broke the covenant. They "spake against God, and against Moses" (Nm. 21:5) and "fiery serpents" went among them to destroy them (v. 6). When they once again met God's conditions through repentance, God healed all who looked to the brazen serpent on the pole (a picture of Calvary, see Jn. 3:14). He was still the Great Physician who healed all who looked to Him.

Other Old Testament scriptures which show God's willingness to heal the sick are:

> And ye shall serve the LORD your God, and he shall bless thy bread, and thy water; and I will take sickness away from the midst of thee.
>
> —EXODUS 23:25

> And the LORD will take away from thee all sickness, and will put none of the evil diseases of Egypt, which thou knowest, upon thee; but will lay them upon them that hate thee.
>
> —DEUTERONOMY 7:15

> That thou mayest love the LORD thy God, and that thou mayest obey his voice, and that thou mayest cleave unto him: for he is thy life, and the length of thy days: that thou mayest dwell in the land which the LORD sware unto thy fathers, to Abraham, and to Jacob, to give them.
>
> —DEUTERONOMY 30:20

> Many are the afflictions of the righteousness: but the LORD delivereth him out of them all.
>
> —PSALM 34:19

> Because thou hast made the LORD, which is my refuge, even the most High, thy habitation; There shall no evil befall thee, neither shall any plague come nigh thy dwelling.
>
> —PSALM 91:9–10

> Bless the LORD, O my soul, and forget not all his benefits: Who forgiveth all thine iniquities; who healeth all thy diseases. ["Who healeth all" is just as permanent as "Who forgiveth all."]
>
> —PSALM 103:2–3

He sent his word, and healed them, and delivered them from their destructions.

—PSALM 107:20

My son, attend to my words; incline thine ear unto my sayings: Let them not depart from thine eyes; keep them in the midst of thine heart. For they are life unto those that find them, and health to all their flesh.

—PROVERBS 4:20–22

Other Old Testament examples of healing are:

- Miriam healed from leprosy (Nm. 12:12–15)
- People healed from the plague (2 Sm. 24:25; Nm. 16)
- A widow's son raised from the dead (1 Kgs. 17:17–24)
- The Shunammite woman's son raised from the dead (2 Kgs. 4:18–37)
- Naaman healed from leprosy (2 Kgs. 5:1–15)
- Hezekiah's life extended fifteen years (2 Kgs. 20:1–11)
- Job healed of his sore affliction (Jb. 42:10–13)

The question of divine healing in the Old Testament is not at all uncertain or doubtful. That Jehovah was the Physician of the Israelites is clearly evidenced by the above examples, together with numerous other promises. The only questions that might arise would be: May God be expected to heal others besides Israel? When God declared Himself to be "Jehovah thy Physician" in Exodus 15:26, did He mean that His healing ministry was to be in a permanent capacity? How can we know that this covenant of healing applies to any but to the nation of Israel, and in that day only?

The answer to these important questions is found in a study of the compound names of Jehovah. The names of God are expressive of Himself and were chosen for that purpose. Some things in God's plan never change and never cease to exist because they are the manifestation of the very nature of God. The Lord never ceases to do some things because they are the acts resultant from His very character. God does what He does because He is what He is. "I am the LORD, I change not," declares Malachi 3:6. James says of the Lord, "Every good gift and every perfect gift is from above, and cometh down from the Father of lights, with whom is no variableness, neither shadow of turning" (Jas. 1:17). The name Jehovah is God's name when He is dealing in covenant relationship with His people. It means "the eternal, self-existent, unchanging God." There are seven compound names which, along with the name Jehovah, reveal His covenant relationship with Israel. Because He never changes, these names also reveal His redemptive relationship to His people today. Note these seven compound names of Jehovah:

- Jehovah-Jireh: "the Lord will provide" (Gn. 22:14)
- Jehovah-Nissi: "the Lord our Banner" (Ex. 17:8–15)
- Jehovah-Shalom: "the Lord our Peace" (Jgs. 6:24)
- Jehovah-Raah: "the Lord our Shepherd" (Ps. 23:1)
- Jehovah-Tsidkenu: "the Lord our Righteousness" (Jer. 23:6)
- Jehovah-Shammah: "the Lord is present" (Ez. 48:35)
- Jehovah-Rapha: "the Lord thy Physician" (Ex. 15:26)

The Jehovah of the Old Testament is the same as Jesus in the New Testament. Compare the following set of Scripture verses, "A voice of one crying!—In the desert, prepare ye the way of Jehovah, make smooth in the waste plain a highway for our God" (Is. 40:3, ROTHERHAM). "For this is He who was spoken of through Isaiah the prophet, saying a voice of one crying aloud! In the wilderness prepare ye the way of the Lord, straight by making his paths" (Mt. 3:3, ROTHERHAM). For whom was John preparing the way? Isaiah calls Him Jehovah. Note also Jeremiah's words, "Lo! days are coming declareth Jehovah, when I will raise up to David a righteous bud and he shall reign as king and prosper, and shall execute justice and righteousness in the land. In his days shall Judah be saved, and Israel abide securely—and this is his name where by he shall be called—Jehovah our Righteousness" (Jer. 23:5–6, ROTHERHAM). Now who is it who shall reign as King on the throne of David? Is it not the Lord Jesus Himself? Who is it that is the Lord our Righteousness? Is it not Christ the Lamb of God, who died for our sins that He might be "made unto us...righteousness" (1 Cor. 1:30)?

Jehovah never changes. What the Lord's name, by its meaning, reveals Him to be is what He will always continue to be. Every one of the seven compound names of Jehovah are given to reveal some aspect of the Lord's eternal relationship to His people. Therefore, what He revealed Himself to be to Israel by His name, so He will be to His Church through Jesus Christ.

	TO ISRAEL	TO THE CHURCH
Jehovah-Jireh	"the Lord will provide" (Gn. 22:14)	"My God shall supply all your need according to his riches in glory by Christ Jesus" (Phil. 4:19).

	TO ISRAEL	TO THE CHURCH
Jehovah-Nissi	"the Lord our Banner" (Ex. 17:15)	"His banner over me was love" (Sg. 2:4). "Greater love hath no man than this, that a man lay down his life for his friends" (Jn. 15:13).
Jehovah-Shalom	"the Lord our Peace" (Jgs. 6:24)	"For he is our peace" (Eph. 2:14)
Jehovah-Raah	"the Lord our Shepherd" (Ps. 23:1)	"I am the good shepherd" (Jn. 10:11).
Jehovah-Tsidkenu	"the Lord our Righteousness" (Jer. 23:6)	"Christ Jesus, who of God is made unto us…righteousness" (1 Cor. 1:30).
Jehovah-Shammah	"the Lord is present" (Ez. 48:35)	"I will never leave thee, nor forsake thee" (Heb. 13:5).
Jehovah-Rapha	"the Lord thy Physician" (Ez. 15:26)	"The prayer of faith shall save the sick, and the Lord shall raise him up" (Jas. 5:15).

It is therefore beyond dispute that if Jehovah has remained constant in all the relationships revealed by His names through the Old Testament centuries and up through the present Church age, He must have continued constant in His relationship as Healer of the body. If He is still our Provider, our Banner, our Peace, our Shepherd, the Ever-present One, and our Righteousness, then He is still our Great Physician—"The same yesterday, and to day, and for ever?" (Heb. 13:8).

B. Healing in the ministry of Jesus

We are still dealing with the topic of the will of God relative to healing those who come to Him. There can be no doubt that it was God's will to heal His people in Old Testament times. We now wish to find the revelation of His will for those of us who live in the New Testament era. First, we will learn from the ministry of Jesus.

There is certainly no better way to find God's will regarding physical healing than by a close study of the ministry and teachings of the Lord Jesus, as recorded in the Gospels. Jesus was the expression of the Father's will. In His entire life and ministry He was "the Word," speaking out the will of God (Jn. 1:1). He said, "For I came down from heaven, not to do mine own will, but the will of him that sent me" (Jn.

6:38). He literally acted out the will of God. Therefore, when we see Jesus healing the multitudes who came to Him, we see the Father revealing His will. "The Father that dwelleth in me, he doeth the works" (Jn. 14:10). The healing of the sick was done, then, as a revelation of God's will for man. Thomas Holdcroft concludes:

> A total of twenty-seven individual miracles of healing credited to Jesus are to be found in the Scriptures, as well as ten occasions recording the general healing of large numbers of people. His ministry dealt with a wide variety of human aliments: demon possession, sickness, disease, accident, and even death…In each instance, Jesus freely and frankly presented Himself as an object of faith to be sincerely believed. In the face of such an impressive ministry of healing, it is truly remarkable that He should promise His disciples, "Greater works than these shall [ye] do" (John 14:12). In ministering to physical needs, our Lord healed by a word, by a touch, and by physical anointing; He healed those near at hand and at a distance, He healed on the Sabbath, He healed both individuals and groups at large. Among the twenty-seven instances of healing, there are seven cases in which a demon was cast out; on eleven occasions friends brought the sufferer; on six occasions the patient himself made an appeal; on three occasions our Lord performed the healing while at a distance. He healed eight persons by a touch; He healed seven by speaking a word; three were healed in a ceremony in which He spat and touched the patient; and in one instance He healed by effecting a gradual cure (John 4:52—"He began to amend").[5]

The following is a list of the individual healings performed by Jesus during His ministry here on Earth, as recorded in the four Gospels:

INCIDENT OF HEALING	MATTHEW	MARK	LUKE	JOHN
Narrated in one Gospel only:				
Two blind men	9:27–31			
Dumb demoniac	9:32–33			
Deaf and dumb man		7:31–37		
Blind man healed		8:22–26		

---

5 Leslie Thomas Holdcroft, *Divine Healing: A Comparative Study* (Springfield. MO: Gospel Publishing House, 1967), 13–14.

INCIDENT OF HEALING	MATTHEW	MARK	LUKE	JOHN
Widow's son raised from the dead			7:11–16	
Woman bowed over			13:11–17	
man with dropsy			14:1–6	
Ten lepers			17:11–19	
Ear of servant of the high priest			22:50–51	
Nobleman's son				4:46–54
Impotent man at Bethesda				5:2–15
Man born blind				9:1–38
Lazarus raised from the dead				11:1–45
Narrated in two Gospels:				
Demoniac in synagogue, Capernum		1:23–27	4:33–36	
Centurion's servant	8:5–13		7:1–10	
Blind and dumb demoniac	12:22–23		11:14	
Syrophoenician woman's daughter	15:21–28	7:24–30		
Mary Magdalene		16:9	8:2	
Narrated in three Gospels:				
The leper	8:2–4	1:40–45	5:12–15	
Peter's mother-in-law	8:14–15	1:29–31	4:38–39	
Man with legion of demons	8:28–34	5:1–20	8:26–39	
Palsied man	9:2–8	2:1–12	5:17–26	
Woman with issue of blood	9:20–22	5:25–34	8:43–48	

INCIDENT OF HEALING	MATTHEW	MARK	LUKE	JOHN
Jairus' daughter raised from the dead	9:23–26	5:35–43	8:49–56	
man in synagogue with withered hand	12:9–13	3:1–5	6:6–11	
Demoniac child	17:14–21	9:14–29	9:37–43	
Blind Bartimaeus (two blind men in Matthew's account)	20:29–34	10:46–52	18:35–43	

In addition to these, there are the following occasions when Jesus healed many at one time: Mt. 4:23–25; 8:16; 12:15; 14:14; 14:34–36; 15:30; 19:2; 21:14; and Lk. 6:17–19. These are inspiring occasions, for we read that there were at times multitudes who came or were brought for healing, and in these accounts we read such expressions as, "He healed all that were sick," "and He healed them all," "and He healed their sick," "and as many as touched Him were made perfectly whole."

As impressive as this list of marvelous miracles is, John tells us, "And many other signs truly did Jesus in the presence of his disciples, which are not written in this book" (Jn. 20:30); also, "And there are also many other things which Jesus did, the which, if they should be written every one, I suppose that even the world itself could not contain the books that should be written" (Jn. 21:25).

It is a remarkable thing—and one worthy of a great deal of consideration—that Jesus healed everyone who came to Him or who was brought to Him for healing. In addition to the great variety of needs that were presented to Him individually, there were those times, as we have noted above, when there must have been huge multitudes of sick folk brought to Him. Yet, He never turned one of them aside. He never refused to heal anyone. You would expect that there might have been a few, or even one, to whom He would say, "I am sorry. It is not my will or my Father's will to heal you." There is no recorded record in the Scriptures of any such statement, or even the suggestion of it. One would have expected that if it were not God's will to heal all who came to Him for healing in the church age, there would have been some suggestion of this in the ministry of Jesus. Yet, how fortunate that such was not the case, for if Jesus had refused even one, millions of those who do not immediately receive the healing they seek would claim exemption on the basis of that one.

C. Healing in the ministry of the disciples

So much was it God's will to heal the sick in the days when Jesus ministered on Earth that He extended this ministry to His disciples, giving them power to heal the sick, raise the dead, and cast out demons. The ministry of Jesus, while He was here in the flesh, was almost entirely limited to the sphere of His physical presence. Thus, the blessed influence of His compassion and power was greatly enlarged by enduing others with the same divine ability. "And when he had called unto him his twelve disciples, he gave them power against unclean spirits, to cast them out, and to heal all manner of sickness and all manner of disease" (Mt. 10:1).

1. *The Twelve given power and sent forth*

> And he called unto him the twelve, and began to send them forth two by two; and gave them power over unclean spirits. And they went out, and preached that men should repent. And they cast out many devils, and anointed with oil many that were sick and healed them.
>
> —MARK 6:7, 12–13

> And when he had called unto him his twelve disciples, he gave them power against unclean spirits, to cast them out, and to heal all manner of sickness and all manner of disease.... These twelve Jesus sent forth, and commanded them, saying.... as ye go, preach, saying, The kingdom of heaven is at hand. Heal the sick, cleanse the lepers, raise the dead, cast out devils: freely ye have received, freely give.
>
> —MATTHEW 10:1, 5, 7–8

2. *The Seventy given power and sent out.* "And after these things the Lord appointed other seventy also, and sent them two and two before his face....And into whatsoever city ye enter....heal the sick that are therein" (Lk. 10:1, 8–9). The results of this commission were quite evident: "And the seventy returned again with joy, saying, Lord, even the devils are subject unto us through thy name" (Lk. 10:17). Jesus seemed not at all surprised at this report, and that the demons were subject unto His name. He said, "I beheld Satan as lightning fall from heaven. Behold, I give you power to tread on serpents and scorpions, and over all the power of the enemy: and nothing shall by any means hurt you. Notwithstanding in this rejoice not, that the spirits are subject unto you; but rather rejoice, because your names are written in heaven" (Lk. 10:18–20).

The disciples were not to be sparing in their use of the healing power given to them. Matthew 10:8 is very significant in revealing God's will to heal not a few, but many. Jesus said, "Freely ye have received, freely give." Undoubtedly the power given to the Twelve and to the Seventy is the same power Jesus promised as a permanent possession and that was received by the Church on the Day of Pentecost (Jn. 14:16–17; Lk. 24:49; and Acts 1:8).

D. Healing in the Early Church

The book of Acts opens with the writer, Luke, calling attention to his "former treatise," the Gospel of Luke, in which he gave an account "of all that Jesus began both to do and teach" (Acts 1:1). Christ's ministry on Earth is described as what He taught and did. The latter word must certainly refer to His miracles of healing. We are told here that during those years of ministry before His death, burial, resurrection, and ascension, Jesus began "to do and teach." The strong inference is that He continued to do the same after His return to the Father. This He accomplished through His disciples—all believers who are members of His body. Christ, the living Head, still ministers through the Church, His body. The book of Luke is one man's inspired record of what Jesus "began both to do and teach" in His earthly ministry, while the book of Acts is his inspired account of that which Jesus continued to do and teach after His ascension on high. We then recognize the book of Acts as a further revelation of God's will relative to healing the sick.

If Christian believers are members of the body of Christ, of which Christ is the motivating, guiding Head, then what Christ did while He was bodily present on the earth, He should be continuing to do through the members of His spiritual body. When Peter said to the lame man at the Beautiful Gate of the temple, "In the name of Jesus Christ of Nazareth rise up and walk" (Acts 3:6) and then reached out "and...took him by the right hand, and lifted him up," it was as though Jesus Christ reached out and touched him. If Christ had been physically present and able to touch the lame man, he certainly would have been made whole and able to walk. Why not the same when one of His body, Peter, touched the afflicted in the name of Jesus? The multitude rushed to Solomon's porch "greatly wondering" at the miracle (v. 11). Peter said, "Ye men of Israel, why marvel ye at this... The God of Abraham, and of Isaac, and of Jacob, the God of our fathers, hath glorified his Son Jesus.... God hath raised [him] from the dead" (vv. 12–13, 15). In other words, Peter was saying, "Jesus is alive. He is not dead. Why then should He not be still manifesting the same power and miracles He performed before His crucifixion?" This, the living Christ working through His body, the Church, is the true picture of Christian ministry today. This is demonstrated in the following examples from the book of Acts:

HEALING PERFORMED THROUGH THE APOSTLES

The lame man (Peter)	Acts 3:1–10
Many healed (Peter)	Acts 5:12–16

Wonders and miracles (Stephen)	Acts 6:8
Revival in Samaria (Philip)	Acts 8:5–8
Aeneas (Peter)	Acts 9:32–35
Tabitha (Dorcas) raised from the dead (Peter)	Acts 9:36–42
Crippled man at Lystra (Paul)	Acts 14:8–10
Paul raised up at Lystra	Acts 14:19–20
Demon cast out (Paul)	Acts 16:16–18
Special miracles (Paul)	Acts 19:11–12
Eutychus (Paul)	Acts 20:7–12
On the isle of Melita (Paul)	Acts 28:8–9

Nothing has been changed since those apostolic days as far as God's provisions for the needs of mankind are concerned. Christ has died and risen again, the Holy Spirit has been poured out, and the Great Commission is still in force. The ravages of sin and its dire results are still manifest in our world today. Physicians, with all their knowledge and dedication, are still baffled by afflictions and diseases. No one can prove that the God who never changes has ever altered His will concerning the healing of disease. He is *Jehovah-Rapha*—"I am the LORD that healeth thee" (Ex. 15:26).

VI. HEALING THROUGH THE CHURCH AGE

Dr. A. J. Gordon quotes Dr. Gerhard Uhlhorn as saying, "Witnesses who are above suspicion leave no room for doubt that the miraculous powers of the apostolic age continued to operate at least into the third century."[6] Dr. Gordon then makes the important comment:

> Prove that Miracles were wrought, for example, in the second century after Christ, and no reason can be thereafter urged why they might not be wrought in the nineteenth [and we add "the twentieth"] century. The apostolic age, it must be admitted, was a peculiarly favored one. So long as the men were still living who had seen the Lord, and had companied with Him during His earthly ministry, there were possible secrets of power in their possession that a later generation might not have. It is easy to see, therefore, that this period might be especially distinguished by the gifts of the Spirit. And yet the Saviour seems to be careful to teach that there would be an augmenting rather than a diminishing of supernatural energy after His departure. "But

---

6 Dr. Gerhard Uhlhorn, *Conflict of Christianity with Heathenism,* 196, as quoted in Adoniram Judson Gordon, *Ministry of Healing* (Harrisburg, PA: Christian Publications), 58.

ye shall receive power after that the Holy Ghost is come upon you." "Verily, verily I say unto you, he that believeth on me the works that I do shall he do also, and greater works than these shall he do; because I go unto my Father." But, conceding certain marked advantages possessed by the immediate followers of Christ, if we find in history that there is no abrupt termination of miracles with expiration of the apostolic age, then we must begin to raise the question why there should be any termination at all, so long as the Church remains, and the ministry of the Spirit is perpetuated.[7]

Indeed, history shows that healing by the direct power of God continued through the entire Church age to the present time.

Note the testimonies of some of the Church fathers:

Writing in A.D. 165, more than sixty-five years after the death of John, the last of the apostles, Justin Martyr, said, "For numberless demoniacs throughout the whole world and in your city, many of our Christian men, exorcising them [casting out] in the name of Jesus Christ, who was crucified under Pontius Pilate, *have healed, and do heal,* rendering helpless and driving the possessing devils out of men, though they could not be cured by all the other exorcists, and those who used incantations and drugs" (emphasis added).[8]

Writing in A.D. 192, Irenaeus declared, "Those who are in truth the disciples receiving grace from Him do in His name perform miracles so as to promote the welfare of others, according to the gift which each has received from him....Others still heal the sick by laying their hands upon them, and they are made whole. Yea moreover, as I have said, the dead even have been raised up, and remained among us for years."[9]

Writing in A.D. 216, Tertullian said, "For the clerk of one of them who was liable to be thrown upon the ground by an evil spirit was set free from his affliction, as was also the relative of another, and the little boy of a third. And how many men of rank, to say nothing of the common people *have been delivered from devils and healed of diseases*" (emphasis added).[10]

Writing in A.D. 250, Origen testified, "And some give evidence of their having received through their faith a marvelous power by the cures which they perform, invoking no other name over those who need their help than that of the God of all things, and of Jesus...For by these means we too have seen many persons freed from

---

7   Gordon, 58–59.

8   Justin Martyr, *Apol.,* 1, Ch. 6, as quoted in Gordon, 60.

9   Irenaeus, *Versus Heretics,* 1, Ch. 34, as quoted in Gordon, 60.

10   Tertullian, *Ad. Scap.* IV, 4, as quoted in Gordon, 60–61.

grievous calamities, and from distractions of mind, madness, and countless other ills which could be cured neither by men or devils."[11]

Writing in A.D. 275, Clement of Alexandria said, "Let them [young ministers], therefore, with fasting and prayer, make their intercessions, and not with well arranged, and fitly ordered words of learning, but as men who have received the gift of healing confidently, to the glory of God."[12]

Writing in A.D. 429, Theodore of Mopsuestia declared, "Many heathen amongst us are being healed by Christians from whatever sickness they have, so abundant are miracles in our midst."[13]

In A.D. 500, Gregory the Great (believed to be the first pope) gave away his inherited fortune and became a missionary to the Britons, praying for the people and anointing them with oil in the name of the Lord, quoting James 5:14–15.

John Wesley, speaking of the period after Constantine, said, "The grand reason why the miraculous gifts were so soon withdrawn was not only that Faith and Holiness were well nigh lost, but that dry formal orthodox men began to ridicule whatever gifts they had not in themselves, and to decry them all as either madness or impostures."[14]

From Gregory's day until the Reformation, the world went through a dark age, both in respect to the progress of spiritual things and the advancement of learning. But with the dawn of the Reformation returned the evidence of God's supernatural works.

The following is an excerpt from *The Confessions of Faith* of the Waldenses, a deeply spiritual sect of Christians in the twelfth century who were the followers of Peter Waldo: "Concerning this anointing of the sick, we hold it as an article of faith and profess sincerely from the heart that sick persons, when they ask it, may lawfully be anointed with the anointing oil by one who joins with them in praying that it may be efficacious to the healing of the body, according to the design and end and effect mentioned by the apostles; and we profess that such an anointing performed according to the apostolic design and practice, will be healing and profitable."[15]

Count Zinzendorf, a bishop of the Moravian movement (United Brethren), a close friend of John Wesley and a deeply sincere man with a burden for world evangelization, said of his church, "To believe against hope is the root of the gift of Miracles, and I owe this testimony to our Beloved Church, that Apostolic powers are there mani-

---

11 Origen, *Contra Celsum B.*, III, Ch. 24, as quoted in Gordon, 61.

12 Clement of Alexandria, *Epis. C.*, XII, as quoted in Gordon, 61.

13 Theodore of Mopsuestia, *Christlieb; Modern Doubt*, 321, as quoted in Gordon, 61.

14 John Wesley, *The Journal of the Rev. John Wesley, A.M.*, ed. Nehemiah Curnock (London: Epworth Press, 1938), I–IX.

15 *Johannis Lukawitz Waldensia Confession*, 1431, as quoted in Gordon, 65.

fested. We have undeniable proofs thereof. In the healing of maladies in themselves incurable, such as Cancer, Consumption, and when the patient was in the agonies of death, all by means of a prayer or word."[16]

The following excerpts are from John Wesley's diary:

- March 19, 1741—"...Judith Williams, who was in grievous pain of both body and mind. After a short time of prayer, we left her. But her pain was gone...her body so strengthened that she immediately rose, and the next day went abroad." (17)[17].

- October 3, 1756—"My disorder returned as violent as ever; but, I regarded it not while I was performing the service at Snowfields in the morning, nor afterwards at Spitalfields; till I went to the Lord's Table to administer. A thought came into my mind, 'Why do I not apply to God in the beginning rather than the end of an illness?' I did so, and found immediate relief." (IV, 188)[18].

- September 2, 1781—"I believe it my duty to relate here what some will esteem a most notable instance of enthusiasm. Be it so or not, I aver the plain fact. In an hour after we left Taunton, one of the chaise-horses was on a sudden so lame that he could hardly set his foot to the ground. It being impossible to procure any human help, I knew no remedy but prayer. Immediately the lameness was gone, and he went just as he did before."[19]

John Wesley was certainly not an ignorant fanatic, but a learned man, a graduate of Oxford University. The great revival which God entrusted to him actually saved England from moral and civil ruin. He was one of the outstanding characters of history, either religious or secular. If his testimony be disregarded, then no human testimony can be regarded as of value. He has given undeniable witness of God's mighty power in bodily healing and of the truth that the day of miracles is definitely not passed.

In this brief review of history, an array of witnesses has been presented whose unquestionable testimonies should remove any doubt that divine healing has continued from the Old Testament days, during Christ's lifetime, the days of His disciples and apostles, after the apostles' death, the early Church fathers, and down through the ages to our own generation. *Jehovah Rapha*—the Lord thy Physician—is

---

16 A. Bost, *History of the United Brethren,* I, 17, as quoted in Gordon, 66–67.

17 Wesley, II, 437.

18 Ibid., IV, 188.

19 Ibid., VI, 334.

"the same yesterday, to day, and for ever" (Heb. 13:8). Thus God has shown His willingness to heal in every age of the world's history. Innumerable miracles of healing in the present day bear witness that His will has not changed to this present hour. The Bible and history are in perfect agreement on this point.

VII. Healing and the Atonement

We learned in our study of soteriology that the word *atonement* literally means "covering." It is an Old Testament word that signifies what an Israelite received as he brought his prescribed offering to the priest for his sin. His sins were covered until the blood of Jesus Christ would be shed for the remission, not merely the covering, of his sin (Heb. 10:1–18). However, it has become quite common in theological circles to use this word *atonement* in a broad manner as referring to the fullness of the sacrifice which Jesus made on Calvary and all that was accomplished for believers there. It is in this larger sense that the word is here used as we discuss divine healing and the atonement.

The most positive answer to the question concerning God's will for healing today is found in the relationship between divine healing and the atonement. No doubt is entertained regarding Christ's ability to heal, but the heart of the matter centers around the question, did Christ make special provision for the healing of the body? Is this blessing included in the atoning sacrifice which He made on Calvary's cross? We believe the Bible teaches that this is so, and Thomas Holdcroft agrees: "Healing is not so much an end in itself; it may rather be seen as the appropriation of one more vital aspect of the total victory of Jesus Christ."[20]

A. Atonement was made for healing in the Old Testament.

Leviticus 14:1–32 describes the method by which an Israelite who was afflicted with leprosy could be healed. Six different times the expression, "The priest shall make an atonement for him," is used in this passage (vv. 18–21, 29, 31). The ceremonial instructions given to the priests and people in Old Testament times are recognized to be types of the sacrifice and provisions made by Jesus Christ on the cross. This suggests that Jesus also made atonement for sicknesses when He was offered as a sacrifice for us.

Numbers 16:46–50 describes a great plague that was running rampant through the camp of Israel because of their sin. The plague was stayed and the people were healed when an atonement was made for them (vv. 46–47).

---

20 Holdcroft, 40.

Numbers 21:5–9 recounts the occasion when, because of the sins of the people of Israel, "fiery serpents" went out among the people, causing affliction and death. Healing was wrought when Moses erected a serpent of brass upon a pole, and those who had been bitten looked upon it. According to John 3:14–15 we read, "And as Moses lifted up the serpent in the wilderness, even so must the Son of Man be lifted up: That whosoever believeth in him should not perish, but have eternal life." The serpent of brass upon the pole was clearly a type of Christ's sacrifice upon the cross, and we may expect physical healing as we look in faith to Him, even as the Israelites of old found deliverance looking at the brazen serpent.

Job 33:24–25 reads, "Then he is gracious unto him, and saith, Deliver him from going down to the pit: I have found a ransom. His flesh shall be fresher than a child's: he shall return to the days of his youth." The word *ransom* literally means "atonement." It is significant that this promise deals plainly with a physical blessing of healing and strength and that the word *atonement* is used here.

B. Forgiveness of sins and healing of diseases go hand-in-hand in the Bible.

In the healing covenant of the Old Testament, Exodus 15:26, it is definitely stated that if the children of Israel would "diligently hearken unto the voice of the Lord...and wilt do that which is right in his sight, and wilt give ear to his commandments, and keep all his statutes," the Lord would put none of the diseases of Egypt upon them and would be their healer. Thus, healing and health were based on obedience to the Lord. This was also exactly the basis for the forgiveness of sin under the Mosaic economy, putting healing and the forgiveness of sins on the same basis in the Old Testament. In the New Testament, forgiveness of sins and healing are also on the same basis—faith in the sacrifice of Christ on Calvary.

Note also two other passages, one each from the Old and New Testaments, where this close relationship is seen: "Bless the LORD, O my soul, and forget not all his benefits: Who forgiveth all thine iniquities; who healeth all thy diseases" (Ps. 103:2–3); "And the prayer of faith shall save the sick, and the Lord will raise him up; and if he have committed sins, they shall be forgiven him" (Jas. 5:15).

Mark 16:16–18 reads, "He that believeth and is baptized shall be saved...And these signs shall follow them that believe; In my name...they shall lay hands on the sick, and they shall recover." Notice that the belief that results in salvation is joined with that of healing for the sick. No Christian would doubt that the phrase "He that believeth and is baptized shall be saved" applies to anyone in every age of the Christian dispensation. Why should not "these signs shall follow them that believe" likewise apply to anyone in every age of the Christian era?

C. Redemption from the curse of the Law

The key verse in this consideration is Galatians 3:13: "Christ hath redeemed us from the curse of the law, being made a curse for us: for it is written, Cursed is every one that hangeth on a tree." What is the curse of the Law? The answer is found in Deuteronomy 28:15–68. In the first fourteen verses of this chapter, Moses enumerates the blessings of obedience of the Law. Then, starting with verse 15 he lists the curses that would come because of disobedience. It is significant that, among other things, the following physical diseases and afflictions are mentioned: consumption (tuberculosis), fever, inflammation, extreme burning, emerods (tumors), scabs, itching, madness, blindness, ailments of the knees and legs, great plagues of long continuance, sore sicknesses of long continuance, all the diseases of Egypt, as well as every other sickness and plague not written in the book of the Law. These were the curses of the Law, but "Christ hath redeemed us from the curse of the law" (Gal. 3:13). Therefore, Christ has redeemed us from sickness. How did He do this? Upon the cross of Calvary, for we read in the same verse, "Cursed is every one that hangeth on a tree." Thus, in a way which we do not fully understand, the Lord substitutionally bore our sicknesses on the cross.

D. Isaiah 53

The great redemption chapter of the Old Testament, Isaiah 53, teaches that Christ bore our sicknesses as well as our sins on Calvary.

Through the eye of prophecy, Isaiah describes the events which were to take place on Calvary hundreds of years after he wrote. Verse 4 reads, "Surely he hath borne our griefs, and carried our sorrows." The word translated "griefs" is the Hebrew *choliy*, which means "sicknesses." In Deuteronomy 7:15 we read, "The LORD will take away from thee all sicknesses [*choliy*]." This same word is translated "sicknesses" in Dt. 28:61; 1 Kgs. 17:17; 2 Kgs. 1:2; 8:8; 2 Chr. 16:12; and 21:15.

The word rendered "sorrows" in Isaiah 53:4 is the word *mak'ob*. This word is translated "pain" in Job 14:22, 33:19, and Jeremiah 51:8.

Thus the literal translation of Isaiah 53:4 is, "Surely he hath borne our sicknesses, and carried our pain." Rotherham's translation reads, "Yet surely our sicknesses he carried, and as for our pains he bore the burden of them." Young's Literal Translation reads, "Surely our sicknesses he hath borne, and our pains he hath carried them." The margin of the Revised Standard Version gives the words "sicknesses" and "pains," as does the New American Standard Bible.

Notice also the verbs in this fourth verse of chapter 53. The word "borne" is the Hebrew verb *nasá*, and the word "carried" is the Hebrew *cabal*. The Hebrew verb *nasá* means to bear in the sense of suffering punishment for something. "And if a soul sin...he...shall bear [*nasá*] his iniquity" (Lv. 5:17). "And he [Christ] was numbered with the transgressors; and he bare [*nasá*] the sin of many" (Is. 53:12). How did

Christ bear our sins? Vicariously, as our substitute. If He bare our sins vicariously, He must also have borne our sicknesses (v. 4) in the same way. The same verb (*nasá*) is used for both.

The verb "carried" (*cabal*) also means to bear something as a penalty or chastisement. "Our fathers have sinned...and we have borne [*cabal*] their iniquities" (Lam. 5:7). "He [Christ] shall see the travail of his soul, and shall be satisfied...for he shall bear [*cabal*] their iniquities" (Is. 53:11). How did Christ bear our iniquities? The same way as our sins—as our substitute. In the very same way, then, He also bore our pains (v. 4).

If there could be any doubt with regard to this translation and interpretation, it must be forever removed as we turn to Matthew 8:16–17, for here we have the Holy Spirit's own interpretation of Isaiah 53:4: "When the even was come, they brought unto him many that were possessed with devils: and he cast out the spirits with his word, and healed all that were sick: That it might be fulfilled which was spoken by Esaias the prophet, saying, Himself took our infirmities, and bare our sicknesses."

Isaiah continues to describe the scene about Calvary in verse 5: "But he was wounded for our transgressions, he was bruised for our iniquities: the chastisement of our peace was upon him, and with his stripes we are healed." The word *stripes* is literally "bruise." It signifies the entire wounding or bruising of Christ, including the stripes that were laid on His back, the buffeting, the plucking out of His beard, the nails driven into His hands and feet, the crown of thorns on His brow, and the spear thrust into His side. All of His bodily sufferings were in order that we might be healed. Peter bears this out when he quotes Isaiah 53:5: "Who his own self bare our sins in his own body on the tree, that we, being dead to sins, should live unto righteousness: by whose stripes ye were healed" (1 Pt. 2:24). Lest it might be thought that Peter was referring to spiritual healing, it is noted that the word *healed* is the Greek *iaomai,* a verb that always speaks of healing in the New Testament in connection with healing of physical ailments.

E. The Passover and the Lord's Supper

The Passover and the Lord's Supper both clearly teach that provision was made not only for spiritual deliverance but for bodily health and strength as well. The blood of the lamb, which was slain on the night of the first Passover in Egypt, was sprinkled on the lintel and the doorposts of every Hebrew house to insure the sparing of the life of the firstborn, who represented the entire family. The body of the lamb was eaten so that the people might receive physical strength for the journey which lay before them (Ex. 12:7–8).

Paul says, "For even Christ our passover is sacrificed for us" (1 Cor. 5:7). Here again, the type, the lamb, is fulfilled in the antitype, Christ. The significance of the Passover in the Old Testament is carried on for us in the observance of the Lord's Supper, or the communion service. Why did Jesus make a distinction between the bread and the cup? Why did He differentiate between His body and His blood? It would seem that He wanted His followers to realize that there was a difference in the provisions made by each. As in the Passover observance, the blood is for the forgiveness of sin and the sparing of life, while the body is for the health and strength of the physical man.

Paul has this great truth in mind in writing to the church at Corinth (1 Cor. 11:23–30). The Corinthian church was making a feast out of the Lord's Supper, and Paul rebuked them for the manner in which they were desecrating this ordinance. He said, "For he that eateth and drinketh unworthily [in an unworthy manner], eateth and drinketh damnation [condemnation] to himself, not discerning the Lord's body. For this cause many are weak and sickly among you, and many sleep" (1 Cor. 11:29–30). This condition of sickliness and premature death among the Corinthians was due to the fact that they had not discerned the Lord's body. There are many Christians today who have not realized the efficacy of the Lord's body for their physical strength and healing. Some may have already died for this same reason. By failing to realize the provision made for their body—that "with his stripes we are healed" (Is. 53:5)—they have not appropriated by faith what He made available. Thomas Holdcroft declares:

> The conclusion to be drawn from the foregoing facts is that healing was provided by Christ's atoning death on Calvary, and it is appropriated by the exercise of faith. It is not something to be earned, nor something to be coaxed from an unwilling God. Healing is an accomplished fact for every afflicted child of God, and the only requirement or condition imposed by God is that believing faith must be exercised. Healing is not a special favor, an award, or a providential gift dependent upon the benevolence; it is a special provision of Christ's atonement available to all who meet the sole condition of appropriation. In being an integral part of the finished work, healing is delivered from all capriciousness or uncertainty.[21]

VIII. Why Jesus Healed the Sick

Many false notions are being spread abroad concerning the healing ministry of Jesus while He was here on Earth. Some of these are merely the reasonings of men, often of those who do not believe that Christ can be expected to heal today. Some of these

---

21 Holderoft. 48.

unscriptural ideas have to do with the reasons why Jesus healed the sick during His earthly ministry. The following three reasons are most popularly advanced: to demonstrate His power, to vindicate His claim to deity, and to initiate the preaching of the gospel.

With regard to the first of these—to demonstrate His power—let it be observed that there is no scriptural evidence of this. Jesus most certainly did not go about performing miracles just to show that He could. If He merely wished to manifest His power, He would not have needed to heal everyone who came to Him for healing. A few outstanding demonstrations would have been all that would have been necessary. He had all power in heaven and in Earth, but He did not use it to show that it was His. In fact, this was one area of His life in which He was the most completely in full yieldedness to the will of His Father. To have all power and yet use it only for the glory of God showed how completely He was dedicated to the Father's will. Certainly there was a purpose far more important behind each miracle than the mere show of power!

Regarding the second claim—to vindicate His claim to deity—there is some scriptural basis. When the scribes questioned Jesus' ability to forgive sins, He said to them, "For whether is easier, to say, Thy sins be forgiven thee; or to say, Arise, and walk? But that ye may know that the Son of Man hath power on earth to forgive sins [a prerogative of Deity alone], (then he saith to the sick of the palsy,) Arise, take up thy bed, and go unto thine house" (Mt. 9:5–6). One other incident suggests this same basic thought.

> Now when John had heard in prison the works of Christ, he sent two of his disciples, And said unto him, Art thou he that should come, or do we look for another? Jesus answered and said unto them, Go shew John again those things which ye do hear and see: The blind receive their sight, and the lame walk, the lepers are cleansed, and the deaf hear, the dead are raised up, and the poor have the gospel preached to them.
> —MATTHEW 11:2–5

However, it seems that this is not the only, or even the most important, reason why Jesus healed the sick. The fact is that all the miracles Jesus performed convinced only a few that He was their Messiah, the Son of God. Multitudes cried out while He was hanging on the cross, "If he be the King of Israel, let him now come down from the cross, and we will believe him…for he said, I am the Son of God" (Mt. 27:42–43).

There is very sincere doubt regarding the third reason—to initiate the preaching of the gospel. Some have added the thought that the miracles were used for this purpose until the New Testament was written, and now these are no longer necessary. This latter idea is without scriptural foundation, a purely gratuitous thought. It is true that the performance of great miracles did draw multitudes to Jesus, but it is questionable that He did these mighty works principally to draw crowds. In fact, on more than one occasion, He commanded the healed person to tell no one about it (Mt. 8:4; 12:15–16; Mk. 7:36; 8:26; Lk. 8:56). On some occasions He led the needy out of the town, where the populace would have been, before He healed him (Mk. 7:33; 8:23).

A close study of Christ's miracles of healing shows that in the majority of these, a reason is given why they were performed. These may be grouped in five or six classifications. We shall not presume to declare all that was in the Lord's mind, but will confine ourselves to what is plainly stated in the record.

A. Because of the promises of His Word

"And [He] healed all that were sick: That it might be fulfilled which was spoken by Esaias the prophet, saying, Himself took our infirmities, and bare our sicknesses" (Mt. 8:16–17).

B. In order to reveal His will

"And he entered again into the synagogue; and there was a man there which had a withered hand. And they watched him, whether he would heal him on the sabbath day; that they might accuse him. And he saith unto the man which had the withered hand, Stand forth....And when he had looked round about on them with anger, being grieved for the hardness of their hearts, he saith unto the man, Stretch forth thine hand. And he stretched it out: and his hand was restored whole as the other" (Mk. 3:1–3, 5). (See also Luke 14:1–6.)

C. To manifest the works of God

"Jesus answered, Neither hath this man sinned, nor his parents: but that the works of God should be manifest in him" (Jn. 9:3). "Now a certain man was sick, named Lazarus, of Bethany....When Jesus heard that, he said, This sickness is not unto death, but for the glory of God, that the Son of God might be glorified thereby" (Jn. 11:1, 4).

D. Because of compassion

On at least six occasions we are told that Jesus healed because He had compassion on those who were afflicted. This was true of vast multitudes (Mt. 9:35–36; 14:14); of two blind men (Mt. 20:34); a leper (Mk. 1:41); the maniac of Gadara (Mk.

5:19); and the widow of Nain whose son Jesus raised from the dead (Lk. 7:13). F. F. Bosworth has pointed out:

> Modern theology magnifies the power of God more than it magnifies His compassion.... But the Bible reverses this, and magnifies His willingness to use His power more than it does the power itself. In no place does the Bible say that "God is power," but it does say, that "God is love." It is not faith in God's power that secures His blessings, but faith in His love and in His will.[22]

> It is not what God can do, but what we know He yearns to do, that inspires faith.[23]

> Hundreds needing healing have come or written to us, saying, concerning their need of deliverance, "the Lord is able;" but their teaching, as well as their lack of teaching, have kept them from knowing that the Lord is willing. How much faith does it take to say "the Lord is able?" The devil knows God is able, and he knows He is willing; but he has kept the people from knowing this latter fact.[24]

E. Because of faith not only in His ability, but also His willingness

1. *Sometimes the faith of others, rather than the sick person*

a) The centurion's servant—Mt. 8:5–13

b) The nobleman's son—Jn. 4:46–53

c) The four who brought the palsied man—Mk. 2:1–12

d) The Syrophoenician woman's daughter—Mt. 15:21–28

Many other cases could be cited: Mt. 9:32–33; 12:22–23; Mk. 5:35–43; 7:32; 8:22–26; and Jn. 5:1–15.

2. *Sometimes the faith of those who needed the healing*

a) The woman with the issue of blood—Mk. 5:25–34. "For she said, If I may touch but his clothes, I shall be whole" (v. 28). She had no Scripture to guide her in this. The idea started within her own heart. The healing came entirely in response to her own faith. Jesus said, "Thy faith hath made thee whole."

b) Two blind men—Mt. 9:27–31. "Jesus saith unto them, Believe ye that I am able to do this? They said unto him, Yea, Lord. Then touched he their eyes, saying, According to your faith be it unto you" (vv. 28–29).

---

22 Bosworth, 63–64.

23 Bosworth, 62.

24 Ibid., 64.

c) A leper—Mt. 8:2–4.

d) Ten lepers—Lk. 17:11–19.

In the following two cases there was a combination of the faith of those who came and the compassion of Jesus: a leper (Mk. 1:40–45) and two blind men (Mt. 20:29–34).

In these cases where the reason for the healing is plainly stated, the vast majority were healed either because of definite, positive faith or because of the compassion of the Lord. There is not a word in the Bible to indicate that the Lord's compassion has ever lessened or that God has ever ceased to respond to the faith of those who come.

In addition to the cases listed under the above six reasons for healing, the following five incidents are recorded. In these, no reason is stated. Perhaps we are to conclude that they were simply the result of the sovereign will of Christ to overcome the work of the devil: Mt. 8:14–15; 8:28–34; Mk. 1:23–27; Lk. 7:11–16; and 13:10–13.

IX. WHY CHRISTIANS SHOULD SEEK DIVINE HEALING

A. Because it is a solemn command

When God has expressly declared that He is the healer of His people, both in His Word and in living example, are they at liberty to treat this ministry of His with complacent indifference? Fine Christian people are often heard to say, "Yes, I think it is a beautiful truth. It must be delightful to live such a life of momentary dependence upon God. But then, you know, few have such faith." It is no advantage to ourselves, nor any glory to God, to say that others can have what we do not venture to possess. This is dishonoring to God—He is no respecter of persons. If He did, it would be a sin (Jas. 2:9), and God does not sin. We have a solemn responsibility to God to receive all that He can and will do for us.

God has declared Himself as the healer of His people (Ex. 15:26, 23:25; Dt. 30:20; Ps. 103:3). Shall we obey and trust Him or not? Some may use other means and get healing, but is this God's plan for us? Some ask God to bless the means. If we have faith for that, why not for a real healing? It is not being said that God does not sometimes bless means, but such believers are not standing on covenant ground. They are simply taking their place with the rest of the world.

The point that must be settled is, what does God want His children to do? Are they free to choose? Will our Father be as pleased with us if we fall short of His command as if we fulfill it?[25]

---

25 The above thoughts have been taken from Mackenzie, Chapter 5.

B. Because of the spiritual blessing it will bring

Let it not be forgotten that Satan is the source of disease, and that sickness is not simply a physical condition, but the reflection of a spiritual condition. Sin caused sickness; Satan caused sin. Then we must seek a means of deliverance that will not only deal with the physical manifestation but with the spiritual condition and with the enemy who has caused it.

Whenever a Christian receives healing from the supernatural touch of God, there is always a glorious spiritual blessing that accompanies it. This proves that there is a spiritual condition behind the disease. James says, "And the prayer of faith shall save the sick, and the Lord shall raise him up; and if he have committed sins, they shall be forgiven him" (Jas. 5:15). Here is the spiritual result.

Of course, if merely getting well of our sickness is the thing for which we are striving, then any device is legitimate. But those who seek to dwell deep in God see a deeper meaning to the afflictions of the flesh. They seek to learn spiritual victory through their sufferings and the defeat of the enemy.

Jesus learned obedience by the things which He suffered: "Though he were a Son, yet learned he obedience by the things which he suffered" (Heb. 5:8); "For it became him...to make the captain of their salvation perfect through sufferings" (Heb. 2:10).

Realizing, then, the spiritual nature of disease; that Satan is behind it; and that God wants to teach His children something and accomplish a spiritual result in them, believers must look to God for the victory. They will learn nothing spiritual by the use of means—not even by asking God to bless the means.

C. Because it is glorifying to God

Some have taught that there are sicknesses which are for the glory of God. There is no scripture which states this concept. A very simple study will show that glory to God was brought, not while the persons were sick, but when they were healed. See the following: the palsied man let down through the roof (Mt. 9:8), the multitudes (Mt. 15:31), the raising of the widow's son at Nain (Lk. 7:16), the woman bowed over for eighteen years (Lk. 13:13), and the grateful leper (Lk. 17:15–16). In regard to the sickness of Lazarus, where Jesus said, "This sickness is not unto death, but for the glory of God" (Jn. 11:4), it is quite plain that no one gave any glory to God until after Lazarus was raised from the tomb. Prior to this, the disciples were confused, Mary and Martha were full of sorrow, and the friends of the family were full of doubt. "And some of them said, Could not this man, which opened the eyes of the blind, have caused that even this man should not have died?" (Jn. 11:37). The glory came to God after Lazarus was raised from the dead. "Then many of the Jews which...had seen the things which Jesus did, believed on him" (Jn. 11:45). God wants to be glorified in our healing. Our service is richer, our testimony clearer, if we have experienced the touch of God upon our body. Healing magnifies the name of Jesus.

X. Methods of Administering Divine Healing

It has been noticed, in relation to other spiritual experiences, that God is a God of variety. His methods are not stereotyped by any means. This is true also in relation to the manner in which divine healing is administered. The following are six different ways in which people receive healing from the Lord.

A. Pray for yourself.

James 5:13 says, "Is any among you afflicted? let him pray." Apparently, it is scriptural to pray for yourself when afflicted.

B. Ask someone else to pray for you.

James 5:16 instructs, "Pray one for another, that ye may be healed." Any sincere Christian who believes can pray for another. No ministerial credentials nor special gifts of the Spirit are necessary.

C. Call for the elders of the church.

James 5:14–16 has often been called the New Testament healing covenant.

> Is any sick among you? let him call for the elders of the church; and let them pray over him, anointing him with oil in the name of the Lord: And the prayer of faith shall save the sick, and the Lord shall raise him up; and if he have committed sins, they shall be forgiven him. Confess your faults one to another, and pray one for another, that ye may be healed. The effectual fervent prayer of a righteous man availeth much.

This should be the regular procedure for those in fellowship with a local church. These verses clearly teach that God is no respecter of persons, but that all may be healed. The promise stipulates, "Is any sick among you?" There is no discrimination whatever. It is God's will to heal any and all who will call on Him. "The prayer of faith" would be that prayer offered by the elders. There is a responsibility resting upon them. The sick exercises his faith when he calls for the elders. The elders pray the prayer of faith. Some have gone so far as to say that the elders were supposed to massage the sick person with oil, and this was the cause of his recovery. There certainly is no oil known to medical science which can guarantee healing, regardless of what the affliction is. The text does not say that the oil healed the sick. Some associate the oil with Hezekiah's poultice of figs, as if it were a means of healing (2

Kgs. 20:7). It was the prayer of faith, and even then it says, "And the Lord shall raise him." We believe the oil is a symbol of the Holy Spirit, who quickens our mortal body (Rom. 8:11). It is amazing how people can have more faith in a little oil or in a bunch of figs than they do in the power of God!

D. By laying on of hands

"These signs shall follow them that believe; In my name…they shall lay hands on the sick, and they shall recover" (Mk. 16:17–18). It should be carefully noted here that no mention is made of anointing with oil or of praying for the sick. All that is said is that those who believe shall lay their hands on the sick in the name of Jesus. This is the method which Jesus used on a number of occasions. In the following Scriptures, Jesus is said to have touched the sick or laid His hand or hands upon them: Mt. 8:15; Mk. 6:5; 8:23, 25; Lk. 4:40; 5:13; and 13:13. Today, when the believing one lays his hands on the sick in the name of Jesus, it is as though the hands of Jesus were laid thereon.

E. Special miracles through handkerchiefs and aprons

"And God wrought special miracles by the hands of Paul: So that from his body were brought unto the sick handkerchiefs or aprons, and the diseases departed from them, and the evil spirits went out of them" (Acts 19:11–12). These were special miracles in that there were no scriptural instructions concerning them. Paul must have simply been guided by the Holy Spirit in this matter. Many Churches have followed a similar pattern and have given out small pieces of cloth over which prayer has been made, and sometimes they have been anointed with oil. Some most remarkable miracles have been reported from the use of this method. It is understood that the prayer cloth has no virtue in itself, but provides an act of faith by which one's attention is directed to the Lord, who is the Great Physician.

F. Spiritual gifts of healing

"For to one is given by the Spirit…the gifts of healing" (1 Cor. 12:8–9). "God hath set some in the Church…then gifts of healings" (1 Cor. 12:28). Inasmuch as this subject is covered thoroughly under the gifts of the Spirit, it will not be elaborated on here. Two things are of special interest. First, this is the only gift of the Spirit which is in the plural. Suggested reasons for this are given in the study of the gifts. Second, in the list of healings previously listed in this chapter that were wrought through the apostles and recorded in the book of Acts, it is of interest that in no case did the apostles pray for the sick to be healed. In several cases, there was prayer about the sick person, but the healing seemed to be administered by the power which had been given them for this ministry. They probably had the gifts of healing described in 1 Corinthians 12.

XI. Why Are Some Not Healed?

If the Lord is Jehovah our Physician and never changes, if healing is provided in the atonement of Jesus Christ, if sickness is the work of the devil and Jesus was manifested to destroy the works of the devil, if God is all-powerful, and if the Lord is full of compassion, why then are not all who are prayed for instantly healed of their diseases? We must conclude that the fault does not lie with God. It must be with man, either in the one prayed for or in those who pray. One should realize, however, that the healing of the body, as marvelous as that is, is not the most important thing that can happen to a person. Salvation and spiritual growth are greater than physical health, and there, no doubt, are times when the spiritual blessing must be given precedence over the physical. We thoroughly believe that God wants His children to enjoy both benefits to the full, but sometimes hindrances do come in the way. Why some are not immediately healed is explained by the following suggested reasons.

A. Some seek healing before salvation.

Divine healing is one of the covenant blessings from the Lord. It is for the children of the kingdom, the members of the family of God. As our heavenly Father, He has taken a solemn responsibility to provide for His own. This is not true concerning those who, because of their unbelief, are outside the family fold. This is not to say that God will not sometimes heal those who are unsaved. Experience has taught that this is so, but there is no promise which the unsaved can claim. God is very merciful, and he does cause "his sun to rise on the evil and on the good, and sendeth rain on the just and on the unjust" (Mt. 5:45). Still, the seeker cannot come with any degree of positive faith. Perhaps the Lord heals an unsaved person because He knows this will lead to his salvation. However, the rule would seem to be that one should accept Jesus Christ as his Savior and Lord and commit his life to the will of God before seeking healing for his body.

B. Some seek healing for wrong purposes.

The Lord does not heal simply that people may be more comfortable or that they may use their health in selfish, worldly pursuits. James says, "Ye ask, and receive not, because ye ask amiss, that ye may consume it upon your lusts" (Jas. 4:3). Healing should be for the glory of God and for His service.

C. Some look to the minister rather than to Christ.

While it is true that God uses human channels to bring to pass His marvelous works, it is important that the one seeking healing look beyond the channel to the Source and realize that no minister can heal anyone. Jesus alone is the Great Physician. While it is true that Peter said to the lame man at the temple gate, "Look on us" (Acts

3:4), in order to get his attention, he immediately directed the man's attention away from himself with the words, "Silver and gold have I none; but such as I have give I thee: In the name of Jesus Christ of Nazareth rise up and walk" (Acts 3:6).

D. Disobedience

As we have noted from Exodus 15:26, healing is conditioned on obedience to the Word and the will of God. If one has been disobedient regarding commitments made to the Lord or is resisting God's will in his life, it is doubtful if he can expect to be healed.

E. Because of some unconfessed sin

Healing is not a reward for personal holiness. It comes by the grace of God, as all other blessings purchased at the cross, but known sin in the believer's life will hinder faith and the reception of what the Lord has provided. "If I regard iniquity in my heart, the Lord will not hear me" (Ps. 66:18). "Confess your faults one to another, and pray one for another, that ye may be healed" (Jas. 5:16).

F. Because of unbelief

1. *In the one who prays.* "The prayer of faith shall save the sick" (Jas. 5:15). "These signs shall follow them that believe" (Mk. 16:17).

2. *In the one prayed for.* "He that cometh to God must believe that he is, and that he is a rewarder of them that diligently seek him" (Heb. 11:6).

G. Failure to stand in faith until the answer comes

"For ye have need of patience, that, after ye have done the will of God, ye might receive the promise" (Heb. 10:36). While those to whom Jesus and the early disciples ministered received healing virtually immediately, there seem to be times when there is a delay in the manifestation of the victory. Daniel experienced a dramatic delay when he sought the Lord for twenty-one days. After this time, the word of the Lord came to him:

> Fear not, Daniel: for from the first day that thou didst set thine heart to understand, and to chasten thyself before thy God, thy words were heard, and I am come for thy words. But the prince of the kingdom of Persia withstood me one and twenty days: but, lo, Michael, one of the chief princes, came to help me; and I remained there with the kings of Persia. Now I am come.
> —DANIEL 10:12–14

Disease comes from Satan, and there will be times when he will seek to hinder the deliverance. We need to believe God's Word and stand in faith until the answer is manifested.

XII. How to Retain Divine Healing

Millions of God's people around the world are bearing testimony to a personal experience of the healing touch of the Lord Jesus upon their body in answer to believing prayer. The vast majority of these have found that this has been a permanent deliverance. Experience shows, however, that in some cases the symptoms have returned, and because these people did not know what to do, they lost the healing God had wrought. This has caused considerable bewilderment and not a little unbelief.

Does the Bible give any example of this? No, it does not, and we are thankful for this. If it did, some would say it is scriptural to lose your healing. If the Bible contained only one account of a person losing his healing, many would forget about the innumerable multitudes who were healed by Jesus and would hide behind the one who lost his, just as multitudes of cases of awful diseases are justified because of Paul's "thorn in the flesh." How readily the human heart grasps at an excuse for unbelief!

If symptoms of a physical infirmity from which a believer has been healed return, this does not mean that he was not healed in the first place. There is nothing wrong with what God does, but human beings are responsible individuals and can either cooperate with God's will or resist it. Retaining healing requires yielding to the will of God. It is all too easy to put the blame on God and say, "Maybe I was not really healed after all." If God is willing to heal, then it certainly is God's will that healing be retained. The answer to this problem lies not in God but in the individual soul.

There are two principal reasons why Christians lose their healing. The first is because of willful sin. Soon after healing the man at the Pool of Bethesda, Jesus found him and said to him, "Behold, thou are made whole: sin no more, lest a worse thing come unto thee" (Jn. 5:14). Apparently, some sin was responsible for the man's affliction, and Jesus warned that continued sin would result in even greater suffering. Willful sin could be depriving many today of gracious healings God has imparted. This does not mean that perfection of life is necessary for one to continue to enjoy the blessing of his healing, but it does mean that a Christian cannot live in known sin and keep the victory which God has given. We are not healed to live for the devil.

The second and more prevalent reason why some lose their healing is that faith wavers. Healing is received by faith, and if faith wavers, healing will waver. We retain what we receive from God in the same manner in which we receive it. Many times it is necessary to contend for our faith. There is an enemy who would accuse us and rob us of what God does in our behalf: "Whom resist steadfast in the faith" (1 Pt. 5:9). One of Satan's chief occupations is to rob people of their faith. "Then cometh the devil, and taketh away the word out of their hearts, lest they should believe" (Lk. 8:12). Once you lose your faith, your experience will soon follow. The following seven practical suggestions are given as to how to retain healing:

A. Keep in an atmosphere of faith.

Associate with those who believe. Faith will respond to the atmosphere with which it is surrounded. Listening to those who doubt and criticize will discourage faith. Every Christian needs the refreshment and spiritual strength that comes from the worship and study services of a good, spiritual Church.

B. Keep praising the Lord for what He has done.

One needs to realize that he has been the recipient of the marvelous grace of God. He did not deserve the healing he received. Let the glory and gratitude of God's goodness ever continue to thrill your heart. It is dangerous to think you are in any wise worthy.

C. Keep testifying of what God has done.

Keep telling others of God's gracious goodness to you. This must be done with a real sense of humility, without the thought that receiving healing from the Lord makes you better than others. Some have lost miraculous healings because they failed to testify of the deliverance God wrought for them.

D. Feed your faith on the Word of God.

Do not look to the one who prayed for you. God may have used him, but he is help-less apart from the Lord Jesus Christ. He was only the channel; God did the work. "Faith cometh by hearing, and hearing by the word of God" (Rom. 10:17). Note the importance of reading and studying the Word! Quote the promises of healing every day. "I am the LORD that healeth thee" (Ex. 15:26). "Himself took our infirmities and bare our sicknesses" (Mt. 8:17). "By whose stripes ye were healed" (1 Pt. 2:24). Believe what God says, not what you feel.

E. Contend in faith for your healing.

Sometimes the devil will tell a child of God that he is not saved. The best way to answer such a charge is to realize that the devil is a liar. "When he speaketh a lie, he speaketh of his own: for he is a liar, and the father of it" (Jn. 8:44). Tell him that God says, "Believe on the Lord Jesus Christ, and thou shalt be saved" (Acts 16:31). Tell him, "I believe; therefore, I am saved." Quote Romans 10:9, which says, "If thou shalt confess with thy mouth the Lord Jesus, and shalt believe in thine heart that God hath raised him from the dead, thou shalt be saved." Tell the enemy, "I believe in my heart and confess Jesus as Lord, so I am now saved." No one objects to this method of silencing the doubts that Satan would put in the believer's heart with regard to his salvation. Why not deal with the symptoms of doubt regarding healing in the same manner? If you want to know if you are saved, you look to the Word, not to yourself and your feelings in the matter. If you want to know if you are healed, look to what God says about it in His Word. Do not hesitate to take a firm stand on God's unfailing promises.

F. Walk in obedience to God's will—His Word.

We are saved to serve and obey the Lord. We are healed to serve and obey the Lord. God's will is revealed in His Word. Faith, along with all the blessings it brings, flourishes in the pathway of obedience.

G. Start, and continue, service to the Lord.

Do not be selfish with what God has given. Use the health and strength He has imparted to you in His work. Find a place of service in His Church and be faithful to it. Faithfully bring your tithe into His storehouse. Bring others to the Lord. There are multitudes who need God's saving and healing power. God has healed you by imparting His life to you. Live wholly for God and enjoy the fullness of what He has done for you.

XIII. Divine Life for the Body

The closer we draw to the Lord and the more our faith reaches out to claim all the promises of God, the more clearly we see that Christ Jesus provided for us a complete salvation, not only to die by, but to live by. It is a salvation that embraces the entire man—spirit, soul, and body. "For in him dwelleth all the fullness of the Godhead bodily. And ye are complete in him" (Col. 2:9–10). Jesus said, "I am come that they might have life, and that they might have it more abundantly" (Jn. 10:10). This life that He has provided includes His life for our bodies. Aimee Semple McPherson once wrote, "Divine healing…is not performing a ceremony, it is not wringing a petition from the heavens by the logic of faith and the force of your will, but it is the inbreathing of the life of God. It is the living touch which none can understand except those whose senses are exercised to know the realities of the world unseen."[26]

---

26 Aimee Semple McPherson, from the author's notes.

Divine healing is divine life in the physical body. It is part of that life that is in Christ. Paul testified to Christ's life in him in his letter to the Galatians, saying, "I am crucified with Christ: nevertheless I live; yet not I, but Christ liveth in me: and the life which I now live in the flesh I live by the faith of the Son of God, who loved me, and gave himself for me" (Gal. 2:20). Moses, of old, testified to this experience: "That thou mayest love the LORD thy God, and that thou mayest obey his voice, and that thou mayest cleave unto him: for he is thy life, and the length of thy days: that thou mayest dwell in the land which the LORD sware unto thy fathers, to Abraham, to Isaac, and to Jacob, to give them" (Dt. 30:20).

Here is a passage that is most explicit concerning the life of Christ in the mortal body: "Always bearing about in the body the dying of the Lord Jesus, that the life also of Jesus might be made manifest in our body. For we which live are alway delivered unto death for Jesus' sake, that the life also of Jesus might be made manifest in our mortal flesh" (2 Cor. 4:10–11). This does not only mean spiritual life in our unseen spirit, but His life in our very flesh, that is, the mortal part of us—the physical body. This is blessed identification with Christ to the effect that the mortal body is bene-fited thereby. Paul is not talking about a new kind of living, but a new kind of life. "For we are members of his body, of his flesh, and of his bones" (Eph. 5:30). "Know ye not that your bodies are the members of Christ?" (1 Cor. 6:15). It is His life—the life of the Head—that flows through the body: "He would grant you…to be strength-ened with might by his Spirit in the inner man….And…that ye might be filled with all the fulness of God" (Eph. 3:16, 19). Triumphant faith will not allow this infilling of life to be limited to spiritual needs alone. Think of the power of the fact "that your body is the temple of the Holy Ghost which is in you" (1 Cor. 6:19). Some people are not content to live in a dirty, broken-down house. They immediately clean it up and strengthen its structure. When the Holy Spirit comes in, if we will yield to Him, He will cleanse and heal the temple of the Christian's body.

Kenneth MacKenzie describes the relationship of God's life and Spirit and the body:

> Divine Healing is just Divine Life. It is the union of our members with the very body of Christ, and the inflowing life of Christ in our living members. It is as real as His risen and glorified body.
>
> It is as reasonable as the fact that He was raised from the dead and is a living man with a true body and a rational soul today at God's right hand. That living Christ belongs to us in all His attributes and power. We are members of His body, of His flesh, and His bones. If we can only believe it, we may live upon the very life of the Son of God.[27]

---

27 Mackenzie, 56–57.

No longer are we in bondage to the old sentiment that the body is a miserable tenement in which we endure our confinement until at last we are released. But it becomes the scene of the sanctifying inworking of the Holy Spirit, which, pressing into every niche of our being, permeates the whole with His Holy energy, and insures the possession and experience of Christ's very life.[28]

XIV. Answers to Objections

In this chapter, most of the objections to the doctrine of divine healing have been anticipated and have been answered in substance, but because of rather widespread opposition to the doctrine of divine healing by traditional teachers, there remains a need for answers to their common objections.

It is not that the objections are formidable, but that the Foursquare ministry needs to be able to give a ready answer to every objector without hesitation or confusion. Not only must the teacher of healing be able to meet the objectors themselves, but he must be able to remove the objections from the minds of sick people who have been taught against divine healing.

The arguments, however, should not be presented unless there are real objectors present or there are doubts in the minds of people. It is far better to teach healing in a positive manner, dealing with the scriptural promises and teachings, than to teach it in a controversial manner.

The objections take many forms, but they may all be covered under twelve headings. Some of the twelve objections may overlap, but there is a real sense in which each differs and requires a different answer or explanation.

A. The day of miracles has passed.

The above conclusion has come to be universally accepted. In fact, many believe that the Bible teaches the idea of an age of miracles. One risks his reputation for sanity in many quarters by even suggesting the possibility of a modern miracle. Yet in an age when science is performing virtual miracles, it is strange that those who believe in God should doubt that the omnipotent One can and does at times perform works that are above the usual working of natural law.

There are two classes of people who object to miracles: the *rationalist*, who does not believe that miracles have ever taken place and who believes that God has always limited His works to natural laws of the universe that are known by man; and the *traditionalist*, who believes that miracles were confined in an age or dispensation of miracles, after which God would work only by natural laws. The great trouble

---

28 Ibid., 59–60.

with both of these classes is that they have made natural law too narrow. They have confined law within the narrow bounds of a definition made by modern natural scientists who have not investigated outside the laboratory. There are laws, such as the law of faith, which the natural scientist has not investigated, yet remain sure and uniform as any so-called natural laws. Further, they are amply proved by Church history. It is a fault of many natural scientists to admit as evidence only what will prove their presuppositions.

If the testimonies of miracles in Church history are discarded, then the reliability of all history is in question and one must believe only what he himself has seen.

The philosophy of the rationalist can be disproved by proving just one miracle. There is one miracle which has as much weight of evidence as any historical event and which certainly cannot be disproved—the resurrection of Jesus Christ. When Jesus died on the cross, the disciples were completely disheartened. The women went out to embalm His body as a last respect to the memory of His remarkable life. The men went back to their trades with their hopes blasted. There never would have been a Christian religion without a resurrection. Moreover, the disciples repeatedly testified unequivocally to the resurrection of Christ in the very place where the events of the Lord's death and resurrection took place. If the testimonies were not true, the Jewish leaders could easily have proved their contentions to be false. Then, too, the disciples had nothing to gain by preaching the Resurrection, unless they knew it to be true. Rather, they had everything to lose. The Gospel writers were honest, intelligent men who were willing to die for their resurrection doctrine. Therefore they were, beyond question, sincere. Now there was no possibility of their being mistaken in what they saw, because Christ appeared to many on several occasions and they are in agreement about what transpired (Acts 1:1–3). There is no historical event more firmly founded on evidence, none more obviously real, than Christ's resurrection, which was the miracle of miracles. Whoever denies this miracle must be prepared to doubt all history.

Now, if there has been one miracle, there can be thousands of miracles with equal probability. If Jesus rose from the dead, why should it be improbable that the same power would quicken and heal the sick bodies of God's children (Rom. 8:11)?

To the traditionalist, we answer that there is no such scriptural distinction as an age of miracles. The Bible recognizes seven dispensations, or ages, which are as follows: innocence (Gn. 1:28), conscience (Gn. 3:23), human government (Gn. 8:20), promise (Gn. 12:1), law (Ex. 19:8), grace (Jn. 1:17), and kingdom (Eph. 1:10). In every one of these dispensations, there are recorded events—miracles—which would be considered contrary to the working of natural law. Why should God consider it expedient to permit miracles in each dispensation except the present one? Where is the statement in the Bible that miracles would cease to be performed? Does not the

Bible, on the contrary, represent God and Christ as being eternally the same (Mal. 3:6; Heb. 13:8; Jas. 1:17; Ps. 107:27)?

Beyond question, healing is in the Atonement (see Section VII), and certainly the benefits of the Atonement extend throughout the present age of grace.

One of the strongest arguments in favor of the continuance of miracles is that they did in fact continue, according to some of the most revered saints and writers of Church history. (See Section VI.) Does not the statement of Luke in Acts 1:1–3 strongly infer that the works of Jesus were to continue under the operation of the Holy Spirit? He refers to the Gospel of Luke as the book relating the things which Jesus began to do and teach. (Compare also Jn. 14:12 and Mk. 16:17.)

If the age of miracles is past, then the same objectors would have to conclude that the possibility of conversion no longer exists, because conversion is as miraculous and supernatural as divine healing.

Some contend that healing was only a sign permitted in the first century to attest to the supernatural character of Christianity and that now healing is no longer necessary because the truths of Christianity have been confirmed. While some kinds of special miracles have been used as signs, it is clearly revealed that Jesus healed not only as a sign, but because He had compassion upon the people in their painful state (Mk. 1:41; Mt. 9:35–38; 14:14; and 20:34). Who can say that Jesus is less compassionate today? Then, too, does not each new century, or even generation, have its doubters and skeptics who oppose Christianity? Does not each generation need signs also to attest the preaching of a religion which claims to be supernatural in its origin and results? Every age is an age of miracles for those who have faith in God. Faith says "all things are possible" (Mt. 19:26).

B. Why are many Christians not healed?

Victorious living is for all Christians, but all do not live victoriously. Salvation is in the Atonement, but not all are saved. The fruit of the Spirit is intended for every Christian life, but many are lacking much in fruit-bearing. Every promise of God's Word is accompanied with a provision, and the provision must be met by the seeker before the blessing comes. In healing, the provision is faith. Where the seeker does not have faith for healing, the healing is not, as a rule, forthcoming.

There are other reasons also, besides lack of faith, for failure to receive healing. One of these is wrong teaching. There are many patient, pious Christians in traditional churches who are sick and who do not receive healing because they are taught by their pastors that divine healing is not for today or that it is of satanic origin. Naturally, these people accept their sickness as a necessary evil of earthly life and try to be patient until they can put off this earthly frame, but if many of these people were taught the great truth of vicarious healing, they would believe and receive bodily health. As the Word declares, "Ye have not, because ye ask not" (Jas. 4:2).

Moreover, some Christians are sick because they constantly disregard the laws of nature. One cannot expect to tempt God and have His favor. Those who live so as to unnecessarily imperil their bodily health suffer the consequences and are not likely to recover until they cease living wrongly. Such cannot protest that healing does not work, for healing is promised to those who live in the will of God (Jn. 5:14).

Again, medical science has been so exalted that most persons think of it as the sole source of healing benefit. Medical science has indeed made great advances and is a very worthy and needful profession, but it is not the sole source of healing benefit. If all Christians would recognize God as a source of healing, there would be more faith and consequently less sickness among believers.

It is a mistake to judge the teaching of God's Word by the degree of success attained in any age. If every Christian were sick, it would not change the plain teaching of God's Word. It would indicate only that men were failing to meet God's requirements. But all Christians are not sick! On the contrary, there are thousands who are, by faith, availing themselves of the Atonement's provisions and receiving divine healing from the throne of grace.

C. Why not also believe in raising the dead and other miracles promised in Mark 16?

Let it be noted, first of all, that raising the dead is not mentioned in the Great Commission of Mark 16. It is true that the twelve disciples, when sent on a preaching tour to announce the kingdom, were commanded to raise the dead (Mt. 10:8), but this was not the permanent commission given to the Church. The Church is not commanded to raise the dead, neither is such a promise given to the Church. The Church is, however, instructed to lay hands on the sick, and it is promised that the sick will recover (Mk. 16:18; Jas. 5:14–16). There is a difference between special miracles and covenant miracles. Special miracles were performed as a sign to meet special circumstances, such as turning water to wine, walking on the sea, calming the storm, and multiplying the loaves and fishes. These special miracles are not promised to the Church. Miracles such as divine healing, regeneration, the Spirit baptism, and the provision of needs, however, are promised and may be claimed by God's people on the strength of the promises. Special miracles are for special times and circumstances, but covenant miracles are for the whole age of grace. Now this does not mean that special miracles will never occur in this day. It means only that they cannot be claimed on the strength of any promise. Special circumstances in any age may give rise to special miracles, and there have been many of such recorded in Church history. Faith is powerful and may bring Providence to man's aid in many ways not specifically promised. There are many verified cases of the dead being raised in modern times because of a powerful faith that would not surrender to death.

Now regarding taking up serpents and drinking poisons, these are included in the Great Commission and are to be expected by the Church whenever circumstances warrant. Missionaries constantly witness to the working of these promises. Many such are constantly facing the peril of poisonous water, but God gives protection so that they are not harmed. Of course, it would be tempting God to deliberately drink poison or handle poisonous reptiles when there existed no purpose or need for so doing. Such would not be faith, but presumption or intrepidity. Regarding the speaking with new tongues, this phenomenon is also part of the Great Commission, and it is promised to the Church in several places, including 1 Corinthians 12:10, 30; Acts 2:4; 10:46; 19:6; and Isaiah 28:11.

It is plain that the above objection is no objection at all, because believers in the Foursquare doctrine do believe in all the miracles mentioned. They accept them as blessings for the Church by promise (except raising the dead), and they do not consider it an incredible thing that God should raise the dead, if circumstances warranted.

D. Now that medical science is perfected, God expects His people to use medicine for healing.

The objection stated above is in error for three reasons:

- *There was a developed medical science in Bible times.* As early as 400 B.C. there was a scientific practice of healing. Hippocrates (460–370 B.C.), the father of medicine, developed the science of medicine to a relatively high state. Some of his technique is still practiced today. Greece, Egypt, and Rome had many competent practitioners in Jesus' time. The Jews who adhered to the health regulations of the law of Moses lived under hygienic conditions not greatly excelled today, because the law of Moses was given of God in order to preserve a holy nation for the purpose of carrying out His plan of redemption.
- *Medical science today is not able to cure all sickness.* The medical science of today is still in an experimental stage and is unable to cure scores of diseases with which thousands are afflicted. There are actually several common diseases and afflictions which are at present on the increase, notwithstanding all the medical activity. If Jesus healed in His day because medicine was impotent in comparison to the healing power of God, He will heal yet today, because medicine is still impotent in so many kinds of sickness.
- *Divine healing has nothing to do with the competence or incompetence of a natural healing science.* Divine healing is principally a spiritual blessing provided by the Atonement, not merely a matter of physical cure. If medical science could cure every sick person on Earth, it

would not make divine healing void. When medicine heals the body, the physician receives the credit, but when one is healed by the power of a personal, loving heavenly Father, the glory goes to God. That person healed is blessed spiritually and strengthened in faith.

One might likewise reason that sociology is now in a more advanced state and that as a consequence one does not now need divine regeneration. The fact is that some extreme liberals do reason in this manner, but the Atonement alone can satisfy the sin question for God. Reformation does nothing about past sin, nor does it establish a covenant fellowship between God and man. Divine healing is a part of the Atonement, the physical benefit of the new birth, and both benefits of the work of Calvary are intended as permanent for the entire age of grace. Neither salvation nor healing are conditioned upon the improvement of natural sciences. Natural sciences are good and will always be needed, but God's best way is the way of faith in matters of which the Scriptures make promise.

E. If divine healing always worked, no Christian would ever die.

It is not claimed by exponents of divine healing that death can be perpetually averted, nor was such a claim made by the apostles, who certainly practiced divine healing with miraculous results. It is claimed only that the faithful believer may have divine health within the normal life span. Such a full life is described in Job 5:26. The same Bible that teaches divine healing also sets a limit on the length of man's life. (Ps. 90:10; Heb. 9:27). Therefore, healing is provided for man, but only within the allotted lifespan. It is not meant, however, that man, though being a mortal body, should live in pain and suffering, nor that he should die by an affliction. Faith will secure for the believer a life of divine health and vigor, and when death comes at the appointed time, it can be without great suffering or disease. Of course, imperfect faith and disobedience frequently hinder this ideal physical state, but this provision is valid, notwithstanding, and is actually appropriated by many believers.

Even if perpetual life could be secured by divine healing, it would not be desirable in this present body, even in its most healthy state. The mortal body of Jesus was subject to natural fatigue, weariness, and other penalties of mortality. Divine health is a marvelous blessing for this present sojourn, but the redeemed believer's aim is fixed on the heavenly city, the immortal life in a glorified eternal body.

F. There are cases of failure in the New Testament.

Much is made of Paul's thorn in the flesh by opponents of divine healing. The fact is that no one knows the exact character of his thorn, so it cannot be proved that the thorn was sickness. Whatever the thorn was, Paul was delivered from it (Gal.

4:13–15; 2 Cor. 1:8–10). If the difficulty mentioned by Paul in Galatians 4:13–16 was sickness, it was not a permanent sickness, because he had it only "at first."

That Paul had no permanent serious affliction is quite easily proved by two facts: First, Paul's strenuous life of travel and labor could not have been carried on, had he been seriously afflicted. When it is considered that Paul constantly traveled under trying conditions; organized Churches; suffered stonings, floggings, shipwrecks, and imprisonments; sustained himself by working with his own hands; and that he was always joyful and confident, it would not appear likely that he was suffering with a serious sickness. Second, Paul mentioned all his difficulties in 2 Corinthians 11:23–33, and not once does he mention a disease. The word translated "painfulness" in verse 27 means literally (in the Greek) "travail." If Paul had had a serious sickness, he would have mentioned it in this list.

Some point to Galatians 4:15 as proof that Paul had an eye disease. However the words, "Ye would have plucked out your eyes and have given them to me," are a figure of speech, such as, "You would have given me your right arm." Furthermore, the theory of oriental eye disease is not consistent with Paul's great activity. There is another passage in which Paul refers to his thorn as a buffeting (2 Cor. 12:7). A buffeting infers repeated blows, not a permanent state of sickness.

Regarding Epaphroditus, his case supports divine healing, rather than raising an objection. Epaphroditus was sick indeed, but God healed him (Phil. 2:25–27). It is not claimed that believers will never be sick under any circumstances. When believers overtax their bodies or disobey the laws of nature, they are likely to be sick, but when they turn to the Lord for healing, they receive it. Epaphroditus became sick as the result of a very strenuous journey from Philippi to Rome, but God delivered him, a fact which supports the healing doctrine.

The reference to the case of Trophimus is so brief that little can be gathered from it. Paul did, it is true, leave Trophimus sick (2 Tm. 4:20), but nothing is known about the faith of this obscure worker. Who can say that he was not healed soon after, for healing is not always instantaneous. Certainly such a brief reference is not sufficient to overthrow the great fund of Scripture in support of divine healing. Finally, the interpretation of the Scripture rests upon its promises and teachings and not upon anything which happened to persons, for no matter how sure and simple are God's provisions for man's needs, there will always be failures on man's part.

G. Divine healing is taught only by false cults.

This statement is far from being true. Wesley, Luther, and Zinzendorf taught and practiced divine healing. They were the leaders of the Methodist, Lutheran, and Moravian churches, and certainly none would doubt that these are orthodox churches. Those who teach healing today, along with the saving power of the blood of Jesus and the deity of Christ, are no more unorthodox than were the above-mentioned church leaders when they taught divine healing.

It is true that several false cults teach a kind of healing, but their doctrines of healing are far from being similar to the orthodox, biblical doctrine. The fact is that Satan has taken advantage of the Church's failure to preach the whole gospel by advancing healing cults that deny the efficacy of the blood and the deity of Christ. The result is that many sick people are lured into false cults when their bodily healing should have been met within the true Church. That false healing cults are able to survive and steadily grow is proof that they offer something greatly desired by multitudes of people. Jesus always had compassion on the multitudes and healed their sick, and Jesus is the same today and forever. It is a great tragedy that the true Church should send the suffering away empty handed with a shallow excuse that God's power no longer works.

Furthermore, the healing taught by most of the false cults is not divine healing, but mind-over-matter, or psychic, healing. Physicians have admitted that mental healing is truly scientific in many respects, but even so, it is only natural healing. When one is healed by Christian Science, God is not credited with the recovery. The healing cults recognize God as only a principle and not a person. When one is healed by a principle, that is natural, not divine, healing. The teachers of orthodox divine healing believe that the sick are healed by the direct power of a personal God who has compassion upon suffering mankind. In cult healing, the existence of sin and sickness is denied, but in orthodox healing, sin and suffering are admitted to be real. However, Christ, the personal Savior of the world, is recognized as the Victor over every foe of man.

Finally, Satan has frequently counterfeited God's true blessings. The fact that some false cults imitate divine healing is not a sign that all healing is false. On the contrary, it is some indication that there is a true divine healing.

H. Divine healing puts more emphasis upon the body than upon the soul.

If this objection is to be admitted, then the same objection must be made of the ministry of Jesus, because the greater part of His ministry was devoted to healing the sick. Likewise, it would necessitate objection to the ministry of the apostles, for the book of Acts records healing miracles in all the revivals (Acts 8:5–8; 9:36–42; 14:6–10; 16:16–18; 19:11–12; 28:7–9). Now, if the Lord Jesus and the disciples could preach and practice divine healing without fear of over-emphasizing bodily needs, then the same may be done at any time, provided the procedure is kept scriptural and the teaching is properly balanced. Of course, it is possible to give too much emphasis to any doctrine, but this is not necessarily so. Salvation for the soul and healing for the body are inseparable benefits of Christ's atoning work. They should be preached together as aspects of the same message (Is. 53:4–5; 1 Pt. 2:24). To omit the healing message is to preach a partial gospel. The good news of salvation also concerns the mortal body, which has been redeemed by a price (1 Cor. 6:19–20).

It is a shame to suppose that divine healing imparts only a physical blessing. The benefit received from a healing touch is as much spiritual as it is physical. In divine healing, the recipient is made to feel the nearness and providential care of a personal Savior and Lord. His faith is strengthened, and he is made doubly aware of the great love of God. It is true that faith mainly concerns the unseen, but while man is in a temporal world, he needs and benefits from God's material provision of blessing. Many who regularly pray for financial blessing or providential care and protection scorn divine healing, but there certainly is no difference in principle between one kind of benefit or the other. If the believer is not to pray for healing because it over-emphasizes the material, then he must never pray for employment, money, food, clothing, protection, or any other material benefit. If man profits in sickness, he would profit in poverty or misery also. The early Christians practiced poverty far more than they suffered affliction of body.

Finally, let it be cautioned that healing ought never to be preached apart from redemption of the soul and other fundamental truths of the gospel. Healing is not a gospel of itself; it is one aspect of the gospel of Christ. Neither is the gospel complete which omits the healing message. In addition, it is wise to conduct healing instruction meetings before the sick are prayed for. This is in order that the proper relationship of healing to the gospel may be thoroughly understood and also in order that only those who are yielded to God and possess some faith are prayed for publicly. Further, it should always be made plain that no power for healing is possessed by the one who prays, but that it is God's power and mercy (Acts 3:12–13).

I. If God created herbs and drugs, does He not expect man to use them for healing?

It is true that God created all herbs and plants, but He did not thereby sanction every use to which man would put their extractions. God created the poppy, but He did not sanction every use to which opium would be put. God created the tobacco plant, but He did not intend that man should use the plant for drawing nicotine into his body. Tobacco nicotine does make a splendid insecticide for killing harmful insects, but it should not be used to kill human beings. Now while some herbs were, no doubt, created with a view to the therapeutic use for mankind as a whole, it does not follow that they are the only source of healing, nor that healing by drugs is the best source of healing. God is merciful to all humanity, saved and unsaved, just and unjust. He has provided mercy even for those who do not recognize Him as Lord, but cannot God provide a better and more direct healing for those who are in close fellowship with Him?

The Bible does command the use of oil in praying for the sick, also figs and wine in one case each, but none of these is recommended as a drug for healing. The Bible nowhere recommends drugs or physicians for the redeemed. On the island of Melita, Paul prayed for the father of Publius and many other sick people who were healed by God's power, yet Luke, who was a physician, was present with Paul. If God wanted the believer to call a physician, why did not Luke administer drugs to the people of the island (Acts 28:8–9)?

Oil is commanded for anointing in James 5:14–16, but it is clearly stated that it is the prayer of faith which saves the sick and the Lord who raises him up, not the oil. Furthermore, would God permit an inspired apostle to recommend oil for the healing of all sicknesses? Anyone knows that, while oil may perform certain minor benefits, it is certainly not a cure-all. It is not a panacea for all man's physical ills. The oil is to be used as a symbol only in praying for the sick. The anointing typifies the work of the Holy Spirit, who is the agent in healing. When a king or priest was inaugurated in Israel, he was anointed with oil, which did him no physical good but which was symbolic of the Spirit of God who was thereafter to direct his reign or ministry. The oil in healing indicates that the healing is performed by the Spirit of God and by not the elder who prays.

The account of Hezekiah's illness and healing is recorded in 2 Kings 20:1–11. In this account, it is clear that the poultice of figs was not the source of the healing. Hezekiah prayed and received assurance from God that he would be healed and would receive a fifteen-year extension on his life before the figs were applied. God witnessed to His promise by causing the sundial to go backward ten degrees. It is obvious that Hezekiah put his sole trust in the power of God, for if figs had had such a curative value, he would have trusted the figs at once. If figs are curative to the extent of being able to save life, why does not medical science of today exploit their power? Furthermore, the recommendation of this poultice was made by Isaiah and not the Lord. If God had inspired the recommendation, it was only an act of obedience, such as Naaman's dipping in the River Jordan or Jesus' anointing of the blind man's eyes with clay.

Paul recommended that Timothy drink wine in the place of water (1 Tm. 5:23). It is contended by some that the wine was prescribed as a remedy for Timothy's stomach trouble. One wonders if all the opponents of divine healing would recommend that all their members suffering with stomach ailments cease drinking water in favor of wine. If the water available were fit for drinking, it is certain that it would have been better for the stomach than wine. Nothing is better for health than the generous use of pure water, but it is likely that the water where Timothy resided was impure and harmful and was therefore doing harm to his health. The wine was only a substitute for water, where good water was not available. Had wine been intended as a medicine, it would have been prescribed in addition to water. The fact that water was forbidden proves that the local water was the source of his problem.

Physicians are frequently mentioned in the Bible, but certainly nothing is said of their replacing divine healing. Moses was educated in all the ways of the Egyptians, a people learned in the use of herbs, but not once does he prescribe any medicine for the Israelites. On the contrary, God promised him that obedience would assure the whole nation of divine health.

J. The miracles recorded in Matthew 8:16–17 completely fulfilled the prophecy of physical healing in Isaiah 53:4–5.

This objection is answered by two arguments:

- The words translated "took" and "bore" are used of both bodily healing and soul salvation, and used in the same sense. If Jesus' first healings completely fulfilled the prophecy that Christ would take our infirmities and bear our sicknesses, then the first conversions would completely fulfill the prophecy that Christ would "bear the sin of many" (Is. 53:11–12).
- The word *fulfilled*, as it is used in the Bible to mark fulfillments of Old Testament prophecy, does not infer in its use that the event marked is the complete fulfillment and that there will be no such similar events following. (See the discussion of this matter in Section VII.)

K. If healing is in the Atonement, Christians who are sick must conclude that they are sinners.

If some Christians are sick, it does not mean that they are necessarily sinners. They may be either ignorant of the healing blessing, lacking in faith at present, or careless about definitely asking God for healing. Salvation is in the Atonement, but that some do not receive salvation does not mean that Christ did not die for them. Men are not saved until they exert faith and call upon the Lord. Healing is provided by the Atonement, but it is received, like salvation, only by those who recognize the provisions and seek the blessing. Faith is the requisite for receiving healing, and some Christians are weak in active faith. We are saved by grace through faith, but we achieve many differing degrees of practical holiness and divine blessing, though perfect victory and blessing are provided for every saint by the Atonement.

There are many who are morally upright and spiritually devout but, because of the lean teaching which they receive, are unaware of the full provision of Calvary. When they are sick, they resort to medical remedies when divine healing is available for the asking, if they had known or cared to ask for it. No, sick Christians are not sinners any more than others in this present imperfect state; they are merely underprivileged by wrong teaching. As James said, "Ye have not, because ye ask not" (Jas. 4:2).

L. Failure by many to receive healing weakens the faith of the whole Church.

Hebrews 11:1 defines faith as follows: "Faith is the substance of things hoped for, the evidence of things not seen." Faith is not dependent upon sight nor circumstances. Faith believes, even when it cannot see. While faith is strengthened somewhat by seeing the working of God, faith will not be shipwrecked if it does not see. The fact overlooked in this objection is that faith always brings to pass what it desires. If the Church has faith, its faith will bring things to pass. Jesus never fails, and where prayer, accompanied by faith, is offered for the sick, there will be signs following. The Word of God assures that such will be so (Mk. 16:17). No one contends that everyone who is prayed for will be healed, but most believers must know that there will be some failure when there is a provision to be met—faith—by those who seek healing.

The opponents of divine healing are opponents because they have no faith in the supernatural power of God. Lack of faith in the supernatural is lack of faith in the very heart of Christianity, which is not a mere ethical society, social order, or fraternal brotherhood, but a supernatural religion vitalized by the Holy Spirit. Those who believe in healing understand it sufficiently to know that not all for whom prayer is offered will be healed, for accountable reasons. Those who do not believe in a supernatural Christianity have no vital faith to lose, although they may otherwise be very splendid and pious persons.

THE DOCTRINE OF THE CHURCH

Ecclesiology

Introduction

I. *Church*—Its Meanings
- **A.** *Kuriakos*
- **B.** *Ekklesia*

II. Uses of the Term *Church* in the New Testament
- **A.** The universal body of Christ
- **B.** The local church
- **C.** House churches
- **D.** The collective Church
- **E.** The churches acting in concert

III. Uses of the Term *Church* Not Found in the New Testament
- **A.** Not used of a building
- **B.** Not used for a denomination

IV. The Officers, Ministers, and Leaders of the Church
- **A.** Apostles
- **B.** Prophets
- **C.** Evangelists
- **D.** Pastors
- **E.** Teachers
- **F.** Elders, presbyters
- **G.** Bishops, overseers
- **H.** Deacons
- **I.** Ministers
- **J.** Leaders, rulers

V. The Mission of the Church
- **A.** Preaching and teaching
- **B.** Discipleship
- **C.** Fellowship
- **D.** Worship
- **E.** Missions and evangelism
- **F.** Maturity of the believer
- **G.** Ministry in the home
- **H.** Ministry to material needs

VI. The Ordinances of the Church (Sacraments)
    A. Water baptism
    B. The Lord's Supper

VII. The Church as the Body of Christ
    A. Vital relationship to the Head
    B. Unity of the body
    C. Importance of each member in the body
    D. Submission in the body
    E. The body of Christ and the local Church
    F. Body ministry

VIII. The Church and the Kingdom of God
    A. The meaning of the word *kingdom*
    B. Is the kingdom of God present or future?
    C. Is the kingdom inward and spiritual or outwardly visible?
    D. Are the Church and the kingdom of God identical?
    E. Is the kingdom of heaven different from the kingdom of God?

IX. Other Metaphors of the Church
    A. The Church as the Lord's family
    B. The Church as a fellowship of believers
    C. The Church as a team of athletes
    D. The Church as the Lord's army
    E. The Church as the Lord's flock
    F. The Church as the Lord's school
    G. The Church as a servant or steward
    H. The Church as a building
    I. The Church as a mystery
    J. The Church as the Lord's field
    K. The Church as a royal priesthood
    L. The Church as the bride of Christ
    M. The Church as the Lord's embassy
    N. The Church as the pillar and ground of truth
    O. The Church as the Lord's sanctuary
    P. The Church as pilgrims
    Q. The Church as the Way
    R. The Church as the Lord's inheritance
    S. The Church as the Lord's masterpiece
    T. The Church as the light of the world
    U. The Church as the salt of the earth
        1. *Salt preserves.*

CHAPTER EIGHT

The Doctrine of the Church

Ecclesiology

INTRODUCTION

ECCLESIOLOGY IS THE study of the Church in its nature, ordinances, ministry, mission, and government.

In recent times there has been a renewed interest in the study of the doctrine of the Church. Every age has had its particular doctrinal emphasis. Our age is no exception. Many contemporary theologians and Bible scholars are saying that we need to restudy the doctrine of the Church in order that we may understand what the Church is and what its mission is in today's world. Several contemporary movements, such as the ecumenical and the Charismatic movements, have contributed to a resurgence of interest in the New Testament pattern of the Church. A revival of the spirit of worship among Foursquare Gospel and other Pentecostal Churches has been accompanied by strong concern to better understand the life, ministry, and leadership of the New Testament Church.

Since the Church is the divinely constituted body through which the gospel is preached and believers are nurtured, the careful study and clear understanding of it are obviously important. The best place to begin such a study is with definitions of key terms.

I. *CHURCH—ITS MEANINGS*

A. *Kuriakos*

The English word *church* is derived from the Greek word *kuriakos*, which means "belonging to the Lord." This word which is never applied to the Church in the New Testament period, although it is found twice in the New Testament as an adjective applying to the Lord's Supper and to the Lord's day (1 Cor. 11:20; Rv. 1:10). In post-apostolic times, the Greeks used the term *kuriakos* to designate the church building. The evolution of the Greek *kuriakos* to the English word *church* can be seen in the Scottish term for a church, *kirk*. The only words in the New Testament used to designate a building as a place of worship are *temple* and *synagogue* (Acts 5:42; Jas. 2:2, RSV).

B. *Ekklesia*

In the English New Testament, the word *church* is used invariably to translate the Greek word *ekklesia* (Mt. 16:18; 18:17; Acts 2:47; 9:31; 13:1; 14:23; 15:22; 16:5; 20:17, 28; Rom. 16:4–5; 1 Cor. 12:28; Eph. 5:23–29; Col. 1:18; Rv. 1:4, 11). The word *ekklesia* means "an assembly of the people." The term is derived from two Greek words, *ek,* meaning "out from," and *kaleo,* which means "to call." Originally, "the ones called out" had reference to the legislative body of citizens of the Greek republic who were called from their communities to serve the country. When we refer to a session of the state assembly, we are using the word *assembly* in exactly the same way the Greeks used the term *ekklesia.*

By New Testament times, when Jesus employed the word *ekklesia* to designate the body He would build, the word borrowed meaning from at least two sources: the Jewish use of the word in the Greek Old Testament (Septuagint), where it referred to the congregation of Israel; and the Greek employment of the word to refer to any assembly of people, whether a constituted body or an unorganized mob. An example of the Jewish use is found in Acts 7:37–38: "This is that Moses...that was in the church in the wilderness with the angel which spake to him in the mount Sina, and with our fathers: who received the lively oracles to give unto us." The Jewish use of the word *ekklesia* usually translates the Hebrew word *qahal,* which was the Old Testament word for the congregation of Israel in the wilderness. An example of the Greek use of *ekklesia* is found in Acts 19: "Some therefore cried one thing, and some another: for the assembly [*ekklesia*] was confused; and the more part knew not wherefore they were come together" (v. 32); "But if ye inquire any thing concerning other matters, it shall be determined in a lawful assembly [official legislative body]" (Acts 19:39).

There is no doubt that Jesus chose the word translated "Church" because it had been used to designate God's people, but the word in the popular mind merely meant "assembly." Because the Hebrew word translated *ekklesia* was sometimes rendered "synagogue," there may have been a purpose in the choice of the first in order to avoid confusion of the Church with the synagogue of Israel. When Jesus said, "And upon this rock I will build my church" (Mt. 16:18), He placed emphasis not on the word *Church,* but on the word *my.* The Church is unique not because it is called a Church, but because it is the assembly of believers who belong to Jesus, who constitute His body.

II. USES OF THE TERM *CHURCH* IN THE NEW TESTAMENT

A. The universal body of Christ

The universal Church is composed of all genuine Christian believers of all ages, both on Earth and in paradise—the total body of Christ. The total universal Church will be assembled at the Marriage Supper of the Lamb (Rv. 19:6–9), which will follow the rapture of the Church. The following passages apply to the universal Church: Mt. 16:18; Eph. 3:10, 21; 5:23–32; and Col. 1:18, 24. Hebrews 12:23, which also refers to the universal Church, is especially poignant: "To the general assembly and church of the firstborn, which are written in heaven, and to God the Judge of all, and to the spirits of just men made perfect."

B. The local church

The local church is composed of Christian believers identified with a constituted body, worshiping in one locality (Rom. 16:1; Col. 4:16; Gal. 1:2, 22; Acts 14:23). The members of a local church constitute the Church even when they are not assembled, which fact can be seen in Acts 14: "And when they were come, and had gathered the church together, they rehearsed all that God had done with them" (v. 27). All genuine believers are members of the universal body of Christ; however, all faithful believers are to be identified with a local church where they assemble for worship, fellowship, and service with some regularity (Heb. 10:24–25). Christians cannot properly be believers in isolation, for they are not believers only; they are also disciples, brethren, and members of a body. The following statement is from the Foursquare *Declaration of Faith:*

> We believe that having accepted the Lord Jesus Christ as personal Savior and King, and having thus been born into the family and invisible body or church of the Lord, it is the sacred duty of the believer, whenever this lieth within his power, to identify himself with, and labor most earnestly for the up-building of God's kingdom with the visible church of Christ upon earth.[1]

C. House churches

In New Testament times there were no church buildings. Believers met for worship wherever facilities were made available to them. Often they met in homes of believers: "Aquila and Priscilla salute you much in the Lord, with the church that is in their house" (1 Cor. 16:19). When the church in a given community was very large, there were many house churches (1 Cor. 14:23). However, the church of that community was considered one, and they all came together as often as possible. In small communities, one house church may have accommodated the entire body (Col. 4:15). One reason why the churches usually had a plurality of elders was perhaps that there were several house churches within the total body in the given community. In Acts 20, the apostle Paul called together the elders of the church in Ephesus: "And from Miletus he sent to Ephesus, and called the elders of the church" (Acts 20:17). The church in

---

1 Aimee Semple McPherson, *Declaration of Faith* (International Church of the Foursquare Gospel, n.d.), 22.

Ephesus was one, but the large number of elders (pastors) suggests that the Church often met in homes because of the lack of large Church buildings. All of these house churches were, however, one church of Ephesus, as is indicated by verse 28 of the same chapter: "Take heed therefore unto yourselves, and to all the flock, over the which the Holy Ghost hath made you overseers, to feed the Church of God, which he hath purchased with his own blood." Every local Church was considered to be the physical manifestation of the universal Church in that community (Rom. 16:5, 23; 1 Cor. 16:19; Phlm. 1:2).

D. The collective Church

There are several New Testament passages in which reference is made to the visible Church on Earth as one Church: 1 Cor. 10:32; 15:9; Gal. 1:13; and Phil. 3:6. In Acts 9:31, where reference is made to the peace which the Church experienced after Saul's conversion, the Authorized Version reads *churches*, but in the Greek text, as well as in other versions, the word is singular: "So the *church* throughout all Judaea and Galilee and Samaria had peace, being edified; and, walking in the fear of the Lord and in the comfort of the Holy Spirit, was multiplied" (Acts 9:31, RV, emphasis added).

In several passages, the word *church* is used generically, that is, referring to the church generally (Mt. 18:17; 1 Tm. 3:15; 1 Cor. 12:28).

E. The churches acting in concert

There are those who contend that the local churches were autonomous, subject only to the local leadership which was selected by the vote of the congregation. There is no doubt that the local churches had much liberty. Certainly, they were not ruled rigidly by a central hierarchy, a fact demonstrated by the council on doctrine and practice recorded in Acts 15. However, that the churches acted in concert and followed apostolic leadership is made clear by a number of Scripture passages: Acts 14:23; Rom. 16:4; 1 Cor. 14:33; 16:19; 2 Cor. 11:28; and Ti. 1:5. Paul instructed local churches on doctrine, practice, and government. He sent greetings on behalf of groups of churches of an area, and he appointed elders over churches or instructed fellow-workers to appoint officers. Paul wrote to Titus ordering, "For this cause left I thee in Crete, that thou shouldest set in order the things that are wanting, and ordain elders in every city, as I had appointed thee" (Ti. 1:5).

III. Uses of the Term *Church* Not Found in the New Testament

A. Not used of a building

The Greek word *ekklesia*, which is translated "church," always has reference to people; it never has reference to a building. Today, one might say, "There is a white church at the corner of Fourth and Main." When the Bible speaks of the church at Ephesus, it refers to the congregation of Christian believers at Ephesus. Inasmuch as no church buildings were built until the third century, no word was coined to refer to one. When church buildings were built, a different word (*kuriake*), meaning "the Lord's house," was used to refer to them. On the other hand, the use of one word to describe both the building and the congregation is a natural development. Calling the building a church is a figure of speech called metonymy, in which the container is used to refer to the contents or a part used to speak of the whole. The same is found in 1 Corinthians 11:26: "For as often as ye...drink this cup." (We do not drink the cup itself, but the contents.) No harm is done in calling the sanctuary a church as long as one keeps in mind the real nature of the Church.

B. Not used for a denomination

During New Testament times, no groups of Christians arose with separate name identities similar to modern denominations. Therefore, the word *church* did not come to be appended to the names of leaders or doctrinal tenets, as in Lutheran Church or Baptist Church, to identify distinct ecclesiastical organizations. The ideal condition for the Church on Earth would, no doubt, have been one of universal unity in doctrine and organization. However, when the main ecclesiastical body departed from Scripture in doctrine and practice, it was inevitable that there would be reformations rejected by the parent system, forcing the faithful to form distinct bodies. Since every widespread revival has brought reaction by the established church leadership, the formation of newly created organizations to preserve doctrinal soundness and spiritual life have been virtually unavoidable. The ecumenical movement has endeavored to bring the denominations to a corporate reunion, but when it has been accomplished, it has been at the expense of doctrinal and spiritual fullness. A faith and practice acceptable to all has been a least common denominator. Denominations may have been God's way of preserving revival and missionary fervor. The members of denominational churches, however, must keep in mind that the Church, which is the body of Christ, is composed of all true believers. These believers must be united in spirit to carry forward the gospel of Christ in the world, for all will be caught up together at the coming of the Lord. It is certainly a Bible-based truth that local churches should band together for fellowship and missions (2 Cor. 8:1–19, 23–24; Ti. 1:5).

IV. The Officers, Ministers, and Leaders of the Church

The amount of scriptural material relative to the organization and leadership of the apostolic Church is not large. The titles borne by New Testament Church leaders were more descriptive of their ministries than of their office and rank. Since the first members and leaders of the Early Church were Jews familiar with the synagogue, they patterned church organization somewhat after that of the synagogue. In fact, in one New Testament passage, the Christian assembly is called a synagogue (Jas. 2:2, ASV, YOUNG'S, BAS).

That there was organization in the New Testament Church is clearly seen from the following:

(1) When problems arose in certain ministry activities, leaders were appointed to administer those activities (Acts 6:1–7).

(2) The disciples met regularly for worship, at first, every day. Later, they met on the first day of the week (Acts 2:46–47; 5:42; 20:7; 1 Cor. 16:2).

(3) Diligence was given to the appointment of proper leadership (Acts 1:23–26; 14:23; Ti. 1:5).

(4) Qualifications for elders (bishops) and deacons are set forth in some detail (1 Tm. 3:1–13; 5:1, 17–22; Ti. 1:5–9; 1 Pt. 5:1–4; Acts 6:1–7; 20:28–35).

(5) Each church had the authority to discipline or exclude certain members (Mt. 18:17; 1 Cor. 5:1–5; 2 Thes. 3:6–16; 1 Tm. 1:18–20).

(6) Members are admonished to respect and obey church leaders (1 Thes. 5:12–13; Heb. 13:7, 17, 24).

(7) Missionaries are sent forth by the church with official sanction (Acts 13:1–3).

(8) A council was convened in Jerusalem to settle for the whole Christian Church a dispute over doctrine and practice (Acts 15:1–35).

It is not easy to classify the various ministers and officers mentioned in the New Testament. Several terms that we take for titles, such as *pastor, elder,* and *bishop,* are probably different ways of describing the same function. Some terms like *minister* and *deacon* are different translations of the same Greek word, *diakonos.* Some offices, such as that of the apostle and prophet, are strictly by divine appointment of the exercise of a spiritual gift, while other offices are by human election or appointment and based upon specified qualifications. Pastors and teachers may be two kinds of ministers, or the terms may simply represent two functions of one office. In spite of the difficulties involved, effort will be made to analyze each New Testament office.

A. Apostles

The first exponents of the Christian gospel were the apostles, who were also God's first ministry gift to the Church.

> And when it was day, He called unto Him his disciples: and of them He
> chose twelve, whom He named apostles.
>
> —LUKE 6:13

And as they went through the cities, they delivered them the decrees for to keep, that were ordained of the apostles and elders which were at Jerusalem.

—ACTS 16:4

And He gave some, apostles; and some, prophets; and some, evangelists; and some, pastors and teachers; For the perfecting of the saints.

—EPHESIANS 4:11–12

Ye...are built upon the foundation of the apostles and prophets, Jesus Christ himself being the chief corner stone.

—EPHESIANS 2:19–20

The word *apostle* is a transliteration of the Greek word *apostolos,* which means "a messenger" or "one sent forth with orders." The original apostles were those whom Jesus chose to be with Him, whom He personally commissioned and sent forth (Mt. 10:2–4; Lk. 22:14). They were twelve in number. When Judas Iscariot betrayed the Lord, leaving only eleven, another apostle was chosen in his place (Acts 1:15–26). The names of the twelve apostles are written in the twelve foundations of the new Jerusalem (Rv. 21:14).

The requirements for apostleship were: to have been with the Lord (Acts 1:21–22); to have been a witness of the Resurrection (Acts 1:22); to have seen the Lord (1 Cor. 9:1); and to have wrought signs, wonders, and mighty deeds (2 Cor. 12:12).

The foundational apostles were a fixed number of twelve. There are others, however, who are called apostles, such as Paul, who was given a vision of the Lord, was called personally by Jesus to be the apostle to the Gentiles (Rom. 11:13; 1 Cor. 9:1) and twelve times declared himself to be an apostle; James, the brother of Jesus (1 Cor. 15:7); Barnabas (Acts 14:14); certain kinsmen of Paul (Rom. 16:7); and certain unnamed apostles (1 Cor. 15:7). Apparently the term *apostle* came to be used in a wider sense for those who had been with Jesus (including the Seventy, the one hundred twenty who followed Him, etc.) and especially of those who seemed to have a special commission to found new churches. The terms *apostle* and *missionary* have the same meaning. That the term *apostle* was used in the wider sense is obvious from the fact that there were those who falsely claimed to be apostles (2 Cor. 11:13; Rv. 2:2). If only the original Twelve had been recognized as apostles, no one else could have made a claim to apostleship. It is important to keep clear the distinction between the original apostles and those who were called apostles in the wider meaning of the term. Closely identified with the Twelve would be men like Paul, Mark, Luke, James, Jude, and the writer of Hebrews, all of whom were used by the Spirit to write the New Testament.

Discussion often arises of whether there could be modern apostles. It would depend upon the meaning given to the word *apostle.* Obviously the Church can have only one foundation. After the close of the New Testament Canon, no additional apostolic writers have been commissioned to add to Scripture. However if the term *apostle* is used in the wider sense of one commissioned of the Lord to open new mission fields, whose ministry is accompanied with signs and wonders, it would not be an inappropriate use of the word. Nevertheless, it should be kept clear that apostles are a gift from God, commissioned by Him. The Church was never authorized to create apostles. No apostolic succession was ever established. When Jesus, the chief Shepherd, returns, He will come to crown pastors (elders), not apostles (1 Pt. 5:1–4). Peter, who was certainly an apostle, happily identified with the elders (1 Pt. 5:1). Perhaps the End Times will be marked by pastors who evangelize their whole areas.

B. Prophets

The Church is said to be built upon a foundation of apostles and prophets (Eph. 2:20): "And He gave some, apostles; and some, prophets" (Eph. 4:11). While the prophets were next in rank to the apostles, they were subject to the apostles (1 Cor. 14:37). Paul seemed to give the gift of prophecy the highest priority among the spiritual gifts (1 Cor. 14:1–3). Prophecy is defined by Paul as follows: "But he that prophesieth speaketh unto men to edification, and exhortation, and comfort…he that prophesieth edifieth the church" (1 Cor. 14:3–4). This definition is demonstrated in Acts 15: "And Judas and Silas, being prophets also themselves, exhorted the brethren with many words, and confirmed them" (v. 32). A less frequent function of the prophet was that of predicting the future. On two occasions, a prophet named Agabus predicted future events (Acts 11:27–29). His prediction of a future famine enabled the church to make preparation to assist the poor in Judaea. Later Agabus predicted Paul's imprisonment by the Jews in Jerusalem, a prediction that came to pass, although Paul made no attempt to avoid the trouble (Acts 21:10–15). Prophecy had a vital function in relation to Timothy's enablement for ministry (1 Tm. 4:14). In his sermon on the Day of Pentecost, Peter identified Joel's prophecy from Joel 2:28 with the Spirit's outpouring on the Church: "And it shall come to pass in the last days, saith God, I will pour out of my Spirit upon all flesh: and your sons and your daughters shall prophesy" (Acts 2:17).

The gift of prophecy remains in effect in the Church today, where spiritual gifts are recognized. The spirit of prophecy is manifested in much Pentecostal preaching.

C. Evangelists

The evangelist is less easy to identify in the New Testament because almost everyone did the work of evangelism. Philip is the only one actually called an evangelist (Acts 21:8). Judging from Philip's ministry in Samaria, an evangelist is one whose ministry is directed primarily toward winning the unsaved: "Then Philip went down to the city of Samaria and preached Christ to them" (Acts 8:5, NKJV). It is noteworthy that his soul-winning ministry was accompanied with miracles and signs. Afterward, Philip was called to preach to one man in the desert, the Ethiopian treasurer, whom he led to Christ. It is interesting to note that as much space is taken to tell of the one man's conversion as is taken to narrate the Samaritan revival story. Timothy is not called an evangelist, but Paul admonishes him to do the work of an evangelist (2 Tm. 4:5). In the Greek, the word *evangelist* is derived from the verb that is translated "to preach the gospel." An evangelist, then, is one whose chief goal is to preach the gospel with the object of soul-winning.

The ministries of the apostle, the prophet, and the evangelist were ministries to the Church in general. Those that follow are ministries to the local church.

D. Pastors

While the term *pastor*, used to refer to the spiritual leader of the local church, is found only once in the New Testament (Eph. 4:11), it will be treated fully here for two reasons: it is the term most commonly used in the Church today, and the pastoral metaphor is employed in several passages (1 Pt. 5:2–4; Acts 20:28–29; Jn. 10:1–16; 21:15–17; Heb. 13:20; 1 Pt. 2:25; Mk. 6:34; 1 Cor. 9:6–7). The favorite terminology of Jesus to express His relationship to the people was as the Shepherd and sheep. It is natural, therefore, that those entrusted with the care of the Lord's flock should be called pastors.

It is difficult for people of the Western world to understand the intimate relationship that existed between the Palestinian shepherd and his sheep. No word could have better expressed the loving care and mutual trust that should exist between the spiritual leader and his congregation than the word *pastor*. Other synonyms for pastoral office are used more frequently in the New Testament, but the title that has persisted is that of pastor.

E. Teachers

Teachers are the fifth category of ministry gifts bestowed upon the Church by the ascended Lord (Eph. 4:11). It is not absolutely clear whether the term *teacher* represented a distinct office or merely a function of apostles and pastors (elders). That teaching was a distinct ministry is indicated by the fact that there were prophets and teachers in the church at Antioch (Acts 13:1) and that teachers are listed along with apostles and prophets as offices which God had set in the Church (1 Cor. 12:28). On the other hand, in Ephesians 4:11 *teacher* is not preceded by a definite article, as are the other offices. Therefore, the term may merely indicate teaching as a function of pastors (in the role of pastor-teachers). Teaching is listed as a spiritual gift in Romans 12:6–7; therefore, it might be exercised by any believer who is so gifted. Paul refers to himself as one "appointed a preacher, and an apostle, and a teacher of the Gentiles" (2 Tm. 1:11). Paul admonishes Timothy, a pastor, to exercise a teaching ministry (2 Tm.

2:2). The Great Commission strongly infers that teaching is of primary importance in the ongoing work of the Church: "Go ye therefore, and teach all nations, baptizing them in the name of the Father, and of the Son, and of the Holy Ghost: teaching them to observe all things whatsoever I have commanded you" (Mt. 28:19–20). Although teaching was a part of nearly all of the New Testament ministries, there were those whose primary calling was that of teaching the Word of God. Undoubtedly, there are those today whose ministry could be best identified as that of a teacher.

F. Elders, presbyters

Elder was a title borrowed from the synagogue and from the congregation of Israel. The term is used in the New Testament about thirty times, all with reference to the elders of Israel. The Hebrew word for "elder" was *zaqen,* which referred to an older man. The Greek word *presbuteros* has the same meaning, and is the source of our word *presbyter.* When Paul had founded a number of churches in Asia, he appointed elders to be in charge of them (Acts 14:23). The elder was equivalent to the pastor and was the most common title for the person in charge of a local church (Acts 20:17, 28; Ti. 1:5; 1 Pt. 5:1–4). The elders were supported materially by their congregations, which were exhorted by the apostle Paul to grant double honor to the elders who ruled (governed or directed) their churches well. Worthy of very special honor were those elders who labored in preaching and teaching (1 Tm. 5:17–19). Since the word *elders* is usually plural, it is assumed that each church had several elders, the probable reason being that larger congregations had to meet often in smaller groups in homes of members (1 Cor. 11:20; 16:15, 19). Some have reasoned from the passage in 1 Timothy 5:17 that there were both ruling elders and teaching elders. The elders were men of faith and spiritual power, for the sick were directed to seek them out for anointing with oil and the prayer of faith.

> Is any sick among you? let him call for the elders of the church; and let them pray over him, anointing him with oil in the name of the Lord: And the prayer of faith shall save the sick, and the Lord shall raise him up; and if he have committed sins, they shall be forgiven him.
>
> —JAMES 5:14–15

G. Bishops, overseers

The Authorized Version translates the Greek word *episkopos* (from which is derived our word *episcopal*) with the English word *bishop.* A better translation of the word would have been "overseer," which is the literal meaning. The Church of England's influence can be seen in the use of the word *bishop.* In the New Testament, *bishop* and *elder* are names for the same office, as can be seen clearly from a comparison of Titus 1:5–6 with 1:7–9, and Acts 20:17 with 20:28, where the word *overseer* is from the same Greek word translated "bishop" in other passages. In New Testament times the bishop or overseer was over one church. It was not until the second century that the bishop or overseer came to be over several churches. After the passing of the apostles, there probably was a need for more extensive organization. It is regrettable that this trend led to the Roman hierarchy. (See also 1 Tm. 3:1–10, a passage in which qualifications for the office of overseer [elder, pastor] are set forth.)

H. Deacons

The Bible makes it quite clear that the two set offices of the local church were those of the elder and the deacon. Deacons are mentioned directly in only two passages (Phil. 1:1; 1 Tm. 3:8–13). However, rather detailed qualifications for deacons are set forth in the same chapter where the qualifications for overseers are given. The Scriptures do not delineate the duties of deacons in the later New Testament church, but it is taken for granted that their duties had to do with the management of the charities and business affairs of the churches. The word *deacon* is from the Greek word *diakonos,* which means "servant." The deacons, then, served the church in such a way as to free the elders for prayer and the ministry of the Word.

The first deacons were probably the seven who were chosen in the sixth chapter of Acts to serve tables and administer the charities to the widows of the Jerusalem church. They are not called deacons in Acts 6, but the verb form of the word deacon is found in the clause, "Their widows were neglected in the daily ministration" (Acts 6:1). Two of the seven, Philip and Stephen, were also preachers, so it must not be assumed that deacons performed only menial tasks.

I. Ministers

The word *minister* comes from the same Greek word that is translated "deacon," but there are a number of passages where the word *diakonos* cannot refer to the office of the deacon. For instance, Paul, writing to the Corinthians, said, "Who then is Paul, and who is Apollos, but ministers by whom ye believed, even as the Lord gave to every man?" (1 Cor. 3:5). And again, to the Ephesian church, "Whereof I was made a minister, according to the gift of the grace of God given unto me by the effectual working of his power" (Eph. 3:7). Paul refers to himself as a minister five times, and several times refers to his younger workers as ministers. The term apparently emphasizes the servanthood role of the preacher. The goal of the spiritual leaders is that of equipping the saints for ministry (Eph. 4:12). All saints are expected to minister (verb), but the title *minister* (a noun) is in every case used only of those called to spiritual leadership. When the pastor is called the minister, the title *minister* is being used in a perfectly scriptural way.

J. Leaders, rulers

The words *rule* and *ruler* are used several times in the Authorized Version to designate church leaders (Rom. 12:8; 1 Tm. 5:17; Heb. 13:7, 17, 24). The New American Standard Version employs the words *lead* and *leader*, which seem more appropriate. "Remember those who led you, who spoke the Word of God to you....Obey your leaders, and submit to them; for they keep watch over your souls, as those who will give an account....Greet all your leaders and all the saints" (Heb. 13:7, 17, 24, NASB).

There are some who are prone to depreciate leadership in the Church. That duly-constituted and recognized leadership is a biblical teaching is undeniable: "And we beseech you, brethren, to know them which labour among you, and are over you in the Lord, and admonish you; And to esteem them very highly in love for their work's sake" (1 Thes. 5:12–13).

V. THE MISSION OF THE CHURCH

A. Preaching and teaching

The primary mission of the Church is declared in the Great Commission, which Jesus gave to the apostles before His ascension. A form of the commission is found in all four Gospels and in the book of Acts, each writer reporting only a selected part of the total commission. Therefore, it will be necessary to examine all five occurrences of Jesus' charge to the Church in order to grasp the full scope of it.

Mark emphasizes the Church's mission to preach the gospel: "Go ye into all the world, and preach the gospel to every creature" (Mk. 16:15). The importance of preaching may be indicated by the fact that the words for preaching are found more than 115 times in the New Testament. There are two principal Greek words translated "to preach": *kerusso,* which means "to...herald" (as a royal proclamation), and *euaggelizo* which means "to bring good news." Each of the above words occurs more than fifty times. In addition to preaching as a mission of the Church, Mark also accents the supernatural power of the Holy Spirit that would accompany the preaching of the gospel (Mk. 16:17–20).

The part of the Great Commission reported in Luke's Gospel also emphasizes preaching: "And that repentance and remission of sins should be preached in his name among all nations, beginning at Jerusalem. And ye are witnesses of these things. And, behold, I send the promise of my Father upon you: but tarry ye in the city of Jerusalem, until ye be endued with power from on high" (Lk. 24:47–49).

Luke's Gospel discloses some of the content of the Church's preaching when it says, "Repentance and remission of sins should be preached in his name." This content can be summarized as follows: unbelievers are called upon to repent of sins, the offer of the gospel is forgiveness of sins, and the Church's preaching is in the name of Jesus (salvation from sin is by virtue of the redeeming work of Jesus). Luke records, both in his Gospel and in Acts, the Lord's charge regarding the necessary preparation for preaching: "But ye shall receive power, after that the Holy Ghost is come upon you: and ye shall be witnesses unto me both in Jerusalem, and in all Judea, and in Samaria, and unto the uttermost part of the earth" (Acts 1:8). (See also Jn. 20:21–23.)

According to both Luke and Acts, Jesus commissions the Church's preachers to be His witnesses. They are not to preach the gospel as hearsay, but to herald what they have experienced firsthand: "That which we have seen and heard declare we unto you, that ye also may have fellowship with us: and truly our fellowship is with the Father, and with his Son Jesus Christ" (1 Jn. 1:3). (See also Lk. 24:48; Acts 1:8; 10:40–43; 1 Cor. 1:17–24; 9:16.)

Matthew's account of the Great Commission emphasizes the teaching mission of the Church.

> All authority has been given to Me in heaven and in earth. Go therefore and make disciples of all the nations, baptizing them in the name of the Father and of the Son and of the Holy Spirit, teaching them to observe all things that I have commanded you, and lo, I am with you always, even to the end of the age.
> —MATTHEW 28:18–20, NKJV

The dual ministry of the Church of preaching and teaching is evident throughout the book of Acts:

> And daily in the temple, and in every house, they ceased not to teach and preach Jesus Christ.
> —ACTS 5:42

> And they were continually devoting themselves to the apostles' teaching.
> —ACTS 2:42, NASB

> And when he [Barnabas] had found him [Saul], he brought him unto Antioch. And it came to pass, that a whole year they assembled themselves with the church, and taught much people.
> —ACTS 11:26

(See also Acts 15:35; 18:11; 20:20; 28:31.)

Preaching is the recruiting and motivating ministry of the Church; teaching is the maturing ministry. Through preaching, new babes are born into God's family; through teaching, the babes are matured from milk to strong meat. It could be said that the Church's work is twofold: winning and weaning (1 Cor. 3:1–2; Heb. 5:12–14).

B. Discipleship

The Great Commission in Matthew's Gospel charged the Church to "go…and teach all nations" (28:19). The Greek word translated "teach" is *matheteuo,* from the noun *mathetes,* which means "disciple." A mission of the Church is that of discipling all nations. Discipling is more than teaching. One may teach by communicating a system of precepts, but one disciples another by demonstrating truth with example. It is possible to tell others how to be victorious, but he who disciples others shows them, by example, the victorious life. Those who merely teach have pupils, but those who disciple make followers—first of Jesus, then of the teacher. Paul said, writing to the Thessalonians:

> For our gospel did not come to you in word only, but also in power, and in the Holy Spirit and in much assurance, as you know what kind of men we were among you for your sake. And you became followers of us and of the Lord, having received the word in much affliction, with joy of the Holy Spirit, so that you became examples to all in Macedonia and Achaia who believe.
> —1 THESSALONIANS 1:5–7, NKJV

The great strength of the local church is its Christian community life. All learn from one another, draw strength from one another, and grow together under a Spirit-filled ministry.

C. Fellowship

A mission of the Church is to sustain a fellowship of believers. The Early Church was rich in fellowship: "And they continued steadfastly in the apostles' doctrine and fellowship" (Acts 2:42). The Greek word for "fellowship" is *koinonia,* which means "joint participation" or "communion." The passage in Acts goes on to define fellowship as, "And all that believed were together, and had all things in common" (Acts 2:44). The biblical word *fellowship* is frequently misunderstood and misapplied. In terms such as *fellowship circle, fellowship hall,* and *fellowship day,* the meaning of *fellowship* is related usually to games, dining, and social interaction. The above-mentioned activities, when they conform to biblical ethics, are perfectly innocent and useful to the life of the Church, but when we reserve the biblical word *fellowship* to refer to them, we sadly reduce our concept of fellowship *(koinonia).* The following are scriptural uses of *koinonia:* "The fellowship of the ministering to the saints" (2 Cor. 8:4—charities); "They gave to me and Barnabas the right hands of fellowship" (Gal. 2:9—acceptance into the body); "And to make all men see what is the fellowship of the mystery" (Eph. 3:9—participation in the body); "For your fellowship in the gospel" (Phil. 1:5—participation in salvation); and "If any fellowship of the Spirit"

(Phil. 2:1—unity which the Spirit effects). Perhaps the apostle John, in his first letter, summarizes the clearest applications of biblical fellowship.

> That which we have seen and heard declare we unto you, that ye also may have fellowship with us: and truly our fellowship is with the Father, and with His Son Jesus Christ...If we say that we have fellowship with Him, and walk in darkness, we lie, and do not the truth: But if we walk in the light, as He is in the light, we have fellowship one with another.
>
> —1 JOHN 1:3, 6–7

Fellowship is, first of all, having a common relationship to the Father and the Son in the body of Christ, where we are united by the Spirit in bonds of love, unity, and singleness of purpose. This fellowship of believers extends to all mutual activities that are God-honoring, including dining together in the fellowship hall.

D. Worship

Jesus said that the Father seeks the worship of those who will worship Him in spirit and in truth (Jn. 4:23). An important mission of the Church is to promote and sustain an atmosphere conducive to worship, prayer, and praise: "But ye are a chosen generation, a royal priesthood, an holy nation, a peculiar people; that ye should shew forth the praises of him who hath called you out of darkness into His marvellous light" (1 Pt. 2:9).

In the Old Testament, the worship of God was usually accompanied by the offering of animal sacrifices. The New Testament Church offers to God the sacrifice of praise: "By Him therefore let us offer the sacrifice of praise continually, that is, the fruit of our lips giving thanks to his name (Heb. 13:15). "I urge you therefore, brethren, by the mercies of God, to present your bodies a living and holy sacrifice, acceptable to God, which is your spiritual service of worship" (Rom. 12:1, NASB).

It is one of the works of the Holy Spirit to assist the believer in prayer, intercession, worship, and praise: "Likewise the Spirit also helps in our weaknesses. For we do not know what we should pray for as we ought, but the Spirit Himself makes intercession for us with groanings which cannot be uttered" (Rom. 8:26, NKJV).

An important aid in worship for the Spirit-filled believer is his prayer language, by which he is able to worship God more perfectly than he could by the sole means of the human intellect: "For he who speaks in a tongue does not speak to men but to God...however, in the Spirit he speaks mysteries....He who speaks in a tongue edifies himself" (1 Cor. 14:2, 4, NKJV). A spirit of worship, prayer, and praise—almost without exception—has brought revival, renewal, and growth to the Church.

E. Missions and evangelism

The Great Commission implied world evangelization. Jesus intended that the gospel should be carried beyond Jerusalem, Judea, and Samaria. The gospel was good news for all nations, even for "the uttermost part of the earth" (Acts 1:8). However, it took a devastating persecution to scatter the gospel and the evangelists as far as Antioch (Acts 8:1; 11:19–20). The Church has frequently needed special urging to get on with her assigned task. William Carey, called the father of modern missions, had to overcome strong resistance before he was freed to take the gospel to India. The fact cannot be urged upon the Church too strongly that all nations have not yet been discipled and the uttermost part of the Earth has not been reached. Paul, the great missionary, challenged the Church with his testimony.

> Through mighty signs and wonders, by the power of the Spirit of God; so that from Jerusalem, and round about unto Illyricum, I have fully preached the gospel of Christ. Yea, so have I strived to preach the gospel, not where Christ was named, lest I should build upon another man's foundation: But as it is written, To whom he was not spoken of, they shall see: and they that have not heard shall understand.
>
> —ROMANS 15:19–21

(See also 2 Cor. 10:14–16; Is. 52:10.)

F. Maturity of the believer

The Church has not completed her mission with making converts. A great part of the New Testament pertains to teaching, edifying, and maturing the believer. Paul explains very clearly the Lord's purpose for His body, the Church:

> And He gave some as apostles, and some as prophets, and some as evangelists, and some as pastors and teachers, for the equipping of the saints for the work of service, to the building up of the body of Christ; until we all attain to the unity of the faith, and of the knowledge of the Son of God, to a mature man, to the measure of the stature which belongs to the fullness of Christ. As a result, we are no longer to be children...but...we are to grow up in all aspects into Him, who is the head, even Christ.
>
> —EPHESIANS 4:11–15, NASB

The Bible speaks of growth and maturity in and by means of the following: prayer (Col. 4:12); the Word of God (1 Pt. 2:2); the exercise of faith (1 Thes. 3:10); patience in testing (Jas. 1:2–4; 1 Pt. 1:7); love (1 Thes. 1:3; Col. 3:14; 1 Jn. 2:5; 4:12); grace

(2 Pt. 3:18); Christian works (Heb. 13:21); spiritual gifts (Rom. 1:11). (See also Heb. 6:1; 1 Cor. 3:1–2; 2 Tm. 2:15.)

G. Ministry in the home

The mission of the church extends into the home and concerns the life of the family, which fact is clear from the following:

1. *Jesus had great concern and love for children (Mk. 10:13–16).*

2. *In his epistles, Paul gives special instructions for all members of the Christian family (Eph. 5:33–6:4; Col. 3:18–21).*

3. *The promise of the Holy Spirit was unto believers and their children (Acts 2:39).*

4. *When Paul made converts, he followed by witness to, or baptism of the whole family (Acts 16:15, 34; 18:8).*

5. *Church elders and deacons were required to have well-regulated families (1 Tm. 3:4–5, 12; Ti. 1:6).*

6. *Many of the early churches were home churches, where the gospel influenced the whole family life (Col. 4:15; Rom. 16:5; 1 Cor. 16:19; Acts 21:4–5, 8–9).*

H. Ministry to material needs

The Early Church had a sincere concern for the material needs of men, especially the Christian family. This social concern arose, no doubt, from the teaching of Jesus (Mt. 25:34–46; Lk. 10:25–37). The Church is not charged to preach a social gospel, but the Church cannot escape the social implications of the biblical gospel. The Foursquare Church, inspired by the works of the founder, has from the beginning maintained a commissary, from which millions have been ministered to materially. The following biblical examples demonstrate that such ministry follows a scriptural precedent:

1. *The church in Jerusalem maintained a food service for widows, and in a time of crisis chose special leadership from among the most spiritual men to solve the problems (Acts. 6:1–7).*

2. *Dorcas of Joppa's ministry was that of sewing garments for the poor and widowed. When she died, Peter raised her from the dead, returning her to her work of charity (Acts 9:36–42).*

3. *In a time of famine in Judea, the Christians of Antioch sent financial assistance to a man (Acts 11:27–30).*

4. *During a later crisis, Paul and his workers took collections in all the Gentile churches for the poor saints in Jerusalem.* Much of the book of 2 Corinthians relates to these collections. The passage "God loveth a cheerful giver" (2 Cor. 9:7), refers to giving for material needs (2 Cor. 8–9).

5. *Special instructions for the care of widows is given in Paul's letter to Timothy (1 Tm. 5:3–10).*

6. Christ's work of redemption is for the whole person—spirit, soul, and body.

The Church is the Lord's instrument for implementing His provided blessing. The Church, as well as individual believers, must reflect the compassion of Jesus, which is often best expressed in sharing with the less fortunate. James wrote:

> If a brother or sister be naked, and destitute of daily food, And one of you say unto them, Depart in peace, be ye warmed and filled; notwithstanding ye give them not those things which are needful to the body; what doth it profit? Even so faith, if it hath not works, is dead, being alone.
>
> —JAMES 2:15–17

VI. THE ORDINANCES OF THE CHURCH (SACRAMENTS)

The ordinances of the local church are outward rites or symbolic observances commanded by Jesus, which set forth essential Christian truths. The term *ordinance* comes from the Latin word *ordo,* which means "row" or "order." It is by this etymology that the word means "an authoritative decree or direction." The ordinances are sometimes called sacraments. The word *sacrament* originally had as a meaning "an oath of allegiance," often taken by newly enlisted soldiers. The ordinances observed by the Protestant churches are two in number, namely water baptism and the Lord's Supper. These ordinances are considered outward signs of an inward work or, otherwise stated, visible signs of an invisible work of grace.

While only two ordinances were clearly and unmistakably commanded by Jesus, it is interesting to note that during the history of the Church as many as twelve outward observances have been referred to as sacraments. The Roman Catholic Church observes seven sacraments: baptism, confirmation, Eucharist (mass), penance, extreme unction (anointing with oil of the sick), marriage, and orders (ordination of priests and consecration of nuns). However, the early Church fathers generally recognized baptism and the Lord's Supper as the major sacraments. It was not until the twelfth century that Peter Lombard (1100–1164), in his *Book of Sentences,* defined the number of sacraments as seven, and it was not until the Council of Florence in the year of 1439 that the seven sacraments were formally decreed by the Roman Church. It is important to observe that for more than a thousand years after Christ, no recognized Christian author declared the number of ordinances to be seven.

A. Water baptism

That Jesus established water baptism as an ordinance is made clear in the Great Commission, as reported by both Matthew and Mark (Mt. 28:19; Mk. 16:16). Jesus Himself set an example for His Church by submitting to baptism by His forerunner, John the Baptist (Mt. 3:13–17). Peter reechoed the command to be baptized in his sermon on the Day of Pentecost (Acts 2:38, 41). Throughout the book of Acts, the apostles observed the ordinance, baptizing their converts (Acts 8:12, 36–38; 9:18; 10:47–48; 16:15, 33; 18:8; 19:5–6; 22:16). The spiritual significance of water baptism is taught in the epistles (Rom. 6:3; 1 Cor. 10:2; Gal. 3:27).

1. *The manner of water baptism is by immersion.* This is seen in the meaning of the Greek word *baptizo,* which clearly means "to immerse," even by the admission of scholars whose churches sprinkle and by the biblical description of the manner of Jesus' baptism in the river Jordan.

2. *The formula for water baptism is clearly stated in the Great Commission as "in the name of the Father and of the Son and of the Holy Spirit."* Statements about being baptized "in the name of Jesus" omit the longer formula and emphasize the Christian baptism as distinct from John's baptism. The following from the Foursquare *Declaration of Faith* affirms belief in the doctrine of water baptism and explains the significance of the ordinance:

> We believe that water baptism in the name of the Father and of the Son and of the Holy Ghost, according to the command of our Lord, is a blessed outward sign of an inward work, a beautiful and solemn emblem reminding us that even as our Lord died upon the cross of Calvary so we reckon ourselves now dead indeed unto sin, and the old nature nailed to the tree with Him; and that even as He was taken down from the tree and buried, so we are buried with Him by baptism into His death; that like as Christ was raised up from the dead by the glory of the Father, even so we should walk in newness of life.[2]

B. The Lord's Supper

Jesus, at His last Passover, instituted the ordinance of the taking of the bread and the fruit of the vine as a memorial of His atoning death: "This is my body which is given for you: this do in remembrance of me" (Lk. 22:19). In the book of Acts, the observance of the Lord's Supper is referred to as the breaking of bread. While the disciples frequently broke bread as a love feast of fellowship, the feast was concluded with the Lord's Supper (Acts 2:42, 46; 20:7, 11; 27:35). The clearest evidence that the Church observed the Lord's Supper as a sacrament is found in the teaching of the apostle Paul in 1 Corinthians:

> For I have received of the Lord that which also I delivered unto you, that the Lord Jesus the same night in which he was betrayed took bread: and when he had given thanks, he brake it, and said, Take, eat: this is my body, which is

---

2 McPherson, 15.

broken for you: this do in remembrance of me. After the same manner also he took the cup, when he had supped, saying, This cup is the new testament in my blood: this do ye, as oft as ye drink it, in remembrance of me. For as often as ye eat this bread, and drink this cup, ye do shew the Lord's death till he come.

—1 CORINTHIANS 11:23–26

(See also 1 Cor. 10:16–21; 11:20–22, 27–34.)

1. *Observe the following points relative to the nature of the Lord's Supper.*

a) It is an act of obedience to the Lord's command. Whatever the blessings derived from the observance of the ordinance, it is kept out of obedience to the Head of the Church (1 Cor. 11:23–25).

b) It is a memorial to the atoning death and shed blood of Jesus (1 Cor. 11:24; Lk. 22:19).

c) It is a proclamation, an act of confession by the Church, of faith in the efficacy of Christ's atoning work: "Ye do shew the Lord's death" (1 Cor. 11:26).

d) It is a statement of anticipation of the return of Christ to finalize His redeeming work: "Ye do shew the Lord's death till He come" (1 Cor. 11:26).

e) It is an experience of communion with the Lord in which the participant receives by faith the strength and blessing of fellowship with the Savior: "The bread which we break, is it not the communion [*koinonia*] of the body of Christ?" (1 Cor. 10:16).

f) It is a communion (*koinonia*) of believers at the Lord's table and a statement of the oneness of the body of Christ (1 Cor. 10:17).

2. *Regarding the nature of the element of the Lord's Supper, there are four views:*

a) Transubstantiation, the view of the Roman Catholic Church. According to this view, the elements, when blessed by the priest, are changed into the actual, physical body and blood of Jesus. This view is contradicted by experience, for it has never been shown by any test that the elements are anything but bread and the fruit of the vine. It is also contradicted by logic, for Jesus was still in His physical body when He instituted the ordinance and said of the bread, "This is my body."

b) Consubstantiation, held by Martin Luther. According to this view, the elements are unchanged, but the actual body and blood of Jesus are present with the elements. These views are nowhere upheld by Scripture. Further, they encourage superstition and overemphasize the physical over the spiritual blessings of the Lord's Supper.

c) The observance of the supper is merely a memorial act that mediates no blessing. This is the other extreme to the Catholic and Lutheran views.

d) Calvin and the majority of the reformers held that the elements, when received by faith, mediate to the believer the spiritual benefits of Christ's death. The elements in themselves are only tokens, but when received by faith, real communion with the

Lord is experienced and the benefits of that communion may be mediated. This seems to be the more scriptural view (1 Cor. 10:16; 11:27–29).

A word needs to be said about the warning against "eating and drinking unworthily" (1 Cor. 11:27–29). Many believers who have misunderstood these warnings have abstained from the Lord's Supper unnecessarily. It should be noted that *unworthily* is an adverb modifying the verbs *eateth* and *drinketh* and has to do with the manner of partaking, not with the unworthiness of the persons. The warning referred to the greedy and intemperate manner of the Corinthians, described in 1 Corinthians 11:20–22. No one is worthy in himself to have communion with Jesus, but we have the privilege by virtue of the atoning work which the elements symbolize. However, participants need to examine themselves in relation to their manner of taking and their attitude toward other believers. Participants, furthermore, should be certain to discern the Lord's body and not partake in an irreverent or frivolous manner. Partaking in faith can bring great blessing, even spiritual and physical healing (1 Cor. 11:29–30).

The Foursquare *Declaration of Faith* states, regarding the Lord's Supper:

> We believe in the commemoration and observing of the Lord's supper by the sacred use of the broken bread, a precious type of the Bread of Life, even Jesus Christ, whose body was broken for us; and by the juice of the vine, a blessed type which should ever remind the participant of the shed blood of the Savior who is the true vine of which His children are the branches; that this ordinance is a glorious rainbow that spans the gulf of the years between Calvary and the coming of the Lord.[3]

VII. The Church as the Body of Christ

While wise, Spirit-directed organization helps the Church to carry out her mission, the Church is not by nature an organization, but rather, an organism. The Church is a living being whose divine life is provided by the indwelling Spirit of Christ (Rom. 8:9).

A. Vital relationship to the Head

The Lord Jesus, after His earthly mission, ascended to the right hand of the Father, but in a real sense He is still in the world manifested through His body, the Church. Paul expresses this relationship as follows: "And hath put all things under his feet, and gave him to be the head over all things to the church, Which is his body, the fulness of him that filleth all in all" (Eph. 1:22–23).

---

3 McPherson, 15–16.

The Church is Christ's body, by which He fulfills His earthly mission. The last two verses of Mark's Gospel express dramatically the relationship of Christ to the Church: "The Lord Jesus therefore, on the one hand, after talking with them was taken up into heaven, and sat down on the right hand of God; they on the other hand, going forth, proclaimed on every side, the Lord coworking, and confirming the Word through closely following signs" (Mk. 16:19–20, ROTHERHAM).

Jesus returned to the Father, but just before He left He promised, "Lo, I am with you alway" (Mt. 28:20). He is with us, as a head is with a body. He is still working on Earth more powerfully than before (Jn. 14:12). The members of His Church are His arms and legs and mouth. The Church is the extension of the Lord Jesus Christ. Jesus expressed this relationship with a different metaphor in John 15: "I am the vine, ye are the branches: He that abideth in me, and I in him, the same bringeth forth much fruit: for without me ye can do nothing" (Jn. 15:5).

The branches are to the vine what the body is to the head. In fact, the branches are the body of the vine. As the branches of the vine bear fruit, so the work of Christ in the world must be done by the body (the Church). But also, as the branches can do nothing severed from the vine, so the body can accomplish nothing without the life and direction of the Head (the Lord Jesus).

B. Unity of the body

One of the strongest emphases of the body metaphor is that of the unity of the many members of the Church. The Church (body) of Christ is no merely a collection of individuals who subscribe to its philosophy. Rather, the Church is an organism, of which the members are interrelated parts. Paul describes the unity of the Church in 1 Corinthians 12:

> But now hath God set the members every one of them in the body, as it hath pleased him.... But now are they many members, yet but one body. And the eye cannot say unto the hand, I have no need of thee.... And whether one member suffer, all the members suffer with it; or one member be honored, all the members rejoice with it.
> —1 CORINTHIANS 12:18, 20–21, 26

There are many ministries in the Church, but they are all coordinated by the Spirit to achieve the purpose of the equipping of the saints for service (Eph. 4:12). There are many gifts of the Spirit, but they are all exercised in harmony to accomplish one end: the edifying of the body of Christ (1 Cor. 12:4–7; 14:5, 12, 26). There are many methodologies employed by the Church, but they all share the goal of preaching the gospel of the kingdom in all the world for a witness (Mt. 24:14; 28:19–20; Mk. 16:15).

C. Importance of each member in the body

No member of the body of Christ is unimportant or unnecessary.

> And the eye cannot say unto the hand, I have no need of thee: nor again the head to the feet, I have no need of you. Nay, much more those members of the body, which seem to be more feeble, are necessary.... That there should be no schism in the body; but that the members should have the same care one for another.
>
> —1 CORINTHIANS 12:21–22, 25

Dr. F. F. Bruce, commenting on the above-quoted passage, remarks, "No member is less a part of the body than any other member: all are necessary. Variety of organs, limbs and functions is of the essence of bodily life. No organ could establish a monopoly in the body by taking over the functions of the others. A body consisting of a single organ would be a monstrosity."[4]

D. Submission in the body

There are many members of the body of Christ; but there is but one Head, the Lord Jesus Christ. The members cannot function properly without full submission to the Head, who provides direction to the whole body: "And hath put all things under his feet, and gave him to be head over all things to the church" (Eph. 1:22; see also 1 Cor. 12:4–7). There are four respects in which the Christian believer must practice submission:

1. *Submission to God and to His Son Jesus (Eph. 5:24; Heb. 2:8; 12:9; Jas. 4:7).*

2. *Submission to the God-appointed leaders of the Church (Heb. 13:17; 1 Cor. 16:16; Phil. 2:12; 1 Thes. 5:12–13).*

3. *Submission one to another in Christ (Eph. 5:21–6:9; 1 Pt. 5:5).*

4. *Submission to rulers of society, when such submission does not require disobedience to the plain teaching of Scripture (Acts 4:19–20; 5:29; Rom. 13:1–7; 1 Pt. 2:13–17).*

E. The body of Christ and the local church

The universal body of Christ consists of the total number of genuine Christian believers of all ages, in heaven and on Earth. It needs to be pointed out, however, that the New Testament Scriptures address all earthly believers as functioning members of some local church. Unfortunately, there are many professing Christians who think of themselves as belonging to the mystical body of Christ, who believe that local church

---

4 Frederick Fyvie Bruce, *The New Century Bible Commentary; 1 and 2 Corinthians* (Grand Rapids, MI: Wm. B. Eerdmans Publishing Company, 1978).

relationship is optional or unnecessary. The following facts argue for the needs of local church relationship:

1. *Jesus assumed that His people would be related to a local church.* Because the Church's founding was yet future, Jesus refers to it by name only twice. The second reference pertained to cases of disagreements between brethren, in which Jesus instructed, "And if he shall neglect to hear them [witnesses], tell it unto the church: but if he neglect to hear the church, let him be unto thee as an heathen man and a publican" (Mt. 18:17). It is obvious that a church that can arbitrate disputes among believers is a local church to which members are in submission in the Lord.

2. *All the epistles of the New Testament are addressed to local churches or to leaders of local churches.*

3. *All ministries, which are God's gifts, are given to the local bodies to equip saints for ministry to one another.* Apostles, prophets, evangelists, pastors, and teachers can minister only to saints who assemble together in fellowship (Eph. 4:11–16).

4. *Believers are commanded by Jesus to partake of the holy Communion together until His return* (1 Cor. 11:23–26).

5. *The operation of the gifts of the Spirit can function only in a local body.* Speaking of the operation of the gifts, Paul said, "Seek that ye may excel to the edifying of the church" (1 Cor. 14:12).

6. *As members of the body of Christ, believers are related not only to Christ, the Head, but they are related one to another in the body.* "So we, being many, are one body in Christ, and every one members one of another" (Rom. 12:5). An arm that decided to sever all relationship with the rest of the body would be useless, even though it had communication with the head, for it would need blood pumped by the heart and purified by the lungs and kidneys (1 Cor. 12:14–17).

7. *We are told that God places members in the body as it pleases Him* (1 Cor. 12:18).

8. *In order for Christians to carry out the commission of Christ, there must be fellowship, growth of the visible church, and the mutual work of evangelism and worldwide missions (Acts 2:41–47; 11:26–30; 13:1–3).*

F. Body ministry

The concept of the Church as the body of Christ has been given new emphasis in recent years. This new emphasis has led to important insights for worship and ministry. Too often ministry has been viewed as coming exclusively from a rostrum or pulpit and only by designated clergy. When ministry is so conceived, the members of the congregation become merely spectators, whose only activity is that of filling the pews. The Bible picture of body life does not support such a limited view of ministry. God has, indeed, placed spiritual leadership in the Church to preach and teach, but the object of their preaching, teaching, and pastoral care is that of perfecting the saints to minister one to another and to the world:

> And He Himself gave some to be apostles, some prophets, some evangelists, and some pastors and teachers, for the equipping of the saints for the work of ministry, for the edifying of the body of Christ, till we all come to the unity of the faith and of the knowledge of the Son of God, to a perfect man, to the measure of the stature of the fullness of Christ; that we should no longer be children...but, speaking the truth in love, may grow up in all things into Him who is the head—Christ.
>
> —Ephesians 4:11–15, NKJV

From this concept of body ministry as expressed by the apostle Paul, several facts are clear:

1. *It is the Lord's intention that every member of the body of Christ should have a ministry.* Every member of a human body contributes to the preservation, growth, health, and activity of that body. If some members do not function, disease results. Many of the ills of the Church have been the result of a non-functioning membership. To achieve total participation in the work and worship of the Church, God has provided spiritual leadership to equip and mature the saints, and the gifts of the Spirit to empower and give direction to them. (The Bible mentions some thirty gifts of the Spirit, which have been treated specifically in Chapter 6, The Doctrine of the Holy Spirit; Section VI, "The Gifts of the Spirit.")

2. *The central purpose of body ministry is that of the edification of the whole Church (Eph. 4:12).* The test of the value and validity of body ministry and of the exercise of the gifts is in whether they edify the body of Christ. Peter wrote, "As every man hath received the gift, even so minister the same one to another, as good stewards of the manifold grace of God" (1 Pt. 4:10). Ministry and gifts are a stewardship. The believer's gift is not given primarily for his edification. It is a stewardship for others, for the church family.

3. *When the whole body ministers in unity and love, the result is spiritual and numerical growth.* "From whom the whole body, joined and knit together by what every joint supplies, according to the effective working by which every part does its share, causes growth of the body for the edifying of itself in love" (Eph. 4:16, NKJV). Much is being said today about church growth. Optimum growth of the Church cannot be accomplished by the efforts of church leaders, pastors, evangelists, and missionaries alone. Ideal growth results only when the entire Church ministers.

4. *When the whole Church ministers, there must be present the adhesive force of love.* Unless total Church participation is motivated by and carried out in a spirit of love and submission to leadership, the growth accomplished may be transient and the

ministry performed may be less than edifying. "Since you have purified your souls in obeying the truth through the Spirit in sincere love of the brethren, love one another fervently with a pure heart" (1 Pt. 1:22, NKJV). (See also, 1 Cor. 13; Gal. 5:13; Eph. 3:17–19; 4:2–3, 15–16; Phil. 2:1–5; Col. 3:12–15; 1 Thes. 5:12–13.)

VIII. THE CHURCH AND THE KINGDOM OF GOD

The phrases *kingdom of heaven* and *kingdom of God* are found more than eighty times in the New Testament. The kingdom of God is obviously an important subject. Several questions arise, however, in relation to the identity and manifestation of the kingdom of God: What is meant by the word *kingdom*? Is the kingdom of God an inner spiritual reality, or is it an outwardly visible rule? Who are the subjects of the kingdom? Are the kingdom of God and the kingdom of heaven identical? What relationship does the Church have to the kingdom of God? Is the kingdom of God present or future? These and other questions will be addressed and, as far as possible, answers from Scripture will be supplied.

A. The meaning of the word *kingdom*

The Greek word *basileia,* from which the word *kingdom* is derived, has two principle meanings: a king's "right or authority to rule over a kingdom" and "the territory subject to the rule of a king." W.E. Vine defines *basileia* as follows: *"Basileia* is primarily an abstract noun, denoting sovereignty, royal power, dominion, e.g., Rv. 17:18, translated 'which reigneth,' lit. 'hath a kingdom'...then, by metonymy, a concrete noun, denoting the territory or people over whom a king rules, e.g., Mt. 4:8; Mk. 3:24."[5] In the Greek Old Testament, *basileia* translates the Hebrew word *malkuwth,* which likewise has the two meanings "royal, reign" (Dn. 1:1) and then the kingdom or realm of a king. The word *kingdom* is used most frequently in the New Testament with the first meaning of "reign" or "royal power." Regarding the meaning of the word *kingdom*, Dr. Ladd says, "The primary meaning of the New Testament word for kingdom, *basileia,* is 'reign' rather than 'realm' or 'people.' A great deal of attention in recent years has been devoted by critical scholars to this subject, and there is practically unanimous agreement that 'regal power, authority' is more basic to *basileia* than 'realm' or 'people.'"[6]

---

5 William Edwy Vine, *Expository Dictionary of New Testament Words* (Old Tappan, NJ: Fleming H. Revell Publishing Company, 1958), 294–296.

6 George E. Ladd, *Crucial Questions About the Kingdom of God* (Grand Rapids, MI: Wm. B. Eerdmans Publishing Company, 1977), 78.

B. Is the kingdom of God present or future?

The kingdom of God is both present and future. The kingdom, meaning the realm of God's people of all dispensations over which Christ will reign in righteousness, is yet future. It will begin with the second coming of Christ (2 Tm. 4:1; Rv. 11:15). The kingdom as the reign or royal power of God is present in the redeeming work of Jesus, who came to destroy the works of the devil. Dr. Ladd states:

> The kingdom has come in that the powers of the future kingdom have already come into history and into human experience through the supernatural ministry of the Messiah which has effected the defeat of Satan. Men may now experience the reality of the reign of God. In the future eschatological kingdom Satan will be utterly destroyed, cast into a lake of fire and brimstone (Rv. 20:10) that men may be freed from every influence of evil. However, God's people need not wait for the coming of the future kingdom to know what it means to be delivered from Satanic power. The presence of Christ on earth had for its purpose the defeat of Satan, his binding, so that God's power may be a vital reality in the experience of those who yield to God's reign by becoming the disciples of Jesus. In Christ, the kingdom, in the form of its power, has come among men.[7]

C. Is the kingdom inward and spiritual or outwardly visible?

The future (eschatological) kingdom will be an outwardly manifested kingdom over which Christ will reign in power and glory. It will prevail over the whole earth and will fulfill the Old Testament prophecies to the faithful remnant of Israel concerning the Messiah's reign upon the throne of David (Is. 9:6–7; 11:1–10; 24:23; 32:1; Dn. 2:44; 7:18, 27; Mi. 4:7). The New Testament saints will rule and reign with Christ as kings and priests (Mt. 25:21, 23; 1 Tm. 6:14–15; Rv. 5:9, 10; 19:14–16; 20:4–6). The one-thousand-year reign of Christ over the earth is known as His millennial reign. Although the word *millennium* does not occur in the Bible, it is the Latin word for "thousand years" (Rv. 20:4–6).

On the other hand, the present (soteriological) kingdom of Christ is spiritual and invisible, for it consists of the kingship, power, and authority of Jesus as Savior and destroyer of Satan. That the kingdom of Jesus was spiritual is made clear by two statements of Jesus. In the first, in answer to the Pharisees' question about when the kingdom would come, He said, "The kingdom of God cometh not with observation: Neither shall they say, Lo here! or, lo there! For, behold, the kingdom of God is within you [or, in your midst]" (Lk. 17:20–21). In the second, to Pilate, who asked Him if he was a king, He answered, "My kingdom is not of this world" (Jn. 18:36). Jesus goes on

---

7 Ibid., 91.

to say, however, that He was born to be a king over the realm of divine truth and that "every one that is of the truth heareth my voice" (Jn. 18:37). Jesus said to Nicodemus, "Except a man be born again, he cannot see the kingdom of God…Except a man be born of water and of the Spirit, he cannot enter into the kingdom of God" (Jn. 3:3, 5). The born-again ones enter into His kingdom of the divine, saving truth of the gospel. Jesus' present kingdom on Earth is a kingdom of gospel, a fact which relates to the reason why the gospel is called the gospel of the kingdom (Mt. 4:23–24; 9:15; 24:14; Mk. 1:14; Lk. 4:43). (See also Acts 1:3; 8:12; 19:8; 28:23, 31.) Those who accept the gospel of Jesus also accept Him as sovereign Lord and Master and enter into His kingdom, becoming citizens of heaven (Phil. 3:20, NIV, NASB). The gospel is the central message of Jesus' present kingdom or kingship, but this is not an abstract or passive gospel. Instead, it is a dynamic gospel that is "the power of God unto salvation" (Rom. 1:16). Writing to the Thessalonians about the gospel, Paul said, "For our gospel did not come to you in word only, but also in power and in the Holy Spirit and with full conviction" (1 Thes. 1:5, NASB). The result of Paul's preaching to the Thessalonians was that they "turned to God from idols to serve the living and true God" (1 Thes. 1:9). That the believer presently enters the kingdom of God is clearly declared: "For He delivered us from the domain of darkness, and transferred us to the kingdom of His beloved Son" (Col. 1:13, NASB). Jesus plainly declared that He brought the kingdom into this present age in the form of dominion over Satan and his realm of darkness: "But if I with the finger of God cast out devils, no doubt the kingdom of God is come upon you" (Lk. 11:20). The spiritual nature of the present reign of God is affirmed by Paul in Romans 14:17, which says, "For the kingdom of God is not meat and drink; but righteousness, and peace, and joy in the Holy Ghost."

D. Are the Church and the kingdom of God identical?

The final and complete manifestation of the eschatological kingdom of God is yet future; but the power, authority, and message of the kingdom were introduced into the present age by Jesus and bestowed upon the Church, to whose apostles He said, "Upon this rock I will build my church…And I will give unto thee the keys of the kingdom of heaven" (Mt. 16:18–19). The kingdom of God as a domain of God is yet to come, but the kingdom as dominion has already broken into the present age, since the Church exercises the power of the kingdom. The Church is not identical to the kingdom of God, for the kingdom is larger than the Church. However, the Church is the present instrument of the kingdom and will inherit the kingdom (Jas. 2:5; 2 Pt. 1:11).

The ultimate kingdom of God will include, not only the Church, but the Old Testament saints, the regathered remnant of Israel, and the righteous nations that will be a part of the millennial reign of Jesus (Mt. 25:32–33; Rv. 20:4; Is. 66:18–23; Jer. 3:16–18; 23:3–6; 31:10–12; Zec. 14:8–9).

E. Is the kingdom of heaven different from the kingdom of God?

Some Bible scholars (including the Scofield Chain Reference Bible editors, see foot-notes on Mt. 3:2) teach that *the kingdom of heaven*, found only in Matthew, usually refers to professing Christendom; while *the kingdom of God*, used by Mark, Luke, and John, refers to God's sovereign reign. There is no doubt that Jesus, in His parables, sometimes extends the kingdom concept to include the sphere of outward profession (tares and wheat, Mt. 13:24–30). Nonetheless, a close comparison of the two terms, *kingdom of God* and *kingdom of heaven*, as they are used in all four Gospels, will show that they have the same meaning. For instance, in the Beatitudes, Matthew's Gospel says that the poor will inherit the kingdom of heaven, while in Luke's Gospel he writes that they will inherit the kingdom of God (Mt. 5:3; Lk. 6:20). In Matthew, the disciples are sent forth to preach that the kingdom of heaven is at hand, while in Luke they announce that the kingdom of God is at hand (Mt. 10:6–7; Lk. 9:2). (See also Mt. 4:17.) In the very context where Jesus refers to the parables (including that of the tares and wheat) as teaching the mysteries of the kingdom, Matthew's Gospel refers to them as mysteries of the kingdom of heaven (13:11), while in Mark's Gospel (4:11) they are mysteries of the kingdom of God. In one passage in Matthew, Jesus uses both terms in the same figure of speech with exactly the same meaning (Mt. 19:23–24). In one sentence, "It is hard for a rich man to enter the kingdom of heaven;" in the next, "It is easier for a camel to go through the eye of a needle than for the rich man to enter the kingdom of God" (NIV). It is obvious from these comparisons that the terms *kingdom of heaven* and *kingdom of God* were completely interchangeable in usage.

IX. OTHER METAPHORS OF THE CHURCH

The metaphors of the Church as the body of Christ and as a holy nation, treated above, were given special consideration: the Church as the body of Christ because of its scriptural prominence and contemporary application; the Church as a holy nation or kingship because of differences in interpretation of the word *kingdom*. However, the metaphors applied to the Church in Scripture are many, and properly so, because no one metaphor can fully express the relationship of believers to Christ, to one another, and to the world. Treatment will be given to twenty-four additional metaphors, each of which adds something to the total concept of the Church.

A. The Church as the Lord's family

Jesus introduces us to the family relationship, teaching us to pray, "Our Father which art in heaven" (Mt. 6:9; Lk. 11:2). God, the Father of our Lord Jesus Christ, is also our Father. Jesus prayed using the Aramaic word *abba*. According to Romans 8:15, the believer cries out in the spirit of adoption, "Abba, Father." If we, together with our Lord Jesus, call God our Father, then Jesus is our elder Brother in the family of God (Heb. 2:10–11). The author of Hebrews declares that believers are members of God's family: "But Christ was faithful as a Son in the household of His own Father, and we are members of this household [family, BECK] if we hold on to the end" (Heb. 3:6, PHILLIPS). As families are normally proud of the family name, so the church family exults in the Father's name (Eph. 3:14–15). As families receive an inheritance from the father, so the Church awaits the heavenly Father's promised inheritance (Rom. 8:17). As good families observe a certain pattern of conduct, so there is a given standard of behavior for God's household (1 Tm. 3:15). In the Old Testament, the father of each household was, in effect, the priest over the household (Nm. 7:2). Jesus has become the High Priest over God's Church family (Heb. 2:17–18; 10:21–23).

The idea of the Church as God's family and household is derived from the Old Testament, where God's people are the house (family) of Israel, a nation grown from the family of Jacob, nurtured through family culture. That the Church is called God's family and household testifies to the basic importance of the family as a societal institution. In the New Testament, especially in Acts, much is made of the effect of the gospel upon entire families: Acts 2:46; 5:42; 12:12; 16:15, 33–34; 21:8–9; 1 Cor. 1:16; 16:15; and 2 Tm. 4:19.

Although in the Old Testament God is spoken of as the Father of the whole house of Israel (Is. 5:7; Ps. 98:3), He is never referred to as the Father of an individual. Apparently, calling God Father is a privilege reserved for believers in Jesus Christ the Son.

B. The Church as a fellowship of believers

The Greek word for "fellowship," meaning "a company of equals or friends," is *koinonia*. It came to be applied to those belonging to a society. *Koinonia* was applied to the Church as those having a common salvation through a common faith in God and in His Son Christ Jesus: "That which we have seen and heard we declare to you, that you also may have fellowship with us; and truly our fellowship is with the Father and with His Son Jesus Christ" (1 Jn. 1:3, NKJV). (See also 1 Cor. 1:9.) As soon as the Church came into being, a strong fellowship of faith, worship, and service was established: "And they continued steadfastly in the apostles' doctrine and fellowship, and in breaking of bread, and in prayers" (Acts 2:42). The metaphor of the family stresses the idea of a common Father. The metaphor of the fellowship stresses the idea of a common mission, purpose, worship, and action.

In America there is a strong inclination to privacy and individualism, but the Great Seal of the United States contains the motto, *E Pluribus Unum*, meaning, "In many, one"—one nation indivisible. Only a strong sense of unity makes a great society. The Church is God's new society, held together by the unity of the Spirit. Luke says about the apostolic Church: "And all that believed were together, and had all things common [*koinos*]" (Acts 2:44). The book of Ephesians is the New Testament epistle in which the doctrine of the Church is most fully developed. Ephesians does not use the word *koinonia,* but it is the only New Testament book to use the term *unity* (Eph. 4:3–6, 13). The Church as God's *koinonia* stresses the idea of a society whose primary characteristics are unity and love. One practical expression of the Church's love was that of sharing with the needy. *Koinonia* is sometimes translated "communicate," with the meaning of extending material help to the poor and to those overtaken by misfortune (Phil. 4:14; 1 Tm. 6:18; Heb. 13:16; Acts 2:45; 2 Cor. 8:4; 9:13; Gal. 2:10; Rom. 12:13). The Church's *koinonia* (also translated "communion") is celebrated at the Lord's Supper, which symbolizes our common redemption by Christ's atoning death on the cross (1 Cor. 10:16–17; 11:23–34). John R. W. Stott, in a commentary on Ephesians, wrote concerning its message:

> The letter focuses on what God did through the historical work of Jesus Christ and does through His Spirit today, in order to build His new society in the midst of the old. We have been raised from spiritual death, exalted to heaven and seated with Him there. We have also been reconciled to God and to each other. As a result, through Christ, and in Christ, we are nothing less than God's society, the single new humanity which He is creating and which includes Jews and Gentiles on equal terms. We are the family of God the Father, the body of Jesus Christ His Son, and the temple and dwelling place of the Holy Spirit. Therefore we are to demonstrate plainly and visibly by our new life the reality of this new thing which God has done: first by the unity...of our common life, secondly by the purity and love of our everyday behaviour.[8]

C. The Church as a team of athletes

Athletic events were as common in the Greek and Roman world as they are today. Paul, who was a keen observer, frequently used the athletic metaphor (1 Cor. 9:24–26; Gal. 2:2; 5:7; Phil. 2:16; 2 Tm. 2:5; 4:7; Heb. 12:1; 1 Tm. 6:12). The passage with the athletic metaphor that best applies to the Church is, "That ye stand fast in one spirit, with one mind striving together for the faith of the gospel" (Phil. 1:27). The Greek word translated "striving together" is *sunathleo,* from *athleo,* meaning to "contend for a prize," and *sun,* which means "with" or "together." Paul wants to hear from the Philippians that they are in unity, playing as a team. The Church's greatest advancement and growth has not been the result of individual efforts, but the result of the mutual effort and teamwork of the whole family of God. If Christian believers

---

8 John R. W. Stott, *God's New Society, The Message of Ephesians* (Downers Grove, IL: Inter Varsity Press, 1980), 24–25.

are like a team of athletes, they will display such characteristics as dedication, team-work, cooperation, self-denial, self-control, and unity.

D. The Church as the Lord's army

The idea of the Church as an army would probably not be a pleasant one for many, particularly for young people. However, the Bible often refers to the battle against the powers of darkness in which the Church is engaged. Some of our aversion to the military metaphor is removed when we remember that "the weapons of our warfare are not carnal, but mighty through God to the pulling down of strong holds;) Casting down imaginations…and bringing into captivity every thought to the obedience of Christ" (2 Cor. 10:4–5). The believer is further exhorted, "Put on the whole armour of God, that ye may be able to stand against the wiles of the devil. For we wrestle not against flesh and blood, but against principalities, against powers, against the rulers of the darkness of this world, against spiritual wickedness in high places" (Eph. 6:11–12). The Church is engaged in a real warfare, but Christ is our Captain and we are assured of victory. In fact, Satan is already a defeated foe (1 Tm. 1:18; 2 Tm. 2:3–4; Eph. 6:10–17; 1 Cor. 9:7; 1 Pt. 2:11; Rv. 19:11–21; 20:7). The Church on Earth is called the Church militant; the Church in heaven is called the Church triumphant.

E. The Church as the Lord's flock

The pastoral metaphor is a very familiar one. The spiritual leader of the local church is usually called the pastor and the congregation is frequently referred to as the flock. The first eighteen verses of the tenth chapter of John speak of Christ as the Good Shepherd and of His followers as the sheep of His fold. Although the word *pastor* as the spiritual leader is found only once in the New Testament, both Paul and Peter give vivid examples of the pastoral metaphor: "Take heed therefore unto yourselves, and to all the flock…to feed [shepherd] the church of God" (Acts 20:28); "Feed [shepherd] the flock of God which is among you…being ensamples to the flock: and when the chief Shepherd shall appear, ye shall receive a crown of glory that fadeth not away" (1 Pt. 5:2–4). Peter would well remember the words of Jesus, spoken after the Resurrection, which were three times repeated: "Lovest thou me?" "Feed my lambs," and "Feed my sheep" (Jn. 21:15–17). (See Ps. 23:1; 80:1; 100:3; 2 Sm. 7:7; Jer. 31:10; Mk. 6:34; Eph. 4:11; Heb. 13:20; Rv. 7:17.)

F. The Church as the Lord's school

More than fifty times Jesus is called or referred to as Master or Teacher (both from the Greek word *didaskalos,* from the verb *didasko,* which means "to teach") or Rabbi. The Gospels have much more to say about Jesus as a teacher than as a preacher. That the local Church was intended to be a teaching place is clearly inferred by the Great

Commission: "Having gone, then, disciple all the nations, baptizing them into the name of the Father, and of the Son, and of the Holy Spirit, teaching them to observe all things whatsoever I commanded you; and behold, I am with you all the days until the completion of the age" (Mt. 28:19–20, IGEB). (See also NIV, NASB, NKJV, RSV, JB, etc. on Mt. 28:19.) Jesus used two different words for "teach" in His commission. The first is *matheteuo* (28:19), meaning to make disciples; and the second *didasko* (28:20), which is the common word for "to teach." The emphatic term in the commission is *make disciples*. *Go* and *teaching* are participles which are subordinate to the main verb, *make disciples*. Making disciples involved both teaching and preaching, but it required more, namely, bringing the adherents to a level of discipleship to which the teachers had been brought. Teaching and preaching may often fall on deaf ears, but he who disciples brings his followers by word and example to be like himself. However, we do not make men our disciples, but disciples of Jesus.

Jesus' method of discipling is clearly revealed in a passage in Mark's Gospel: "And He went up on the mountain and called to Him those He Himself wanted, and they came to Him. Then He appointed twelve, that they might be with Him and that He might send them out to preach, and to have power to heal sicknesses and to cast out demons" (Mk. 3:13–15, NKJV). In this passage, Mark lists three aspects of making disciples: "that they might be with Him" (learning by example), "that He might send them out to preach" (learning to communicate), and "and to have power to heal sicknesses and to cast out demons" (learning to minister). None of these aspects is learned by mere verbal instruction. The pupil must imbibe of his master's spirit, as Elisha took upon himself the mantle of his teacher, Elijah. The word *disciple* was the first name given to the early Christians (Acts 11:26). The crowning virtue that characterizes one as a disciple of Jesus is that of love (Jn. 13:35) (See also Mk. 8:34; Jn. 1:43; 21:19–22; Lk. 5:11, 27–28; 1 Thes. 1:6–7; 1 Pt. 2:21; 5:3; 1 Tm. 1:16; 4:12; Ti. 2:7).

G. The Church as a servant or steward

The principal words of church life are words of servanthood: *minister* or *ministry*, from the Greek *diakonos; diakonia*, which refers to servants of God and the service they perform (probably originally "one who served tables" [Jn. 12:26]); *servant*, from *doulos*, meaning "slave" (Mt. 24:45; 25:14; Gal. 5:13); and *steward*, from *oikonomos*, who was the servant who managed the household and its affairs (Lk. 12:42; 1 Cor. 4:1–2; Ti. 1:7; 1 Pt. 4:10). Two other words translated "minister" are *huperetes*, which originally meant a servant who rowed a ship (Acts 13:5), and *leitourgos*, meaning a public minister or a servant who served the community at his own expense (Rom. 15:16).

That all Christian officers, ministers, workers, and leaders are servants is clearly seen from the following:

(1) The example Jesus set by assuming the place of a servant (Mk. 10:42–45; Mt. 20:27–28).

(2) The spirit of the world is to lord it over other people, but the Lord's ministers serve one another (1 Pt. 5:3; 1 Cor. 9:19; Gal. 5:13; Lk. 22:24–28).

(3) The believer's service is a stewardship of which he will give account (Mt. 25:14–30), and the greatest virtue in stewards is to be found faithful (1 Cor. 4:1–2; Mt. 25:21).

(4) Believers are to be in subjection to one another, and to those who are placed over them in the Lord. Furthermore, leadership and guidance are ministries in themselves (Eph. 5:21; 1 Thes. 5:12; Acts 20:28; 1 Pt. 5:2–3; Heb. 13:7, 17, 24).

(5) Paul, who had apostolic authority, called himself a "servant of Jesus Christ" (Rom. 1:1).

(6) Words expressing servanthood are used more than three hundred times in the New Testament.

(7) The charge to all mature believers is to minister, that is, to serve one another (Eph. 4:12).

H. The Church as a building

The metaphor of the Church as a building is suggested in the following Scripture passages: 1 Cor. 3:9–15; Eph. 2:20–22; Mt. 16:18; 21:42; 1 Pt. 2:4–7; Lk. 6:46–49; Acts 4:11; Rom. 15:20; and Ps. 118:22. From these Scriptures, a number of architectural figures are derived:

(1) Christ is the foundation and the chief Cornerstone of the Church. It is worthy of note that Psalms 118:22, "The stone which the builders refused is become the head stone of the corner," quoted by Peter in 1 Peter 2:7, is found five times in the New Testament (Mt. 21:42; Mk. 12:10–11; Lk. 20:17; Acts 4:11). (See also Is. 8:14; 28:16; Dn. 2:34–35; Rom. 9:32–33.)

(2) Believers are the building materials or "lively stones" (1 Pt. 2:5).

(3) Ministers are said to be builders, Christ being the Master Builder and Architect.

(4) There are no isolated "stones;" all are built into the building.

(5) Believers must take heed as to what kinds of materials they are and how they build (1 Cor. 3:9–15).

I. The Church as a mystery

One of Paul's strongest concepts of the Church was that of the Church as a mystery. It must be noted that the Bible word *mystery* has a different meaning from that attached to it in modern English. In ancient Greece, the mysteries were secrets of the mystery religions, revealed only to those initiated into them. The secrets were not mysterious in the modern use of the term; they were clearly understandable by the initiated. In this sense, Paul is explaining that God's mysteries are truths that may be known only by divine revelation concerning redemption and the Church, but they are clearly revealed to believers in the Scriptures. One of these mysteries is the Church, which was not revealed in the Old Testament. The prophets predicted that God would bless the Gentiles, but they did not reveal that Gentile believers would share equally with Israel in the body of Christ.

To be specific, that the Gentiles are fellow-heirs and fellow-members of the body, as well as fellow-partakers of the promise in Christ Jesus through the Gospel (Eph. 3:4–6, NASB; Col. 1:25–27). Paul considered that God had given him a special ministry to declare the doctrine of the Church as mystery (Eph. 3:3–4). The glory of this mystery is said to be the truth and fact of "Christ in you, the hope of glory" (Col. 1:27).

J. The Church as the Lord's field

The Bible frequently employs the agricultural metaphor. Paul wrote to the Corinthian church, "Ye are God's husbandry [field]" (1 Cor. 3:9). In God's field (the church) there are planters, cultivators, and reapers, but it is really God who gives the increase. Workers must not quarrel over their relative importance; God calls and places each in his divinely determined office. The workers are indispensable, but the divine Husbandman gives the vine its life and growth (Jn. 15:1–2). Diligent work in God's field brings reward. As Paul wrote to Timothy, "The hardworking farmer ought to be the first to receive his share of the crops" (2 Tm. 2:6, NASB). The agricultural parables in Matthew 13 speak of the seed (the Word), different soils (hearers of the Word), and varying degrees of yield: thirty, sixty, and one hundredfold (Mt. 13:3–8, 18–23).

K. The Church as a royal priesthood

Peter introduces the metaphor of the Church as a royal priesthood:

> You...are being built up a spiritual house, a holy priesthood, to offer up spiritual sacrifices acceptable to God through Jesus Christ.
>
> —1 PETER 2:5, NKJV

> But you are a chosen generation [race], a royal priesthood, a holy nation, His own special people, that you may proclaim the praises of Him who called you out of darkness into His marvellous light.
>
> —1 PETER 2:9, NKJV

The Church no longer needs priests, in the Old Testament sense, to offer up animal sacrifices. Christ Jesus has made, once for all, the perfect atoning sacrifice of

Himself for our redemption. The Church, however, offers up spiritual sacrifices of praise, worship, and thanksgiving to God (Heb. 13:15). The Church also intercedes and prays for rulers and all mankind (1 Tm. 2:1–4).

One of the great truths of the Church is that of the priesthood of all believers. Every believer in Christ has access to the throne of God by the merits of Jesus: "For through Him we both have access by one Spirit to the Father" (Eph. 2:18, NKJV). (See also Heb. 4:14–16.)

As priests, believers have been given a ministry of reconciliation: "God...has given us the ministry of reconciliation...and has committed to us the word of reconciliation. Now then, we are ambassadors for Christ, as though God were pleading through us: we implore you on Christ's behalf, be reconciled to God" (2 Cor. 5:18–20, NKJV). In consecration, the believer offers himself to God as a living sacrifice, holy and acceptable (Rom. 12:1). Other sacrifices which the believer offers to God are brotherly love (Eph. 5:1–2), good works (Heb. 13:16), material possessions to assist others (Heb. 13:16), and ministry for others (Phil. 2:17).

L. The Church as the bride of Christ

One of the most attractive metaphors of the Church is that of the Church as the bride of Christ. This metaphor is used by John the Baptist (Jn. 3:29), by the apostle Paul (2 Cor. 11:2; Eph. 5:21–32), and by the apostle John (Rv. 19:7–9). There is a strong relationship between this metaphor and that of the Church as the body of Christ. The following applications may be drawn from the analogy of the Church as Christ's bride:

(1) It provides a pattern for relationship between Christian husbands and wives.

(2) Wives are to be in submission to their husbands as the Church is to Christ and as believers are one to another (Eph. 5:21–22), not because the wife is inferior, less worthy, or less capable. Responsibility for spiritual leadership in the home must be established, therefore the husband is assigned that responsibility, which he bears with the indispensable support of the wife.

(3) Husbands are to love their wives as Christ loves the Church, as much as they love themselves, and even enough to die for her (Eph. 5:25–29. If both wives and husbands comply with this pattern, no one is disadvantaged in the marriage relationship.

(4) This figure portrays the great love which Christ has for His Church as His own bride and which the Church experiences waiting for the coming of the Bridegroom.

M.The Church as the Lord's embassy

Paul calls himself the Lord's ambassador: "I am an ambassador in chains" (Eph. 6:20, NKJV). He also includes the believers with himself in this ambassadorship: "Now then, we are ambassadors for Christ" (2 Cor. 5:20). Several applications may be made from this figure. First, we are the ambassadors of our King, who dispatches us on a divine mission of peace. The second is that of an ambassador delivered on behalf of his sovereign terms for peace (Lk. 14:31–32), for the Church announces to the world the terms of reconciliation to God, which are faith in Christ and surrender to Him as Lord. The Lord has given to the Church the ministry of reconciliation (2 Cor. 5:18–21).

N. The Church as the pillar and ground of truth

The Church supports the truth of the gospel and lifts it on high. Paul wrote to Timothy concerning the Church: "But in case I am delayed, I write so that you may know how one ought to conduct himself in the household of God, which is the Church of the living God, the pillar and support of the truth" (1 Tm. 3:15, NASB). In the following verse, Paul went on to give what may have been a poetic doctrinal expression of the mystery of godliness, which was widely used in the early Church (v. 16). The Church is to safeguard sound doctrine and to lift it on high by the proclamation of the gospel and by exemplary conduct.

O. The Church as the Lord's sanctuary

A number of Scripture passages support the metaphor of the Church as a sanctuary or temple. From those passages, practical applications are made: The Lord does not abide in buildings made with hands, but in His people as a Church (Acts 17:24–25; 1 Cor. 3:16; 1 Kgs. 8:27; Is. 66:1–2). The Church is the Lord's sanctuary, and He dwells where His people are gathered together in His name (Mt. 18:20). The temple was a sanctuary, a holy separated building, dedicated exclusively to the worship and service of God; likewise the Church is the temple of the Holy Spirit, the sanctuary where the Lord dwells. It is because of this that the members of the Church are called saints or holy ones (1 Cor. 3:17; Eph. 2:21–22; 1 Pt. 2:4–5).

Peter says of the believers, "As living stones, are being built up a spiritual house" (1 Pt. 2:5, NASB). In the figure, stones are part of a building, but they are *living* stones that therefore form part of a household or family—and not just any family or any building, but a sanctuary and dwelling place for the Lord.

P. The Church as pilgrims

This metaphor defines the Church's relationship to this present world with the following applications: (1) Believers are not really at home in this world, nor are they to be "conformed to this world" (Rom. 12:2). Their true citizenship is in heaven (Phil. 3:20). (2) Believers are said to sojourn here as pilgrims and strangers (Heb. 11:13). (3) The Church members, though pilgrims, are commissioned to witness to this world and to win citizens for Christ's kingdom from the world (1 Pt. 2:11–12;

Col. 1:12–14; Acts 1:8). (4) The believers' goal is the coming city of God, as described in Hebrews 13:14: "For here we have no continuing city, but we seek one to come."

Q. The Church as the Way

In the book of Acts, the life of the Church is called the Way and believers are called "those of the way": "And desired of him letters to Damascus to the synagogues, that if he found any of this way, whether they were men or women, he might bring them bound unto Jerusalem" (Acts 9:2). The Church as the body of Christ is the Way, for Christ is the Way, the Truth, and the Life. No one comes to the Father except by Him (Jn. 14:6). The following things are stated about the Way in the book of Acts: the way of God is a persecuted way (22:4); it is often spoken evil of (19:9); it is called heresy by some (24:14); Paul confessed joyfully to Felix that he was of that Way (24:14); when the Church is mighty in witness and in power as it was in Ephesus, it will cause "no small stir," for the way of God will be a disturbing element in a society ruled over by the powers of darkness (19:23).

R. The Church as the Lord's inheritance

In the first chapter of Ephesians, Paul makes the remarkable statement, "That ye may know what is…the glory of his inheritance in the saints" (Eph. 1:18). This is often interpreted to refer to our inheritance, but a careful reading shows that the verse refers to the Lord's inheritance, which is the saints or the Church. In verses 11 and 14, the same truth is found. Although the Authorized Version renders verse 11, "In whom also we have obtained an inheritance," the American Standard Version reads, "In whom also we were made a heritage." The great Greek scholar B. F. Wescott renders Ephesians 1:11, "We were also made God's portion."[9] The Living Bible translates verse 11, "Because of what Christ has done, we have become gifts to God that He delights in." F. F Bruce, commenting on the American Standard Version's rendering of that verse, says:

> "In whom we were made a heritage"—This is a preferable rendering to… "in whom we have obtained an inheritance." Both statements are true, but the apostle is thinking here of "God's own possession" (verse 14), "His inheritance in the saints" (verse 18). So, in Old Testament days, it was revealed that the Lord's portion is His people; Jacob is the lot of His inheritance (Dt.

---

9 Brook Foss Westcott, *Saint Paul's Epistle to the Ephesians* (Grand Rapids, MI: Baker Book House, 1979), 14.

32:9). In Christ, then, we have been admitted to the ranks of the chosen people, the holy heritage of God.[10]

(See also 1 Pt. 2:9–10; Ex. 19:5–6; Dt. 14:2; 32:9; Mal. 3:17.)

S. The Church as the Lord's masterpiece

Since Ephesians is the epistle about the Church, many of the metaphors of the Church will be found in it. In Ephesians 2 Paul states, "For we are His workmanship, created in Christ Jesus unto good works" (Eph. 2:10). The Greek word translated "workmanship" is *poiema,* meaning "that which has been made." It is the word from which we get the English word *poem.* The Church is God's masterpiece of creation. When the Church, which is created for good works, is perfected, it will portray its Maker and Creator, Christ Jesus the Lord. "When he shall appear, we shall be like Him; for we shall see him as he is" (1 Jn. 3:2). It should be noted that all the pronouns in Ephesians 2 are plural: "We are God's workmanship" (v. 10). The Church is God's masterpiece, a mosaic of all His people in a designed, collective work (Phil. 1:6; 2:13; Eph. 3:10; Col. 1:28–29; Heb. 13:21; 2 Cor. 5:17).

T. The Church as the light of the world

In the Sermon on the Mount, Jesus said, "Ye are the light of the world. A city that is set on a hill cannot be hid" (Mt. 5:14–16). The figure of the Church as light suggests the following: the believers, who are the children of light, give witness to Christ, the true Light of the world (Jn. 8:12). This means that the believer's light is a reflected light; like the light of the moon, he reflects the light of Christ. Ephesians 5:14 says literally, "Christ will shine on you" (NIV). The book of Revelation calls the local Churches lampstands (Rv. 1:20, NKJV). No matter how blessed it is to minister one to another, believers must not forget that their primary mission is that of illuminating the darkness of the world (Mt. 5:16). The believer's witness is twofold: witness by words and witness by works (1 Pt. 2:12).

U. The Church as the salt of the earth

What did Jesus mean when He said, "Ye are the salt of the earth?" (Mt. 5:13). The following applications seem to be indicated:

1. *Salt preserves.* The Church preserves and reinforces the qualities of goodness, honor, justice, and mercy in a society that tends to corrupt.

2. *Salt inhibits corruption.* The Church restrains the corrupting influences, and the good works of the Church rebuke evil.

---

10 Frederick Fyvie Bruce, *The Epistle to the Ephesians* (Westwood, NJ: Fleming H. Revell Publishing Company, 1961), 33.

3. *Salt gives zest and flavor.* The Church gives a zest and distinctive flavor to its surroundings. However, it is not said to be the "sugar of the earth." Savor must be important to the figure, for believers are warned not to lose their savor, lest the salt be cast out and trodden under foot (Mt. 5:13).

(a) The Church is not only to salt the world, but it must also maintain its saltiness within itself to restrain selfish ambition, quarrelsomeness, etc. (Mk. 9:49–50; Lk. 14:34).

(b) Paul seems to interpret *salt* to mean wisdom or spiritual zest in speech, that is, speech that is not dull or insipid (Col. 4:6).

V. The Church as the Lord's fishery

Jesus said to His disciples, "Come after me, and I will make you to become fishers of men" (Mk. 1:17). This figure derives from the fact that the first disciples were fishermen. Employing a ready metaphor, He called them to become fishers of men. The Church is commissioned to catch men for Christ's kingdom, but in a good sense, for in Luke 5:10 the words "catch men" mean literally to "take men alive." Men caught for Christ receive a new quality of life. If the Church does not catch men for Christ, Satan will snare them (2 Tm. 2:25–26). The merely nominal Church, as in the parable of the dragnet, tends to catch some who are not true believers (Mt. 4:18–20; 13:47).

W. The Church as a crucible

The life of the Church is a life of faith. To be genuine, faith must be tested. God lets our faith be tested and tried in order that He may approve it. God can bless only the faith that has been proved genuine by testing. In 1 Peter 1:6–7, the phrase "the trial of your faith" is literally "the approval [by trial] of your faith." The Greek word for "trial" is *dokime*. The testing and approval of the believer's faith is said to be more precious than the testing and approval of gold. Like gold, faith must be put in the crucible to be proved and purged by the fire (1 Pt. 4:12–17; Jas. 1:3).

The believer's very life in the Christian fellowship of the Church puts him to a testing to love all the brethren, to walk in faith and obedience, to submit to Christ and to one another, and to draw upon the ministry of the Word in times of adversity (Prv. 17:3; 27:21). Peter declares that judgment begins at the household of God (1 Pt. 4:17). The Greek words *dokime, dokimazo, dokimos, dokimion*, which are used thirty-nine times in the New Testament, are words describing the work of the assayer with his crucible. In the life of the Church, believers are in God's crucible, being tested and approved (1 Thes. 2:4; 2 Cor. 10:18; Jas. 1:12.)

X. The Church as the wild olive branch

The Church, described as the wild olive branch, has been grafted into the tree of God's redeeming purpose, replacing rebellious Israel. This is not, however, a permanent displacement. When the Church has been completed, God will yet deal with and fulfill His promises to the remnant of Israel (Rom. 11:16–24; Jer. 11:16–17).

THE DOCTRINE OF ANGELS

Angelology

Introduction

I. Angelology

    A. Definition

    B. The origin of angels

    C. The nature of angels

        1. *Not corporeal*

        2. *A company, not a race*

        3. *Number*

        4. *Abode*

        5. *Personalities*

        6. *Wisdom and power*

    D. The classifications and organization of angels

        1. *The good angels*

        2. *The evil angels*

II. Demonology

    A. The reality of demons

    B. The origin of demons

        1. *The disembodied spirits of a pre-Adamic Earth*

        2. *The offspring of angels and antediluvian women*

        3. *The fallen angels*

    C. The nature of demons

        1. *Their strength*

        2. *Their wisdom*

        3. *Their character*

    D. The purpose of demons

    E. The activities of demons

        1. *Opposing the saints*

        2. *Inducing departure from the Faith*

        3. *Encouraging formalism and asceticism as the result of false teaching*

        4. *Backing all idol worship*

        5. *Causing various physical afflictions*

        6. *Accomplishing God's purposes sometimes*

    F. Demon possession

        1. *The reality of demon possession*

2. *Is there demon possession today?*
3. *The casting out of demons*
4. *The occult and demon possession*
5. *The Christian and demon possession*

III. Satanology
A. Importance of this doctrine
B. The reality of his existence
1. *Doubt of his existence*
2. *Scriptural record of his existence*
C. His personality
D. His origin
E. His character
F. His names and titles
1. *Lucifer*
2. *Satan*
3. *Devil*
4. *Serpent*
5. *Dragon*
6. *Beelzebub or Beelzebul*
7. *Belial*
8. *Tempter*
9. *Wicked, evil, or lawless one*
10. *Prince of this world*
11. *Prince of the power of the air*
12. *God of this world or age*
13. *Deceiver*
14. *Accuser*
15. *Angel of light*
16. *Murderer*
17. *Father of lies*
18. *Roaring lion*
19. *Destroyer*
G. His defeat
1. *Cast out of his exalted position in heaven*
2. *Cursed in the Garden of Eden*
3. *Defeated by Christ in the wilderness temptation*
4. *Judged at the cross of Calvary*
H. His destiny
1. *To be finally cast out of heaven*

      2. *To be confined to the bottomless pit*

      3. *To be consigned to the lake of fire*

I. The believer's course of action regarding Satan

      1. *Recognize Satan's limitations*

      2. *Realize Satan's power is limited by the will of God*

      3. *Realize Satan has been conquered*

      4. *Remember the believer has One who intercedes in his behalf*

      5. *Practice unceasing vigilance*

      6. *Deny Satan any foothold*

      7. *Put on the whole armor of God*

CHAPTER NINE

THE DOCTRINE OF ANGELS

Angelology

INTRODUCTION

THERE IS AN order of celestial beings which occupy a position quite distinct from that of either God or man. Far below the Godhead, they nevertheless dwell in an estate above that of fallen man. According to A. T. Pierson:

> God is the all-presiding, all-pervading, uncreated Spirit. Between Him and man there lies an intermediate realm, inhabited by a higher order of intelligences, neither pure spirit like God, nor so physically constituted as man. They are called angels, because they appear in Scripture as messengers of God to man.[1]

And according to Pearlman:

> With lightning speed and noiseless movement they pass from place to place. They inhabit the spaces of the air above us. Some we know to be concerned with our welfare, others are set on our harm. The inspired writers draw aside the curtain and give us a glimpse of this invisible world, in order that we may be both encouraged and warned.[2]

The only source of information we have of their existence and activities is the Holy Scriptures; mysticism and philosophy have no word of authority whatever. The Sadducees, a prominent group in the Jewish Sanhedrin at the time of Christ, did not believe in angels: "For the Sadducees say that there is no resurrection, neither angel, nor spirit" (Acts 23:8). Inasmuch as all our information about them comes from the Bible, we do well to learn from all that it says about them, but we must not go beyond that which is revealed. That they occupy a prominent place in God's providential administrations is indicated by the frequency of their mention in the Bible. The Old

---

1 Arthur Tappan Pierson, *The Bible and Spiritual Life* (New York: Gospel Publishing House, 1908), 166.

2 Myer Pearlman, *Knowing the Doctrines of the Bible* (Springfield, MO: Gospel Publishing House, 1939), 79.

Testament refers to them 108 times, while the New Testament mentions them 165 times. Satan was once a great angel, and we believe that demons are probably fallen angels. Whether holy or unholy, the spirit-beings are designated as angels. "And there was war in heaven: Michael and his angels fought against the dragon; and the dragon fought and his angels" (Rv. 12:7). Under the general title of angelology we will deal with three areas of consideration: holy angels, fallen angels (demons), and Satan. Thus, we will study angelology, demonology, and Satanology.

I. ANGELOLOGY

A. Definition

The word *angel*, whether taken from the Hebrew *mal'ak* of the Old Testament or from the Greek *aggelos* of the New Testament, means "messenger." The holy angels are messengers of God, while fallen angels are the messengers of Satan—"the god of this world."

B. The origin of angels

In distinction from God, the angels are created beings. They have not existed from all eternity. "Thou, even thou, art LORD alone; thou hast made heaven, the heaven of heavens, with all their host...and the host of heaven worshippeth thee" (Neh. 9:6). "Praise ye him, all his angels: praise him, all his hosts....Let them praise the name of the LORD: for he commanded, and they were created" (Ps. 148:2, 5). "For by him were all things created, that are in heaven, and that are in earth, visible and invisible, whether they be thrones, or dominions, or principalities, or powers: all things were created by him, and for him" (Col. 1:16). Angels indeed are among the invisible things which God created. As to exactly when they were created, the Scripture is not explicit. It is believed that it is most probable that they were created on the first day of Creation, immediately after the creation of heaven. Genesis 1:1 says, "In the beginning God created the heaven and the earth," and Job 38:7 says that "the sons of God shouted for joy" when He laid the foundations of the earth. Thus they were there when the earth was created.

C. The nature of angels

1. *Not corporeal*

a) They are spirits. They do not have bodies in the sense that man does. They are said to be spirits. "Who maketh his angels spirits; his ministers a flaming fire" (Ps. 104:4). "Are they not all ministering spirits, sent forth to minister for them who shall be heirs of salvation?" (Heb. 1:14). In Luke 24:39, Jesus said, "A spirit hath not flesh and bones, as ye see me have," but this does not mean that they are not real, individual creatures, both finite and special. However, they stand in a freer relation to time and space than man. Many can be present at one time in a very limited space. "And Jesus asked him, saying, What is thy name? And he said, Legion: because many devils were entered into him" (Lk. 8:30). They are certainly not omnipresent. Each is only in one place at one time.

b) They are not to be worshiped. Except on those very special occasions when God chooses to allow men to see them, angels are invisible to human sight and men are unconscious of their presence. It has been suggested that the reason that they are mostly invisible is because of the human tendency to worship them. The Scripture plainly warns against such a practice. We must not worship the creature rather than the Creator (Rom. 1:25). "Let no man beguile you of your reward in a voluntary humility and worshipping of angels, intruding into those things which he hath not seen, vainly puffed up by his fleshly mind" (Col. 2:18). This is a practice of the gnostic heresy.

> And I fell at his feet to worship him. And he said unto me, See thou do it not: I am thy fellowservant, and of thy brethren that have the testimony of Jesus: worship God: for the testimony of Jesus is the spirit of prophecy.
>
> —REVELATION 19:10

> And I John saw these things, and heard them. And when I had heard and seen, I fell down to worship before the feet of the angel which shewed me these things. Then saith he unto me, See thou do it not: for I am thy fellowservant, and of thy brethren the prophets, and of them which keep the sayings of this book: worship God.
>
> —REVELATION 22:8–9

c) Angels have, on numerous occasions, assumed the form of human bodies. "Be not forgetful to entertain strangers: for thereby some have entertained angels unawares" (Heb. 13:2). Such a thing as this verse suggests could not be possible if they did not appear as men. Many occasions when this became a reality are enumerated throughout the Scriptures. Here are just a few:

> And there came two angels to Sodom at even; and Lot sat in the gate of Sodom: and Lot seeing them rose up to meet them; and he bowed himself with his face toward the ground.
>
> —GENESIS 19:1

> And in the sixth month the angel Gabriel was sent from God unto a city in Galilee, named Nazareth, To a virgin espoused to a man whose name was Joseph, of the house of David; and the virgin's name was Mary.
>
> —LUKE 1:26–27

And seeth two angels in white sitting, the one at the head, and the other at the feet, where the body of Jesus had lain.

—JOHN 20:12

And the angel of the Lord spake unto Philip, saying, Arise, and go toward the south unto the way that goeth down from Jerusalem unto Gaza.

—ACTS 8:26

And, behold, the angel of the Lord came upon him, and a light shined in the prison: and he smote Peter on the side, and raised him up, saying, Arise up quickly. And his chains fell off from his hands. And the angel said unto him, Gird thyself, and bind on thy sandals. And so he did. And he saith unto him, Cast thy garment about thee, and follow me.

—ACTS 12:7–8

d) The angel of the Lord. The expression *the angel of the Lord*, which is used throughout the Old Testament, seems to have a very special significance in relation to the presence of God. It would seem that this person is the second person of the Godhead, Christ Himself in preincarnate presence. A few of these outstanding occasions are here listed.

The angel of the Lord appeared to Hagar as she was fleeing from the house of Abraham (Gn. 16:7–14). Four times in this passage the expression *the angel of the Lord* is used, but in verse 13 we read, "And she called the name of the LORD that spake unto her, Thou God seest me: for she said, Have I also here looked after him that seeth me?" Hagar recognized this angel of the Lord as God.

He appeared to Abraham when he was about to slay his son Isaac (Gn. 22:11–18). It was God who told Abraham to go offer his son, and when Abraham lifted up the knife to do so, "The angel of the LORD called unto him out of heaven, and said, Abraham, Abraham...Lay not thine hand upon the lad, neither do thou any thing unto him: for now I know that thou fearest God, seeing thou hast not withheld thy son, thine only son from me" (vv. 11–12). The phrase "from me" most definitely refers to God.

He appeared to Moses out of the bush which burned, but was not consumed (Ex. 3:2–5). In verse 2 of this passage we read that the angel of the Lord appeared to Moses "in a flame of fire out of the midst of the bush." In verse 4, this same person is called God: "God called unto him out of the midst of the bush, and said, Moses, Moses."

He showed himself to Gideon as he was threshing a little wheat behind the winepress, hiding it from the Midianites (Jgs. 6:11–23). In verse 12 we read of the angel of the Lord appearing to Gideon. In verse 14 we are told, "And the LORD looked upon him, and said, Go in this thy might."

Judges 13:2–23 gives the account of several visits to Manoah and his wife (the parents of Samson) by one who is variously called the angel of the Lord, an angel of God, and the man of God. Twelve times these expressions are used of this One, but in verse 22 we read, "Manoah said unto his wife, We will surely die, because we have seen God."

As Elijah was fleeing from Jezebel, who had threatened to take his life, he was weary and slept under a juniper tree, and the angel of the Lord brought him food (1 Kgs. 19:5–7).

Second Kings 19:35 recounts how, as the Assyrian army surrounded the city of Jerusalem, the angel of the Lord in one night smote 185,000 of the Assyrian soldiers.

2. *A company, not a race.* Angels were all created at one time, and there is no propagation among them. They do not die; thus there is no increase or decrease in their numbers. Jesus made it quite plain that they do not marry.

> And Jesus answering said unto them, The children of this world marry, and are given in marriage: But they which shall be accounted worthy to obtain that world, and the resurrection from the dead, neither marry, nor are given in marriage: Neither can they die any more: for they are equal unto the angels; and are the children of God, being the children of the resurrection.
> —Luke 20:34–36

Angels are referred to in the masculine gender, which is always used of those in whom there is no sexual distinction. Though we read of the sons of God, we never read of the sons of angels.

3. *Number.* Their great numbers are indicated in the following Scriptures: "But ye are come unto mount Sion, and unto the city of the living God, the heavenly Jerusalem, and to an innumerable company of angels (Heb. 12:22; "Thinkest thou that I cannot now pray to my Father, and he shall presently give me more than twelve legions of angels?" (Mt. 26:53); "And I beheld, and I heard the voice of many angels round about the throne and the beasts and the elders: and the number of them was ten thousand times ten thousand, and thousands of thousands" (Rv. 5:11). Ten thousand times ten thousand is one hundred million. Thousands of thousands could not be less than four million. So you have a minimum total of 104 million angels! No doubt the main thought being conveyed by all these verses is that within the comprehension of man their number is innumerable. God, who knows all things, knows the number of angels.

4. *Abode.* While angels are often depicted as ministering in God's behalf to saints here on Earth, it seems their main abode is in heaven (Mt. 22:30). "And suddenly there was with the angel a multitude of the heavenly host praising God, and saying,

Glory to God in the highest, and on earth peace, good will toward men. And it came to pass, as the angels were gone away from them into heaven" (Lk. 2:13–15). "And he saith unto them, Verily, verily, I say unto you, Hereafter ye shall see heaven open, and the angels of God ascending and descending upon the Son of Man" (Jn. 1:51).

Jesus spoke of "the angels which are in heaven" (Mk. 13:32), and Paul wrote, "But though we, or an angel from heaven, preach any other gospel unto you" (Gal. 1:8). It would seem that the angels have a special place in which to dwell in heaven. Jude writes of "the angels which kept not their first estate, but left their own habitation" (Jude 6).

5. *Personalities.* Angels possess every feature of personality. They are individual beings. They are rational beings: "My lord is wise, according to the wisdom of an angel of God, to know all things that are in the earth" (2 Sm. 14:20); "Which things the angels desire to look into" (1 Pt. 1:12). They render intelligent worship: "Praise ye him, all his angels: praise ye him, all his hosts" (Ps. 148:2). They possess emotions: "Likewise, I say unto you, there is joy in the presence of the angels of God over one sinner that repenteth" (Lk. 15:10). They are moral beings created with the ability to know and do that which is right or wrong. They have been rewarded for obedience and punished for disobedience: "For if God spared not the angels that sinned, but cast them down to hell, and delivered them into chains of darkness, to be reserved unto judgment" (2 Pt. 2:4); "And the angels which kept not their first estate, but left their own habitation, he hath reserved in everlasting chains under darkness unto the judgment of the great day" (Jude 6). There was a time of probation during which the angels could choose to obey God or to disobey. Those who disobeyed were cast out, while those who obeyed were confirmed in their stand for God. We do not read of any angels falling after the period of probation passed.

6. *Wisdom and power.* The angels are represented as having superhuman wisdom and intelligence. "But of that day and hour knoweth no man, no, not the angels of heaven, but my Father only" (Mt. 24:36). This implies that angels' knowledge is above man's: "My Lord is wise, according to the wisdom of an angel of God, to know all things that are in the earth" (2 Sm. 14:20); "Art thou come to destroy us? I know thee who thou art; the Holy One of God" (Lk. 4:34). Though the knowledge of angels is great, they are not omniscient. There are certain things they would like to know: "Which things the angels desire to look into" (1 Pt. 1:12).

Much is said in the Scripture concerning the power and strength of the angels, though nowhere is it indicated that they are omnipotent. Their power is derived from God. "They are unable to do those things which are peculiar to Deity—create, act without means, or search the human heart."[3] "Bless the LORD, ye his angels, that

---

3 Lewis Sperry Chafer, *Systematic Theology* (Dallas, TX: Dallas Seminary Press, 1947), II, 15.

excel in strength, that do his commandments, hearkening unto the voice of his word" (Ps. 103:20). "Whereas angels, which are greater in power and might, bring not railing accusation against them before the Lord" (2 Pt. 2:11). "And to you who are troubled rest with us, when the Lord Jesus shall be revealed from heaven with his mighty angels" (2 Thes. 1:7). Disciples were delivered from prison by angels. "But during the night an angel of the Lord opened the doors of the jail and brought them out" (Acts 5:19, NIV). "Suddenly an angel of the Lord appeared and a light shone in the cell. He struck Peter on the side and woke him up. 'Quick, get up!' he said, and the chains fell off Peter's wrists" (Acts 12:7, NIV). It has been estimated that the stone which was placed in front of the Lord's tomb could have weighed four tons, yet we read, "There was a violent earthquake, for an angel of the Lord came down from heaven and, going to the tomb, rolled back the stone and sat on it" (Mt. 28:2, NIV). In Revelation 20:1–2, John tells us, "And I saw an angel come down from heaven, having the key of the bottomless pit and a great chain in his hand. And he laid hold on the dragon, that old serpent, which is the Devil, and Satan, and bound him a thousand years." The angels are spoken of as being subservient to Christ. They are "his mighty angels" (2 Thes. 1:7). "Who is gone into heaven, and is on the right hand of God; angels and authorities and powers being made subject unto him" (1 Pt. 3:22). "And ye are complete in him, which is the head of all principality and power" (Col. 2:10).

D. The classifications and organization of angels

Generally speaking, all angels may be classified under two headings: good or evil angels. We shall consider the good, or holy, angels.

1. *The good angels*

a) An apparent variety among them

(1) Different positions or offices—Comparing the following three verses of Scripture, it seems there are five different positions or offices of authority among the angels: thrones, dominions, principalities, authorities, and powers. "Far above all principality, and power, and might, and dominion" (Eph. 1:21); "For by him were all things created, that are in heaven, and that are in earth, visible and invisible, whether they be thrones, or dominions, or principalities, or powers" (Col. 1:16); "Angels and authorities and powers being made subject unto him" (1 Pt. 3:22). Just what each of these designations indicates is not made clear in the Scripture. It is not easy for us to comprehend heavenly organization.

> All that we know is, that there is foundation for the main idea—that there is
> no dull and sating uniformity among the inhabitants of heaven—that order
> and freedom are not inconsistent with gradation or rank—that there is glory
> and a higher glory—power and a nobler power—rank and a loftier rank,
> to be witnessed in the mighty scale. As there are orbs of dazzling radiance

amidst the paler and humbler stars of the sky, so there are bright and majestic chieftains among the hosts of God, nearer God in position, and like God in majesty, possessing and reflecting more of the Divine splendour, than their lustrous brethren around them.[4]

The most important point of all as we consider just what these various ranks may signify is that Jesus is high above them all; He has no equal and no superior.

(2) Cherubim—Whether this term indicates a special position or an exalted service rendered by those who bear this name is uncertain. Cherubim first appear at the entrance to the garden of Eden: "So he [God] drove out the man; and he placed at the east of the garden of Eden Cherubims...to keep the way of the tree of life" (Gn. 3:24). Over the ark of the covenant in the holy of holies of the tabernacle in the wilderness, two golden cherubims were wrought as part of the mercy seat (Ex. 37:6–9; 2 Kgs. 19:15). They are also said to have been woven into the beautiful inner veil of the tabernacle and temple (Ex. 26:1). Ezekiel refers to them nineteen different times. It is believed that they are synonymous with the "living creatures" of Revelation 4:6–5:14 (NKJV, a better translation than "beasts," from the Authorized Version). From these and other references it would seem that the cherubims particularly have to do with the righteousness and majesty of the throne of God.

(3) Seraphim—The word *seraphim* means "the burning ones." They are mentioned only in Isaiah 6. They are seen by the prophet as standing above the throne of God, each having six wings, and they are occupied with praising God, crying one to another, "Holy, holy, holy, is the LORD of hosts; The whole earth is full of His glory" (v. 6). One of the seraphim, in response to Isaiah's confession of the uncleanness of his lips, flew with a live coal from off the altar and touched the prophet's lips saying, "Lo, this hath touched thy lips; and thine iniquity is taken away, and thy sin purged" (v. 7). This prepared Isaiah for the service to which God was about to call him. This would appear to be a very significant part of the ministry of the seraphim. Dr. C. I. Scofield, in his Bible notes on this incident, speaks of the necessity of cleansing before service: "The Cherubim may be said to have to do with the altar, the Seraphim with the laver."[5]

(4) Michael and Gabriel—These two are distinct among the angel hosts, for they are the only two whose names are mentioned. Michael is mentioned on four different occasions in the Scripture. "And at that time shall Michael stand up, the great prince which standeth for the children of thy people" (Dn. 12:1). The name Michael means

---

4 John Eadie, *Commentary on the Epistle to the Ephesians* (Grand Rapids. MI: Zondervan Publishing House, 1883), 102.

5 Cyrus I. Scofield, *The New Scofield Reference Bible* (New York: Oxford University Press, 1967), 718.

"who is like God?" He is spoken of as the one who stands up—probably in defense—of the people of Israel. "But the prince of the kingdom of Persia withstood me one and twenty days: but, lo, Michael, one of the chief princes, came to help me" (Dn. 10:13). In this same connection, verse 21 speaks of "Michael your prince." If it is true, as many Bible teachers believe, that there are angelic personalities who oversee certain nations, such as the Prince of Persia and the Prince of Grecia, then Michael could be thought of as the Prince of Israel (Dn. 10:21). In Jude's epistle we read, "Yet Michael the archangel, when contending with the devil he disputed about the body of Moses, durst not bring against him a railing accusation, but said, The Lord rebuke thee" (Jude 9). Here Michael is called an archangel. He is the only one to whom this designation is applied. If he is the only one, then perhaps he will be the one to speak at the second coming of the Lord: "For the Lord himself shall descend from heaven with a shout, with the voice of the archangel, and with the trump of God" (1 Thes. 4:16). In Revelation 12:7–9 we learn more about the warring capability of Michael:

> And there was war in heaven: Michael and his angels fought against the dragon; and the dragon fought and his angels, And prevailed not; neither was their place found any more in heaven. And the great dragon was cast out, that old serpent, called the Devil, and Satan, which deceiveth the whole world: he was cast out into the earth, and his angels were cast out with him.

Gabriel, signifying "warrior of God," is never designated in the Bible as an archangel, but he has often been called one. He is mentioned four times in the Scripture, always as the bearer of great tidings concerning God's purposes. In Daniel 8:15–27 he informed Daniel of events concerning the End Times. In Daniel 9:20–27 He revealed to Daniel the meaning of the vision he had concerning the seventy weeks. As Zacharias, the priest and father of John the Baptist, was burning incense in the priest's office, Gabriel appeared to him and said unto him, "Fear not, Zacharias: for thy prayer is heard; and thy wife Elisabeth shall bear thee a son, and thou shalt call his name John....I am Gabriel, that stand in the presence of God; and am sent to speak unto thee, and to shew thee these glad tidings" (Lk. 1:13, 19). Gabriel's preeminent position is indicated by the words, "that stand in the presence of God." John was to be the forerunner of our Lord's coming and the one who should baptize Him in the Jordan. Gabriel's greatest message was his announcement to the Virgin Mary of the birth of the Lord Jesus Christ and His part in the kingdom of God, sitting upon the throne of David (Lk. 1:26–38).

b) The ministry of the good angels

(1) In relation to God

(a) Giving worship and praise—The principal, and possibly most important, ministry of the good angels is that of worshiping and offering unceasing praise to God, for He is worthy:

> And I beheld, and I heard the voice of many angels round about the throne and the beasts and the elders: and the number of them was ten thousand times ten thousand, and thousands of thousands: Saying with a loud voice, Worthy is the Lamb that was slain to receive power, and riches, and wisdom, and strength, and honour, and glory, and blessing.
>
> —REVELATION 5:11–12

> And again, when he bringeth in the firstbegotten into the world, he saith, And let all the angels of God worship him.
>
> —HEBREWS 1:6

> And one cried unto another, and said, Holy, holy, holy, is the LORD of hosts: the whole earth is full of his glory.
>
> —ISAIAH 6:3

> Bless the LORD, ye his angels, that excel in strength, that do his commandments, hearkening unto the voice of his word. Bless ye the LORD, all ye his hosts; ye ministers of his that do his pleasure.
>
> —PSALM 103:20–21

One thing seems to be certain: angels never draw attention to themselves, but always ascribe glory to God. Angels were present at the time of Creation and joined together in song at this great event: "Where wast thou when I laid the foundations of the earth.... When the morning stars sang together, and all the sons of God shouted for joy?" (Jb. 38:4–7).

(b) Bringing God's law to His people—"Who have received the law by the disposition of angels, and have not kept it" (Acts 7:53). "Wherefore then serveth the law? It was added because of transgressions, till the seed should come to whom the promise was made; and it was ordained by angels in the hand of a mediator" (Gal. 3:19). "For if the word spoken by angels was stedfast, and every transgression and disobedience received a just recompense of reward" (Heb. 2:2).

(c) Executing God's judgments upon His enemies—"And immediately the angel of the Lord smote him, because he gave not God the glory: and he was eaten of worms, and gave up the ghost" (Acts 12:23). Thus was Herod smitten after he gave a great oration at Caesarea. The people said, "It is the voice of a god, and not of a man," and Herod did not give God the glory (Acts 12:22). "And it came to pass that night, that the angel of the LORD went out, and smote in the camp of the Assyrians an hundred fourscore and five thousand: and when they arose early in the morning, behold, they were all dead corpses" (2 Kgs. 19:35).

(d) Gathering together God's elect at Christ's second coming—"And they shall see the Son of Man coming in the clouds of heaven with power and great glory. And he shall send his angels with a great sound of a trumpet, and they shall gather together his elect from the four winds, from one end of heaven to the other" (Mt. 24:30–31).

They stand before the gates of the New Jerusalem, which had, "A wall great and high, and had twelve gates, and at the gates twelve angels" (Rv. 21:12). Thiessen suggests that "they will apparently serve as a kind of honorary body of sentinels, as if to guarantee that nothing that is unclean or defiled will ever enter that city."[6]

They are seen pouring out the bowls of wrath in Revelation 16: "And I heard a great voice out of the temple saying to the seven angels, Go your ways, and pour out the vials of the wrath of God upon the earth" (v. 1).

(e) Assisting on the Day of Judgment—"Let both grow together until the harvest: and in the time of harvest I will say to the reapers, Gather ye together first the tares, and bind them in bundles to burn them: but gather the wheat into my barn.... The enemy that sowed them is the devil; the harvest is the end of the world; and reapers are the angels" (Mt. 13:30, 39). God's angels will be the reapers who will separate the believers from the unbelievers. They know the difference between the wheat and the tares. "So shall it be at the end of the world: the angels shall come forth, and sever the wicked from the just, And shall cast them into the furnace of fire: there shall be wailing and gnashing of teeth" (Mt. 13:49–50). "And to you who are troubled rest with us, when the Lord Jesus shall be revealed from heaven with his mighty angels, In flaming fire taking vengeance on them that know not God, and that obey not the gospel of our Lord Jesus Christ" (2 Thes. 1:7–8). Between chapters 7 and 20 of the book of Revelation, angels are mentioned as having part in God's judgments no less than fifty-seven times. If any wonder how God will bring all men to the judgment, he has only to remind himself of the multitude of mighty angels whom the Lord will use for this purpose. Nothing can thwart this ministry of the angels, and there will be no mistakes made.

(2) In relation to Christ—The angels have shown, and continue to show, a great interest in the person and ministry of Jesus Christ. A great deal is involved in the words of Paul when he wrote, "And without controversy great is the mystery of godliness: God was manifest in the flesh, justified in the Spirit, seen of angels" (1 Tm. 3:16). Some fifteen distinct references in relation to Jesus Christ are attributed to angels' ministrations:

---

6 Henry Clarence Thiessen, *Introductory Lectures in Systematic Theology* (Grand Rapids, MI: Wm. B. Eerdmans Publishing Company, 1949), 207.

- The birth of His forerunner, John the Baptist, was announced to John's father by an angel (Lk. 1:11–13).
- Mary was informed by the angel Gabriel that she should be the mother of the Savior (Lk. 1:26–38).
- Joseph was assured by an angel that "that which is conceived in her is of the Holy Ghost" (Mt. 1:20).
- Angels brought the tidings of His birth to the shepherds in the fields at Bethlehem (Lk. 2:8–15).
- Joseph was warned by an angel to take Mary and the young child to Egypt to escape from Herod (Mt. 2:13).
- Joseph, again directed by an angel, was instructed to return to the land of Israel after the death of Herod (Mt. 2:19–20).
- Angels ministered to our Lord after His wilderness temptation (Mt. 4:11).
- Jesus told Nathaniel that he would see angels ascending and descending upon Himself (Jn. 1:51).
- An angel from heaven strengthened Him in the Garden of Gethsemane (Lk. 22:43).
- Jesus said He could ask the Father and He would send more than twelve legions of angels to protect Him if necessary or desirable (Mt. 26:53).
- An angel rolled back the stone from before the sepulchre and spoke to the women who came to the tomb (Mt. 28:2–7).
- Angels were present at the time of Christ's ascension (Acts 1:11).
- In His glorified position, angels render Him supreme homage as their Lord (1 Pt. 3:22).
- Angels will accompany the Lord when He comes the second time (Mt. 16:27; 25:31).

(3) In relation to believers—It is of the utmost importance that believers understand the ministry of angels in their behalf, that their faith might be encouraged regarding this gracious provision God has made for them. It is surprising to find a number of commentators expressing their belief that the ministry of angels to men ceased at the ascension of Christ, not to be resumed until His return to Earth. This is difficult to understand in relation to Hebrews 1:14, where we are told, "Are they not all ministering spirits, sent forth to minister for them who shall be heirs of salvation?" This certainly applies to believers today.

The following are some of the many ministrations angels have performed in behalf of God's people in Old Testament times, the time of our Lord's dwelling on Earth, and during the early Church days. There is no reason to believe that they have ceased to do similar things today.

(a) Protecting from accidental harm—"For he shall give his angels charge over thee, to keep thee in all thy ways. They shall bear thee up in their hands, lest thou dash thy foot against a stone" (Ps. 91:11–12). When we know as we are known, we will understand who it was that delivered us from times of disaster and harm.

> And when the morning arose, then the angels hastened Lot, saying, Arise, take thy wife, and thy two daughters, which are here; lest thou be consumed in the iniquity of the city. And while he lingered, the men laid hold upon his hand, and upon the hand of his wife, and upon the hand of his two daughters; the LORD being merciful unto him: and they brought him forth, and set him without the city.
>
> —GENESIS 19:15–16

(b) Delivering from their enemies—"The angel of the LORD encampeth round about them that fear him, and delivereth them" (Ps. 34:7). Elisha and his servant experienced this very blessing.

> And when the servant of the man of God was risen early, and gone forth, behold, an host compassed the city both with horses and chariots. And his servant said unto him, Alas, my master! how shall we do? And he answered, Fear not: for they that be with us are more than they that be with them. And Elisha prayed, and said, LORD, I pray thee, open his eyes, that he may see. And the LORD opened the eyes of the young man; and he saw: and, behold, the mountain was full of horses and chariots of fire round about Elisha.
>
> —2 KINGS 6:15–17

Here is a beautiful example of the words: "The chariots of God are twenty thousand, even thousands of angels" (Ps. 68:17). "My God hath sent his angel, and hath shut the lions' mouths, that they have not hurt me: forasmuch as before him innocency was found in me; and also before thee, O king, have I done no hurt" (Dn. 6:22). "And when Peter was come to himself, he said, Now I know of a surety, that the Lord hath sent his angel, and hath delivered me out of the hand of Herod, and from all the expectation of the people of the Jews" (Acts 12:11).

(c) Encouraging in times of extreme trial—When Elijah was fleeing from the threats of Jezebel: "And as he lay and slept under a juniper tree, behold, then an angel touched him, and said unto him, Arise and eat" (1 Kgs. 19:5). As Jacob was fleeing from the wrath of his brother Esau:

And he dreamed, and behold a ladder set up on the earth, and the top of it reached to heaven: and behold the angels of God ascending and descending on it. And, behold, the LORD stood above it, and said, I am the LORD God of Abraham thy father, and the God of Isaac: the land whereon thou liest, to thee will I give it, and to thy seed.

—GENESIS 28:12–13

Twenty years later, as Jacob was returning to meet his brother Esau, he was filled with fear in anticipation of the reception he might receive from Esau. But we read of a host of angels meeting him, no doubt to greatly encourage him: "And Jacob went on his way, and the angels of God met him. And when Jacob saw them, he said, This is God's host: and he called the name of the place Mahanaim [meaning 'two hosts, or two bands']" (Gn. 32:1–2). Paul, in the midst of the storm at sea that threatened the lives of all on board, cheered his fellow sailors with these words:

And now I exhort you to be of good cheer: for there shall be no loss of any man's life among you, but of the ship. For there stood by me this night the angel of God, whose I am, and whom I serve, Saying, Fear not, Paul; thou must be brought before Caesar: and, lo, God hath given thee all them that sail with thee.

—ACTS 27:22–24

(d) Granting wisdom and guidance—Joseph was perplexed regarding giving Mary a bill of divorcement: "But while he thought on these things, behold, the angel of the Lord appeared unto him in a dream, saying, Joseph, thou son of David, fear not to take unto thee Mary thy wife: for that which is conceived in her is of the Holy Ghost" (Mt. 1:20). (See also Mt. 2:13, 19–20.) Philip was directed to win the Ethiopian eunuch to the Lord: "And the angel of the Lord spake unto Philip, saying, Arise, and go toward the south unto the way that goeth down from Jerusalem unto Gaza, which is desert" (Acts 8:26–27). Cornelius, the Roman centurion, was praying and "saw in a vision evidently about the ninth hour of the day an angel of God coming in to him, and saying unto him, Cornelius.... Thy prayers and thine alms are come up for a memorial before God. And now send men to Joppa, and call for one Simon, whose surname is Peter" (Acts 10:3–5).

(e) Escorting the soul at death—Concerning Lazarus, the beggar, we are told: "And it came to pass, that the beggar died, and was carried by the angels into Abraham's bosom: the rich man also died, and was buried" (Lk. 16:22). Many a great saint of God has testified at the moment of his departure from this life of being conscious of the presence of heavenly beings around him.

(f) Rejoicing over salvation—That the angels are vitally interested in believers is evidenced by their rejoicing at the repentance of each sinner: "Likewise, I say unto you, there is joy in the presence of the angels of God over one sinner that repenteth" (Lk. 15:10). No doubt they also rejoice as Jesus confesses the faith of these believers in the presence of the angels: "Also I say unto you, Whosoever shall confess me before men, him shall the Son of Man also confess before the angels of God: But he that denieth me before men shall be denied before the angels of God" (Lk. 12:8–9).

(g) Concerning guardian angels—There is no scriptural authority for the age-old idea that each person, as soon as he is born, is assigned a special guardian angel who will attend and watch over that one throughout his lifetime. The two verses of Scripture that have often been used as evidence do not provide enough evidence for this notion. "Take heed that ye despise not one of these little ones; for I say unto you, That in heaven their angels do always behold the face of my Father which is in heaven" (Mt. 18:10). Many interpretations of this verse have been offered. The following seems to be a plausible explanation, and one which brings in the other verse often used to support the doctrine of individual guardian angels.

> All of course depends on the interpretation of "angel." At the first glance it would seem that these little ones have angels in heaven. There is a passage in Acts 12:15 which is the key to solve the difficulty here. When Peter, rescued by an angel, led forth miraculously from the prison house, knocked at the door of a praying assembly and Rhoda maintained that Peter stood outside, they said, "It is his angel." They believed that Peter had suffered death and that his angel stood outside. What does "angel" mean in this passage? It must mean the departed spirit of Peter. This fact throws light on the passage before us. If these little ones, who belong to the kingdom of heaven, depart, their disembodied spirits behold the Father's face in heaven; in other words, they are saved.[7]

The Scripture is very clear with regard to the ministry of angels in behalf of all believers, but it does not teach individual guardian angels.

(h) Ministering to believers—There has been much confusion between the ministry of angels and that of the Holy Spirit toward believers within the Church today. Billy Graham has these interesting things to say:

> Angels do not indwell men, the Holy Spirit seals them and indwells them when He has regenerated them. The Holy Spirit is all-knowing, all-present,

---

7 Arno Clemens Gaebelein, *The Gospel of Matthew* (New York: Publication Office, Our Hope, 1910), 83–84.

and all-powerful. Angels are mightier than men, but they are not gods and they do not possess the attributes of the Godhead. Not angels, but the Holy Spirit convicts men of sin, righteousness and judgment (John 16:7). He reveals and interprets Jesus Christ to men, while angels remain messengers of God who serve men as ministering spirits (Heb. 1:14). So far as I know, no Scripture says that the Holy Spirit ever manifested Himself in human form to men. Jesus did this in His incarnation. The glorious Holy Spirit can be everywhere at the same time, but no angel can be in more than one place at any given moment. We know the Holy Spirit as spirit, not flesh, but we can know angels not as spirits alone but sometimes also in visible form.[8]

It would seem that angel ministrations are especially related to temporal matters, while the Holy Spirit ministers to believers with regard to spiritual things. Again, according to Billy Graham, "The Holy Spirit not only guides and directs believers, but also performs a work of grace in their hearts, conforming them to the image of God to make them holy like Christ. Angels cannot provide this sanctifying power."[9]

(i) Learning from the Church—Though they are extremely wise, they are not omniscient, and thus it would be natural to suppose that they are continually learning, especially with regard to the things of God. This fact is made clear in the Scripture. For ages, the angelic host has been worshiping and praising God for His holiness and the greatness of His power in creation, but with the manifestation of the gospel of the grace of God, a whole new sphere of God's greatness and character—His infinite love and marvelous grace—has been revealed. Thus the angels desire to know more of this great salvation.

> Of which salvation the prophets have enquired and searched diligently... Searching what, or what manner of time the Spirit of Christ which was in them did signify, when it testified beforehand the sufferings of Christ, and the glory that should follow. Unto whom it was revealed, that not unto themselves, but unto us they did minister the things, which are now reported unto you by them that have preached the gospel unto you with the Holy Ghost sent down from heaven; which things the angels desire to look into.
>
> —1 PETER 1:10–12

Furthermore, God's disciplines and dealings with the Church have provided a marvelous revelation to the angels of His manifold wisdom: "To the intent that now

---

8 William Franklin Graham, *Angels: God's Secret Agents* (Garden City, NY: Doubleday Pocket Books, 1975), 42–43.

9 Ibid., 53.

unto the principalities and powers in heavenly places might be known by [or through] the church the manifold wisdom of God" (Eph. 3:10). No doubt the angels will enjoy the prospects revealed in Ephesians 2:7: "That in the ages to come he might shew the exceeding riches of his grace in his kindness toward us through Christ Jesus."

j) Availing oneself of the ministry of angels—Nowhere are we instructed to pray to angels and request their help. Their ministrations are directed in our behalf by the Lord Himself. Thus, if we would experience the benefits and blessings of these ministering spirits, we must keep close to our Lord. The great promise of Psalm 91, "He shall give his angels charge over thee, to keep thee in all thy ways" (v. 11), is given to those who dwell "in the secret place of the most High" and "abide under the shadow of the Almighty" (v. 1). Again, we are instructed by the promise, "The angel of the LORD encampeth round about them that fear him, and delivereth them" (Ps. 34:7). Let us reverently fear Him and abide in His presence! Remember they are "ministering spirits, sent forth to minister for them who shall be heirs of salvation" (Heb. 1:14). May we ever conduct ourselves as those who are children in the household of our heavenly Father: "And if children, then heirs; heirs of God, and joint-heirs with Christ" (Rom. 8:17).

2. *The evil angels.* While it is inspiring and most encouraging to learn of God's great guardian angels watching over and ministering to those who are the redeemed children of the Lord, it is also very important to recognize the reality and presence, in this area of our spiritual warfare, of a vast host of enemy spirits whose purpose seems to be to thwart all spiritual progress. One of the fundamental maxims of warfare has always been study the enemy. We would be very unwise if we did not do this in this most important of all areas—that of spiritual conflict.

a) Their existence. The Bible clearly states the fact of their existence. It contrasts them with those angels who have continued to do the will of God: "And the angels which kept not their first estate, but left their own habitation" (Jude 6); "For if God spared not the angels that sinned, but cast them down to hell" (2 Pt. 2:4). They are recognized as agents of God's judgment upon an evil people, in this case the people of Egypt: "He cast upon them the fierceness of his anger, wrath, and indignation, and trouble, by sending evil angels among them" (Ps. 78:49) They are pictured as in the service of Satan: "Depart from me, ye cursed, into everlasting fire, prepared for the devil and his angels" (Mt. 25:41); "And there was war in heaven: Michael and his angels fought against the dragon; and the dragon fought and his angels....and his angels were cast out with him" (Rv. 12:7, 9).

b) Their identity. There are those who make a difference between evil, or fallen, angels and demons, but it would seem a great number of Bible teachers have come to believe that the evil angels are the demons of which the Bible has much to say. We recognize that the Bible is not explicit with regard to this point, but with what evidence from the Scripture we have, this explanation seems to be the best supported and most clearly authenticated. With this in mind, we shall consider the subject of demonology.

II. DEMONOLOGY

The subject of demonology occupies a fairly substantial place in the revelations of Holy Scripture. It would seem wise for us to learn what the Scripture has made clear without endeavoring to trespass into areas that God has not revealed. The Authorized Version has somewhat obscured the subject by a poor translation of the words *daimonion* and *daimon,* rendering them as "devil" or "devils." The Revised, and other later versions, have properly translated these as "demons." There is only one devil—*diabolos*—while there are multitudes of demons.

A. The reality of demons

Jesus recognized their reality. "And if I by Beelzebul cast out demons, by whom do your sons cast them out? Consequently they shall be your judges. But if I cast out demons by the Spirit of God, then the kingdom of God has come unto you" (Mt. 12:27–28, NASB). "Heal the sick, raise the dead, cleanse the lepers, cast out demons; freely you received, freely give" (Mt. 10:8, NASB). "And these signs will accompany those who have believed: in My name they will cast out demons, they will speak with new tongues" (Mk. 16:17, NASB).

The Seventy believed in their reality. "And the seventy returned with joy, saying, 'Lord, even the demons are subject to us in Your name'" (Lk. 10:17, NASB).

The apostle Paul recognized their reality. "No, but I say that the things which the Gentiles sacrifice, they sacrifice to demons, and not to God; and I do not want you to become sharers in demons" (1 Cor. 10:20, NASB). "But the Spirit explicitly says that in later times some will fall away from the faith, paying attention to deceitful spirits and doctrines of demons" (1 Tm. 4:1, NASB).

B. The origin of demons

After God, the Creator of all things, had finished His work of creation, He pronounced that it was all good: "And God saw every thing that he had made, and, behold, it was very good" (Gn. 1:31). It seems quite certain from this verse that the demons were not created sinful. If, as we are assuming, the demons are angels "which kept not their first estate, but left their own habitation" (Jude 6); and are those referred to when we read, "For if God spared not the angels that sinned, but cast them down to hell" (2 Pt. 2:4), then we can conclude that they were once perfect, sinless beings. The cause of their fall and how they became demons has been the subject of much conjecture. Three principal theories have been advanced by conservative Christian scholars endeavoring to demonstrate scriptural authority.

1. *The disembodied spirits of inhabitants of a pre-Adamic Earth.* Merrill Unger has written the following:

> A pre-Adamite race is thought of as existing on the original earth (Gn. 1:1), under the governorship of Satan in his unfallen state, as "the anointed cherub that covereth" (Ez. 28:14). This pristine sphere is, moreover, viewed as the scene of Satan's revolt (Is. 14:12–14), and the invasion of sin into the moral universe, resulting in an awful cataclysm which reduced it to chaos (Gn. 1:2). The members of the pre-Adamite race, whom Pember describes as being "men in the flesh," were somehow involved in the rebellion, and, in the ensuing catastrophe, suffered the loss of their material bodies, becoming "disembodied spirits," or demons. The oft-recorded fact that demons are continually seizing upon the bodies of men to try to use them as their own is taken as confirmatory evidence that demons are disembodied spirits, and that their intense desire for re-embodiment indicates that the intolerable condition of being unclothed, for which they were not created, is so overpowering that they will even enter the bodies of swine (Luke. 8:32).[10]

2. *The offspring of angels and antediluvian women.* This theory is based on an interpretation of Genesis 6:1–2, 4:

> And it came to pass, when men began to multiply on the face of the earth, and daughters were born unto them, That the sons of God saw the daughters of men that they were fair; and they took them wives of all which they chose.... There were giants in those days; and also after that, when the sons of God came in unto the daughters of men, and they bare children to them, the same became mighty men which were of old, men of renown.

What some believe is taught here is that there was a totally unnatural cohabitation between evil spirit-beings and the women of that day. Those who hold this view believe that this sin is the explanation of why some fallen spirit-beings are confined in chains while others are allowed to go free. Jude speaks of some who are "reserved in everlasting chains under darkness unto the judgment of the great day" (v. 6). The nature of the sin of which these "angels who kept not their first estate" were guilty is compared to Sodom and Gomorrah, where the sexual sins of these cities caused them to be destroyed by fire and brimstone. Jude 7 goes on to designate the sins of these evil angels as fornication, so we know these were sins of the flesh. He further describes

---

10 Merrill F. Unger, *Biblical Demonology: A Study of the Spiritual Forces Behind the Present World Unrest* (Wheaton, IL: VanKampen Press, 1952), 42–43.

their deeds as "going after strange flesh," referring, it is believed, to the unnatural relationship between spirits and women. As a result of these great sins, God's wrath was manifest, and He sent the Flood in judgment. The bodies of the monstrous offspring of these unions, according to the theory, were destroyed in the Flood, and their disembodied spirits became demons. This purports to show why demons desire to enter into human bodies, inasmuch as they have experienced embodiment and are unhappy in their disembodied state.

If all this could possibly be true, why were the spirits of those who were born to these unholy unions allowed to go free instead of being consigned to sheol (the same as hades in the New Testament), as were the other wicked antediluvians? "The wicked will return to sheol, even all the nations who forget God" (Ps. 9:17, NASB). "The rich man also died, and was buried. And in hell he lift up his eyes, being in torments" (Lk. 16:22–23). "And the sea gave up the dead which were in it, and death and Hades gave up the dead which were in them; and they were judged, every one of them according to their deeds" (Rv. 20:13, NASB). (See also Ez. 32:17–24.)

This position hinges on the meaning of *the sons of God*. In the New Testament, this expression refers to those who have become the sons of God through the new birth: Jn 1:12; Rom. 8:14–16; and 1 Jn. 3:1–2. In the Old Testament, the expression is used five times: twice in Genesis 6:2–4 and three times in Job, where Satan, an angelic being, is classed with the sons of God (Jb. 1:6; 2:1; 38:7). One of the principal objections to this theory is taken from Jesus' words in Matthew 22:30 and Mark 12:25, where the teaching seems to be that angelic beings are sexless. Jesus said that they neither marry nor are given in marriage. To counteract this statement of Jesus, it is claimed that this fact may be true of unfallen angels in heaven, but not of fallen angels. Unger says that to claim such knowledge "is to assume, it would seem, a degree of knowledge of fallen angelic nature which man does not possess."[11]

Many who deny the possibility of interrelationships between the evil spirits and the daughters of the human race believe the term *the sons of God* refers to the descendents of the godly line of Seth with the women of the descendents of Cain. This may well be an oversimplification of the problem, for it raises almost as many difficulties as it meets. On what basis could the descendents of Seth be called the sons of God? Because of his creation in the image of God, Adam could be well-called a son of God. But when Adam bore Seth, it is said he "begat a son in his own likeness, after his image" (Gn. 5:3). Adam was a fallen man—a sinner—when Seth was born in his likeness. Both Seth and Cain were born outside the garden of Eden to parents who were sinful by nature. Though in practice Cain may have gone into deeper depths of sin than Seth, neither, apart from the grace of God, could be called sons of God. The

11 Unger, 50.

more obvious difficulty with this explanation is the reason why the union of these two families would result in the birth of unusual offspring, as suggested by the words, "When the sons of God came in unto the daughters of men, and they bare children to them, the same became mighty men which were of old, men of renown" (Gn. 6:4). Also note the words from verse 4: "There were giants in the earth in those days." These are called *nephilim* here and in Numbers 13:33.

3. *The fallen angels.* This view comes from the fact that a number of Scriptures refer to a great host of spirits who are variously designated as under the authority of Satan: "Beelzebub, the prince of demons" (Mt. 12:24, NIV); "the devil and his angels" (Mt. 25:41); "the dragon…and his angels" (Rv. 12:7, 9). Inasmuch as these spirit beings who follow under Satan's leadership must have been created by God (and we know He did not create them evil), they must have fallen from their created, perfect condition, possibly at the time of Lucifer's revolt. In keeping with the fact that Satan, in his unfallen position, was called the "star of the morning" (Is. 14:12, NASB and others), many have thought that no less than one third of the angels followed in Lucifer's fall and now are the demon hosts (Rv. 12:4). Some of the angels who "kept not their first estate" (Jude 6), have been cast "down to hell [*Tartarus*]" and are kept in "chains of darkness, to be reserved unto judgment" (2 Pt. 2:4). Just why some of these fallen angels are bound, while others are free to cooperate with Satan in his opposition to God, is not made clear in the Scripture.

In examining this whole subject, we are forced to recognize difficulties in upholding any of these positions beyond controversy. We therefore conclude that God has not chosen to reveal the answer to the question of the origin of demons. There would be no practical, and for that matter no spiritual, purpose in His so doing. That the Bible makes the fact of their existence very clear is sufficient to make it important for us to know what it reveals about their nature, their evil designs and methods, as well as our defense against them. Let us concentrate, then, on what we do know about them, while not giving them more prominence than their positions merit.

C. The nature of demons

Many things which have been said about angels' nature are true of demons, in that they appear to be fallen angels. They are spirit personalities and are incorporeal. From some of their activities it would seem they desire to indwell men and, if not permitted, even choose to enter swine (Mt. 8:31).

1. *Their strength.* They are strong. It is evident that they are no match for Jesus, but they are stronger than men.

> And when he was come out of the ship, immediately there met him out of the
> tombs a man with an unclean spirit, Who had his dwelling among the tombs;
> and no man could bind him, no, not with chains: Because that he had been

often bound with fetters and chains, and the chains had been plucked asunder by him, and the fetters broken in pieces: neither could any man tame him.

—MARK 5:2–4

2. *Their wisdom.* Though they are far from omniscient, their wisdom is above that of man's. They do know much concerning the authority and deity of Christ, nor of their own eternal doom:

And, behold, they cried out, saying, What have we to do with thee, Jesus, thou Son of God? art thou come hither to torment us before the time?

—MATTHEW 8:29

And they went into Capernaum; and straightway on the sabbath day he entered into the synagogue, and taught.... And there was in the synagogue a man with an unclean spirit; and he cried out, Saying, Let us alone; what have we to do with thee, thou Jesus of Nazareth? art thou come to destroy us? I know thee who thou art, the Holy One of God.

—MARK 1:21, 23–24

And the evil spirit answered and said, Jesus I know, and Paul I know; but who are you?

—ACTS 19:15

Thou believest that there is one God; thou doest well: the demons also believe, and tremble.

—JAMES 2:19

3. *Their character.* They are wicked, unclean, and vicious: "And when he was come to the other side into the country of the Gergesenes, there met him two possessed with devils, coming out of the tombs, exceeding fierce, so that no man might pass by that way (Mt. 8:28); "And when he had called unto him his twelve disciples, he gave them power against unclean spirits, to cast them out" (Mt. 10:1).

There even seem to be degrees of wickedness among them.

When the unclean spirit is gone out of a man, he walketh through dry places, seeking rest, and findeth none. Then he saith, I will return into my house from whence I came out; and when he is come, he findeth it empty, swept, and garnished. Then goeth he, and taketh with himself seven other spirits more wicked than himself, and they enter in and dwell there: and the last state of that man is worse than the first.

—MATTHEW 12:43–45

D. The purpose of demons

The overall purpose of the demons seems to be twofold: they seek to hinder the purposes of God and to extend the power of Satan. Satan's desire to rule and to be "like the most High" has not changed from its initial expression in Isaiah 14:13–14. His conduct in the wilderness temptation of Jesus is a positive evidence of this arrogant spirit, as he even sought to influence Christ to worship him (Mt. 4:9). Under his control, the hosts of demons are interested in fostering this very plan.

E. The activities of demons

1. *Opposing the saints.* They constantly oppose the saints in their endeavors to live godly lives and to serve the Lord: "For our struggle is not against flesh and blood, but against the rulers, against the authorities, against the powers of this dark world and against the spiritual forces of evil in the heavenly realms" (Eph. 6:12, NIV); "Wherefore we would have come unto you, even I Paul, once and again; but Satan hindered us" (1 Thes. 2:18). Inasmuch as Satan is not omnipresent, many of the activities of the devil must be carried out by demons.

2. *Inducing departure from the Faith.* "Now the Spirit speaketh expressly, that in the latter times some shall depart from the faith, giving heed to seducing spirits, and doctrines of devils [demons]" (1 Tm. 4:1).

3. *Encouraging formalism and asceticism as the result of false teaching*

> Now the Spirit speaketh expressly, that in the latter times some shall depart from the faith, giving heed to seducing spirits, and doctrines of devils; Speaking lies in hypocrisy; having their conscience seared with a hot iron; Forbidding to marry, and commanding to abstain from meats, which God hath created to be received with thanksgiving of them which believe and know the truth.
>
> —1 TIMOTHY 4:1–3

4. *Backing all idol worship*

> What say I then? that the idol is any thing, or that which is offered in sacrifice to idols is any thing? But I say, that the things which the Gentiles sacrifice, they sacrifice to devils [demons], and not to God: and I would not that ye should have fellowship with devils [demons]. Ye cannot drink of the cup of the Lord, and the cup of devils [demons]: ye cannot be partakers of the Lord's table, and of the table of devils [demons].
>
> —1 CORINTHIANS 10:19–21

Paul, in discussing the question of offering meats to idols and whether it was right for Christians to then eat this meat, has already said, "We know that an idol is nothing in the world, and that there is none other God but one" (1 Cor. 8:4), but he warns that behind the idols is a demon. If the Corinthian Christians ate the meat which had been offered to the idols, they would be in danger of having fellowship with demons. It is difficult to understand how the multiplied millions who have worshiped and do worship idols could find any spiritual satisfaction in bowing down and pledging allegiance to something made by human hands. However, the realization that there are demon spirits behind the idols makes it clear that there is a spiritual communion there and that Satan and his hosts have succeeded in deceiving the multitudes. Revelation 9:20 also points out the association between demons and idolatry: "And the rest of the men which were not killed by these plagues yet repented not of the works of their hands, that they should not worship devils [demons], and idols of gold, and silver, and brass, and stone, and of wood: which neither can see, nor hear, nor walk."

5. *Causing various physical afflictions.* It is in the power of demons to cause dumbness (Mt. 9:32–33), blindness (Mt. 12:22), insanity (Lk. 8:26–35), suicidal mania (Mk. 9:22), personal injuries (Mk. 9:18), and various defects and deformities (Lk. 13:11–17).

6. *Accomplishing God's purposes sometimes.* As Unger explains:

> Demons are the instruments for executing God's plans for punishing the ungodly (Ps. 78:49). Wicked Ahab was punished for his crimes by a "lying spirit" which Jehovah put in the mouth of all his prophets to lead them to disaster at Ramoth Gilead (1 Kings 22:23). Demons lure the God-resisting armies of Armageddon to similar catastrophe (Rv. 16:13–16). Satan and his ministers also effect God's plans for chastening the godly. Satan's sifting but accomplished the Lord's winnowing, as in the case of Peter (Luke 22:31). Job is brought through Satanic testing to a place of spiritual enlargement and refinement (Job 42:5–6). The incestuous believer at Corinth is delivered "unto Satan for the destruction of the flesh, that the spirit might be saved in the day of the Lord Jesus" (1 Cor. 5:5). Hymenaeus and Alexander are "delivered unto Satan, that they may be taught not to blaspheme" (1 Tm. 1:20).[12]

F. Demon possession

1. *The reality of demon possession.* Despite the fact that many modern scientists are trying to do away with the idea that demon possession ever existed, the Bible is explicit that such was the case.

---

12 Unger, 70.

a) As seen in the ministry of Jesus. Demon-possessed people were brought to Jesus. He dealt with them by casting out the demons.

> When the even was come, they brought unto him many that were possessed with devils: and he cast out the spirits with his word.
>
> —MATTHEW 8:16

> And when he was come out of the ship, immediately there met him out of the tombs a man with an unclean spirit.... And the unclean spirits went out, and entered into the swine: and the herd ran violently down a steep place into the sea.
>
> —MARK 5:2, 13

> As they went out, behold, they brought to him a dumb man possessed with a devil [demon]. And when the devil [demon] was cast out, the dumb spake: and the multitudes marveled, saying, It was never so seen in Israel.
>
> —MATTHEW 9:32–33

Jesus most certainly believed that He cast the demons out of those individuals. He made this fact of His ministry a proof of His divine mission. When the Pharisees accused Him of casting out demons by Beelzebub, the prince of demons, He showed them the foolishness of such a claim: "And if Satan cast out Satan, he is divided against himself; how shall then his kingdom stand? And if I by Beelzebub cast out devils [demons], by whom do your children cast them out? therefore they shall be your judges. But if I cast out devils [demons] by the Spirit of God, then the kingdom of God is come unto you" (Mt. 12:26–28). So much did He believe that demons were real and that He was casting them out, He warned those who were criticizing Him for this work that they were bordering on the unpardonable sin.

b) As seen in the ministry of the Early Church. Further scriptural testimony to the reality of demon possession may be found in the apostolic commission that came from the lips of the Lord Himself. "And he said unto them, Go ye into all the world, and preach the gospel to every creature.... And these signs shall follow them that believe; In my name shall they cast out devils [demons]" (Mk. 16:15, 17).

(1) Early apostles—This was fulfilled in the ministry of the early apostles: "There came also a multitude out of the cities round about Jerusalem, bringing sick folks, and them which were vexed with unclean spirits: and they were healed every one" (Acts 5:16).

(2) Philip the Evangelist

> And the people with one accord gave heed unto those things which Philip spake, hearing and seeing the miracles which he did. For unclean spirits, crying with loud voice, came out of many that were possessed with them: and many taken with palsies, and that were lame, were healed.
>
> —ACTS 8:6–7

(3) The apostle Paul

> And it came to pass, as we went to prayer, a certain damsel possessed with a spirit of divination met us, which brought her masters much gain by soothsaying: The same followed Paul and us, and cried, saying, These men are the servants of the most high God, which shew unto us the way of salvation. And this did she many days. But Paul, being grieved, turned and said to the spirit, I command thee in the name of Jesus Christ to come out of her. And he came out the same hour.
>
> —ACTS 16:16–18

The reality of demon possession is clearly evidenced by the dramatic events recorded in Acts 19:13–16. Here seven professional traveling exorcists sought to use the name of Jesus in casting out demons, as they had seen Paul do, but they suffered at the hands of the possessed man, departing naked and wounded.

c) In relation to Christ's redeeming work. It has been noted that there seems to be an increase of demon activity during the life and ministry of our Lord Jesus here on Earth. This could well be, in that Satan's avowed opposition is against the Seed of the woman (Gn. 3:15). It is also plausible when it is realized just why Jesus came to Earth. This is succinctly summarized by John: "For this purpose the Son of God was manifested, that he might destroy the works of the devil" (1 Jn. 3:8). There will be a similar increase in the activity of demons in the world at the close of this age, and on into the Great Tribulation. "Now the Spirit speaketh expressly, that in the latter times some shall depart from the faith, giving heed to seducing spirits, and doctrines of devils [demons]" (1 Tm. 4:1).

d) As contrasted with demon influence. All demon activity does not result in demon possession. There is a vast difference between demon possession and demon influence. In the former, the body is entered and a dominating control is gained, while in the latter, a warfare from without is carried on by suggestion, temptation, and influence. These must be "the fiery darts of the wicked" (Eph. 6:16).

e) As opposed to sickness. The Scripture makes it very clear that all sickness, though originally the result of sin and Satan, is not caused by demon possession and is not an indication that one is possessed. Thus the practice of some, who in ministering to the sick always try to cast out a demon, is not biblical procedure. Note how the Word of God distinguishes between the two, both in cause and in method of deliverance. In Jesus' ministry, "He cast out the spirits with his word, and healed all that were sick" (Mt. 8:16). Again a clear distinction is made in Jesus' message to Herod: "And he said unto them, Go ye, and tell that fox, Behold, I cast out devils [demons], and I do cures to day and to morrow" (Lk. 13:32). "Now when the sun was setting, all they that had any sick with divers diseases brought them unto him; and he laid his hands on every one of them, and healed them. And devils [demons] also came out of many, crying out, and saying, Thou art Christ the Son of God. And he rebuking them suffered them not to speak" (Lk. 4:40–41). It should be noted that Jesus laid hands on the sick, but He rebuked the demons. Again, the distinction is clear in His commissioning the Twelve: "And gave them power and authority over all devils [demons], and to cure diseases" (Lk. 9:1). Demons are expelled; diseases are healed. There is a vast difference between healing and exorcism.

2. *Is there demon possession today?* There seems to be no reason why the devil should not be as active today through his army of demons as he has been in former, particularly Bible, days. Dr. John Nevius, a Presbyterian missionary to China from 1854 to 1892, made a careful and unbiased study of demon phenomena in Shantung Province and presents unequivocal evidence of widespread demon possession in modern pagan China. Unger refers to the findings of Dr. Nevius in the following paragraph:

> What is striking in the accounts given by Dr. Nevius is their close correspondence with the cases of demon possession as recorded in the New Testament. For example, the subject at the time of possession passes into an abnormal state (cf. Mark 9:18). During the transition he is frequently thrown into a violent paroxysm, falling senseless on the ground or foaming at the mouth (cf. Mark 9:18; Luke 9:39, 42). During the attack he evidences another personality, his normal personality for the time being wholly or partially dormant (cf. Mark 5:7). The new personality presents traits of character utterly foreign to those characteristic of the demonized in his normal condition, and this change of character is practically always in the direction of moral impurity (cf. Luke 8:27). Many people while being demon possessed display a superhuman knowledge. Frequently they appear to know the Lord Jesus as a divine person and show a fear of him (cf. Luke 8:31). They sometimes converse in foreign languages, of which in their normal condition they are totally ignorant.[13]

---

13 Dr. John Nevius, *Demon Possession and Allied Themes,* 5th edition, 9–94, as quoted in Unger, 87.

Missionaries from many lands bring similar testimonies.

It may be asked why we do not see this sort of manifestation in the United States more often. Demons are very wise and able to adapt themselves to the cultural environment of place and age. In an educated and highly cultured community, they do not reveal the grosser aspects of their manifestations. They are able to not only reveal themselves as a "roaring lion" (1 Pt. 5:8), but also as "an angel of light" (2 Cor. 11:14). Their presence may be unsuspected, but their purpose in opposing God is often accomplished, even in moral and exemplary lives. It is possible that some highly educated individuals who oppose the Word of God in a sophisticated rationalism are tools of demons in a more efficient manner than those who suffer the cruder manifestations of demon activity, as seen in heathen countries. Many times only the spiritual gift of "discerning of spirits" can detect their presence (1 Cor. 12:10) .

3. *The casting out of demons.* It is not the purpose of this book to go into a detailed study of this phase of ministry. In an excellent chapter of the book *Pentecostal Doctrine* (edited and published in England by the Rev. Percy Brewster), George Canty, evangelist in the Elim Pentecostal Church, says the following:

> A Christian service when no demons are cast out is not necessarily a failure as some suggest, which indicates an obsession with one small aspect of Satanic activity. Nevertheless, Jesus insists that casting out demons is part of the gospel commission (Mark 16:15–20; Luke 9:1–2; 10:1, 17; Matthew 10:8). Remarkably, nothing is said about this in John's Gospel or in any apostolic letter, though they frequently urge the preaching of the gospel as a continuation of Christ's own work. He was "manifested to destroy the works of the devil" (1 John 3:8), and "went about doing good, and healing all that were oppressed of the devil" (Acts 10:38), as should we.
>
> This work, in recent years, has been called for by the increased interest in the occult, spiritism, Satanism and experiments in magic. The effects upon people have been typical. People become aware of "presences" near them in an unpleasant sense, with unnerving apparitions, nightmares, supernatural hauntings, voices, impulses that cannot be refused, depressions, tendencies to suicide, constant fear, inner urges to commit violence or murder, fits, unendurable tensions, sexual obsessions, hysteria, and so on. Sheer madness or death can be the ultimate result. That there is a call to care for those who are in this distressed state is obvious, and there should be a special alertness to discern such needs.
>
> No precise instructions for dealing with foul spirits are laid down in the New Testament, therefore the manner in which Christ and the apostles acted has to be our guide. From it we make the following points.

The name of Jesus is the primary secret... Christ's great commission said, "In my name shall they cast out devils" (Mark 16:17). Paul rebuked a spirit in the words: "I command thee in the name of Jesus Christ to come out of her" (Acts 16:18), just as Peter, when healing the lame man, said, "In the name of Jesus Christ of Nazareth rise up and walk" (Acts 3:6, cf. 3:16; 4:10).

Carefully note, however, that there is danger in tackling spirits with the name of Jesus used merely as a magic formula, since it could merely provoke them, as in the case of the sons of Sceva. The vital element is not the formula, but the presence of Jesus in the life of the person casting demons out. He himself should be a true representative of Christ, a person "in Christ," accepting the Lord's authority.

In that case, the formula is not perhaps so important. The pronunciation of the name over the possessed person was partly a testimony to those who observed what was happening. The sons of Israel cast out spirits by various names, so, when the lame man was healed, the authorities at once were curious as to which name was used (Acts 4:7). The fact is that demons left people when the name of Jesus was not uttered (Acts 5:15–16; 19:11–12). Peter raised Dorcas from the dead without mentioning Jesus (Acts 9:40), just as Paul brought blindness on Elymas the sorcerer without invoking the name (Acts 13:9–11), and in the same way healed the cripple at Lystra (Acts 14:9–10). Christ has given us a certain "power of attorney," to act in His behalf, or "in His name," without necessarily quoting the name constantly. Indeed we are told, "Whatsoever ye do, in word or deed, do all in the name of the Lord Jesus, giving thanks to God and the Father by him." Obviously, this does not mean that we must be constantly repeating His name for every act. We act for Him, on His behalf—"Ye serve the Lord Christ." In the same way, we baptise in the name of Jesus—that is on His authority. The actual formula to be used is clearly laid down in Matthew 28:19. The casting out of demons does not require a barrage of words with voluminous repetitions of the word "Jesus" or "Christ." We have authority, and can use it, as "ambassadors" (2 Cor. 5:20), but we must avoid treating it as a "magic" incantation, like a piece of abracadabra or spell. When we utter "Lord Jesus Christ" it indicates that he is the Lord of the one who speaks, otherwise we are like the sons of Sceva, unknown to the spirits.

The particular "method" is of very small consequence. Some may lay hands upon the patient; some feel that they should not. There is no actual record of deliverance from demons by the laying on of hands, but most instances make no mention at all of what was actually done. If it was of any importance, we would have clear instances or some instructions about it.

In one case, Jesus asked the spirits their name and they replied "Legion" (Mark 5:9). From this, some have said that it is necessary to do it always, but this rule was not followed by Paul in the cases quoted already. One wonders what is the use if the spirits are lying spirits? They could lie about their identities for the sake of putting us off.

There is nothing, either, in Scripture about coughing up or spitting out demons. A demon is a spirit and as such is invisible. Nor are we given any encouragement to hold conversations with demons. Once they are known to be there, they should be told to leave. Jesus "suffered not the devils to speak, because they know Him" and He charged unclean spirits "that they should not make him known" (Mark 1:34; 3:11–12). Certainly, spirits suffer from egotism and nothing pleases them better than to be the center of interest.

In this connection, nobody was ever given a special gift for "exorcism," only for discernment, as part of the protection of the church, chiefly against false teachers with lying and deceitful doctrines of demons. Nobody manifested a ministry exclusively for dealing with demons. This would draw attention more to Satan than to Christ. Preoccupation with this sphere of things is a kind of tribute to the power of Satan. "The end of our conversation" says Hebrews 13:7–8, is "Jesus Christ the same yesterday, today and for ever," which hardly can be said of some whose continual thought is about "the powers of darkness."

If "method" does matter, it would be at another level. While it may be possible to cast out a demon, very often a person needs more than this. They need deeper help, in fact. Life situations, strong temptations, affecting the willingness of a person to give up their sin, cannot be ignored. Unless sin is forsaken, then, as Jesus said, the last state of that man may be worse than the first, for the devil will return with several more. It is the will of a man which makes a way in for the devil, and therefore repentance is required as well as exorcism. Patient pastoral interest may have to be taken to get down to the roots of a man's trouble, of which demon possession is not the cause but the result or symptom. It is wrong to assume that a particular evil in a man's life is the result of demon control. It is more likely that the evil was there first, permitting the entry of Satanic power.

Again, "method" must not underestimate the power of the Word of God. The preaching of the gospel is deliverance—it is the power of God in itself "unto salvation" (deliverance). It could well be that great conversions are sometimes straightforward cases of the Word of God overcoming Satan in a man's life. It would be absurd to think of a great conversion of a man leaving him with demons still in his heart. Can a man be saved through faith in the gospel and then need a second experience to save him from Satan? From what was he saved in the first instance? "The anointing breaks the yoke."

Discernment should not only detect demons, but also detect when there are no demons. It is quite common for people to have hypochondriac tendencies. They insist that they have an illness, but they are really quite well and live to a good old age. There may be psychological motives present, unrealised by the patient himself, such as finding illness useful for his own schemes or to attract attention or sympathy. That the condition extends to simulated demon-possession is obviously likely. Where there is a ministry to the demon-troubled, it automatically suggests to some that they also have such a condition. Their very fear of it can bring on pseudo-symptoms, especially if they are told that they may be possessed.

For this reason it become extremely dangerous to tell people that they are victims. It is much easier to create the idea than to get rid of it. Some go from healer to healer wanting deliverance but getting no better, simply because it is not realised that they are not possessed, but are the victims of suggestion, either auto-suggestion or imposed by some other person. This again calls for careful counseling. If a person has sufficient confidence in the counsellor, a cure may be wrought by saying directly, "You have no demon."

Demons themselves enjoy having attention paid to them, and tend to turn up where they are talked about a great deal. Demonhunters also, exhibiting their fancied powers in some pride, can annoy Satan. He in turn oppresses those who provoke them by their efforts at exorcism. This is perhaps the modern lesson to be learned from Jude's warning that even the archangel Michael showed a healthy respect for the dignity of the devil and said merely, "The Lord rebuke thee." Some call Satan names; this is neither Scriptural nor wise. The powers of hell should not be provoked nor should we daily with them. They should be commanded to leave if they confront us, and that should be the end of the matter, if we believe God…That the Church will be called upon more and more to cleanse people from foul spirits may be likely, but the preaching of the gospel is the main means, and this should be the prior activity of all God's servants.[14]

4. *The occult and demon possession.* Satan has become very bold of recent years, and the occult has been receiving a great deal of public attention. It almost seems incredible that, even in so-called Christian lands, spirit worship should be so prevalent. Information about such things is obtainable at any bookstand. In the foreword to his book *I Believe in Satan's Downfall,* Michael Green says:

> Satan worship, fascination with the occult, black and white magic, astrology and horoscopes, seances and tarot cards have become the rage. Ouija boards and levitation are to be found in many schools. Despite our professed sophis-

---

14 George Canty in *Pentecostal Doctrine,* ed., Rev. Percy Brewster (Cheltenham, England: Grenehurst Publishers, 1976), 252–257.

tication, there is today in the West a greater interest in the practice than for three centuries.[15]

The term *occult* means "hidden from view" and has to do particularly with magic, fortune-telling, and spiritism. According to Michael Green, "Magic is the attempt to bring the spirit world under one's knowledge and control. It is the precise opposite of religion, which seeks surrender to the divine, not control over it, and operates by faith not knowledge."[16] Further, it is an endeavor to "conjure up spirits of the universe that are alien to God Almighty."[17] Such methods as telepathy, clairvoyance, clairaudience, ESP, automatic writing, charms, and magic healing are employed. Fortune-telling uses palmistry, tarot cards, crystal gazing, psychometry (in which the practitioner holds a personal object of the enquirer), and astrology. Spiritism, falsely called spiritualism and identical with ancient necromancy, is the attempt to communicate with the spirits of the dead.

All of these practices were severely condemned in the Bible: "Do not turn to mediums or spiritists; do not seek them out to be defiled by them" (Lv. 19:31, NASB); "As for the person who turns to mediums and to spiritists, to play the harlot after them, I will also set My face against that person and will cut him off from among his people" (Lv. 20:6, NASB); "There shall not be found among you anyone who makes his son or daughter pass through the fire, one who uses divination, one who practices witchcraft, or one who interprets omens, or a sorcerer, or one who casts a spell, or a medium, or a spiritist, or one who calls up the dead. For whoever does these things is detestable to the LORD; and because of these detestable things the LORD your God will drive them out before you" (Dt. 18:10–12, NASB); "And when they say to you, 'Consult the mediums and the wizards who whisper and mutter,' should not a people consult their God? Should they consult the dead on behalf of the living" (Is. 8:19, NASB).

Believers are warned against having anything whatever to do with all such practices, even though some of them appear outwardly to be quite innocent. There is no doubt that much trickery is practiced in these areas, but it must be realized that there are demon spirits who ever seek to deceive and to enslave those who give themselves to such practices. Familiar spirits are simply demons who have been familiar with a person in his lifetime and who impersonate the departed friend or loved one in the unholy atmosphere of the modern seance. It is not by accident that witchcraft and immorality are so often mentioned in the same Scripture: "Now the works of the

---

15 Michael Green, *I Believe in Satan's Downfall* (Grand Rapids, MI: Wm. B. Eerdman's Publishing Company, 1981), 9.

16 Ibid., II.

17 Ibid., 118.

flesh are manifest, which are these; Adultery, fornication, uncleanness, lasciviousness, Idolatry, witchcraft" (Gal. 5:19–20); "Neither repented they of their murders, nor of their sorceries, nor of their fornication, nor of their thefts" (Rv. 9:21). Spiritism was a capital offence in Israel: "You shall not allow a sorceress to live" (Ex. 22:18, NASB).

5. *The Christian and demon possession.* Much has been said and written about the possibility of Christians becoming demon possessed. While one should not blind himself to the presence and power of demonic forces in the world and be ignorant of Satan's devices (2 Cor. 2:11), he must not underestimate the great salvation and deliverance which God has wrought for him in Christ Jesus. He must ever encourage and strengthen himself in the fact that Christ "spoiled principalities and powers," and "made a shew of them openly, triumphing over them in it" (Col. 2:15).

Christ is the stronger one mentioned in Luke 11:21–22: "When a strong man armed keepeth his palace, his goods are in peace: But when a stronger than he shall come upon him, and overcome him, he taketh from him all his armour wherein he trusted, and divideth his spoils."

When the Lord called Saul of Tarsus on the road to Damascus, He sent him to both Jew and Gentile, "To open their eyes, and to turn them from darkness to light, and from the power of Satan unto God" (Acts 26:18). The effect of the gospel is described: "Who hath delivered us from the power of darkness, and hath translated us into the kingdom of his dear Son" (Col. 1:13).

John says that if a man has been born of God, "That wicked one toucheth him not" (1 Jn. 5:18). Jesus said, "Behold, I give unto you power to tread on serpents and scorpions, and over all the power of the enemy: and nothing shall by any means hurt you" (Lk. 10:19). "Repentance to the acknowledging of the truth" means, says Paul, "that they may recover themselves out of the snare of the devil, who are taken captive by him at his will" (2 Tm. 2:25–26).

Paul asks, "What concord hath Christ with Belial…And what agreement hath the temple of God with idols?" Then he assures us, "For ye are the temple of the living God" (2 Cor. 6:15–16). The statement is that the believer is His temple. Is God going to allow that which is His—and that in which He dwells—to be occupied by demons of Satan? If the Christian's body is "the temple of the Holy Ghost which is in you" (1 Cor. 6:19), can a demon and the Holy Spirit dwell in the same house? Would God allow it? Has Christ provided a great deliverance for us, or has He not? In cases where it is mentioned that sicknesses were caused by demons (Mt. 4:24; 9:32–33; 10:1; Mk. 1:32; 3:15; Lk. 6:17–18; 9:1, etc.), there is no indication whatever that these individuals were in right relation to God.

This does not mean that the child of God is totally immune from Satan's power. We have deliverance from Satan as long as we live in Christ's victory over him. This we do by faith and obedience. When Jesus told Peter, "Satan hath desired to have you, that he may sift you as wheat," He did not pray that he would not be allowed to do so, but He prayed that Peter's faith would not fail (Lk. 22:31). Disobedience and persistent waywardness provide the enemy grounds from which He can attack and influence the Christian. We are admonished, "Do not give the devil a foothold" (Eph. 4:27, NIV). Ananias and Sapphira are solemn examples of those who permitted Satan to fill their heart and "to lie to the Holy Ghost" (Acts 5:3).

The Lord is fully acquainted with the constant wrestling in which the Christian is engaged, and so He has provided the necessary armor for his constant victory (Eph. 6:12–18). Special note should be taken of the fact that the armor is of God's provision, and the believer is admonished to *take* the armor, not to make it. The Scripture does not indicate that these spiritual conflicts which the Christian has with the enemy are the result of demon possession. Satan and his cohorts are external foes, and they are looking for opportunities to attack us from their dwelling in the atmosphere around us.

Much misunderstanding has arisen from a wrong interpretation of the word *spirit* as it is sometimes used in the Bible. A statement adopted by the General Presbytery of the Assemblies of God states:

> Some, for example, teach that since the Bible speaks of a spirit of cowardly fear, any deliverance from fear must be by the casting out of an evil spirit or demon of fear. But an examination of the same passage (2 Timothy 1:7) shows it speaks also of a spirit of power, of love, and of a sound mind or self-control. If people interpret fear to be an evil spirit needing to be cast out, to be consistent they would need to beseech three good spirits to come in. The fallacy of this reasoning is obvious. Love and self-control are fruits of the Holy Spirit in our lives. By a spirit of love and of self-control is meant the attitudes that result from our cooperation with the Holy Spirit. Actually, the word "spirit" in many cases means an attitude or a disposition. David spoke of a broken spirit (Psalm 51:17); Solomon of a humble spirit (Proverbs 16:19); Paul wanted to come to Corinth, not with a rod, but with love and a meek or gentle spirit (1 Corinthians 4:21). Peter spoke of the adorning of the heart with the imperishable gift of a meek and quiet spirit (1 Peter 3:4), actually meaning a quiet disposition. This is in line with the frequent use of the word "spirit" for one's own spirit and its expressions (Haggai 1:14; Acts 17:16; 1 Corinthians 2:11, etc.). Thus, unless the context shows that an independent spirit-being is meant, it seems best to take most phrases such as a haughty spirit, a hasty spirit, a spirit of slumber, a spirit of jealousy, etc., to be sins of the disposition or lusts of the flesh (Galatians 6), and not demons. A serious danger in considering all these sins of the disposition to be demons is that the individual may feel no responsibility for the actions and feel that the necessity for repentance is removed. Actually, the Bible calls men to re-

pent of these things and to put off these attitudes. The great conflict within us is not between the Holy Spirit and demons, but between the indwelling Holy Spirit and the flesh (that is, all the sensory apparatus that tends toward sin).[18]

In concluding this section on demonology, let it be stated again that demons thrive on publicity. Like their leader Satan, they are proud and selfish and seem to delight when attention is paid to them. The wise servant of God will not publicize their activities, or seek to instill fear in the hearts of Christians concerning them. To the child of God who is walking in the light of God's Word and firmly rejoicing in our Lord's victory over them, believing God's promises of triumph, there need to be no fear of demons. They are spirits of darkness and we are children of light. There is not enough darkness in the whole world to put out one little light. Let us "walk in the light, as he is in the light" (1 Jn. 1:7)! There are almost three hundred references to angels in the Word of God and only approximately eighty to devils and demons. In other words, there are more than three times as many references to angels in the Bible than there are to demons. Why, then, do some people spend three times as much time talking about demons as they do about angels? The angels are our friends. Let us think and talk about them, rather than our enemies the demons. Demons are unclean and impure. Paul admonishes us, "Finally, brethren, whatsoever things are true, whatsoever things are honest, whatsoever things are just, whatsoever things are pure, whatsoever things are lovely, whatsoever things are of good report; if there be any virtue, and if there be any praise, think on these things" (Phil. 4:8).

III. SATANOLOGY

A. Importance of this doctrine

Though Satan should never be given undue prominence, it is important that the place given to him in Scripture be realized. There is no one other individual except the Father, the Son, and the Holy Spirit that is afforded so prominent a place in the Bible from its very beginning to its end as the character whom we know as Satan, the devil. Of no one else are we so minutely informed concerning his origin, his fall, his character and work, his influence, and his ultimate judgment and destiny. We can be deeply thankful for this revelation of him and his host of demons. Heathen lands have been enveloped in the grossest darkness and basest superstitions and practices

---

18 Taken from a pamphlet published by the Gospel Publishing House, Springfield, Missouri, called "Can Born-Again Believers Be Demon Possessed?" This is the statement approved as the official statement of the Assemblies of God by the General Presbytery in May, 1972 (see pp. 9–10).

because they lack the clear teachings concerning him that the Scriptures afford. We need not be ignorant of his devices.

B. The reality of his existence

1. *Doubt of his existence.* It has become quite popular to speak of him as a mere figure of speech, a metaphorical personification of evil, or a delusion of unsound minds. Interestingly, this is true only in Christian lands where the name of his Conqueror (Jesus) is known. It is certainly to Satan's advantage to have his presence denied so that he may be enabled to work more subtly in deceiving mankind, disarming their prejudices and fears. Chafer has well said:

> It may be observed that figures of speech are not created angels who sin and serve in realms of darkness and are doomed to a final and dreadful judgment at the hand of God. A metaphor would hardly enter a herd of swine and precipitate their instant destruction. Nor would a metaphor offer the kingdoms of this world to the Lord of glory, asserting that those kingdoms were delivered unto it and that it gave them to whomsoever it would.[19]

2. *Scriptural record of his existence.* Satan, his Hebrew name, is only mentioned, expressly, on five occasions in the Old Testament. On the first occasion (Gn. 3:1–15), he is seen in the guise of the serpent who tempted Eve and caused the first sin on this earth. In 1 Chronicles 21:1 we read, "And Satan stood up against Israel, and provoked David to number Israel." He appears in Job on two occasions, where he is seen "when the sons of God came to present themselves before the LORD, and Satan came also among them," and there ensued those dramatic confrontations between Satan and God that led to the variety of trials to which Job was subjected (Jb. 1:6–12; 2:1–7). The final place is in Zechariah 3:1–2:

> And he shewed me Joshua the high priest standing before the angel of the LORD, and Satan standing at his right hand to resist him. And the LORD said unto Satan, The LORD rebuke thee, O Satan; even the LORD that hath chosen Jerusalem rebuke thee: is not this a brand plucked out of the fire?

However, in the New Testament he is referred to as Satan or the devil about seventy-two times. This apparent discrepancy between the Old and the New Testaments can probably be accounted for by Genesis 3:15: "And I will put enmity between thee and the woman, and between thy seed and her seed; it shall bruise thy head, and thou shalt bruise his heel." When Christ, the seed of the woman, was born of the flesh and

---

19 Chafer, II, 34.

came to accomplish His great victory over Satan and purchase redemption at Calvary, the devil became manifestly active in a greater degree than prior to this event.

C. His personality

The personality of Satan is a fact which is pointedly denied by the rationalists of our time, but those who accept the Bible as the inspired Word of God have no difficulty accepting this truth, along with all that the Scriptures reveal. The Bible speaks of the personality of Satan as fully as of any other person referred to in it. Indeed, if we did not believe in the personality of Satan from what the Bible records, it would be difficult to believe in the personality of the Lord Jesus. Actually, we would not be able to trust the Scriptures at all. All of the characteristics of personality are ascribed to Satan. He is constantly referred to as a personal being. Personal pronouns are applied to him (Jb. 1:8, 12; 2:2–3, 6; Zec. 3:2; Mt. 4:10; Jn. 8:44). Personal attributes are ascribed to him, including a will (Is. 14:13–14) and knowledge (Jb. 1:9–10, and personal acts are performed by him (Jb. 1:9–11; Mt. 4:1–11; Jn. 8:44; 1 Jn. 3:8; Jude 9; Rv. 12:7–10).

D. His origin

Much of the scriptural teaching regarding Satan's origin is covered under the doctrine of hamartiology, which should be studied in this connection. Satan, along with the other angels, as we have noted in a previous section of this study (see Section I.B. of Angelology), was created by God: "Praise ye him, all his angels: praise ye him, all his hosts...Let them praise the name of the LORD: for he commanded, and they were created" (Ps. 148:2–5).

God did not create the devil, as we know him today. Everything God made was declared good (Gn. 1:31). Ezekiel 28:12–19 gives a detailed picture of the beauty and wisdom with which Satan was originally created. This passage speaks of him as "full of wisdom, and perfect in beauty...every precious stone was thy covering...Thou art the anointed cherub that covereth...Thou wast perfect in thy ways from the day that thou was created." Isaiah 14:12–17 gives us his name before he fell. He was called Lucifer, which means "the morning star." It is, literally, "lightbearer." He is pictured to us as the highest angel of God's creation. The mystery is how such a wise and beautiful being could have fallen to such depths as to now be the vilest being in the universe.

Isaiah 14 tells of his fall and the reason for it. It all began when Lucifer lifted his will above that of God Almighty: "I will ascend into heaven, I will exalt my throne above the stars of God: I will sit also upon the mount of the congregation, in the sides of the north: I will ascend above the heights of the clouds; I will be like the most High" (vv. 13–14). Heaven had been heaven because there was only One who reigned, and none thought to oppose His will. Thus harmony and peace prevailed.

Then came the moment of rebellion, and five times this beautiful, anointed cherub voiced his will in opposition to that of God. Chafer says, "Feeble indeed is the power of the human imagination to picture the crisis in this universe at the moment when the first repudiation of God took place in heaven."[20] What caused such an unthought-of happening? Pride and selfish ambition!

Paul, in writing to Timothy concerning the qualifications for officers in the early church, insists that such a person must not be a novice, "Lest being lifted up with pride he fall into the condemnation of the devil" (1 Tm. 3:6). Lucifer, in his selfish pride, sought to rise above the sphere in which he was created and above the purpose and service assigned to him. As a result of this rebellion, Lucifer was cast out of the heavenly realm and office which he had held. "Yet thou shalt be brought down to hell, to the sides of the pit" (Is. 14:15). Thus the prophet cries, "How art thou fallen from heaven, O Lucifer, son of the morning! how art thou cut down to the ground, which didst weaken the nations!" (Is. 14:12).

Jesus said, "I beheld Satan as lightning fall from heaven" (Lk. 10:18). Some commentators believe that these words were prophetic and refer to that which is recorded in Revelation 12:9: "And the great dragon was cast out, that old serpent, called the Devil, and Satan, which deceiveth the whole world: he was cast out into the earth, and his angels were cast out with him." Others hold to the position that these words of Jesus look back to that historic judgment of Lucifer, when he was expelled from heaven and became Satan.

As to whether Satan still has access to heaven, we have noted already, "When the sons of God came to present themselves before the LORD...Satan came also among them. And the LORD said unto Satan, Whence comest thou? Then Satan answered the LORD, and said, From going to and fro in the earth, and from walking up and down in it" (Jb. 1:6–7). The fact Satan had previously been walking up and down the earth would lead us to believe that he, along with the sons of God, was here before the throne of the Lord in heaven. As the accuser of our brethren, he did have access to heaven (Rv. 12:10). One thing is certain: after he was expelled for his wicked pride and rebellion, he never had access to his former position of honor and influence.

If the question be pressed as to how a holy being in a holy place could originate the first sin and himself suffer such a fall, the reply is that, as the devil, he is self-made. In some way that is unexplained and perhaps unintelligible to us, he originated his own sin: "Thou hast said in thine heart, I will..." (Is. 14:13).

---

20 Chafer, II, 47.

E. His character

One of Satan's greatest assets in opposing the work of the Lord is his deceptiveness. Down through the centuries, he has posed in roles that have caused men to think of him in any way other than his true character, thus making it easier for him to lead them away from God. F. C. Jennings has said:

> In considering the person of Satan, it may be well first to look at the common, vulgar, popular idea, such as is still held by the masses of Christendom, and such as is made the basis, or one of the bases, for the rejection of his very existence by many of the "learned" of the day. The lowest possible, and yet the most widespread conception we have is in what one may term the stage idea, as we constantly see it on the posters in our streets. A human form, with leering face, characterized by a grin of low cunning, horns, hoofs, and forked tail; utterly obscene, and provoking nothing but contempt, ridicule, and disgust.[21]

The Bible certainly does not present such a picture of him. If he came in such a guise, no one would follow him. Satan's dominant purpose is not, as the popular belief is, to be unlike God. His transcendent objective is to "be like the most High" (Is. 14:14). The Scriptures give a great number of different names and descriptive titles to Satan. The following nineteen are listed so that the variety of his approaches may be seen and much of his true character may be revealed.

F. His names and titles

1. *Lucifer.* This was his title in heaven before his rebellion and fall. "How art thou fallen from heaven, O Lucifer, son of the morning!" (Is. 14:12). The latter phrase is literally, "star of the morning" or "morning star." It signifies "lightbearer." The Bible indicates that Lucifer occupied an exalted position in the heavens, possibly second only to the Trinity itself. It is well to remember this in our thinking of him, for he, no doubt, has not lost all of the dignity which was his then. We must be warned that he does not come to us as a hideous creature out of hell, but as one who formerly occupied the heights. Thus, his appeals will sometimes seem to be high and lofty.

2. *Satan.* This name accentuates his activities as the adversary. The name Satan is used fifty-six times in the Old and New Testaments. It pictures his malicious and persistent attempts to hinder God's program. As such, he is opposed to everything and every person that is good. He is the adversary of both God and man. First Peter 5:8 speaks of "your adversary the devil." Paul writes to the Thessalonian church and

---

21 Frederick Charles Jennings, *Satan, His Person, Work and Destiny* (Neptune. NJ: Loizeaux Brothers), 12.

tells the saints there, "Wherefore we would have come unto you, even I Paul, once and again; but Satan hindered us" (1 Thes. 2:18).

3. *Devil.* Revelation 20:2 uses four names for Satan: "And he laid hold on the dragon, that old serpent, which is the Devil, and Satan." The name devil particularly signifies "slander and accuser." Satan is pictured in this role as he, through the serpent, accuses God to man: "And the serpent said unto the woman, Ye shall not surely die: For God doth know that in the day ye eat thereof, then your eyes shall be opened, and ye shall be as gods, knowing good and evil" (Gn. 3:4–5). In Revelation 12:10 we read of Satan as "the accuser of the brethren" being "cast down, which accused them before our God day and night." Thus he accuses man to God. "Devil," referring to Satan himself, occurs thirty-five times in the New Testament.

4. *Serpent.* Satan is first seen in his activity on Earth as a serpent (Gn. 3:1–15). Paul, in 2 Corinthians 11:3, says, "But I fear, lest by any means, as the serpent beguiled Eve through his subtilty, so your minds should be corrupted from the simplicity that is in Christ." One must not think of the serpent, as mentioned in Genesis 3, as the slithering, crawling creature we know it today. This action came only as a result of the curse upon it, when God said to the serpent, "Because thou hast done this, thou art cursed above all cattle, and above every beast of the field; upon thy belly shalt thou go, and dust shalt thou eat all the days of thy life" (Gn. 3:14). Prior to the curse, the serpent must have walked upright and been a most beautiful creature. Nor must we think of the serpent as a mere animal. This could not be, for he is said to speak, and speech is a characteristic of the spirit, which a serpent does not possess. We conclude that some spirit, Satan, took possession of the serpent, speaking, arguing, and reasoning. Revelation 12:9 and 20:2 speak of "that old serpent…the Devil." This name denotes crookedness, deceitfulness, and guile.

5. *Dragon.* In Revelation 20:2 Satan is specifically identified as "the dragon, that old serpent, which is the Devil, and Satan." Also in Revelation 12:9 we read, "And the great dragon was cast out, that old serpent, called the Devil, and Satan, which deceiveth the whole world: he was cast out into the earth, and his angels were cast out with him." Verse 7 of the same chapter tells us, "There was war in heaven: Michael and his angels fought against the dragon." The word *dragon* is literally "sea monster." The name is thought to refer to his great power. This is clearly seen in Revelation 13:2: "And the beast which I saw was like unto a leopard, and his feet were as the feet of a bear, and his mouth as the mouth of a lion: and the dragon gave him his power, and his seat, and great authority."

6. *Beelzebub or Beelzebul.* "If they have called the master of the house Beelzebub, how much more shall they call them out of his household" (Mt. 10:25). Jesus is speaking here of the Pharisees calling Him by this name: "But when the Pharisees heard it, they said, This fellow doth not cast out devils, but by Beelzebub the prince of the devils" (Mt. 12:24). The name originally signified "lord of flies," but the Jews

later changed it to "lord of the dunghill." As Beelzebub, Satan is particularly seen as the prince of the demons. This name suggests the vast host of demon spirits over which Satan rules as their prince.

7. *Belial.* This name is often used of evil men who are designated as children of Belial (Dt. 13:13; Jgs. 20:13; 1 Sm. 10:27; 30:22). The name means "good for nothing" and indicates worthlessness.

8. *Tempter.* "And when the tempter came to him, he said, If thou be the Son of God, command that these stones be made bread" (Mt. 4:3). "For this cause, when I could no longer forbear, I sent to know your faith, lest by some means the tempter have tempted you, and our labor be in vain" (1 Thes. 3:5). While God tests men for their good so that they may learn and become stronger thereby, Satan tempts men for the purpose of destroying them. As tempter, he constantly incites men to sin.

9. *Wicked, evil, or lawless one.* Any of these names bears witness to the character of Satan. Though his ways may be varied and deceiving, they are always for a wicked and evil purpose. "We know that we are of God, and the whole world lies in the power of the evil one" (1 Jn. 5:19, NASB). Second Thessalonians 2:8 is variously translated: "Then shall be revealed the lawless one" (ASV); "Wickedness Incarnate" (TCNT); "The embodiment of disobedience" (GSPD.); and "Representative of lawlessness" (WMS). "Then cometh the wicked one, and catcheth away that which was sown in his heart" (Mt. 13:19). "The field is the world; the good seed are the children of the kingdom; but the tares are the children of the wicked one" (Mt. 13:38). John twice declares, "And ye have overcome the wicked one" (1 Jn. 2:13–14).

10. *Prince of this world.* Three times Jesus ascribed this name to Satan: "Now is the judgment of this world: now shall the prince of this world be cast out" (Jn. 12:31); "Hereafter I will not talk much with you: for the prince of this world cometh, and hath nothing in me" (Jn. 14:30); "Of judgment, because the prince of this world is judged" (Jn. 16:11). This title speaks of Satan's rule and influence over governments of this world—world politics. Business and society are under his domain. Satan has a throne: "I know where you dwell, where Satan's throne is" (Rv. 2:13, NASB). During Jesus' temptation in the wilderness when the devil offered Him "the kingdoms of the world, and the glory of them" (Mt. 4:8), Jesus did not deny Satan's right to offer these to Him. God gave Adam dominion over the earth (Gn. 1:26), but by disobeying the word of the Lord and hearkening to Satan, man forfeited his right to rule and sold his dominion to the devil. In the book of Job, as the Lord asked Satan where he had been, his reply was, "From going to and fro in the earth, and from walking up and down in it," as though he ruled over it (Jb. 1:7). But let it be clearly noted that Satan is never called the king of this world. He is designated as its prince, but he is still under the dominion of God, who reigns Supreme, and must recognize the One who is above him.

11. *Prince of the power of the air.* This suggests his rulership over those spirit-beings who shared his sin: "When in time past ye walked according to the course of the world, according to the prince of the power of the air, the spirit that now worketh in the children of disobedience" (Eph. 2:2). "For our struggle is not against flesh and blood, but against the rulers, against the powers, against the world forces of this darkness, against the spiritual forces of wickedness in the heavenly places" (Eph. 6:12, NASB). (See also Mt. 12:24; 25:41; Rv. 12:7.)

12. *God of this world or age.* "In whom the god of this world [age] hath blinded the minds of them which believe not, lest the light of the glorious gospel of Christ, who is the image of God, should shine unto them" (2 Cor. 4:4). The previous two titles, prince of this world and prince of the power of the air, refer to powers of rulership. Royalty is a civil dignity and political glory. In seeking to be like the Most High, Satan aspired to religious leadership, and so this title "god of this age" speaks of his rulership in this realm. Indeed, it may be that here is his most devastating attack against God. As a religious leader, a god, he attends religious gatherings (Jb. 1); he has his teachings, "doctrines of devils" (1 Tm. 4:1); his meeting places, such as the synagogue of Satan (Rv. 2:9); his sacrifices, "The things which the Gentiles sacrifice, they sacrifice to devils, and not to God" (1 Cor. 10:20); and ministers, "Therefore it is no great thing if his ministers also be transformed as the ministers of righteousness; whose end shall be according to their works" (2 Cor. 11:15). These ministers sponsor all kinds of materialistic and humanistic religions and, no doubt, are responsible for the multitudinous cults abroad in the world.

We quote an apt passage from F. C. Jennings on this very theme:

> In this present system of things looked at morally and away from God, he (Satan) so arranges not merely the politics of earth, or its immoralities, but its religion—for this is necessarily the force of this title "God" as in contrast with "prince"—as to suit his own ends. He so weaves the course of this age: its religious forms, ceremonies, external decencies, respectabilities, and conventionalities to form a thick veil, that entirely hides "the glory of God in the face of Jesus Christ," which consists in righteous mercy to penitent sinners only. This veil is not formed by evil-living, depravity, or any form of what passes as evil amongst men; but by cold formality, heartless decency, proud self-complacency, highly esteemed external respectability, and we must add, church-membership—all without Christ. It is the most fatal of all delusions, the thickest of all veils, and the most common. It is the way that, because it is religious, respectable, decent "seems right unto a man but the end thereof

is death"; for there is no Christ, no Lamb of God, no Blood of Atonement in it.[22]

13. *Deceiver.* If there is any name appropriate for this archenemy of God it is this—the deceiver: "And the devil that deceived them was cast into the lake of fire" (Rv. 20:10); "And the great dragon was cast out, that old serpent, called the Devil, and Satan, which deceiveth the whole world: he was cast out into the earth" (Rv. 12:9); "And he laid hold on the dragon, that old serpent, which is the Devil, and Satan, and bound him a thousand years, And cast him into the bottomless pit, and shut him up, and set a seal upon him, that he should deceive the nations no more, till the thousand years should be fulfilled" (Rv. 20:2–3). Having learned nothing from his one-thousand-year incarceration in the bottomless pit (literally, "the abyss"), Satan, as soon as he is loosed, goes "out to deceive the nations which are in the four quarters of the earth, Gog and Magog, to gather them together to battle: the number of whom is as the sand of the sea" (Rv. 20:8). This is his last great attempt to deceive the nations into thinking they can triumph over God Almighty and that it will be to their advantage to follow the prince of this world. The only possible way Satan could influence anyone to forsake God and follow him would be to deceive him. No one would knowingly march under Satan's banner.

14. *Accuser.* "For the accuser of our brethren is cast down, which accused them before our God day and night" (Rv. 12:10). Not satisfied with directing his subtle energies and forces against the saints personally, he even presumes to accuse them before their God unceasingly. Imagine the arrogance of one who, in the presence of God Himself, would accuse those who have been redeemed through the precious blood of God's own Son.

The classic example of this is Job, whom Satan dared to say would curse God to His face if the hedge were lifted and he, Satan, were allowed to touch his possessions (Jb. 1:10–11). The Lord knows who are His, and Christians need never fear that His hand of protection will ever be lifted from them, except perhaps temporarily and, even then, for their good. Notice the triumphant notes of victory that accompany this great proclamation of the accuser's downfall: "And I heard a loud voice saying in heaven, Now is come salvation, and strength, and the kingdom of our God, and the power of his Christ" (Rv. 12:10).

15. *Angel of light*

For such are false apostles, deceitful workers, transforming themselves into the apostles of Christ. And no marvel; for Satan himself is transformed into an angel of light. Therefore it is no great thing if his ministers also be trans-

---

22 Jennings, 29–30.

formed as the ministers of righteousness; whose end shall be according to their works.

—2 Corinthians 11:13–15

This is, perhaps, the greatest role of deceptiveness which Satan plays. He poses as a spiritual helper to lead those who need help out of their darkness, yet his only purpose is to guide them into ever-increasing darkness, deceiving them under the impression that they are coming more and more into the light. How true the words of Jesus, "If therefore the light that is in thee be darkness, how great is that darkness!" (Mt. 6:23).

16. *Murderer.* Jesus Himself said to the Jews, "Ye are of your father the devil, and the lusts of your father ye will do. He was a murderer from the beginning" (Jn. 8:44). What a contrast to our Lord, who said, "I am come that they might have life, and that they might have it more abundantly" (Jn. 10:10)! Satan has been a murderer from the beginning, for he is the originator of sin, and sin brings death. Thus, in tempting men to sin, he is promoting death.

17. *Father of lies.* In John 8:44, Jesus describes the devil, saying, "He...abode not in the truth, because there is no truth in him. When he speaketh a lie, he speaketh of his own: for he is a liar, and the father of it." Again, the chief characteristic of Satan is seen. He is a deceiver and lies are his favorite devices. Satan does not specialize in coal-black lies that are quite apparent. His stock in trade are the gray-white variety, with just enough truth in them to trick the unwary. There was a measure of truth in what he said to Eve. She and Adam did come to know good and evil by eating of the tree, but they had no power to do the good, nor to resist the evil. Satan will even use Scripture, as he did with Jesus (Mt. 4:6), but always to misquote or misapply it. When you read something that Satan says, look for the lie in it. He cannot speak the truth.

18. *Roaring lion.* "Be sober, be vigilant; because your adversary the devil, as a roaring lion, walketh about, seeking whom he may devour" (1 Pt. 5:8). Satan is pictured as a serpent to denote his subtlety, but as a lion to express his fierceness and strength. The word rendered "roaring" is used especially of the cries of wild beasts when ravenous with hunger.

19. *Destroyer.* "And they had a king over them, which is the angel of the bottomless pit, whose name in the Hebrew tongue is Abaddon, but in the Greek tongue hath his name Apollyon" (Rv. 9:11). Both of these names, Abaddon or Apollyon, mean "destroyer."

G. His defeat

Though allowed to continue his activities in the earth, Satan is a defeated foe. He has already suffered much under the hand of the God, whom he dared to oppose. It is very helpful for the Christian in his daily conflicts with the world, the flesh, and the devil to recognize and rejoice in the defeats Satan has had to endure.

1. *Cast out of his exalted position in heaven.* Immediately after his seven bold "I will" assertions recorded in Isaiah 14:12–14, his fall is announced: "Yet thou shalt be brought down to hell [sheol], to the sides of the pit" (Is. 14:15). It could well be that Jesus was referring to this event when He said, "I beheld Satan as lightning fall from heaven" (Lk. 10:18). Though there is indication in the Scripture that Satan has some access to the presence of God when he accuses the brethren (Rv. 12:10), Satan never regained the lofty position he once had.

2. *Cursed in the Garden of Eden*

> And the LORD God said unto the serpent, Because thou has done this, thou art cursed above all cattle, and above every beast of the field; upon thy belly shalt thou go, and dust shalt thou eat all the days of thy life: And I will put enmity between thee and the woman, and between thy seed and her seed; it shall bruise thy head, and thou shalt bruise his heel.
> —GENESIS 3:14–15

Though this curse was directed against the creature that Satan had possessed in his approach to Eve—and the serpent has ever since slithered on its belly—the reference to the enmity certainly goes beyond the creature to Satan himself. This is a curse against the devil that has never been lifted, nor ever will be. In spite of all his boldness, Satan must realize he carries the weight of this curse upon himself at all times.

3. *Defeated by Christ in the wilderness temptation.* Three times the tempter sought to turn Christ aside from His divine mission here on Earth, and three times Jesus unsheathed the sword of the Spirit, the Word of God, and declared, "It is written" (Mt. 4:3–10). Never would Christ, in any wise, depart from the purposes of God, as expressed in His Word. The result was, "Then the devil leaveth him, and, behold, angels came and ministered unto him" (Mt. 4:11).

4. *Judged at the cross of Calvary.* Just prior to His condemnation and crucifixion, as He knew He was on His way to the cross, Jesus said, "Now is the judgment of this world: now shall the prince of this world be cast out" (Jn. 12:31). Referring to this same event on Calvary, Jesus prophesied that the Holy Spirit would convict of judgment. Then He explained, "Of judgment, because the prince of this world is judged" (Jn. 16:11). Through His death on the cross, Jesus destroyed "him that had the power of death, that is, the devil" (Heb. 2:14). Paul speaks in glowing terms of the victory over Satan at the cross: "And having spoiled principalities and powers, he made a shew of them openly, triumphing over them in it" (Col. 2:15).

If Satan's defeat was so triumphant at Calvary, it may be wondered why he is still on the scene and allowed the measure of freedom which is his to harrass the Church of Jesus Christ. Even after the Cross, Satan is still called the prince of the power of the air and the god of this world. There is a vast difference between a judgment that is passed and the carrying out of the penalty. There is no doubt of the judgment rendered against Satan at the Cross, but for good reasons best known to Himself, God has seen fit to allow the enemy a degree of freedom. It certainly is not for lack of power that God has not dispensed with the devil already. The time for his final dispersal will come; its time has already been set.

H. His destiny

1. To be finally cast out of heaven

> And there was war in heaven: Michael and his angels fought against the dragon; and the dragon fought and his angels, And prevailed not; neither was their place found any more in heaven. And the great dragon was cast out, that old serpent, called the Devil, and Satan, which deceiveth the whole world: he was cast out into the earth, and his angels were cast out with him.
> —REVELATION 12:7–9

From this time on, his wickedness will be confined to this earth.

2. To be confined to the bottomless pit

> And I saw an angel come down from heaven, having the key of the bottomless pit and a great chain in his hand. And he laid hold on the dragon, that old serpent, which is the Devil, and Satan, and bound him a thousand years, And cast him into the bottomless pit, and shut him up, and set a seal upon him, that he should deceive the nations no more, till the thousand years should be fulfilled: and after that he must be loosed a little season.
> —REVELATION 20:1–3

At the beginning of the millennial reign of Christ, Satan will be bound in the bottomless pit—literally, "the abyss." It would seem logical to presume that the demon hosts will be there with him. They are cast out of heaven with him (Rv. 12:9), so it would seem they would be bound with him in the Abyss. After the thousand years is finished, he is to be loosed for a little season, at which time he will conduct his last campaign of deceit. The rebellious army which he will gather will be destroyed with fire from God out of heaven (Rv. 20:7–9).

3. Consigned to the lake of fire. "And the devil that deceived them was cast into the lake of fire and brimstone, where the beast and the false prophet are, and shall be tormented day and night for ever and ever" (Rv. 20:10). Having ended his work—the

last group of human beings having been tested—Satan will then be consigned by Almighty God to the lake of fire, where he will be tormented forever.

I. The believer's course of action regarding Satan

1. *Recognize Satan's limitations.* It is never wise to underestimate the devil. He is a sly and skillful foe. He has had almost six thousand years of experience dealing with mankind. But neither should one overestimate his abilities. He has certain very definitive limitations. These should be fully known so that one will not be overwhelmed by him.

a) He is not omnipotent. He has great power—more than any man. Only our God is all-powerful, and Satan is no match for Him.

b) He is not omniscient. He has a very keen intellect, and from experience knows many things, far more than men. But again, only God is all-knowing.

c) He is not omnipresent. Satan has an individual personality and is only in one place at one time. Because of the great number of the demons under his control, it seems as if the devil is everywhere at the same time. Many of the so-called attacks by the devil are only the activity of one of his assisting demons. Only God is always everywhere.

d) The devil cannot bestow life, nor raise anyone from the dead. The Authorized Version's rendering of Revelation 13:15 reads, concerning the beast, the Antichrist, "And he had power to give life unto the image of the beast." This passage is better rendered, "There was given to him to give breath to the image of the beast" (NASB).

2. *Realize that Satan's power is limited by the will of God.* This is clearly seen in the story of Satan, God, and Job. Satan's accusation in Job 1:10 reads, "Hast not thou made an hedge about him, and about his house, and about all that he hath on every side?" Satan could touch none of Job's possessions, nor his person, until God gave him permission (Jb. 2:4–6). Jesus said to Peter, "Simon, Simon, behold, Satan hath desired to have you, that he may sift you as wheat" (Lk. 22:31). The implication is that Satan could not have Peter for this purpose without the Lord's permission.

3. *Realize he has been conquered.* "For this purpose the Son of God was manifested, that he might destroy the works of the devil" (1 Jn. 3:8). Satan is a conquered foe, overcome by none other than our Lord Jesus Christ. Nowhere are Christians told to fight the devil. Our Lord did that once for all on the cross. Our part is to claim, by faith, and stand in His victory. "Resist the devil"—do not fight him—and he is the one who "will flee from you" (Jas. 4:7). First Peter 5:9 explains how this is to be done: "Whom resist stedfast in the faith." Faith in the account of Christ's victory over the devil and faith in God's promises is the secret of victory. Jesus made Satan's tactics quite clear in the parable of the sower and the seed. Some of the seed, Jesus said, fell by the wayside and the fowls of the air devoured it. Interpreting this, Jesus explained, "Those by the way side are they that hear; then cometh the devil, and taketh away the

word out of their hearts, lest they should believe and be saved" (Lk. 8:12). The devil knew that if the Word were allowed to remain in the hearts of the hearers it would bring forth faith: "So then faith cometh by hearing, and hearing by the word of God" (Rom. 10:17). Faith in God's Word is the secret of the believer's daily triumph. F. C. Jennings sums up this truth when he says:

> This then suggests very clearly the root-aim of his attacks: it is always to destroy faith in God; and our side of the conflict is to maintain that faith in spite of everything he can bring against it. So the apostle Peter says "whom resist steadfast in the faith;" and our apostle's (Paul's) joyful swan-song is: "I have fought a good fight, I have finished my course, I have kept the faith" (2 Tm. 4:7); and he passes back the word to us "fight the good fight of faith" (1 Tm. 6:12).[23]

4. *Remember the believer has One who intercedes in his behalf.* This is beautifully illustrated in the following verse: "And the Lord said, Simon, Simon, behold, Satan hath desired to have you, that he may sift you as wheat: But I have prayed for thee, that thy faith fail not" (Lk. 22:31–32).

5. *Practice unceasing vigilance.* "Be sober, be vigilant; because your adversary the devil, as a roaring lion, walketh about, seeking whom he may devour" (1 Pt. 5:8). Another version translates the same verse, "Exercise self control, be watchful" (TCNT). The believer, knowing Satan's malice, cunning, and power, will make it his supreme concern to be watchful.

6. *Deny Satan any foothold.* "Neither give place to the devil" (Eph. 4:27). The admonition is that the believer must not give the devil any place within his life where he might gain a place, or opportunity, for attack. Jesus could say, "The prince of this world cometh, and hath nothing in me" (Jn. 14:30). There was no place in Jesus where Satan could get a foothold.

7. *Put on the whole armor of God.*

> Wherefore take unto you the whole armor of God, that ye may be able to withstand in the evil day, and having done all, to stand. Stand therefore, having your loins girt about with truth, and having on the breastplate of righteousness; And your feet shod with the preparation of the gospel of peace; Above all, taking the shield of faith, wherewith ye shall be able to quench all the fiery darts of the wicked. And take the helmet of salvation, and the

---

23 Jennings, 140.

sword of the Spirit, which is the word of God: Praying always with all prayer and supplication in the Spirit.

—EPHESIANS 6:13–18

The Lord has provided a complete set of armor, that the Christian may be protected from every fiery dart of the wicked one, but the believer must put on this armor—all of it. The omission of any one part may be fatal to one's Christian life and testimony.

THE DOCTRINE OF LAST THINGS

Eschatology

Introduction

I. Death
- **A.** Physical death
- **B.** Spiritual death
- **C.** Eternal death

II. The Intermediate State
- **A.** Of the wicked
- **B.** Of the righteous
- **C.** False views of the intermediate state
  1. *Purgatory*
  2. *Soul sleeping*
  3. *Spiritism*

III. The Second Coming of Christ
- **A.** The importance of His coming
- **B.** The nature of His coming
  1. *What the second coming is not*
  2. *What the second coming is*
- **C.** The time of His coming
- **D.** The signs of His coming
  1. *The regathering of Israel in Palestine*
  2. *Perilous times*
  3. *The rise of communist Russia*
  4. *The rise of communist China*
  5. *Armaments and modern war potential*
  6. *Progress in transportation and science*
- **E.** The Rapture of the Church
  1. *Its any-moment occurrence*
  2. *Various rapture theories*
- **F.** Christ's return to rule—the revelation

IV. The Tribulation
- **A.** The word *tribulation* in Scripture
  1. *Trials and persecutions of believers throughout the Church age*

2. *Period of tribulation for Israel prophesied by Daniel*
3. *God's final wrath upon the Antichrist and the Gentile nations who follow him*
- **B.** Daniel's dream and vision
- **C.** Principal events of the Tribulation

V. The Antichrist
- **A.** The word *antichrist* in Scripture
- **B.** The identity of the Antichrist
- **C.** The titles of the Antichrist
- **D.** The works of the Antichrist

VI. The Resurrection
- **A.** The fact of the Resurrection
  1. *In the Old Testament*
  2. *In the New Testament*
- **B.** The nature of the Resurrection
  1. *The resurrection of believers*
  2. *The resurrection of unbelievers*
- **C.** The time of the Resurrection

VII. The Millennium
- **A.** Its relation to the second coming
  1. *Post-millennialism*
  2. *Amillennialism*
  3. *Pre-millennialism*
- **B.** Its relation to Israel
- **C.** Its relation to the nations
- **D.** Its relation to the Church
- **E.** Life and conditions on the millennial earth

VIII. The Judgments
- **A.** Of the believers
- **B.** Of the Gentile nations
- **C.** Of national Israel
- **D.** Of the wicked dead
- **E.** Of Satan and the fallen angels

IX. The Final Destinies
- **A.** The future destiny of the unrighteous
- **B.** The final destiny of Satan, the fallen angels, and the Antichrist
- **C.** The future state of the righteous

CHAPTER TEN

The Doctrine of Last Things

Eschatology

Introduction

THE TERM *ESCHATOLOGY* comes from two Greek words: *eschatos*, meaning "last," and *logos*, which means "subject matter." Therefore, eschatology is the doctrinal study that deals with the last events of sacred history, including all that is beyond this life and this age, as well as the final events of this present age. However, the term *eschatological* is frequently applied to this entire age, for:

- Peter, on the Day of Pentecost, declared that the Spirit's outpouring fulfilled Joel's prophecy concerning the last days (Acts 2:16–21);
- the Church already enjoys certain powers of the kingdom age and the world (age) to come (Lk. 17:21; Mt. 16:19; Heb. 6:5);
- since the Church expects the any-moment coming of the Lord, every moment is eschatological (Rom. 8:23; 1 Cor. 1:7; Lk. 12:35–36; 1 Thes. 1:10);
- since Christ the Son of God is the end or goal of all things in God's plan of redemption, the coming of the Son incarnate introduced the last days: "Hath in these last days spoken unto us by His Son, whom He hath appointed heir of all things" (Heb. 1:2);
- since the spirit of antichrist is already working in anticipation of the final conflict, John said, "Little children, it is the last time: and as ye have heard that antichrist shall come, even now there are many antichrists; whereby we know that it is the last time" (1 Jn. 2:18).

Even though it is important to note that this age is in a real sense an eschatological age, the study in this section will include the present age only in two aspects: that of the present state of the dead and that of the latter-time signs of the Lord's coming.

I. Death

The Scriptures speak of three kinds of death: physical death, spiritual death, and the second or eternal death.

A. Physical death

Physical death is the separation of the soul from the body and constitutes the transition from the visible world to the invisible. For the believer, it marks his entrance into paradise and into the presence of Christ Jesus (2 Cor. 5:1, 8; Phil. 1:23). For the unbeliever, death is his entrance into hades (Lk. 16:22–23; Mt. 10:28; Rv. 20:13). Physical death is not the end of existence, but only a change in the state of existence. For the believer, physical death is the ultimate effect of sin and the last effect of sin to be canceled by Christ's redeeming work (Rom. 5:12–15; 1 Cor. 15:26). Although all men die physically, the atoning death and resurrection of Christ have robbed death of its sting for the believer (1 Cor. 15:54–57; 2 Tm. 1:10; Heb. 2:9, 14–15; 9:15); in fact, the Christian can triumphantly declare that, for him, "to die is gain" (Phil. 1:21).

B. Spiritual death

Spiritual death is separation from God, both in this world and in the world to come. For example, Adam died as a result of his disobedience in accordance with the warning of God: "For in the day that thou eatest thereof thou shalt surely die" (Gn. 2:17). His death (exclusion from the garden) did not consist of immediate physical decease, though his state of mortality began then. Instead, his death was spiritual death. When Jesus said, "Let the dead bury their dead" (Mt. 8:22), he meant "let the spiritually dead bury the physically dead." In speaking of the spiritually dead, He was making reference to those separated from God by unbelief. Paul, writing to the Ephesians, said, "And you he made alive, who were dead in trespasses and sins" (Eph. 2:1, NKJV). Formerly, as sinners, they existed in spiritual death, but when they came to Christ, they were made alive. When one comes into fellowship with God through faith in Christ, he passes from "death unto life" (1 Jn. 3:14).

At the final Great White Throne Judgment of unbelievers, which takes place after the thousand years (the Millennium), the wicked dead will still exist and stand before God in judgment. Although they will be able to stand judgment, their state is called death because they are alienated from God (Rv. 20:13–15). (See also Rv. 3:1; 1 Tm. 5:6.)

C. Eternal death

When those who are dead in trespasses and sins die physically and are unrepentant, they enter into the state of eternal death. James refers to this death, explaining how it may be averted: "Let him know, that he which converteth the sinner from the error of his way shall save a soul from death" (Jas. 5:20). Clearly, eternal death is not cessation of existence; it is an everlasting punishment. Paul warns of this eventuality in 2 Thessalonians 1:7–9:

> The Lord Jesus shall be revealed from heaven with his mighty angels, In flaming fire taking vengeance on them that know not God, and that obey not the gospel of our Lord Jesus Christ: Who shall be punished with everlasting destruction from the presence of the Lord, and from the glory of his power.

At the final Great White Throne Judgment all the wicked dead will be cast into the lake of fire, a sentence which is called the "second death" (Rv. 20:13–15). The eternal death is described in Scripture as eternal or everlasting fire (Jude 7; Mt. 18:8; 25:41), eternal punishment (Mt. 25:46), eternal judgment (Heb. 6:2), everlasting destruction (2 Thes. 1:9), and eternal damnation (Mk. 3:29). Although the English words *everlasting* and *eternal* have slightly different theological meanings, they both have the same meaning in the New Testament, for both words are derived from the same Greek word, *aionios,* which means "eternal" and "without end." When applied to God, the word signifies "without beginning or end."

II. THE INTERMEDIATE STATE

The intermediate state is that state of the soul between physical death and the resurrection. For the believer, the resurrection will occur at Christ's coming. For the unbeliever, it will not occur until after the Millennium at the Final Judgment.

A. Of the wicked

When unbelievers die, they go at once to hades, which is the abode of the wicked dead. Before Christ, the righteous and the wicked went to sheol, which had two compartments separated by an impassable gulf (Lk. 16:22–31; Gn. 37:35; Dt. 32:22; Ez. 32:23–24, NASB). In the Old Testament, the Hebrew word *sheol* is variously translated "hell" and "the grave." In the New Testament, the "lowest part of sheol" is called in Greek *hades.* This carries over from the Septuagint version, where the Hebrew word *sheol* is translated with the Greek word *hades.* The word in Hebrew for the final state of perdition or lake of fire was *gehenna,* properly translated "hell" (Mk. 9:43, NASB). (The name *gehenna* was a figurative term borrowed from the perpetual fires that burned refuse in the Valley of Hinnom near Jerusalem.) Since the wicked do not go to their final perdition until after the Last Judgment when they are cast into the lake of fire, the word *hell* should not be used to describe the present state of the wicked dead. As far as is known, no one is at present in hell, which is the lake of fire. The wicked are at present in hades, awaiting the resurrection of judgment. Hades is, however, a place of suffering, as is seen in the account of the rich man and Lazarus (Lk. 16:23; 1 Pt. 3:19).

B. Of the righteous

The intermediate state of the righteous is called paradise. Jesus said to the dying thief, "To day, shalt thou be with me in paradise" (Lk. 23:43). After the resurrection of Jesus, the abode of the righteous was transferred from sheol to paradise. Jesus personally descended into sheol to "lead captivity captive" (Eph. 4:8). He spent "three days and three nights in the heart of the earth" (Mt. 12:40—apparently sheol is located in the heart of the earth; also Eph. 4:9–10; Nm. 16:33.) Jesus did not go into the abode of the wicked in sheol or hades, but to the part known as Abraham's bosom. He emptied sheol of the righteous, taking them with Him to paradise (Ps. 16:10; Acts 2:27).

When the righteous die, they go immediately to be in the presence of Christ Jesus. Paul spoke of "having a desire to depart, and to be with Christ; which is far better" (Phil. 1:23). That Paul expected at death to go at once to the Lord's presence is confirmed by his inspired words to the Corinthians: "We are confident, I say, and willing rather to be absent from the body, and to be present with the Lord" (2 Cor. 5:8). When Lazarus died, he went immediately to Abraham's bosom, which was the name the Jews gave to the abode of the departed faithful. Lazarus was conscious and comforted. The rich man wanted Abraham to send Lazarus to witness to his living brothers, showing that both were in a state of conscious activity. Perhaps no thought is more comforting to believers than to know that at death they will go to be with Jesus. The apostle spoke the following words of hope: "For God did not appoint us to wrath, but to obtain salvation through our Lord Jesus Christ, who died for us, that…we should live together with Him. Therefore comfort each other and edify one another" (1 Thes. 5:9–11, NKJV).

C. False views of the intermediate state

There are several false but widely held views of the intermediate state. Some have no scriptural basis whatever, and others are based upon an incorrect interpretation of Scripture. Three of these will be treated here.

1. *Purgatory.* The Roman Catholic and Greek Orthodox Churches teach that those members who have lived imperfect lives must spend some time in purgatory in order that their sins and imperfections may be purged. Depending upon the seriousness of their offenses, the length of time spent in purgatory may last a few hours or centuries, terminated only by the Last Judgment. According to the Catholic Church, the time in purgatory may be shortened by gifts or services rendered to the Church or by prayers or masses sponsored by relatives. The doctrine of purgatory cannot be supported by Scripture. The doctrine is based upon a passage taken from

the Apocrypha, found in 2 Maccabees 12:41–43. The apocryphal books were not a part of the canon of Scripture. They are included in Catholic Bibles, perhaps because of their support of doctrines not supported by the canonical Scriptures. No reference in Scripture to the intermediate state makes any reference to purgatorial sufferings. Furthermore, the concept of purgatory violates the clearly scriptural teaching of the sufficiency of the blood of Christ to cleanse sin and of salvation by grace through faith (Heb. 10:10–23; Eph. 2:8–10; Rom. 3:24–28; 5:1–2, 9–10; 8:31–39; 10:8–11; 1 Jn. 2:1–2; 3:1–2).

2. *Soul sleeping.* This is the teaching that after death the soul rests in an unconscious state until the Resurrection. This doctrine is held by the Seventh-day Adventists, the Jehovah's Witnesses, and several smaller groups. The arguments advanced to support the doctrine of soul sleep are: the Bible often refers to death as sleep (1 Thes. 4:13–14; Jn. 11:11–14); it is assumed that the soul cannot function apart from the body and therefore will not awaken until joined with the body at the resurrection; and, it seems inappropriate that the righteous should enjoy heavenly bliss or the unrighteous suffer in hades until after the Judgment (Heb. 9:27).

The arguments for soul sleep stated above will be answered in the same order:

a) The use of the term *sleep* to describe death is a figurative and euphemistic expression to emphasize the fact that the deceased person still lives. W. E. Vine explains:

> The metaphorical use of the word "sleep" is appropriate, because of the similarity in appearance of a sleeping body and a dead body; restfulness and peace normally characterize both. The object of the metaphor is to suggest that, as the sleeper does not cease to exist while his body sleeps, so the dead person continues to exist despite his absence from the region in which those who remain can communicate with him.[1]

Furthermore, the account given by Jesus of the state of the rich man and Lazarus immediately after death demonstrates clearly that their souls were not sleeping in unconsciousness (Lk. 16:22–31). See also Paul's statement to the Philippians: "Having a desire to depart, and to be with Christ, which is far better" (1:23).

b) Paul's treatise on death in 2 Corinthians makes it clear that the spirit of man can function apart from the body.

> Therefore, being always of good courage, and knowing that while we are at home in the body we are absent from the Lord—for we walk by faith; not by sight—we are of good courage, I say, and prefer rather to be absent from the

---

1 William Edwy Vine, *Expository Dictionary of New Testament Words* (New York: Fleming H. Revell Publishing Company, 1958), 81.

body and to be at home with the Lord. Therefore also we have as our ambition, whether at home or absent, to be pleasing to him.

—2 CORINTHIANS 5:6–8, NASB

He states that "being at home with the Lord" means absence from the body. Furthermore, the apostle's ambition was to be pleasing to the Lord, whether in the body or absent from it. If being absent from the body meant soul sleep, why would he be concerned about being pleasing to the Lord after death? A sleeper could hardly be unpleasing to Him. If Paul expected to sleep after death, his ambition to please would have applied only to existence before death. Since he expected to be conscious after death, he expected to please the Lord by praising Him (Rv. 7:9–10; also Heb. 12:23; Rv. 6:9–11; Eccl. 12:7.)

c) Answering the assumption that men must await the Judgment before enjoying bliss or suffering punishment, Louis Berkhof remarks, "The day of judgment is not necessary to reach a decision respecting the reward or punishment of each man, but only for the solemn announcement of the sentence, and for the revelation of the justice of God in the presence of men and angels."[2] Jesus said, "He who believes in Him is not judged; he who does not believe has been judged already, because he has not believed in the name of the only begotten Son of God" (Jn. 3:18, NASB). There will be a believer's judgment concerning rewards for service, but not concerning his salvation. One's salvation is conditioned only on faith in Jesus (1 Cor. 3:12–15; 2 Cor. 5:10).

3. *Spiritism.* Spiritism teaches that the living may communicate with the dead, and the dead with the living, usually through the agency of a medium. There is no evidence in the Bible to suggest that there can be legitimate communication between the living and the dead. In fact, the Scriptures unequivocally forbid any attempt to do so (Lv. 19:31; 20:6, 27; Dt. 18:9–12; Is. 8:19–20; 1 Chr. 10:13–14). There are two explanations for spiritist phenomena: they are produced by deceptive manipulations, as has often been proved, or they are produced by lying spirits (1 Kgs. 22:22–23; 1 Tm. 4:1). In Acts 16, Paul delivered a girl from a spirit of divination (*puthon*) by which she was able to bring great gain to her exploiters (Acts 16:16–19). Without doubt, evil spirits often deceive people who consult mediums by imitating the voice or appearance of deceased loved ones. Seeking biblical support, spiritists often cite the case of the witch of Endor bringing up the spirit of Samuel (1 Sm. 28:7–20). However, that case can be no encouragement for spiritism, for Saul was punished with death for disobeying the Lord by consulting a familiar spirit (1 Chr. 10:13–14). Some scholars believe that Samuel actually appeared to Saul, but if he did, it was by a special permis-

---

2 Louis Berkhof, *Systematic Theology* (Grand Rapids, MI: Wm. B. Eerdmans Publishing Company, 1941), 689.

sion of the Lord to pronounce judgment upon Saul for his disobedience. Moses and Elijah also appeared on the Mount of Transfiguration, but again, this was only by a rare, special permission in order to represent the Law and the prophets and to confirm that Christ Jesus was the goal of Old Testament Law and prophecy: "Two men, Moses and Elijah, appeared in glorious splendor, talking with Jesus. They spoke about His departure, which He was about to bring to fulfillment at Jerusalem" (Lk. 9:30–31, NIV). The Greek word for "departure" is *exodon,* the root of our English *exodus.* Just as Moses delivered Israel from bondage through the exodus from Egypt, so Christ, by the exodus of the Cross and Resurrection, delivered mankind from the bondage of sin. The appearance of Moses and Elijah was a token of messianic fulfillment (Mt. 17:1–8; Mk. 9:2–8.) The Bible lends no encouragement to consultation with the dead. Christ is the "Lord both of the dead and the living" (Rom. 14:9). If He ever permits the dead to appear, it will be to signal some strategic event of sacred history. If we need comfort or guidance, we have the Word of God and the Spirit of God.

III. The Second Coming of Christ

For the majority of those who will read and study this book, the subject of the second coming of Christ is a doctrine of major importance. About the second coming, the Foursquare *Declaration of Faith* says:

> We believe that the second coming of Christ is personal and imminent; that He will descend from Heaven in the clouds of glory…and that at this hour, which no man knoweth beforehand, the dead in Christ shall rise, then the redeemed that are alive and remain shall be caught up together with them in the clouds, to meet the Lord in the air, and that so shall they ever be with the Lord; that also seeing that a thousand years is as a day with the Lord, and that no man knows the hour of His appearance, which we believe to be at hand, each day should be lived as though He were expected to appear at even, yet that in obedience to His explicit command, "Occupy till I come," the work of spreading the gospel, the sending forth of missionaries, and the general duties for upbuilding the Church should be carried on as diligently, and thoroughly, as though neither ours nor the next generation should live in the flesh to see that glorious day.[3]

---

3 Aimee Semple McPherson, *Declaration of Faith* (Los Angeles, CA: International Church of the Foursquare Gospel, n.d.), 21–22.

A. The importance of His coming

If the importance of a Bible subject can be judged by the frequency of reference to it, the second coming of Christ is, indeed, a subject of primary importance. Christ's coming is mentioned more than three hundred times in the New Testament—an average of once in every twenty-five verses. In Paul's epistles there are more than fifty references to the Second Advent. It has been said that there are eight times more verses concerning the second coming of the Lord than there are those that concern His first coming. Whole books (1 and 2 Thessalonians, Revelation) and whole chapters (Mt. 24, 25; Mk. 13; Lk. 21) are devoted to this subject. Jesus Himself often referred to His coming again and urged His followers to watch and to be ready. In fact, believers are urged to be ready for the Lord to come again about fifty times in the New Testament. In five New Testament passages, the believer's posture is said to be that of waiting for the coming of the Lord: "Ye turned to God from idols to serve the living and true God; And to wait for his Son from heaven" (1 Thes. 1:9–10). (See also Rom. 8:23–25; 1 Cor. 1:7; Gal. 5:5; Jas. 5:7.) The hope of the second coming was connected by Jesus with both ordinances of the Church. The apostles were commanded to make disciples, baptizing them and teaching them with the assurance: "And, lo, I am with you always, even to the end of the age" (Mt. 28:20, NASB). Paul, quoting Jesus, gave the apostolic pattern for the observance of the Lord's Supper, saying: "For as often as ye eat this bread, and drink this cup, ye do shew the Lord's death till he come" (1 Cor. 11:26). (See also Mt. 26:26–29; Lk. 22:17–20.)

The hope of the second coming provides the motivation for practical Christian living: for brotherly love (1 Thes. 3:12–13); for holiness (Rom. 13:12–14; 1 Thes. 3:13; 5:23; 1 Jn. 3:3; Ti. 2:11–13); for faithful meeting together for worship (Heb. 10:25); for faithfulness in Christian service (1 Tm. 4:13–16; 2 Tm. 4:1–2; 1 Pt. 5:2–4); for a continued passion for souls (1 Thes. 1:9–10; 2:11–12, 19–20); and for comfort in time of bereavement (1 Thes. 4:14–18). So important is the second coming to the Church, the bride of Christ, that it is called the blessed hope: "Looking for that blessed hope, and glorious appearing of the great God and our Saviour Jesus Christ" (Ti. 2:13).

B. The nature of His coming

How are we to understand the term *second coming*? In what manner will Christ come the second time? Before answering these questions, it will be helpful to discuss several false explanations of the meaning of the second coming.

1. *What the second coming is not*

a) It is not the death of the believer. Christ's coming is at our resurrection, not at our death (1 Thes. 4:16–17). Death is the believer's departure to be with Christ, not His coming for the believer (Phil. 1:23). Christ's coming is the defeat of death, not the occurrence of it (1 Cor. 15:51–54). Death is an enemy (1 Cor. 15:26), but the Lord's coming is our blessed hope (Ti. 2:13).

b) Christ's second coming is not the coming of the Holy Spirit on the Day of Pentecost. Jesus promised to send another Comforter (Jn. 14:16). Therefore, His coming and that of the Comforter could not be identical. Furthermore, most of the references to Christ's coming were written after Pentecost and were indicated as being yet future (Acts 3:19–21). None of the phenomena prophesied to accompany Christ's parousia happened on the Day of Pentecost.

c) Christ's second coming was not the destruction of Jerusalem in A.D. 70. The destruction of Jerusalem by Titus may have been referred to as a type of latter-day events during the Tribulation, but there was no coming of the Lord to catch up His Church that happened simultaneous with that event (Mt. 24:15–23; Lk. 21:24–28.) Titus' destruction of Jerusalem scattered Israel, but Christ's coming will mark the gathering of Israel (Jl. 3:16–18).

d) Christ's second coming is not conversion. If this were true, His coming would not be a second one, but one of millions of comings. "So Christ was sacrificed once to take away the sins of many people; and He will appear a second time, not to bear sin, but to bring salvation to those who are waiting for Him" (Heb. 9:28, NIV). According to Paul, the believer waits for the Lord's coming after conversion, not before it (1 Thes. 1:9–10). Attention will be directed now to a positive definition of the nature of the Lord's second coming.

2. *What the second coming is*

a) The second coming of Christ is a literal coming or return. Since the coming is a second one, it will be as literal as His first coming. There is no evidence in Scripture that Christ's return, which He Himself promised, would be a figurative one. The Old Testament has more references to Christ's second coming than to His first. Prophecies of His first coming were fulfilled literally, so there is no doubt that the prophecies concerning His second coming will be fulfilled literally.

b) The Lord's coming will be a personal return. "I go to prepare a place for you. And if I go and prepare a place for you, I will come again, and receive you unto myself; that where I am, there ye may be also" (Jn. 14:2–3). Christ's coming cannot be a figurative reference to some other being or to some spiritual experience of the believer, because the angels said to the disciples when Christ ascended to heaven, "This same Jesus, which is taken up from you into heaven, shall so come in like manner as ye have seen him go into heaven" (Acts 1:11).

c) From the above quoted reference (Acts 1:11), it is clear that the Lord's coming will be a visible, bodily coming. The angel also said that He would return "in like manner as ye have seen him go into heaven." They saw Him ascend in a glorified, yet visible and tangible body; He will return in the same manner. "Behold, He cometh with clouds; and every eye shall see Him" (Rv. 1:7).

C. The time of His coming

Jesus said regarding the time of His return, "But of that day and hour knoweth no man, no, not the angels of heaven, but my Father only" (Mt. 24:36). Some scholars contend that Jesus and His disciples expected His coming to be within the first generation. But in the parable of the talents Jesus said, "After a long time the lord of those servants cometh" (Mt. 25:19). Since the parable was about the coming of the kingdom, the term *long time* seems to hint of a considerable delay in the coming. Peter could not have expected an immediate coming, for he said:

> Knowing this first, that there shall come in the last days scoffers...saying Where is the promise of His coming?...beloved, be not ignorant of this one thing, that one day is with the Lord as a thousand years, and a thousand years as one day. The Lord is not slack concerning his promise...but is longsuffering to us-ward, not willing that any should perish, but that all should come to repentance.
>
> —2 PETER 3:3–4, 8–9

Jesus also said, "And this gospel of the kingdom shall be preached in all the world for a witness unto all nations; and then shall the end come" (Mt. 24:14). When the Thessalonian church became upset by the belief that the Great Tribulation had already begun, Paul exhorted them not to be soon shaken in mind: "For that day shall not come, except there come a falling away [departure] first" (2 Thes. 2:3). On the other hand, Jesus warned, "Watch therefore: for ye know not what hour your Lord doth come" (Mt. 24:42). Even though there are clear indications that the Lord's return would not occur until after an extended period of evangelization, the Church was taught to be ready for an any-moment appearance of the heavenly Bridegroom (Mt. 24:44, 48, 50; 25:13; Mk. 13:35–37; Ti. 2:12–13; Jn. 3:3). The apostle Peter, who sat at the feet of Jesus, strongly urged the recipients of his second epistle to look for "the coming of the day of God" (2 Pt. 3:12). "Since all these things will be dissolved, what manner of persons ought you to be in holy conduct and godliness, looking for and hastening the coming of the day of God" (2 Pt. 3:11, NKJV). Peter adds the thought that we may actually hasten the coming day. The Church certainly is not to sit by passively waiting for a set day that will end this dispensation. The Church is working together with the Lord to accomplish His work, which must be done before He returns in glory. Commenting on the above quoted verse from Peter, Michael Green says:

> Christians are expected to look for the coming of the Lord; had not Jesus Himself told them to watch? But this does not mean pious inactivity. It means action. For wonderful as it may seem, we can actually "hasten it on"

(NEB) (not "hasting unto" as in KJV). In other words, the timing of the advent is to some extent dependent upon the state of the Church and of society. What a wonderfully positive conception of the significance of our time on earth. It is no barren waiting for "finis" to be written. It is intended to be a time of active cooperation with God in the redemption of society... The Rabbis had two apt sayings: "It is the sins of the people which prevent the coming of the Messiah. If Jews would genuinely repent for one day, the Messiah would come," and "If Israel would perfectly keep the Torah for one day, the Messiah would come."[4]

Is it possible that God sees time in the terms of tasks accomplished rather than earthly calendars? We cannot hasten or delay God's program, but it is possible that we may do so in relation to our time frame. In any case, looking for the Lord does not mean folding our arms, but rather putting our hand to the plow and to the sickle.

While no one knows the time of Christ's coming, we are given signs by which we may recognize the emergence of the last times.

D. The signs of His coming

In answer to questions put to Him by some of the disciples, Jesus revealed a number of signs of coming events (Mt. 24; Mk. 13; Lk. 21). Some of the events Jesus described would happen in the first century, some would come on progressively during the church age, but still others would happen just before and during His coming in power and glory. A very careful reading of Christ's Olivet discourse, recorded in all three synoptic gospels, is necessary in order to properly arrange the sign events in a time sequence. It is suggested that the readers consult good evangelical commentaries for detailed exegesis. In the epistles, a number of passages describe conditions that would prevail in the latter days: 1 Tm. 4:1–3; 2 Tm. 3:1–7; 1 Thes. 5:1–3; 2 Thes. 2:1–12; Jas. 5:1–8; and 2 Pt. 3:1–10. Latter-day signs are of two kinds, primary signs and secondary signs. The primary signs are those that are declared explicitly to be evidences of the near approach of the Day of the Lord, and the secondary signs are inferential. That is, they are events or conditions that would have to precede the explicit signs in order for them to happen. For instance, in Revelation it is said that the Beast out of the earth (the Antichrist) would cause everyone to receive a mark or number, without which no one could buy or sell. In order for such control over humanity to be exercised, there would have to exist a mechanism by which such total control could be expedited. With half the world's peoples ruled by totalitarian

---

4 Michael Green, *The Second Epistle General of Peter and the General Epistle of Jude: An Introduction and a Commentary* (Grand Rapids, MI: Wm. B. Eerdmans Publishing Company, 1976), 140.

governments and with most of the rest of society subject to numbered identification and computerized records of financial transactions, the environment now exists for the Beast's appearance. Many students of prophecy view the present environment as a sign of the last days. There are many such inferences drawn from modern developments, scientific advancement, military capability, and international alignments that are legitimate indicators of where the hands are on the prophetic time clock. The following are some of the world conditions that prophetic scholars look for as signs of the latter days:

1. *The regathering of Israel in Palestine.* As far back as the time of Moses, God predicted that Israel, if disobedient, would be scattered throughout all nations (Dt. 28:64). He also promised that He would regather His people out of all nations, bringing them back into their land (Dt. 30:3; Is. 2:2–5; 11:11–16; Ez. 36:8, 24; 37:11–12; 38:8). In the Old Testament, there are prophecies concerning two regatherings. They would be regathered from Babylonia after seventy years captivity (Jer. 25:11–12), but in this first captivity they were not scattered throughout all nations, nor was their return complete and permanent. The passages cited above with regard to the second regathering refer to a complete and permanent regathering, ending in a rule of peace and righteousness. The second scattering of Israel into all nations is prophesied by Jesus in Luke 21: "And they [Israel] shall fall by the edge of the sword [A.D. 70], and shall be led away captive into all nations: and Jerusalem shall be trodden down of the Gentiles, until the times of the Gentiles be fulfilled" (21:24). The phrase "times of the Gentiles" refers to the period symbolized by the image Nebuchadnezzar saw in a dream interpreted by Daniel (Dn. 2:24–45), a period during which a succession of Gentile rulers would dominate Europe and the Middle East, including Palestine. Daniel himself had a dream in which he saw these same Gentile rulers represented by four beasts, the last of which ruled "until the Ancient of days came...and the time came that the saints possessed the kingdom" (Dn. 7:22). Paul seems to refer to the term "times of the Gentiles" in Romans 11:25–27:

> For I would not, brethren, that ye should be ignorant of this mystery....that blindness in part happened to Israel, until the fulness of the Gentiles be come in. And so all Israel shall be saved: as it is written, There shall come out of Sion the Deliverer, and shall turn away ungodliness from Jacob: For this is my covenant with them, when I shall take away their sins.

On May 14, 1948, the regathered Jews declared a portion of Palestine to be the independent state of Israel. This in itself did not fulfill specifically the prophecies concerning Israel's regathering, for the regathering has still been in unbelief of the deity of Christ. But after nearly two thousand years of exclusion from their land, Israel's existence as a state may very well set the stage for the final act.

2. *Perilous times.* Paul describes social conditions in the last days:

> But realize this, that in the last days difficult days will come. For men will
> be lovers of self, lovers of money, boastful, arrogant, revilers, disobedient
> to parents, ungrateful, unholy, unloving, irreconcilable, malicious gossips,
> without self-control, brutal, haters of good, treacherous, reckless, conceited,
> lovers of pleasure rather than lovers of God; holding to a form of godliness,
> although they have denied its power... among them are those who enter into
> households and captivate weak women weighed down with sins, led on by
> various impulses, always learning and never able to come to the knowledge
> of the truth.
>
> —2 Timothy 3:1–7, NASB

Of course such men as Paul describes have always existed; but when the depravity
that he describes characterizes a whole society, such a condition signals the approach
of the end of this age. When the currently-prevalent conditions of selfishness, sexual
perversion, crime, violence, lack of conscience, and rebellion against biblical morality
are contemplated, one is not surprised that many Bible scholars view modern society
as a doomsday society.

3. *The rise of communist Russia.* In Ezekiel 38 and 39, the prophet prophetically
describes a nation or nations that will come against Israel when she is regathered in
her own land. He says, "Son of Man, set your face toward Gog of the land of Magog,
the prince of Rosh, Meshech, and Tubal, and prophesy against him, and say, 'Thus
says the Lord GOD, "Behold, I am against you, O Gog, prince of Rosh, Meshech
and Tubal"'" (Ez. 38:2–3, NASB). The Hebrew name *Rosh* is translated "chief" in the
Authorized Version, but Hebrew scholars agree that in this context it is a proper
name and should be rendered as such, as is done in the American Standard, New
American Standard, New King James, and Amplified Versions. It is quite clear that
the above is a reference to Russia. Meshech is Moscow; Tubal is Tobolsk; and Rosh
is Russia. Authority for this identification comes from the Hebrew Lexicon of Dr.
William Gesenius, who defines Rosh in the following description:

> *Rosh* Ezekiel 38:2–3; 39:1; proper name of a northern nation, mentioned
> with Tubal and Meshech; undoubtedly the "Russians," who are mentioned
> by Byzantine writers of the tenth century, under the name *hoi ros* (Greek)
> dwelling to the north of Taurus, and described by Ibn Fosslan, an Arabic
> writer of the same age, as dwelling on the river Wolga.[5]

---

5 William Gesenius, *Hebrew and Chaldee Lexicon to the Old Testament Scriptures* (Grand
Rapids, MI: Wm. B. Eerdmans Publishing Company, 1974), 752.

Russia only became a world power with a goal of world conquest after World War I in 1917. With the Middle East being the chief oil source of the world, a status coveted by Russia, and with Russia at odds with Israel, an ally of the United States, it is neither impossible nor unthinkable that Moscow would invade regathered Israel at some near future date, especially in the light of the prophecy in Ezekiel 38 and 39. According to Ezekiel's prophecy, God will send a fire to destroy Russia, and the defeat will be so complete that the massive invader will leave behind weapons of war in such a quantity that it will take seven years to dispose of them. The dead will be so numerous that it will take Israel seven months to bury them. At the turn of the century there was no state of Israel, and Russia would have had no motive for invading Palestine. The rise of modern communist Russia and the establishment of the state of Israel now make possible the circumstances needed for the fulfillment of Ezekiel's prophecy, which was predicted to happen in the latter years.

4. *The rise of communist China.* In Revelation 16, there is a passage which makes reference to the kings of the east: "And the sixth angel poured out his bowl upon the great river, the Euphrates; and its water was dried up, that the way might be prepared for the kings from the east" (Rv. 16:12, NASB). The river Euphrates is also mentioned in Revelation 9 in connection with a prophecy that an army of two hundred million would be released, resulting in the death of a third part of mankind (Rv. 9:13–21). The river Euphrates was considered the boundary between East and West. Many prophetic scholars see the rise of modern China, now with nuclear weapons, as an inferential sign of the latter days.[6]

5. *Armaments and modern war potential.* Just before Jesus returns with His saints to claim His kingdom, the earth will be the scene of the greatest war of all time, called Armageddon. It will be the final conflict of this dispensation. At the turn of this century, a war of the proportion of Armageddon was difficult to conceive. Now with the development of atomic weapons, the destructive power of which has already been witnessed, another world war would beyond doubt be the last war, bringing about the destruction of mankind. In that sense, the modern war potential is a latter-day sign, because only the coming of Jesus can prevent total destruction. The Lord must come to save us from ourselves.

6. *Progress in transportation and science.* In the last chapter of Daniel's prophecy this word of the Lord is recorded: "But you, Daniel, shut up the words and seal the book until the time of the end; many shall run to and fro, and knowledge shall increase" (Dn. 12:4, NKJV). This prophecy seems to indicate that in the End Times there will be a notable acceleration in travel and in the acquisition of knowledge. Many who write about latter-day signs point to Daniel's prophecy, quoted

---

6 Hal Lindsey, with C. C. Carlson, *The Late Great Planet Earth* (Grand Rapids, MI: Zondervan Publishing House, 1970), 81.

above, as a sign that the end is approaching. Until the nineteenth century, there was very little change in the way people traveled. Abraham could get from one place to another about as rapidly as Shakespeare could. Until the turn of the twentieth century, the average person traveled in a vehicle drawn by animals. Today, travelers span continents in jet planes in a matter of hours and space travel will eventually offer speeds that permit individuals to circle the globe faster than Abraham could get to the next village.

The increase in knowledge has been equally spectacular. Until the invention of the printing press and the discovery of the New World, the sum of human knowledge was not appreciably greater than it was in the Golden Age of Greece and Rome. The Renaissance was really only the rediscovery of the cultures of ancient Greece, Egypt, Arabia, and China. Today's scientists have split the atom, developed nuclear power, successfully cloned animals, traveled to the moon, photographed the planets at close range, and computerized all statistics and most of industrial production. It has been estimated that three-fourths of all present knowledge has been acquired in the last fifty years and that seventy percent of modern medicines and surgical procedures have been developed since World War II. Three-fourths of all the scientists who have ever lived are alive today. With the use of computers, in an hour a modern engineer can duplicate the lifetime work of an engineer working before 1940. In an atmosphere of exploding scientific advancement and of declining morality and ethics, Jesus must come and rule to save us from ourselves.[7]

It should be pointed out, however, that only the general inferential signs and conditions in society are to be looked for before the Rapture of the Church. The explicit signs are prophesied to happen during the Tribulation, in connection with the Lord's return in judgment. No specific sign must happen before the Bridegroom comes for the bride. His appearing, as in the parable of the ten virgins, should be expected at all times.

E. The Rapture of the Church

1. *Its any-moment occurrence.* A number of events are associated with the end of the age. Jesus promised His disciples, "I will come again, and receive you unto myself, that where I am, there ye may be also" (Jn. 14:3). Paul wrote, "The dead in Christ shall rise first: Then we which are alive and remain shall be caught up together with them in the clouds, to meet the Lord in the air" (1 Thes. 4:16–17). Jesus spoke also of great tribulation: "For then shall be great tribulation, such as was not since the beginning of the world to this time, no, nor ever shall be" (Mt. 24:21). This Great Tribulation is described in detail in Revelation 6–19. (See also Dn. 12.) The tribula-

---

7 See Tim LaHaye, *The Beginning of the End* (Tyndale, 1972); H. Leo Eddleman, *Last Things* (Zondervan, 1969); and A. E. Bloomfield, *Signs of His Coming* (Bethany Fellowship, 1962).

tion will be caused by Satan, through the agency of one called variously the Beast (Rv. 13:1), the Antichrist (1 Jn. 2:18), the "man of sin" and the "son of perdition" (2 Thes. 2:3), and the "little horn" (Dn. 7:8). The Great Tribulation will be concluded by the Battle of Armageddon and the revelation of Jesus as King of kings, who will come with His armies of saints to bring judgment upon the Beast and his followers (Rv. 19:11–21). The Great Tribulation is followed by the millennial reign of Christ, the Final Judgment, and the eternal state (Rv. 20–22).

Which of these events will happen first? Will it be the coming of Jesus or the revelation of the Antichrist? If the Bible is to be taken in a natural sense, it seems that the first event for which the believer waits is the blessed hope (Ti. 2:13)—the Rapture of the Church:

> Here we have a definite message from the Lord. It is that those who are still living when He comes will not in any way precede those who have previously fallen asleep [died], one word of command, one shout from the archangel, one blast from the trumpet of God and the Lord Himself will come down from heaven! Those who have died in Christ will be the first to rise, and then we who are still living will be swept up with them into the clouds to meet the Lord in the air. And after that we shall be with Him forever.
> —1 THESSALONIANS 4:15–18, PHILLIPS

The apostle Paul, since he was the apostle to the Gentile church, was given a special revelation from the Lord Himself regarding the details of the Rapture and its relationship to the resurrection.[8]

In a passage in 1 Corinthians, Paul again speaks of the Rapture of the Church together with the bodily resurrection of deceased believers: "Behold, I tell you a mystery; we shall not all sleep, but we shall all be changed, in a moment, in the twinkling of an eye, at the last trumpet; for the trumpet will sound, and the dead will be raised imperishable, and we shall be changed" (15:51–52, NASB). When the Lord comes for His Church, not only will the living saints be raptured, their bodies will be changed into glorified, imperishable bodies. The believer will become like Jesus in body and spirit (1 Jn. 3:2–3).

Another reference to the Rapture made by Paul is found in 2 Thessalonians: "Now we beseech you brethren, by the coming of our Lord Jesus Christ, and by our gathering together unto him" (2:1). There is a probable additional reference to the Rapture in the next verse: "That day [the Day of the Lord] shall not come, except there come a falling away first" (v. 3). The Greek word translated "falling away" may

---

8 See Roy Hicks, *Another Look at the Rapture* (Tulsa, OK: Harrison House, 1982), where an extended treatment is made of Paul's special insight into the Rapture.

also have the meaning "departure" (see 2 Cor. 12:8, "depart"). The word in Greek has the definite article, which means that it refers to an event known by the recipients. Since the whole subject is about the Rapture and the concern of the Thessalonians that they were already in the Tribulation, the rendering "departure" is a reasonable one.[9]

Without doubt, the New Testament, especially Paul's writings, is very clear about a rapture of the living believers at Christ's coming. All evangelicals are agreed that a rapture will occur, but they are not in agreement about when the Rapture will occur in relation to the tribulation period described in the book of Revelation. While this book will identify itself with the pre-Tribulation Rapture position, which is the historic position of our Church, the authors refrain from radical dogmatism in the presentation of the position, recognizing the fact that godly and scholarly teachers take other positions.

2. *Various Rapture theories*

a) The post-Tribulation Rapture theory. Those who hold this theory believe that the believers will go through the Tribulation and that the Rapture will occur simultaneously with, or immediately before, the Lord's coming in judgment. They hold that the Rapture of the Church and Christ's return to rule are simply different aspects of a single event that will happen at the end of the Great Tribulation, just before the defeat of the Beast and his followers and the beginning of the Millennium. The best contemporary advocates of the post-Tribulation Rapture are Dr. George E. Ladd, in *The Blessed Hope*[10] and *A Theology of the New Testament;*[11] and J. Barton Payne, in *Encyclopedia of Biblical Prophecy.*[12]

(1) The principal arguments advanced in favor of the post-Tribulation Rapture position are as follows:

(a) The coming of Christ is variously described but nowhere said to be two events separated by a seven-year (or three-and-one-half-year) interval of tribulation.

(b) Jesus' answer to His disciples regarding the signs of the End Times indicated that a period of unequalled tribulation (Mt. 24:3–22) would precede His coming. Other passages also predict tribulation for God's people (Jn. 15:18–19; 16:33).

(c) The Resurrection is identified with the Rapture, yet Revelation 20:4–6 puts the first resurrection after Christ's return to rule and just before the Millennium, signaling that the Rapture and Revelation must happen together. (See also Dn. 12:1–2.)

---

9 See Kenneth S. Wuest, *The New Testament, an Expanded Translation* (Eerdmans, 1972) 486; also Roy Hicks, *Another Look at the Rapture* (Harrison House, 1982), 45–49.

10 George E. Ladd, *The Blessed Hope* (Grand Rapids, MI: Wm. B. Eerdmans, 1957).

11 Ladd, *A Theology of the New Testament* (Grand Rapids, MI: Zondervan, 1977).

12 J. Barton Payne, *Encyclopedia of Biblical Prophecy* (New York: Harper & Row, 1973).

(2) The following considerations argue against the post-Tribulation Rapture position:

(a) The tribulation period is not a Church period, but is the final week of Daniel's vision regarding God's dealing with Israel: "Seventy weeks are determined upon thy people and upon thy holy city, to finish the transgression, and to make an end of sins, and to make reconciliation for iniquity, and to bring in everlasting righteousness (Dn. 9:24, see also 25–27). It is a time of God's dealing with Israel and of His wrath upon the godless nations (Rv. 6:15–17). The tribulation period is called by Jeremiah "Jacob's trouble" (Jer. 30:4–7).

(b) Paul declares regarding the Church, "For God hath not appointed us to wrath, but to obtain salvation by our Lord Jesus Christ" (1 Thes. 5:9). The Church has suffered and will suffer many trials and tribulations, but not the great day of His wrath.

(c) The Lord has promised the faithful that they will be kept from that hour of wrath: "Because thou hast kept the word of my patience, I also will keep thee from the hour of temptation, which shall come upon all the world, to try them that dwell upon the earth" (Rv. 3:10). (See also 2 Pt. 2:9; Lk. 21:34–36.)

(d) Nowhere in the book of Revelation after chapter 4 is the Church mentioned specifically until chapter 19, where the Church is seen in heaven as the bride of Christ. Many scholars identify the Church with the twenty-four elders who are in heaven throughout the Apocalypse. These elders are arrayed in white with crowns of victory on their heads, symbols of the redeemed. The Tribulation saints (those who are saved during the Tribulation and martyred) are seen as a group only in heaven. The righteous who are seen on Earth are the 144,000, who are said to be Jews (Rv. 7:1–8; 14:1–5). Furthermore, if the Church is to be on Earth during the Tribulation, why is witnessing assigned to the two witnesses, who are apparently Jews (Moses and Elijah, Rv. 11:1–14)?

(e) The Rapture and the final coming cannot happen simultaneously, nor hardly on the same day, for two important events separate the Rapture and the resurrection of the saints from Christ's coming to Earth to rule—the Believers' Bema Judgment of Rewards and the Marriage Supper of the Lamb (Rv. 19:5–9; 1 Cor. 3:11–15; 2 Cor. 5:9–11).

(f) Since the Church age terminates with the beginning of the Tribulation (Daniel's seventieth week, Dn. 9:27; "the fullness of the Gentiles," Rom. 11:12, 25–27), the Church plays no more part in earthly affairs until the Millennium.

(g) Regarding the resurrection recorded in Revelation 12, referred to as the first resurrection, careful reading will reveal that the resurrected ones mentioned are those who are beheaded during the Tribulation. No mention is made of the saints of the entire Church age, who must have been raised up at the time of the Rapture before the Great Tribulation. Daniel 12:1–2 places the resurrection of the Old Testament saints at the end of the Tribulation, but John does not mention it in Revelation 20. Christ is called the "firstfruits of them that slept" (1 Cor. 15:20). At Christ's resurrection, a number of saints arose from the dead (Mt. 27:52–53). In Revelation 11:11–12, the two witnesses are resurrected. The resurrection of the Tribulation saints is recorded in Revelation 7:12–17. Apparently all those who are resurrected before the Millennium are a part of the first resurrection, while those who are raised after the Millennium are raised unto judgment and perdition (Rv. 20:13, 15).

(h) The strongest argument for a pre-Tribulation Rapture is the fact that throughout the New Testament, exhortation is given to look for and wait for the coming of Jesus (Mt. 24:42–43; 25:13; Mk. 13:35; 1 Thes. 5:6; Ti. 2:13; Heb. 9:28). Jesus promised, "And if I go and prepare a place for you, I will come again, and receive you unto myself; that where I am, there ye may be also" (Jn. 14:3). Here Jesus' coming is for the purpose of receiving the Church unto Himself and taking her to a place in the Father's house. This coming cannot be the same as His coming with the Church to Earth, as the post-Tribulationists contend. The blessed hope of an imminent coming of Jesus is one of the strongest incentives to practical godliness and diligent service (Ti. 2:12–14; 1 Jn. 3:3). If the Tribulation must come first before the Rapture, along with the manifestation of the Antichrist, who will look for a coming of Jesus until many of the events of the Apocalypse have transpired? The parable of the faithful and unfaithful servants, recorded in Matthew 24, teaches the tragic result of failing to recognize and prepare for Christ's return, making the excuse, "My lord delayeth his coming" (24:44–51).

The principal proponents of the pre-Tribulation position are Dr. C. I. Scofield, *Scofield Study Bible*;[13] Dr. John F. Walvoord, *The Rapture Question*[14] and *The Revelation of Jesus Christ*;[15] Dr. Kenneth S. Wuest, *Prophetic Light in the Present Darkness*;[16] Dr. J. Dwight Pentecost, *Prophecy for Today*;[17] Dr. Henry C. Thiessen, *Lectures in Systematic Theology*;[18] Dr. Mark G. Cambron, *Bible Doctrines*;[19] W. E. Vine, *The Epistle to the Thessalonians*;[20] Herbert Lockyer, *All the Doctrines of the*

13 C. I. Scofield, *Scofield Study Bible* (Oxford: Oxford University Press, 1967), footnotes.

14 John F. Walvoord, *The Rapture Question* (Findlay, OH: Dunham, 1957).

15 Walvoord, *The Revelation of Jesus Christ* (Chicago, IL: Moody Press, 1972).

16 Kenneth S. Wuest, *Prophetic Light in the Present Darkness* (Grand Rapids, MI: Eerdmans, 1956).

17 J. Dwight Pentecost, *Prophecy for Today* (Grand Rapids, MI: Zondervan, 1961).

18 Thiessen, *Lectures in Systematic Theology* (Grand Rapids, MI: Eerdmans, 1961).

19 Mark G. Cambron, *Bible Doctrines* (Grand Rapids, MI: Zondervan, 1973).

20 Vine, *The Epistle to the Thessalonians* (London: Pickering & Inglis).

Bible;[21] Dr. Gerald B. Stanton, *Kept From the Hour*;[22] Dr. Charles C. Ryrie, *The Ryrie Study Bible*[23] and *Dispensationalism Today*.[24]

b) The mid-Tribulation Rapture theory. As the term *mid-Tribulation* reveals, it describes the position of those who teach that the Church will be raptured after the first half of Daniel's seventieth week (Dn. 9:27). Most of those who hold this view, however, claim to be pre-Tribulation rapturists because they do not interpret the first half of the seven-year Tribulation period as being a time of great tribulation or wrath.

(1) The principal points of this theory are:

(a) The last trumpet, mentioned in connection with the Rapture in 1 Corinthians 15:52, is identified with the seventh trumpet sounded in Revelation 11:15, which occurs in the middle of the Tribulation (Rv. 11:2–3). If the two trumpets are identical, then the Rapture occurs in the middle of the Tribulation.

(b) Since the Church is raptured before the Great Tribulation (the last three and one-half years), the Church escapes the wrath mentioned in 1 Thessalonians 5:9 and the "hour of temptation" described in Revelation 3:10.

(c) The resurrection of the two witnesses in Revelation 11:11–12 is declared to be a reference to the Rapture and resurrection of the Church or to happen simultaneously with the Rapture.[25]

(2) The following arguments may be advanced in opposition to the mid-Tribulation Rapture position:

(a) The trumpets in 1 Corinthians 15 and Revelation 11 are not the same. Paul's "trump of God" is a trumpet call of victory over death; John's seventh trumpet is the seventh in a series of announcements of judgment upon the wicked and final triumph over Satan's reign.

(b) The entire seventieth week of Daniel is Jewish in character, therefore the Church does not belong in any part of it. God's wrath is also poured out in the first half of the tribulation period (Rv. 6:12–17). (See also 1 Thes. 5:9; Rv. 3:10; 2 Pt. 2:9.)

(c) The two witnesses appear to be Jewish from the Old Testament symbols—the temple, olive trees, and lampstands (Zec. 4:3, 12), withholding rain, and smiting with plagues (Ex. 7:20; 8:1–12:29; 1 Kgs. 17:1; 18:41–45; 2 Kgs. 1:10–12; Jas. 5:17–18). If the Church were on the earth, why would God assign Jewish prophets to the mission

---

21 Herbert Lockyer, *All the Doctrines of the Bible* (Grand Rapids, MI: Zondervan, 1964).

22 Gerald B. Stanton, *Kept From the Hour* (Grand Rapids, MI: Zondervan, 1956).

23 Charles C. Ryrie, *The Ryrie Study Bible* (Chicago, IL: Moody Press, 1978).

24 Ryrie, *Dispensationalism Today* (Chicago, IL: Moody Press, 1981).

25 See J. Oliver Buswell, *A Systematic Theology of the Christian Religion* (Grand Rapids, MI: Zondervan Publishing House, 1963), II, 456.

of witnessing to the nations? Until the end of the Church age, it is the Church's mission to witness to all nations. Dr. Buswell believes, however, that the Church age and the tribulation period will overlap three and one-half years.[26]

(d) The same objection can be made to the mid-Tribulation Rapture position that is made to the post-Tribulation position; that is, that the mid-Tribulation position removes the any-moment expectation of Christ's coming. The Tribulation period begins with the Antichrist's making a covenant with the Jews, an event that could not be concealed. If the Church is going through any part of the tribulation period, Christ cannot come for His Church until the Tribulation has begun with the Antichrist's covenant to restore the daily sacrifice (Dn. 9:27). Both of the theories discussed above require us to look for the Antichrist's coming before Christ's coming.

c) The partial rapture theory. Those who hold to a partial rapture base their belief on passages such as Hebrews 9:28, Luke 21:36, 1 John 2:28, and Matthew 25:1–13, which are interpreted to mean that believers who are not looking for Him, who are not counted worthy, who have something in their lives that might make them "ashamed before Him at His coming," or that do not have oil (taken to be a symbol of the fullness of the Spirit) will be left behind to go through the Tribulation. Advocates of this theory believe that only those believers who are fully worthy will go up in the Rapture. The following considerations argue against the partial rapture theory:

(1) First Thessalonians 4:16 says, "The dead in Christ shall rise first." If all who have died in Christ will be resurrected, certainly all who are alive in Christ will be raptured. Certainly the Lord will not wait until the generation alive at His coming to make distinctions between believers who are worthy and those who are not.

(2) Furthermore, in 1 Corinthians 15:51, Paul says: "Behold, I shew you a mystery; We shall not all sleep, but we shall all be changed." All who are in Christ will be changed at His coming. This of course does not include the unregenerate who are only professing Christians.

(3) If only the worthy are to be caught up, who will go? Who can claim worthiness in himself? Our standing with God is based on the righteousness of Christ, not our righteousnesses, which are "filthy rags" (Is. 64:6).

(4) Every believer ought to be filled with the Spirit, but the purpose of that fullness is not to make us worthy, which is accomplished by the blood of Jesus, but to equip us with power for service (Acts 1:8). To interpret the oil in the parable of the ten virgins as symbolic of the fullness of the Spirit violates sound principles for the interpretation of parables, since both the wise and the unwise had oil at the beginning.

(5) Proponents of the partial rapture theory, as well as those who believe that the Church must go through some or all of the Tribulation, contend that tribulation is

---

26 Ibid., 453.

necessary to purify the Church and make her ready for the Bridegroom. This belief contends for a kind of Protestant purgatory. And if the saints alive at the end of the age need purging by tribulation, it would seem that the Lord would need to resurrect the dead saints for a period of tribulation previous to their rapture. An absurd thought, of course!

F. Christ's return to rule—the revelation

At the Rapture, Christ comes for His saints; at His revelation, He comes with His saints. At the Rapture, He comes in the air; at His revelation, He comes to Earth to rule in power and glory. The Rapture is followed by the Believers' Judgment of Rewards and the Marriage Supper of the Lamb; the revelation is followed by the defeat of the Antichrist and the wicked nations, as well as the establishment of His millennial kingdom (Rv. 19, 20). "And Enoch also, the seventh from Adam, prophesied of these saying, Behold, the Lord cometh with ten thousands of His saints" (Jude 14). (See Dn. 7:9–10, 21–22; Is. 11:1–4; 63:1–3.) According to Revelation 19, the steps in Christ's return to rule are:

1. *The heaven is opened and Christ appears riding on a white horse with a crown on His head and with garments dipped in blood.* His name is announced to be the Word of God (vv. 11–13; also Jn. 1:1).

2. *He is accompanied by armies of saints, also riding on white horses.* A sharp sword issues from His mouth to smite the wicked nations. His title is revealed to be King of kings and Lord of lords (vv. 14–16).

3. *An angel announces His readiness for battle against the Beast and his armies, which gather to oppose the Lord.* The Beast's armies are crushed. The Beast, the false prophet, and all those who have taken the mark of the Beast or worshiped his image are cast into the lake of fire (vv. 19–21; Dn. 8:25).

4. *An angel from heaven casts Satan, called the old serpent, the dragon, and the Devil, into the bottomless pit, where he is imprisoned for a thousand years (Rv. 20:1–3).*

5. *The Tribulation saints are raised and, together with the Church saints, reign with Christ for a thousand years (Rv. 20:4; Mt. 25:21; 2 Tm. 2:12; Rv. 5:9–10).*

IV. THE TRIBULATION

A. The word *tribulation* in Scripture

In the Bible, the word *tribulation* is used in at least three different ways:

1. *To apply to the trials and persecutions that the Christian believers will suffer throughout the Church age as a result of their identification with Christ:* "In the world ye shall have tribulation: but be of good cheer; I have overcome the world" (Jn. 16:33). John, in his first epistle, explains why we suffer with Christ in this world: "Therefore

the world knoweth us not, because it knew Him not" (1 Jn. 3:1). (See also 2 Thes. 1:4; Acts 14:22; Rom. 12:12; Eph. 3:13; 2 Cor. 7:4.)

2. *To apply to a special period of tribulation for Israel, prophesied by Daniel (9:24–27).* Jeremiah also makes reference to the same period, calling it "Jacob's trouble" (Jer. 30:7–9). Jesus describes the Great Tribulation (Mt. 24:21) and confirms its application to Israel by the use of terms such as *Judea, the sabbath day,* and *the abomination of desolation* (Dn. 9:27), which refers to the desecration of the altar of the Jewish temple by the Antichrist.

3. *To apply to God's final wrath upon the Antichrist and the Gentile nations that follow him (Rv. 6:12–17), called the great day of His wrath.* It is very important that the three different applications of the word *tribulation* be clearly distinguished. The fact that believers must be ready to suffer trials and tribulations throughout the Church age (Acts 14:14) does not mean that the Church must go through the Great Tribulation and the final hour of God's wrath. God has promised to keep the Church saints from (Greek, *ek,* "out of") the Tribulation period (Rv. 3:10; 1 Thes. 5:9). Furthermore, the Great Tribulation, which is Daniel's seventieth week of the seventy-week period determined for dealing with Israel (Dn. 9:24–27; 12:8–13), is not a part of the Church age. When the fullness of the Gentiles comes, as Paul explains in Romans 11:25, the Church will be raptured and God will turn again to effect the salvation of national Israel (Rom. 11:24, 26; Rv. 7:4–8; Rv. 11, 12).

B. Daniel's dream and vision

Daniel also prophesied about times of world domination by Gentile nations (Nebuchadnezzar's image—Dn. 2:31-44; Daniel's dream of four beasts—Dn. 7:1-14). The four parts of the image and the four beasts represented four successive Gentile empires, the last of which was to be the Roman Empire. According to the dream of the image, the Roman Empire would be revived in the form of ten kingdoms, represented by the ten toes of the image. According to the vision of the four beasts, the fourth would have ten horns among which a "little horn," symbolizing the Antichrist, would come forth. In both the dream and the vision, the Son of Man will come in the time of the fourth empire to punish the nations and to set up His everlasting kingdom (Dn. 2:31-35; 7:8-14; 12:1-3). In Matthew 24 and in Luke 21, Jesus makes clear that the Great Tribulation will include Daniel's seventieth week of God's dealing with Israel and His final wrath against Satan and the wicked Gentile nations that serve him. (See also Zec. 14:1-4; Rv. 16:14-16; 19:19.)

C. Principal events of the Tribulation

1. *The removal of the Church and the restrainer of evil (2 Thes. 2:1, 7–8)*

2. *Restoration of the daily sacrifice in a rebuilt temple by covenant with the Antichrist (Dn. 9:27)*

3. *Outpouring of judgments resulting from the opening of the seven seals (Rv. 6:1–8:1)*

4. *Outpouring of judgments from the sounding of the seven trumpets (Rv. 8:6–11:15)*

5. *The taking away of the daily sacrifice by the Antichrist and the setting up of the abomination of desolation (Dn. 9:27; 12:10–11; Mt. 24:15).* (This happens in the middle of the seven years, which are divided into two parts, each three and one-half years long: Rv. 11:2–3, Dn. 9:27, 12:11, and Rv. 12:14. The latter half is considered to be the Great Tribulation.)

6. *Increased persecution of Israel (Rv. 12); 144,000 Jews from the twelve tribes are sealed (Rv. 7:1–8); an innumerable company of Tribulation saints from all nations, converted during the Tribulation, are taken to heaven (Rv. 7:9–17)*

7. *Total control by the Beast and the false prophet; the introduction of the mark of the Beast and his number with compulsory worship of the Beast's image (Rv. 13)*

8. *The judgments resulting from the outpouring of the seven vials of wrath (Rv. 15–16)*

9. *Judgment upon the harlot, mystery Babylon (Rv. 17–18), who probably represents apostate religion.* (After the Rapture of the true Church, organized religion with a "form of godliness but denying the power thereof" [2 Tm. 3:5] will become increasingly corrupt, even aligning herself with the Beast's government.)

10. *Gathering of the kings of the East and armies of the Antichrist (Beast) to make war with the remnant of Israel, resulting in the Battle of Armageddon (Rv. 12:17, 16:12–16)*

11. *Celebration of the Marriage Supper of the Lamb (Rv. 19:6–9)*

12. *Christ returns with His armies of saints to confront the Beast and his armies, and the Beast's armies are destroyed by the brightness of Christ's coming (Rv. 19:14–21; 2 Thes. 2:8).*

13. *The Beast and the false prophet are cast into the lake of fire (Rv. 19:20).*

14. *Satan is cast into the bottomless pit (the Abyss) for one thousand years (Rv. 20:1–3).*

V. THE ANTICHRIST

A. The word *antichrist* in Scripture

The word *antichrist* comes from two Greek words: *Christos,* meaning "Christ" or the "anointed one," and *anti,* meaning in this context "against." Thus, the whole word may be taken to mean "the one against Christ, God's anointed." The name of the Antichrist is found only in John's epistles (1 Jn. 2:18, 22; 4:3; 2 Jn. 7), where he is described as one coming in the last time and one whose spirit is already present in the world. The spirit of antichrist will be embodied in the Beast described in Revelation

11:7 and 13:1. The first prophetic reference to the Antichrist is probably found in Genesis 3:15: "And I will put enmity between thee and the woman, and between they seed and her seed." Christ is the seed of woman. The Antichrist is the seed of Satan or the devil, whose name means "slanderer" and who speaks against Christ and against His redeemed.

B. The identity of the Antichrist

The spirit of antichrist has possessed many enemies of God through the ages, such as the king of Babylon, a representation of Satan (Is. 14:4–17). The name "Mystery, Babylon" is borne by the great harlot of Revelation 17:5, for she is the embodiment of anti-God religion. Many anti-Christian rulers and evil men of power have been identified as the Antichrist through history, such as: Nero, Napoleon, Kaiser Wilhelm, Mussolini, Hitler, Stalin, etc. Some of these were no doubt motivated by the spirit of antichrist, but the Antichrist is yet to come. He may be somewhere in the world already, but he will not be revealed until after the Rapture of the Church. Therefore, it is rather futile to try to identify him. The spirit of antichrist will continue to possess any vehicle yielded to Satan.

C. The titles of the Antichrist

1. *The Beast (Rv. 13:1–4, 12–18; 15:2; 16:2; 17:8; 19:19; 20:4, 10)*

2. *The little horn (Dn. 7:8; 8:9).* He shall rise up from among rulers of the revived Roman Empire. The little horn of Daniel 8:9 is Antiochus Epiphanes (170 B.C.), the Syrian ruler who persecuted the Jews and defiled the temple in the time of the Maccabees (Macc. 1:10–47). Because of this, he is a type of antichrist.

3. *The man of sin (2 Thes. 2:3).* He will be history's vilest embodiment of sin and rebellion.

4. *The son of perdition (2 Thes. 2:3).* The Antichrist will be Satan's tool to seduce men and consign them to the realm of the lost.

5. *The wicked one (2 Thes. 2:8).* The word *wicked* is from the Greek term *anomos*, which means "a violator of the law." He totally opposes every law of God.

6. *The willful king (Dn. 11:36–45).* While Jesus prayed, "Not my will, but thine, be done" (Lk. 22:42), the Antichrist will oppose God's will and do his own will. He is the inspirer of all those who do their own thing.

7. *The foolish shepherd (Zec. 11:15–17).* Jesus is the Good Shepherd who preserves, but the Antichrist is the worthless shepherd who devours.

D. The works of the Antichrist

1. *He is the last ruler of the revived Roman empire (Dn. 7:8; Rv. 13:1).*

2. *He will appear on the scene as a proponent of peace who is tolerant of religion (Dn. 9:27; Rv. 6:2; Dn. 8:25; 1 Thes. 5:3).*

3. He will arise after the Rapture of the Church and at the beginning of the seventieth week of Daniel when God sets His hand to deal again with national Israel, and he will make a covenant with the Jews to restore the daily sacrifice (Dn. 9:24–27).

4. After three and one-half years, in the middle of the Tribulation, he will cast off all pretense of toleration, break his covenant with the Jews, cause the daily sacrifice to cease, and begin his persecution of Israel (Rv. 13:7–8).

5. One of his heads will receive a deadly wound, then be miraculously healed, causing the wonderment and worship of the whole world (Rv. 13:3–4).

6. As the man of sin and lawless one, he will blaspheme God, then require the worship of all men with the threat of death (Rv. 13:7–8).

7. The third member of the satanic trinity of the dragon, the Beast, and the false prophet arises. The false prophet exercises miraculous power to deceive, causes men to worship the Beast, creates an image of the Beast to which he gives life, and causes all men to take a mark or number of the Beast in order to buy or sell (Rv. 13:11–18).

8. During the Tribulation, the Beast sponsors the great harlot, who represents apostate religion, but finally the Beast, together with the ten kings who rule with the Beast, utterly destroy the scarlet woman (Rv. 17). The woman is said to be "that great city, which reigneth over the kings of the earth" (Rv. 17:18). The city is situated on "seven mountains" (Rv. 17:9). (Scholars are divided as to whether the city is Rome or Babylon.)

9. The Beast gathers his subject nations together to make war with the Lamb at the Battle of Armageddon, where he is utterly defeated and cast, together with the false prophet, into the lake of fire (Rv. 16:16; 17:14; 19:19–20).

VI. THE RESURRECTION

Almost all religions teach the immortality of the soul, but the Bible teaches the redemption of and the survival of the total person—spirit, soul, and body. The ancient Greeks believed in life after death for the soul, but since the body was the source of all evil, release of the soul from the body was desirable. A heretical Christian sect called the Gnostics shared this concept, derived from Greek philosophy. The Bible does not teach that the physical body is the source of evil. The Pauline term *flesh* refers to man's sinful and selfish nature which, while it manifests itself through actions of the body, derives from a "carnal mind" (Rom. 8:6–7). By taking our human body (the "likeness of sinful flesh"), Christ "condemned sin in the flesh" (Rom. 8:3). Christ, by His incarnation, death, and resurrection, redeemed the total person who is in Christ, giving him a hope of a bodily resurrection that will occur at the Rapture of the Church. "For since by man came death, by man came also the resurrection of the dead. For as in Adam all die, even so in Christ shall

all be made alive. But every man in his own order: Christ the firstfruits; afterward they that are Christ's at His coming" (1 Cor. 15:21–23).

A. The fact of the Resurrection

The fact of the Resurrection is taught in both the Old and the New Testaments:

1. *In the Old Testament*

a) By affirmation: "For I know that my Redeemer lives, and He shall stand at last on the earth; And after my skin is destroyed, this I know, That in my flesh I shall see God" (Jb. 19:25, NKJV). "As for me, I will behold thy face in righteousness: I shall be satisfied, when I awake, with thy likeness" (Ps. 17:15). (See also Ps. 16:9–11; Dn. 12:2.)

b) By prophecy: "Thy dead men shall live, together with my dead body shall they arise. Awake and sing, ye that dwell in dust: for thy dew is like the dew of herbs, and the earth shall cast out the dead" (Is. 26:19). (See also Hos. 13:14.)

c) By typology: Events such as Joseph's deliverance from the pit are descriptive of death and resurrection (Gn. 37:20–36), as are Isaac's return from the altar of sacrifice (Gn. 22:5–14), and Jonah's deliverance from the great fish (commonly called a whale) (Jon. 2; Mt. 12:40).

d) By example: The Old Testament contains several examples of persons who were raised from the dead (1 Kgs. 17:17–24; 2 Kgs 4:32–35; 13:20–21). While these are cases of resuscitation rather than resurrection (for those who were raised died natural deaths later), they demonstrate God's power and disposition to restore dead bodies to life.

2. *In the New Testament*

a) By affirmation: "So also is the resurrection of the dead. It is sown in corruption; it is raised in incorruption: It is sown in dishonor; it is raised in glory: it is sown in weakness; it is raised in power" (1 Cor. 15:42–43). (See also Mt. 22:30–32; Jn. 5:21; Acts 23:6–8; 26:8, 23; 2 Tm. 1:10; 1 Pt. 1:3.)

b) By prophecy: "Marvel not at this: for the hour is coming, in which all that are in the graves shall hear his voice, And shall come forth; they that have done good, unto the resurrection of life; and they that have done evil, unto the resurrection of damnation" (Jn. 5:28–29). (See also Jn. 6:39–40, 44, 54; Lk. 14:13–14; 20:35–36; 1 Cor. 15; Phil. 3:11, 21; 1 Thes. 4:14–16; Rv. 20:4–6, 13–15.)

c) The New Testament also contains examples of persons raised from the dead. They were not resurrections such as will occur at the second coming and at the Last Judgment, for they later died and will experience the final resurrection just as others. However, they were prefigures of the final resurrection.

On the other hand, the resurrection of Jesus was the true and ideal resurrection. When Jesus arose, He became "the firstfruits of them that slept" (1 Cor. 15:20). His resurrection was the guarantee of all resurrections of believers: "But God....raised us up together, and made us sit together in heavenly places in Christ Jesus" (Eph. 2:4, 6). (See Jn. 11:41–44, Lazarus; Lk. 8:41–56, Jairus' daughter; Lk. 7:12–15, the widow's son; Mt. 27:52–53, Old Testament saints.)

B. The nature of the Resurrection

The Resurrection will be universal. Not everyone has eternal life, but everyone does have eternal existence. All persons will be resurrected, the just to eternal life and the unjust to eternal condemnation. All will be raised, but not all at the same time (Jn. 5:28–29).

1. *The resurrection of believers (1 Thes. 4:13–18; 1 Cor. 15:50–57; Rv. 20:4–6).* The resurrection of the Church occurs at the coming of Jesus, immediately prior to the Rapture (1 Thes. 4:16). The believers' resurrection is called the first resurrection: "Blessed and holy is he that hath part in the first resurrection: on such the second death hath no power" (Rv. 20:6). It has been taught by some that there will be one general resurrection of the dead and one judgment at which just and unjust are judged. Jesus sometimes mentioned the two resurrections and judgments in the same passage, but a careful reading will reveal that Jesus was not speaking of one general resurrection: "And shall come forth; they that have done good, unto the resurrection of life; and they that have done evil, unto the resurrection of damnation" (Jn. 5:29). Notice that one is a resurrection of life, while the other is a resurrection of condemnation. They are not the same, nor do they occur at the same time, as Paul and John both elucidate.

It is normal for prophetic perspective to view several related future events as if they were one event. With similar prophetic language, the first and second comings of Jesus are merged in the same passage in Old Testament prophecy (Is. 9:6–7; 61:1–3; Dn. 12:2). New Testament writers sometimes allude to both the Rapture and final coming in the same reference (1 Thes. 3:13). Both Paul and John make it clear that the saints' resurrection (including the saved remnant of Israel and the Tribulation saints) takes place at Christ's coming and before the Millennial Reign (1 Cor. 15:51–52; Rv. 20:4–6; Dn. 12:1–2).

That the saints' resurrection is selective is seen in a remarkable statement of the apostle Paul: "That I may know Him, and the power of His resurrection, and the fellowship of His sufferings, being made conformable unto His death; If by any means I might attain unto the resurrection of the dead" (Phil. 3:10–11). If there is only one general resurrection for the just and the unjust, would Paul aspire to attain to it? A more literal translation reveals Paul's full meaning: "If by any means I might advance to the earlier resurrection, which is from among the dead" (Phil. 3:11, ROTHERHAM). The Greek preposition *ek* means "out from." Paul desired to be in the group that would be resurrected at the time of the Rapture, those who would be taken selectively out from among the general mass of the dead, those who would be raised in the earlier resurrection (the first resurrection, Rv. 20:6). The Greek word for "resurrection" is *exanastasis* (used only once in the New Testament). The use of *exanastasis* and the word *ek* ("from among," in Phil. 3:11, ROTHERHAM) in this passage gives added emphasis to the idea that the resurrection of the Christian believers is one in which they are selected for a special awakening. Paul expresses in another place that there will be several orders of resurrection: "But every man in his own order: Christ the firstfruits; afterward they that are Christ's at his coming" (1 Cor. 15:23).

a) It will be a literal bodily resurrection. This is shown by the Resurrection of Jesus. His resurrected body still bore the prints of the nails and the wound of the sword (Jn. 20:26–28); after His resurrection, Jesus had a body of flesh and bones and even took food (Lk. 24:36–43). On the other hand, the body of Jesus was sufficiently glorified that His disciples did not always recognize Him at once. His appearances show that His body was not subject to normal physical limitations (Jn. 20:19, 26).

Paul speaks of death as a sowing of the body as a farmer sows seed. The seed dies, but it contains a life principle by which nature brings forth a new plant of the same genus, species, and variety as the original seed. That our resurrection will be literal does not mean that all the same molecules of our dead bodies will be recovered. In fact, our body cells are replaced a number of times during our life span without our losing personal identity. One may be certain that God will recover from the dust a body with a definite relationship to one's earthly body, yet transformed and fashioned to one's new environment (Phil. 3:21). Believers' bodies will be changed (1 Cor. 15:52), but each will have a relationship to the earthly body. It appears from the identification of Moses and Elijah on the Mount of Transfiguration and of Jesus after His resurrection that our resurrection bodies will retain their personal identity. The resurrection body will not be the earthly body merely resuscitated; but the likeness of the earthly body glorified.

At the Resurrection, cemeteries will be turned into harvest fields (1 Cor. 15:42–44), and out of the planted earthly bodies, the Lord will raise up resurrection bodies that are identified with the earthly body, but which are transformed with a likeness to Christ's resurrection body.

b) The resurrection body will be God-given. "But God giveth it a body as it hath pleased him" (1 Cor. 15:38). This is in answer to a hypothetical question, "How are the dead raised up? and with what body do they come?" (1 Cor. 15:35). How a dead body can be raised and glorified cannot be conceived by human intellect. Christ's resurrection is the great miracle of our gospel. We do not explain it. We accept it as divine revelation in the same manner we accept bodily resurrection as a miracle of divine power and wisdom. If we accept Christ's resurrection (which is one of the best-attested events of history), we should have no problem with the acceptance of our final resurrection, for we shall be raised up by the same omnipotent God who raised up Jesus from the dead.

c) The believer's resurrection body will be immortal and incorruptible (1 Cor. 15:42). The Scriptures never speak of the immortality of the soul. The believer now has eternal life, but he dwells in a mortal body. All men have eternal existence. Only believers who shall experience the first resurrection will receive immortal and incorruptible bodies (1 Cor. 15:42).

d) The resurrection body will be a celestial body (1 Cor. 15:40). Our earthly bodies are suited to this present earthly environment. The resurrection body will be suited to our new heavenly environment. It will be equally suited to both the new heavens and the new earth, as well as to the millennial earth. Like the body of Jesus, it will be able to come and go between heaven and the earth.

e) The resurrection body will be a powerful body. "It is sown in weakness; it is raised in power" (1 Cor. 15:43). The contrast here expressed indicates that the new capacities of the resurrection body will be inconceivably and inexpressibly greater than those of any earthly human body. The events recorded of angels are a preview of the capacities of resurrected saints (Mt. 22:29–30).

f) The resurrection body will be a glorious body. "It is sown in dishonor; it is raised in glory" (1 Cor. 15:43). The resurrected body will be as glorious as the decaying earthly body can be inglorious. Jesus promised, "Then shall the righteous shine forth as the sun in the kingdom of their Father" (Mt. 13:43). The above words of Jesus suggest for the saints the glory that He manifested on the Mount of Transfiguration: "And was transfigured before them: and his face did shine as the sun, and his raiment was white as the light" (Mt. 17:2). Jesus prayed for us, "And the glory which thou gavest me I have given them; that they may be one, even as we are one "(Jn. 17:22). After speaking of the Resurrection, Daniel said, "And they that be wise shall shine like the brightness of the firmament; and they that turn many to righteousness as the stars for ever and ever" (Dn. 12:3).

2. *The resurrection of unbelievers (Rv. 20:5, 12–14; Jn 5:28–29; Dn. 12:2; Acts 24:15).* The Bible does not reveal specifically the state or nature of the resurrection bodies of the unrighteous, but it may be assumed that they will be bodies subject to corruption or ruin. Jesus said, "And fear not them which kill the body, but are not able to kill the soul: but rather him which is able to destroy [Greek, *apollumi,* 'to destroy' or 'put out of the way entirely') both body and soul in hell [Greek, *gehenna*]" (Mt. 10:28). The bodies of the unrighteous dead will suffer utter ruin eternally (2 Thes. 1:8–9). The unrighteous are not resurrected at the time of Christ's second coming, but after the millennial reign of Christ (Rv. 20:5).

C. The time of the Resurrection

The order of resurrections is as follows:

1. *The resurrection of Jesus (Mt. 28:1–10; Mk. 16:1–14; Lk. 24:1–39; Jn. 20:1–17)*

2. *A resurrection of saints of the Old Testament (Mt. 27:52–53)*

3. *The resurrection of the church saints at the Rapture (1 Thes. 4:16; 1 Cor. 15:52)*

4. *The resurrection of the two witnesses of Revelation 11:12 during the Tribulation period*

5. *The resurrection of the saints of Israel and of the Tribulation saints who are witnesses for Christ and who do not worship the Beast (Rv. 20:4–6; Dn. 12:1–2).*

6. *The resurrection of the unrighteous.* This will occur after the millennial reign of Christ. They will be resurrected to stand before the great white throne (Rv. 20:5, 11–14).

VII. THE MILLENNIUM

The word *millennium* is not found in the Bible; however, the thousand-year period of Christ's rule over the earth is mentioned six times in Revelation 20. The word *millennium* is derived from Latin words which simply mean "thousand years." The Millennium will be a period during which Satan will be bound in the Abyss: "And he laid hold on the dragon, that old serpent, which is the Devil, and Satan, and bound him a thousand years" (Rv. 20:2). The binding of Satan prepares the earth for the millennial reign of Christ, who comes to Earth, as described in Revelation 19, as King of kings and Lord of lords (vv. 15–16). The resurrected Church saints, together with the Tribulation saints, will reign with Christ in His millennial kingdom: "And they lived and reigned with Christ a thousand years.... but they shall be priests of God and of Christ, and shall reign with him a thousand years" (Rv. 20:4, 6). (See also Rv. 19:7–10, 14.)

A. Its relation to the second coming

There are three theories about the time relationship of the Millennium to the second coming:

1. *Post-millennialism.* This theory puts the Millennium before the coming of Jesus. According to this theory, which is based on an interpretation of the parables of the leaven and the mustard seed, the Church will gradually overcome war and evil in the world through the preaching of the gospel and the promotion of social justice. After that point, Christ will come. Post-millenarians believe that universal peace and righteousness will be accomplished by the Church gradually, rather than by the coming of Christ in power. Two world wars in the last century, together with increasing crime, violence, and the threat of a nuclear holocaust have largely disproved this optimistic theory.

2. *Amillennialism.* Amillenarians spiritualize all references relative to Christ's reign and apply them to His spiritual rule over the hearts of believers. The Old Testament prophecies concerning Christ's ruling on the throne of David are likewise applied to the Church. All promises to Israel are fulfilled by blessings upon the Church, inasmuch as the Church is the spiritual Israel. According to the amillennial theory, a national Israel has no further destiny that differs from that of the other nations. Paul's teaching about the natural and wild branches of the olive tree in Romans 11 quite clearly refutes the spiritual or figurative interpretation of Israel.

3. *Pre-millennialism.* Pre-millenarians interpret Scripture literally, or better, naturally. Differences in the method of interpretation of prophecy lead to differences in theory. When one departs from a natural interpretation of Bible prophecy, he then can only speculate. If everything is a symbol rather than a real event, the symbols can be made to mean anything the interpreter wants them to mean. Taking the book of Revelation and the kingdom prophecies naturally, the pre-millenarian believes that when Christ comes again, He will then—and only then—establish His reign of peace and righteousness over the earth. He believes in a literal rule of Christ on the promised throne of David, when He, together with the redeemed of the Church age, will reign over the regathered and saved remnant of Israel and the righteous Gentile nations. The pre-millenarian does not confuse Israel with the Church, nor the Church age with the millennial age. For him, the schedule of future prophetic events is:

a) the Rapture
b) the Tribulation
c) the final coming of Christ as King
d) the millennial reign of Christ on Earth
e) the eternal state of a new heaven and a new Earth.

B. Its relation to Israel

Among the millennial family of nations, the nation of Israel will occupy the central place.

> When the most High divided to the nations their inheritance, when he separated the sons of Adam, he set the bounds of the people according to the number of the children of Israel. For the LORD's portion is his people; Jacob is the lot of his inheritance. He found him ... he led him about, he instructed him, he kept him as the apple of his eye.
>
> —DEUTERONOMY 32:8–10

It was revealed to Mary by the angel that Jesus was destined, as the promised Messiah, to reign upon the throne of David.

> He shall be great, and shall be called the Son of the Highest; and the Lord
> God shall give unto him the throne of his father David: And he shall reign
> over the house of Jacob for ever; and of his kingdom there shall be no end.
>
> —LUKE 1:32–33

It is true that the Church has entered into the spiritual blessings first given to Israel (Eph. 1:18, 3:6; 1 Pt. 2:9–10), but that fact does not change God's purpose for national Israel (Is. 61:1–62:4; 66:7–24; Rom. 11:13–28). It seems clear that Israel will be the ministers and missionaries to all the nations during the Millennium, directing the Gentile inhabitants of the earth to serve and worship the Lord (Is. 61:4–11). While Israel will have the preeminence among the nations during the millennial reign of Christ, the Church in her glorified state will sit in judgment over the tribes of Israel (Mt. 19:28; Lk. 22:29–30).

C. Its relation to the nations

At the coming of Christ to reign, there will be a judgment of Gentile nations, referred to in Matthew as the sheep and goat nations (Mt. 25:31–36). The sheep nations are judged apt for kingdom blessing on the basis of their treatment of the Lord's "brethren" (Israel). That there will be Gentile nations on the millennial earth is clear from Revelation 20:7–8; Isaiah 2:1–5; 11:5–10; 60:1–5; and Zechariah 14:16–21. It was revealed to Daniel in a vision that the Christ would have dominion over a kingdom that would include all nations:

> I saw in the night visions, and, behold, one like the Son of Man came with
> the clouds of heaven, and came to the Ancient of days, and they brought him
> near before him. And there was given him dominion, and glory, and a king-
> dom, that all people, nations, and languages, should serve him: his dominion
> is an everlasting dominion, which shall not pass away.
>
> —DANIEL 7:13–14

D. Its relation to the Church

The Church will bear a different relationship to the millennial kingdom than either the restored nation of Israel or the Gentile nations. The latter will be earthly peoples, and even though they will live under the ideal conditions of an earth freed from the curse, they will have mortal bodies and will pursue normal earthly occupations. There will be universal peace, justice, and holiness because of the sovereign rule of Christ, but there will not be absolute perfection in the earthly inhabitants (Is. 11:4; 65:20; Zec. 14:17–19). On the other hand, the Church and all saints who have had part in the first resurrection will rule and reign with Christ (Rv. 2:26–27; 3:21; 5:9–10; 20:6). They will not be confined to the earth, for they have glorified bodies and they will have access to heaven and Earth (Rv. 19:6–14; Mt. 22:30–31; Lk. 20:35–36). Jesus said to His disciples, "In my Father's house are many mansions [abiding places];" then He added, "I go to prepare a place for you, And if I go and prepare a place for you, I will come again, and receive you unto myself" (Jn. 14:2–3). Paul spoke of his hope of a better place than this earth: "Having a desire to depart, and to be with Christ; which is far better" (Phil. 1:23). When the apostle said "for me to die is gain" (Phil. 1:21), he meant gain over life at its best, not at its worst, for he had just declared, "for to me to live is Christ." The believer, even now, is seated together with Christ in heavenly places (Eph. 2:6). Therefore, in our resurrected state, we will always occupy heavenly places, even while we are sharing rule over the earth with Christ (Mt. 25:21; Lk. 19:17–19). That the Church saints will be equipped for both heavenly and earthly environments is suggested by three things: (1) The saints in the resurrected state will be like the angels (Lk. 20:35–38), and angels often ministered to men on Earth. (2) Jesus, after His resurrection, appeared to His followers on Earth for forty days. (3) At the death of Jesus, many saints arose from their graves and appeared unto many persons (Mt. 27:52–53).

E. Life and conditions on the millennial earth

1. *Christ's millennial reign will be characterized by universal justice and righteousness (Jer. 23:5–6; Is. 11:3–5; 52:1; Ps. 72:1–8).*

2. *All the earth will be under the righteous discipline of King Jesus, and all who disobey will be disciplined (Zec. 14:16–21).*

3. *There will be peace among all the nations during the millennial rule of Christ (Ps. 72; Is. 2:4; 9:5–6; 32:1, 17–18; Mi. 5:4–5).*

4. *There shall be happiness and joy in His kingdom (Is. 9:2–4; 25:6–9; 35:10).*

5. *In Christ's kingdom, the people of the nation of Israel will enjoy health and longevity (Is. 35:5–6; 65:20–22).*

6. *On the millennial earth there will be great material prosperity (Ps. 72:15–16; Am. 9:13–15; Zec. 3:10; 8:12).*

7. *Under Christ's reign, the earth will be freed from the curse (Rom. 8:19–22; Is. 55:13; 41:18–19).* With the removal of the curse, wild animals will lose their ferocity (Is. 11:6–9; 65:25; Ez. 34:25, 28; Hos. 2:18).

VIII. THE JUDGMENTS

All men will stand before the judgment bar of God in order that His righteousness may be vindicated: "And it is appointed unto men once to die, but after this the judgment" (Heb. 9:27). The psalmist declared: "Righteousness and justice are the foundation of Thy throne" (Ps. 89:14, NASB). God's holiness and justice require that all sin be punished and that all right be upheld: "Far be it from Thee to do such a thing, to slay the righteous with the wicked, so that the righteous and the wicked are treated alike. Far be it from Thee! Shall not the Judge of all the earth deal justly?" (Gn. 18:25, NASB). Man's conscience witnesses to the fact all good and evil are known by God and recorded in His indelible record: "These...shew the work of the law written in their hearts, their conscience also bearing witness, and their thoughts the mean while accusing or excusing one another;) In the day when God shall judge the secrets of men by Jesus Christ according to my gospel" (Rom. 2:15–16). All men have sinned (Rom. 3:10–23), therefore all are deserving of condemnation. The clearest picture of the demands of God's holiness and justice is seen in the Cross. God is also a God of love, but in order for His mercy to be bestowed upon sinners, their sins had to be laid upon His redeemer Son and there upon the cross be judged and punished. The infinite Savior bore the sinners' guilt in order that believing ones identified with Jesus might be freed from condemnation (Rom. 8:1).

There is an erroneous idea held by some that there will be one general day of reckoning on which all beings, just or unjust, will be judged. The Bible speaks of a number of judgments. *The Scofield Bible,*[27] in the footnotes for Revelation 20:12, lists seven separate judgments. In the following section, these judgments will be treated under five categories: the judgment of the believer, the judgment of the nations, the judgment of national Israel, the judgment of the wicked dead, and the judgment of Satan and the fallen angels.

A. Of the believers

There are three aspects to the believer's judgment. His first judgment took place at the cross: "Now is the judgment of this world: now shall the prince of this world be cast out. And I, if I be lifted up from the earth, will draw all men unto me" (Jn. 12:31–32). In reality, the Cross is the judgment of all sin and of all sinners, including Satan. At the cross, the believer pleads guilty, confesses his sin, and identifies himself with Jesus, his substitute and Savior: "If we confess our sins, He is faithful and just to forgive us our sins, and to cleanse us from all unrighteousness" (1 Jn. 1:9). Having been judged at the cross, the faithful will not stand judgment relative to their salvation, but rather relative to their rewards for service (Jn. 3:18; 5:24; Rom. 8:1, 33; 1 Thes. 5:9). The second aspect of the believers' judgment is his continuing self-judgment. Paul wrote, "For if we would judge ourselves, we should not be judged. But when we are judged, we are chastened of the Lord, that we should not be condemned with the world" (1 Cor. 11:31–32). This is a part of the sanctifying work of the Holy Spirit in the believer's life (Rom. 15:16; 1 Thes. 5:14–23; 2 Thes. 2:13; 1 Jn. 1:7–2:2).

---

27 Scofield, *The Scofield Bible* (Oxford: Oxford University Press, 1967), footnotes for Rv. 20:12.

The believer's judgment before the judgment seat of Christ is not a judgment of condemnation, but that of determining the believer's awards. It will take place at the coming of Christ (1 Cor. 4:5). Two passages give details relative to the believer's judgment:

> Every man's work shall be made manifest: for the day shall declare it, because it shall be revealed by fire; and the fire shall try every man's work of what sort it is. If any man's work abide which he hath built thereupon, he shall receive a reward. If any man's work shall be burned, he shall suffer loss: but he himself shall be saved; yet so as by fire.
> —1 CORINTHIANS 3:13–15

> For we must all appear before the judgment seat of Christ; that every one may receive the things done in his body, according to that he hath done, whether it be good or bad [worthless].
> —2 CORINTHIANS 5:10

In his life and service, each believer is building upon the foundation of Christ Jesus. He must answer before Christ's tribunal (the Bema Judgment) to have his works tested as a basis for recompense. His service may be revealed to be gold, silver, and precious stones; or to be hay, wood, and stubble. The latter will not stand the test in the crucible of Christ's glory. If what he has built on the foundation of Christ Jesus is worthless, he will still be saved, because salvation is by faith not works, but his works will bring him no awards or crowns: "Look to yourselves, that we lose not those things which we have wrought, but that we receive a full reward" (2 Jn. 8). (See also 1 Jn. 2:28; Rv. 3:11). If what he builds on Christ is good, he will receive a reward and God's statement of approval: "Well done, thou good and faithful servant" (Mt. 25:21). It seems clear that the believer's Bema Judgment occurs at the time of the Rapture, for the Marriage Supper of the Lamb takes place before Christ returns with the saints (Rv. 19:7–9), and the voice from the throne declares of the bride, "His wife hath made herself ready" (v. 7). Her readiness indicates that she has passed beyond judgment.

The believer's special rewards are called crowns. They are four in number.

1. *The crown of rejoicing.* "For what is our hope, or joy, or crown of rejoicing? Are not even ye in the presence of our Lord Jesus Christ at his coming? For ye are our glory and joy" (1 Thes. 2:19–20). Paul considered his converts his crown of rejoicing. Note that he expected to receive his crown at the coming of Jesus. This is the soul-winner's crown.

2. *The crown of righteousness.* Paul expected to receive the crown of righteousness as a reward for, as he says in 2 Timothy 4:7–8, his good fight, keeping the faith,

and finishing his course. This is the winner's crown from the athletic metaphor (1 Cor. 9:25–27: "But I keep under my body...lest...when I have preached to others, I myself should be a castaway" [v. 27]).

3. *The crown of life.* "Blessed is the man that perseveres under trial, because when he has stood the test, he will receive the crown of life" (Jas. 1:12, NIV). This is the martyr's crown, for it is promised to those who are faithful unto death (Rv. 2:10); but those who live prepared to die for their witness receive it also.

4. *The crown of glory.* This is the crown for pastors and elders: "And when the chief Shepherd shall appear, ye shall receive a crown of glory that fadeth not away (1 Pt. 5:4). The Greek word for "crown" is *stephanos.* It was often used to refer to the crown made of olive or laurel branches and awarded at athletic games. Though those crowns soon faded, the crown of glory that the Lord will give to His undershepherds will outlast the ages.

B. Of the Gentile nations

In Matthew 25, Jesus declares that He will gather all nations before Him to be judged at the time of His coming (Mt. 25:31–46). At the end of the Tribulation and before He begins His millennial reign, Jesus will separate the nations as a shepherd would separate sheep from goats. It seems from what follows that the basis of judgment will be the treatment rendered to His brethren, the righteous remnant of Israel who will be Christ's witnesses during the Tribulation (Rv. 7; 11:1–12). These will be the Gentiles who survive the Tribulation, who do not bow to the Beast. They will become the nations that the Old Testament prophets predicted would inhabit the earth during the kingdom age (Is. 11:10).

C. Of national Israel

The Old Testament prophets predict a time of trial and judgment for the remnant of Israel in preparation for the kingdom (Ez. 20:33–38; Dn. 12:1–2). Jesus, in Matthew 24, speaks of the Great Tribulation as a time of trial and judgment for Israel. Since the Tribulation, which will be Daniel's seventieth week, will be an ordeal for Israel, it will constitute a final judgment upon the nation to meet out justice and to purge a remnant for the Messiah's reign upon the throne of David (Dn. 9:24–27; Rv. 12).

D. Of the wicked dead

This is known as the Great White Throne Judgment. It will not take place until after the millennial reign of Christ.

> And I saw a great white throne, and him that sat on it, from whose face the earth and the heaven fled away; and there was found no place for them. And I saw the dead, small and great, stand before God; and the books were opened;

and another book was opened, which is the book of life: and the dead were judged out of those things which were written in the books, according to their works. And the sea gave up the dead which were in it; and death and hell delivered up the dead which were in them: and they were judged every man according to their works. And death and hell were cast into the lake of fire. This is the second death.

—REVELATION 20:11–14

This describes the Final Judgment of all the wicked dead. The judge will be Christ Jesus, to whom God has assigned all judgment (Acts 17:31). The judged are the wicked dead who did not have part in the first resurrection, which took place at the time of the Rapture of the saints (1 Thes. 4:16; 1 Cor. 15:52). The judgment is on the basis of works. There will be a difference in the severity of judgment (Lk. 12:46–48). However, the mildest degree of being lost is a dreadful fate. These will have spurned every offer of God's mercy in Christ Jesus. Therefore, their names are not found written in the Book of Life.

E. Of Satan and the fallen angels

At the end of Christ's thousand-year reign, Satan will be released from his prison for a brief season. He will go forth to deceive the nations, but this rebellion (his last) will end with the fiery destruction of the rebels and Satan's being cast into the lake of fire forever (Rv. 20:10). Several Bible passages refer to a Final Judgment of fallen angels (Is. 24:21–22; 2 Pt. 2:4; Jude 6). It is usually assumed that the fallen angels will be judged at the same time Satan is judged. According to Paul, the saints will participate in the angels' judgment (1 Cor. 6:3).

IX. THE FINAL DESTINIES

No teaching is clearer than that of a final destiny for all men beyond this present life on earth.

And these go away into everlasting punishment, but the righteous into eternal life.

—MATTHEW 25:46, NKJV

And I give unto them eternal life; and they shall never perish.

—JOHN 10:28

In flaming fire taking vengeance on them that know not God, and that obey not the gospel of our Lord Jesus Christ: Who shall be punished with everlasting destruction from the presence of the Lord, and from the glory of His power.

—2 THESSALONIANS 1:8-9

Quite clearly, the righteous will enjoy everlasting life and bliss in the presence of the Lord, while the unrighteous will suffer everlasting punishment and separation from the Lord. The future abode of the righteous will be heaven (2 Cor. 5:1; 1 Pt. 1:4). The future abode of the unrighteous will be hell (*gehenna*; Mk. 9:43–44; Rv. 20:14).

A. The future destiny of the unrighteous

The Authorized Version refers to the final abode of the unbeliever as hell. The English word *hell* translates several Hebrew and Greek words that have reference to different stages of existence after death. It sometimes designates the place of departed spirits or the intermediate state, which in Hebrew is called *sheol* and in Greek is called *hades*. In the New Testament, "hell" more often translates *gehenna*, which symbolizes the final, eternal perdition. (Gehenna was the refuse dump in the Valley of Hinnom, where fires burned unendingly.) The wicked are kept in hades until the Final Judgment, after which they are cast into the lake of fire. "Hell" once translates *tartaroo*, where the wicked angels were cast (2 Pt. 2:4). After the Millennium, all the wicked dead are resurrected, and after the Great White Throne Judgment are cast into the lake of fire (Rv. 19:20; 20:10, 14–15; 21:7–8).

1. *The final condition of the wicked is presented in the following descriptions:*

a) Separation from God (Lk. 13:25, 28; 2 Thes. 1:9)

b) Outer darkness (Mt. 22:13; 2 Pt. 2:4, 17; Jude 6, 13)

c) Eternal or unquenchable fire (Mt. 18:8; Mk. 9:43–46, 48; 2 Pt. 3:7; Jude 7)

d) Everlasting contempt (Dn. 12:2)

e) Everlasting torment (Rv. 14:10–11)

f) Eternal punishment (Mt. 25:46)

g) Everlasting destruction or perdition (ruin) (2 Thes. 1:8–9; Phil. 3:18–19; Mt. 7:13; Rom. 9:22; 2 Pt. 3:7)

h) Where the worm dies not (Mk. 9:44)

i) The wrath of God (Rom. 2:5, 8–9; 1 Thes. 1:10)

j) Retribution, or punishment proportionate to the evil (2 Cor. 11:14–15; 2 Tm. 4:14; Rv. 18:6; 22:12)

k) The second death (Rv. 20:14; 21:8)

2. *Several theories have been proposed that deny that the punishment of the wicked is unending.*

a) Annihilationism. According to this theory, the wicked are punished for an age and then are annihilated. Annihilationists contend that the Greek word *aionios,* derived from *aion,* which means "period of time, age," has the meaning of "age-long" (that is, lasting for one age) rather than "everlasting." However, *aionios* is the strongest word in the Greek language to express the idea of endlessness. Furthermore, *aionios* is the very word used to express the eternity of God, of the Holy Spirit, and of the life of the believer. By the reasoning of the annihilationist, if punishment of the wicked is only an age long, then the life of God and of the believer is only an age long. In Matthew 25:46, the punishment of the unrighteous and the life of the righteous is expressed by the same word, *aionios.* At the beginning of the thousand years, the Beast and false prophet are cast into the lake of fire. At the end of the thousand years, Satan is cast into the same lake of fire: "where the beast and false prophet are and ["they," plural] shall be tormented day and night for ever and ever [literally, into the ages of the ages]" (Rv. 20:10). They have spent the millennial age in perdition, and after that they share Satan's doom into the ages of the ages. Obviously their punishment is more than an age long.

b) Universalism. According to universalists, punishment will bring about a change of heart on the part of the wicked, and finally they, including Satan himself, will be saved. However, the Word says that after a millennium in the Abyss, when released, Satan immediately leads a rebellion against God and against His saints. A thousand years of imprisonment does not change the deceiver one iota. The Beast and false prophet do not change after a millennium in the lake of fire (Rv. 19:20, 20:10). The rich man in hades finds a great gulf fixed between himself and Abraham's Bosom, and he pleads for a messenger from the realms of the dead to warn his brothers of the dangers of hell. The reply is that the Law and the prophets are their only avenue of salvation, and that if his brothers rejected God's Word, no messenger from the dead would be able to avert their same destruction (Lk. 16:22–31).

However frightening the prospect of eternal perdition may be, we may be certain that God's righteous judgment will be vindicated. This is assured by the great extent to which God went in sending His Son to die for us. The grace and love of God are beyond measure. If there had been a way for men to be saved without the ordeal of the Cross, God would not have subjected His Son to it. The Cross demonstrates not only the love and mercy of God, but also the sinfulness of sin. The wicked are consigned to hell only after a judgment in which the books are opened and just sentences are pronounced. The severity of perdition will not be the same for all. The punishments of the wicked will vary in severity, just as the rewards of the righteous will differ in glory (Lk. 12:47–48; 1 Cor. 3:12–15). Every man's conscience will witness to the rightness of God's final judgments.

B. The final destiny of Satan, the fallen angels, and the Antichrist

Inasmuch as the final destiny of Satan, the wicked angels, and the Antichrist has already been treated under the section on their judgment and under the final destiny of the wicked, it will not be necessary to give further treatment to their final fates, other than to cite the passages of Scripture where the subject is revealed: Mt. 25:41; Jude 6; 2 Pt. 2:4; Rv. 19:20; 20:1–3, 10; Is. 14:14–15; and 24:21.

C. The future state of the righteous

The eternal state of the believer is life through and with the Lord Jesus Christ: "And this is the record, that God hath given to us eternal life, and this life is in his Son. He that hath the Son hath life; and he that hath not the Son of God hath not life" (1 Jn. 5:11–12). Eternal life is not merely eternal existence, since all men, righteous and unrighteous, will exist eternally. Eternal life in this context refers not merely to the duration of life, but rather to the quality of life. The believer has Christ's life, because he has Christ within (Gal. 2:20; Col. 1:27). Life in Christ is the present possession of the believer as well as his future hope. It is spoken of as the future state of the believer only in the sense that when Christ comes, eternal life is beyond forfeiture (1 Jn. 3:2; Rv. 2:10).

Whether in paradise reigning with Christ in His millennial kingdom or inhabiting the New Jerusalem, the believer will abide in the presence of Jesus in his Father's house. Life in the Father's house is assured by the promise of Christ, who has prepared a place for us there (Jn. 14:2–3) through His atoning work on Calvary's cross. The eternal abode of the believer then, is a home in heaven. But what kind of place did Jesus prepare?

1. *Heaven is the place where Jesus, our Savior, is* (Jn. 14:2–3; Acts. 7:56; 2 Cor. 5:2; Phil. 1:23).
2. *Heaven is an ample place.* "In my Father's house are many mansions [abiding places]" (Jn. 14:2–3).
3. *Heaven is a better place* (Heb. 10:34; 11:16).
4. *Heaven is an ideal place.* We are taught to pray, "Thy will be done in earth, as it is in heaven" (Mt. 6:10).
5. *Heaven is a place of inheritance.* The believer will receive an inheritance because he is a joint-heir with Christ (1 Pt. 1:4; Rom. 8:17).
6. *Heaven is a place of reward* (Mt. 5:12; 6:20; 19:21; Lk. 12:33; Col. 1:5; 2 Tm. 4:8).
7. *Heaven is a place of praise* (Rv. 19:1).
8. *Heaven is a place of beauty, splendor, and glory* (Rv. 21–22).
9. Heaven is a joyful place (Rv. 21:4; Mt. 25:21, 23; Lk. 15:7, 10; Heb. 12:2).
10. *It is a place of personal identity.*

After death, the rich man and Lazarus retained their personal identity. Moses and Elijah were still identifiable when they appeared to Jesus on the Mount of Transfiguration (Mt. 17:2–3). After the resurrection, Jesus was recognized by His followers. Our names are written in the Book of Life, and names signify identity and personality (Phil. 4:3). The fact that believers will have their resurrected bodies in heaven demonstrates that God's redeeming work extends to the total person. We will not lose personal identity in heaven. On the contrary, our personalities will be raised to the highest level of personal being. The best of Earth's relationships in the body of Christ will endure in heavenly life.

> I Jesus have sent mine angel to testify unto you these things in the churches. I am the root and the offspring of David, and the bright and morning star. And the Spirit and the bride say, Come. And let him that heareth say, Come. And let him that is athirst come. And whosoever will, let him take the water of life freely.... He which testifieth these things saith, Surely I come quickly. Amen. Even so, come, Lord Jesus.
>
> —REVELATION 22:16–17, 20

INDEX OF AUTHORS
AND PERSONS

A

Abba, 33, 70, 114, 240–241, 253, 281, 317, 453

Abel's offering, 185

abiding in Christ, 298–301, 303–304, 306

ability, God-given, 315

Abraham's bosom, 484, 526, 562

abyss, 513, 516, 546, 553, 562

accepting Jesus as Savior, 239

access to God, 167, 209

accuser, 508, 510, 513

acquittal, 227

Adamic nature, 95, 142

administrations, 333, 351, 471

Adonai, 66–68, 70, 90, 106

adoption, 70, 74, 82, 136, 184, 195, 212, 240–242, 253, 366, 453

adultery, 77, 169, 236, 249, 273, 297, 360, 503

adversaries, 221

adversary, 143, 509, 514, 518

advocate, 19, 106, 116, 289

afflictions, 365, 370, 372, 378, 387, 393, 400, 413, 494

agapao, 80

agape, 80

age of accountability, 197

agnosticism, 62

àhab, 79

aion, 562

aionios, 525, 561–562

Alexandrian manuscript, 35

Alexandrian version, 37

all-knowledge of God (omniscient), 82

almighty God, 21, 52, 60, 66–67, 72, 90, 96, 100, 113, 134, 155, 163, 272, 487, 502, 507, 513, 517

ambassadors, 194, 287, 331, 460–461, 499

ambition, 159, 162, 464, 508, 528

American Standard Version, 44–45, 436, 462

Amillennialism, 554

Angel of Jehovah, 90, 127

angel of light, 143, 498, 513–514

Angel of the Lord, 90–91, 94, 275, 474–475, 477, 480, 483–484, 487, 506

angelology, 472

aggelos, 472

angels,
  cherubim, 478
  definition, 472
  evil, 159–160, 180, 472, 476–477, 479, 487–488, 490–491, 506, 508, 510, 557, 560–562
  final destiny of, 562
  good, 471–477, 479–482, 484–487, 505, 507, 510, 525, 528, 531
  instruction of, 157
  judgment of, 560
  ministry of, 478, 480, 482–483, 486–487, 515, 556
  organization, 477
  origin, 472, 488, 491, 507
  references to, 71, 74, 100, 121–122, 126, 140, 157, 184, 196, 208, 213, 260, 302, 341, 472, 476–477, 481–487, 490, 505, 507, 531–532, 552, 556
  seraphim, 77, 478

angels, doctrine of, 471
  angelology, 472
  demonology, 488
  Satanology, 505

anger, 169, 178, 245, 306–307, 330, 370–372, 397, 487

annihilationism, 561

anointed one, 101, 546

anointing, 23, 101, 116–117, 131, 249–250, 278, 285, 287, 298, 301, 313, 321, 324–325, 327–328, 332, 337, 343, 349–350, 353, 358, 382, 389, 401–402, 418, 434, 442, 500
  of the Spirit, 249, 278, 287, 323, 325, 327–328, 332, 343, 349–350
  with oil, 101, 116–117, 131, 337, 389, 401–402, 418, 434, 442

anomos, 547

another Comforter, 72, 92, 111, 209, 288, 290, 531

anthropology, 121, 183

anthropos, 121

anti, 546

Antichrist, 97, 99, 517, 523, 533, 538, 541,

INDEX OF SCRIPTURES

James